The Greenwood
Encyclopedia of Daily Life

4 17th AND 18th CENTURIES

The Greenwood Encyclopedia of Daily Life

A Tour through History from Ancient Times to the Present

Joyce E. Salisbury
GENERAL EDITOR

Peter Seelig
VOLUME EDITOR

GREENWOOD PRESS
Westport, Connecticut • London

Library of Congress Cataloging-in-Publication Data

The Greenwood encyclopedia of daily life : a tour through history from ancient times to the
 present / Joyce E. Salisbury, general editor.
 p. cm.
 Includes bibliographical references and index.
 Contents: v. 1. The ancient world / Gregory S. Aldrete, volume editor; v. 2. The medieval
world / Joyce E. Salisbury, volume editor; v. 3. 15th and 16th centuries / Lawrence Morris,
volume editor; v. 4. 17th and 18th centuries / Peter Seelig, volume editor; v. 5. 19th
century / Andrew E. Kersten, volume editor; v. 6. The modern world / Andrew E. Kersten,
volume editor.
 ISBN 0–313–32541–3 (set: alk. paper) — ISBN 0–313–32542–1 (v. 1: alk. paper)
— ISBN 0–313–32543–X (v. 2: alk. paper) — ISBN 0–313–32544–8 (v. 3: alk. paper)
— ISBN 0–313–32545–6 (v. 4: alk. paper) — ISBN 0–313–32546–4 (v. 5: alk. paper)
— ISBN 0–313–32547–2 (v. 6: alk. paper)
 1. Manners and customs—History—Encyclopedias. I. Salisbury, Joyce E.
GT31.G74   2004
390—dc21   2003054724

British Library Cataloguing in Publication Data is available.

An online version of *The Greenwood Encyclopedia of Daily Life* is available from
Greenwood Press, an imprint of Greenwood Publishing Group, Inc. at:
http://dailylife.greenwood.com (ISBN 0–313–01311–X).

Library of Congress Catalog Card Number: 2003054724
ISBN: 0–313–32541–3 (set)
    0–313–32542–1 (vol. 1)
    0–313–32543–X (vol. 2)
    0–313–32544–8 (vol. 3)
    0–313–32545–6 (vol. 4)
    0–313–32546–4 (vol. 5)
    0–313–32547–2 (vol. 6)

First published in 2004

Greenwood Press, 88 Post Road West, Westport, CT 06881
An imprint of Greenwood Publishing Group, Inc.
www.greenwood.com

Printed in the United States of America

The paper used in this book complies with the
Permanent Paper Standard issued by the National
Information Standards Organization (Z39.48–1984).

10 9 8 7 6 5 4 3 2 1

Everyday life consists of the little things one hardly notices in time and space. . . . Through the details, a society stands revealed. The ways people eat, dress, or lodge at the different levels of that society are never a matter of indifference.

~Fernand Braudel, *The Structures of Everyday Life*
(New York: Harper and Row, 1979), 29.

ADVISORY BOARD

Mark C. Carnes
Ann Whitney Olin Professor of History
Barnard College

Davíd Carrasco
Neil L. Rudenstine Professor of Latin American Studies
Harvard Divinity School

B. S. Chandrababu
Reader in History
Madurai Kamaraj University

Toyin Falola
Frances Higginbothom Nalle Centennial Professor in History
The University of Texas at Austin

Jacqueline Murray
Dean of Arts
University of Guelph

CONTENTS

Contents

TOUR GUIDE: A PREFACE FOR USERS

What did people, from the most ancient times to the most recent, eat, wear, and use? What did they hope, invent, and sing? What did they love, fear, or hate? These are the kinds of questions that anyone interested in history has to ask. We spend our lives preoccupied with food, shelter, families, neighbors, work, and play. Our activities rarely make the headlines. But it is by looking at people's everyday lives that we can truly understand history and how people lived. *The Greenwood Encyclopedia of Daily Life* brings into focus the vast majority of human beings whose existence is neglected by the standard reference works. Here you will meet the anonymous men and women of the past going about their everyday tasks and in the process creating the world that we know.

Organization and Content

The Greenwood Encyclopedia of Daily Life is designed for general readers without a background in the subject. Articles are accessible, engaging, and filled with information yet short enough to be read at one sitting. Each volume provides a general historical introduction and a chronology to give background to the articles. This is a reference work for the 21st century. Rather than taking a mechanical alphabetical approach, the encyclopedia tries something rather more elegant: it arranges material thematically, cascading from broad surveys down to narrower slices of information. Users are guided through this enormous amount of information not just by running heads on every page but also by "concept compasses" that appear in the margins: these are adapted from "concept mapping," a technique borrowed from online research methods. Readers can focus on a subject in depth, study it comparatively through time or across the globe, or find it synthesized in a way that provides an overarching viewpoint that draws connections among related areas—and they can do so in any order they choose. School curricula have been organizing research materials in this fashion for some time, so this encyclopedia will fit neatly into a modern pedagogical framework. We believe that this approach breaks new ground in the structuring of reference material. Here's how it works.

Level 1. The six volumes of the encyclopedia are, naturally, arranged by time period: the ancient world, the medieval world, 15th and 16th centuries, 17th and 18th centuries, the 19th century, and the modern world.

Level 2. Within each volume, information is arranged in seven broad categories, as shown in this concept compass:

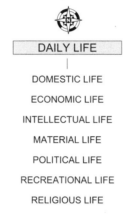

DAILY LIFE

DOMESTIC LIFE

ECONOMIC LIFE

INTELLECTUAL LIFE

MATERIAL LIFE

POLITICAL LIFE

RECREATIONAL LIFE

RELIGIOUS LIFE

Level 3. Each of the introductory essays is followed by shorter articles on components of the subject. For example, "Material Life" includes sections on everything from the food we eat to the clothes we wear to the homes in which we live. Once again, each category is mapped conceptually so that readers can see the full range of items that make up "Material Life" and choose which ones they want to explore at any time. Each volume has slightly different categories at this level to reflect the period under discussion. For example, "eunuchs" appear under "Domestic Life" in volume 2 because they served a central role in many cultures at that time, but they disappear in subsequent volumes as they no longer served an important role in some households. Here is one example of the arrangement of the concepts at this level (drawn from the "Domestic Life" section of volume 1):

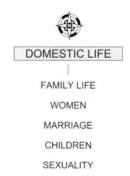

DOMESTIC LIFE

FAMILY LIFE

WOMEN

MARRIAGE

CHILDREN

SEXUALITY

Level 4. These conceptual categories are further subdivided into articles focusing on a variety of representative cultures around the world. For example, here users can read about "Children" in Egypt, Greece, medieval Europe, and 16th-century Latin America. Here is an example of a concept compass representing the entry on money in Ancient India:

ECONOMIC LIFE
|
MONEY
|
Mesopotamia

Egypt

Greece

Rome

India

The articles at each level can stand alone, but they all also offer integrated information. For example, readers interested in food in ancient Rome can focus right in on that information. If curious, they can look at the next conceptual level and learn how Roman food compares with that of other cultures at the same time, or they can see how food fits into material life in general by looking at the highest conceptual level. Readers may also decide to compare ancient Roman food with menus in Italy during the Renaissance; they need only follow the same process in another volume. Readers can begin at any of the levels and follow their interests in all directions: knowledge is linked conceptually in these volumes, as it is in life. The idea is to make it easy and fun to travel through time and across cultures.

This organization offers a number of advantages. Many reference works provide disparate bits of information, leaving it to the reader to make connections among them. More advanced reference tools assume that readers already have the details and include articles only on larger conceptual issues. *The Greenwood Encyclopedia of Daily Life* assumes no previous knowledge but recognizes that readers at all stages benefit from integrated analysis. The concept-mapping organization allows users to see both the details of the trees and the overall shape of the forest. To make finding information even easier, a cumulative subject index to the entire encyclopedia appears at the end of each volume. With the help of detailed running heads, concept compasses, and an index, anyone taking this "Tour through History" will find it almost impossible to get lost.

This encyclopedia is the work of many contributors. With the help of advisory boards, specialists in daily life around the world wrote the detailed articles in the "level 4" concept category. Many of these experts have published books in Greenwood's award-winning "Daily Life through History" series, and their contributions were crafted from those books. Each volume's editor wrote all of the many higher-level conceptual articles that draw connections across the topics, thus providing a consistent voice and analysis throughout the volume.

Coverage

The chronological coverage of this encyclopedia is consistent with the traditional organization of history as it is taught: the six volumes each take on one of the standard periods. But in reality, history is messy, and any strictly chronological organization has flaws. Some societies span centuries with little change, whereas others change rapidly (usually because of cross-cultural interactions). We have addressed these questions of change and continuity in two ways. Sometimes, we introduce cultures in one volume, such as the Australian Aborigines in volume 1, and then we do not mention them again until they were transformed by colonial contact in volume 4. In these entries, readers are led by cross-references to follow the story of the Australian indigenous peoples from one volume to another. At other times, cultures have experienced enough change for us to introduce many new entries. For example, volume 5, devoted to the 19th century, includes many entries on Muslim lands. But some aspects of the 19th-century Muslim world (e.g., education) had long remained largely unchanged, and in these instances readers are led by cross-references to entries in earlier volumes. This network of cross-references highlights connections and introduces users to the complexities of change and continuity that form the pattern of the social fabric.

We also depart from the chronological constraints of each volume when describing cultures that left few written records. Borrowing from anthropological methods, we sometimes (cautiously) use evidence from later periods to fill in our understanding of earlier lives. For example, colonial observers have at times informed our description of earlier indigenous cultures in many parts of the world.

The geographic scope of this encyclopedia reflects the relatively recent recognition that culture has always operated in a global context. In the Stone Age, bloodstone from Rhum, an inaccessible island off the stormy coast of Scotland, was traded throughout Europe. Domesticated plants and animals from Mesopotamia spread to Africa through Nubia in the third millennium B.C.E., and throughout the ancient world the trade between China and the Mediterranean was an essential part of life. Global history is woven throughout these volumes.

We do not attempt to document every one of the thousands of societies that have arisen throughout history and around the world. Our aim—to provide a general reference source on everyday life—has led to a careful focus on the most studied and representative cultures of each period. For example, ancient India is introduced in volume 1 and then reappears in the complexities of a global society in volumes 5 and 6. Nubia, the path from Egypt to sub-Saharan Africa, is introduced in volume 1, but the range of African cultures is addressed in depth in volume 4 and again in volume 6. Muslim cultures are introduced in volume 2 with the birth of the Prophet, reappearing in volume 3 with the invigorated society of the Turks and then again in volumes 5 and 6 with modern Muslim states. This approach draws from archaeological methods: we are taking deep samples of cultures at various points in time. The overall picture derived from these samples offers a global perspective that is rich and comprehensive. We have covered every area of the world from Australia and the South Pacific to Viking Scandinavia, from indigenous cultures to colonial ones, from age-old Chinese civilization to the modern United States.

Another issue is that of diversity within some dizzyingly complex regions. Africa, China, Polynesia, and India, for example, all contain many cultures and peoples whose daily life is strikingly diverse. Rather than attempt exhaustiveness, we indicate the range of diversity within each entry itself. For instance, the many entries on Africa in volume 4 recognize that each society—Yoruba, Swahili, Shona, and all the others—is unique, and each entry focuses on the cultures that best represent trends in the region as a whole.

The United States is yet another complex region. It grew from its inception with a mingling of European, Native American, African, and other cultural groups. Instead of treating each individually, we combine them all within the entries on the United States. For example, as volume 4 discusses Colonial New England, it weaves a description of Native American life within the entries showing the full range of social interaction between native peoples and colonists. This organization recognizes the reality that all these groups grew together to become the United States.

Features

This work has been designed by educators, and pedagogical tools help readers get the most out of the material. In addition to the reader-friendly organization already described, we have added the following special features:

- *Concept compasses*. Each section of each volume contains a concept compass that visually details the contents of that section. Readers are immediately able to see what topics are covered and can decide which ones they want to explore.
- *Illustrations*. The illustrations drawn from primary sources are in themselves historical evidence and are not mere ornament. Each shows some aspect of daily life discussed in the text, and the captions tell what the picture illuminates and what readers can see in it.
- *Maps*. Maps give readers the necessary geographic orientation for the text. They have been chosen to reinforce the global perspective of the encyclopedia, and readers are consistently offered the view of the parts of the world under discussion.
- *Chronologies*. In addition to geography, students can quickly lose track of the chronology of events. Each volume offers a list of the major events of the periods and of the cultures covered in the volumes. These chronologies serve as a quick reference that supplements the historical introduction.
- *Snapshots*. The fascinating details of the past engage our curiosity. Each volume is scattered with boxed features that highlight such evidence of past life as a recipe, a song, a prayer, an anecdote, or a statistic. These bits of information enhance the main entries; readers can begin with the snapshot and move to more in-depth knowledge or end with the details that are often designed to bring a smile or a shocked insight.
- *Cross-references*. Traditional brief references point readers to related entries in other volumes, highlighting the changes in daily life over time. Other "See" references replace entries and show readers where to find the information they seek within the volume.
- *Primary documents*. The encyclopedia entries are written to engage readers, but nothing brings the past to life like a primary source. Each volume offers a selection of documents that illustrate the kinds of information that historians use to re-create daily life. Sources range widely, from the unforgettable description of Vikings blowing their noses in a water basin before they wash their faces in it to a ration book issued by the United States government during World War II.

- *Bibliography.* Most entries are followed by a section called "For More Information." These sections include recommended readings, as one might expect in a bibliographic attachment, but they often provide much more. For this media age, the authors recommend Web sites, films, educational videos, and other resources.
- *Index.* Even in the 21st century, a comprehensive index is essential. Concept compasses lead readers from one topic to the next, but an index draws connections among more disparate entries: for example, the history of the use of wine or cotton can be traced across many volumes and cultures. A cumulative index appears in each volume to allow fast and easy navigation.

The Greenwood Encyclopedia of Daily Life: A Tour through History from Ancient Times to the Present has been a labor of love. At the end of the day, we hope that readers will be informed and entertained. But we also hope that they will come to a renewed appreciation of an often-spoken but seldom-felt reality: at the most basic level all humans, across time and space, share concerns, pleasures, and aspirations, but the ways these are expressed are infinite in their range. The six volumes of this encyclopedia reveal both the deep similarities and the fascinating differences among people all over the world. We can participate in our global village more intelligently the more we understand each other's lives. We have also learned that people are shown at their best (and sometimes their worst) in the day-to-day activities that reveal our humanity. We hope readers enjoy taking this tour of people's lives as much as we have enjoyed presenting it.

~Joyce E. Salisbury

Acknowledgments

I would like to thank the following people for their valuable and, more often than not, indispensable assistance: this volume's talented contributors, who provided each entry with its substance; the helpful staff and freelance editors at Greenwood Publishing and at Impressions Book and Journal Services, Inc.; and Professor Joyce E. Salisbury, who, as the general editor of the series, contributed greatly to its original framework and who, as a professor of the humanities, has inspired me with her engaging commitment to excellent scholarship and excellent teaching.

~Peter Seelig

1

HISTORICAL OVERVIEW

The Global Perspective

Globalism is a widely used term today, referring to the interconnectedness of distant and divergent cultures around the world. The history of the 17th and 18th centuries reflects the movement toward globalism. While the following historical overview emphasizes the basic political, economic, social, and military themes and events that characterized the eight regional subjects covered in this volume, it also stresses their interconnectedness.

The entries that comprise the main part of this volume focus on the events, activities, ideas, and physical objects that constituted people's daily lives in eight cultural groupings from the 17th and 18th centuries: sub-Saharan Africa, colonial Australia, the French and British colonial frontiers in North America, 18th-century England, 17th- and 18th-century France, 18th-century Japan, colonial New England, and Western oceanic exploration ("Life at Sea").

Within these eight groupings were even more distinct cultures. For example, the vast region of Africa that lies south of the Sahara was as diverse culturally as it was geographically. Similarly, the many Native American tribes occupying New France and British America, including New England, exhibited great diversity. Indeed, differences based on ethnicity, religion, class, language, and other factors resulted in the partitioning of the social landscapes of all the eight regional and cultural groupings.

Given this vast array of divisions, the reader could conclude that these many cultures and subcultures existed as disconnected, separate entities. In reality, the 17th and 18th centuries were years of expanding and intensifying cultural relations.

By 1600, Europe's great powers, including England and France, had come to focus on the Atlantic Ocean as a way to establish themselves on other continents. The reasons for this outward push were manifold, but it is certain that Europe's expansion would not have been possible had it not been for the maritime technology and oceangoing vessels that European powers at the time possessed.

Making their way across the Atlantic and Pacific Oceans, these vessels spearheaded much of Europe's commercial, military, and colonial drive. England and

France established North American colonies. In the Pacific, England and France also made efforts to colonize Australia, with England triumphant.

Extensive commercial relations arose between European and African merchants, and these transactions included the buying and selling of enslaved Africans, many of whom found themselves in North America and Europe. By 1800, Europe continued to engage Africa in primarily commercial relations, although outright colonization was not far off.

Interestingly, 18th-century Japan's self-imposed prohibition on most contact with outsiders enabled Japanese to avoid Europe's colonial and commercial expansion. As with Africa, this relative autonomy would undergo significant shifts during the 19th century.

At this point, a historical overview of each of the eight cultural regions discussed in this volume will help to balance the global perspective of the 17th and 18th centuries.

England

The hundred years preceding the 18th century were indeed trying for the English and greatly influenced 18th-century life on the island nation. In 1642, civil war broke out between the supporters of the king, Charles I (r. 1625–49), and those of Parliament, an assembly of influential men whose interests frequently clashed with the king's wishes. By 1649, Charles had suffered military defeat and was beheaded. England became a republic; that is, no monarch—no king or queen—held power. Over the next few years, a military government ruled England until, in 1660, Charles II, the son of Charles I, restored the monarchy (the Stuarts) and successfully negotiated with Parliament over religious, military, and financial matters. Two political parties evolved from these dynamic circumstances: the Whigs, who resolved to weaken the crown, and the Tories, a party dedicated to the defense of the Stuart Restoration (Weisser, 69–74).

In 1685, Charles II died, and his son, James II, acquired the crown. As king, James managed to infuriate both Parliament and many English with his toleration of Catholics and his failure to negotiate with other political institutions. James's eldest daughter, Mary, was the wife of William of Orange of the Netherlands, and both were Protestant. Invited by Parliament to replace James, William sailed to England and effectively exiled his father-in-law to continental Europe. England now had two new rulers—William and Mary—and the Glorious Revolution (1688), as this transfer of power was called, acquired a prestigious reputation for parliamentary monarchy, the preservation of tradition, Protestant Christianity, and Whiggish politics (Weisser, 77–80).

England during the 18th century witnessed an expansion of its economy, population, and imperial territory, as well as of parliamentary rule. In the realm of economics, industry not only grew but also became more efficient, as coal steadily

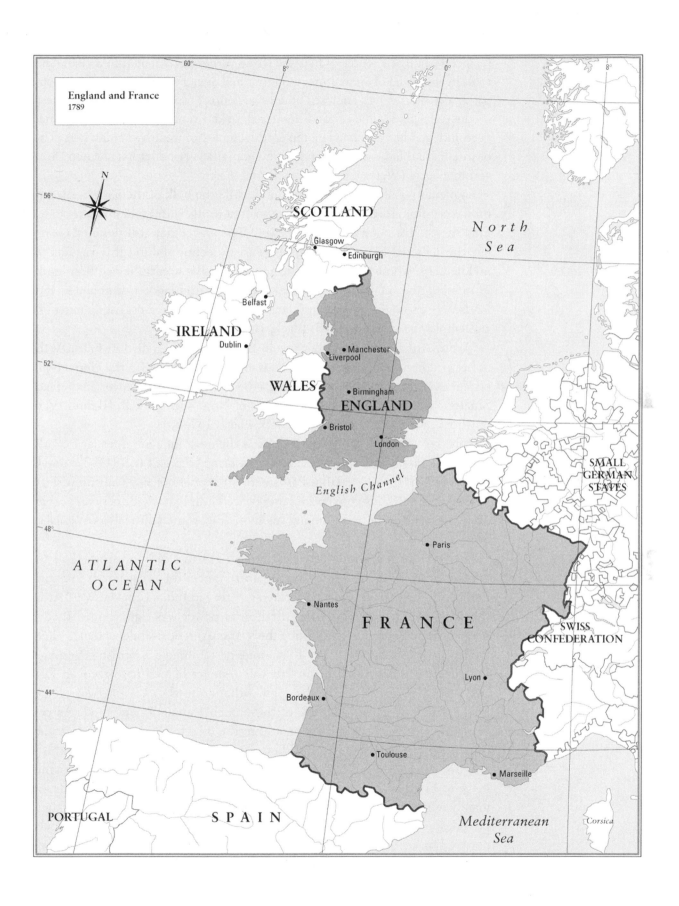

England and France
1789

SCOTLAND

Glasgow
Edinburgh

North
Sea

Belfast

IRELAND

Dublin

WALES

Manchester
Liverpool

ENGLAND

Birmingham

Bristol

London

English Channel

ATLANTIC
OCEAN

Paris

FRANCE

Nantes

SMALL
GERMAN
STATES

SWISS
CONFEDERATION

Lyon

Bordeaux

Toulouse

Marseille

PORTUGAL

S P A I N

Mediterranean
Sea

Corsica

replaced wood as a source of fuel and steam power developed into a viable industrial tool. In the realm of agriculture, land that had once been fragmented in a communal pattern of sharing was enclosed under the control of a single owner. As a result, the productivity and value of land increased, as did rents, and farmers who had once been independent became laborers in the employ of wealthy landowners. The ranks of intellectual labor also expanded, including lawyers, doctors, teachers, financiers, and managers (Weisser, 97–99; Black, 164–65).

England's population grew apace, and while the bulk of the population inhabited rural or semirural areas, England was also urbanizing, with London as the centerpiece. English social structures evolved as well. The aristocracy still retained great power, but the material basis of that power was in decline. Filling this vacuum was the middle class, whose fidelity to trade and productive wealth helped their ranks grow in number and influence. Meanwhile, agrarians and laborers dominated the social landscape, earning relatively little and lacking security against the vagaries of health and employment (Weisser, 83; Black, 167).

Queen Anne, who began her rule of England in 1702, died in 1714. With all 17 of her children dead, her closest Protestant relatives, living in the German province of Hanover, became the heirs to the crown. Thus, the Hanoverians replaced the Stuarts, furnishing England with a series of kings, George I, II, III, and IV, the last of whom died in 1830 (Weisser, 81–83; Black, 157–60).

Robert Walpole, a Whig politician, was the most influential leader in Parliament during the first half of the 18th century, assisting George I (r. 1714–27) and George II (r. 1727–60) while leading Parliament in support of fiscal restraint, legislative moderation, religious convention, and peaceful diplomacy. Bribery and other forms of corrupt patronage were among his most important political tools (Black, 158–59).

England was not always at peace. From 1743 to 1748 and from 1754 to 1763, England waged two victorious wars against France, the great power in continental Europe. In the process, England secured territory in India, Canada, West Africa, and the West Indies. England's concentration of power was significantly, though only temporarily, compromised following the War of American Independence (1775–83). England's defeat and loss of the 13 colonies destabilized the British government, but the effective statesman William Pitt the Younger helped it to recover. Pitt again aided King George III during the conflict that erupted in 1793 between France and England following the outbreak of the French Revolution in 1789. As power in France shifted from the revolutionaries to the dictator Napoleon, the conflict continued with little abatement until France's total defeat in 1815. During this stretch of years, the French military constituted a considerable military and economic challenge to England, although France waged its wars primarily on European soil, ultimately relinquishing the sea-lanes to the British Royal Navy. Thus, from these years of widespread death and suffering, England entered the 19th century doubly empowered by a growing empire and a rapidly industrializing economy that was second to none (Weisser, 85; Black, 162–76).

France

In 1661, Louis XIV became king of France and came to represent absolute monarchy—that is, absolute rule by a king or queen. On the domestic front, Louis XIV boosted the efficiency of revenue collection and expenditure, subdued aristocratic rivals for power, and carefully aligned France's Catholic Church with the government. On the international front, a decade of peaceful coexistence gave way to successful military expansion (1673–88) but ended with military disappointments (1688–1715). Nevertheless, France had managed to acquire and settle part of Canada, at the time referred to as New France (Haine, 55–61).

During the 18th century, economic and population growth strengthened France's material standing. French society was, in the main, an agricultural one, characterized by peasants who worked the land. A small minority of the population comprising a nobility and clergy enjoyed the benefits of privilege, such as freedom from much taxation. In the middle was a growing and rather flexible middle class (the bourgeoisie) (Haine, 63–64).

After Louis XIV died in 1715, France suffered from military defeats (resulting in the surrender of New France in North America to England) and government deficits. Before he could attempt to resolve the situation, the new king, Louis XV, died of smallpox in 1774. His successor, Louis XVI, opted for a conciliatory stance since any attempt to tax the rich and powerful met with their obstinate refusals (Haine, 63–67).

In May 1789, King Louis XVI hoped to avert a crisis by meeting with the Estates-General, a consultative body representing the three "estates": the clergy, the nobility, and the masses (peasants, urban laborers, and especially, the bourgeoisie). A complex association of opposition groups from all three estates forced the king to recognize a single body, the National Assembly, the members of which immediately declared their intention to have a constitution composed for France. The French Revolution was underway (Haine, 71–76).

Between 1789 and 1791, the French monarchy relinquished significant power to nonmonarchical governmental bodies, which abolished the system of aristocratic and clerical privileges while affirming the equality of men, the importance of the people in determining legitimate government, and the rights of religious expression, free speech, and property ownership. Still, inequality continued to exist, as those able to vote had to be (1) male, (2) adult, and (3) substantial taxpayers. Many citizens had no vote and thus little influence over government (Haine, 77–79).

In a frenzy of revolutionary nationalism and fear, France declared war on Austria on April 20, 1792. From this date forward, France was, with only brief interludes, at war with the rest of Europe and England until 1815. Growing numbers of radicals who came under the influence of this same frenzy questioned the need for a monarchy at all and had the king jailed and later executed, the monarchy abolished, and a republican form of government instituted. Revolutionary France's conflict with Europe had, at least in the propaganda, become a war to liberate Europe's masses from monarchs, aristocrats, and clerics (Haine, 80–84).

Counter-revolutionary threats from abroad and within France inspired the new, republican government to impose a reign of terror across the country, marked by a surge in executions throughout the country. By the summer of 1794, the Reign of Terror had succeeded in containing the menace of domestic and foreign opposition. As a sense of security returned, moderates, known as Thermidorians, were able to put an end to the Reign of Terror. From 1795 until 1799, they participated in a new government (the central body of which was the Directory), prosecuted the war in Europe, fended off monarchical forces that hoped to reestablish a feudal order in France, and stifled radical "Jacobins" who revered the Reign of Terror. Yet this balance of power collapsed before the manipulations of the soon-to-be dictator Napoleon and his allies (Haine, 84–87).

Napoleon Bonaparte had become a national hero thanks to his widely praised military acumen in the French army. At the same time, the Directory's popularity had been ebbing in face of both a downturn in the economy and a new anti-French coalition led by England and Russia. Napoleon took advantage of the French government's vulnerability and seized power on November 19, 1799 (known as the 18th Brumaire). This coup enabled him to amass dictatorial powers, which he did by skillfully meshing the popular symbols of the French Revolution with a concentration of power that mirrored Louis XIV's absolute rule decades earlier. Napoleon, who declared himself emperor in 1804, effectively quashed opposition by using secret police, censorship agencies, a top-down bureaucracy, and clerical bureaucrats. Napoleon's selection of men from the nobility and bourgeoisie appeased a good number of potential opponents at the same time that his famous Civil Code, which rationalized the legal system, recognized in a formal way the abolition of feudalism, the sacredness of private property, the principle of equality before the law, and freedom of religion (Haine, 88–92).

The domestic stability of France was a direct consequence of the country's continued military success throughout the rest of Europe, for victory in battle translated into the spoils of war. The French navy, however, was woefully outmatched when it came to the British Royal Navy, and Napoleon's attempts both to invade England and then to cut off England's trade failed. A guerilla war in Spain, disputes with the Pope, and a disastrous invasion of Russia in 1812 all combined with the baleful effects of a worsening economy at home to bring about Napoleon's eventual downfall at the Battle of Waterloo in 1815. France emerged with the restoration of its monarchy, this time with Louis XVIII as king. Nonetheless, the French were not the same as they had been in 1789. Accustomed to at least the pretense of representative government, France was torn between republican rhetoric and feudal traditions. Moreover, France found that its imperial conquests and industrial output were considerably behind those of its archrival, England. These domestic and international concerns continued to shape France's development throughout the 19th century (Haine, 93–99).

Life at Sea

Europe's early modern and modern oceanic exploration began on the Iberian Peninsula, shared by Spain and Portugal. From 1400 to 1600, incentives as diverse as wealth, knowledge, religious fervor, and nation building encouraged a desire to explore the world's oceans. Technological advances, the competence of seamen and officers, and the strength of armed galleys and sailing ships made these explorations possible (Reynolds, 105–9).

After 1419, Portugal financed early southward explorations along the west coast of Africa in search of slaves and gold. By the 1520s, Portuguese and Spanish explorers had rounded the tip of Africa, sailed to the Caribbean (Columbus, in 1492) and to India, and circumnavigated the globe. Ultimately, Spain held sway over much of the Americas, as well as the Philippines. Portugal maintained a significant commercial presence not only along the West African and East African coasts, but also in Brazil, India, and the Orient. These successes inspired jealousy among other European powers, and soon the Dutch, English, and French were raiding Portuguese and Spanish galleons while building their own navies. By the end of the 16th century, Spain was steadily losing its capacity to compete with its neighbors on the open seas (Reynolds, 122–44).

The Protestant Netherlands, sometimes called Holland, led Europe in maritime commerce during the first three-quarters of the 17th century. The Dutch did so by organizing their naval commerce and aligning it with the wealth of investors. One outgrowth of such investment was the Dutch East India Company, which vied with the Portuguese in the Far East for commercial dominance. The Protestant Netherlands eventually controlled the Eastern sea-lanes and thus a profitable trade in spices, silks, and precious metals (Reynolds, 145–71).

As Dutch naval supremacy made itself felt, the French and English grew wary. During the late 17th century, France expanded its ports and maritime schools, established itself in India, and widened its presence in Canada ("New France") and the Caribbean. England, too, expanded its presence in North America, the West Indies, and India. The English, however, differed significantly from the French in that the English, living on the island of Great Britain, necessarily relied on the high seas. The French did not, and perhaps could not, share this enthusiasm because of their land-oriented location on the European continent (Reynolds, 172–78).

The English therefore concentrated their energies on unseating the Dutch as masters of maritime commerce. Beginning in 1652, the English fought the Dutch in the Anglo-Dutch Wars, and by 1674, the Dutch no longer menaced England's economic prosperity. Indeed, England allied itself with the Dutch to preempt an even greater threat to English security—France. In 1692, Louis XIV, king of France, de-

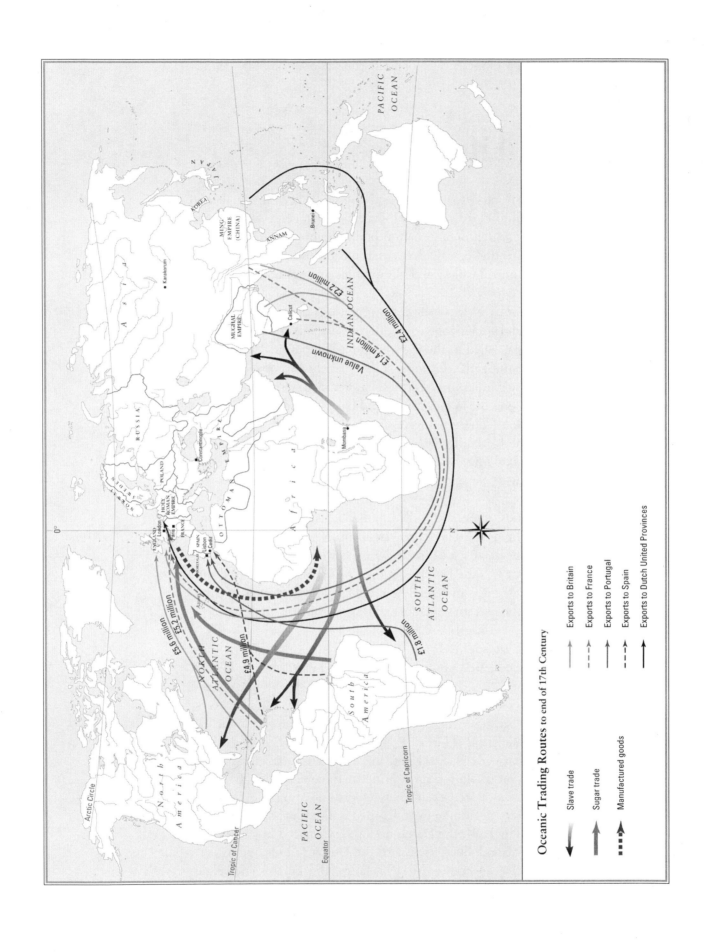

Oceanic Trading Routes to end of 17th Century

Slave trade

Sugar trade

Manufactured goods

↑ Exports to Britain

↑ Exports to France

↑ Exports to Portugal

↑ Exports to Spain

↑ Exports to Dutch United Provinces

cided to assemble a naval fleet with which to invade England. The English triumphed over the French, and from this point forward, French policy began to shift away from direct competition with England's navy. Thus, by the 1720s, England ruled the seas. Spain still laid claim to most of Latin America; Portugal to Brazil; and the Dutch to Eastern India. France's possessions were scattered but did include the sparsely settled New France (Reynolds, 188–210).

During the 18th century, England developed lucrative commercial relations with its colonies and continued its maritime explorations, including those of the Pacific island-continent of Australia. Naval warfare was also common to the 18th century, typically pitting the English against the French. Naval power influenced both the Seven Years' War (1756–63), at the end of which France ceded New France to the English, and the War of American Independence (1775–83), which left the 13 North American colonies independent of England, thanks in part to French naval intervention (Reynolds, 211–75).

In 1793, revolutionary France declared war on England. Throughout the prolonged conflict, French leaders including Napoleon hoped that a French-led naval fleet could spearhead a successful invasion of England; but each time the French made such an attempt, English naval strategy confirmed its supremacy. By 1815, England and its allies had defeated France. The British had learned the strategic importance of naval dominance and was intent on using its newly acquired territories of Capetown, Malta, and Mauritius to strengthen its commercial empire based on trade among India, the Middle East, and Europe (Reynolds, 289–318).

The Colonial Frontier of North America

North America's colonial frontiers pitted the settlements of New France against the neighboring British-American colonies. The history of France's attempts to colonize Canada began with Jacques Cartier, who, upon trying to reach Asia by sailing west on the Atlantic Ocean, instead reached Newfoundland in 1534. From there, he sailed up the Gulf of the St. Lawrence River, hopeful that the passage would lead to the Pacific Ocean and thus to Asia. Unsuccessful from this perspective, Cartier made two subsequent voyages in 1535 and 1541. By the time of the second voyage, the French king was interested in transforming the region that Cartier was exploring into the colony of New France. For more than 60 years, however, France was largely unsuccessful in this regard, and only scattered fishermen and fur traders occupied this French territory in North America. Nevertheless, the French managed to upset the English colonists along their frontiers, and the armed conflict that resulted would, with few interruptions, characterize relations between New France and the British colonies (McNaught, 42–45).

In 1608, a proponent of New France, Samuel de Champlain, established a trading post at Quebec and endorsed the presence there of a company monopoly. In 1627, the French king authorized the existence of The Company of One Hundred Associates, which received from the crown the right to own, develop, and govern land in New France, in exchange for which right the company would furnish New France with 4,000 settlers, a vibrant Catholic foundation, and effective company government (McNaught, 48–52).

Champlain thought it wise to ally New France with the local natives and consequently befriended the Hurons of Ottawa and the Algonquins of the St. Lawrence Valley. As it turned out, the Iroquois were, with regard to warfare, superior to both the Hurons and the Algonquins. The Iroquois allied themselves with the English, thus posing a constant threat to New France (McNaught, 52).

Inclement weather, poor agriculture, Indian hostilities, and difficult transportation hampered the colony's settlement. By 1663, New France could claim only 2,500 settlers. This state of affairs was unacceptable to King Louis XIV. Concluding that The Company of One Hundred Associates had failed to fulfill its contractual obligations, he ordered regular French troops from Europe to secure the borders of New France. The king also decided that the company had failed as a governing entity. Therefore, a Sovereign Council consisting of a governor, a bishop, an intendant, and four local officials would attend to the well-being of the New French community. By 1700, New France had a colonial population of 7,000, and land cultivation had doubled (McNaught, 61–69).

Quebec was the center of New France, playing the simultaneous roles of military stronghold, commercial port, government capital, and religious hub. Along the frontier, however, existed wild and daring young men who escaped the control of French officials, marrying Native American women and selling furs to the French and English, alike. More official ventures into unexplored regions led the French to the Mississippi River, threatening the English settlements in the east (McNaught, 73–80).

It was not the French, however, but the English who made the greatest inroads in the pursuit to colonize North America. A failed settlement on Roanoke Island in the late 16th century was followed by Jamestown in Virginia. Organized by the London Company with permission from the English crown, Jamestown suffered at first from Native American attacks, incompetent company rule, and insufficient foodstuffs, but the cultivation of tobacco soon brought an irresistible source of revenue for the settlers, who waged war against the Indians in the area during the 1620s, virtually eliminating the Native American threat from the region. Still, the London Company failed to satisfy the English Crown, which made Jamestown and Virginia a royal colony in 1624. On the basis of this settlement sprung a populous and diverse colony (Unger, 27–31).

To finance its North American settlement at Jamestown, the Virginia Company issued a lottery in London to raise funds. © Library of Congress.

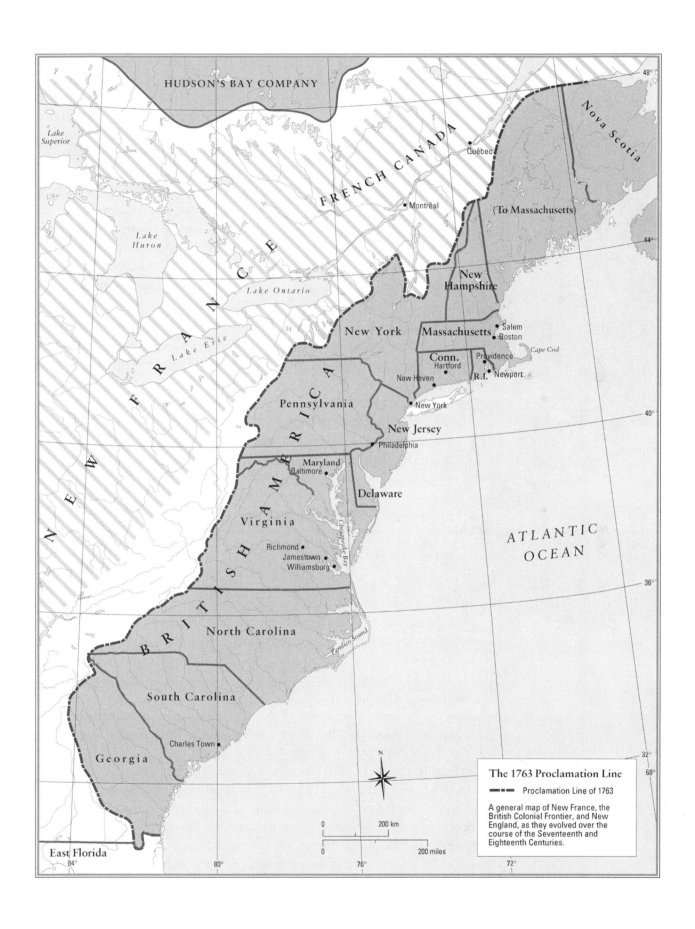

HUDSON'S BAY COMPANY

Lake Superior

Lake Huron

Lake Ontario

Lake Erie

NEW FRANCE

FRENCH CANADA

Québec

Montréal

Nova Scotia

(To Massachusetts)

New Hampshire

New York

Massachusetts

Salem

Boston

Conn.

Hartford

Providence

Cape Cod

New Haven

R.I.

Newport

BRITISH AMERICA

Pennsylvania

New York

New Jersey

Philadelphia

Maryland

Baltimore

Delaware

Virginia

Chesapeake Bay

ATLANTIC OCEAN

Richmond

Jamestown

Williamsburg

North Carolina

Pamlico Sound

South Carolina

Charles Town

Georgia

East Florida

N

0   200 km

0   200 miles

The 1763 Proclamation Line

▬ ▬ ▬ Proclamation Line of 1763

A general map of New France, the British Colonial Frontier, and New England, as they evolved over the course of the Seventeenth and Eighteenth Centuries.

English, Dutch, Swedes, Germans, French Protestants (Huguenots), and Scotch-Irish came to the British colonies for a host of reasons. Some sought adventure; others hoped to escape debt. Some were orphans with no choice; others hoped to amass great wealth in the new land. A significant number came to North America to establish communities that reflected their religious ideals. Because not all colonists could pay for the transatlantic voyage, some contracted to work as servants in North America for a stipulated number of years in return for passage to the colonies. Not all colonists made the trip voluntarily. Some were convicts unwanted in England. Others were African slaves. The first slave seems to have arrived in the colonies in 1619. By 1759, slaves of African descent constituted one-fifth of the colonial population (Unger, 32–36).

This picture of a German plate from Pennsylvania shows the importance that dance held for settlers in the North American colonies. © Philadelphia Museum of Art.

Communities in the middle colonies were dispersed over a broad area that included New York, New Jersey, and Pennsylvania, where farmers cultivated grains and ground them into flour. The south's hot and humid climate kept settlements there sparsely populated. The survival of Maryland, Virginia, the Carolinas, and Georgia depended on the slave labor that went into the cultivation of tobacco, rice, indigo, and grains. In general, the middle colonies and the south (along with New England, discussed separately) depended on a lively import-export trade, including the slave trade (Unger, 45–58).

Colonial government varied from one colony to the next but followed a general pattern that consisted of an executive branch, headed by a governor; a legislature, divided into two chambers; and local governing bodies at the town and county levels. To vote or hold office, adult males in most colonies had to be proprietors or make minimum tax payments. Overall, the English government was relatively accommodating to the wishes and needs of the white settlers in its North American colonies. Militarily, however, the colonies were in a nearly perpetual state of conflict with the native populations (Unger, 65–97).

The English competed with the French for dominance in North America, as well. The French and Indian War (1754–63) ultimately ended France's hopes of developing a powerful North American colony. The Treaty of Paris (1763) that ended the conflict granted New France to England, effectively placing a large French-speaking population under British rule. Nonetheless, a more formidable threat to English claims in North America emerged: the growing desire among colonists for freedom—even independence—from English rule. This perceived threat was perhaps the most important necessary condition underpinning the American War for Independence (1775–83), from which emerged the United States of America (McNaught, 39–42; Unger, 65–97).

Colonial New England

New England became the most famous of all the early British-American colonial regions in North America. The central motivation behind New England's Plymouth settlement hinged on a group of Puritans who were convinced that the Church of England (the Anglican Church) was corrupt. In exchange for agreeing to develop land in North America, these Puritans received official English permission to settle the region. In 1620, they sailed from England and reached an area near Cape Cod Bay, which they called Plymouth. In 1640, only 1,000 settlers lived there, but that number grew to 3,000 by 1660. However, a larger and more prosperous New England settlement, the Massachusetts Bay Colony, eventually encompassed Plymouth (McInerney, 21–22; Unger, 41).

Formed in 1629, the Massachusetts Bay Company involved a group of Puritans who, although skeptical of any outright separation from the Church of England, hoped to found a vibrant Puritan community beyond the Church's shadow. They arrived in New England in 1630 and, under the governorship of John Winthrop, established a thriving community. In 1640, the Massachusetts Bay Colony counted 9,000 settlers in its midst. The community leaders patterned the colony's social and political structure on rigid and narrow religious precepts. Not a few settlers left (or fled) the Massachusetts Bay Colony for other areas (Unger, 44).

Relations between the Massachusetts Bay Colony and the Native Americans were even less friendly. The Pequot War suppressed Indians in the Connecticut region during the 1630s. During the 1670s, King Philip led the Wampanoags and their allies, the Narragansetts of Rhode Island and the Nipmucks of Connecticut, on a war spree against the European settlers. In 1678, tribes in Maine and New Hampshire also rose up against the colonists, who nevertheless successfully crushed the native threat in the area (Unger, 55–56).

The New England economy depended on the fur, fishing, and whaling industries, as well as on textiles, shipbuilding, and commerce, including the slave trade. Because of the region's rocky soil, New England agriculture tended to focus on self-sufficiency. Early in the Massachusetts Bay Colony's history, a profound religious concern with sin and purity shaped most economic motivations. Over time, however, themes of wickedness and salvation gave way to those of investment and profit, although renewed zeal for Protestant concerns occasionally surfaced to counteract the fading religiosity (Unger, 68–87).

New England's population was quite homogeneous early on, consisting principally of Puritans from east-central England. Over time, new immigrants from different parts of England, Great Britain, and Europe itself arrived in New England by ship.

Blacks in New England numbered 12,000 by 1760, and New England slaves were common laborers, seamen, household servants, and artisinal assistants (Unger, 56–58).

The Massachusetts Bay Colony enjoyed a great deal of freedom from British intervention. England, however, finally decided to force a new charter on the colonists and required them in 1691 to accept the oversight of a crown-appointed governor, who, in this role, would supervise colonial legislation and reduce the number of formal ties between government rule and Puritan prescriptions. As the 18th century progressed, the New England colonies grew rapidly, and relative prosperity was obtainable and even common among white settlers. Despite these general advantages, discontent among the colonists increasingly directed itself against British interventions in colonial affairs. The English victory against New France at the end of the French and Indian War (1754–63) meant that colonists would have to accept the burden of new and increased taxes, a proposition that prompted many prominent New England residents in the city of Boston and elsewhere to protest. These protests eventually resulted in open and armed rebellion and, finally, in a declaration of independence (1776). The War of American Independence (1775–83) concluded with New England representing no longer a collection of British colonies but a region in the United States of America (Unger, 91–97).

Africa South of the Sahara

The most remarkable European contact with sub-Saharan Africa during the period covered in this volume first occurred up and down the African west coast. Beginning in the 1470s, Portuguese explorers had sailed these routes hoping to circumvent commercial intermediaries in North Africa and then to acquire precious metals such as gold. By the 16th century, the Atlantic slave trade had become lucrative for European commercial interests, and trading posts along the west coast of Africa enabled African rulers to supply the Portuguese with captured warriors from rival tribes. This traffic in human cargo depleted many regions in sub-Saharan Africa of young men and women, ultimately contributing to a significant decline in the region's economic productivity (Shillington, 170–76).

In West Africa, there were a number of significant cultures, including the Songhay, Borno, Hausa, Ife, Oyo, Dahomey, and Asante. The Muslim Songhay, which depended on trans-Saharan trade and revenue from their salt mines, suffered from fragmentation, commercial competition, and invasions. The Songhay consequently split into separate kingdoms. The 17th and 18th centuries were less divisive for the Borno, among whom Islam spread alongside a profitable market in slave trading. In addition, the Borno received tribute from Hausa city-states. These states practiced agriculture, industry, and trade and relied extensively on slave labor to build their vibrant cities. During the 18th century, Islam spread among the Hausa and spurred criticism of government corruption. The Ife Kingdom comprised a community of

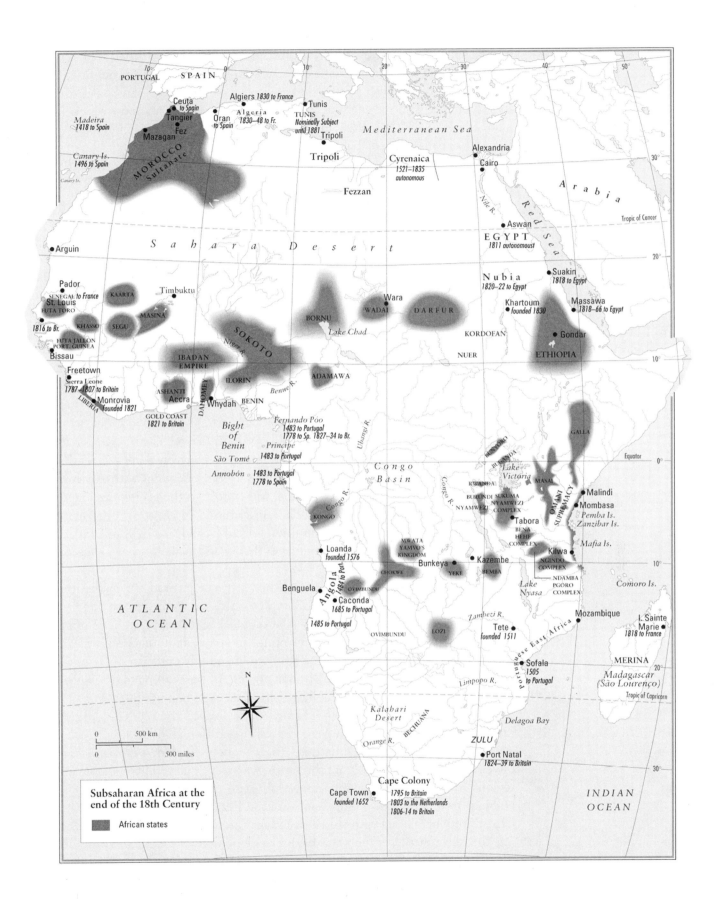

PORTUGAL   SPAIN

Madeira
1418 to Spain

Ceuta
to Spain
Tangier
Fez
Mazagan

Algiers *1830 to France*
Oran
to Spain
Algeria
1830–48 to Fr.
Tunis
TUNIS
*Nominally Subject
until 1881*
Tripoli

Mediterranean Sea

Alexandria
Cairo

Tripoli

Cyrenaica
*1521–1835
autonomous*

A r a b i a

MOROCCO
Sultanate

Canary Is.
1496 to Spain

Canary Is.

Fezzan

Nile R.

Red Sea

Tropic of Cancer

Arguin

S a h a r a   D e s e r t

Aswan

EGYPT
1811 autonomous†

Nubia
1820–22 to Egypt

Suakin
1818 to Egypt

Pador
SENEGAL *to France*
St. Louis
FUTA TORO

KAARTA

Timbuktu

Wara
WADAI   DARFUR

Khartoum
founded 1830

Massawa
1818–66 to Egypt

1816 to Br.
KHASSO   SEGU

MASINA

BORNU
Lake Chad

KORDOFAN

NUER

Gondar

FUTA JALLON
PORT. GUINEA
Bissau

SOKOTO

ETHIOPIA

Freetown
Sierra Leone
1787–1807 to Britain
LIBERIA   Monrovia
founded 1821

IBADAN
EMPIRE

ILORIN

ADAMAWA

Niger R.

ASHANTI
Accra
Whydah   BENIN
GOLD COAST
1821 to Britain

DAHOMEY

Benue R.

*Bight
of
Benin*

Fernando Póo
*1483 to Portugal
1778 to Sp. 1827–34 to Br.*

*Principe
1483 to Portugal*

São Tomé

GALLA

Equator

Ubangi R.

*Annobón   1483 to Portugal
1778 to Spain*

*C o n g o
B a s i n*

BUGANDA
*Lake
Victoria*
MASAI

KONGO

Congo R.

RWANDA
BURUNDI   SUKUMA
NYAMWEZI   NYAMWEZI
COMPLEX

Malindi
Mombasa
Pemba Is.
Zanzibar Is.

OMANI
SUPREMACY

Congo R.

Tabora

BENA
HEHE
COMPLEX

Mafia Is.

Loanda
founded 1576

MWATA
YAMVO'S
KINGDOM

Bunkeya

Kazembe
YEKE   BEMBA

Kilwa
NGINDO
COMPLEX

Benguela

Angola
1484 to Port.

CHOKWE

OVIMBUNDU
Caconda
1685 to Portugal

1485 to Portugal

OVIMBUNDU

LOZI

*Lake
Nyasa*

NDAMBA
PGORO
COMPLEX

Comoro Is.

Zambezi R.

Tete
founded 1511

Mozambique

L. Sainte
Marie
1818 to France

*ATLANTIC
OCEAN*

Limpopo R.

Sofala
*1505
to Portugal*

Portuguese East Africa

MERINA

*Madagascar
(São Lourenço)*

Tropic of Capricorn

N

*Kalahari
Desert*

BECHUANA

Delagoa Bay

ZULU

*Indian
OCEAN*

Orange R.

Port Natal
1824–39 to Britain

0   500 km
0   500 miles

Cape Colony
Cape Town
founded 1652
*1795 to Britain
1803 to the Netherlands
1806–14 to Britain*

Subsaharan Africa at the
end of the 18th Century

African states

Yoruba-speaking farmers, hunters, and traders living in small villages. The Oyo, who cultivated grains and traded with other Yoruba-speaking communities, used a powerful cavalry to establish an empire based on slave labor and slave sales, in return for which the Oyo received firearms, cloth, and metal. Dahomey, which initially paid tribute to the Oyo, was founded in the early 1600s with its capital in Agbome. Wars of expansion went hand in hand with slave trading, and by 1730, the Oyo paid tribute to Dahomey. The Asante were another West African civilization that practiced territorial expansion during this period, using commercial incentives and military threats to absorb other clans. The Asante wars of expansion continued during the 18th century, ultimately contributing to both the slave trade and the slave labor used to mine the Asantes' considerable gold fields (Shillington, 163–96).

In central and eastern Africa, Kongo profited from the slave trade with the Portuguese but weakened over the course of the 17th century, eventually fragmenting into competing slave-trading communities. Angola was the chief source of slaves not only for the Portuguese but for the English, Dutch, and French, as well. The widening prevalence of firearms in the region bred a greater number of wars throughout the 18th century, thus encouraging the sale of captives as slaves. The Lunda of Mwata Yamvo and of Kazembe dealt in trade and cultivated American crops such as maize and cassava, which the Portuguese had introduced to the area. A result, in part, of the efforts of one man, Changamire Dombo, the Mutapa Empire succeeded in recovering from both internal disputes and Portuguese exploitation. Strong-arm tactics enabled the Changamires to collect tributes (food, cattle, ivory, skins) and to place mining and trade under royal control. Relying on domestic markets, the Changamires agreed during the 18th century to have dealings with African representatives of the Portuguese. Agriculture was central to the economies and cultures of Buganda, Bunyoro, Nkore, Rwanda, and Burundi. In contrast, the Maasai were pastoralists who, as separate communities, settled Uganda, Kenya, and Tanzania. As with so many other African communities, their trade in slaves became a prominent source of revenue (Shillington, 197–211).

In southern Africa, the Dutch established settlements along the cape, leading to the Dutch and Khoi War of 1659. Dutch colonization expanded, as did slavery, so that, by the early 1700s, there were 25,000 black slaves opposite a community of 21,000 whites. The Khoisan had three options: retreat, fight, or surrender. Although they practiced all three options, the Khoisan eventually opted to work for the Boer (Dutch) settlers. Further inland, Khoisan chiefdoms were falling to black Nguni and Xhosa forces, which eventually collided with the white Boers (Shillington, 212–24).

In the north and east of sub-Saharan Africa existed the related civilizations of Ethiopia, Nubia, and Funj. In Makurra, Christianity had given way to Islam, and Arabs and Nubians had intermarried. Their economy included the capture and enslavement of non-Muslims from the south, who were sold to Egypt and neighboring regions of Asia. The Funj were non-Arabs who eventually gave way to Christian Nubians from Alwa. Also Christian were the Ethiopians, particularly in the north. Christianity here fused with feudal structures throughout the 17th century, and during the subsequent century, the Ethiopian monarchy weakened as the Christian nobility assumed more power (Shillington, 163–67).

Japan

In 18th-century Japan, symbolic power emanated from and was accorded to the emperor at his court in Kyōto, while real authority rested with a military strongman (a shōgun) working as a national leader of sorts. From 1603 to 1867 and thus throughout the 18th century, power in the shōgunate was exercised by the Tokugawa family, which ruled from Edo (later called Tokyo) with the aid of an expansive militarized bureaucracy called the *bakufu*. At the regional level existed a series of feudal lords, or daimyō, who, while largely self-governing in their respective territories, owed allegiance to the Emperor and, hence, to the shōgun. Some among the daimyō earned the trust and valuable favor of the shōgun, whereas others remained outside the shōgun's select circle of advisors and administrators. Given the peaceful and hermetic existence that Japan enjoyed throughout the 18th century, the warrior class of samurai was, in fact, an administrative class, manning the bureaucratic machinery of the state (Tames, 87–88).

Japan was very urbanized by this time. Edo boasted a population of one million, and Ōsaka, 400,000. Artisans and businessmen were two prominent classes in these and other cities. Although some of these individuals amassed sizable fortunes, religious and philosophical traditions based on Confucianism earned those involved in commerce a curious blend of wealth and disdain. The Tokugawa government hesitated to sully its honor by taxing this wealthy class. Most of the Tokugawa revenue derived, instead, from the taxes imposed on the peasantry, taxes that included a substantial percentage of the peasants' harvests—usually about 40 to 50 percent. An underclass called *eta* and *hinin* existed. Many were not even considered human, and their lowly status was typically hereditary, passed on from one generation to the next (Hane, 29–40).

Tokugawa rule during the 18th century highlighted the important aspects of its political, economic, and social history. The fifth Tokugawa shōgun, Tsunayoshi, ruled from 1680 to 1709 and ushered in a period during which urban culture thrived. Nevertheless, debt threatened the viability of the *bakufu*, and Tsunayoshi's recourse to education and Confucian principles failed to solve his financial woes. The next shōgun, Ienobu (r. 1709–12), relied on a Confucian scholar named Arai Hakuseki to create a healthy balance between expenditure and revenue. Hakuseki's measures included an effort to stem the flow of precious metals out of Japan. As with his predecessor, however, Ienobu ended his term as shōgun still shy of success (Hane, 28).

The next important shōgun was Yoshimune (r. 1716–45), who pioneered the Kyoho reforms. His goal was to boost government revenue, and to this end, he promoted the expansion of land under cultivation. He reasoned that the more crops that were harvested, the more the peasants could be taxed. The Kyoho reforms could be punitive, as with the stipulation that prohibited peasants from leaving their villages for urban areas. Yoshimune also imposed sumptuary laws (prohibitions or limits

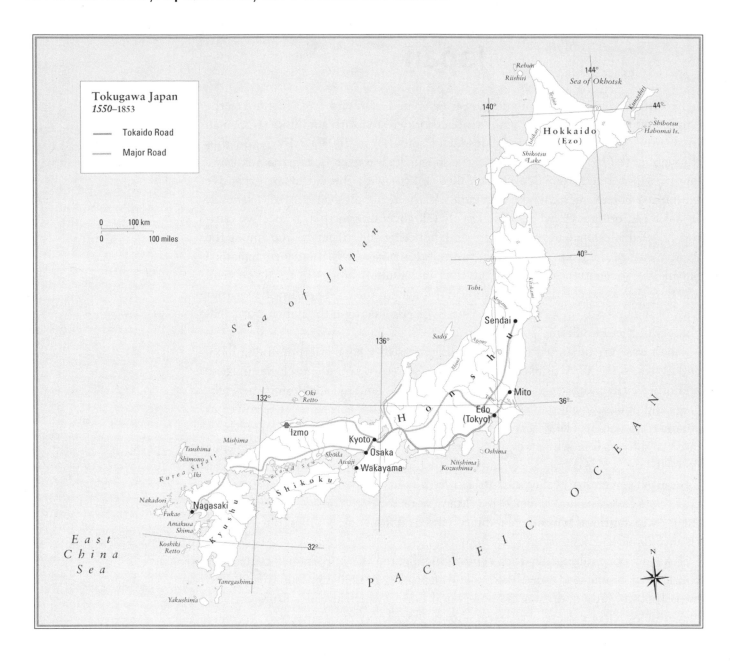

on the purchase of luxury goods) on wealthy individuals and censored literature to heighten the moral sensitivity of Japanese (Hane, 28).

The tenth shōgun was Ieharu, who, from 1760 to 1786, allowed his senior advisor, Tanuma Okitsugu, to exercise most of the shōgunate's power. He avoided traditional solutions such as decreased expenditures, compulsory frugality, and expanded agriculture. Instead, the advisor reformed Japan's monetary system, sold off monopolies, taxed the business class, and encouraged the expansion of exports. But Okitsugu was selfish and corrupt, and his era had the misfortune of ending in conjunction with devastating famines in 1783 and 1787, as well as with inflation and rioting. Ieharu died and Okitsugu was thrown out of office, replaced in 1786 by the grandson of Yoshimune, Ienari. Shōgun Ienari's advisor was Matsudaira Sadanobu, a revered feudal lord who had made an honorable and successful effort to prevent his peasants from starving during the 1783 crisis. As advisor, Sadanobu confronted Japan's crises with the Kansei Reforms, a collection of traditional measures (decreased expenditure, increased frugality), social welfare (price controls, rice reserves, income distribution, low-interest rates for the poor, vocational education for the unemployed), and legislated morality (restricted prostitution, prohibition of mixed bathing). All these efforts failed to resolve Japan's deeply rooted economic troubles, and Sadanobu resigned after six years. Ienari remained shōgun until 1837. Perhaps not surprisingly, these years witnessed a growing disenchantment with failed reforms and legislated morality, accompanied by a growing hedonistic disposition among the elite. Although reforms continued, the 19th century would bring to a close the period of Tokugawa Japan's self-imposed seclusion, as Europe forced its way into the Japanese homeland and mentality (Hane, 45–47).

Colonial Australia

Several European nations eyed Australia, but England successfully absorbed the continent into the British Empire, and along with it, a native population—the Aborigines—that had inhabited the island for at least 60,000 years. By 1600, Aborigines existed in highly structured clans and tribes, which, although interrelated, were usually detached from one another. Thus their languages were so diverse as to be incomprehensible between tribes. By the 18th century, these communities of Aborigines were scattered throughout Australia. The Aborigines focused on hunting, fishing, and animal husbandry, as well as on food gathering. Land, for the Aborigines, was endowed with the spirits of ancestors, and for this reason, wars of conquest were nonexistent—one clan or tribe had little interest in the spirits of a foreign clan or tribe. Instead, Aboriginal wars evolved from acts of vengeance or jealousy over a woman. Women were important workers in each clan,

Here, an Aboriginal warrior undergoes trial by ordeal to establish his standing in the community. © Perry Casteneda Library.

and husbands often shared with one another their multiple wives (Clarke, 1–16).

Europeans first heard Australia designated "Terra Australis Incognita," meaning "The Unknown South Land." It was widely believed that this unexplored territory was suited for cash crops and other profitable ventures. Therefore, exploratory voyages on behalf of the Portuguese, Dutch, Spanish, French, and English set out for this fabled land of opportunity. During the 1600s, the Dutch called Australia "New Holland." However, it was the English buccaneer William Dampier who established the first extended settlement on the continent. Over the subsequent decades, France endorsed voyages into the Pacific, prompting England to follow suit, this time with

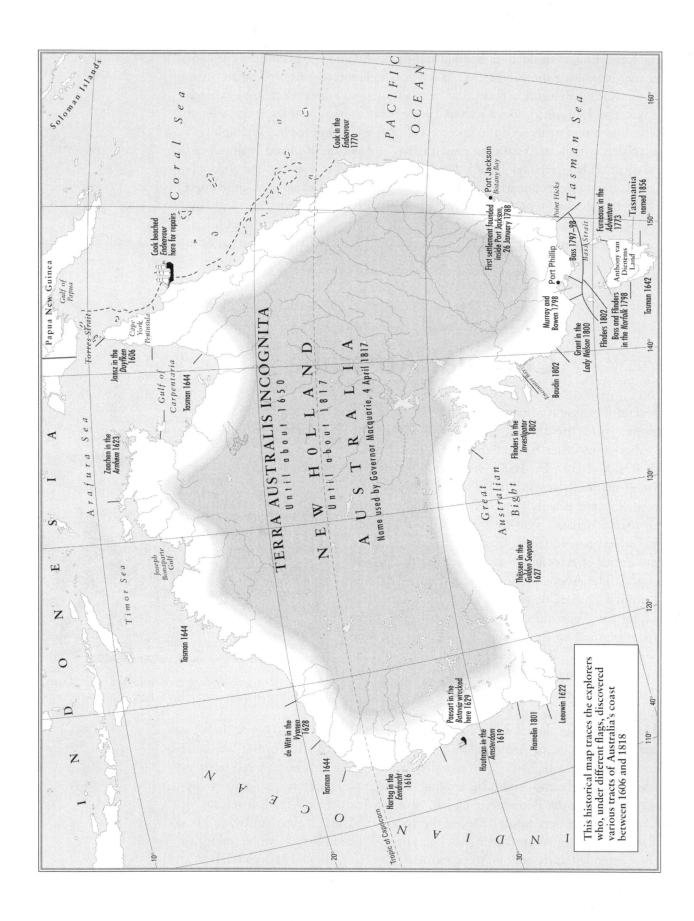

PACIFIC OCEAN

Cook in the *Endeavour* 1770

Cook beached *Endeavour* here for repairs

Port Jackson

Botany Bay

First settlement founded inside Port Jackson, 26 January 1788

Point Hicks

Tasman Sea

Bass 1797–98

Bass Strait

Furneaux in the *Adventure* 1773

Tasmania named 1856

Anthony van Diemen's Land

Tasman 1642

Port Phillip

Murray and Bowen 1798

Flinders 1802

Bass and Flinders in the *Norfolk* 1798

Grant in the *Lady Nelson* 1800

Baudin 1802

Coral Sea

Solomon Islands

Papua New Guinea

Gulf of Papua

Torres Strait

Cape York Peninsula

Jansz in the *Duyfken* 1606

Zeachen in the *Arnhem* 1623

Gulf of Carpentaria

Tasman 1644

I N D O N E S I A

Arafura Sea

Timor Sea

Joseph Bonaparte Gulf

Tasman 1644

TERRA AUSTRALIS INCOGNITA
Until about 1650

NEW HOLLAND
Until about 1817

A U S T R A L I A
Name used by Governor Macquarie, 4 April 1817

Flinders in the *Investigator* 1802

Great Australian Bight

Thijssen in the *Gulden Seepaar* 1627

de Witt in the *Vyanen* 1628

Tasman 1644

Hartog in the *Eendracht* 1616

Pelsart in the *Batavia* wrecked here 1629

Houtman in the *Amsterdam* 1619

Hamelin 1801

Leeuwin 1622

I N D I A N

O C E A N

Tropic of Capricorn

10°

20°

30°

40°

110°

120°

130°

140°

150°

160°

This historical map traces the explorers who, under different flags, discovered various tracts of Australia's coast between 1606 and 1818 the famed explorer James Cook. His expedition on the HMS *Endeavour* brought Cook to Australia's east coast, which he promptly called "New South Wales" in the name of the English Crown, King George III. In 1772, France claimed the western coast in the name of King Louis XVI. During the 1780s, however, it was England—not France—that put to work a plan to settle Australia. Curiously, however, these early settlers were English prisoners, sent to the colony as laborers whose mission was to develop the profitability of the land (Clarke, 21–23).

Australia's Botany Bay was one such settlement. In 1786, the government selected a retired British spy, Arthur Phillip, to command a fleet from England to Botany Bay. On board the fleet's vessels were 568 male prisoners and 191 female prisoners (with 13 children), as well as a good number of sailors, marines, officers, and others. The goal was to use prison labor for textile production. By 1788, "New South Wales" covered one-half of the Australian continent, although this claim was made largely in theory. In practice, the Second Fleet did not arrive until 1790, carrying 733 additional convicts (500 of whom were sick). Animals, crops, tools, clothing, and (not surprisingly) enthusiasm were in short supply (Clarke, 23–25).

The English explorer James Cook claims New South Wales (later, Australia) for England. Unknown, *Captain Cook's Landing at Botany AD 1770*, a7890396. National Library of Australia.

While the white settlers dealt with these frustrations, the Aborigines in the vicinity suffered a far more devastating fate. Lacking immunity against the diseases that the European settlers released into the environment, Aborigines quickly succumbed to the ravages of smallpox. Settlers discovered their corpses in coves throughout the area. The death rate among these Aborigines was perhaps as high as 50 percent (Clarke, 25–26).

The colonial settlement steadily evolved into a unique economy wherein the officers, being the only settlers to possess money, purchased the goods of visiting supply ships. Once Phillip left the colony, the commanding officers distributed tracts of land to their subordinates, who, in turn, furnished the convict workers with clothing and foodstuff. Collectively, the soldiers became known as the Rum Corps, and the convicts acquired a sordid reputation for indolence, promiscuity, and alcoholism (Clarke, 26–29).

British Australia continued to operate under a loosely organized group of officers, soldiers, and convicts until William Bligh, famous for his exploits on and off the HMS *Bounty,* arrived at the colony in 1806 as the governor of New South Wales. His mission was to eradicate the use of rum as a medium of exchange. The offending (and offended) members of the Rum Corps placed Bligh under arrest and declared their intention to manage the colony. However, troops loyal to the Crown soon put an end to the Rum Rebellion. Over the coming decades, Australia would expand its population and its economy, with important consequences for its settlers, the Aboriginal population, and the rest of the world (Clarke, 28–29).

~*Peter Seelig*

Chronology of the 17th and 18th Centuries

1400s	Portuguese develop advances in maritime technology
1492	Christopher Columbus discovers a "new world"
1530	Christianity penetrates Benin in West Africa
1571	Portugal establishes its first African colony in Angola
1580	Spain absorbs Portugal
1588	English defeat the Spanish Armada
1600s	Portuguese, Dutch, and English explorers discover Australia
1601	First French trading post in North America established at Tadoussac
1607	English establish a colony at Jamestown, Virginia
1608	French establish a post at Quebec along the St. Lawrence River in Canada
1609	Samuel de Champlain involves North American French settlers in warfare with Native Americans
1614	Dutch establish a trading post in New Amsterdam (New York)
1620	John Smith names the North American territory he explores "New England"
1625	West African kingdom of Dahomey is founded
1626	English colonists establish a settlement at Salem, Massachusetts
1628	Massachusetts Bay Company is organized in England
1630	John Winthrop and 900 colonists arrive in Salem and move to Charlestown; Boston becomes the seat of government for Massachusetts Bay

1633	Maryland is established as an English colony; the French monarchy approves a large grant of land in New France (Canada) for The Company of One Hundred Associates
1636	Thomas Hooker leaves Massachusetts to found Hartford, Connecticut; Roger Williams founds colony in Rhode Island
1638	Anne Hutchinson is excommunicated by the Puritan church and leaves Massachusetts Bay for Rhode Island
1640	Dutch force the Portuguese out of Malacca
1641	Law legalizing slavery takes effect in Massachusetts
1650	Dutch control trade in the East Indies
1652	Rhode Island declares slavery illegal; Dutch establish their first settlement in South Africa
1652–54	First Anglo-Dutch War
1656	First Quakers arrive in New England
1659	Two Quakers are hanged in Boston
1661–1715	Reign of Louis XIV, king of France; the French monarchy reaches the peak of its power
1663	Control of New France transfers from The Company of One Hundred Associates to the Compagnie des Habitants
1664	English capture the Dutch colony in New York
1665–67	Second Anglo-Dutch War
1671	Hostilities between European settlers and Native Americans escalate
1672–74	Third Anglo-Dutch War
1675	Nathaniel Bacon's Rebellion in Virginia
1675–76	King Philip's War, an uprising of the Wampanoag and Narragansett Indians, is fought in New England
1680	Fifth shōgun, Tsunayoshi, comes to power in Japan
1682	Quakers establish Pennsylvania
1684	Charter of the Massachusetts Bay is revoked
1689–97	War of the League of Augsburg, known in America as King William's War
1690	Indians and French attack New York
1691–92	Witchcraft cases in Boston and Salem
1693	Massachusetts Bay governor orders the release of all accused witches
1697	Dojima Rice Exchange founded in Ōsaka, Japan; the English take over part of Nova Scotia (Acadia) from the French
1699	French colonial rule in North America is extended down the Mississippi to Louisiana
1701–14	War of the Spanish Succession, the American phase of which is known as Queen Anne's War (1702–13)
1702	Queen Anne becomes the last Stuart monarch of England
1705	Asante emerges as a strong African empire
1707	Act of Union formalizes the political union of Scotland and England
1709	Sixth shōgun, Ienobu, comes to power in Japan and attempts economic reforms

1713	Seventh shōgun, Ietsugu, comes to power in Japan
1714	Queen Anne dies childless; George I of Hanover succeeds her on the English throne
1715–89	The Enlightenment, an intellectual movement rooted in France, promotes secularism and rationalism
1715–92	Reigns of Louis XV (1715–74) and Louis XVI (1774–92), ineffectual French kings
1716	Eighth shōgun, Yoshimune, comes to power in Japan and attempts economic reforms
1727	George I of Great Britain dies and is succeeded by his son George II
1740–48	War of the Austrian Succession in Europe, the American phase of which is known as King George's War (1744–48)
1741	The Great Awakening, a religious revival, begins in British North America
1744	England declares war against France during the War of the Austrian Succession
1745	Ninth shōgun, Ieshiga, comes to power in Japan
1746	Regular French army units arrive in Quebec
1748	Treaty of Aix-la-Chapelle ends the War of the Austrian Succession
1750	Muslim revival movement expands in western Sudan
1754–63	The French and Indian War, which merges with the wider Seven Years' War (1756–63)
1758	Fortress Louisbourg in New France falls to the English
1760	Tenth shōgun, Ieharu, comes to power in Japan; George II of Great Britain is succeeded by his grandson George III
1763	The Treaty of Paris ends the Seven Years' War; Great Britain acquires former French colonies, including Canada (formerly New France) in North America
1764	British Parliament begins to levy a new series of taxes on the American colonies
1768	James Cook's first voyage to the Pacific
1770	Confrontations between English troops and Massachusetts colonists climax in the Boston Massacre; James Cook annexes New South Wales, Australia, for Great Britain
1772	France annexes Western Australia
1773	Protesting British taxation, New England colonists destroy imported tea during the Boston Tea Party
1775–83	War of American Independence (the Revolutionary War)
1776	American colonies issue Declaration of Independence from the British
1778–83	French support Americans against the British during the War of American Independence
1783	Peace of Versailles ends the American Revolution and recognizes the independence of the United States
1783–86	Tenmei famine in Japan is followed by a series of peasant uprisings (*ikki*)

1784	George III dissolves British Parliament and calls a general election; Swahili city-states come under control of the Omani Arabs
1786	Eleventh shōgun, Ienari, comes to power in Japan; famines and epidemics continue in Japan; French navy is reorganized
1788	British First Fleet reaches New South Wales, Australia
1789	French Revolution begins; feudalism is abolished in France
1789–1801	Japan's Kansei era (Nengo system) ushers in new economic reforms
1790	British Second Fleet reaches New South Wales, Australia
1792	Revolutionary France declares war on Austria; Louis XVI is deposed and France becomes a republic
1793	Revolutionary France declares war on Great Britain on February 1; Reign of Terror begins in France
1794	The Thermidorian reaction in France subdues radical phase of French Revolution
1795–99	The Directory government rules France
1798	British admiral Horatio Nelson defeats the French at the Nile
1799	Napoleon topples the Directory in France and leads a new French government known as the Consulate
1801	Nelson defeats the Danish fleet at Copenhagen
1803	British hinder French attempts to settle Western Australia
1804	Napoleon declares himself emperor of France and institutes new legal code
1805	Nelson defeats the French at Trafalgar but is killed during the battle
1806	The British take over part of South Africa
1808	New South Wales Corps (the Rum Corps) stages a failed rebellion in Australia against the British governor
1812	Napoleon's disastrous invasion of and retreat from Russia
1814	Napoleon abdicates and is confined to the isle of Elba; French monarchy is restored
1815	Napoleon escapes from Elba but is defeated by the British duke of Wellington at Waterloo and exiled to St. Helena
1829	British establish the first free colony in Western Australia

FOR MORE INFORMATION

Black, J. A *New History of England*. Stroud, England: Sutton, 2000.

Clarke, F. G. *The History of Australia*. Westport, Conn.: Greenwood Press, 2002.

Falola, T. *Key Events in African History*. Westport, Conn.: Greenwood Press, 2002.

Haine, W. S. *The History of France*. Westport, Conn.: Greenwood Press, 2000.

Hane, M. *Japan, a Historical Survey*. New York: Scribner, 1972.

Johnson, C. D. *Daily Life in Colonial New England*. Westport, Conn.: Greenwood Press, 2002.

McInerney, D. J. *A Traveller's History of the USA*. New York: Interlink Books, 2001.

McNaught, K. W. *The Pelican History of Canada*. Baltimore, Md.: Penguin Books, 1969.

Olsen, K. *Daily Life in 18th-Century England*. Westport, Conn.: Greenwood Press, 1999.

Perez, L. G. *Daily Life in Early Modern Japan.* Westport, Conn.: Greenwood Press, 2002.

Reynolds, C. G. *Command of the Sea: The History and Strategy of Maritime Empires.* New York: Morrow, 1974.

Shillington, K. *History of Africa.* New York: St. Martin's Press, 1989.

Tames, R. *A Traveller's History of Japan.* New York: Interlink Books, 1993.

Unger, I. *These United States, the Questions of Our Past.* Englewood Cliffs, N.J.: Prentice Hall, 1992.

Volo, J. M., and D. D. Volo. *Daily Life in the Age of Sail.* Westport, Conn.: Greenwood Press, 2002.

Volo, J. M., and D. D. Volo. *Daily Life on the Old Colonial Frontier.* Westport, Conn.: Greenwood Press, 2002.

Weisser, H. *England, an Illustrated History.* New York: Hippocrene Books, 2000.

HISTORICAL OVERVIEW: WEB SITES

http://newark.rutgers.edu/~jlynch/18th/history.html

http://www.bbc.co.uk/worldservice/africa/features/storyofafrica/index.shtml

http://www.fordham.edu/halsall/mod/1695potato.html

http://www.cjn.or.jp/tokvgawa/english/index.html

http://www.mnh.si.edu/africanvoices/

http://www.napoleon.org/en/home.asp

http://www.sonoma.edu/history/reason/

2

DOMESTIC LIFE

The center of daily life is the home and, more important, the people who inhabit our domestic space. Domestic life here is defined as the humans who share our private spaces rather than our friends and acquaintances with whom we interact in the public worlds of work, politics, and sometimes recreation. However, even this definition of domestic life is a little slippery because we include family members within our private sphere even if they live in separate homes and join us for the holidays and celebrations that mark our domestic life. Over time, the definitions of those who are our intimates has changed. Who are the people who might share our domestic life?

The first ties link a married couple with their children. But even these relationships defy clear definition. Throughout history, children have often depended on the kindness of strangers to raise them, whether they were orphaned or fostered or fed by wet nurses. All these people share the domestic intimacy of home life. Furthermore, households have included others outside the nuclear family, from relatives to servants to slaves. In ancient Rome, the head of the family (the *pater familias*) was responsible for family, relatives, slaves, and freed slaves, and he also cared for clients who put themselves in his charge. Families can also include unmarried partners or even roommates who combine living space for convenience or necessity, or concubines who shared the private life of rulers. The relationships that make up domestic life are impossible to define perfectly, but (like art) we recognize them when we see them.

As discussed in this volume, domestic life comprises the categories of marriage, men and women, children, aging and death, and sex. The 17th- and 18th-century cultures of sub-Saharan Africa, colonial Australia, the North American colonial frontier, England, France, Japan, New England, and oceanic exploration ("Life at Sea") receive specific treatment in these categories.

During these two centuries, the concept of love or emotional attachment negotiated a place for itself alongside material concerns. Across all of these geographically and historically distinct cultures, one discovers that food, money, and land represented many of the concerns of prospective spouses, married couples, parents, the dying, and even children. In Yoruba, the union of a couple involved material com-

DOMESTIC LIFE

MARRIAGE

MEN & WOMEN

CHILDREN

AGING & DEATH

SEX

pensation, called bridewealth; in 18th-century England, such compensation was known as a dowry. A husband and wife constituted an economic venture as much as a loving relationship. Children, too, assumed openly material roles, and the number of children in a family, as well as the sex of those children, directly corresponded to work that needed to be done on the farm, in the shop, or in the household. The death of a family member frequently initiated a reassessment of the distribution of the family's wealth and earning potential. Finally, sex—be it out of love or lust—carried with it material considerations. After all, the need for child labor and heirs required copulation. Moreover, prostitution was a source of income for countless people, from Tokugawa Japan to maritime ports around the globe.

A study of domestic life not only includes the people who create a private, emotional sphere but also encompasses the roles they play—including the material functions they fill. This duality was particularly true during the 17th and 18th centuries in the cultures discussed here. In the realm of domestic life, societies define the roles of men, women, and children who share this space. It is here that we learn early on who we are and how we are to act and feel.

~*Joyce E. Salisbury and Peter Seelig*

FOR MORE INFORMATION

Veyne, P., ed. A *History of Private Life*. Vols. 1 and 2. Cambridge, Mass.: Harvard University Press, 1987.

DOMESTIC LIFE
|
MARRIAGE
|
Africa

Colonial Australia

The Colonial Frontier
of North America

England

Japan

New England

Life at Sea

Marriage

Marriage is the combination of two or more individuals who, once united, form close physical and emotional relations. Yet one should be careful not to confuse physical relations with love making, or emotional relations with love.

Today, the terms most often associated with marriage are *emotional love* and *sensual love*. In the 17th, 18th, and early 19th centuries, however, the idea of marriage did not exclusively hinge on sentimental compatibility. Instead, subjects such as work, social standing, wealth, and family and community consent each acted as a powerful factor in any attempt to distinguish an acceptable marriage from an unacceptable one. Thus the position of love as an idea related to marriage was not nearly as binding hundreds of years ago in Africa, colonial Australia, the North American colonial frontier, England, Japan, New England, and the sailing populations of the West as it is in the contemporary West.

A broad outline of the events leading up to, including, and following a marriage ceremony belonging to these bygone eras is fascinatingly similar to our own. However, a more focused analysis of these events suggests the degree to which various marital practices differed from one culture to the next and from our own. For instance, each of the cultures in this volume emphasized the importance of courtship—that is, some preliminary establishment of relations between the future spouses. Yet parents and family groupings were of particular importance during this early stage in the marital process. In Japan during the 18th century, go-betweens acting on behalf of samurai families determined the appropriateness of prospective spouses. The final decision to proceed with a samurai marriage rested on family reputations, wealth, social standing, and physical health. In colonial Australia, the government acted as a pseudo-family and encouraged the institution of marriage among its convict settlers in order to promote stability. Such considerations, which also surfaced in Africa, England, and colonial North America, always represented the unique beliefs and practices of the given society.

Following a successful courtship was the actual wedding, at which a symbolic union—sometimes religious, sometimes civil—would complete the courtship, transforming it into a new, more substantial, and more lasting association. In New England, colonists of the Puritan faith rejected weddings that entailed religious ceremony, preferring to avoid the association of both ornate ritual and earthly relations with holiness. Unlike civil marriages in New England, the Christian peoples of Kongo greatly valued religious unions, preferring to verify a couple's capacity to endure over several years before calling for a Christian wedding.

Finally, the topic of divorce, which is so familiar to Western cultures today, existed in all of the cultures discussed here. Indeed, these cultures prescribed resolutions to the dilemmas of separation and divorce on a number of social, political, and geographical levels. Yet divorces operated according to widely acknowledged conditions that varied from culture to culture. In England, these conditions received expression in Parliament, the approval of which was indispensable if a couple were to divorce. In other words, a dissatisfied husband and wife required the specific approval of the country's legislature, in the form of an act, to obtain a legal separation. Within Native American couples from certain tribes, divorce usually led to the expulsion of the wife from the tribe where her husband and she had been residing.

Sometimes, social and economic circumstances rather than personal incompatibility resulted in the separation of couples. The purchase and sale of slaves in colonial New England were responsible for the splitting of marriages. And men aboard ocean-going vessels could expect to remain out of touch with their wives for months. In fact, it was not unusual for whalers to be absent from their spouses for several years.

Similarities between our ideas about marriage and those of peoples who lived hundreds of years ago typically reside in a general reading of the sequential events related to marriage: courtship, wedding, divorce. However, the purpose of the following entries is centered on an articulation of the particular and unique characteristics of marriage customs in a host of distant cultures. Readers can discover for themselves the vast range of unexpected practices that, while reflecting perceptions of marriage in the past, have influenced our own today.

~Peter Seelig

FOR MORE INFORMATION

Quale, R. G. *A History of Marriage Systems*. Westport, Conn.: Greenwood Press, 1988.

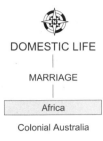

AFRICA

In Africa, marriage represented not simply an important personal relationship between two people but also a complex relationship between clans and among the members of the clan that had been married into. Whether the husband joined the wife's family or vice versa depended on a particular group's social structure, as did both the means by which people could get divorced and the fate of their children. Marriage often represented a lengthy process undertaken in stages over a period of years. Although single men were common, women were seldom unmarried, and except under exceptional circumstances, they had to have a male's protection at all times. Polygamy was therefore common, and the relationship among different wives formed an important part of a given family.

Throughout Africa, the marriage process began with the betrothal. Sometimes this event took place in early childhood, or even by informal agreement before children were born. In all cases, it was concluded soon after puberty. Children usually had no say in whom they were to marry, although in some cultures they did. Among the Yoruba of northern Nigeria, men often proposed through intermediaries, whose task it was to relay a proposal to the girl's parents. The girl's parents then investigated the prospective groom's character and background before taking the matter to a diviner. The diviner determined the prospects for a successful marriage, a key element of which was the number of children the couple would have. If the diviner gave his or her approval, it was considered rude to refuse a proposal, although there were ways.

Engagements often lasted for some time. Among the Bemba of modern Zambia, the groom would move in with the bride's parents for the different stages of the marriage process after a marriage received the blessing of the bride's parents and next of kin. The groom worked for them in order to earn his place in the bride's family. To advance a marriage, the groom had to compensate the bride's family for her work, as well as acquire the rights to her offspring from her clan. This obligation took the form of bridewealth, which, in eastern and southern Africa, people paid in cattle. In other areas, items of food or currency were used. Among the Yoruba, bridewealth was paid in three stages. The first came with the groom's first visit to the bride's parents after the engagement and consisted of kola nuts, yams, and logs for the fire. The second installment, called "love money," was paid before the third year after puberty, with the last, "wife money," coming at marriage. Frequently, the prospective son-in-law had to work for the bride's parents to prove his worth, helping them with farm chores and construction. Women had to avoid their fiancés throughout the course of the engagement.

One issue that arose during an engagement was the role of other wives in a polygamous family. Usually, one wife would have seniority over the others, and sometimes her role included finding other wives with whom to share her duties. Senior wives of the Yoruba played a key role as intermediaries during the required visits of the groom with the bride's parents. Among the different groups of southern Bantu, women could refuse to recognize other wives and force the husband to choose between them. A senior wife might also adopt a new one as a sort of mentor, instructing her in her new life.

Actual marriage rituals varied considerably, and there was typically a period following the marriage when it could be broken off if things did not work out. In Kongo, a prospective bride would have a house to herself where elder women would instruct her in a wife's duties. *Takula,* a red dye symbolizing transitions, played an important part of the rituals. One day, the new husband would send his bride *takula,* roasted chicken, and a needle to symbolize the aspects of her new life. A male relative would send *takula* and a cloth for the woman's loins. At the wedding feast, the bride would offer pieces of *takula* to her husband and parents and then leave the rest at a crossroads. If the couple remained happy after several years, they went to a priest for a Christian marriage. This was not done lightly, however, because of Christian beliefs that marriage should be permanent (Thornton, 82–85).

Women generally retained their own property after a marriage. This tradition led to an interesting situation among the nomadic Tuareg, who lived in the western Sahara. Tuareg women owned their own bed and tent. Shortly before her marriage, a woman's tent was made from a piece cut from that of her mother, and after marriage, the husband went to live there with his wife. According to custom, however, the woman had to join her husband's clan. Thus, after one year of marriage, the man's family came and staged a "surprise" raid on the woman's family, carrying off both the married couple and the tent (Brett and Fentress, 211).

An interesting case of women seeking to retain status as heads of household is "woman marriage," found especially in Dahomey. In these cases, women married younger women, thereby preserving their social status while fulfilling social requirements that they marry. The younger woman remained free to cohabit with the man of her choice. In many societies, marriage continued after death, and the wife either tended her husband's spirit or was inherited by his heirs (July, 110).

Married life varied from place to place, but women were seldom without protection for their rights. In Kongo, where men and women ate separately, women kept special lids for food dishes. If a woman developed a problem with her husband, she covered his food with the appropriate lid. Ideally, she waited until he had company, so that all knew of his shame. Among the Yoruba, women could leave their husbands for a variety of reasons, including a desire to marry another man. If that happened, the bridewealth was returned. Pleasing the in-laws also remained important. The custom of the Ngoni of southern Africa was that the husband had to avoid his mother-in-law for one year after marriage. At the end of that time, the wife cooked her first meal for her husband, and the mother-in-law shared the meal to show her approval of him (Cutrufelli, 45).

Marriage in Africa was an important part of the social landscape. People defined their status by how large their families were and hence by how much labor they could draw on. Men were the heads of households, and women shared in their spouse's status, but women used their own voices to contribute to the family group and in many areas enjoyed a fair degree of freedom. Both men and women had to follow established customs and were associated with given roles within society. Hence, African marriage ideally represented in some ways a partnership in which people joined together to fulfill certain roles in maintaining and reproducing the family group.

~Brian Ulrich

FOR MORE INFORMATION

Bascom, W. *The Yoruba of Southwestern Nigeria.* Prospect Heights, Ill.: Waveland Press, 1969.

Brett, M., and E. Fentress. *The Berbers.* Malden, Mass.: Blackwell, 1996.

Cutrufelli, M. R. *Women of Africa: Roots of Oppression.* Translated by Nicolas Romano. London: Zed Press, 1983.

Halsall, P., ed. *Internet African History Sourcebook.* 1996. <http://www.fordham.edu/halsall/africa/africasbook.html>, accessed October 23, 2003.

July, R. W. *A History of the African People.* 5th ed. Prospect Heights, Ill.: Waveland Press, 1998.

Thornton, J. K. *The Kongolese Saint Anthony.* Cambridge, England: Cambridge University Press, 1998.

COLONIAL AUSTRALIA

In Australia, which was ostensibly a penal settlement, the sexes were not physically segregated and the society was not a closed one, so the authorities quickly realized the futility of trying to prevent sexual activity. Marriage was thus encouraged among convicts as a means of introducing and maintaining stability. Married convicts could be assigned to each other to form a working family unit, and there is at least one case of the British government agreeing to an early request to pay the passage to New South Wales of the families of two convicts already in the colony.

British authorities offered material incentives to the unattached to encourage marriage. Single convicts were granted 30 acres for cultivation, married couples were given an additional 20 acres, and each child brought another 10. The major impediment to settling down was the gender imbalance in each of the three settlements, New South Wales, Norfolk Island, and Van Dieman's Land (established in 1803). Households containing a husband and wife were the exception rather than the norm. By 1806, only 25 percent of convict women were married, although many others were in stable relationships. Some couples of Catholic or Jewish faiths chose not to be married by Protestant ceremony.

Married life and the resulting families flourished on Norfolk Island, the satellite settlement established in March 1788. By 1791, Reverend Richard Johnson, on his brief visit to the island, had the unions of more than 100 couples formalized. Commandant Phillip King was very concerned to maintain "the harmony of . . . families." In 1794, the same gender imbalance that prevailed in Sydney Cove led to simmering tension between the male convicts and the military. The tension erupted into days of quarrel and riot, and during the subsequent investigation, King appeared to favor the families, provoking the anger of the soldiers. In the face of a possible mutiny, King returned some of the offending soldiers to Port Jackson and reported that they had disrupted convict settlers by "troubling their domestic quiet" (Bladen, 137).

After the wreck in 1790 of the supply ship *Sirius* in the treacherous Norfolk Island waters, another commandant, Robert Ross, decided to reduce the dependency on the public store by engineering family units, starting with marriage. Convicts received an acre of ground and a sow, with two free days to work the land, on condition that they live in groups of no fewer than three, including women and children. He exempted the women from most public work, provided that the males of the group maintain them. Not all women agreed with Ross's definition of family life, but those who left the farms in protest were likely to be punished.

Cohabitation was not confined to convicts, and many officers and officials lived openly with convict women, seeking comfort in family life. Perhaps the most notable instance of this phenomenon involved George Johnston, who arrived in the colony in 1788 as the marine's commander and began an association with Esther Abrahams. The relationship endured until his death in 1823. They had seven children, although they did not marry for 25 years. Some married officers began relationships and established families but abandoned them on leaving the colony.

Marriage, or at least cohabitation, clearly involved more than love. Social engineering in favor of boosting the material foundations of colonial Australia was at the heart of much coupling during the period.

~Valda Rigg

FOR MORE INFORMATION

Bladen, F., ed. *Historical Records of New South Wales.* Vols. 1, 2, and 6. Sydney: Government Printer, 1892. Facsimile edition, Marrickville: Southwood Press, 1978.

Frost, A. *Arthur Phillip 1738–1814: His Voyaging.* Melbourne: Oxford University Press, 1987.

National Library of Australia. *Australian History on the Internet.* <http://www.nla.gov.au/oz/histsite.html>, accessed October 23, 2003.

Robinson, P. *The Hatch and Brood of Time: A Study of the First Generation of Native-Born White Australians, 1788–1828.* Vol. 1. Melbourne, Australia: Oxford University Press, 1985.

Tench, W. *1788: Comprising A Narrative of the Expedition to Botany Bay [1789] and A Complete Account of the Settlement at Port Jackson [1795].* Edited by Tim Flannery. Melbourne: Text Publishing, 1996.

THE COLONIAL FRONTIER OF NORTH AMERICA

Among Native Americans and colonists alike, courtship and marriage balanced family and community expectations on the one hand with individual preferences on the other. Although both the Native Americans and the colonists typically regarded consent as important, if not necessary, rules with deep historical and cultural roots indicated the appropriateness or inappropriateness of a given marital arrangement. Families and, in particular, the parents of the prospective spouses exerted a forceful, although not unbreakable, influence over the likelihood of any marriage, and this influence was, more often than not, of an economic nature. When a marriage worsened, separation and divorce were two possible solutions.

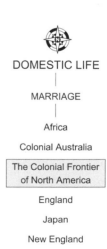

Although Native American parents arranged many marriages, the parties concerned do not appear to have been forced to marry without their consent. Nonetheless, tribal traditions dictated the existence of a formal courtship procedure. These customs seem to have differed from tribe to tribe but usually involved the giving of presents. Among the Algonquians, a prospective husband presented his intended with a trumpline, a kettle, and a firelog. These gifts were based on practical considerations and represented very little in the way of romance. The woman's acceptance of these gifts signified her acceptance of her role as a wife. The woman gave her intended husband only a bag of tobacco and sweet sumac leaves. As Indian men almost always had a pipe in their mouths or hands, the tobacco may have signified their position as husband.

Polygamy was common among many tribes. The Algonquians recognized two types of wives, one of which was subservient to the other. It was into this former class that many white women captives were placed if they married a warrior. In some tribes, blood relationship was scrupulously regarded. One did not marry a relative or a member of one's own clan. However, a widower might marry his dead wife's sister or some other female relation. A widow might be required to do the same thing with regard to her dead husband's brothers. If she had no children and was still young, however, she might be allowed to seek a husband elsewhere.

It would be a mistake to think that these concepts concerning matrimony were hard and fast rules. Many variations existed even within a single clan. Among the Iroquois, for instance, both polygamy and polyandry (many husbands for one woman) were practiced. In some nations, men had wives at every location where they hunted, yet some clans recognized marriages only among their members. Divorce was recognized in different ways. Couples might agree to stay together only as long as they were happy; others agreed to separate only for a good cause. A man who abandoned his wife might have to face retaliation from her relations, and a woman who left her husband for another man without both his consent and the approbation of the clan matrons could have a bad time of it. In this regard, the clan matrons served in place of a divorce court, deciding whether the cause warranted the separation.

Among colonists, marriage was presumed for all adult men and women. Communities feared that unmarried mothers would not be able to provide for themselves and would ultimately be a drain on the community. If pregnancy occurred outside of marriage, the couple could either wed or face the wrath of the community. Consequently, contemporary records show a remarkable number of "early-term births" six or seven months after their parents were married.

When it came to the selection of a wife, a man searched for a woman with a good temper and a virtuous demeanor. Certainly, a woman who was fair of face was desirable, but given the demographics of the time, good looks were most likely a secondary consideration. Men outnumbered women in 17th-century settlements, a situation that persisted into the 18th century and remained true even longer on the frontier.

Naturally, some men sought a woman who came with a dowry or an annual allowance. Such a quest might even receive support from a young man's family hoping to improve its own situation with a judicious union. Generally, once a woman married, all of her property and money came under the control of her husband.

When a man became interested in a woman, he had to move carefully, or he risked gossip and possibly legal action. Custom dictated that he speak to both the young woman's parents and his own in advance of any active courtship. Any disagreement between the young man and his parents over his selection of a bride-to-be often led to a polarization and family tensions. Usually, however, the only influence that his parents had over his actions was based on economics. Failure to select a young woman acceptable to his parents could prompt them to withhold a marriage gift or even to limit a future inheritance.

If the consent of a willing young woman's parents was not attained beforehand, the young man risked being brought into court for stealing the affections of their daughter. British colonial records reveal numerous instances of young men being fined for such offenses. If a young woman was of age, however, she could not legally be prevented from marrying her suitor. As with the young man, her parents' major weapon was financial.

Once married, a man was required to provide for his wife and children. A husband and wife might have labored together for the benefit of the entire family, but when financial hardship loomed, both the courts and the community looked to the husband to supply a remedy. In his 1712 sermon "The Well-Ordered Family," Benjamin Wadsworth reminds husbands of their divine mandate to "contrive prudently and work diligently that his Family, and his Wife particularly, may be well provided for."

This obligation continued through divorce, illegitimacy, and even after his death. Children born outside of wedlock were usually left unrecognized until their father's death, at which time they might be remembered in a will. However, many illegitimate children found themselves at odds with their legitimate siblings even when a favorable will was outstanding. The courts tended to uphold the rights, and desires, of the eldest legitimate son in most cases where there was friction between siblings over an estate.

The themes of courtship, consent, social procedure, family approval, and separation and divorce were common to both Native American and colonial marital practices (Volo and Volo, 43–44, 121–24).

FOR MORE INFORMATION

Berkin, C. *First Generations: Women in Colonial America.* New York: Hill, 1926.
Boorstin, D. J. *The Americans: The Colonial Experience.* New York: Random House, 1958.
Volo, J. M., and D. D. Volo. *Daily Life on the Old Colonial Frontier.* Westport, Conn.: Greenwood Press, 2002.

ENGLAND

Marriage in 18th-century England revealed a general preoccupation with courtship, weddings, and divorce. The social status of the families involved—in particular,

their wealth—was a principal factor in determining who married whom. However, parental control, physical and emotional attraction, and age each played an important role. Weddings were typically family and community affairs but could also be secret events. Naturally, not all marriages succeeded, and some were positively unbearable. When marriages failed, separations could be obtained, although often with great difficulty, through formal and informal means.

Marriage usually took place only when the courting couple could afford to set up house on their own, so the average age of marriage was relatively late, about 25 to 27. Moreover, 10 to 20 percent of the population never married.

Early in the century, people of property arranged marriages for their sons and daughters. It was common for families to decide on a union, haggle over the financial ramifications of the marriage, and then present it to the prospective bride and groom, who were given an opportunity to meet and to veto the match if they found it too distasteful. Typically, fathers of the potential bride offered, along with their daughters, a sum of money called a dowry to help the couple get started in life. By 1800, however, the dowry had lost some of its importance. Although parents still threatened to withdraw financial support for a son or daughter who married against their wishes, young people met at assemblies, balls, and spas, chose their own spouses, sometimes presented the choice to their parents for approval or veto, and then began a round of haggling over the financial settlements.

As the burden of choosing a spouse moved from parents to children, parents rushed to offer advice. Most authors agreed that looks were desirable and tempting but often misleading. The result was a confusing series of pronouncements. For instance, women were to learn how to dress well, walk well, and look pretty without seeming artificial, coquettish, provocative, or unduly concerned with fashion. There is ample evidence, however, that money continued to be a prime criterion in the choice of a spouse, rivaling sexual attraction for preeminence.

Below the middle class, most of the control over courtship remained, as it had always been, in the hands of the courting couple. There were no great estates to dispose of, no huge dowries to foster parental influence, and for the most part, less chaperonage, since both parties were likely to be out of the house and working by age 15 or 16. Couples met at fairs, in the workplace as fellow servants, or at church. Often, they were longtime acquaintances. In many cases, courtship was a prolonged affair.

The ideal wedding began with securing the community's permission to wed, in the form of obtaining a license or publishing the banns, in which an announcement of the wedding was read aloud on three successive Sundays at church. The couple then went to church, and a clergyman married them. In theory, the groom could be as young as 14 and the bride as young as 12, but usually they were about twice this age. The bride and groom recited their vows, and the groom gave the bride a ring. Grains of wheat were scattered for fertility, and pieces of the wedding cake were passed through the bride's ring and fed to the unmarried, that they might be married soon. Then there was as much festivity as the bride's family could afford. The guests kissed the bride, played practical jokes, sang obscene songs, danced, and ate.

After the ceremony and the feast, the bride and groom were escorted to their home and left alone to consummate the marriage, while, outside, the revelers sang dirty songs and shouted insinuations about what was going on in the bedroom.

In practice, not every wedding proceeded as just described. An informal contract marriage could help those wanting to circumvent parental objections, to avoid the embarrassments of banns or of drunken guests, or to spare the expense of an official license and certificate.

For those who needed a more official ceremony, there was the clandestine marriage, considered binding by both church and state. A typical clandestine marriage offered speed, economy, and secrecy and involved neither a license nor a church setting. No banns were proclaimed, a clergyman read a standard service, and usually no license was issued. By the 1740s, perhaps as many as 15 to 20 percent of marriages were conducted clandestinely.

In 1753, Lord Chancellor Hardwicke pushed a marriage act through Parliament that banned contract and clandestine marriages once and for all. A legal marriage had to be performed in church with banns or a license and parental consent for any party under the age of 21.

The act contained several loopholes. The most colorful loophole, as it turned out, was the Scottish one. Scotland, the marriage and inheritance customs of which differed from England's, was exempted entirely from the act. Because one peculiar clause in the act made a false statement of place of residence legal on a marriage license, a man and woman desperate to be married could sneak away to Scotland, lie about being residents of the parish, and be married quietly far from home.

The most typical attitude toward marriage evinced in 18th-century literature and visual art is one of sly, collegial misery. Shrewish wives and oafish husbands are a dime a dozen. One author compares jail favorably to marriage, noting that while he was in the Bridewell, he was untroubled by the demands of his "freakish wife" and "lawless brats." A similarly bitter tone can be found in the works of female authors.

The Marriage Ceremony Performed in Mr. B's Own Chapel (Pamela Is Married), by Joseph Highmore, engraved by Antoine Benoist, 1745. Notice the servant in the background making an informal visit to the proceedings. © Tate Gallery, London/Art Resource, NY.

Women could ask for a separation on the grounds of cruelty, although the suit could be denied if they had offered any provocation, disobedience, or bad temper at any time in the marriage. Divorce was possible by private act of Parliament, but getting such an act passed could be difficult, time consuming, and expensive; this method was therefore reserved for the very rich and very determined. Only 13 such divorces were granted between 1700 and 1749. Successful petitions never exceeded 10 per year. Once a divorce was granted, both parties were free to remarry.

Either as a prelude to a divorce petition or as an end in itself, some couples sought a judicial separation from an ecclesiastical court or drafted a private separation agreement themselves. Both types of separation, while not allowing the partners to re-marry, did get them into separate houses. Divorce would not become a legal alternative for the majority until 1857. In the meantime, the working classes found their own ways around the law. Some, often with the community's tacit consent, moved apart and took up with new partners. If community approval was not forth-coming, some unsatisfied spouses simply abandoned their old families and contracted bigamous marriages in other towns. Bigamy was, until the 1790s, a hanging offense.

Marriage, then, was a complicated arrangement, and courtship, not to mention the wedding and the marriage itself, easily became a source of conflict. For the well-off, social and family concerns over a potential marriage often overshadowed the physical and emotional attraction of the individuals to be married. Material concerns also affected the decisions of the not so wealthy. Whatever the type of wedding (and, in some cases, the type of separation), marriage was a standard and basic way for individuals both to associate and to survive in society (Olsen, 31, 35–41, 43–47).

To read about marriage in Chaucer's England, see the Europe entry in the section "Marriage" in chapter 2 ("Domestic Life") of volume 2 of this series.

FOR MORE INFORMATION

Lynch, J. *Eighteenth Century Resources.* <http://newark.rutgers.edu/~jlynch/18th/>, accessed October 10, 2003.
Olsen, K. *Daily Life in 18th-Century England.* Westport, Conn.: Greenwood Press, 1999.
Sense and Sensibility. Directed by Ang Lee. Videocassette, 1995.
Stone, L. *Road to Divorce: A History of the Making and Breaking of Marriage in England.* Oxford: Oxford University Press, 1995.

JAPAN

As in the feudal West, marriage in 18th-century Japan was not viewed as the union of two people in love or even as a permanent monogamous estate. Marriage was a social combination of two corporations (usually called families). All in all, it was a legal arrangement for goals other than emotional or sexual gratification. The selection of a spouse, weddings, divorces, and even widowhood reflected social pre-rogatives rather than sentimental ones.

In Japan, as in many societies, "trial" marriages were fairly common. Prospective brides came to live with the family of the boy, and some sexual experimentation was allowed, with the general understanding that if pregnancy resulted, the wedding ceremony would follow immediately. Commonly, the young girl served the patriar-chal family as a servant for a year until her first menstrual period at about age 13 or 14. If the arrangement did not suit both parties, then the girl would return home and could be betrothed and married to another without any stigma resulting from the loss of virginity.

In the countryside in particular, social standards did not place much stock in bridal virginity and accorded young people some premarital license. Of greatest importance was proven fecundity, namely, pregnancy. The purpose of marriage, after all, was the production of children and therefore of heirs. Among the samurai (warrior administrators), however, more attention was paid to chastity before marriage, and prospective brides could be and sometimes were rejected if they were not virgins.

Among peasants, the only ceremony was the traditional *sansankudo* (three sips from three cups), which is descriptive of the simple ritual. The bride and groom exchanged three thimble-size sake (rice wine) cups in turn, which were consumed in three sips each. Upon completion of this public ceremony, the couple was considered married, and everyone at the wedding then celebrated the union with food and drink.

Among samurai and some *chōnin* (city folk) of substance, the ritual extended to a week of ceremony. A go-between made the actual match after investigating each prospective family's history, financial standing, social reputation, and even the possibility of some hereditary disease. The go-between acted as guarantor should either family be displeased after the wedding.

If both parties were agreeable, a betrothal was announced and there would be an exchange of gifts, since both dowry and bride-price were common in Japan, depending on the relative social and economic station of the respective families. Sometimes the gifts were converted to actual money. The samurai upper-class *sansankudo* took place in the same fashion as did the simple peasant wedding.

Commonly, the bride wore a white kimono, as well as a peculiar triangular hat that was supposed to hide the "horns of jealousy," white being the color of death and mourning. The color symbolized that, with regard to her natal family, the bride had died. To assure everyone of that symbolism, the bride's name was blotted out of the *koseki* (family register) and then was entered into that of her husband's *koseki*. Such a ceremony was commonly performed on the third day after the marriage and was called "returning home," when she was formally received in her natal home as a guest. Of course, if the husband-to-be was about to be adopted into his wife's household (in order to avoid a concentration of land in his father's family), all of the wedding rituals were altered, since the bride was to remain at home.

In those cases, when a young man married and brought his wife not to his natal family's home but to hers, the wife's father would "retire" from the active headship of the *ie* (household). Symbolically, the previous head and his wife would move out of the main room of the house, exchanging rooms with the new head and his new wife. Thus, the bride's family adopted its daughter's husband as the family scion. Most often, the young man assumed the name of his wife's family, but sometimes a conflation of both names was allowed. A Yamamoto adopted into the Matsumura family, for example, could become a Yamamatsu.

Many people were never allowed to marry. This method of birth control reduced the number of excess children who could not inherit. Only one son per peasant household was allowed to take a wife. All others were forbidden to marry unless they could provide their own land. Some did this by marrying women whose parents did not have sons. The young man would be adopted into his in-laws' household and bear their name. Young women who did not marry often joined the ranks of servant girls or of prostitutes and geisha (female servant-entertainers).

At this time, any remaining sibling in the house would move out as well. Obviously, this was a rupture in the old social order, one that was not taken lightly.

In Japan, divorce was possible without the attendant social and economic catastrophes that characterized it in other societies, such as China. Men could divorce their wives relatively easily and on very minor pretexts. Incompatibility characterized most grounds for divorce in 18th-century Japan, including such problems as the new bride being "lazy," too talkative, or inconsiderate, but most of all, "childless." What this really meant was that she had not given birth to a boy within a reasonable time (usually two years). She was then unceremoniously returned to her natal family. The fact that any dowry had to be returned with her often served as a deterrent to divorce.

Because children were the property of the household patriarchy, a divorced woman returned to her natal household without them. But being childless, she was unencumbered and could therefore be married off relatively easily. More commonly, returned wives were sold into concubinage or prostitution.

Not surprisingly, it was more difficult for women to divorce their husbands. If her natal family was more prominent than her husband's family, however, the divorce became much easier. A woman could divorce a husband who had gone insane, who had become a criminal, or more rarely, who abused her or the children. Also, there was a little-used escape at Kamakura. Since 1285, the Zen temple of Tokei-ji was known as the "divorce temple" because wives who could abscond there received sanctuary. If they remained cloistered there for three years (later reduced to two years), then the *bakufu* (Japan's national military government) would grant them a divorce. Still, only rarely did more than 20 or 30 women take refuge in the temple at any given time.

Childless widows could and did remarry. Widows with children had to remain in the households of their deceased husbands if they wanted to remain with their children. Among the *chōnin* and peasantry, divorce and widow remarriage were much more common than within the samurai class. Scarcely a rural village existed that did not contain several women who had been married more than once.

A marriage in 18th-century Japan revealed the degree to which social stability and material welfare dominated thinking not only among peasants but also within the ranks of the samurai and *chōnin* (Perez, 241, 254–56).

To read about family life in Japan in the 20th century, see the Japan entry in the section "Family Life" in chapter 2 ("Domestic Life") of volume 6 of this series.

FOR MORE INFORMATION

Dunn, C. J. *Everyday Life in Traditional Japan.* Tokyo: Tuttle, 1969.

Japan Information Network. <http://www.jinjapan.org/index.html>, accessed October 23, 2003.

Perez, L. G. *Daily Life in Early Modern Japan.* Westport, Conn.: Greenwood Press, 2002.

NEW ENGLAND

A look at courtship and marriage in colonial New England reveals that they were not different in most ways from traditional practices in England at the time but that

they were markedly different from those of our own time. The entire process followed a rather fixed series of events: a contract showing intent to marry; a public announcement of the contract, called a publishing of the banns; the marriage ceremony; and a celebration following the ceremony. In the event of a failed marriage, divorce was possible. Marriage between New England slaves was markedly different from marriages between whites, and Native Americans living in the New England region also maintained a unique set of marital customs.

With few exceptions (as in the case of a few powerful chiefs), marriages among native peoples were monogamous. Intermarriage within the greater family was strongly discouraged, and there is ample evidence, in tributes and the frequent refusal to remarry after a mate died, that these unions were often strong and affectionate. Divorce, however, was not forbidden or unknown. Usually, the dissolution of an unsuccessful union was accommodated when the female left her husband and joined another village. Family planning was enabled with the use of plants consumed to prevent conception or cause abortion.

In colonial New England, young unmarried men and women did not pair off to socialize with one another just for the pleasure of each other's company. Instead, a man typically arranged to pay a visit to the young woman's house only after talking the matter over with his father, who may have suggested the visit after consultation with the young woman's parents. In some cases, the two fathers discussed the details of the marriage for months before the two young people even had a first conversation with each other.

Parents whose children were of different social classes did not broach a discussion of marriage. Just as it was imperative to remain in the station to which God had placed one, so was it equally imperative to marry someone of the same class. Because no one could marry without parental permission, and because one could run away with one's forbidden beloved only to a lonely and dangerous wilderness, elopements of "star-crossed" sweethearts of different classes seem to have been rare in New England.

It was hoped and understood that love or affection would follow the meeting of two prospective colonial spouses. The courtship leading up to the contract consisted of business discussions over the exact property contributions that the families of the bride and groom would contribute to the marriage. The father of the groom often deeded a portion of his land to the couple and sometimes agreed to build a house for them on the land.

A marriage contract, once drawn up and signed, was as legally binding as any other contract regarding property. Any attempt to withdraw from the contract could result in litigation over a breach of contract.

The publication of the banns, announcing that the marriage contract had been made, is today similar to placing an engagement announcement in a local paper. For the colonial New Englander, the publication of the banns was an absolute requirement, without which the marriage could not take place. One effect of this tradition was to thwart clandestine marriages, which might allow one of the marriage partners either to evade his or her marital responsibilities or even to attempt a bigamous marriage.

The courtship following the espousal was often a critical period when the prospective husband and wife who knew little of each other were expected to learn to be fond of each other. Although sex between espoused couples was not officially approved of, it was sometimes condoned.

Unlike the Catholic Church and the Church of England, the Puritans of New England did not regard marriage as a sacrament or holy ceremony. Thus, these colonists legally prohibited ministers from performing marriage ceremonies, which were, instead, the responsibility of public officials—magistrates. Not until 1686, with the loss of the charter and the interference in colonial life by the British Crown, were ministers allowed to perform ceremonies.

In keeping with its secular nature, the wedding ceremony usually took place in the house of the bride rather than in church. The ceremony seemed to avoid the formal nature of repeated vows that are customary in ceremonies today. Instead, the gathering was informal and often consisted of the spontaneous remarks of the guests regarding marriage and the couple. The groom's family paid for the wedding feast.

Although the guests expected alcoholic drinks to be served at any wedding feast, presumably little or no toasting of the bride or groom took place: that ritual was an officially despised practice because it was regarded as an impetus to heavy drinking and drunkenness. There was probably also no dancing, which was frowned on and even outlawed in "public houses," that is, in inns and taverns.

Despite the success of many colonial marriages, some of them were unhappy and ended in annulment or divorce, both of which were legal in colonial New England. The legal termination of a marriage could occur when it was discovered that the couple's marriage was not legal in the first place or when one or the other partner failed to live up to the marriage contract.

Records show that divorces cut across class lines and that, although Massachusetts had no divorce laws as such, between 1639 and 1692 it granted at least 27 divorces, 13 of them for desertion or adultery. The Plymouth colony granted six divorces, five of them for adultery.

In the south, marriage between slaves was not legalized or formalized, but New Englanders encouraged marriage between slaves. Slave couples got acquainted at church meetings, socials such as house raisings, and holidays celebrated on the village common. Courtship was convenient for a couple who shared the same master, for the couple could visit with each other whenever there was a lull in work. But with so few slaves being employed on a single farm, the likelihood of this happening was remote. If a couple living at different locations fell in love, the man had to obtain a pass to pay court to the woman at her master's house.

Before the wedding of two slaves took place, the masters of both the man and the woman had to agree to the union and also arrive at a prenuptial agreement, settling matters such as ownership and support of any child. After these matters were settled, banns were published, and a ceremony was performed (usually in the living room of one of the masters), followed by a wedding feast.

Many factors, each related to one another, formed a network of rules and customs according to which Native Americans, Europeans, and slaves in colonial New England each entered into the institution of marriage (Johnson, 109–12, 115–16, 134, 152).

FOR MORE INFORMATION

Johnson, C. D. *Daily Life in Colonial New England*. Westport, Conn.: Greenwood Press, 2002.
Koehler, L. *A Search for Power: The "Weaker Sex" in Seventeenth-Century New England*. Urbana: University of Illinois Press, 1980.

LIFE AT SEA

Marriage between a sailor and a woman entailed a number of unique and harsh realities. Both partners often had to endure extended periods of loneliness, as the husband went out to sea while the wife remained on land. In some cases, wives joined their husbands aboard merchant and naval vessels, but this life lacked normalcy and ease, as well. A sailor-husband and his wife also had to concern themselves with the uncertainties of pay, the threat of poverty, and the dangers that press gangs posed not only for unlucky seamen but also for their wives.

A seaman's wife had to endure a life of loneliness and uncertainty. Naval wives tolerated months of prolonged absence from their husbands, but merchant seamen's wives often had to resign themselves to marital separation for a year or more. The wife of a whaling captain, however, was one of exceptional trial. As the economics of whaling demanded larger and larger ships, which drew men farther away from their homes, the voyages became extremely lengthy, lasting four or five years.

It was not unusual for whaling families to have three or four children, each the interval of a whaling voyage apart. Many a man set sail an expectant father only to return years later to learn that his child had died at age two or three, never knowing the comfort of the father's strong embrace or basking in the warmth of his loving smile. Couples who had been married 10 years could count their time together in months. An 18th-century gravestone on Martha's Vineyard stoically paints the picture of a couple both dead after less than a year of marriage, she in childbirth and he at sea.

In some coastal New England towns, widowhood and separation while the men were on voyage created populations that were largely female. At one point in time on Nantucket, women outnumbered men four to one. Women ran the shops, kept their husband's books, and marketed the exotic goods in which their absent spouse dealt. So ubiquitous was the presence of women in business that the main street of commerce was nicknamed "Petticoat Row."

Yet some women wanted a more normal life. They wanted to live in a home with their husbands, no matter how abnormal that home might be. Recalling the time her husband was away on a cruise, one wife wrote, "At home though it appeared to some I knew no sorrow then, alas they could not see my feelings nor will they ever know of the many bitter hours I have experienced."

Nonetheless, life aboard ship could be very lonely for captains' wives. Most men enjoyed their wife's company for a stroll on deck, and many showed their wives how to take readings and other elements of navigation. There were, however, long periods of time when the captain's attention was entirely consumed by the running of the ship.

It was important for a wife to be present when her husband was paid. Seamen's wages seldom amounted to much, and they were quickly exhausted. Even if a wife did get some of her spouse's pay before he spent it, it was not likely to last for very long unless there was a good deal of prize money to be distributed.

As for a seaman's pay in the navy, the usual practice aboard a man-of-war was to pay the crew just before they sailed. During the 18th century, the British navy provided a means by which men might remit the money to their families through government agents. A man had only to sign a simple legal instrument naming the beneficiary of his remittances. These legislated policies had the advantage of making naval service more attractive to married men.

The number of impoverished seamen's families was an oppressive presence in most seaport towns. Supplementing the pittance they received from their husbands was not easy for most wives. Women of this period were generally prohibited from participating in many of the exclusively male trades that paid well. Domestic service offered the most possibilities for women, but there were always few open positions. Those who resorted to begging could be arrested, jailed, and whipped for the offense.

Economic conditions in English seaports were so bad that some seamen's wives resorted to prostitution to avoid exposing their children to the dangers of the workhouses, where infant mortality among children under one year of age ran as high as 70 percent. Once a wife and any child were transported home, their prospects were not much better unless they had relatives who could provide for them or assist them in finding work.

The numerous seaport towns of England making up the greater Portsmouth and Plymouth areas were deluged with a destitute population, seamen's families, owing its status to British naval practice. The demands for crews to man British ships drove press gangs into coastal towns, "pressing" men into naval service. During the height of the seamen shortage (1803–15), press gangs went so far as to intercept merchant ships returning to port and siphon off their most experienced seamen to serve in the navy without ever stepping on dry land. Some men simply disappeared until word was sent from the processing ships to their distraught families.

This cruel system left many women and children in the most desperate of situations. Wives seldom knew when their husbands would return. Even if they did, seamen had no right to shore leave, and getting to the ship was not easy for a family without the resources to pay for transportation.

Separation, loneliness, awkward circumstances, poverty, and impressments constituted the greatest hardships that sailor-husbands and their wives and families endured. Yet at least one marriage of the period resulted from these very difficulties. An 1802 London journal contained an interesting report of a marriage between two sailors. The couple "had been old shipmates . . . during most part of the war, where the lady bore a most conspicuous part in the different actions in which the frigate was engaged. She was always an attendant in the surgeon's department and waited upon Jones (the bridegroom) in his wounded state. An attachment took place which ended in their union" (Volo and Volo, 24–25, 110, 159–61).

FOR MORE INFORMATION

Stark, S. J. *Female Tars: Women aboard Ship in the Age of Sail.* Annapolis, Md.: Naval Institute Press, 1996.

Volo, D. D., and J. M. Volo. *Daily Life in the Age of Sail.* Westport, Conn.: Greenwood Press, 2002.

Men and Women

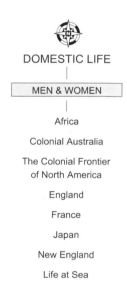

In this section, the focus is on the roles of men and women, from the 17th century into the 19th century, in Africa, colonial Australia, the North American colonial frontier, England, France, Japan, New England, and Western seagoing cultures. Each entry provides an indication of the similarities and differences that mark cultures off from one another. On the other hand, cross-cultural similarities in gender roles provoke more questions than they do answers.

One fundamental distinction that repeatedly surfaces in the following entries concerns public versus private spheres. The public sphere includes, but is not limited to, outdoor work, commerce, government, and law. In contrast, the private sphere chiefly relates to domestic affairs—activities occurring in and around the household and away from places and positions of open (though not at all unrestricted) activity.

In the cultures discussed here, men tended to dominate the public sphere, and women preponderated in the private sphere, while significant overlap and exceptions blurred the public-private opposition without effectively contradicting it.

There are numerous examples of culturally specific gender roles that divided along public and private lines. In 18th-century England, respectable women were increasingly enjoined to stay at home and practice "feminine arts" that included music, drawing, and needlework. Those women who, out of economic necessity, had to find work were socially and materially penalized for their efforts, insofar as they failed to conform to norms of respectability and typically received poorer wages than men for the same work performed. In France, the level and type of education that were available to women became—in part, a result of the promptings of the Enlightenment—a matter of intense debate.

Western oceanic exploration during these centuries provides a glaring example of the public-private distinction. The men aboard ship, be they officers or common seamen, frequently treated women as a collective nuisance, relegating them to their husband's quarters or to the orlop deck below the waterline, where they remained hidden and cut off from the official and essential tasks that men assumed elsewhere on the ship.

A similarly disproportionate presence of men in the public sphere characterized African, colonial Australian, colonial North American, French, and Japanese societies. And yet the patterns of belief and practices that set men apart from women varied significantly, depending on the culture. Take agricultural work, for example. In England, men usually sowed seeds and harvested crops, whereas certain African societies assigned the tasks of sowing seeds and harvesting crops to women.

Despite the occurrence of notable and even surprising cross-cultural variations in the gender roles of men and women, it is difficult to lose sight of the prevailing division of such roles along public and private lines. Perhaps a longing to explore not only forbidden lifestyles but also the possibilities of the self prompted a few women to affect a transformation of their gender—women such as Mary Lacy, who, under the pseudonym of William Chandler, inhabited the distinctly masculine role of a sailor on the high seas for more than a decade. Although tension existed between conformity and deviance in public and private spheres, the influence of existing gender-related standards remained inescapable for most. Consequently, situating a person's daily life at a specific time and place is key to any profound exploration of the roles of men and women in society.

~*Peter Seelig*

FOR MORE INFORMATION

Kent, S., ed. *Gender in African Prehistory*. Walnut Creek, Calif.: AltaMira Press, 1998.
Veyne, P., ed. *A History of Private Life*. Vols. 1 and 2. Cambridge, Mass.: Harvard University Press, 1987.

DOMESTIC LIFE
|
MEN & WOMEN
|

Africa

Colonial Australia

The Colonial Frontier
of North America

England

France

Japan

New England

Life at Sea

AFRICA

In Africa, men and women had separate roles in all aspects of life. However, these roles often had equal importance in the maintenance of families and communities. At the same time, women often possessed fewer rights than men in the political and legal arenas, and in many areas they had no identity other than those of daughter, wife, or mother. Women's greatest importance came in areas where they played key roles as religious or spiritual figures, positions from which they could exercise as much actual power as the generally male political leaders. At the level of the individual household, people considered men to be the primary authority figures, although women were not entirely without protection and power of their own.

All Africans remained bound in important respects to the lineage of their birth. In patrilineal societies, male relatives became the permanent core of the family, while in matrilineal ones, women took on that role, and men joined the women's family. Marriage remained less important than lineage and often represented a form of negotiation between the spouses. Within a given marriage, however, men retained a dominant role. Even in cultures wherein women could initiate divorce, it usually remained easier for men to do so, especially because women were economically dependent on their husbands. Whereas in matrilineal societies women could draw on the immediate support of female relatives, men had the power to initiate sex and control their immediate family, and both men and women considered beating an acceptable punishment for wives who failed in their duties. In some areas, genital mutilation robbed women of their sexuality. Among the Yao people of the Lake Malawi area, an example of a matrilineal society, men mediated disputes and sought to serve the interests of their female relatives, with women determining by their allegiance which uncle or brother possessed the greatest influence (Hay and Stichter, 77).

Families also divided work according to sex, with the males generally performing those tasks that required the most demanding physical labor. Education by age was gender specific and geared toward the tasks that children would perform during their adult lives in their society. In some areas, men cleared the fields whereas women cultivated and harvested the crops. In other areas, men performed such farm labor while women engaged in making crafts and food preparation. Men usually defended and acquired new land, sometimes through military means. In some parts of Africa, women engaged in trade; in other areas this responsibility fell to the men. In the Niger valley, men held certain jobs, such as blacksmiths, but only women of certain lineages could become potters. Thus, although one cannot deny the importance of women as producers of more labor, both men and women made crucial contributions to the work that was necessary for the sustenance of the community.

Division by sex also applied to the realm of government and social organization. Among the hunting-and-gathering societies of central and southern Africa, women took charge of getting water, small animals, and berries, as well as of caring for children. Men handled larger hunting projects. In West Africa, women often had control of whatever constituted their affairs in society, be it trade, agriculture, crafts, or something else. Among the Yoruba, one woman who sat on the king's council held responsibility for all women's matters in a kingdom, whereas other societies had both parallel and equal governing structures for men and women.

Under certain circumstances, women had authority over men. Among the Kom people of modern Cameroon, for example, the women of a community meted out *anlu*, one of the most feared penalties. *Anlu* served as a punishment for men who insulted their parents, beat a pregnant woman, caused a woman to become pregnant in fewer than two years after her last childbirth, committed incest, abused an elderly woman, or unfairly attacked someone's genitals in a fight. When people were abused in this manner, they let out a high-pitched call, which the women of the village echoed before they came to help. The accused pleaded his case before the head woman of a compound, who then discussed the matter with female elders. Some men accepted a fine and apology as punishment. For those who did not, the women gathered around the man's compound, danced and mocked the offender, defecated and urinated in his water containers, and pelted him with stones and fruit. Most men admitted defeat after several weeks of such treatment. If the women accepted the man's pleas for mercy, he was bathed naked in a stream to purify him and was given food. Otherwise, he had to leave the community. Men could not appeal the verdicts of women in such matters (Hay and Stichter, 167).

Men served as the rulers of most African states, but exceptions did exist. One of the greatest rulers of the 17th century was the woman Anna de Sousa Nzingha. In 1623, Nzingha negotiated a peace treaty that ended decades of war between her homeland of Ndongo, in modern Angola, and Portugal. When she succeeded her brother as ruler the following year, however, she began protesting Portuguese violations of the treaty, made Ndongo a refuge for escaped slaves, and encouraged Africans to rebel against Portuguese control. In 1626, she was deposed and replaced by a Portuguese puppet. Undaunted, she fled to the nearby kingdom of Matamba, conquered it about 1630, and continued to wage war against Portugal until a new treaty was signed in 1656. To this end, she made an alliance with the Dutch, an agreement that was the first of its kind between an African and European power.

Both men and women wielded influence through religion, as well. Male and female priests were found throughout Africa, as were male and female spirit mediums. In Muslim areas, women could become religious scholars and mystics, although they could not rise to the most prestigious positions in the religious or political establishments. Many feared that certain women were practitioners of witchcraft.

Both men and women in Africa played important roles in society, with the exact division of responsibilities depending on the society. Men and women performed important work inside and outside the home and played a role in decision making for the community. People's responsibilities in life depended largely on their sex and on the specific conceptions that each tribe held in relation to maleness and femaleness. The distribution of these gender roles affected everything from childhood tasks and education to the councils and powers one acquired as an adult. During their old age, both men and women could, before the respectful gaze of the community, look back upon a constructive and consequential life.

To read about women in Africa in the 20th century, see the Africa entry in the section "Women" in chapter 2 ("Domestic Life") of volume 6 of this series.

~Brian Ulrich

FOR MORE INFORMATION

Cutrufelli, M. R. *Women of Africa: Roots of Oppression*. Translated by N. Romano. London: Zed Press, 1983.

Halsall, P., ed. *Internet African History Sourcebook*. 1996. <http://www.fordham.edu/halsall/africa/africasbook.html>, accessed October 23, 2003.

Hay, M. J., and S. Stichter, eds. *African Women South of the Sahara*. 2nd ed. New York: Longman, 1995.

Kent, S., ed. *Gender in African Prehistory*. Walnut Creek, Calif.: AltaMira Press, 1998.

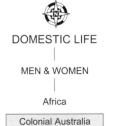

COLONIAL AUSTRALIA

Because all males in colonial Australia were part of an exclusively penal society, constant regulation blurred the distinction between public and private life. Freeman and prisoner alike functioned domestically under the continuing gaze or scrutiny of authority, although not always under strict regulation.

Of the 213 male officials who arrived with the First Fleet, only 27 had wives with them, and the ratio was 548 male convicts to 188 female convicts. There were several different European male groups in the settlement—convicts, emancipated convicts, and later, free settlers, military men, their officers, and government officials. Men's roles were defined by their place within these groups.

The major role of the first 548 male convicts in Port Jackson and Norfolk Island (9 male convicts were sent there on February 15, 1788) centered on work both for the public good and for the atonement of their crimes, and this tenet pervaded their domestic life. On their arrival in January 1788, the convicts' immediate and urgent task was to establish shelters and stores for the population. Work gangs were formed from which the convicts could select their own overseer. The gangs undertook jobs such as rush cutting, shingle making, and road building. Because many of these men were from urban slums and had few vocational skills, the initial settlement suffered from a critical short-

On the eve of their forced departure to Botany Bay in Australia, these two male convicts are bidding farewell to their English sweethearts. Unknown, an5577509. Rex Nan Kivell Collection, National Library of Australia.

age of artisans for the public building work required. However, by June, Watkin Tench could report in his journal that thatched or shingled storehouses and a hospital, even though temporary, were finished, while military barracks and many huts were nearing completion. Still, Governor Phillip had to write in July to the Home Office in England, requesting the urgent dispatch of male bricklayers and carpenters.

Establishing a reliable food source was also paramount, and men began clearing and felling the heavily wooded shorelines. Fish being an accessible food source, some men occupied their time with fishing duties. The commencement of vegetable gardens and crop fields was of the utmost importance, and many men were put to work hoeing and digging, but the combination of inadequate and inappropriate tools and the lack of agricultural experience hindered their efforts.

"Returns of Labour" at Sydney, Parramatta, and Toongabbie in 1797 and 1799 show men employed in myriad roles that included wheelwrights, shipwrights, watchmen, tailors, shoemakers, blacksmiths, coppersmiths, cutlers, coopers, sawyers, masons, laborers, a few elderly men as hut keepers, and an executioner. Although many of these men were ostensibly prisoners, they were not imprisoned and they received pay for their work. Provided they worked diligently at their tasks, these laborers could spend some of their own time either working their own small farms or hiring their labor to others. Not all administrators favored the task system. In 1800, Paterson described the system to Viscount Castlereagh as "an irredeemable evil" because it allowed efficient workers more time to make their own profits than to contribute to public labor, while the indolent and inefficient did not exert themselves for the public good.

Most convicts were encouraged to establish their own small farms, and paroled men (those with a "ticket of leave") could lease, or acquire through grant, land for cultivation. Along with free settlers, many convicts were involved in the small-scale farming of food and cash crops and in the raising of livestock. Cases existed of women gaining land, but these women were not thought capable of performing hard labor.

Four companies of marines comprising 213 men arrived in 1788. Those who brought their wives or who selected female convicts enjoyed the comforts of domestic life, while convict servants attended to others.

The marines left the colony in 1791 and were replaced by a specifically formed regiment, the New South Wales Corps. Although many of its officers also dedicated themselves to personal commercial ventures, the military played a major part in countering outbreaks of convict dissent and Aboriginal resistance to white encroachment. After the transportation to New South Wales of many of the 1798 Irish rebels, the government used the corps to implement suppression during several periods of suspicion that centered on, sometimes without merit, this particular convict population. It was ruthlessly effective in quelling a serious uprising of mostly Irish convicts at Castle Hill (sometimes known as Vinegar Hill) in 1804. The corps was recalled in 1809 because of the officers' role in the illegal usurpation of Governor Bligh in 1808.

> ### 📷 Snapshot
>
> **The First Fleet of Convicts to Australia**
>
> The First Fleet, which transported convicts from England to Australia, arrived at its destination in January 1788. Among the passengers were
>
> • Long, William, First Mate, fell into the sea at Portsmouth and was saved
> • Read, Ann, drank mercury instead of water and fell ill
> • Hill, Henry, sailor, jumped ship at Rio
> • Squires, Second Mate, caught sleeping with convict women
>
> Of the 1,350 people aboard the fleet's 11 ships, 48 died during the eight-month voyage. (King, 1, 26)

Over two decades, men were government officials, including Governors Phillip, Hunter, King, Bligh, and Macquarie, as well as Administrators Grose, Paterson, Johnston, and Foveaux, all of whom exercised ultimate authority. Other official roles for men included the judge advocate, the magistrates who presided over minor offences and made sentences, surgeons, and a handful of ministers, priests, and chaplains. It was in these roles, not available to women, that men were expected to implement the mechanics for the maintenance of public order and welfare.

During the period 1788–1810, men outnumbered women by almost 10 to 1, and this numerical inequality, in addition to the authorities' perception of women, was a limiting factor in women's roles. Although the seamlessness that women experienced between the public and domestic spheres was similar to that of men, it was women who were usually assigned to domestic roles.

At the outset, the first governor, Arthur Phillip, realized the difficulties of the gender imbalance. In May 1788, he wrote England stating that it was "absolutely necessary" to send more women to the colony. However, by June 1790, although conceding that women (and children) were "undoubtedly necessary," he claimed that women were a "deadweight" on the more productive male workers. Even in 1810, the enlightened Macquarie was still claiming that women in the colony were a "drawback."

This view surfaces repeatedly in official sources, written by males, and few documented female voices exist to illuminate women's roles from their own perspectives. One administrator, Paterson, claimed that while London and Irish women were "depraved and abandoned," some women from the English counties were "making themselves very useful . . . in domestic concerns and rearing stock" (Bladen, vol. 6, 150). It was in these domestic and nurturing roles that women, according to the authorities, were considered to be most useful. In 1806, Governor King stated that although 1,216 of the colony's 1,412 women were doing no public labor, their domestic labor was "providing for their families" and saving expense on the public purse.

One of the first tasks allocated to women was the collection of shells, which were to be ground for lime, but this task was soon given to men. Women were then ordered into cooking, sweeping, laundry work, light clearing, and making shingles and pegs for housing. As in Sydney, the women of Norfolk Island were assigned to remove the ever-present grubs from struggling crops.

As subsequent fleets arrived, men were permitted to select women as wives and partners before the women even disembarked from their ships and regardless of the women's choice. This unofficial practice was not ended until 1810, on instruction from the Home Office. Those few who were left without male partners and "protectors" were designated as hut keepers to guard against daytime robbery or were ordered to make men's clothing. In 1790, Watkin Tench observed that all of the 50 women in the Rose Hill settlement were employed in the manufacture of clothing. Beginning in 1801, girls in the Female Orphan School received training in the domestic skills of sewing and spinning.

Later, when the livestock supply improved, women tended to household hens and pigs. Dairying tasks included milking and butter and cheese making, which could be difficult and futile in the extremes of the Australian summer. As agriculture improved, maize and, later, wheat were used for baking. Gathering fuel for the fires was also a necessary domestic task.

For most women, the most obvious means of survival were marriage, cohabitation, and prostitution. Although women (and men) could be assigned to their spouses, unattached women were often assigned as servants to men who sought their sexual, as well as domestic, services, whether willingly given or not (Daniels, 72). Those of more independent mind and higher spirits were labeled "troublesome" or of "abandoned character." The authorities resorted to punishments in an attempt to bring them under control, or, after 1803, to confinement in the "Female Factory," above the jail at Parramatta. There, the unlucky women were ordered to undertake public work of a domestic nature such as laundry, needlework, and cloth making; and it was from this institution that men could select servants and wives.

The reproductive role of women was of critical importance to the colony's development. Women bearing children were exempted from manual labor. Tench attributed the encouraging birth rate to the "salubrious climate," adding that "women who certainly would never have bred in any other climate here produced as fine children as ever were born" (Tench, 235).

With the benefit of female- (and male-) assigned servants, the wives of officers and officials enjoyed a more privileged domestic life than other female settlers, acting as hostesses within their small circle. A few of these women took a more active role, as did the astute and adept Elizabeth Macarthur, who managed estate affairs during the two absences from the colony of her husband, Captain John Macarthur of New South Wales Corps.

As colonial Australia grew, the records revealed many more examples of women undertaking roles beyond their domestic milieu, roles such as farmers, shopkeepers, innkeepers, tutors, and traders. Of particular note is that during the 1788–1810 period, women enjoyed the advantage of being less likely than men to suffer imprisonment or corporal punishment.

To read about children and family life among Australian Aborigines, see the Australian Aboriginal entries in the sections "Family Life" and "Children" in chapter 2 ("Domestic Life") of volume 1 of this series.

~*Valda Rigg*

FOR MORE INFORMATION

Bladen, F., ed. *Historical Records of New South Wales.* Vols. 1–6. Sydney: Government Printer, 1892. Facsimile edition, Marrickville: Southwood Press, 1978.

Daniels, K. *Convict Women.* St. Leonards, Australia: Allen and Unwin, 1998.

Frost, A. *Arthur Phillip 1738–1814: His Voyaging.* Melbourne: Oxford University Press, 1987.

Government of New South Wales. *Index to Bench of Magistrates Cases, 1788–1820.* <www.records.nsw.gov.au/indexes/benchofmag/introduction.htm>, accessed October 23, 2003.

King, J. *The First Fleet.* South Melbourne: Macmillan, 1982.

National Library of Australia. *Australian History on the Internet.* <http://www.nla.gov.au/oz/histsite.html>, accessed October 23, 2003.

Tench, W. *1788: Comprising A Narrative of the Expedition to Botany Bay [1789] and A Complete Account of the Settlement at Port Jackson [1793].* Edited by Tim Flannery. Melbourne: Text Publishing, 1996.

THE COLONIAL FRONTIER OF NORTH AMERICA

Along North America's colonial frontier, Native American women generally worked longer and harder at a greater number of tasks than did their male counterparts. Colonial men and women also performed different roles, with the wife occupying herself with household tasks, including the care of children. Pregnancy accounted for the basic contours of a married woman's life cycle. Unmarried women, on the other hand, came to be designated as "spinsters." Exceptions and overlap, however, did exist, accounting for a good number of women who were savvy in fields typically associated with male accomplishments.

Native American men and women who were about to be married often exchanged gifts with each other, indicating their future roles as husband and wife. The *trumpline*, which a Native American woman wore across the forehead to support loads carried on the back, showed that she would carry heavy objects; the kettle, that she would cook; and the firelog indicated that she would not only provide the firewood but would do everything else required to establish a household as well. She was also expected to cultivate the fields, to carry game, to transport bark sheets used to mark wigwams, and to make and repair moccasins.

An observer of Native American culture noted that "the men glory in their idleness." Certainly, the husband's duties were limited, "save for hunting, fishing, and war." Among the Algonquians, the husband was also required to build and repair the family dwelling, while among the Iroquoian nations, the husband moved into an established dwelling with his wife's relations, and it is unclear whether he was required to help them in its upkeep.

Colonial men and women on the frontier spent most of their time living and working side by side. A wife was expected to manage the household and to care for the children, but she was also expected to help in the economic affairs of her husband, acting as his representative or even as his surrogate if the situation warranted. A husband was expected to provide for his family and to guide and educate his children. The daily routines and tasks of a husband and a wife were frequently quite distinct, but the spouses worked toward a common goal, the well-being of the family. A husband and wife, and in fact all family members, were interdependent. Each and every member was expected to contribute to the welfare of the family unit as their gender, age, and ability permitted.

Generally, the selection of a career was a prerequisite in a man's attempts both to assert his freedom from childhood and to establish himself as an adult. Only after a man had chosen a career and was financially solvent was he able to contemplate marriage and children. If he came from a family of wealth, a man had numerous employment options within certain expectations. In 17th-century British America, he was expected to choose an occupation useful to God, his community, and his family. As the 18th century progressed, however, considerations became more secular. Decisions regarding who would farm, who would be apprenticed, or who would be sent for advanced schooling were made to benefit the family as a whole. These determinations were not always equitable from the individual's point of view, but individuality was of secondary importance in relation to the greater good—the welfare of the family. Those young men who had few family connections or wealth were subject to serving out their lives as laborers. Of course, in America, one could strike out into the forests to carve out a farm; but as settlements grew, farming opportunities became more limited, and more young men were forced farther into the wilderness to find sufficient land on which to establish a farmstead of their own.

Women did not benefit from the choices, limited though they were, that men enjoyed. Generally, women on the frontier maintained the fire, cooked and preserved food, sewed and repaired clothing, cultivated the vegetable garden, cleaned and laundered, and assisted their spouse in any way they could. The few occupations open to women produced little income. In marriage, a woman en-

Frontispiece for Daniel Defoe's *The History of Colonel Jack*. Defoe's story concerns a Londoner given to thievery who makes the transatlantic voyage to the North American colonies, where he promptly earns a fortune as a plantation owner. © The British Library.

tered a cycle of pregnancy, birth, and nursing that set the bounds of her life for the remainder of her child-bearing years. For many women, 20- to 30-month intervals stretched from the birth of one child to that of the next. This population explosion in the house required that a large number of people be fed.

Women who remained unmarried often lived with other relatives. If a woman was not the female head of a household, then she found herself occupying an awkward position in the family scheme. Many of these women made their contribution by spinning flax and wool. They would spin for their own household and could also bring in additional income by spinning for other families. It is from this practice that the term *spinster* came to refer to an older, unmarried woman.

Colonial law permitted women more freedom than the common law of England. Benjamin Franklin wrote to his wife as he set sail for England, "I leave Home and undertake this long Voyage more cheerful, as I can rely on your Prudence in the Management of my affairs; and education of my dear child." Women in the colonies were permitted to act as agents for their absent or busy husbands, and many did. In fact, colonial wives were expected to assist their husbands in any way that they could. Samuel Sewall reported the following information in his diary: "gave my Wife the rest of my cash £4.3 &8 and tell her she shall now keep the Cash; if I want I will borrow of her. She has a better faculty than I at managing Affairs: I will assist her."

One of the most striking differences between the colonies and England in such matters concerned the transfer of real estate. In the colonies, both the husband and the wife executed the deed by which the title passed. Moreover, in certain cases, a wife would be asked to verify her signature and attest that it had been given voluntarily and without undue duress from her husband. Thus, the strictures that bound men and women to culturally prescribed roles were not always accepted or applied (Volo and Volo, 43, 121, 122, 124–25, 148).

FOR MORE INFORMATION

Berkin, C. *First Generations: Women in Colonial America.* New York: Hill, 1926.
Boorstin, D. J. *The Americans: The Colonial Experience.* New York: Random House, 1958.
Volo, J. M., and D. D. Volo. *Daily Life on the Old Colonial Frontier.* Westport, Conn.: Greenwood Press, 2002.

DOMESTIC LIFE
|
MEN & WOMEN
|
Africa

Colonial Australia

The Colonial Frontier
of North America

England

France

Japan

New England

Life at Sea

ENGLAND

Within the family, men and women occupied different legal, occupational, and public roles. These different roles implied an underlying difference between the sexes, and insofar as marital, legal, economic, and political power surfaced in daily life, men enjoyed more authority and more control than did women. Still, the presence of such disparity has often concealed the active and powerful actions of women from all walks of life who dealt with personal, family, and social realities from day to day.

The most intimate relations between men and women arose in marriage, which was, among other things, a legal institution. Once married, a woman became a ghost or shadow in the eyes of the courts. According to Sir William Blackstone, the concept was simple: "[I]n marriage husband and wife are one person, and that person is the husband," with "the very being, or legal existence, of the woman . . . suspended during marriage." Nothing in her husband's home technically belonged to her, nor could she give anything away or bequeath anything in a will without his consent. Her children were his to dispose of as he pleased. There was no such thing as marital rape under the law; a man was entitled to have sex with his wife whenever he chose. He could send her to a private madhouse. He could confine her to her home against her will. He could beat her as long as he used a stick no bigger in circumference than his thumb; hence the phrase "rule of thumb."

The sex of an adult family member, as interpreted by 18th-century English society, indicated the occupational tasks for which he or she was responsible. Men tended to earn most of the income, and women tended to do most or all of the housework, but plenty of women earned money and performed tasks similar to men's. On farms, men did the hardest physical tasks—clearing, plowing, sowing seed, harvesting, and threshing—with the help of sons or hired laborers. Women, with the help of daughters or domestic servants, cooked, brewed ale, knitted, carded wool, washed, taught young children, gardened, made butter and cheese, sewed, and kept chickens for eating and egg production.

Women might help in the fields at harvest time or do factory work, although their wages for these jobs tended to be about half to two-thirds of men's. In shop-keeping families, men and women alike helped out in the store. In artisanal families, the wife was principally responsible for the housekeeping, but she might also oversee the workers while her husband was away and even inherit the business when her husband died.

The crushing economic realities of the 18th century made it imperative for many women to work at something outside the family home or trade. Most hoped to work during their youth, save enough money to marry, and then settle into a life of housework only. But many, from ambition or necessity, worked outside the home all their lives. There were huge numbers of women in domestic service and prostitution and small numbers of female coffeehouse proprietors, butchers, artists, weavers, toll-gate collectors, coal dealers, preachers (chiefly among the Quakers but to a lesser extent among the Methodists), boxers, patent-medicine makers, and mill owners.

However, one of the trends noted by contemporaries was the gradual disappearance of respectable work for middle-class women. Anxious to imitate the rich, more and more middle-class wives hired servants to do the housework. At the same time, men were providing competition, sometimes overwhelming competition, in traditionally female fields, including midwifery, embroidering, and hairdressing. Few female occupations opened to compensate for these losses. Women were still forbidden entry to Parliament, the bar, institutionalized medicine, the Anglican clergy, and the magistracy. That left them not with occupations but with hobbies: music, drawing, needlework, and artistic or social patronage.

Perhaps the only significant field newly open to women was that of the arts. Women became actresses, playwrights, and novelists. Some founded and edited newspapers. Of course, the prospect of obtaining such a vocation was extremely poor, not least of all because of the stigma attached to women and professions.

Some women, too, took an interest in public affairs, although for genteel women it was an extremely delicate business. Advocacy of a particular candidate was acceptable only if he was a husband, relative, or close family friend. Georgiana, the duchess of Devonshire, discovered this restrictive norm when she supported Charles James Fox for the Westminster seat in 1784. The press and the caricaturists, who implied that she was unnatural and that Fox was her lover, savaged her repeatedly in print. To emphasize the masculine nature of the political arena, the galleries of Parliament were forbidden to women in 1778. Lower-class women, who had more freedom of action, often participated in bread riots and street demonstrations.

There was a very definite idea of a private sphere that women inhabited and tended. Lady Mary Wortley Montagu thought a woman's learning ought to be hidden. However, a few people, mostly women, argued in favor of a wider sphere for women. Mary Wollstonecraft wrote in *A Vindication of the Rights of Woman,* "I wish to persuade women to endeavour to acquire strength, both of mind and body, and to convince them that the soft phrases, susceptibility of heart, delicacy of sentiment, and refinement of taste, are almost synonymous with epithets of weakness."

The regulation of legal, household, and occupational roles in an 18th-century English family revealed the powerful influence of the perceived differences between men and women. A man's or a woman's life—its general contours as much as its particular concerns—operated within a framework of competing interests that frequently reflected ideas of what it meant to be male or female (Olsen, 9, 33–35, 43).

To read about women's roles in Chaucer's England, see the Europe entry in the section "Women" in chapter 2 ("Domestic Life") of volume 2; for women's roles in Elizabethan England, see the England entry in the section "Women's Roles" in chapter 2 ("Domestic Life") of volume 3; and for the roles of men and women in Victorian England, see the Victorian England entries in the sections "Men" and "Women" in chapter 2 ("Domestic Life") of volume 5 of this series.

DOMESTIC LIFE

|

MEN & WOMEN

|

Africa

Colonial Australia

The Colonial Frontier
of North America

England

France

Japan

New England

Life at Sea

FOR MORE INFORMATION

Hufton, O. *The Prospect before Her: A History of Women in Western Europe, 1500–1800.* New York: Knopf, 1996.

Lynch, J. *Eighteenth Century Resources.* <http://newark.rutgers.edu/~jlynch/18th/>, accessed October 10, 2003.

Olsen, K. *Chronology of Women's History.* Westport, Conn.: Greenwood Press, 1994.

———. *Daily Life in 18th-Century England.* Westport, Conn.: Greenwood Press, 1999.

FRANCE

In the 17th and 18th centuries, a growing number of French intellectuals began to question the existence of inequalities between men and women. While intellectuals had begun to deal with some of these issues during the Renaissance, the debate over these issues, often referred to as the "querelle des femmes" or "woman question," reached a fever pitch by the middle of the 18th century. The baron de Montesquieu's *Persian Letters* (1721), for example, used the social status of women as a measure of the general level of enlightenment within a society. Taking Montesquieu's ideas even further, in her *Declaration of the Rights of Woman and Citizen* (1792), Olympe de Gouges argued for the extension to women of French revolutionary freedoms and political rights. Of course, not all historical examples of male and female roles hinged on the theories of elite and privileged intellectuals. Many women simply performed work—not infrequently outside the home—that was materially required of them given the economics of the time.

The new urgency for this debate can be related to a number of trends. Perhaps first and foremost, scientific investigation paved the way for a reconsideration of gender roles. After all, the new rationalism, typified by the thoughts and writings of René Descartes, had seemed to indicate that bodies and minds were not inextricably linked. For this reason, Cartesian rationalism indicated that the mind had no gender and that all minds were equally capable of grasping reality. Adding to the argument in favor of equality, the social psychology of John Locke had suggested that the *tabula rasa*, or "blank slate," was the most logical parallel to the unformed human mind. If humans came into the world with no innate ideas, then gender might not be a determining factor in one's intelligence, personality, or capabilities. The new science thus provided a basis upon which 18th-century intellectuals could reconsider the necessity of distinctions between men and women in political, social, and economic life. If all minds were equal, on what basis were male and female bodies differentiated?

Etching by Jean Duplessi-Bertaux, from the series *Beggars*. Many French women received an income outside the home. The woman pictured here is a road sweeper. © Library of Congress.

Writers arguing for and against women's emancipation contributed to an explosion of publishing, with pamphlets, plays, and treatises that attempted to answer the question of difference by making a case for the superiority, inferiority, or equality of women to men. Those who argued that females were naturally subordinate to males also tried to demonstrate that restrictions on women's rights to own property, conduct business, and participate in political life were warranted. These polemicists, who often based their arguments on the biblical account of Creation found in Genesis, argued that women were lustful and idle creatures of whim, the restraint of whom ought to be the task of unemotional and rational men.

Writers who opposed women's subordination, on the other hand, used the newly developing language of human rights to argue that as persons, women, as men did, had claims to equal treatment and would, if properly educated, be as capable as men in contributing to public life. Some writers went even further and argued that women were not merely equal to men but even morally superior, capable of greater self-sacrifice and more control over their passions. The poor education of young women was a primary target of these writers, for all of them recognized that legal equality would be nearly meaningless without education as a basis for women's advancement in society.

One of the most influential writers to enter into this debate was François Fénelon, whose *Treatise on the Education of Girls* (1687) represented an attempt to negotiate a middle ground between the two camps. In his book, Fénelon argued neither that women's education would result in a greater enlightenment of society nor that the less girls knew, the better off everyone would be. Although Fénelon advocated a more developed course of study than was usually provided to girls, he also argued that women should educate their daughters themselves, so that the girls would avoid both corruption and overeducation and would thus become, in the end, better wives and mothers.

The popularity of Fénelon's writing outlines the generally accepted limit of even tolerant attitudes toward women's emancipation. Even those who argued for the moral superiority of the female believed that different spheres of influence, appropriate to men's and women's natural abilities, ought to serve as the basis for social organization. Even the most radical writers to address "the woman question" rarely argued that the empirical model could justify complete social and political equality.

Scientific study of the human mind did not exist in a vacuum, of course. There were also political and social reasons for people to be increasingly concerned about the status of women. The mistresses of Louis XV (1715–74), for example, were known to advise him on foreign policy even as he let much of the rest of the government degenerate into factions. The most notorious example was that of the marquise de Pompadour, whose political influence with the king lasted nearly 20 years. Eventually, Madame de Pompadour encouraged Louis XV to sign an alliance with Austria, France's most notorious enemy, angering much of the country and contributing to the growing sentiment that women's political, social, and sexual influence needed to be limited.

Additionally, the feminine space of the salon had become more influential. Although aristocratic salons, which were intended to provide training in courtly behavior, had existed since the 16th century, the critical public sphere expanded in the 18th century, and so too did the influence of the salon. Previously, a few noble women had welcomed select guests and facilitated conversation between them. Now, hostesses, who were still women of influence, not only facilitated conversation but also acquired a reputation for wit and banter while promoting the careers of their favorites. Not infrequently, these philosophical liaisons between hostess and favorite were also sexual in nature, prompting opponents of the salons to charge that these gatherings could better be characterized as influential brothels. The philosopher Jean-Jacques Rousseau, no stranger to salon life himself, also criticized the salons, declaring in a letter to a fellow philosopher, "Every woman at Paris gathers in her apartment a harem of men more womanish than she" (Rousseau, 101).

The fact that even "enlightened" men were uncomfortable with the influence that women could wield in their position as hostess should demonstrate both the promise and limits of women's emancipation in 18th-century France. Some women had power and influence, but these women's very existence sparked an opposition that represented the limitations of their society.

~Jennifer J. Popiel

FOR MORE INFORMATION

Goodman, D. *The Republic of Letters: A Cultural History of the French Enlightenment.* Ithaca, N.Y.: Cornell University Press, 1994.

Harth, E. *Cartesian Women: Versions and Subversions of Rational Discourse in the Old Regime.* Ithaca, N.Y.: Cornell University Press, 1992.

Landes, J. B. *Women and the Public Sphere in the Age of the French Revolution.* Ithaca, N.Y.: Cornell University Press, 1988.

Lynch, J. *Eighteenth Century Resources.* <http://newark.rutgers.edu/~jlynch/18th/>, accessed October 10, 2003.

Rousseau, J.-J. *Politics and the Arts: Letter to D'Alembert on the Theatre.* Translated by Allen Bloom. Ithaca, N.Y.: Cornell University Press, 1960.

Spencer, S. *French Women and the Age of Enlightenment.* Bloomington: Indiana University Press, 1984.

Trouille, M. S. *Sexual Politics in the Enlightenment: Women Writers Read Rousseau.* Albany: State University of New York Press, 1997.

JAPAN

The prevailing view of the relations between women and of men created important distinctions between the sexes, distinctions that greatly affected the lives of rural and urban Japanese during the 18th century.

The most famous treatise on Tokugawa-era women is commonly attributed to Kaibara Ekiken, who must be otherwise considered a friend and apologist of the common people. This moralist tract, "Greater Learning for Women," begins with a brief explication of the proper role and status of women in a moral society: "Seeing that it is a girl's destiny, on reaching womanhood, to go to a new home, and live in submission to her father-in-law and mother-in-law, it is even more incumbent upon her than it is on a boy to receive with all reverence her parent's instructions."

From this perspective, women appeared only as second-class citizens, and then really only in relationship to their husbands. It was implied that a woman had three obediences in the course of her life. As a child, she was to be obedient to her father; as a wife, she owed fealty to her husband; and as a widow, she was to obey her adult son.

Neo-Confucianism deemed women to be both morally incompetent and the source of emotional attachment, which was the only "sin" in Buddhism. Not only were women intrinsically immoral, therefore, but they were also the cause of immorality in men. Witness Kaibara's explanation: "The five worst maladies that afflict the female mind are: indocility, discontent, slander, jealousy, and silliness. Without any doubt, these five maladies infest seven or eight out of every ten women, and it is from these that arises the inferiority of women to men."

Obviously, any social philosophy that begins its consideration of women in this manner has little—and cold—comfort to give them in terms of their normal expected relations with men. Women were admonished to be long-suffering, forgiving, patient, honest, circumspect, industrious, modest, thrifty, and obedient—in short, to exemplify all those ideals that leaders advocated in their pets, their children, and their servants.

One practical outcome of such beliefs involved civil behavior. Women were expected to bow to everyone, even to their husbands, fathers, and parents-in-law. The female bow was supposed to be graceful and demure. Young women learned to bow in a kind of coquettish sideways simper while covering their lower face with an unfurled fan. Serving girls were required to proffer the serving tray as they extended their bodies in a kind of cat stretch while on their knees. Geisha (female servant-entertainers) studied upward of 20 different bows, each appropriate to the station of one's customers and to the occasion. Even common prostitutes were expected to know at least a dozen bows.

Female submissiveness, however, was not universal. Successful and influential women usually used their supposed weaknesses to control weak-minded men. If they were deemed to be overly emotional, they used emotion to gain what they wanted. If they were esteemed for their physical beauty, they forced men to suffer to win their favors. If they were expected to be silly and incompetent in dealing with business matters, they bested the male merchant by employing wiles and intelligence that were never to be expected of a woman. In short, women used what few powers were allotted to them.

Peasant women were very important to agricultural endeavors. They were often in the fields alongside the men. For certain tasks, women were in fact preferred over men. Commonly, gangs of peasant women transplanted rice seedlings communally. Plowing and other farm tasks could be done separately, but collective teams of women almost always transplanted together.

Men who were not actively involved in other agrarian tasks would toss the bunches of seedlings to the women, shore up paddy ridges, dredge irrigation canals, or provide a rhythmic accompaniment for the job. Traditional "call-and-response" work songs lightened the drudgery. The women, to the collective enjoyment of all, rhythmically answered the men's double-entendre calls. Women could make ribald jokes about their sex lives or make suggestive taunts to the men; the time seemed to slip by faster, and the work seemed not as tiring.

Peasant women, like their *chōnin* (city folk) counterparts, traditionally performed several cottage industrial and by-employment jobs, as maids, in the silk sheds, or in the embroidery, weaving, and tailoring establishments of the fan-, umbrella-, and paper-making factories. Many young women worked away from their families as maids, hairdressers, waitresses, or "hostesses" in the public restaurants, tea and sake shops, and theaters in the licensed quarters of the large cities. In times of bad economic fortune, particularly in famines, many young farm girls were enslaved into prostitution.

Frequently, *chōnin* women worked side-by-side with their family's menfolk in artisanal and business endeavors. Few artisan-class women were allowed to ply their husband's or their father's trade if the job happened to be public and required physical strength. When city work was performed indoors (and thus outside the public eye), then women excelled in arts and crafts, many of which required dexterity, ingenuity, and aesthetic sensibility.

Some women, however, openly practiced traditionally male roles for male relatives who either could not or would not handle such tasks. Women sold and bought goods, collected debts, and kept the accounts of artisan families. Hen-pecked husbands were common stock characters in the theater, so much so that only a few words of dialogue were necessary to establish that the presence of women running the family household was not particularly rare.

Ironically, of the four official socioeconomic classes of the era, women in the top class suffered the most. That is partially because they were held to a higher moral standard than their peasant and *chōnin* sisters, but it was also because of the nature of their husbands' work. Samurai men produced nothing but administration, which required a fair amount of technical education. Even if a samurai woman could learn to read and write the complex Sino-Japanese writing system, she never would be allowed to apply her learning to the actual work of government.

The writings of Kaibara did not represent unusual or radical ideas. During the 18th century, Japanese society in general acknowledged certain concepts of masculinity and of femininity, privileging the former over the latter. Consequently, relatively inflexible and pervasive conceptions of gender affected the countryside as much as they did the cities (Perez, 166, 250, 267–70).

To read about the roles of men and women in Japan in the 20th century, see the Japan entries in the sections "Men" and "Women" in chapter 2 ("Domestic Life") of Volume 6 of this series.

FOR MORE INFORMATION

Japan Information Network. <http://www.jinjapan.org/index.html>, accessed October 23, 2003.

Perez, L. G. *Daily Life in Early Modern Japan.* Westport, Conn.: Greenwood Press, 2002.

Smith, T. C. *Nakahara: Family Farming and Population in a Japanese Village, 1717–1830.* Stanford, Calif.: Stanford University Press, 1977.

NEW ENGLAND

New England men and women had particular roles in family life, and these roles functioned not so much according to a person's sex but to the cultural stipulations of the society in which men and women lived. Native Americans, white colonists, and black slaves all contended with different and powerful obligations regarding the duties of men and women.

In most Native American families, women did all the work, except hunting and breaking up the fields for the first planting. Women cared for the domesticated animals, grew the crops, put up the houses and cleaned them, gathered wild berries, fruits, and medicines, ground the corn, and otherwise prepared the food. The women administered most of the medical treatments.

In a New England Indian village, the mother's day began as she made the all-important fire; fed the baby, who was placed in a cradle board hanging on the wall;

and cooked the morning meal, usually the most important of the day. The rest of her work for the day involved securing the necessary corn from an underground storage area, where it had been placed in the summer and fall, and grinding it for mush or bread. With her store of dried blueberries and the cornmeal she had ground, she would make small cakes on the hearth in the center of the house. Having finished the day's food preparation, she might turn her hand to making rope for fishing nets.

The father and older sons might do some ice fishing or go through the complicated, arduous process of making wooden bowls. A block of wood was charred and scraped until the bowl reached the desired shape. The laborious process usually took more than one day. When it was finished, it was smoothed with sand and then polished with bear fat.

At the end of the day, several men and women of the Indian village got together in one wigwam to visit, smoke, and entertain themselves with stories. Finally, each family returned to its own wigwam, banked the fires, and turned in under skins for a night's sleep.

In fair weather, native populations in New England participated in many more outdoor activities. The men did more hunting and fishing from canoes, and the women planted or hoed vegetables; collected herbs, fruits, and nuts; and collected clay and molded it into pots, strengthening and decorating them with dried sea shells, then drying them, and later baking them.

In New England white families, the male was generally expected to exercise authority and the wife to assume a submissive role. The final decisions with regard to finances and property were his. The hiring and disciplining of servants, for example, were his roles. He decided about the purchase or sale of any land. He decided how property was to be distributed when his own children married, and he decided how property was to be distributed in his will. Nevertheless, in many marriages, the husband made decisions only after consultation with his wife.

The laws of New England clarified the conditions that the culture expected in a marriage. From their marriage, a husband and wife could expect a peaceful life (that is, no violent behavior or abusive language), sexual union and faithfulness, economic support (a husband owned property and supported the wife, and the wife had an obligation to help maintain and increase her husband's property by using it wisely and by working hard), and a life lived together; that is, no decision on the part of either husband or wife to live in a separate house was acceptable.

Love was not considered necessary before a marriage took place. Nor was love between husband and wife ever to be greater than their love for God. Moreover, public displays of love and affection were not typical of New England couples. Nevertheless, it was thought that husbands and wives did learn to love each other after marrying, if they did not already do so, and letters and diaries show that many New England couples loved each other passionately.

Whether they were wives or employees, women's work was, with few exceptions, domestic, involving the rearing and education of young children; house cleaning; the growing, gathering, preserving, preparing, and serving of food; and most aspects of providing cloth and clothing—spinning, carding, weaving, and sewing.

It was also the wife's job to support the work of the family, aside and apart from domestic chores. Women helped with most farm chores, and many supported the work of the family as tradesmen or artisans, for they were expected to be their husband's helpmate in whatever calling he pursued. Women in colonial New England were found working as blacksmiths, silversmiths, tinworkers, shoemakers, shipwrights, tanners, gunsmiths, barbers, printers, butchers, and shopkeepers.

Although a woman's work and business were always subordinate to her husband's, and although her position was always determined by her husband's position, many women were expected to have complete control in running the family business when their husband was away. Wives also assumed the running of the family business when their husband died.

A number of women of modest means had their own small but thriving businesses. In at least one instance, when a wife's small business became more lucrative than her husband's larger enterprise, he borrowed money from her.

Although colonial New England women could not initiate a business without the sponsorship of a male, she was allowed, even expected, to protect and enlarge any business of her husband or father while either was alive or after their deaths. For example, during the early 1770s, women ran an amazing 10 percent of the Port of Boston's mercantile firms.

White masters in New England widely influenced the roles of men and women in slave families. Slaves devoted a great deal of their time and energy to chores, be they domestic or public. As in the south, slave families often fragmented when a master sold a husband or wife, mother or father, or a son or daughter to a faraway estate. When New England slave families lived together, they often lived with the master's family, sometimes occupying the entire second floor of the house; and many New England masters were eager—for economic, religious, or other reasons—to support a union between a black man and woman who were slaves.

Colonial New England society was, in fact, an association of overlapping societies, as diverse in their general features as they were in their specific duties and proscriptions that governed the daily lives of men and women (Johnson, 67–68, 112–13, 134, 141, 151–54).

FOR MORE INFORMATION

Cott, N. F. *The Bonds of Womanhood: "Woman's Sphere" in New England, 1780–1835.* New Haven, Conn.: Yale University Press, 1977.

Johnson, C. D. *Daily Life in Colonial New England.* Westport, Conn.: Greenwood Press, 2002.

LIFE AT SEA

Men and women, whether married or not, often shared one another's company aboard ship. Whereas men's roles principally derived from their duties as seamen or as officers, the roles of the wives of these men were enormously restricted. Never-

DOMESTIC LIFE
|
MEN & WOMEN
|
Africa

Colonial Australia

The Colonial Frontier
of North America

England

France

Japan

New England

Life at Sea

theless, husbands and wives made do with their circumstances, each in ways acceptable to society. Some women, however, reversed traditional norms and played the roles of seamen and pirates, often with great accomplishment.

One widely documented superstition on the high seas resulted in a strong opposition to having women aboard ships. This particular obsession was an outgrowth of the belief that witches had power over the winds and could therefore bring forth deadly storms. This adverse attitude toward women was not confined to simple, uneducated sailors. British admiral Cuthbert Collingwood wrote in 1808, "I never knew a woman brought to sea in a ship that some mischief did not befall the vessel."

In reality, however, the tradition of taking women to sea was, by the 18th century, well established in the British Royal Navy and persisted through the mid-19th century, despite written regulations to the contrary. It became customary for wives of lower-ranking officers to accompany their husbands to sea, and prior to 1815, some seamen were allowed to bring their wives, as well.

Living conditions for women at sea were harsh. Seamen's wives had virtually no privacy. Whatever few possessions the women brought with them had to be stored in their spouse's sea chest. They were forced to share their husband's hammocks in the cramped quarters common to the entire crew. Once the hammocks were stowed away at 8 A.M., the women often congregated on the orlop deck. Below the waterline and without gunports, this was a dark and oppressive place. The time passed slowly for them when their main task was to keep out of the way. If they could acquire a tub in which to wash, the women did laundry.

Late in the day, the men generally had time to relax. Wives would be permitted at this time to join their husbands on deck for dancing and entertainment. The women joined in other recreational activities such as shipboard plays and skits, which often took place at this time.

The tradition of taking women to sea was, by the 18th century, well established.

Warrant officers' wives were in a somewhat improved situation in that they shared their husbands' small, canvas-sided cabins located on the sides of the lower deck. This enabled them to have some meager amount of privacy and even permitted the possession of some furniture. These women would have employed their time sewing garments for themselves and their husbands and attending to any mending that was needed. Because warrant officers' wives were much more likely to know how to read than seamen's wives, many of them passed part of the day reading and writing journals. They also formed maternal relationships with cabin boys, who acted as servants to the wives, polishing shoes, running errands, preparing special dishes, and such.

Evenings were often the favorite time for the wives. They walked the now quiet decks with their husbands, talking and making plans. Back in their cabin, they played cards, dominoes, and backgammon, or they passed the time reading. It was common for one family member to read aloud while others listened.

Not all of a wife's time at sea was spent in what might be considered idle labor. Even a captain's wife had to deal with the realities of life at sea. Nineteen-year-old Mary Ann Patten was on a honeymoon voyage when her captain-husband fell ill with "brain fever" and was rendered both blind and deaf. With the first mate incarcerated for insubordination and the second mate lacking skill in navigation, Mary, now pregnant with their first child, accepted her husband's charge to take command of the ship. Not only was Mary—who had carefully studied her husband's calculations during the early months of their journey—able to navigate the ship home, but she safely guided it through a harrowing rounding of Cape Horn, as well.

There are verified accounts from the late 17th through the early 19th centuries of over 20 women who joined the British Royal Navy or Marines and successfully passed themselves as men. A number of these women served honorably for years before they were discovered. In 1815, a London newspaper reported, "Among the crew . . . it is now discovered was a female African who served as a seaman in the Royal Navy for upwards of eleven years."

These women, if they were small in stature, yet strong and athletic enough to perform the assigned work, could easily be taken for young men. The disguise would be even more complete if the women could sustain rough language and were willing to chew tobacco. Moreover, clothing did much in this period to establish the trade, wealth, and sex of the wearer. If you dressed as a merchant, it was assumed that you were a merchant. People did not presume to dress out of their station, and proper women simply did not don male attire.

While a sailor's life was generally more restrictive than that of a civilian man, it offered incredible freedom to a woman. In her disguise at sea, the woman received pay equal with that of men, and she was free to dispose of it as she saw fit. Mary Lacy, who served as William Chandler from 1759 to 1771 in the Royal Navy, rose from a carpenter's servant to a fully qualified shipwright. Such an opportunity would never have been offered to her as a woman. Women were commonly prohibited from many trades or paid less for the same work. Of course, some women probably identified emotionally with men. They were not only successful in their disguises; they were comfortable living as a male.

A few women gained notoriety and infamy as female pirates. Although they dressed as men, the gender of these women was no secret. Any woman who successfully commanded men and ships under a variety of hostile circumstances must have been both highly skilled and especially charismatic. The best-known female pirates were Ann Bonny and Mary Read, who fully engaged in pirate attacks and robberies. They were captured, tried, and found guilty of piracy. Upon being sentenced to death by hanging, the women revealed the scandalous fact that each of them was pregnant. Granted a reprieve due to their circumstances, Mary died of fever shortly after being imprisoned. Ann Bonny's fate was not recorded and remains a mystery.

While a mariner's role as a husband and father frequently yielded to the requirements of working and organizing an oceangoing vessel, wives concentrated their attention on domestic tasks, even when aboard ship. Still, there were some women who, for varied reasons, joined merchant and naval crews disguised as men, or, with no disguise at all, led pirate ships (Volo and Volo, 155–58, 162, 164–65, 170–73).

FOR MORE INFORMATION

Druett, J. *Hen Frigates: Wives of Merchant Captains under Sail*. New York: Simon and Schuster, 1998.

Stark, S. J. *Female Tars: Women aboard Ship in the Age of Sail.* Annapolis, Md.: Naval Institute Press, 1996.

Volo, D. D., and J. M. Volo. *Daily Life in the Age of Sail.* Westport, Conn.: Greenwood Press, 2002.

Children

Between 1600 and 1800, children occupied no less an important place in societies than they do today. Their importance, however, took on sharply distinct characteristics. Whereas contemporary Western societies tend to espouse the sanctity of childhood innocence, such tendencies were, several hundred years ago, somewhat less discernible along North America's colonial frontier; in England, France, Japan, and New England; and on American and European oceangoing vessels. Variation, however, existed within each culture.

Children who came from agricultural families in early modern Japan lived more relaxed and leisurely childhoods than did their peers in Japan's numerous and large cities. Similarly, if children living in 18th-century England belonged to an impoverished, urban family, then those children could expect to work as little adults in factories, as chimney cleaners, or even as contributors of human teeth (their own) for the manufacture of dentures. Not so for English children born and raised in a socially and economically privileged family from the countryside. The advantages of such a situation meant that instead of spending a childhood in factories and squalid metropolitan dwellings, these children could expect to grow up in a relatively comfortable environment, which included not only the material trappings of wealth but also the flattering beliefs of social, moral, intellectual, and emotional superiority that served to distinguish the well-off from the rabble.

Along North America's colonial frontier, settlers' children were practical and hardworking helpers in the difficult outposts of European colonization. In colonial New England, free white children worried far less than did black slave children about a master who could sell off his slaves whenever he so desired. The social biases associated with the color of one's skin and the economic effects of slavery fused together to create a socioeconomic system (slavery in colonial New England) that burdened some children (enslaved blacks) with concerns that never bothered the minds of other children (free whites).

And yet children were not simply urban or rural, rich or poor, free or chattel. They were also boys and girls. Distinctions between boys and girls—distinctions that varied from one culture to another—fall under the category of gender roles. Not all well-off English children, for instance, could expect to lead similar lives. Well-off English boys found themselves rushed off to schools and occupied with Latin, Greek, mathematics, rhetoric, and other intense studies, while well-off English girls practiced more feminine arts in preparation for as early and as lucrative a marriage as would be possible.

Boys and girls in Japan also grew up within the context of gender-specific expectations. Boys had very factual or descriptive names, indicating their order of birth, their appearance ("red nose"), or perhaps later, their profession. Japanese girls, on the other hand, had names such as Chrysanthemum or Spring, which, on the whole, connoted far more delicate and pleasing impressions than did Red Nose.

In North America, many Native American boys hunted and fished while girls followed the more peaceful routine of foraging for berries and other items. Even aboard sailing ships in deep ocean waters, the sons and daughters of officers received significantly different treatment. Sons could stay aboard ship, studying both the classics and the rough language and mannerisms of sailors. Girls, however, would not stay on a vessel for very long, given the harmful effects that uncouth men of the seas could have on a young lady.

Religious and ethical beliefs affected childhood as well. In New England, particularly during the 17th century, Puritan communities and families considered children to be evil and damned, unworthy of God's love, and a definite threat to the little spiritual purity that the community might possess. Hence, adults encouraged children to avoid games and other leisure activities, emphasizing instead the importance of hard work and religious education. On the other hand, French intellectual trends led to an increased emphasis on the innocence of children and on the need for parents, guardians, and teachers to nurture the uncorrupted minds of youth.

Work and play affected children in a multitude of cultures and circumstances. Still, an overall picture of the daily lives of children reveals sharp contrasts in the content of those lives. These contrasts corresponded to social, economic, gender, and religious beliefs and institutions.

~Peter Seelig

FOR MORE INFORMATION

Colón, A. R. *A History of Children: A Socio-Cultural Survey across Millennia*. Westport, Conn.: Greenwood Press, 2001.

THE COLONIAL FRONTIER OF NORTH AMERICA

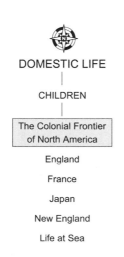

The birth and maturation of Native American and colonial children reveal several important themes common to these two, general cultures. Communities tended to take a significant interest in the young, either in the form of relatives or neighbors. Children occupied their time between games and chores, with the distinction between the two not always as apparent as one would imagine: knife throwing and doll playing, for instance, accustomed children to the responsibilities of hunting and child rearing. Of significant note is the vision quest, or spiritual exploration, that Native American boys and girls undertook at the onset of puberty. This quest offered adolescents a sense of purpose while subtly preserving the influence of their elders.

Each Native American child belonged to the clan of his or her mother and lived in a clan house with his or her mother's relations. While this situation did not disqualify the father from taking a critical role in the life of his children, the most important males in a boy's life were undoubtedly his mother's brothers, his maternal uncles. These would be the ones who instructed him in the skills that he would need as an adult.

Besides practice with the bow and arrow or throwing tomahawks and knives, Native American children played at a number of games. In good weather, running, jumping, and climbing contests abounded, as they would among any group of children. A remarkable development was the vigorous and unrestrained game known to the Jesuits as lacrosse. Played with a long-handled net and a leather ball, lacrosse pitted two teams in a contest to score the ball through a goal. The game could cover many acres of ground and involve many hundreds of players. Winter games included a form of ice hockey without skates and a game known as Indian snakes, in which a long stick was propelled along an icy trench. Many of these games involved both adults and children playing together.

Puberty was an important time in the life of a child, as it marked, more distinctly than it does for teens today, the passage from childhood to adulthood. The search for a protecting or guiding spirit through the experience of a metaphysical vision was an important part of this transition. The vision quest was common to most Native American peoples, but unlike the nations of southwestern North America, the tribes of the northeastern quarter seem to have eschewed the use of mind-altering drugs in the process. However, tobacco may have been burned as a ceremonial offering to ensure success.

Young men generally embarked upon their vision quest when their maternal uncles thought that their nephews were fit in terms of physical and behavioral maturity. Then, in the isolation of a wooded spot, cliffside, or mountaintop of some mystical importance, a young man would fast alone for up to 10 days. The physical stress created by the denial of food and water usually brought on a hallucination or vision. In this state, he would search for a guardian spirit, usually represented by an animal totem, that he would follow for his entire life. During his quest, the young man might put together a small bag of totems or special items of meaning to himself.

The timing of the vision quest was somewhat less problematic for young women. At the onset of her first menstrual period, a young woman would seclude herself in the same type of shelter as that used by the women of the tribe for giving birth. Here she would fast, denying herself food and drink, until her unseen guardian would make a dream visitation and give her directions for her duties as an adult.

A young person who was favored by a vision could have an experience with a clear meaning or might have to consult a shaman, or wise man, regarding an unclear experience. By this means, the relations of the young could effectively direct the efforts of their adolescents. Nonetheless, young persons who, during their vision quests, garnered the favor of many spirit helpers were considered fortunate. Young men, or in some tribes young women, who were so favored could themselves become shamans. After a successful vision, the young person painted his head red as a sign of having reached adult status.

Among colonists, the birth of a child was not only a momentous occasion for the family but a community event, as well. At the first stage of labor, the husband would send for the midwife, who would be on hand for the birth and remain with the family for a brief interval afterward. Other female friends and relatives would also attend to assist in the birth.

All frontier children were breast-fed until they were weaned as toddlers. A mother who was incapable of producing enough milk for her child needed to find a wet nurse as a substitute. Nonetheless, the newborn infant was often given to another woman to nurse for the first few days. The nurse was also available to help with complications following childbirth. It was not uncommon for a nurse to remain with both the mother and child for an extended interval.

Frontier children were expected to become productive contributors to the family as soon as they were able. Only in infancy were they treated simply as children with no responsibilities. As early as the age of three, children were given simple chores. Not only did such work facilitate among children a sense of responsibility, but it also kept them occupied. Young children gathered goose feathers, picked berries, and helped process food. Older children plaited straw, weeded the garden, and knitted stockings.

Playthings were few and simple. Boys played with marbles, balls, whistles, small boats, toy soldiers, wooden animals, and whatever else a loving father might carve from a piece of wood by a winter's fire. Girls mimicked their mother's activities playing with whatever bowls and spoons were not in use. They played with dolls made from scraps of fabric or pieces of wood. Many dolls were more like a log with a face than a baby's image. Outside, children used their imaginations and nature's playthings to fashion garlands of flowers, small boats of leaves and pods, and whistles from blades of grass. As children grew older, chores increased with ability and made greater demands on children's playtime. Thus a large, healthy family was a tremendous resource to a colonial farmer.

From birth and infancy through adolescence and young adulthood, children of both Native American and colonial backgrounds participated in family and community traditions. Work and play, as well as an emphasis on a sense of purpose and guidance, characterized these children's lives (Volo and Volo, 42–43, 125, 128).

> *Snapshot*
>
> **Children in New France**
>
> In both the English and French colonies of North America, children were accused of rebellious behavior. In New France, juveniles were called "les petits sauvages" (little savages) because they smoked pipes in public, were uncivil toward ladies, and pranced about on their horses with great impertinence. (Bennett, 149–50)

FOR MORE INFORMATION

Bennett, P. W., ed. *Canada: A North American Nation.* Whitby, Ontario: McGraw-Hill Ryerson, 1989.

Earle, A. M. *Child Life in Colonial Days.* New York: Macmillan, 1940.

Volo, J. M., and D. D. Volo. *Daily Life on the Old Colonial Frontier.* Westport, Conn.: Greenwood Press, 2002.

ENGLAND

Eighteenth-century English children played, worked, studied, and eventually achieved independence from their parents, although the exact nature of each of these activities often reflected a child's sex and socioeconomic status. The life of a child is very revealing to cultural historians, since England was a nation of children. Over 45 percent of its people were under age 20, and 25 percent were under age 10. Although infant mortality was very high, it was offset by a prodigious birthrate. The birth of a child, however, was fraught with risk.

In the 18th century, if labor did not progress, or began too early or too late, mother or child or both were often doomed. Cesarean sections were performed rarely, usually only when the mother had died during delivery or seemed certain to do so, since the resulting abdominal infection was almost 100 percent fatal. There were changes in obstetrical care besides the introduction of forceps. Chief among them was the shift from female midwives to male obstetricians. By the end of the century, male doctors had attained supremacy in the field.

A woman's lying-in, or labor, was a busy affair. Once the baby was born, it was often fed liquor, or a "comforter" of butter and sugar. When mother and child were well enough, the former returned to society by being churched, and the latter was introduced to society by being christened.

Those who survived the ordeal of birth had some of their hardest work ahead of them. Childhood ailments claimed a large number of children before their fifth birthday (60 percent in London in 1764), and those illnesses that failed to kill often scarred or attracted treatments that were even worse. A child might have to survive teething problems, tapeworms, chicken pox, whooping cough, smallpox, lead poisoning, thrush, measles, and mumps, while being bled, swaddled, and dosed with belladonna, syrup of poppies (opium), quinine, rum, gin, brandy, laxatives, and patent medicines. Children wore amulets of such ingredients as mistletoe and elk's horn, had hare's brains smeared on their gums while teething, and were given enemas for worms. A particularly drastic worm remedy involved inserting a piece of pork on a string into the rectum and drawing it out slowly to lure the worms.

The baby's nourishment might come from several sources. In well-off families, parents would likely turn their babies over to a wet nurse, a servant whose one qualification was an abundant supply of milk. In richer families, the wet nurse lived in the baby's family home; in middle-class families, the baby lived with the wet nurse until weaned. From the middle of the 18th century, however, there was an increasing tendency for even middle- and upper-class women to nurse their own babies. Mother's milk was inefficiently supplemented with pap (bread or flour soaked in milk, water, or beer) and possets (moistened flour and sugar, sometimes flavored with extracts of almonds or violets). Babies were fed with pewter or wooden pap bowls and spoons.

Prior to the 18th century, children were viewed as small, unruly adults. This perception was reflected both in the ferocious chastisements to which they were subjected and in their clothes, which were almost exactly like those of adults. During the 18th century, however, there was an increasing tendency to view childhood as a special state of innocence, during which children could be molded and shaped by love and education. During the second half of the century, there were ample signs that things were changing. The increase in maternal breast-feeding was one example of a more hands-on approach to parenting. Fathers and mothers proudly played with their children and commissioned more portraits of them, and children began addressing their parents by informal, affectionate names like "mama" and "papa." Children were dressed in looser, less-formal clothes. Discipline in many families became less harsh, even lax.

There were special activities and products for children, including oral tales of fairies and children's books. Children's songs and rhymes included variations that are still familiar today, like "Hush-a-bye baby, on the tree top," "Jack and Gill," and "Hickere, Dickere Dock."

Parents also bought toys for their children, including rattles, small tops, dolls, wagons, and sports equipment. They played hoops, trap-ball, and barley-break. Play, in short, was one part mischief, one part organized game, and one part pretending to be an adult—in preparation for courtship, the marriage market, and the founding of a family of one's own.

Life for children was not all play and fun. Whether early or late in the 18th century, some families were simply dreadful. Parents had near-total control over their children. Many parents still expected silence and unquestioning obedience. In poorer families, children were put to work by age four or five. They helped with laundry, farm chores, textile work (such as spinning and carding wool) done at home, factory work, and shop-keeping. London's urchins worked as crossing sweepers or chimney sweeps. Some children had teeth sold to make dentures for the rich. Some were abandoned or orphaned and turned to prostitution and thievery. The revolution in attitudes toward childhood was a slow and gradual one, indeed, for it was accompanied by an acceptance, even an enthusiasm, for child labor.

Among the wealthy, there was an early dispersal of children, with boys (and sometimes girls) being sent to boarding schools. The boys then went to a university, perhaps, or traveled abroad, while the girls were married off as soon as possible. Girls were not admitted to the great public schools (or to most grammar schools). Nor were they allowed to attend any of Britain's universities.

For many, financial independence and marriage marked the end of childhood and, at the same time, the beginning of a new family and new children. The varied expectations and possibilities surrounding birth, play, school, and work helped to shape the lives of young people in 18th-century England (Olsen, 31–32, 51–55, 269–70).

To read about children in Chaucer's England, see the Europe entry in the section "Children" in chapter 2 ("Domestic Life") of volume 2; for Elizabethan England, see the England entry in the section "Children" in chapter 2 ("Domestic Life") of volume 3; and for Victorian England, see the Victorian England entry in the section "Children" in chapter 2 ("Domestic Life") of volume 5 of this series.

FOR MORE INFORMATION

Ford, B. *The Cambridge Cultural History of Britain, Eighteenth-Century Britain.* Cambridge, England: Cambridge University Press, 1992.

Lynch, J. *Eighteenth Century Resources.* <http://newark.rutgers.edu/~jlynch/18th/>, accessed October 10, 2003.

Olsen, K. *Daily Life in 18th-Century England.* Westport, Conn.: Greenwood Press, 1999.

DOMESTIC LIFE
|
CHILDREN
|
The Colonial Frontier
of North America

England

France

Japan

New England

Life at Sea

FRANCE

In 17th-century France, parents from all walks of life routinely shipped their newborn children off to be nursed and cared for by complete strangers, who would swaddle the babies and hang them on hooks in the wall so that the nurses could go about their daily work without the burden of their charges. Child-rearing manuals of the period demonstrate that it was the rare mother who visited her children, even if she had the leisure and means to do so. Those who did visit were generally less worried about the conditions in which their children lived than about ensuring that their payments were being used for a child who was still alive. Nurturing concern was not encouraged, nor was it seen as socially relevant.

By the early 19th century, the tables had turned. Tributes to breast-feeding and "natural" mothers made nurturing a priority. Children were no longer seen as beasts tainted by original sin but as unique individuals in need of personal attention and love. Not surprisingly, mothers who refused to fulfill their God-given obligations to breast-feed, love, and educate their children could find themselves castigated by husbands, neighbors, or even legislators who wished to protect the health of the future citizens.

The change from the older view was driven by philosophers of the 18th century. These philosophers, people such as Jean-Jacques Rousseau and Louis-René Caradeuc de la Chalotais, claimed that children were "noble savages" who would naturally exhibit rational thought and perform good actions if removed from the constraints placed on them by society. As Rousseau claimed in book one of *Emile*, his treatise on education, "God makes all things good; man meddles with them and they become evil." These ideas rapidly caught on. On the eve of the revolution in France, the noblewoman Madame de Staël claimed, "Everyone has adopted Rousseau's physical system of education. A sure system has permitted no disagreement. . . . He has succeeded in restoring happiness to childhood" (Rousseau, xl, 5).

Childhood had begun to have its virtues, distinct from those of adulthood. Primary among them was an assumed "naturalness" and innocence, a distance from and a corresponding lack of corruption by society. As this shift occurred in the perception of childhood and children's needs, a selflessly nurturing and domestic mother displaced a distant and controlling father as the ideal parent for early childhood. Women were often (although not always) seen as uniquely capable of giving young children the love and attention that they would need to become moral adults. No longer was the well-being of the family the sole responsibility of the male bread-winner and official head of the household. In the 17th century, women of any social class had been able to justify sending their children far from home to a wet nurse or for a convent education. By 1800, however, a woman who danced the night away at a ball while a nurse watched over the child in the family home would be berated for her "unnatural tendencies." Women were expected to stay home with their children to love and nurture them.

Once people came to believe that children were naturally capable of rationality and good actions with a proper upbringing, the ideal education became less a matter of having children memorize prayers and decline Latin verbs and more of searching out the most appropriate subjects and methods for each child as a member of a modern society. While the "unenlightened" system was primarily intended to train children to be good Christians and to form consciences that would behave with respect for accepted moral standards, the new education promoted a second goal alongside the first, that of creating valuable citizens. A practical curriculum based on reading French authors, spending time in physical exercise such as gymnastics, and exploring the natural sciences made education constructive and concrete instead of philosophical and based on a Latin ideal. Instruction that would prepare children for an earthly future became essential.

A central part of this practical preparation involved care for the child's body—physical education—as a necessary base for moral education. As the quotation from Madame de Staël indicates, few parents joined the philosophical debates on education or virtue, but many focused on implementing practical components to the physical system of education. In 1700, advice manuals had warned parents to make certain that their children did not crawl before walking; allowing such "bestial" action might

Engraving by Jean-Baptiste Simonet after Moreau le Jeune. The French peasant family idealized here enjoys good housing and clothing. Notice the tender bustle of children and animals, as well as the affectionate parenting skills of the father. © Perry Casteneda Library.

prevent the child from ever becoming civilized. Instead, parents used leading strings, which were ribbons tied around the children's waists or sewn to the shoulders of their clothing. When such children were tempted to drop to all fours and move by crawling, adults could pull them back to a standing position and encourage them to walk—much like a puppet on a string. Swaddling clothes and corsets also kept children firmly upright and molded their bodies into a more adult form.

In a backlash against this physical coercion, 18th-century children's fashions reflected an attempt to be "natural," and clothing became looser and less restrictive. The swaddling and corsets that had restricted children gave way to more freeing styles that allowed children to roam and explore. Soon, things earlier regarded as frivolous, such as the time spent taking long walks, playing with toys, or inventing games with friends, were cast in a new light. Walks provided an ideal time to teach natural science and to fortify a child's body, while games of all sorts allowed the young mind to relax and opened new pathways for thought. A growing emphasis on toys was part of a new focus on both play and relaxation as necessary activities, especially for children of the leisure classes. All of these changes meant that by the end of the 18th century, children were far likelier to live at home, have a great deal of contact with their mothers, and enjoy freedom to move and play than had been the case in 1650.

~Jennifer J. Popiel

FOR MORE INFORMATION

Ariès, P. *Centuries of Childhood: A Social History of Family Life.* Translated by Robert Baldick. London: J. Cape, 1962.

Bloch, J. *Rousseauism and Education in Eighteenth-Century France. Studies on Voltaire and the Eighteenth Century, vol. 325.* Oxford: Voltaire Foundation, 1995.

Ehrenreich, B., and D. English. *For Her Own Good: 150 Years of the Experts' Advice to Women.* New York: Doubleday, 1978.

Gélis, J. "The Child: From Anonymity to Individuality." In *A History of Private Life,* edited by Philippe Ariès and Georges Duby, vol. 3., *Passions of the Renaissance,* edited by Roger Chartier, translated by Arthur Goldhammer. Cambridge, Mass.: Belknap, 1989.

Hardyment, C. *Dream Babies: Three Centuries of Good Advice on Child Care.* New York: Harper and Row, 1983.

Hunt, D. *Parents and Children in History: The Psychology of Family Life in Early Modern France.* New York: Basic, 1970.

Lynch, J. *Eighteenth Century Resources.* <http://newark.rutgers.edu/~jlynch/18th/>, accessed October 10, 2003.

Rousseau, J.-J. *Emile, or On Education.* Edited by Peter D. Jimack. Translated by Barbara Foxley. London: Everyman, 1993.

Shorter, E. *The Making of the Modern Family.* New York: Basic Books, 1975.

JAPAN

Although children in Japanese cities seemed to enjoy more freedom and leisure than children in agricultural areas, the family life of both centered on productivity—that is, on vocational aptitude. The principal concern of parents, in particular, and of the community, in general, involved the contribution that children could make to their households, villages, cities, and superiors.

Neither Buddhism nor Shintō ("The Way of the Gods") considered infanticide a "sin." Because Buddhism taught that life is an illusion and that a person's goal was to return to the great whole, infanticide was just an acceleration of the process of reincarnation. In fact, one of the telling euphemisms used for infanticide was "sending back," implying that the baby was sent back to Buddha. Shintō was quiet on the subject.

Folktales tell of midwives who, in attended births, came prepared with a bowl of water. If the "correct" sex was born, then the baby was washed in the bowl. If the "wrong" sex appeared, the baby was immersed and drowned in the water. The bowl was called the "sending-back bowl."

Not only females were killed; if the birth order was inappropriate, or one already had too many boys, male babies were sometimes killed as well. Reprehensible and disgusting as this is to our sensibilities and morality, Japanese had little if any moral aversion to the practice. It was one of the major methods of family planning.

Peasant families needed at least one son to perpetuate the household. Because of high infant mortality resulting from disease and malnutrition, many families wanted to have two sons as a kind of social security. But more commonly, after being assured of one son, girls were preferable. Girls could be hired out, married out, or even sold.

Naming children was a curious feature to 18th-century Japanese customs. Villager children were commonly known only by a "common name." The firstborn son was almost always named Taro ("big boy") or Ichiro ("first boy"), the second Jiro ("second son"), and the third Saburo ("third son"). Because most families did the same, the resulting comedy of errors was reminiscent of Charlie Chan's "Number One Son." Typically, some sort of descriptive word or phrase ("big-foot," "red nose," "tall") or reference to the boy's father ("Taro's son") helped to differentiate the various Taros within the village. In the market towns, a merchant might refer to one by one's village, such as Murayama ("Mountain Village") Taro, or according to one's special occupation ("rice-mat Jiro," "sedge-hat Saburo").

In the 18th century, girls were often named according to some aspiration. Female names took on flights of fancy as girls were named Haru (Spring), Kiku (Chrysanthemum), or Mitsu (Abundance).

Once children had grown up a bit, adults expected them to participate in household and village tasks. This responsibility was particularly true in agricultural areas. Although peasants used several ingenious scarecrows to protect the village crops, children were often saddled with the task of keeping birds away from the ripening grain. In particular, peasant children used a tool called "pulling boards" (*hiki-ita*), consisting of long lengths of twine attached to several clacking boards. One child could pull and release several strings alternately to startle birds all over the field.

Within the merchant households of *chōnin* (city folk), the needs of the business frequently dictated the composition of families and the proximity of children to their parents. Because the merchant needed assurance that an adult male could both succeed him in business at any time and thereby protect the family inheritance, he often could not wait until his own son became an adult. The merchant would therefore apprentice his son to another merchant household and then adopt his chief clerk as his own heir.

When boys (and often girls as well) were apprenticed at the age of seven or so and went to live with other merchant families, they would receive room and board, one or two sets of clothes per year, and often a little spending money. In return, they would serve their masters, first by drudgery and later as an apprentice in the specialty of the business concern. After 20 years or so, the merchants could adopt them as heirs or set them up in a branch business. In the meantime, the young man's or woman's natal family was doing the same with another set of adoptees. Often, the adopted heir would in turn adopt the natural son of his adopted father.

Chōnin children had their own games and amusements, but the significant advantage to living in the cities was that children were not commonly employed in hard labor or apprenticed until they were teenagers. Stories and accounts abound concerning the relatively carefree lives of *chōnin* children.

Children everywhere did enjoy some free time. Young girls looked forward to the Doll Festival (Hina Matsuri) on March 3, when ornate dolls were displayed in tiers in the main room of the home. In the 18th century, the dolls still represented the evils of the year, and so they were ceremoniously tossed into swift-running rivers. In most areas, however, the dolls were elaborately costumed, representing the noble courtiers at the emperor's palace. They also represented the growth and maturity of girls in the household, who were toasted with a round of *mirin*, a sweetened, cooking sake.

The first week of the fifth month was Boy's Day (*tango no sekku*), when young boys were given gifts of bows and arrows and kites. Carp streamers were also flown to bring good fortune; it was believed that boys were like carp, which prefer to swim upstream against the current.

If a newborn infant in 18th-century Japan escaped the widespread practice of infanticide, then he or she could look forward to a life governed by the material needs of the community. *Chōnin* children, while enjoying more free time than peasant children, had to adapt to the unavoidable requirements of the business class. Similarly, peasant children, from an early age, helped their elders in their village's year-round agricultural duties (Perez, 17–18, 66–67, 157, 167, 239–40, 247, 253).

To read about children and family life in Japan in the 20th century, see the Japan entry in the section "Children" in chapter 2 ("Domestic Life") of volume 6 of this series.

FOR MORE INFORMATION

Dunn, C. J. *Everyday Life in Traditional Japan*. Tokyo: Tuttle, 1969.
Japan Information Network. <http://www.jinjapan.org/index.html>, accessed October 23, 2003.
Perez, L. G. *Daily Life in Early Modern Japan*. Westport, Conn.: Greenwood Press.

DOMESTIC LIFE
|
CHILDREN
|
The Colonial Frontier
of North America

England

France

Japan

New England

Life at Sea

NEW ENGLAND

The day-to-day lives of children in colonial New England varied according to many factors, none of which was more crucial than the culture into which the children were born. The prominence and character of work and play were different for Native American children, white colonial children, and children who were the black slaves of white masters.

For Native Americans, a typical winter day began with the family's need for fire, food, and water. All three might be provided by the older children of the family, one of whom fetched firewood while another fetched water from the village spring, and the third killed some small game such as a rabbit or squirrels for the family breakfast. Native boys did more hunting and fishing from canoes, while the girls gathered berries.

As the children grew older, they adopted the customs of their elders, customs that very often prescribed certain types of thought and behavior depending on the roles that the particular tribe attributed either to men or to women.

Children of white New England families during the colonial period divided their time between work and play. However, New England colonists often regarded free play as suspicious. Puritans deemed many games to be heathenish, immoral, and a waste of time, and such games in the hands of religiously immature children might well be dangerous for them.

The typical New England view of nature also affected child's play. Untamed nature was looked on as spiritually perilous. A child who spent too much time playing in nature could come under the influence of Satan. Indeed, Puritans believed that God had damned all mortals, including infants and children, to hell as retribution for the sinful actions of Adam and Eve. Only a few "elect"—that is, a few individuals spared from hell by virtue of the generous intervention of Jesus—would avoid eternal damnation, and these elect could not be children who die young.

This last doctrine was a matter much contested among Puritan congregations. However, the official answer from the Puritan clergy was that, in the first place, infants and little children were not innocent. They were depraved from the moment of conception, and they would go to hell. Although God might have elected some for salvation, all members of the elect had to secure their salvation by going through a personal journey of spiritual humility known as justification. Children who died did not live (obviously) beyond their youth and consequently never had an opportunity to undertake the ritual of justification. Therefore, they went to hell. The Puritans offered some concessions at this point, however: they taught that children who died young were consigned to an easier room of hell.

In part because of these religious conceptions specific to 17th-century New England culture, adults did not encourage children to prolong the time of childhood games but ushered them as quickly as possible into a somber and useful adulthood where they worked at an early age on the farm and in the household. The urgency of bringing children to God also meant that a substantial amount of time not spent in work had to be spent instead on Bible study and religious education. These more serious activities shortened the playtime of colonial children.

Many young people of 12 or 13 became apprentices when their parents contracted them out to artisans and employers to do work. The duty of their artisan-employers was to feed and lodge them, to teach them to read and write if necessary, and most important, to teach them a trade. Apprentices were under an obligation to work for their master. Boys were usually apprentices of artisans, merchants, and professionals such as lawyers and physicians, while girls were apprentices in households to learn spinning and weaving. The most famous apprentice of colonial New England, who left an account of his days, was Benjamin Franklin, whose father had apprenticed him out to Benjamin's brother James, a Boston printer and journalist.

From Franklin and other sources, we know that the establishment of an apprenticeship required a formal, legal contract. Under usual circumstances, the apprentice who decided to leave his master before the allotted time expired broke the law and could be pursued like a runaway slave. Franklin was able to run away from his brother without consequences only because his contract had been legally suspended after his brother's arrest by the British authorities.

We also learn an unhappy fact about apprentice life from Franklin. It was the rare apprentice who was not ill treated by his master. Often, apprentices were housed abominably, not fed adequately, worked far too hard, and beaten.

Any child of a slave couple in colonial New England legally belonged to the mother's master. However, unlike the situation in the south, where so many hands were required in farming expansive acreage, children were often considered to be burdensome to the master, who was only too eager to have someone else assume responsibility for them.

Black slaves frequently married Indian slaves, free Indians, or free blacks. In such cases, the fate of the children depended on the mother's situation. If she were the free person in the union, the children would be free. If she were the slave, her children would be slaves.

As in the south, slave families were often broken up when mother or father was sold to someone who lived far away. And as in the south, the death of an owner often meant that his estate, including his slaves, was divided up or sold off indiscriminately. Newspaper advertisements reveal that mother and children were separated at the whim of the owner. In some cases, infants considered burdensome were given away, occasionally even before they were born. The Boston newspapers carried the ads—for example, "A fine Negro child of a good healthy breed to be given away—inquire of the printer" (from the *Boston Weekly News Letter* of June 26, 1760), and "a fine healthy female child to be given away" (from the *Boston Gazette* or *Weekly Advertiser*, June 25, 1754).

Slave children, more than the children of Native Americans or white settlers, suffered from the threat and the reality of familial separation. Native American children worked from an early age, as did their white counterparts. However, the Puritan insistence on the natural depravity of infants and children resulted in a particularly rigid and punishing cultural ethos for growing up in colonial New England (Johnson, 6–8, 12, 68–69, 129, 141, 152–53, 169–70).

FOR MORE INFORMATION

Boorstin, D. J. *The Americans: The Colonial Experience*. New York: Random House, 1958.
Johnson, C. D. *Daily Life in Colonial New England*. Westport, Conn.: Greenwood Press, 2002.

DOMESTIC LIFE
|
CHILDREN
|
The Colonial Frontier
of North America

England

France

Japan

New England

Life at Sea

LIFE AT SEA

Children were not strangers to oceanic travel in and around the 17th and 18th centuries. From infancy until young adulthood, children resided on ships as family of crew members and as laborers.

With wives traveling on such extended voyages, whaling captains were sometimes called upon to deliver their own children. Some women managed to return home to await the event; yet others went to sea so that they would be with their husband for the birth. Surely these women missed the buttress of the circle of female relatives and neighbors who normally gathered to assist the doctor or midwife at such a time. Whenever possible, the attempt to provide such support was made. If a ship was in the company of another vessel with a woman aboard, arrangements were made for her to be present. If the time of a woman's "confinement," as it was called, could be synchronized with a visit to a port, the mother-to-be might be left to the care of a missionary or other responsible person until the ship could return.

Caring for a baby shipboard could not have been easy. One solution to this problem was to sew the infant into the crib. This is not as extreme a measure as it perhaps seems. Diapers, or napkins as they were known, were made of flannel, as was much of small children's clothing. Laundering the baby's voluminous wraps was a problem because fresh water was carefully monitored and not always available. Napkins washed in saltwater or dried in salt spray created a surface unsympathetic to the baby's delicate skin. Resourceful mothers used rags, soft paper, or any other gentle material available to line the napkins.

Some parents left one or more of their children in the care of family when they departed for a voyage, although hundreds of children were raised aboard their father's ship. Growing up aboard ship frequently brought times of great trial. It is said that young children who learned to walk while shipboard actually had difficulty walking on land once they got to port and thus reverted to crawling to get around. Shipboard children generally enjoyed good health, although once they returned home, their isolation from other children while on the voyage made them vulnerable to all the childhood diseases from which they had been sheltered.

Despite the bother that the children must have caused aboard ship for the crew, they were often the objects of great affection. "The Men have been mending sails on deck, and I have had the Baby up there. He has been down on the sail, playing with a ball of twine and getting in the Men's way all he could." Crew members made a variety of handcrafted items for shipboard youngsters and tolerated their being underfoot. "The cooper has been making me a bathing tub to bathe the baby in; it is a very nice one. He has taken a great deal of pains with it."

Perhaps having the sound of children about helped the men deal with separation from their loved ones. Seeing the captain's offspring let them imagine what their youngsters could well be doing ashore, and perhaps, in a way, they felt that they were not so far apart.

Living on ship proved one big adventure for most boys, and many became obsessed with it. The rigging made an appealing playground and a perfect place to escape their mother or an annoying sibling. The cook seems to have been a particular favorite of children. The cook could slip the youngsters extra snacks, and he would have a more regular schedule, which could accommodate a small person's questions and desire for companionship. Being such a minority amid so many adults, the captain's children were often spoiled and at times would get out of hand. It was not unusual for the vocabulary of these youngsters to include a striking number of colorful sailors' expressions and swear words.

Parents set time aside to instruct their children. It was not unusual for this to be a responsibility shared by both parents. Once girls reached adolescence, however, it was highly likely that they were left at home for formal schooling. For young women of this time, it was very important to have proper and polished social skills. With no other model than her mother, these were less likely to be complete. Additionally, there was concern for the reputation and virtue of such a young and innocent creature aboard a ship full of men. If aboard ship, little girls tended to be kept closer to mother and indoctrinated in the art of needlework and other acceptable feminine pastimes.

Animals aboard ship offered children opportunities for friendship and hardship. "As I went on deck, the first sight that greeted my eyes was the pigs and chickens running about at large on deck." Carrying live poultry, pigs, and goats was the best way to ensure fresh eggs, meat, and milk. It was not unusual for the children to become attached to the animals, which, in many cases, became their pets. "There were tears in Minnie's eyes this morning, when we went to the breakfast table, to see her Juba on the dish. . . . She thinks Wiggie must be very lonely."

Cabin boys, although unrelated to the passengers and other members of the crew, often assisted the captain's wife and became her responsibility. The women showed their affection for these boys in a variety of ways. Journals report that sometimes the captain's wife altered and repaired a cabin boy's clothes, taught him, and even made sure that his stockings were full for Christmas.

From about 1700 to 1800, children were present aboard all types of wind ships. Children accompanied their parents aboard ships, interacting with the crew, having adventures possible only on the high seas, and still receiving an education throughout. Not all boys aboard ship, however, were simply the sons of a sailor. Cabin boys worked on ships in the absence of any family, although sometimes cared for by the wives of officers (Volo and Volo, 161, 166–69).

FOR MORE INFORMATION

Druett, J. *Hen Frigates: Wives of Merchant Captains under Sail.* New York: Simon and Schuster, 1998.

Volo, D. D., and J. M. Volo. *Daily Life in the Age of Sail.* Westport, Conn.: Greenwood Press, 2002.

DOMESTIC LIFE

AGING & DEATH

The Colonial Frontier
of North America

England

Japan

New England

Life at Sea

Aging and Death

Accompanying the aging process during the 17th and 18th centuries were many changes related to spouses, family, and society. And death resulted in a host of rites and procedures that affected not only the corpse, but the deceased's surviving relatives, as well.

As today, the aging process entailed for many people during the 17th and 18th centuries the loss of a spouse. Along North America's colonial frontiers, female settlers who found themselves widows faced a predicament: how to be independent in a society where female dependence on males was so prevalent. This same dilemma arose for widows in Japan, New England, and England, including those of sailors. The wife of a sailor who died while serving aboard ship faced material destitution. To address the problem, the British Royal Navy implemented a life insurance program of sorts, although it fell short of what was needed. In colonial America and elsewhere, widows could inherit the wealth of their deceased husbands, remarry, or become dependent on their children.

Husbands who lost their wives tended to enjoy greater security. Remarriage was relatively easy. And for those men who reached a ripe old age alongside their wives, retirement was a possibility. In Japan, merchants dreamed of saving enough money to enjoy the leisure of a retirement surrounded by the arts. Similarly, a Japanese village's elders could participate in local government, profiting from the ensuing prestige.

Of course, many people worked into their old age and, indeed, until death. As British sailors aged, they often left the rigors of the Royal Navy for a slightly more relaxed life on merchant ships, where they worked as cooks and sail makers. Japanese villages had at least one diviner, who was typically an older woman. In England, where poverty reigned for a good part of the population, it was not unusual to see the elderly hoping to find work in the miserable workhouses that dotted the land.

With death came a variety of complex funeral arrangements. Some cultures, such as those in England and most North American colonies, buried their dead. In Japan, cremation was characteristic of the burial process. Custom also dictated the response to death of the family and friends of the deceased. In colonial New England, the Puritan aversion toward religious ritual and gilded ceremony meant that religious burial was out of favor, although Puritans did invest time and energy into decorative tombstones.

In contrast, English burials—especially those of the rich—were elaborate and expensive propositions involving many ceremonial fineries, alms, and paid attendants. The poor, on the other hand, made do with what they could afford, which often was very little. In Japan, all funerals took place in Buddhist temples and involved condolence gifts, tablets (like tombstones), and a complex series of postburial mourning rites that reflected the 18th-century Japanese predilection for numbers and vigilant fidelity to ceremonial rites.

Finally, it is important to note that death seemed far more common and capricious during the 17th and 18th centuries than it does for many contemporary cultures in the developed world. Two, three, or four centuries ago, disease and injuries commonly led to serious ailments that, in turn, led to death. Given this familiarity with death and also with brief life expectancies, it was not unusual for a certain acceptance of life's passing to accompany bereavement.

~Peter Seelig

FOR MORE INFORMATION

Veyne, P., ed. *A History of Private Life*. Vols. 1 and 2. Cambridge, Mass.: Harvard University Press, 1987.

THE COLONIAL FRONTIER OF NORTH AMERICA

As colonists in America grew older, they faced new and daunting challenges. Illness and death became more likely, and the death of a spouse left many families emotionally distressed, socially awkward, and materially incomplete. The challenges that widows and widowers faced, however, differed according to sex, and remarriage at an older age was common and not infrequently repeated.

Some families experienced the trauma of losing a father. Legally, the death of the male head of the household meant the dissolution of the family. The archaic term *relict*, used in reference to his survivor, paints an accurate picture of the widow in colonial times. The widow was simply a remnant, a leftover from a relationship that no longer existed. Following the husband's death, household inventories were taken in preparation for the redistribution of resources that would take place. By law, a widow commonly inherited one-third of the household goods. She was also entitled to use or receive income from a third of the real estate for the rest of her life or until she remarried.

In their wills, some husbands made explicit pleas on behalf of their wives. Tristram Coffin directed his son Nathaniel to "take special care [of his mother and] provide for her in all respects." His brothers all contributed a fixed sum annually to help support their mother. If a woman had minor children, as a widow she might be permitted to retain control of the entire estate until her sons came of age. In such circumstances, the courts routinely granted the widow administration of the husband's estate. A study of 93 New Hampshire widows between 1650 and 1730 found that even in the presence of grown sons, 75 to 80 percent of the women obtained joint administration. On some occasions, however, not only did a man manage the estate, but an appointed male guardian received legal custody over her children, as well.

Some widows were hesitant to remarry. For the first time in their lives, they found themselves in control of their finances. William Alexander explained that men "exercised nearly a perpetual guardianship over them (women) both in their virgin and married state, and she who, having laid a husband in the grave, enjoys an independent fortune, is almost the only woman who among us can be called free."

Whereas a widow could be left in a comfortable financial situation, remarriage had its risks. A widow who remarried gave up all her unprotected property to her husband. She would once again have to defer to the generosity of her husband for both her personal needs and those of the household. The widower Samuel Sewall pursued the widow Dorothy Denison, asking her what financial allowance she felt he should bestow on her annually. Despite a generous offer on his part, she refused him, leaving him to note in his diary, "She answer'd she had better keep as she was, than give a certainty for an uncertainty." In addition to her own security and comfort, a widow had to worry about the security of her children's inheritance. If she chose imprudently, her new mate could squander the wealth meant for the children of her prior marriage.

Naturally, many women missed the companionship and emotional support of a spouse, but it was socially acceptable for them to find fulfillment with their children.

It was not unusual for a widow to live with the family of one of her adult children. Even though she would have to acquiesce to her daughter or daughter-in-law as female head of the household, she held a socially acceptable place in the household.

Widowhood for men was different. Dependency on grown children was not as acceptable for a man as for a woman. Many widowers from all economic stations promptly remarried. Loss of a wife affected the entire household negatively. A wife provided essential services to the family, and without her, it functioned poorly. Ironically, death resulting from childbirth was the leading cause of mortality for women. Before the birth of one of her children, Anne Bradstreet composed a poem to her husband acknowledging the risk that loomed: "How soon, my Dear, death may my steps attend." She voiced her concern for the children she would leave behind and bid her husband, "These, O protect from step Dames injury." Husbands, too, worried. Benjamin Bang was concerned about his pregnant wife. In his diary, he noted, "My dearest friend is much concerned being in and near a time of difficulty." He tried to bolster her and dissuade her frightful dreams. Of one such nightmare, he wrote, "I put it off slightly for fear of disheartening her but directly upon it dreamed much the same myself of being bereft of her and seeing my little motherless children about me which when I awoke was cutting to think of."

Besides the emotional loss of a loving spouse and companion, a widower experienced a void in his household. On their deathbeds, many young women urged their husband to remarry. This concern was less out of regard for the husband's happiness than it was for the children's welfare. A mother knew that the vacancy she left would put a tremendous strain on the family. Mary Clap told her husband to "get another Wife as soon as you can, . . . one that will be a good Mother to the Children." Cotton Mather reflected on his widowed state, writing, "My family suffers by it in several instances."

Samuel Sewall's courtship of his third wife, the widow Mary Gibbs, was composed more of legal negotiations than of romantic flirtation. In both letters and personal conversations, the 69-year-old Sewall discussed the monetary effects of the potential union. In his diary, he made note of a conversation: "[H]er sons to be bound to save me harmless as to her Administration; and to pay me £100 provided their Mother died before me: I to pay her £50 per annum during her life, if I left her a Widow." Sewall was concerned because, if a man married a woman before her late husband's estate was settled, he risked becoming liable for the dead man's debts. Mary, naturally, was concerned about burdening her sons financially. Finally, after several letters and meetings between Sewall and Mary's sons, a prenuptial agreement was reached. Sewall agreed to forgo the 100 pounds provided that her sons indemnified him against the debts of their father's estate. However, he did reduce Mary's annual stipend to 40 pounds. The couple was married shortly thereafter (Volo and Volo, 126, 131–33).

FOR MORE INFORMATION

Boorstin, D. J. *The Americans: The Colonial Experience.* New York: Random House, 1958.

Volo, J. M., and D. D. Volo. *Daily Life on the Old Colonial Frontier.* Westport, Conn.: Greenwood Press, 2002.

DOMESTIC LIFE

AGING & DEATH

The Colonial Frontier
of North America

England

Japan

New England

Life at Sea

ENGLAND

Aging had its benefits and its drawbacks in 18th-century England. On the one hand, etiquette recommended that one treat one's elders with respect. On the other hand, getting older meant getting closer to death. Funerals entailed complex rituals, which reflected rigid class structures.

As one aged, one could expect to be treated differently, even by acquaintances and passers-by. For example, it was important to greet acquaintances politely, and when workers greeted each other at their work, they referred to older people as "father" or "mother" even if they were not related; for example, a "Countryman" seeing a wheelwright of his acquaintance greeted him "with the usual Compliment, *Good-Morrow Father Wright, God speed your Labour.*"

Few sources of security existed for an older person who lacked a sufficient income. Workhouses tended to be the last resort of those least able to work: the sick, the handicapped, the mentally retarded, the very young, and the old. It was ironic that those who were older and impoverished wound up in workhouses; workhouses existed, after all, because there was simply not enough well-paid work to go around.

What other options did a poor older man or woman have? There were Poor Law "settlements"—the right to receive parish charity. Enforcement of the Poor Law ultimately resided with the justice of the peace (the local magistrate), who granted certificates for new settlements, and appointed overseers. But they often drove away the elderly, viewing them as a liability rather than as a legitimate person in need.

Prejudice toward older people surfaced in other ways. To some extent, age was an issue in marriage. A husband 10 or 15 years older than his bride would arouse little comment, but significantly larger differences in age, or differences of several years when the woman was the elder, might attract ridicule. In the late 1770s, there was shock and revulsion when historian Catherine Macaulay, age 57, married a man of 21.

Death was a close and constant companion. Birmingham businessman William Hutton received a straightforward appraisal of his chances when, as a child, he lost both his parents. "Don't cry," his nanny told him. "You will soon go yourself." His case was not unusual; average life expectancy fluctuated throughout the century, but it usually hovered in the low- to mid-thirties. This statistic, of course, included children, soldiers and sailors at war, and women giving birth. Those who made it past their young adulthood often led quite long lives.

When death came, it was attended by as much ceremony and display as the family resources permitted. Funerals could be expensive, entailing fees for the beadle, porter, pallbearers, grave digger, and others, as well as mourning clothes for family and servants, alike. Alms were also traditionally distributed to the poor at such a time. The funeral began with a viewing of the corpse, which was usually dressed in a white wool shroud, with its head resting on a wool pillow and covered by a white flannel cloth. The Burial in Wool Act, intended to increase the wool trade, mandated that grave clothes be of wool. Rich families who wanted to circumvent the law had to pay a five pound fine to dress their dead in beautiful clothes, silk stockings, and expensive shoes. The very poor, who could not afford wool shrouds, avoided grave clothes altogether and covered the naked corpse with flowers or hay.

In a genteel family, guests would be issued engraved invitations to the funeral. The guests would receive tokens, including leather gloves (sometimes black for the principal mourners and white for everyone else), mourning rings of varying worth (sometimes containing a bit of the deceased's hair), decorative knots of black ribbons, and a sprig of rosemary, which symbolized remembrance. The procession to church and churchyard would include the parson, wearing a long black gown; an attendant called a mute, who held a black-draped staff; a "feather-man" carrying a "lid of feathers," a tray of black ostrich plumes that he balanced on his head; mourners and attendants on foot, on horseback, or in carriages; and the coffin itself, carried in a hearse drawn by black horses.

The coffin was covered with a long fabric covering called a pall (hence, "pall-bearer"), decorated with the family's coat of arms and topped with several black plumes. The church bells announced the sex and age of the dead, tolling three times for a child, six times for a woman, and nine times for a man.

The poor had only three or four bier carriers in their regular clothes. Even the cost of a small child's funeral—about two guineas—might be beyond them, and their dead were commonly placed in mass graves called "poor's holes," left open to the elements until filled to capacity.

Unfortunately, the troubles of the world did not end with death, or even with burial. "Resurrectionists," who supplied cadavers to medical schools, sometimes unearthed recently buried coffins and stole the bodies inside. To thwart such grave robbers, families buried bodies extra deep, buried them in metal or metal-lined coffins, posted guards, or even on occasion, booby-trapped the gravesites.

If death was a more assertive companion in the 18th century than today, it was sometimes a less-terrifying one. The coarse, straightforward wit of the times accompanied people not only to coffeehouses and clubs but equally to gallows and graves. The one-legged comedian Samuel Foote's epitaph in Westminster Abbey reads as follows:

Here lies one Foote, whose death may thousands save,
For death has now one foot within the grave

(Olsen, 22–25, 38, 259, 274–76).

To read about old age in Chaucer's England, see the Europe entry in the section "Old Age" in chapter 2 ("Domestic Life") of volume 2; for life cycles in Elizabethan England, see the England entry in the section "Life Cycles" in chapter 2 ("Domestic Life") of volume 3 of this series.

FOR MORE INFORMATION

Lynch, J. *Eighteenth Century Resources.* <http://newark.rutgers.edu/~jlynch/18th/>, accessed October 10, 2003.

Olsen, K. *Daily Life in 18th-Century England*. Westport, Conn.: Greenwood Press, 1999.

Plumb, J. H. *England in the Eighteenth Century*. New York: Penguin Books, 1990.

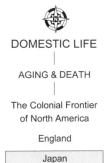

DOMESTIC LIFE
|
AGING & DEATH
|
The Colonial Frontier
of North America

England

Japan

New England

Life at Sea

JAPAN

Many Japanese during the 18th century died at birth or during infancy, whereas others lived into their 80s and 90s. Taken together, the average life expectancy of a Japanese person during the 18th century was about 40 years. As men and women grew older, they encountered new circumstances and expectations. When death came, a host of rituals drawing on religious and other cultural traditions guided the mourning process.

Most Japanese grew old in the context of their household, or *ie*. The head of the *ie* spoke for the household, and the *ie* continued until there was no one to inherit property or title. Heirs therefore had to be obtained. However, it was not unusual for a young man to inherit an *ie* by symbolically disinheriting an elder. For instance, when a young man married and brought his wife home, his father—an older man—might "retire" (*inkyo*) from the active headship of the *ie*. Symbolically, the previous head and his wife would move out of the main room of the house, exchanging rooms with the new head and his new wife. Obviously, this transfer of power and prestige from the old to the young generated a rupture in the social order, one that was not taken lightly by the retired couple.

Symbols of aging manifested themselves in other ways, especially for women. For example, village societies held strong social taboos against older women giving birth. In terms of clothing, the brighter colors of ribbons, combs, or pins were appropriate only to the very young. Older women had to make do with more somber patterned ribbons. Likewise, a distinct hairstyle existed for "retired" (old) women. Very few women dyed their hair (and then only to cover approaching gray); so decorations worn in the hair were the only colorful variations. Older Japanese women sometimes acted as their village's diviner, falling into a trance in order "to channel" the voices of spirits and ancestors.

Older men who retired could benefit from their age. Ōsaka merchants hoped to accumulate enough savings to permit a peaceful retirement. Thereafter, the older merchant could enjoy the arts, literature, and good food and drink.

In many villages, a council of village elders met from time to time to manage village affairs. These men were commonly the heads of the important families in the village. They served as a council to determine tax assessments for the entire village. In some villages, these councils were almost democratic in nature because the heads of virtually every household sat on the council. Of course, many older Japanese had neither the wealth nor the family name to guarantee a comfortable retirement. Indeed, many old men and women labored in fields and in the cities until sickness or injury claimed their lives.

During the 18th century, Japanese funerals could only be conducted at Buddhist temples. The corpse was ritually bathed, the head was shaved, and then the body was wrapped in a plain cotton kimono. The corpse would then be cremated (and soon, considering that bodies were not embalmed or kept refrigerated, except naturally, of course, during the winter). After a short family vigil, when friends and neighbors brought condolence gifts for the family, the ashes were interred in a designated cemetery. The priest would chant special funerary sutras, and then a symbolic vegetarian meal might be shared. The deceased would receive a posthumous Buddhist name, which the priest would write on two commemorative tablets. One tablet was tamped into the earth where the ashes were buried, and the other was given to the family, who ensconced it in their home altar. These ancestral tablets were usually rough, crudely planed laths of wood, although wealthier patrons could buy stone or lacquered wood tablets.

There were two carefully prescribed mourning conventions: the actual mourning period (imi) and the period during which relatives were not to engage in certain acts (buku), such as entering Shintō shrines, wearing brightly colored clothing, eating meat, drinking sake, or, in some areas, trimming one's fingernails or shaving one's head. The length was strictly prescribed for each period, appropriate to one's relation to the deceased. For example, a son was required to keep 49 days of imi and 13 months of buku for his parents. For cousins, one observed 3 days of imi and a week of buku. In-laws merited 10 days of imi and 1 month of buku. Perhaps not too surprisingly, women were to observe 30 days of imi and 13 months of buku for their husbands, but men only observed 20 days of imi and 3 months of buku for their wives.

There were also prescribed visits to the grave at 7, 14, 21, 35, 49, and 100 days after the funeral; then, on the first, third, seventh, thirteenth, seventeenth, twenty-third, twenty-seventh, thirty-third, thirty-seventh, fiftieth, and one-hundredth anniversaries. Grandchildren and great-grandchildren usually had to assume the burden after a while. In practice, the 49- and 100-day visits were the most important because a meal was served at that time. The local priest was usually summoned, or the whole family might pay for a commemorative meal at the temple.

For most peasants who might forget some of these anniversary ceremonies, they could "catch up" either during festivals or by paying a few coppers to have a priest include the neglected dearly departed in his sutra chant.

The temple priests also kept track of the rhythms of the dead, as well. Observing death anniversaries kept both the village safe from offending dead ancestors and the temple in livelihood.

Interestingly, several of Japan's most persistent taboos and superstitions resulted from funerals. For instance, it was thought unlucky to wrap one's kimono right over left or to tie one's kimono sash with two knots instead of one because that was how the corpse was dressed. Handing objects from one set of chopsticks to another recalled the way that bones are picked from cremated ashes. Chopsticks left standing in a bowl of rice were unlucky because that was a dead man's meal. Also, pouring hot water into a cold bath (instead of the reverse) was thought to bring bad fortune because that was how corpses were bathed. And finally, sleeping with one's head pointing north tempted fate because north was the direction of the corpse at the vigil (Perez, 16, 45–47, 63, 97, 131–32, 150–51, 244, 251–55).

FOR MORE INFORMATION

Dunn, C. J. *Everyday Life in Traditional Japan.* Tokyo: Tuttle, 1969.

Japan Information Network. <http://www.jinjapan.org/index.html>, accessed October 23, 2003.

Perez, L. G. *Daily Life in Early Modern Japan.* Westport, Conn.: Greenwood Press, 2002.

DOMESTIC LIFE
|
AGING & DEATH
|
The Colonial Frontier
of North America

England

Japan

New England

Life at Sea

NEW ENGLAND

Death came to New Englanders in many forms. Often, communicable diseases spread rapidly throughout a community, causing the relatively sudden deaths of scores of colonial settlers. The death of a loved one, especially a spouse, created the possibility of remarriage and a host of attendant cultural dictates. Thanks to tombstone carvers, the actual burial of colonial New Englanders took on an artistic aspect with decidedly macabre overtones.

Before the arrival of the Europeans, the native peoples were relatively healthy, their diets and physical activities serving to keep them strong. Europe's devastating diseases—smallpox, malaria, typhus, tuberculosis, bubonic plague, diphtheria, measles, and probably syphilis—were unknown.

With the arrival of the Europeans, however, the good health of Native Americans came to an end. Having no physiological defense against these intrusive germs and viruses, they began dying at alarming rates.

Many New Englanders grew sick and died of diseases and other serious maladies, even though the lack of highly populated and congested cities meant that epidemics were not as bad as in Europe. The illnesses mentioned most often were scurvy, malaria, smallpox, and measles. William Bradford writes that half of the original settlers at Plymouth died of scurvy (and other diseases) within two months of their arrival.

New England also had outbreaks of malaria. One outbreak reported in 1629 and 1630 in Salem took the lives of many citizens and may have been one reason that prompted Governor Winthrop to relocate near Boston, which he considered less unhealthy than Salem.

Sporadic outbreaks of smallpox took their toll on the Massachusetts population, notably in 1660, 1684, 1689, and 1702. The Reverend Cotton Mather, associated with the Salem witch trials, was also a learned scientist and physician and tried to introduce New England to the practice of inoculation. Epidemics of scarlet fever and measles also occurred, including a particularly virulent one in 1688.

Many deaths resulted in a single, surviving spouse. A widow, who in some communities had a legal right to at least one-third of her deceased husband's property, had much to lose in placing that property in the hands of a new husband. Thus, in the case of second marriages, particularly when widows were involved, financial negotiations took place between the couple themselves. Records indicate an unusual situation for widows: while in England, women had no authority to sign contracts, widows in New England had the power to enter into contracts on their own.

The presumed death of an absent mate also resulted in official widowhood. For example, a man who left for a potentially dangerous mission—perhaps into the wilderness to hunt—and did not return within the year might be presumed dead. As a consequence of such a presumption, the missing man's wife was no longer married and was thus free to remarry.

An example of widowhood and remarriage conveys the sense of courtship as an economic negotiation. After Samuel Sewall's wife died, he entered into marriage negotiations with the widow of one of Governor Winthrop's sons. Sewall would have benefited from the handsome estate she inherited from her husband, but when she insisted on him providing her with her own carriage, the negotiations fell apart and the courtship ceased.

There were no last rites and no religious burials, but a symbolic ritual did accompany interment of the dead. From the mid-17th century, tombstone carvers were among the most prolific artists of colonial New England. The central figure found on the 17th-century tombs was a winged skull, signifying the flight of the soul from the earth. The mat area, around the square containing the name and dates of the deceased, was decorated with carvings of leaves and flowers, sometimes Cupid-like figures carrying open books or closed coffins, crossbones, and hourglasses symbolic of the passage of time. Religious themes such as crosses were rare on tombstones. Gradually, the death heads were replaced by highly stylized circular heads (sometimes with heads topped with coifed or curly hair) that seemed to be intended to resemble a particular person and sometimes with a romanticized cherub. In the usual cases, wings continued to be attached to whatever head was drawn. Each community had its own stone carver whose individual touch is identifiable in the cemeteries that display his art.

The poet Edward Taylor enumerated the images found on tombstones in his "Meditation One Hundred and Twelve":

With empty Eyeholes, Butter teeth, bones bare
And spraggling arms, having an Hour Glass
In one grim paw. Th' other a Spade doth hold,
To shew deaths frightfull region under mould.

(Johnson, 25, 103–4, 110, 116, 124–25, 139–40).

FOR MORE INFORMATION

Boorstin, D. J. *The Americans: The Colonial Experience.* New York: Random House, 1958.
Johnson, C. D. *Daily Life in Colonial New England.* Westport, Conn.: Greenwood Press, 2002.

LIFE AT SEA

Over the course of a typical seaman's life, risks of injury, infirmity resulting from the effects of aging, and death all contributed to the emotional, physical, and material risks that faced both him and his colleagues. Some aging or disabled seamen

DOMESTIC LIFE
|
AGING & DEATH
|
The Colonial Frontier
of North America

England

Japan

New England

Life at Sea

continued to work aboard ship as accomplished, though limited, professionals. Others adapted to land but chose to earn their living in seaports, close to newer generations of seamen. Yet again, others suffered cruelly within the walls of "charitable" workhouses. When death came to a sailor, his immediate family, especially any surviving spouse, would hope to benefit from back pay or "dead shares."

Several feasible vocations were available to aging mariners who were not yet ready to retire. It was not uncommon for the cook aboard a merchant or naval vessel to be an older seaman infirmed by age or the loss of a limb. The cook spent most of his time tending the fires in the galley, where he cooked for both the officers in the cabin and the men in the forecastle.

Although most vessels had one set of extra sails that had been made ashore in a sail loft, having someone aboard who could care for the sails was important, if not requisite. At sea, the sail maker was usually an older seaman with sufficient skill in the trade to mend sails worn over the normal course of their use or make them up in an emergency.

Service in a warship was physically taxing in the extreme, and as the experienced man-of-war's men grew older, they became proportionately less attractive to the naval recruiters and press gangs. Unfortunately, in peacetime, there was no market for a maritime labor force composed of men trained to the rigors of the man-of-war. When paid off, experienced and older sailors generally drifted from the navy into the merchant service, where wages and working conditions varied from port to port and master to master.

Many men who were too old or too infirm to serve at sea continued to draw half-pay for decades, a source of security, given the difficulty involved in locating a new source of income when old skills and trades are no longer possible. Still, there were jobs on land at which retired seamen could excel. For instance, boardinghouses made up a large portion of any area of a seaport that

Sailors died in all different manners and degrees of pain, but few had their deaths immortalized in a painting as did Lord Nelson, who fell during the Battle of Trafalgar (1805). © National Maritime Museum, London.

housed sailors. Former seamen, retired from the rigors of the life at sea, ran the most respectable ones. These offered the sailor what he needed most: a decent bed, fair victuals, and a few good drinks.

For some seamen who were aging, retired, or disabled, charitable organizations existed, but often their main strategy was to send these and other poor wretches to workhouses. The first workhouse was established in Portsmouth in 1729. The aged, blind, insane, and diseased were all housed together with the poor. The able-bodied inmates were put to work in the most menial of jobs, such as plaiting straw for sailor's hats or picking apart old rope to make oakum, a hemplike material mixed with tar and used to caulk ship's planking. The proceeds of these labors went to the workhouse so that the inmates of these charities, upon leaving, had neither a nest egg nor a new skill on which to build.

Those who died aboard ship received a burial at sea. The funeral service itself would vary in relation to the standing of the deceased. In 1697, Captain Phenney of the *Septer* died. The following morning, a coffin was made, and at 11:00 A.M., crewmen placed Phenney's corpse into the ready-made casket along with "some iron bullets and coals and what we had to sink him." After prayers were read aloud on behalf of the deceased, a 20-gun salute accompanied the box, body, and weights to the bottom of the sea (Barlow, 476–77).

In either the merchant or naval service, when a seaman was killed by accident or in action at sea, his clothing and effects were auctioned off and the proceeds were given to his widow. The wife of a man who died of disease was less fortunate in that his personal clothing was usually disposed of as being disease ridden. A widow was also eligible to receive her husband's back pay when his ship was finally paid off.

The widows of men killed in major actions were sometimes the beneficiaries of private benefactors or public funds that were raised by subscription in honor of these brave men. Beginning in 1733, every commissioned vessel in the British Royal Navy kept muster rolls containing 2 "widow's men" for every 100 men in the crew. Rated as able seamen, the pay for these phantoms was collected in a pension fund for widows. Known as "dead shares," this policy was expanded in 1695 to include seamen killed in action and finally extended to any seaman serving in the Royal Navy.

Aging, infirmity, and death were constant threats both to the sailors themselves and to their wives and families. Those sailors who could no longer perform their old skills aboard ship would sometimes enjoy the advantages of alternative livelihoods, but many endured humiliating and painful experiences. The death of a seaman was a risk for his family, but various policies dating from the period sought to alleviate the very worst misery (Volo and Volo, 10, 25, 97–98, 109, 158–59).

FOR MORE INFORMATION

Barlow, E. *Barlow's Journal, Vol. II, 1677–1703*. London: Hurst and Blackett, 1934.

Lavery, B. *The Arming and Fitting of English Ships of War, 1600–1815*. London: Conway Maritime Press, 1987.

Volo, D. D., and J. M. Volo. *Daily Life in the Age of Sail.* Westport, Conn.: Greenwood Press, 2002.

DOMESTIC LIFE
|
SEX
|
England

Japan

New England

Life at Sea

Sex

In today's world, sexual behavior is frequently labeled as acceptable, unacceptable, or somewhere in between. The daily patterns of sex in society during the 17th and 18th centuries reveal a similar concern with decency and morality.

In 18th-century England, we find an elevated level of tolerance for certain kinds of behavior and outright hostility directed against other types of behavior. An English gentleman could expect to read and even to hear about the dangers of masturbation. At the same time, he would be attentive to the informal, but widely acknowledged, belief that premarital sex is acceptable, although only in certain carefully delineated situations. He might engage in sexual relations with an inferior such as a maid; or he might frequent a prostitute, so long as he did so with discretion; indeed, he might even spend the night "bundled" up with a girl he hoped someday to marry. Bundling, which occasionally led to sex, was an accepted practice.

Unacceptable in England at the time was homosexuality. If a man or woman flaunted his or her sexual preferences in the wrong place or too openly, he or she could become the victim of a violent and public punishment called a "skimmerton," which was designed to shame the victim under the gaze of his or her peers. Still, certain areas of London were not as dangerous for homosexuals as were others.

By contrast, in 18th-century Japan, the formal and informal rules distinguishing acceptable from unacceptable sexual behavior took on a decidedly more relaxed tone. For example, urban residents—particularly samurai (warrior-administrators)—sought sexual release in homosexual and heterosexual encounters. Wives were not the only source. Japan's extensive and growing sex market included prostitutes and brothels for all tastes and incomes. Curiously, the traditionally masculine warrior ethic that characterized Japan's samurai class did not discourage many from male-male sex.

Japanese government regulation of sexual activity was more concerned with augmenting the profits of the trade in sex and with decreasing disorder in the form of brawls between jealous lovers than it was with enforcing sexual ethics.

Surprisingly, in a society often ridiculed for its sexual prudery and a disdain for sex, the Puritan colonists of New England insisted on the importance, even the necessity, of pleasurable sexual activity. It was necessary, however, that this activity exert itself within the confines of strictly defined and legislated boundaries. Homosexuality, rape, fornication (sex involving unmarried adults), adultery, and other sex acts were outlawed. Being convicted of any one of these crimes carried with it the possibility of public shaming, corporal punishment, or even death.

The sexual activity of American and European sailors triggered a market for prostitutes in ports on both sides of the Atlantic and beyond. Here, too, limits regarding acceptable and unacceptable sex were widely recognized and followed, if not respected. To begin with, prostitution was rarely brought aboard a ship or a vessel. Sex, if it was to be had, was to restrict itself to the brothels and the boardinghouses of ports. Furthermore, reform movements later in the period sought to rid port cities of prostitution. The mechanism by which this cleansing took place involved reformatories for prostitutes.

Two main points appear and reappear in the abstract when considering sexual behavior across cultural borders during the period stretching roughly from 1600 to 1800. First, sexual activity took place in a context of good versus bad—which is to say acceptable versus unacceptable—with a good deal of ambiguity all around. Second, the force, as well as the character, of this opposition varied from culture to culture and within cultures. Therefore, homosexuality was more acceptable in early modern Japan than in 18th-century England, and more acceptable in certain London bars and brothels than elsewhere in the capital. These two main points, taken as an inferred theoretical framework, help to elucidate the almost chaotic assortment of sexual beliefs and practices that the following entries treat.

~Peter Seelig

FOR MORE INFORMATION

Kern, S. *Anatomy and Destiny: A Cultural History of the Human Body.* Indianapolis, Ind.: Bobbs-Merrill, 1975.

ENGLAND

Eighteenth-century England provided men and women with a set of frequently implicit, although identifiable, rules governing sexual relations. "Scientific" notions regarding masturbation and celibacy, for instance, justified a man's premarital sex, itself a well-regulated activity. Manifestations of sexual behavior such as prostitution, homosexuality, and extramarital sex corresponded to quite specific societal expectations and taboos.

In many cases, courtship before marriage was a prolonged affair, meaning that there were several years between puberty and marriage of either celibacy or illicit sexual activity. Some individuals resorted to masturbation. The consensus of medical opinion, however, was that this was an intensely dangerous activity. Dr. James Graham claimed that masturbation could cause "wasting and tottering of the limbs,—idiotism,—horrors,—innumerable complaints—extreme wretchedness—and even death itself." Such dire predictions, combined with a belief that men would suffer injury from too much sexual restraint, made a little discreet fornication a perceived necessity—for men.

There were rules governing a man's pursuit of premarital sex. It was considered permissible to seduce housemaids and even to use a limited amount of force or threat in addition to cajolery; but to be sporting, men had to give their conquests presents or money and to pay for the maintenance of any illegitimate child that resulted.

DOMESTIC LIFE
|
SEX
|
England
Japan
New England
Life at Sea

In practice, many men were unwilling to acknowledge responsibility for their illegitimate offspring, and the inconveniently impregnated maids were often dismissed and driven away from the parish without a good reference.

Lord Sandwich paying attention to a flower-girl; caricature by James Gillray. This cartoon of a nobleman groping a commoner reflects 18th-century England's frequent lampooning of the baser instincts. © Library of Congress.

There was a rise in illegitimate births that cannot be entirely imputed to lecherous masters and hapless maids. The rate of illegitimacy rose from 1.8 percent of all births in 1700 to 5 percent in 1790. One-third of all brides were pregnant at their weddings. The higher illegitimacy rates could have been in part a result of better nutrition, which led perhaps to increased fertility and more conceptions.

Another factor in premarital pregnancy centered on a curious practice that involved a serious couple who might court each other by "bundling." This meant staying together all night in the woman's home. Actual intercourse was discouraged but probably took place in some cases. Also, after an engagement, many families found it quite acceptable for the couple to become sexually active.

Many men chose to get their sexual gratification from prostitutes, who were denounced by doctors, besieged to reform by religious activists, and defended by some as being the safety valve that protected respectable women's virtue. There were more than 10,000 prostitutes in 18th-century London, most of them in their teens.

Some prostitutes offered their services in rooms or brothels; others worked in alleys, coaches, or wherever the customer wanted. The prolific 18th-century writer James Boswell "picked up a strong, jolly young damsel" and had sex with her on the newly opened Westminster Bridge: "The whim of doing it there with the Thames rolling below us amused me very much." For those with very particular tastes, there were specialty brothels and guides to London's prostitutes.

It was mostly to avert sexually transmitted disease that prostitutes and their clients adopted a new form of contraception—condoms—known as "armour" or "English overcoats." Made of sheep's intestines, they were washed, dried, softened by being rubbed with bran and almond oil, and tied at one end with ribbon. Although of dubious effectiveness, some women, for example, who were unmarried or simply unwilling to risk the very real dangers of childbirth resorted to chemicals and plant extracts, in hopes of aborting a fetus. Some believed that drinking heavily or being bled in the feet would do the trick.

Homosexuality certainly existed in 18th-century England. When suspected, homosexuals were exposed to public hostility and ridicule; when found out, their careers and reputations were ruined; when convicted, they were attacked in the pillory and sometimes even killed there.

Despite these obstacles, there was a definite gay presence in 18th-century England. Special brothels and clubs served gay men, who called themselves "mollies" and "queens" (both terms for female prostitutes). There were also lesbians, who attracted attention primarily when they tried to marry other women. Ann Marrow was pilloried in 1777 for dressing as a man and marrying three women; the pelting was so furious that she was blinded in both eyes.

When sex within the marriage grew wearisome or impossible, some people engaged in adultery. A woman in such a position could expect little sympathy in society. The woman was at fault not only if she committed adultery but also if her husband committed adultery. Over the course of the century, fidelity became increasingly fashionable. In the working class, adulterers who carried on shamelessly might find themselves the target of a "skimmerton" or "skimmington," a noisy shaming parade that called attention to their transgression.

The later years of the century saw a growing interest in modesty. Nude bathing was denounced, togas were put on statues, and etiquette books called for more reticence about sex, especially from women. Still, informal rules governing sexual behavior that was variously considered acceptable, not quite acceptable, and not at all acceptable continued to exert their influence, perhaps even more so in contradistinction to the new emphasis on respectability (Olsen, 36–38, 48–51).

FOR MORE INFORMATION

Lynch, J. *Eighteenth Century Resources.* <http://newark.rutgers.edu/~jlynch/18th/>, accessed October 10, 2003.

Olsen, K. *Daily Life in 18th-Century England.* Westport, Conn.: Greenwood Press, 1999.

Stone, L. *The Family, Sex, and Marriage in England, 1500–1800.* New York: Harper and Row, 1977.

JAPAN

During the 18th century, many Japanese displayed a seemingly total disregard for both premarital and extramarital sexual practices and appeared to be casually indifferent to male homosexuality, mixed bathing, open prostitution (of both sexes), common pederasty between Buddhist monks and their juvenile acolytes, and transvestism in the Kabuki theater.

Perhaps because the Japanese religion of Shintō had no strictures against sexual expression, and because Buddhism was a renunciatory religion in the abstract, Japan did not concern itself with sex as "sin." Japan largely ignored the philosophical neo-Confucian strictures against homosexuality. Except for an implied condemnation of incest, Shintō viewed many sexual practices as natural and appropriate human behavior.

The three most commonly used methods of population control were contraception and prenatal and postparturition actions. Methods of birth control other than socially enforced sexual abstinence were common. The so-called rhythm method was not unknown, but coitus interruptus was more common.

Folk medicine had a long history of using herbal concoctions for contraception. Along with coitus interruptus, it appears that Japanese experimented with various forms of condoms. Marriage manuals suggest that the intestines of various animals and fish were used.

DOMESTIC LIFE

SEX

England

Japan

New England

Life at Sea

Chemical compounds to induce abortion were popular and fairly inexpensive, and we know from *bakufu* (national military government) edicts attempting to stop mechanical abortions that they were prevalent, as well. Pictures indicate that the chosen instrument of externally induced abortion was a metal tool resembling a curved knitting needle; but by far the most common means of population control was infanticide.

Homosexuality in medieval Japan was tolerated to such an extent that Japanese were scarcely surprised when they encountered it. Male homosexuality among the samurai class was so common that it became the norm among fighting men. Male prostitutes were commonly available in most inns.

Print by Nishikawa Sukenobu. A man, a male prostitute, and a maid at a brothel in Kyōto. In 18th-century Japan, a wide range of sexual activities existed with greater openness and acceptance than is the case in many contemporary cultures. © Perry Casteneda Library.

The *bakufu* did not make male homosexuality illegal, and the only mention of it in their moral edicts and sumptuary laws concerned brawls or public disturbances outside homosexual brothels or at the stage doors of Kabuki theaters.

Finally, homosexuality among the denizens of the theater was common. Because the *bakufu* forbade women as actors, a professional class of male actors known as *onna-gata* played feminine roles. Although many of those actors were exclusively heterosexual, many were practicing homosexuals.

We have little information about female homosexuality in Japan. It was neither as celebrated nor as overt as male homosexuality was during the period, a fact suggesting that lesbianism was common behind closed doors but never commercialized as was male homosexuality.

Heterosexual practices are the subject of much of Japanese literature. Diaries, letters, and war tales would have been incomplete without candid mention of such human behavior. Officials occasionally condemned these acts because they caused some inappropriate emotional or social attachments or actions; that is, men and women could have sex as long as it did not interfere with their other social roles.

The Tokugawa *bakufu* often tolerated prostitution and the so-called Gay Quarters, sometimes attempting not to regulate morality but to control and even profit from excess.

Virtually every samurai attracted and patronized prostitutes for sexual release and gratification. Licensed castle brothels obtained young women from procurers who kidnapped or purchased them from their families. Young widows, when they could not make another marriage, frequently became concubines or prostitutes. Prostitution had very little in the way of social stigma, and lovers or relatives could "redeem" female prostitutes by repaying their "contract" obligations to the procurers or brothels.

From time to time, the Tokugawa *bakufu* attempted to suppress prostitution, mostly because the brothels were a nuisance to their neighbors. The *bakufu* issued licenses for a fee that became in reality revenue for the *bakufu* coffers. High fences were built around the area, and all customers were disarmed and very carefully controlled. Most large cities had such a quarter. Some, like Ōsaka, had more than one.

Guidebooks tell us that in 1700, there were 308 officially sanctioned prostitutes in Kyōto, 760 in Ōsaka, and 1,750 in Edo. By 1780, the number in Edo had increased to 2,900, and in 1799 it had nearly doubled to 4,972. One must remember that this series of statistics did not include the unlicensed ones who inhabited public baths, massage parlors, teahouses, and sake shops. Stylish young and rich customers ranked their prostitutes, and most guidebooks had convenient rankings for every brothel (Perez, 16–17, 259–63).

FOR MORE INFORMATION

Japan Information Network. <http://www.jinjapan.org/index.html>, accessed October 23, 2003.

Leupp, G. P. *Male Colors: The Construction of Homosexuality in Tokugawa Japan*. Berkeley: University of California Press, 1995.

Perez, L. G. *Daily Life in Early Modern Japan*. Westport, Conn.: Greenwood Press, 2002.

NEW ENGLAND

The topic of sex in colonial New England generally elicited from colonists, not excluding Puritans, a sincere devotion to the pleasures of physical intimacy as long as it occurred within the fixed parameters of marriage. Outside these parameters, sex took on a decidedly sinful hue, and transgressors suffered the punishments fixed by tradition and dogma.

Although we ascribe to the Puritans the prudery of the 19th century, they were open in their acceptance of sex as being a joyful and necessary part of marriage; the final, and indispensable, stage in the completion of the union between a married couple was sexual union. If such a union did not occur for any reason, the marriage was considered to have never taken place. The laws of the various New England settlements reveal that "natural incapacities" or an unwillingness to complete the sexual union was reason for annulling a marriage.

Revealing are the papers of a colonial sailor named Ashley Bowen, who met his wife-to-be after having dreamed of her. He anticipates finding "fair opportunity to examine her real moles and marks with real sweet kisses of real substance of lips and breasts and all the qualifications a young woman could be endowed with to make a man happy."

One of the most graphic examples of the passion of the colonial marriage is that of the poet Anne Dudley Bradstreet to Simon Bradstreet, at one time governor of the Massachusetts Bay Colony. She expresses her feelings in the several poems, replete with sexual connotations, that she wrote about her husband and marriage. She speaks of her children as "those fruits which through thy heat I bore" and her breast as "the welcome house of him my dearest guest," and she declares that "his warmth such frigid colds did cause to melt." Anne went far toward heresy in loving her husband too much. In one of her poems, she compares him with the sun (a symbol of Jesus Christ and God) around which she orbits, suggesting that she not only loved him more than God but also regarded him as equivalent to God.

Despite an acceptance of sex in marriage, some clergymen were under the conviction that lovemaking on the Sabbath, even between husband and wife, was the gravest of sins; and some clergymen were certain that a child born on Sunday was conceived on Sunday. The Reverend Israel Loring of Sudbury, Massachusetts, was especially well known for punishing couples who he thought had made love on the Sabbath. He steadfastly refused to baptize children who were born on Sunday, convinced that they had been conceived on the Sabbath. His policy changed when his own wife gave birth to twins on the Sabbath.

The practice of bundling, particularly in rural households, increasingly came to be an issue at this juncture of the courtship. Bundling was the practice of allowing two unmarried people to lie beneath the bedcovers fully clothed, perhaps with a divider between them. This custom usually took place in the house of the bride-to-be. It was understood that although they lay in the same bed, the male and female were not to have full sexual union. The remoteness of the bride's house in a rural area often made it inconvenient for the groom to visit, and bundling loses something of its daring when one realizes that in most households for many years, there was very little privacy, adults often sleeping in the same room or in both a main room and a loft without a wall or door between them. Still, some theories have it that the increased toleration of bundling increased premarital pregnancies. Another theory is that parents of young people who were reluctant to marry one another often encouraged bundling to heat up the romance and to make them grow more affectionate toward each other.

Although the joys of sex in marriage were anticipated and celebrated, there were as many arrests for sex outside marriage as for any other single crime. Five of the 16 laws carrying the death penalty were sex crimes. With regard to sex outside marriage, magistrates looked into a number of punishable charges. Fornication, or sex between an unmarried couple (including those who were engaged), could result in a fine or worse. On October 6, 1634, John Lee was whipped for several crimes, including enticing the governor's maid to "go with him into the cornfield." On March 7, 1636, William James was set at the bilboes (an iron bar and bolt with shackles) in Boston and in the stocks at Salem and fined for "knowing his wife before marriage."

Adultery, defined as sex between a married woman and a single or married man, could bring with it a penalty of death, although the Massachusetts Bay Colony was reluctant to invoke this punishment. Interestingly, sex between a married man and a single woman was not strictly regarded as adultery or punishable with death. Still, on September 7, 1641, Thomas Owen was to be imprisoned "for his adulterous practices" and sent to stand on the gallows with a rope around his neck for an hour before being returned to prison.

Bestiality and sodomy were punishable by death. One such example occurred on December 10, 1641, when William Hatchet was hanged for having intercourse with a cow.

Rape of an adult was punishable by death or other appropriate punishment, while rape of a child was automatically punished by death.

Also considered a violation of the law was a master's frequent sexual abuse of a servant. The records indicate that the magistrates generally believed the testimony of female servants and strictly dealt with the offenders. For example, a maidservant in John Harris's house complained that Harris and his son, John, had tried to rape her. Her testimony was deemed truthful, and the two men were found guilty. They were whipped 20 stripes each and imprisoned.

The records of colonial New England show a brutality in punishing perceived illicit sex and an insistent invasion into the private lives of the colony's citizens, but they also dispel the stereotype of Puritans as cold, passionless prudes (Johnson, 24, 110–14, 116–17, 167).

FOR MORE INFORMATION

D'Emilio, J., and E. B. Freedman. *Intimate Matters: A History of Sexuality in America*. Chicago: University of Chicago Press, 1997.

Johnson, C. D. *Daily Life in Colonial New England*. Westport, Conn.: Greenwood Press, 2002.

LIFE AT SEA

Prostitution served the carnal requirements of many sailors during the age of sail. These prostitutes tended to work in ports, especially in select taverns and boardinghouses; however, reform movements of the period focused on eradicating this form of sexual relationship that, although characteristic of many parts of 17th and 18th-century Western culture, found a thriving market among mariners.

Prostitution among sailors was typical in the British Empire. A large number of professional prostitutes occupied Portsmouth and Plymouth. Prostitution, which was not illegal, was an institution in most large cities of England at this time. What made it so prolific in these ports was the presence of the British Royal Navy. Although never policy, it was common practice for prostitutes to be brought out to the ships while in port. This was thought to lessen the incidence of desertion. Importing women to the ships was done in foreign ports, as well, especially in the West Indies.

Ships' prostitutes occupied the lowest echelon of their profession, earning so little that they were often not even managed by a madam or pimp. In Plymouth, they rented rooms in the sailors' tavern district near the Quay. They were often forced to share accommodations with other prostitutes or with families of desperately limited means who would tolerate their profession.

Contrary to common perceptions, the women and girls who served as "wenches" and waitresses in taverns and alehouses rarely provided illicit entertainment of a sexual nature. This business was reserved for the bordellos and alleyways of the town. Nonetheless, for as little as a dollar, patrons could bring street prostitutes into the tavern. The owners of these businesses, however, commonly frowned upon this practice, as the authorities could fine them for running a disorderly establishment.

Few, if any, prostitutes remained aboard ships that went to sea. This telling absence was more a function of economics than morality. By the time a ship left port, virtually all of a sailor's money was spent, so that a prostitute's prospect of deriving any financial benefit from a voyage was effectively nil. Additionally, a woman on the lower decks had to depend on a man for her very survival. If she had no husband, she had to find a man who would share both his hammock and his food, as well as serve as her protector.

Boarding establishments in port cities prominently featured a bar, a supply of women of loose morals, or some resident prostitutes. Rooms were furnished with straw mattresses on simple beds, a rough table, and a chair or two. Sailors who frequented these establishments seeking a little sexual diversion sometimes fell victim to conniving characters called crimpers, whose job it was to find crews for ships needing men. Some of the more disreputable boardinghouses overhung the water and contained trap doors so that crimps could easily slip a doped sailor to a waiting boat beneath.

Reform movements of the late 18th and 19th centuries spawned a number of institutions to assist the "wayward women." The Female Penitentiary for Penitent Prostitutes was founded in Stonehouse outside of Plymouth in 1808. Built with private funds after the wretched conditions of the workhouse gained attention, the penitentiary, albeit clean, was austere and constrictive. Inmates were dressed in drab attire, and their heads were shaved. They labored at domestic chores, and those who did not run away generally entered the workforce in domestic service.

The work of prostitutes was a particularly hazardous vocation, but one that thrived in most places where sailors rested from their voyages at sea. The general absence of prostitutes aboard ship made their presence in seaports all the more conspicuous. As a consequence of changing attitudes toward the commercialization of sex, reform movements gained influence in their efforts to eliminate prostitution from the mariners' culture (Volo and Volo, 4–5, 10, 25–26, 156).

FOR MORE INFORMATION

Sturma, M. *South Sea Maidens: Western Fantasy and Sexual Politics in the South Pacific.* Westport, Conn.: Greenwood Press, 2002.

Volo, D. D., and J. M. Volo. *Daily Life in the Age of Sail.* Westport, Conn.: Greenwood Press, 2002.

DOMESTIC LIFE: WEB SITES

http://www.1upinfo.com/country-guide-study/japan/japan87.html
http://www.hoover.archives.gov/exhibits/RevAmerica/1-Who/Fashion.htm
http://www.law.emory.edu/IFL/region/westafrica.html#link4
http://www.royal.gov.uk/output/Page13.asp
http://www.sims.berkeley.edu/academics/courses/is182/s01/assignment1hp.html
http://www.umich.edu/~ece/student_projects/wedding_bride/

3

ECONOMIC LIFE

The basic principle of economic life is that men and women must work to provide for themselves. Of course, throughout history, it has always been that some have had to work harder than others, but this fact does not violate the basic importance of work; it only reveals the complexities of economic life, which includes everything from the production of income to trade to its unequal distribution throughout society. During the 17th and 18th centuries, the spheres of agriculture, industry, trade, and professions intersected one another within—and between—societies. Thus, the economies of colonial Australia and colonial North America, including New England, closely depended on the economies of England, France, and many African societies. Linking them all together were the navies and merchant fleets of Europe and its other colonies. An exception to this intersection of economies was Japan, which quite deliberately cut itself off from almost all trade with foreigners. However, there is one trait of economic life that links these cultures with all others: work.

At the basic level, people work on the land to produce their food and other items they need. However, even at this simplest level, people trade goods among themselves. Thus, economic life moves from the work that we do to the exchange of the products of our labor. This diversification contributes to increasing variety in society, as some who are living in villages and farms work on the land while others move to urban areas that grow ever larger throughout history. The patterns of farm, village, and urban life exist all over the world and help to define the lives of the people who work within them.

Trade, or the exchange of goods, has been as central to human economic life as the production of goods in the centuries preceding and following those covered in this volume. From the beginning of town life in Mesopotamia, the excitement generated within shops lining a street is palpable in the sources. Merchants hawking their wares and shoppers looking for the exotic, as well as the ordinary, form a core of human life. Merchants (and merchandise) have always ranged far beyond local markets as people moved their goods across large areas. Even during the prehistoric late Stone Age, domestic animals native to the Middle East moved down the Nile valley to sub-Saharan Africa, and plants native to the Euphrates valley moved as far east as China. Our global marketplace in the 21st century is only the logical

ECONOMIC LIFE
|
AGRICULTURE
INDUSTRY
TRADE
PROFESSIONS

extension of the constant movement of people and things that goes on as people engage in their economic life.

All societies have been, in part, defined by people at work. They have built societies with divisions of labor, of urban work and rural work, and of class, as some people grow richer than others. To study daily life through history is in large part to understand people at work.

~*Joyce E. Salisbury and Peter Seelig*

FOR MORE INFORMATION

Braudel, F. *The Wheels of Commerce*. New York: Harper and Row, 1979.
Wallerstein, I. M. *Historical Capitalism*. London: Verso, 1983.

ECONOMIC LIFE
|
AGRICULTURE
|
Africa

Colonial Australia

The Colonial Frontier
of North America

England

Japan

New England

Agriculture

From 1600 to 1800, the economies of colonial Australia, North America's colonial frontiers, England, Japan, New England, and sub-Saharan Africa depended primarily on agriculture. This sector of the economy included not only the cultivation of grains, fruits, and vegetables but also the management of livestock ("animal husbandry"). Some of these societies stressed the importance of hunting and fishing, as well. Each society performed agricultural activities in different ways. In some regions, community farming dominated the countryside, while elsewhere, privately owned plots of land were increasingly prominent. In addition, different agricultural traditions gave rise to different methods for preserving the fertility of soil.

England's agricultural output in the 18th century included grains, nuts, fruits, and a celebrated variety of cheeses. Regional diversity characterized England's agriculture. For instance, the Midlands were home to many grain fields. In other regions during the period, shifts in agricultural activity transformed patterns of daily life. In the southern counties, an emphasis on grain notably replaced the more traditional preoccupation with livestock.

In Africa, regional diversity and customs played key roles in agricultural production. In the Great Lakes area, bananas dominated. Central Africa became home to American beans and tobacco crops. Sugarcane and pineapples appeared in other parts of the continent. The diversity resulted from varying climates and soil types.

Early modern Japan possessed three kinds of fields, each suitable for particular crops. Wet rice agriculture dominated the landscape, but upland fields, which were dryer than lowland rice paddies, were appropriate for wheat and sweet potatoes. Residential plots allowed their owners greater discretion in determining which produce was needed.

In colonial Australia, poor soil, droughts, and floods initially hampered crop cultivation; however, sheep breeding there became quite profitable. Along the North American frontier and in New England, Native Americans tended to mix their crops, whereas frontier farmers segregated them according to type. In addition to cultivating crops (especially corn), Native Americans fished and hunted wild game like deer and gathered roots, nuts, and all types of berries. Similar practices appeared throughout sub-Saharan Africa, where hunting, gathering, and fishing not uncommonly accompanied farmwork.

Wherever people lived off the land, the condition of the soil affected the success of agricultural efforts. Thus soil conservation and rehabilitation were vital facets of many agricultural societies, including Japan. Here, villagers improved the fertility of the soil according to several imaginative methods, one of which involved the blending of decaying vegetation, rich in nutrients, with the soil right before seeding.

In England, landowners advanced new, more effective systems of crop rotation, whereby different crops (which required different soil nutrients) grew in select areas. Hence, farmers were able to prevent or reduce the exhaustion of important minerals from the ground. Animal waste also contributed to the replenishment of soil fertility in England.

Agrarians in central Africa burned vegetation and mixed river silt with the earth to fertilize the soil. In East Africa, whole villages moved to a new location after depleting the soil nutrients of their previous location. Africans, too, practiced crop rotation.

Another area of agricultural production that distinguished one society from another concerns the actual farming itself. Japanese villages worked collectively to irrigate, plant, reseed, and harvest crops, as well as to hunt. African farmers in Hausaland worked in extended family units. New England colonists, much like their counterparts in England, were keen on tending their own individually owned plots of land. Indeed, the English farmer ranged from wealthy landowners, who acquired ever-greater tracts of land, to tenant farmers and small freeholders, whose landholdings were sometimes as miserable as their incomes.

The following entries reveal many manners of economic production in the area of agriculture throughout the period and societies covered in this volume. Types of crops, animal husbandry, hunting, gathering, and fishing, as well as land conservation and farming practices, receive particular attention.

~Peter Seelig

FOR MORE INFORMATION

Shaw, T., ed. *The Archaeology of Africa: Foods, Metals, and Towns*. New York: Routledge, 1995.

Slicher van Bath, B. H. *The Agrarian History of Western Europe, A.D. 500–1850*. New York: St. Martin's Press, 1964.

AFRICA

The different types of African agriculture depended on the different climates and cultures found throughout the continent. Most Africans lived in settled communities in which inhabitants of a village worked the surrounding fields, while not a few

others lived a nomadic life with their herds of cattle. Women performed some farm labor in most areas. Some regions saw private ownership of land and resources, whereas, in others, property belonged to the community as a whole. In some areas, hunting, gathering, and fishing represented critical means of providing food for the community. Traditionally, Africans grew only enough crops for local consumption. During the 17th and 18th centuries, however, both the opening of new trade routes across the Atlantic and new cultural contacts led Africans to produce food for export and introduced them to new types of crops, as well.

In the forests of West Africa, people lived in small villages where all the inhabitants were related and spent their lives farming the fields of the surrounding countryside. Men cleared the fields during the dry season, when stumps and brush were burned away. New fields had to be cleared each year, as old ones were allowed to revert to brush in order to replenish their nutrients. Larger trees were left to provide shade to farmworkers. Then the soil was carefully turned so as not to allow the topsoil to blow or wash away. Each farm was about six or eight acres large and was worked by an individual family. Hausaland was similar, in that the extended family worked the land using a large number of hoes to produce such crops as sorghum, maize, and peanuts. The Hausa also had a custom known as the Feast of Thousands, in which people tried to prove that they could get a yield of a thousand sheaves of millet or sorghum, with successful candidates becoming known as "Masters of the Crops" (July, 112–13).

The major crop in the West African forests was yams. In the Great Lakes area and throughout much of the equatorial region, bananas were the main staple. Banana gardens require more labor to set up initially because the ground must be cleared and another crop grown before the soil will support bananas. However, once the banana plants are growing, they can produce 10 times as much food as a similar yam field and require little maintenance. In addition, banana fields do not require standing water and, hence, do not attract the same number of disease-bearing insect pests.

In central Africa, fields were cleared much the same as in other places, and the vegetation was burned to fertilize the soil. In some areas, each extended family had a single field that they farmed by crop association, while in other areas, multiple fields were farmed using crop rotation. In what is now Zambia, large numbers of trees were cut and burned over the soil to increase its richness. Elsewhere, fields were fertilized with silt from the Zambezi or Luapala Rivers. Men and women divided these tasks differently according to the site's environmental conditions. During the 17th and 18th centuries, the equatorial region experienced a farming boom as new American crops such as beans, manioc, and tobacco produced a very high yield that Africans sold the European traders. Unfortunately, these high-yield crops did not lead to a population increase, as the Europeans also traded for large numbers of slaves.

In East Africa, the need to prevent food shortages caused by poor soil and unreliable rainfall shaped many agricultural practices. Farmers grew as many different types of crops as they could so that they would always have something, regardless of the weather in a given year. Using axes, hoes, and sticks, the peoples of East Africa cleared the land, worked its meager resources, and then, when the soil would support no more, moved the village to another location while their old land recovered. Mixed among the farmers were herders, who raised cattle, constantly moving in search of better pasture. Cattle became an important source of wealth throughout the region, and the number of cattle that a family owned determined their prestige. Cattle were exchanged as bridewealth and loans, and in addition to food, people used cattle for clothing, weapons, and tools. During the famines of the early 17th century, farmers whose crops kept failing began having to pay tribute to and recognize the authority of herders who could always travel to find better pastures (Ogot, 831–34).

South of the Zambezi River, the Shona grew millet and sorghum, to which they added sugarcane, pineapples, and other plants introduced by the Portuguese. Most of the latter foods did not become regular staples of the diet and were mainly sold to traders. In the kingdom of Manyika, wheat was grown during April and May, and people may have grown peanuts as well. Farmers used hoes to plow the soil from September until November and commonly burned the brush to create fertilizer. The Shona stored food in bins that were plastered on the inside and sealed to prevent moisture from causing the grain to rot prematurely and that were then kept on rocks or high poles to protect them from termites. People also herded cattle, which held much the same importance as in East Africa. Every year at the beginning of the rainy season, herders moved their flocks to the highlands to prevent disease and then made an annual trek to the lowlands for better pasture. The lowlands also possessed much fish and game. Men fished throughout the year, laying nets made of reeds across the confluence of rivers. Sometimes people would walk downstream and try to drive fish into the nets, as well. Fishing was also important in some river valleys and along the Swahili coast (Ogot, 661–70).

Fire, stone, and muscle went into the forging of this important agricultural tool, the hoe. © Library of Congress.

Hunting and gathering also represented an important means of acquiring food. East Africans without much livestock turned to hunting to supplement their diet. People also hunted to protect both their livestock from predators and their crops from burrowing and grazing animals. Important means of hunting wild animals included trenches, pit traps, nooses, spears, arrows, and dogs. Along the lower Guinea coast, people collected kola nuts from wild trees. People who lived in hunting-and-gathering societies migrated according not only to the seasonal movements of their game but also to the ripening of fruits that they collected. The San peoples of southwestern Africa traveled in groups of 50 to 70, sometimes joining with a group of herders to trade for dairy products. They used hunting implements constructed of stone, bone, wood, or fiber even after iron became available.

Africans thus adapted their agricultural practices to different circumstances, whether they involved the introduction of new crops or traders or the different climates into which they migrated. They learned to adapt in order to survive or even to prevent famines, and they developed means of keeping their flocks free from disease. Hunting, gathering, and fishing also represented important ways of getting food. Both men and women performed vital farm labor depending on the customs of particular groups in different places. In all areas, people cooperated to overcome hardship and make for prosperous communities.

~Brian Ulrich

FOR MORE INFORMATION

Curtin, P., S. Feierman, L. Thompson, and J. Vansina. *African History*. London: Longman, 1995.

Fung, K. *Africa South of the Sahara*. 1994. <http://www-sul.stanford.edu/depts/ssrg/africa/guide.html>, accessed October 23, 2003.

Halsall, P., ed. *Internet African History Sourcebook*. 1996. <http://www.fordham.edu/halsall/africa/africasbook.html>, accessed October 23, 2003.

July, R. W. A *History of the African People*. 5th ed. Prospect Heights, Ill.: Waveland Press, 1998.

Ogot, B. A., ed. *General History of Africa*. Vol. 5. *Africa from the Sixteenth Century to the Eighteenth Century*. Paris: United Nations Educational, Scientific, and Cultural Organization, 1992.

COLONIAL AUSTRALIA

Although it was critical to establish viable agriculture in early colonial Australia, few of the new arrivals had farming experience. Governor Phillip (1786–93) was a typical "gentleman farmer" without much practical knowledge. The convicts having been mostly urban dwellers, only a handful had ever farmed. Nevertheless, the European settlers did not adopt Aboriginal low-impact land management but brought with them the prevailing 18th-century imperialist vision of conquering and taming the land. Other impediments to effective land cultivation included poor equipment and practices, a lack of manure for fertilizer, and scarcity of fresh water. Perhaps of greatest significance was the attempt to re-create European methods of food cultivation, despite the obvious contrasts in topography and climate. During the colonial period, several major floods and droughts spoiled crops and destroyed livestock.

The first site for a garden, Farm Cove, was unsuitable because the soil was poor and exposed to saltwater spray. Another obstacle was the heavily wooded terrain, difficult to clear without proper implements and working animals. The preference for shallow hoeing and digging exposed the sandstone layers, allowing rain to wash away the topsoil and thus rendering the ground infertile (Stephensen and Kennedy, 103). In addition, without adequate means of removal, stumps and roots were often left in the cleared ground, reducing the part of it that was arable by as much as 10 percent. Watkin Tench observed that "immediate subsistence" necessitated "slovenly husbandry" (Tench, 154–55). Plows became available beginning in 1800, but many settlers could not afford them or clung to their shallow tilling methods. Indeed, widespread use of plows was not common until about 1806.

Australian colonists first sowed wheat in 1788, but it was not until 1795 that they produced sufficient crops to sustain the colony. In his detailed study of the Australian wheat industry, Dunsdorfs writes that although wheat was a favored traditional crop, the inexperienced farmers soon realized that maize was better suited both to their rudimentary agriculture and to the climate. Beginning in 1793, officers were entitled to land grants, resulting in a significant increase in wheat fields. Some of these officers established grain monopolies and effectively diverted grain from foodstuffs to the distillation of spirits. Smaller landholders sold their grain to monopolists to settle alcohol debts. One of the most astute of the officers was John Macarthur (also to become one of the wealthiest), who in 1798 allotted almost 500 acres of land at Elizabeth Farm in Parramatta to the cultivation of wheat and to the raising of cattle and sheep. Together with the considerable input of his wife, Elizabeth, John's experimentation with breeding merino sheep gave impetus to the farming of wool in Australia.

In March 1788, a small party was sent to establish a satellite settlement on Norfolk Island. Agricultural production there was so successful at times that the island's farmers were able to provision Port Jackson with foodstuffs. Despite recurring crop problems, including rats, grubs, and parrots, vegetables flourished alongside the small but sufficient grain harvests. Crops of wheat and maize were averaging 20 and 60 bushels per acre, respectively. By 1792, crops such as wheat, maize, potatoes, cabbages, bananas (native and introduced), and a variety of fruits were flourishing in the island's fertile soil; but agriculture in Port Jackson was still a struggling economic pursuit, and people there ran the risk of starvation. However, as the vagaries of the island's climate and the difficulties of its waters emerged, Norfolk's tenuous agricultural prospects became apparent.

By the 1790s, because of low rainfall and the wretched state of both crops and farms, farmers in the Sydney area abandoned cultivation. Settlers gradually pushed out from Sydney in search of more fertile lands. In June 1789, plantings were made at Richmond Hill and the Hawkesbury, although both were subject to frequent flooding; after the failure at Farm Cove, colonists concentrated their efforts at Rose Hill (now Parramatta), 15 miles from Sydney. Two years later, there were still only five settlers at the settlement, which hosted more than four acres under cultivation. The chaplain Richard Johnson, whom Watkin Tench thought "the best farmer in the country" (Tench, 153) had 55 acres of wheat, barley, and oats under cultivation, as well as 30 acres of maize. He kept 20 acres of good, watered land on reserve in anticipation of cattle arriving in the colony. The chronic shortage of cattle hindered efforts to develop a dairy industry, and dairying usually took place on a limited domestic scale.

The most notable Rose Hill farmer was "bred a husbandman," James Ruse, an emancipated convict whom Phillip set up there in 1789 to ascertain how long it would take such a person to become self-sufficient. He was assisted with implements, livestock, shelter, and labor to clear land and was offered a grant of 30 acres, to be called "Experiment Farm." Although given no directions as to how he could achieve self-sufficiency, Ruse realized the problems of surface tilling. He came to rely on a more thorough and slower hoeing technique, clod molding and mulching, which he thought "almost equal to plowing" (Tench, 158). He then left the soil fallow for a short period, turning it again before sowing. By 1791, with the help of his wife, Elizabeth Perry (also a former convict, whom he married in 1790), he could report success. The land was subsequently granted—the first such grant to be made, and one that hinged on the colonialist assumption that Australia was *terra nullius* (land occupied by none).

Although few bothered with experimentation, at least one official attempt was made at pasture improvement. In 1803, Governor King enclosed tracts of 40 acres, which were to be planted with burnet, clover, rye grass, and sainfoin (an herb), "to serve as an example to settlers . . . when pasture becomes scarce" (Bladen, vol. 5, 193). By the start of Lachlan Macquarie's administration in 1810, private agriculture in colonial Australia was so well established that he was able to abolish public farming.

~*Valda Rigg*

FOR MORE INFORMATION

Aplin, G., ed. *A Difficult Infant: Sydney before Macquarie.* Kensington: New South Wales University Press, 1988.

Bladen, F., ed. *Historical Records of New South Wales.* Vols. 1, 2, 5 and 6. Sydney: Government Printer, 1892. Facsimile edition, Marrickville: Southwood Press, 1978.

Dunsdorfs, E. *The Australian Wheat-Growing Industry, 1788–1948.* Carlton: Melbourne University Press, 1956.

Government of New South Wales. *Index to Bench of Magistrates Cases, 1788–1820.* <www.records.nsw.gov.au/indexes/benchofmag/introduction.htm>, accessed October 23, 2003.

Nobbs, R. *Norfolk Island and Its First Settlement, 1788–1814.* North Sydney: Library of Australian History, 1988.

Shaw, A. G. L., ed. *Australian Dictionary of Biography.* Vols. 1–2. Carlton: Melbourne University Press, 1966.

Stephensen, P., and B. Kennedy. *The History and Description of Sydney Harbour.* Sydney: Reed, 1980.

Tench, W. *1788: Comprising A Narrative of the Expedition to Botany Bay [1789] and A Complete Account of the Settlement at Port Jackson [1795].* Edited by Tim Flannery. Melbourne: Text Publishing, 1996.

ECONOMIC LIFE
|
AGRICULTURE
|
Africa

Colonial Australia

The Colonial Frontier
of North America

England

Japan

New England

THE COLONIAL FRONTIER OF NORTH AMERICA

The Native American farmer was not unlike the colonial one. Both followed the annual cycles of preparing the ground and planting, tending, and harvesting the crops as dictated by the seasonal changes in the weather. Colonial agriculture was different in that both men and women tended the crops. Colonists tended to segregate their crops into single-species plots having furrows, while the Indians mixed their corn, bean, and squash plants in hillocks scattered about their fields. The Indians' method was less efficient in terms of space, but their fields were easier to weed and required less-detailed preparation of the soil. Both colonials and Native Americans grew corn, beans, squash, pumpkins, cucumbers, some tubers such as potatoes or yams, and the ubiquitous tobacco plant. Only the Europeans produced wheat, rye, barley, flax, and hay. Colonials grew medicinal plants in small plots near their homes, while Indians generally gathered such plants from the wild.

Growing tobacco saved the southern colonies from extinction once the quest for gold and precious metals had been quelled by failure. Tobacco was used in lieu of cash payments and as collateral for loans. Tobacco bonds, which encumbered the profits of future crops, were even accepted in lieu of taxes; but intensive tobacco farming was hard on the soil, stripping it of valuable nutrients that could not easily be replaced in an era before synthetic fertilizers.

Settlers in the backcountry added new acreage to their farmsteads each year by clearing the land. Those considered the most able farmers cleared the land by cutting down all the trees in early summer, hauling off the valuable logs, and leaving the least valuable wood and branches on the ground until the following spring. These leftovers were scavenged for firewood during the winter, and the remainder was burned in the early spring to complete the clearing. The burning left a layer of fine ash to fertilize and soften the ground between the remaining stumps. The stumps were usually allowed to rot, but they could be pulled after a few years with the help of a team of oxen. Once the stumps were removed, the rocks and boulders could be dragged to the edges of the field on a sledge and dumped. In the winter, these stones could be made up into walls for the enclosure of sheep or cattle, but only on the oldest farms were stonewalls laid up in this manner.

Indian corn was usually planted in a new field, which was commonly prepared by the use of a hoe alone. The hoe and axe were the most widely used farm implements on the frontier. The average farmer devoted most of his fields to hay, which could be planted among the stumps because it was gathered with the use of a hand sickle. The plow could be driven through the open ground between the stumps or in meadows, but it was not generally used until the majority of the stumps, roots, and rocks were removed. The French required that *habitants* (inhabitants) clear about two acres of new ground each year, and English farmers were capable of doing about the same. The average farmer tended about 18 acres of crops on a 100-acre farm. The acreage not put directly into crop production was used as pasture and woodlots or was left as fallow ground to recuperate from several seasons of overfarming. Small kitchen-garden plots, which included a variety of herbs and greens, surrounded the family home.

Both colonials and Indians used seaweed, clam and oyster shells, fish, ashes, and bonemeal to improve their soil. Neither the colonials nor the Indians spent a great deal of time using animal fertilizers, however. This may have been because virgin land was plentiful but also because fertilization was a new idea to the colonists. Not until several decades had passed did the earliest settlers notice a change in the soil that they were farming. At first it had been dark, almost black, but with time its color became lighter, and crop yields fell.

The greatest difference between Native American and European agricultural practices was that of animal husbandry. Native Americans had no conception of the breeding or ownership of animals. The deer, beaver, bear, and moose of the frontier were not owned until they were killed during the hunt. Colonials claimed year-round ownership during the life of their livestock. Moreover, the pigs, cattle, sheep, and horses of Europeans were far different from the wild prey usually consumed by Native Americans.

It can be said that the greatest visible differences between Indian agriculture and colonial farming revolved around hogs and hay. Hogs were of great value to the colonials because they reproduced themselves in large numbers and fed themselves in the brushwood. Unlike sheep and goats, they could hold their own against the depredations of wolves and other carnivores. They required almost no care until the fall slaughter, and they provided meat that preserved well when salted, smoked, or pickled. Besides, pork was much tastier than the preserved beef or mutton from animals that had grazed in the open woodlands. Colonials favored a long-legged variety of hog, somewhat leaner than modern types. The hogs needed to be good walkers because they were often driven in herds to market.

Making hay was a difficult and time-consuming task. The hayfield was cut by hand, dried in the sun, turned to dry the reverse side, and then gathered for storage. Hay could be stored in a barn or loft for winter feeding, or it could be gathered up into a stack or mound. Hay could usually be made from the same field twice a year. It required one cleared acre to produce the hay needed to winter a cow or an ox, and a little more, plus some grain, to winter a horse. Native Americans had no need for hayfields because they kept no livestock, but their abandoned fields quickly became overgrown with grasses and brush. Early settlers often loosed their livestock to graze in these fields, but the native grasses proved less nutritious than European varieties. The animals imported from Europe often brought with them as part of their manure common European grass seeds from their shipboard fodder. These grasses spread naturally in the older settlements, encouraging colonial farmers to import English grass seeds such as bluegrass and white clover to the frontier.

Colonists of the French and British colonies in North America relied on agriculture for sustenance. Although they used the same land and planted, cultivated, and harvested many of the same crops as the Native Americans, European agriculture did not perfectly mirror their agricultural customs. Despite uniquely colonial crops (wheat), meat production (animal husbandry), and land management (hay making), the two civilizations paralleled each other in notable ways (Volo and Volo, 114–17).

FOR MORE INFORMATION

Boorstin, D. J. *The Americans: The Colonial Experience*. New York: Random House, 1958.

Douglas, H. R. *Indian Agriculture in America: Prehistory to the Present*. Lawrence: University Press of Kansas, 1987.

Volo, J. M., and D. D. Volo. *Daily Life on the Old Colonial Frontier*. Westport, Conn.: Greenwood Press, 2002.

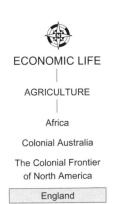

ENGLAND

A developing interplay of tradition and change, continuity and transformation, affected the lives of those involved in agriculture in 18th-century England. Farmers had diverse and demanding jobs. They planted seeds and harvested grain; they bred animals for dairy products, meat, leather, and fabric; and they contributed to cottage industry, which is the household production of textiles and other essential goods. However, these activities gradually underwent changes that would eventually result in profound disruptions in the daily life of agrarians. Legal, economic, and technological developments set the stage for shifts in what farmers produced, how they farmed, and how they lived. The changing characteristics of agricultural production throughout England's diverse counties reflect the sometimes gradual, and sometimes dramatic, mixture of tradition and transformation.

When one thinks of farm life, one typically thinks of fields of grain, corn, potatoes, or other produce. Farm life in England was especially arduous. August was usually the month of the grain harvest, although in some areas it might take place in September or even October. Grain was reaped with scythes. Sheep were shorn without electric shears. Women armed with wooden mallets broke up hardened clods of earth. Domestic servants helped out with harvesting and dairying, and urban workers might migrate to the countryside during harvest to make extra income.

Harvest time was jubilant, followed by feasting, revelry, and courtship; but if the harvest was poor, there might be little joy. In any case, harvest was a prelude to more hard work. Once the grain was in, the work had just begun for the threshers, who beat the stalks against wooden planks with "crab-tree staves" to shake loose the kernels of wheat, rye, or barley. It was sweaty, dusty, and noisy work.

The harvest of various crops—such as walnuts, plums, and pears—continued through the autumn months, even as the rains began. Grain prices dropped as the harvested grain, sold to pay the rents, made its way onto the market. Graziers sold off many of their sheep to farmers and butchers near London, and the price of mutton would drop also.

Winter brought, if not scarcity, then at least less bounty. Farm laborers employed during the harvest now found themselves with less or no work. Those who did have jobs or farms of their own had less to do, and the idleness, combined with the need to stay crowded indoors with one's coworkers or family, must have made people edgier. Nonetheless, there was work to do during the winter. In fact, year-round, those involved in agriculture and animal husbandry often supplemented their earnings by participating in the small-scale production of cloth or clothes, known as cottage industry.

Important innovations in agricultural production were popularized during the 18th century. Enclosure, the result of expensive, privately lobbied acts of Parliament, took a village's commons (communally farmed open land) and parceled it out to individual owners, who could then fence the land and farm it as they chose. Particularly popular during the second half of the century, enclosure created employment, as the owners added ditches, fences, hedges, roads, and outbuildings to their land. It minimized overgrazing and misuse of the land and resulted in a much greater grain output. For cottagers, however, enclosure was a disaster. Enclosure, like its close cousin, engrossing (ousting smaller tenant farmers to combine one's land into larger rented parcels), was perceived as a purely selfish endeavor.

It was the large, easily controlled parcels of land, however, that allowed owners and tenants to introduce new techniques. Some improved the soil by adding lime, clay, or fertilizers. Some followed the example of Lord Townshend, who advocated a fourfold rotation of crops: cereals, root crops, clover, and grasses. Townshend, a booster of turnips for the root-crop phase, earned himself the nickname "Turnip Townshend." Crop rotation enabled animals to be grazed year-round rather than grazed in summer and fed scanty stored fodder in winter; this adaptive practice resulted in healthier animals and more continuous supplies of manure in the fields. More manure meant better soil, which led to better crops the following season. Another agrarian inventor, Jethro Tull, promoted horse hoeing and planting seeds with a drill that he devised rather than by hand. Robert Bakewell inbred his stock for more meat and fat and less bone. Selective breeding and improved feeding more than doubled the average weight of calves, oxen, and sheep sold at Smithfield between 1710 and 1795.

The advantages of these legal, economic, and technological innovations did not benefit all agrarians equally. Wealthy farmers and prominent landowners could earn hundreds or even thousands of pounds a year, but small freeholders, tenant farmers, and "husbandmen" and "country labourers" earned less. A drop in grain prices could mean real hardship. Most agricultural workers—shepherds, plowmen, hop pickers, drovers, threshers, weeders, and others—made just enough to survive.

English agriculture was regionally diverse. Different counties boasted different specialties. However, not all regions, when confronted with external change, were able to maintain their traditional crops and animal products. In the southwest, Devonshire had a reputation for isolation and rurality; and the county's industries included the manufacture of the eponymous cheese at Cheddar. Dorset, primarily agricultural, was also noted for its oysters, mackerel, and sheep.

The southern coastal county of Hampshire was mostly rural, famed for its sheep and bacon. England's western counties included Gloucestershire, where agriculture and animal husbandry led to the raising of sheep and the production of soft cheese and bacon. The northernmost county on the Welsh border was Cheshire. Its staple products were salt, ale, and Cheshire cheese.

In East Anglia, Cambridgeshire occupied part of the marshy area known as the fenland. Thinly populated and even desolate in places, Cambridgeshire was almost wholly agricultural, and its farmers cultivated grain and raised ducks, while suffering heavily from enclosure. The county actually lost population during the century.

Changes in agricultural habits and focus were not unusual in England at this time. In the Midlands, the area as a whole was noted for its grain fields. As the century passed, there was increased grazing of livestock, particularly cattle. Similarly, as southern counties shifted production from livestock to grain, Leicestershire shifted from grain to livestock, particularly the raising of sheep. The agricultural county of Lincolnshire derived little benefit from industrialization, and unlike most of the Midlands, it lost population during the century and suffered during periods of enclosure. In the north, agriculture declined. For instance, Lancashire grew quickly when its faltering agriculture was replaced by booming cotton mills.

Agriculture was a diverse sector of the economy, involving not only grains and other crops but a wide variety of animal products, chiefly for food and fabric. Cottage industry, too, constituted an important economic supplement to farmers, but legal changes including enclosure, an increased emphasis on efficiency in production, and technological innovations requiring important outlays of capital all tended toward a transformation of 18th-century English agriculture in general, as well as of the lives of those who practiced it (Olsen, 72–78, 118, 123–24).

To read about rural life in Chaucer's England, see the Europe entry in the section "Rural Life" in chapter 3 ("Economic Life") of volume 2; for rural life in Elizabethan England, see the England entry in the section "Rural Life" in chapter 3 ("Economic Life") of volume 3; and for the rural environment in Victorian England, see the Victorian England entry in the section "Urban and Rural Environments" in chapter 3 ("Economic Life") of volume 5 of this series.

FOR MORE INFORMATION

Lynch, J. *Eighteenth Century Resources.* <http://newark.rutgers.edu/~jlynch/18th/>, accessed October 10, 2003.

Olsen, K. *Daily Life in 18th-Century England.* Westport, Conn.: Greenwood Press, 1999.

Turner, M. E. *Farm Production in England, 1700–1914.* Oxford: Oxford University Press, 2001.

JAPAN

Although rice was the most predictable crop of 18th-century Japanese farmers, many other crops occupied the time of villagers throughout the countryside. In addition to vegetables, other grains, and cash crops such as cotton, farmers spent the year maintaining their fields and irrigation systems. Agriculture was therefore a precarious endeavor, but Japanese farmers were typically successful in generating the food that they, and the cities, required.

In the 18th century, more than 90 percent of the population resided in the rural countryside and was engaged in agricultural production. Perhaps half of that agricultural effort was to provide food for the rural population; the other half provided either food to Japan's burgeoning urban sector or raw materials to manufacturers and artisans.

In the 1580s, Japanese organized farmland into three types: paddy fields, upland fields, and residential plots. The first was for wet-rice agriculture, meaning that the land was flat enough to hold the water necessary to grow rice. Upland meant fields, being too dry or too steep for the cultivation of rice, that supported other crops such as barley, wheat, millet, and diverse vegetables, herbs, and commercial crops such as cotton. Residential plots belonged to individual households.

All villages were classified into three types: agricultural (*nōson*), mountain (*sanson*), and fishing (*gyoson*). About 80 percent of Japan's villages were *nōson*. Only about 5 percent were engaged in mountain agriculture; the rest drew their sustenance from fishing.

Typically, the villages consisted of small, crudely built houses clumped together to conserve flat agricultural land. Residential land was to be kept to an absolute minimum, and often the villages themselves were directly adjacent to foothills or forests. Because most of Japan was involved in wet-rice agriculture, bodies of water such as rivers, streams, and canals dominated the life of the village. Virtually every village convenience, right, and responsibility was shared communally among the official members of the community. Work, too, was a collective task.

Although the overwhelming majority of Japanese farmers cultivated rice, not many peasants could afford to eat the rice they grew, at least in its polished (white) form. Their daimyō (regional warlords) instructed them to eat other grains (such as barley, wheat, millet, and sorghum) and to turn over to the authorities all their rice as tax. Even if they had some polished rice left over after taxes, most peasants had to sell it to buy other things.

Rice was important to Japanese in part because huge population pressures demanded a high caloric return on human effort expended. Rice is amazingly efficient, returning high yields and requiring that only about 5 percent of a crop be kept for seeds. Wheat, corn, barley, millet, and sorghum all require that 20 to 25 percent of the harvest be kept for seed.

A second reason for the importance of rice in Japan is that when polished, rice absorbs more than twice its weight in water while cooking. Thus, the sheer volume of rice, along with its high carbohydrate content, fools the stomach into thinking that it is full. Unfortunately, the polishing also removes the nutrient bran covering, meaning that polished rice had to be supplemented with vegetables and proteins to provide a nutritious meal.

Growing rice began in the early spring, when farmers would repair dikes, plow the earth, and laboriously spade in what was called "green" fertilizer (the detritus, cut grass, and other vegetation "harvested" in nearby hills and forests). The decaying vegetation would provide the farmland with the nutrients necessary to continue cultivating rice on the same ground that had produced it for hundreds of years. The fields would then be flooded with two to four inches of water.

Once a field had lain under this water for two or three days, farmers would scatter over the fields rice seeds kept from the previous harvest. It took the seeds five to six weeks to germinate into seedlings, during which time the farmers would prepare the rest of their paddy allotment for the integration of other crops.

As soon as the rice seeds had germinated, the farmers would do something that must have seemed counterintuitive to those unacquainted with wet-rice cultivation. They would uproot the seedlings, carefully rinse the roots, and then stack them in bundles throughout the rest of the field. To uproot one's entire crop before it had properly matured was an act of faith, but over time it had become a tradition.

The seedlings were separated and laboriously transplanted, approximately three inches apart in long rows, into the waiting paddy fields. Bent at the waist, ankle-deep in filthy water, the transplanters (often groups of peasant women) stooped down thousands of times to plug each seedling into the muck. Often, the whole village would celebrate the end of the crucial transplantation with a *matsuri* (festival), and winning teams of transplanters would be feted with food and drink.

Harvesting was usually done collectively, with large teams sweeping through several fields at once, cutting the rice stalks low to the ground with scythes and sickles. The harvesters then gathered the stalks into armfuls of sheaves, using a few twisted stalks as ties. Laborers would stand the sheaves out in the field to dry for a week to 10 days and then separate the kernels from the stalk either by using winnowing boards ("dragon's teeth") or by flailing the stalks against a stone or tree. At this point, villagers would store away in dry places an appropriate amount of unhulled rice to be used as seed in the next growing season.

The rest of the kernels of grain would be separated from the protective husks by a number of methods. Commonly, the grain would be tossed lightly into the air so that a slight breeze would carry away the chaff, while the kernels fell to the ground. The resulting grain was called brown rice because it was still encased in its nutrient bran covering. Because brown rice was hard, it did not absorb much liquid and required much heat to prepare; so villagers usually polished it, using pebbles or bones to grind away the bran. The rice was then carefully measured and poured into woven straw bags, where it awaited the tax man.

Prints by Maruyama Okyo, 18th century. In the left-hand image, Japanese peasants prepare the soil for crop cultivation. On the right, peasants harvest the crops. © Cabinet Library Collection.

During the entire rice cultivation season, the farmers also grew all sorts of other crops. Tuber-root vegetables (for instance, carrots, radishes, beets, and potatoes) were important, as were green, leafy vegetables such as cabbage. The cultivation of "dry crops" such as wheat and millet took place in the uplands during the cold months. Soya beans were a major source of protein, especially when made into tofu (bean curd) and shoyu (soy sauce).

Farmers also cultivated a variety of cash crops. The most obvious were the fiber plants necessary for clothing, such as flax for linen, mulberry leaves for silkworms, and cotton. Farmers also grew tea on foothill terraces or on other well-drained tracts of land. Tea bushes grew from transplanted cuttings of older bushes, which, if 10 years old, were considered worn out. Farmers, plucking the tea leaves by hand, prized the "younger" higher leaves. The lower leaves as well as the attached stems were of inferior grade. The bush continued to sprout leaves after each picking, so the harvest was really a periodical gleaning.

Agriculture was a yearlong occupation, involving multiple stages and skills, as well as the cooperation of every member of the village community. Alongside rice (which, when polished, went primarily to Japan's cities) were other grains like wheat, vegetables like potatoes, and cash crops like tea. Given the generally small area and mountainous topography of Japan, the fact that 18th-century Japanese agriculture met the demands of its population is no inconsequential feat (Perez, 130, 163–68, 175).

FOR MORE INFORMATION

Hanley, S. B., and K. Yamamura. *Economic and Demographic Change in Preindustrial Japan, 1600–1868.* Princeton, N.J.: Princeton University Press, 1977.

Japan Information Network. <http://www.jinjapan.org/index.html>, accessed October 23, 2003.

Perez, L. G. *Daily Life in Early Modern Japan.* Westport, Conn.: Greenwood Press, 2002.

NEW ENGLAND

Native Americans grew and harvested crops, hunted wild game, fished, and gathered foods grown in the wild. The colonists of New England were not different in this regard; indeed, the first European settlers, as well as subsequent generations, survived the unpredictable conditions of New England in large part because of the agricultural techniques of Native Americans, which the settlers imitated.

Native Americans fed themselves through cultivating crops, fishing, hunting, and gathering. Corn was the mainstay, but during the colonial period, they also cultivated other vegetables: several kinds of beans, pumpkin, artichokes, and an array of squashes. From the sea, they harvested cod, shad, smelts, swordfish, herring, halibut, bluefish, salmon, oysters, lobsters, crabs, clams, and mussels. They hunted deer, moose, bear, raccoons, rabbits, snakes, turtles, turkeys, and a variety of other birds. From the wild, they harvested wild rice and a variety of fruits and nuts: plums, blackberries, blueberries, cranberries, elderberries, gooseberries, red and black raspberries, strawberries, grapes, watermelon, beechnuts, chestnuts, and hickory nuts.

The chief work to which 90 percent of New England's first settlers believed they were called was farming. The Plymouth settlers got down to the business of planting crops once spring was on the way and the *Mayflower* had returned to England. One tribe of Native Americans instructed them in the art of fertilizing their crop by planting a tiny fish with each seed and kernel. Despite the success with their first crop, the pilgrims continued to starve and to live a marginal existence for several years.

During the first several years in what, for them, was uncharted country, these farmers did the work belonging to many callings. In the 1630s and 1640s, as farms were established in a land where labor was scarce, every farmer had to be his own carpenter (to build houses and outbuildings), mason (to build fireplaces and foundations), trapper (to secure food and hides for the family), and blacksmith (to forge farm implements and kitchen utensils). Farmers in rural areas built their own furniture, tanned leather, made shoes, and even ran stores. They fished, lumbered, and raised livestock. For most women, this involved farmwork of the heaviest kind. Women plowed, planted, tended livestock, slaughtered animals, directed servants, and knew basic carpentry.

The primary aim of most of these early farmers in the 10 years after the establishment of the Massachusetts Bay was to put food on the table and to barter for goods they did not produce, such as cloth. After 1640, goods grown or made on the farm were also exported to Europe and other colonies.

In many New England communities, land was set aside for the communal grazing of livestock. These commons are still in evidence throughout the area today. Certain chores would also be done communally; a community shepherd would watch the livestock, for example, and community milkers would milk the cows. In many instances, gardening was done in common areas, as well.

At critical periods of work on large farms, laborers, including shop owners and artisans, were rounded up by constables, forced to put down their own work, and escorted to work on farms. After all, a large crop had to be harvested before it became ruined. In some communities (for example, Salem, Massachusetts) during the 1630s, workers were also required to devote their time and labor on one day in every month to public projects such as road repair.

During the 17th century, the typical day of a farmworker or the owner of a small farm in central Massachusetts began around 4:30 A.M., when the farmers rose and tended to their livestock. After working in the fields for an hour or two, the farmers quickly ate breakfast and, around seven o'clock, returned to the fields to work for an additional five or six hours, interrupted by a half-hour cider break. From two to three in the afternoon, the farmers ate their dinner, after which they returned to the fields, tended livestock, or repaired tools. From six to seven o'clock, the family ate supper together, and all would retire to bed between eight and nine o'clock.

On New England farms, slaves had to have a greater degree of skill and versatility than they did in the south. For example, they worked a variety of crops, including vegetable gardens and forage crops, as well as flax and hemp. They took care of livestock, did farm repairs, and shoed horses. Rarely were there more than one or two slaves working on a single New England farm. The exception was Rhode Island, where the greater acreage per farm was the task of from 5 to 40 slaves.

Masters frequently assigned farmwork to their indentured servants. The jobs for servants on the farm were varied and included threshing grain, tending livestock, planting crops, slaughtering, herding, tanning hides, husking corn, cutting wood, and felling trees. Farms located on New England's frontier required the hardest work, as wild land had to be cleared of trees, stumps, and boulders before it could be broken up for planting. Women servants cooked, tended children, cleaned house, sewed, spun, wove, preserved foods, tended poultry, and milked.

Some parts of Massachusetts had up to 170 growing days annually. Indian corn continued to be a chief source of grain. It took a long time for wheat to become established in the few areas of New England where it would grow well, and then colonists had to depend on the services of a miller to grind it to a fine texture. Grains such as corn, rye, and oats were more suitable to the New England climate and soil. Early New England farmers also cultivated barley. Hay and oats were the fodder for cattle.

Goats were the first animals imported to New England farms. Cows, also used for milk products and meat, arrived a bit later. By 1640, an average farm in colonial New England had as a food supply about 10 cows and 6 pigs.

The main vegetables that colonial New England farmers grew were turnips, parsnips, beans, cabbage, and pumpkins. More prosperous families added onions, peas, carrots, spinach, asparagus, and beets to their table. The potatoes first imported for planting did not grow well. Not until 1720, when some of the first Irish who immigrated to New England brought potatoes, were they grown successfully. Nor did the settlers eat tomatoes, although they were available, from fear that they were poisonous.

Summer and fall were the seasons for harvesting and preserving vegetables. Farmers took grains, notably dried corn, to the miller for processing into meal and flour. The women also usually did the job of slaughtering and butchering pigs, placing the meat in salt for three or four weeks, and then smoking it. Pumpkins and apples were dried in the fall and stored in the house.

Thanks, in part, to the techniques of Native Americans and the plentiful variety of foods available in the New World, European settlers were able to adapt to their new surroundings and develop a system of agriculture that met the needs of colonial New England and markets abroad (Johnson, 60–61, 67, 99–101, 138–39, 151, 164).

FOR MORE INFORMATION

Innes, S. *Labor in a New Land*. Princeton, N.J.: Princeton University Press, 1983.
Johnson, C. D. *Daily Life in Colonial New England*. Westport, Conn.: Greenwood Press, 2002.

Industry

Industrial production existed throughout the world from 1600 to 1800. Of course, this industry differed considerably from the consolidated and highly mechanized industrial pursuits of the last 150 years. However, the fabrication of goods did display certain features that distinguished it from mere hobby. Cottage industries represented a fragmented and small-scale system of production that augured the consolidated and large-scale systems of the future. The fishing and whaling industries, which involved significant oceangoing crews and vessels, reflected the presence of sizable, international enterprises. Mining, blacksmithing, and textile production had widespread implications for distinct cultural regions such as sub-Saharan Africa, the colonial frontier in North America, Japan, England, and New England. Finally, the existence of industrial systems of production, as any economic system does, corresponded to uneven distributions of tasks and wealth.

Sub-Saharan Africa, the North American colonial frontier, England, Japan, New England, and Western shipping were home to a host of manufacturing systems. One such system concerned cottage industries, which involved an intermediary businessman who acquired and then distributed raw materials to individuals and households that were often located in the countryside or villages. These individuals transformed the raw materials into desired products, which the intermediary later picked up in exchange for some goods or money. Cottage industries were fragmented operations but appealed especially to those farmers who, during the winter months, frequently had little agricultural work and thus few means of support.

In early modern Japan, a familiar cottage industry dealt in the production of silk. Here, village girls worked in silk sheds, where they manipulated cocoons, a dangerous step in the process of fashioning silk.

In England, as in North American colonies (particularly New England), cottage industries contributed to the manufacture of all kinds of goods. However, a notable shift toward large-scale, mechanized industrial production meant that cottage industries were witnessing their twilight. A strong instance of this shift concerned the production of cloth and clothing, which, over the course of the 18th century, steadily altered its natural focus from rural households to urban factories.

Industry also included the oceans. Japan possessed a notable fishing industry, which depended on the oceans rather than on freshwater fish. The whaling industry attracted Russian, and later Dutch, enterprises, but the greatest whalers during the 18th and early 19th centuries concentrated in New England. Towns such as New Bedford and Nantucket became synonymous with whaling and associated products such as whale oil.

A surprising number of parallel industries arose in geographically and culturally distinct societies. A brief summary of African manufactures serves as a case in point. Mining for gold, iron, and copper was part of a prominent tradition in Zambezia and among the Nyiha. Iron deposits in New England and coal, tin, and lead deposits in England also constituted important industries, vital to the coming industrial revolution. In Kongo, blacksmiths forged useful tools, while blacksmiths in Japan, New England, and England were similarly prominent, despite the limited scope of their production. Finally, textiles along the Swahili coast and in Madagascar were comparable (though not equivalent) to textile operations in Japan (noted for its consolidation and factorization of the clothing industry), colonial New England (slowly moving toward mechanization by 1770), and England (where the chief raw materials were wool, silk, and cotton).

Not all industries organized their production methods according to a single blueprint. Administration of Zambezia's mining industry for gold steadily transferred to the state. In contrast, England witnessed a decline in institutions—at least, in worker-organized institutions—that had traditionally managed many aspects of the production process. The influence of guilds (trade organizations) was declining, and unions were illegal.

Not everyone benefited from industry to the same degree. The Nyiha ironworks spawned a powerful aristocracy but banned women from the smelting process. Whereas blacksmiths in Kongo benefited from an honorable reputation for warding off evil, black slaves in colonial New England who worked as skilled blacksmiths found themselves and their offspring legally bound to their masters. And English women, whom English law and custom excluded from many skilled industrial pursuits, were relegated to a few industries, such as hat making.

During the 17th, 18th, and early 19th centuries, industrial production did not resemble the large-scale, electronically mechanized factories of today. Often, these industries were small-scale, with little mechanization beyond a few simple, handheld tools. Yet it was precisely this historical period that marked the beginning of the industrial revolution and the end of premechanized production.

~Peter Seelig

FOR MORE INFORMATION

Innes, S. *Labor in a New Land.* Princeton, N.J.: Princeton University Press, 1983.

Shaw, T., ed. *The Archaeology of Africa: Foods, Metals, and Towns.* New York: Routledge, 1995.

Wallerstein, I. M. *Historical Capitalism* London: Verso, 1983.

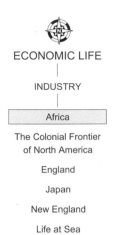

AFRICA

The nature of industry in Africa depended on local resources and conditions. In many areas, such as among the Shona in what is now Zimbabwe, individuals used a number of skills, including agriculture, weaving, and potting. In other places, especially in cities, the presence of long-distance trade opportunities allowed people to specialize in a particular type of industrial work. Mining ranked among Africa's most important industries; however, ironworking, textiles, and other industries were also important, both culturally and economically. Much of the industrial production remained in local hands, with states exercising little or no control.

Before the development of the slave trade, gold represented the primary lure of Africa for Europeans, who sought to eliminate the Saharan traders as middlemen. Along the Lower Guinea coast, the Akan state did exercise control over gold mining and represented a mainstay of rulers' income. At its height, around the year 1700, this region produced two million ounces of gold. Gold was frequently panned from the soils of riverbeds and valleys (Ogot, 404).

Gold production declined sharply in the 18th century, however, possibly because the Africans had exhausted the sources they could reach with nonmechanized methods. The same situation occurred in West Africa, where families mined gold, using open pits 3 to 18 meters deep during the dry season, which was unsuitable for agriculture (Austen, 44, 86).

Gold mining also took place in southern Zambezia, where people mined from August until October as part of the process of clearing the land for agriculture. This time of year proved optimal both because shafts could go deeper as a result of a seasonal drop in the water table and because alluvial deposits from the summer had not been swept away by new floods. For actual mining work, people pried rocks apart with iron gads before using a special tool consisting of a piece of iron on the end of a stick as a pick. They also used fires to heat the rock face and render it easier to crack. Villagers, including women and children, collected alluvial deposits during the mining season. Much of the gold produced went to the state, and when people discovered a new gold deposit, they had to report it to the local chief or face execution. Gold mining in this area declined during the 17th century. Iron, salt, and copper also represented important products mined in Africa (Ogot, 670–74).

Ironworking represented a prestigious occupation throughout much of the African continent, and its process remained a close secret of those who practiced it. Among the Nyiha of East Africa, special rituals formed part of the smelting process, and women were banned from the vicinity of the kiln. Many areas had noble families that claimed blacksmiths as ancestors (Ogot, 874–75).

Among the Mande of the Niger Valley, blacksmiths represented an elite caste believed to possess magical powers. According to legend, the kingdom of Kongo had a blacksmith-king for its founder. Kongolese smiths used a hide stretched over hollow logs for a bellows and pieces of iron for shaping tools. Just as the weapons they forged fought off the enemies of the state, so too could blacksmiths ward off evil. When people became sick, they went to the blacksmith, who blew three bursts of hot air at them from the bellows to drive away evil (Balandier, 109–10).

Different craft industries also became important in Africa during this period, as increasing trade led to increasing specialization in the urban trading centers. Among the Hausa, different groups came to have their own specialties. In the city of Kano, pottery became the province of the Bambadawa, while in Kebbi, the Kebbawa practiced weaving and dyeing. A group known as the Zoromawa produced silver jewelry in several cities. Hausaland also exported sandals, harnesses, saddles, and other leather products (Ogot, 476).

Textile production also ranked among Africa's important industries, especially along the Swahili coast and Madagascar. In Swahili culture, cloth played an important role in marking status and distinguishing the civilized from the uncivilized. Raffia represented a commonly used material and was used in strips just over a meter in length. To make materials more than a meter, the weaver sewed multiple squares together (Mack, 152).

African industry thus represented both an outgrowth of existing culture and a response to the outside world with its demands and possibilities. Frequently, those engaged in crafts or mining also engaged in other forms of labor, most notably agriculture, although in cities people had more freedom to specialize in industrial pursuits. All crafts remained influenced by a given culture, both in the precise importance of figures such as blacksmiths and in the types of designs woven into textiles. Thus, as with so many things, the industrial products of Africa show both the continent's unity and its diversity.

~Brian Ulrich

FOR MORE INFORMATION

Austen, R. A. *African Economic History*. Portsmouth, N.H.: Heinemann, 1987.

Balandier, G. *Daily Life in the Kingdom of Kongo*. Translated by Helen Weaver. London: George Allen and Unwin, 1968.

Fung, K. *Africa South of the Sahara*. 1994. <http://www-sul.stanford.edu/depts/ssrg/africa/guide.html>, accessed October 23, 2003.

Halsall, P., ed. *Internet African History Sourcebook*. 1996. <http://www.fordham.edu/halsall/africa/africasbook.html>, accessed October 23, 2003.

Mack, J., ed. *Africa: Arts and Cultures*. New York: Oxford University Press, 2000.

Ogot, B. A., ed. *General History of Africa*. Vol. 5. *Africa from the Sixteenth Century to the Eighteenth Century*. Paris: United Nations Educational, Scientific, and Cultural Organization, 1992.

THE COLONIAL FRONTIER OF NORTH AMERICA

Industrial production involving factories, conveyer belts, and punch-in cards were not yet representative of the manufacturing process during the 17th and 18th centuries, particularly on the untamed frontiers of North America. Fabricated items, however, did exist, and Native Americans, as well as their colonial neighbors, made, used, and mended all kinds of manufactures, ranging from kitchen utensils to textiles, from iron axes to soap.

ECONOMIC LIFE

INDUSTRY

Africa

The Colonial Frontier
of North America

England

Japan

New England

Life at Sea

It would be an error to suppose that Native Americans valued their archaic methods of toolmaking and weaponry, as modern observers do, from the romantic perspective of the 21st century. Settlers in the 17th century found that Native Americans possessed a surprising abundance of European and colonial manufactured goods and noted the presence of "very good axes . . . and French shirts and coats and razors" among the tribes.

Native Americans were sophisticated in their thinking and vastly pragmatic. In this regard, steel awls and needles were highly valued. Beads for wampum, cut from oyster shells and polished to size, could now be drilled with ease when compared with the laborious process required when using a bone awl. Knives, razors of steel, and axes of iron, which replaced those of stone, were reliable and easy to use and maintain. Woolen blankets and linen cloth were more comfortable and more colorful than animal skins, and the tedious process of weaving mats from marsh reeds, and capes from grasses, was avoided.

A colonial family's attire depended greatly on the skill and industry of the housewife. Men were involved in the early gathering and processing of wool and flax, but it was a woman's job to spin the raw material and fashion it into clothing and linens. In 1656, the Massachusetts General Court passed a compulsory spinning law that detailed weekly spinning quotas and fines for failing to meet assessments. Children helped with textile production as they could. Young girls were set to work sorting, carding, and spinning wool at an early age. Once spun, wool could easily be knitted into caps, stockings, mittens, and dishcloths.

Weaving remained a predominately male occupation, and virtually every community of size had its weaver. Households would bring their spun linen and wool to the weaver to be woven into yard goods. The weaver also would have yard goods of his own production available.

Sewing was also an important activity. Clothing on the frontier was utilitarian, but it still required mending, and growing children always needed something larger to wear. A housewife had to supply her family with all the bed linens and towels they needed. Mastery of the needle was an essential skill for all women at this time. Young girls were taught needle skills at an early age and were expected to master them. While wealthy women may have spent a good deal of time doing fancywork that demonstrated their needle skills in decorative projects, most frontier women engaged in plain sewing.

Textiles were a large part of a family's wealth. Inventories taken for probate commonly listed textiles after landholdings, money, and silver. Clothing was repaired, remodeled, and recycled. Such conservation was not done solely out of frugality; it took less time than making a new garment. When a garment could no longer be used, it would be cut down and remade for a smaller family member.

Although sewing was a regular part of a woman's routine chores, needlework may have been a welcome opportunity for her to sit down and relax while still being productive. The simplicity of the task even allowed it to be done by the limited light of the fire at night. Sewing could be brought along while visiting or done while socializing. Elementary sewing, such as mending and hemming, required little attention and permitted a woman to take part in a conversation or to listen to someone reading as she herself worked.

From time to time, clothing needed laundering, but before the laundry could be done, soap had to be made. Soap was a mixture of animal fat and lye that was boiled together in a kettle for many hours. Lye was obtained by pouring water into a leach barrel filled with hardwood ashes. The water drained through the layers of ash, and the lye trickled out a small opening at the bottom to be captured in a small bucket or tub. Six bushels of ashes and 24 pounds of grease rendered enough lye to make a barrel of a soft textured soap. This soap was very harsh and seldom used for personal hygiene. A hard soap made from the waxy bayberry was more desirable for toilet use.

Life on the frontier did not permit extravagance as far as industrial goods were concerned, and from today's perspective, simple items such as soap and cloth appear far removed from the world of industry. However, such items constitute very basic manufactures, reflecting the relative simplicity of preindustrial methods of production while harkening the imminent industrial revolution (Volo and Volo, 153–56, 171–73).

FOR MORE INFORMATION

Innes, S. *Labor in a New Land*. Princeton, N.J.: Princeton University Press, 1983.
Volo, J. M., and D. D. Volo. *Daily Life on the Old Colonial Frontier*. Westport, Conn.: Greenwood Press, 2002.

ENGLAND

Industry in 18th-century England differed greatly from the massive, mechanized factories of the 19th and 20th centuries. To be sure, there was a noticeable trend toward a greater concentration of both instruments of production and the workers who operated them, but much industry involved the small-scale production of goods in traditional settings (often the home) and with traditional tools. Wages were commonly low, and job security was minimal. Factory work provided a new way to earn a living, with its attendant benefits and drawbacks, but many artisans and unskilled laborers, of either sex or of any age, continued to earn a living outside the new factories: they were metalworkers, woodworkers, shoemakers, bookbinders, and everything in between. Training for a particular skill relied on a system of apprentices, journeymen, and masters. All of this complexity in the manufacturing of goods necessitated some kind of regulating mechanism. Guilds fulfilled this function, although their gradual disappearance temporarily accompanied a rise in unorganized factory labor and a growing faith in economic deregulation.

Some general comments on industry can be made. Wages tended to be higher in London and in the south than in the north, although northern wages rose faster late in the century, when industrialization was well under way. "Combinations" (labor unions) were being made illegal, and guilds were losing their ancient power. Not

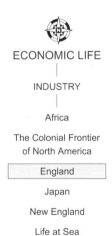

surprisingly, then, workers were often paid irregularly and infrequently—in some cases, only once a year or when they left their employer's service. The workday might be as short as 10 hours or as long as 16; the number of days that were worked varied by trade but in most cases was 6 per week. Unemployment rose during winter (when agricultural laborers had little to do), peacetime (when soldiers had little to do), and the London season (when servants and tradesmen dependent on country gentry had little to do).

Most wages were low, and most jobs offered limited opportunities for advancement. Unskilled and semiskilled workers who did the heavy, dirty jobs—hauling and cleaning, extracting and building—included coal heavers, thatchers, brick makers, sand carriers, fishermen, woodcutters, grave diggers, watchmen, and waiters. There were also miners of coal, tin, and lead, who were susceptible to damps, poisonous gases, and explosions.

A new area of employment was factory work, some of which provided laborers with relative job security and decent wages. In some cases, there were bonuses for especially good work, sickness insurance (paid for by mandatory employee contributions), schools for the employees' children, and even whole mill towns built from scratch. There were also disadvantages to factory work, such as an insistence on punctuality represented by bells and clocking in, dangerous machinery into which children sometimes had to climb to retrieve broken threads, and fines or firing for a variety of infractions, including insubordination, bringing alcohol on the premises, lateness, sleeping, talking, and idleness.

Women participated in every facet of industrial production, although they specialized in certain fields. They were hawkers of food and ballads, washerwomen, lace makers, milliners, needle workers, midwives, spinners, and stocking knitters. Women taught in small schools and were quite often the keepers of jails. Between 1688 and 1775, more than a quarter of jail keepers were widows, who usually inherited their positions from their late husbands.

Craftsmen and artisans who produced industrial goods ranged from humble journeymen employing only their spouses to master manufacturers with hundreds of workers. The average artisan might be a metalworker: a blacksmith, goldsmith, silversmith, nail maker, or file maker (an important trade when all machine parts needed to be hand filed for accuracy). Smiths and smelters needed strength and endurance. Other metalworkers, such as typefounders (makers of printers' type) and scientific instrument makers, used a more delicate touch.

Other industrial workers included builders of various kinds: carpenters, masons, paint makers (who were sometimes poisoned by the lead they used), plasterers, shipbuilders, joiners (who built boxes, sea chests, furniture, and the like), and plumbers.

There were makers of household goods: potters, tanners and leather workers, coopers (who made barrels), wheelwrights, tallow chandlers (who made candles and soap), basket weavers, glassblowers, printers, publishers, bookbinders, and makers of rope, brushes, paper, and toys. Some in the luxury trades included upholsterers, coach builders, jewelers, perfumers, and cabinetmakers. There were thousands of watchmakers, mostly in London, and there were clockmakers all over the country.

Food workers included sugar refiners, maltsters (who roasted barley into malt), distillers, butchers, and brewers.

Textiles were of great importance. Most cherished was wool, which was sheared, carded, and combed before being spun into yarn and finally woven into cloth. At the century's beginning, textile workers did all these steps by hand. Over the next hundred years, the process gradually became mechanized. While hand spinning and weaving survived in some areas, mechanized industrialization threatened it and in the coming century would transform household production of textiles from an industry to a hobby.

Wool was not the only fabric produced in England. Weavers and spinners of silk and cotton furnished their materials to plenty of workers ready to turn these fabrics into clothing: stay makers (makers of corsets), lace makers, tailors, mantua (dress) makers, glovers, stocking knitters, and dyers. Shoemakers were sometimes called cordwainers, after their work with cordovan leather. Some shoe shops were host to well over a hundred workers. Women worked to some extent in most of these trades, but they dominated only a few.

First printed in *Universal Magazine,* 1749. Various steps in the industrial processing of wool. © Library of Congress.

To learn a trade traditionally required that one leave home and pay a fee to live in the home of a master artisan as his apprentice. Apprentices received no salary and worked hard, but they were fed and clothed and given the opportunity to learn the trade. They were bound to the master's service for a fixed number of years, usually seven, and were expected to be celibate during that time. Those who stuck it out became journeymen and then masters themselves with shops of their own.

The governing body of a trade was its guild or, in London, its livery company. Traditionally, the guild controlled entry into the trades to prevent overcompetition. Indeed, aggressive competition was deemed a vulgar violation of the centuries-old guild-based sense of brotherhood in a trade and was considered unnecessary when everyone who mattered could generally agree on a "fair" price.

During the 18th century, however, the old system of guilds and apprenticeship began to dissolve. Legislation governing both apprenticeship and work conditions was repealed, town corporations ceased to enforce their licensing policies, and in the 19th century, apprenticeships disappeared altogether.

The 18th century in England was a period of gradual, sometimes imperceptible, shifts in the area of industrial production. The next century would bring visible and profound changes to the manufacturing of goods. The obsolescence of apprentices and masters, guilds and the cottage industry, small-scale artisans and unmechanized production in present-day England, however, does not mean that these features of the industrial landscape never existed. In the 18th century, a mixture of new and old, of tradition and obsolescence, coexisted in a state of tempered—sometimes anxious—day-to-day work (Olsen, 33, 121–22, 129–30, 134–37).

FOR MORE INFORMATION

Crouzet, F. *The First Industrialists: The Problem of Origins*. Cambridge, England: Cambridge University Press, 1985.

Lynch, J. *Eighteenth Century Resources*. <http://newark.rutgers.edu/~jlynch/18th/>, accessed October 10, 2003.

Olsen, K. *Daily Life in 18th-Century England*. Westport, Conn.: Greenwood Press, 1999.

ECONOMIC LIFE
|
INDUSTRY
|
Africa

The Colonial Frontier
of North America

England

Japan

New England

Life at Sea

JAPAN

Eighteenth-century Japanese industry was as diverse as it was complex. From fishing to the rural cottage industries, from paper production to the manufacture of clothing, the industrial economy of this island nation also generated artisinal products made from metal, wood, stone, and the sap of trees (lacquer).

Being an island nation, Japan obviously had a long history with fishing, which had become an important industry by the 18th century. Buddhism, moreover, never proscribed the eating of fish, as it did meat.

The typhoon season, the craggy coastlines, and the tricky rapid ocean currents made the fishing profession a dangerous one. Divers harvested oysters, clams, mussels, seaweed, kelp, crustaceans, eels, octopus, and squid. Freshwater fish were abundant, but not to the extent of ocean fish.

Cottage industrial work continued as by-employment for villagers. Also known as the "putting-out" system, entrepreneurs provided raw materials to individual villagers who then produced piecework on their own. Later, the entrepreneurs retrieved the work of the villagers in return for a small reimbursement. If the product required more elaborate attention, then the entrepreneurs often transported it to a city artisan who put the finishing touches on the item. All in all, cottage industry was a fragmented affair, quite different from the highly organized and integrated processes of modern industrial production.

Some peasants commuted to nearby towns to do day work, instead of taking materials home as cottage-industry handiwork. The most common such work was silk production. Peasant girls, for example, would work all day in "silk sheds," which were little more than thatched outdoor canopies, constructed to handle what were essentially outdoor tasks out of the hot sun or the rain.

It was here that the village girls engaged in the dangerous and smelly job of boiling cocoons, snatching the boiled cocoons out of the water, and then teasing out the fibrous ends while they were still very hot and wet. Girls would constantly scald their hands and arms, and many became sick from the noxious odor of boiled worms.

Rural day workers made umbrellas, folding fans, and other goods that did not require much skill or specialized expertise in these medium-size towns. The important factors here were cheap, off-season labor and a nearby supply of raw materials, including split bamboo, straw, sedge, and a number of forest products.

Papermaking was another rural occupation. In many areas of the country, peasants made rough sheets of paper during the winter as a kind of cottage by-employment. By the 18th century, the better paper (*washi*) was made in semirural small towns where whole gangs of peasant-artisans worked together in a preindustrial factory. Because the best paper was manufactured in very cold water, the workers spent a great deal of time with their hands or feet in frigid mountain streams.

Almost all farmers made straw products, weaving rice straw into sandals, boots, and platform snowshoes. Peasants made raincoats and snow coats from straw and hemp for their own use. Virtually everyone made conical sedge hats, straw seat cushions, sleeping mats, woven rice bags, and straw ropes.

Clothing, on the other hand, required much more expertise. By the 18th century, almost every village produced enough cotton for its own clothing needs. Villagers carded the cotton and stripped it of seeds by hand, later twisting the strands into simple thread that could be dyed using homemade vegetable dyes. Cloth was woven on simple looms. Not all clothing came from villages, however. Over 100,000 weavers reputedly worked in Kyōto, most working in shops that employed 50 weavers or more. A factory system (*uchibata*) existed that required weavers to sign annual contracts.

Artisinal industry was much different. Here, artisans worked with more skill and at a much more leisurely pace. Their manufactured items were much more refined and "manufactured." Without question, a large percentage of *chōnin* (city folk) workers were involved in semiskilled labor, but the elite artisans predominated.

Blacksmiths created an enormous variety of iron products with an astoundingly small kit of tools. Two or three iron mallets, a small anvil, and a bucket of water were sufficient to turn out most of what the farmers needed. Because Japan had very little iron ore and even less coal, blacksmiths concentrated deficient resources on very small pieces such as knives, hoes, spades, plow tips, hammers, saw blades, sickles, scythes, and a few other odds and ends.

Charcoal, which blacksmiths and other manufacturers required for energy, was processed on site along hillsides. Two types of charcoal were made. *Watan* was produced from several types of wood and was used for home heating and cooking and of course was sold in nearby cities. Commercial charcoal (*kotan*) was produced from *kuri* (chestnut wood) and was used in the production of metal.

Coopers fashioned buckets, barrels, and casks out of wood. Japanese did not use much wooden furniture in their homes, so the only other major employment for carpenters was in house construction and for the wood joinery that went into a few interior furnishings. Japanese joinery, cabinetry, and carved wood products were of very high quality. Because iron nails were very rare, Japanese carpenters cut objects such as cabinets, trunks, and barrels to fit closely together with tabs, inserts, and other interlocking devices that required only a little glue.

Japanese pottery displayed the rough-glazed rustic style made famous by *raku* and *mashiko* artisans. These styles were, by the 18th century, world renowned. Japanese, who were accustomed to having each side dish served individually in tiny saucers and plates rather than bunched together on large plates, created a tremendous market for miniature-sized dishes, which were very often glazed ceramics; but many lacquered wooden ones existed, as well.

Japanese lacquer came from the sap of the *urushi-no-ki* (literally, lacquer tree). The sap was as poisonous when absorbed topically as it was if ingested internally.

Similarly, the fumes of the rendering process were caustic and could be fatal if one did not ventilate the workroom. Virtually anything could be, and was, lacquered. The most common materials were wood, leather, pottery, paper, and cloth. By the 18th century, lacquerware pieces were a major export, especially to Europe via the Dutch. In fact, the lacquering process came to be known as (and is still called) Japanning.

Japan's industrial economy was, during the 18th century, the site of many industries. The fishing industry complemented the efforts of farmers on land. The cottage industry employed many farmers during their spare time in the production of items ranging from umbrellas and fans to silk and paper. More refined industries, usually located in urban areas, incorporated the talents of artisans who, to mention only a few of their doings, fabricated metal jewelry, wood furnishing and homes, ornate pottery, and lacquered items of all kinds (Perez, 169, 171–72, 176–79, 187–88, 192, 203–4, 208–12, 213).

FOR MORE INFORMATION

Hanley, S. B., and K. Yamamura. *Economic and Demographic Change in Preindustrial Japan, 1600–1868*. Princeton, N.J.: Princeton University Press, 1977.

Japan Information Network. <http://www.jinjapan.org/index.html>, accessed October 23, 2003.

Perez, L. G. *Daily Life in Early Modern Japan*. Westport, Conn.: Greenwood Press, 2002.

NEW ENGLAND

Industrial work in the New England colonies, which was typically on a small scale, can be divided into three periods. The first period, from 1630 to 1640, was a time when labor was scarce, and most settlers had to be either jacks-of-all-trades or wealthy enough to hire laborers with varied, though usually not highly specialized, skills. The second period, from 1640 to about 1660, was a time of home industry, when much that was exported was produced in individual households. From the end of the 17th century to the Revolutionary War, artisans and more specialized industrial labor flourished in New England.

Two of the first industries, conducted on a small scale to meet local needs, were sawmills and grain mills. Fairly small sawmills were evidently established in New England as early as 1628. Larger ones, intended to assist in the business of lumber exportation, began contributing to the New Hampshire economy about 1633.

It was imperative that settlers eventually have access to a miller who could grind their grain with a water-powered mill; the grinding of corn or rye by hand resulted in only rough cereal, but a mechanical mill run by a miller could produce the refined bread to which English settlers were accustomed. The first water mill for grinding grain was likely established in Dorchester, Massachusetts, in the late 1620s. In any community, the miller was a pivotal political figure, likely because of the importance of his industrial function.

By the mid-17th century, the collecting of skins and the running of tanneries, especially for shoe leather, were thriving industries. Along with shoe manufacturing came the large-scale manufacturing of wooden shoe heels.

An equally important industry that arose in the first 10 years of settlement was shipbuilding. Shipbuilders worked out of every port city in New England. By 1700, New England had 2,000 vessels on the seas. As in the fur industry, shipbuilding required many kinds of workers: sailors to man the ship, carpenters to build wharves, rope makers, sail makers, blacksmiths, coopers to make barrels, and wheelwrights to make carts and wagons.

One of the most important industries concerned the collection and refinement of bog iron, a valuable metal found at the bottom of swamps, bogs, and ponds. The smelting, forging, and refinement of iron comprised an important industry in Lynn, Massachusetts, from 1643 to 1683. In addition, most household utensils were pewter, which was produced in the New England colonies.

Other growing industries included the manufacture of both gunpowder (so essential in hunting and in arming men for the Indian wars) and brick making, itself requisite to the building industry. Plymouth, in particular, was known for its brick making.

Newbury, Massachusetts, was host to several crucial industries. The discovery of limestone in the mid-17th century had a decisive influence on colonial building. In addition, a wire factory was built in 1667, and numerous factories, called fulling mills, processed cloth to make it thicker.

The whaling industry, which in the 19th century would become the cornerstone of the New England economy, began to flourish in 1713. Whales provided New England households, businesses, and its exporters with oil for light, ivory, and perfume.

Although the British passed laws to prohibit the importation of machinery and manufacturing expertise into the colonies, settlers from Yorkshire, England, were able to transfer machinery and their knowledge of cloth manufacturing to Rowley, Massachusetts, in 1643. Here they set up the first textile mill for the manufacture of cloth and rugs.

Before 1640, settlers imported cloth, hats, gloves, and shoes, but England's Navigation Acts, with their tariffs and commercial prohibitions, began to make trade more difficult. As a result, the Massachusetts Bay legislative bodies foresaw the need for the colonies to produce for themselves much of what they had been importing.

Beginning in 1640, bills were passed to encourage the home production of manufactures such as cloth, shoes, and hats for both domestic consumption and export. During a brief period, the government paid bounties on all cloth made in the colonies, provided incentives to teach servants and children to spin and weave, and equipped numerous households with spinning wheels. Wool production received official encouragement through the establishment both of common grazing areas for sheep and of bounties on wolves, considered to be predators of sheep.

More than 160 different articles were produced in the home to supply colonial needs and in some cases to export. These items ranged from guns to pewter plates, brushes to dishes, and knives to pencils.

Slaves worked in every conceivable industry in New England: shipbuilding, lumbering, forging iron, blacksmithing, tanning, printing, carpentry, barrel making, innkeeping, and distilling. In urban areas especially, black slaves had the responsibility of manager—of warehouses, stores and shops, and even ships. Slaves were very much in evidence in seagoing industries, where they worked at fishing, whaling, trading, and even privateering. Slaves did much menial labor in urban areas, working as helpers, porters, errand carriers, teamsters, and ditch diggers.

Often, black slaves were impressed—that is, forced on board ships as sailors—and many were encouraged to run away from slavery by going to sea. It has been estimated that in the 18th century, after New England had developed whaling as a major industry, half of many of the crews were black slaves.

Colonial New Englanders developed a number of thriving industries during the 17th and 18th centuries. These industries, which manufactured products for consumption both at home and abroad, dealt in lumber (sawmills), grain (grain mills), leather goods, shipbuilding, iron, limestone, whaling, and textiles, to name only the most important. Following the Revolutionary War, many of these colonial industries would continue to expand well into the 19th century (Johnson, 59, 62, 64, 151).

FOR MORE INFORMATION

Innes, S. *Labor in a New Land*. Princeton, N.J.: Princeton University Press, 1983.
Johnson, C. D. *Daily Life in Colonial New England*. Westport, Conn.: Greenwood Press, 2002.

LIFE AT SEA

Whales and cod furnished sailors of the period with two substantial industries, both of which thrived in North America during the 18th and early 19th centuries.

Americans were the unchallenged masters of whaling throughout the world in the 18th and 19th centuries. Yet, in the 13th century, the Basques of France and Spain accomplished the first commercial enterprise in whaling history. At this time, voyages were short. After the whales were caught, the blubber was cut up, packed in barrels, and brought back to land to be "tried out." Later, voyages became longer, and "try-works" were built right on the ships.

The invention of try-works for processing whales at sea is generally attributed to a Basque captain, François Sopite, who erected this mechanism on the deck of his ship. The try-works enabled blubber to be heated in a container placed over a fire on board. The oil was ladled out of the pot, and the remnants of fat were fed to the fire as fuel. These processes remained the predominant methods by which whalers brought home their catch into the 20th century.

The whaling industry during the 17th and 18th centuries comprised a number of simple, violent steps. The whale would be struck with a harpoon attached by a line to drogues, huge pieces of wood two feet square. With the harpoon firmly embedded in its flesh, the animal was forced to expend its energy pulling the drogue through the water. The whalers followed, either under oar power or sail, until they could kill the exhausted animal with lances. They then towed the carcass back to the beach for processing. Heavier whaleboats, better harpoons with a metal head, and more serviceable line led to the development of "fastening on" to the harpoon line and having the whale pull the boat. The practice was dangerous, but it enabled the hunters to keep in closer touch with the whale and make an earlier kill.

In 1611, the Muscovy Company, a chartered company searching for a passage to India through the North Sea, recruited six Basques to lead an unsuccessful whaling expedition of two ships. Dutch merchants, seeing the advantages of the trade, developed small-scale whaling into a large-scale industry. The Dutch, with a bigger European market for their oil, ultimately dominated the industry in Europe and severely restricted English profits.

The Anglo-Americans were not to be so easily dismissed. Colonists in North America began a small whaling industry as early as 1645. In 1690, the Nantucket community, composed of hard-working Quakers, made a concerted effort to develop a whaling industry, and by the end of the 17th century, a growing whaling industry had spread all along the New England coast.

As the New England industry expanded, Anglo-Americans found that they were producing oil and whale by-products beyond their own needs. But they found a ready market in England, where the whaling industry had come to a standstill. In 1774, the American whaling fleet numbered more than 360 vessels and employed almost 5,000 men. Although the Revolutionary War hurt the industry, the spirit of American whale men survived into the 19th century to make them unrivaled around the world.

In 1755, the town of New Bedford began a whaling industry that was to make it the leading whaling community in North America, its greatest days being from 1825 to 1860. In 1850, New Bedford was the richest city per capita in the world. Ships crowded the harbor. The wharves were lined with casks of whale oil covered with seaweed for protection from the hot weather. Whale-oil gaugers trod across the oil soaked ground to test the quality and quantity of the oil. On the cobblestone streets leading down to the waterfront, brick buildings were constructed to house the merchant offices and counting rooms. Banks, insurance underwriters, and law offices established themselves in the heart of the business district. New Bedford's greatest year was 1857, with 10,000 men making their living in the whaling industry.

One of the New England communities that turned to the business of whaling was Nantucket, an island off the coast of Massachusetts. By 1775, the population of Nantucket had risen to 4,500 persons, and 150 vessels called it home. The American Revolution put a halt to whaling, but in the years after the War of 1812, Nantucket rose to its greatest days. At least one whaler entered or left the harbor every week.

From Newfoundland to southern New England, there was a shallow area of the ocean called the banks, which attracted fishermen because of its plentiful supply of cod. This singular cold-water fish could be found in no greater density than on the North American banks. The countries of Europe and North America had been sending fishermen to the banks since before the discovery of America. Vikings,

Basques, Frenchmen, Englishmen, and Americans had all fished the banks, and the right to do so has been incorporated into many international treaties.

The Atlantic cod is the largest species among five related fish: cod, haddock, pollack, whiting, and hake. Cod has the whitest meat of the five types. It has virtually no fat and is more than 18 percent protein. Air dried, sun dried, smoked, or salted, the meat represents 80 percent concentrated protein. It not only lasted longer than other salted fish (such as the herring), but it tasted better and presented a fine flaky texture, which could be restored through soaking.

From the 17th century, the common way to fish for cod was to go to the banks in a ship and then drop off a number of dories, 20-foot deckless boats with two-man crews. Europeans crossed the ocean in large barks built with deck space and large holds. New Englanders and Canadians went out in schooners that could race back and forth to the shore with the catch.

From this brief survey of industry in the world of Western sails, it is clear that whaling and fishing were large-scale industries to which many sailors devoted their lives (Volo and Volo, 19, 21, 42–46).

FOR MORE INFORMATION

Kurlansky, M. *Cod: A Biography of the Fish That Changed the World.* New York: Penguin Books, 1997.

Spence, B. *Harpooned: The Story of Whaling.* New York: Crescent Books, 1980.

Volo, D. D., and J. M. Volo. *Daily Life in the Age of Sail.* Westport, Conn.: Greenwood Press, 2002.

Trade

Commerce, or trade, concerns the financing, movement, and eventual sale of goods. Between 1600 and 1800, sub-Saharan Africa, the North American colonial frontier, England, France, Japan, New England, and Western shipping ventures on the world's oceans took part in commercial activities. These activities typically touched on the themes of currency, finance, monopolies, shopkeepers, and global trade.

Each society possessed a mechanism that allowed individuals to exchange items of value. In some places, money was not used. Instead, barter—an exchange of products—acted as such a mechanism. Throughout Africa, long-distance trading ventures relied on a merchant presenting his item to another merchant in exchange for the latter's item. Quite simply, bartering as a mechanism of exchange had serious limits.

As a result of these limits, currency was widely used throughout, for example, local African markets. Currency acts as a medium of exchange, greatly simplifying the process of exchange. Currencies that circulated in sub-Saharan Africa included crosses, iron bars, and shells, all of which could be exchanged for any number and type of goods.

Colonial traders in North America wanted to get hold of furs and skins that Native Americans were so skilled at acquiring. If an exchange was to take place, some system of barter or a medium of exchange was needed. Many colonial traders opted for shells and beads, which they used as currency with Native Americans in exchange, principally, for beaver furs.

Both England and Japan experienced shortages in currency. During the 18th century, a paucity of coinage limited England's commercial transactions. Japanese reacted in two ways. First, local governments authorized the production of diverse moneys to facilitate local economies. Second, Japan developed an extensive and powerful credit system.

Finance, or the transaction of money and credit on a wide scale, was increasingly central to economic ventures throughout this period. Large cities in Japan were sites of financial traditions and institutions. Because government officials loathed these operations, finance was a largely private affair of businessmen. At the same time, the Japanese government, both local and national, needed money to finance itself. Hence, government officials, after forcing businessmen to offer them loans, often refused to acknowledge the creditor, instead acting as though no loan had ever been made. Despite these strong-arm tactics, Japanese finance remained influential, particularly in Ōsaka, where merchants and artisans dominated the social landscape and where the prominent exchange of rice found its capital.

England, too, saw the growth of financial institutions during the 18th century. London became the center of financial transactions, a transformation facilitated by the growth of banks, insurance companies (fire insurance, shipwreck insurance), and the stock exchange, where entrepreneurs tried to amass enough money and financial influence (capital) to start or expand a company. If successful, investors who purchased stock in the company could expect to receive reimbursements that well exceeded their initial investments. Of course, risk accompanied any purchase of stock in a company; if the company went belly up (as did the South Sea Company), then investors could find themselves completely destitute or, at best, out their initial investment.

Some businesses came to dominate the entire market in which their products were bought and sold. These businesses were monopolies because they monopolized their market (they contended with no significant competition). New England's first colonial government comprised a handful of wealthy merchant-landowners who, by virtue of their political influence, were able to carve out monopolies for their particular commercial endeavors.

European governments issued formal monopolies to businessmen who organized enormous transoceanic fleets for the business of global trade. One such monopoly was the famous East India Company, originating in England but physically active in the coastal city of Bombay, where a giant mercantile fleet was docked. Portugal, Spain, and the Dutch, among others, sponsored mercantile fleets to seek profits in Africa, Asia, the Americas, and islands everywhere.

Alongside such powerful monopolies struggled many small businesses. Small shops specializing in any number of goods appeared and sometimes prospered, sometimes not. Colonial New England was home to many shopkeepers, as were Japan and

England. In 18th-century London, one could find stores specializing in cocoa, flowers, medicine, china, coal, and countless other consumer goods. In France, cafés grew in number and popularity, signifying an important intersection of leisure, beverages, and sociable discourse in a consumer setting.

Of particular note during this period was the slave trade. Africa, North America's colonial frontier, England, France, New England, and Western oceanic shipping formed an integrated and clearly global commercial network based on the trade of humans. African rulers supplied slaves to European and American slave ships, which, in turn, transported their human cargo to various locations, including the West Indies, where the slaves were exchanged for, among other things, rum and molasses. Hundreds of thousands of souls passed through many of England's port cities, contributing mightily to the growth and uneven prosperity of Liverpool and Bristol.

The "triangular trade" in slaves thus represents the most singularly infamous element in the global pattern of commerce. Trade existed in many forms and dealt not just in profit making and sharing, but in human suffering, as well.

~*Peter Seelig*

FOR MORE INFORMATION

Braudel, F. *The Wheels of Commerce.* New York: Harper and Row, 1979.

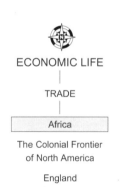

ECONOMIC LIFE
|
TRADE
|
Africa

The Colonial Frontier
of North America

England

France

Japan

New England

Life at Sea

AFRICA

During the 17th and 18th centuries, Africa continued to play an important role in the global economy. For centuries, Arab and Berber caravans had crossed the Sahara Desert, exchanging salt for gold and slaves. The Swahili coast became the site of numerous trading centers through which gold, slaves, and other products were shipped across the Indian Ocean in exchange for cloth, metalwork, and beads from India and the Middle East. When Europeans entered their Age of Exploration, it opened up the Atlantic coast, as well. Slaves came to surpass gold as the major African export, and the slave trade came to have an impact on virtually all areas of African life. At the same time, the means by which trade was conducted remained much the same, with merchants organized into family groups under varying degrees of state control.

Most indigenous African trading networks were organized on a religious basis that furnished them with a common identity. In West Africa, for example, merchants were Muslims just like those with whom they traded across the Sahara. This gave the West African merchants increased status in their communities as members of a cult that belonged to a world wider than a village or local region. Despite this generality, the trading practices of these merchants followed traditional African custom rather than Islamic law, and the principle of kinship continued to organize merchant groups, with junior partners being recruited as clients, slaves, or in-laws to integrate them into a family. In central Igboland, devotees of Chukwu, the "Great Spirit" of the Aro homeland, worked in the same way (Austen, 43, 95).

In the equatorial and southern savanna regions along the Atlantic coast, large-scale trade was mainly organized at the village level. When the agricultural season ended, the men of a village would become merchants and engage in commerce with neighboring regions. Because they had to return to farming, the distance traveled remained small, and goods reached the coast by passing from the merchants of one village or ethnic group to those of another. There were also family-based trading houses that controlled the waterways and transported goods by canoe (Austen, 93–94).

In eastern Africa, the interior was linked to the coastal trading cities by *balowoka*, or "those who crossed the lake." These traders often assumed political power in the regions where they acquired their merchandise. Among them was Kakalala Musawila Gondwe, who crossed Lake Malawi and settled on a plain near the Luanga River, heavily populated with elephants. There, he brought beads, cloth, and shells imported across the Indian Ocean to exchange for ivory. He established himself locally by marrying into influential families and then distributed turbans to local leaders. In cultures influenced by Islam, the turban symbolized a grant of prestige or authority, and hence Gondwe placed himself above the local leaders by symbolically granting them a form of power that he himself possessed. Gondwe's major problem was the preservation of his rights to a ferry at Chilumba, which was threatened by two other immigrants who had risen to power, Katumbi Mulindafwa Chabinga and Katong'ongo Mhenga, known as Mwahenga. Gondwe first succeeded in having a weak leader installed as Katumbi's heir after his death and gave Mwahenga cloth in exchange for allowing him free access to the ferry (Ogot, 635–38).

Because no currency was accepted throughout Africa, trade often took place by bartering based on the relative value of goods in different markets. However, different forms of currency were used in local trade, such as small crosses, iron or brass bars, and brass horseshoe-shaped *manillas*. One of the most important in much of West Africa was the cowry shell, produced in the Maldives and in common use throughout the Indian Ocean basin, China, and Polynesia. To produce this valued object, artisans took the cowries from the sea, left them to die, and afterwards shelled and cleaned them. In Africa, groups of 40 shells, identified by the Portuguese word *toque*, were collected in bags or on strings. Five *toques* made up a *galinha*, and 20 *galinhas* a *cabess*. People carried them on their heads; hence in English, the *cabess* became the "head" (Klein, 111–14).

Although Africa initially lured Europeans with the promise of gold, the colonization of the Americas created a huge new market for slaves. By 1800, slaves had replaced gold as Africa's main export. To purchase slaves, Europeans depended on African rulers who closely taxed and regulated the slave trade and in some cases even established a state monopoly. Historically, Africans became slaves through capture in war, indebtedness, punishment for a crime, or payment in tribute to a more powerful ruler. To meet the growing European demands for slaves, African slave traders also began raiding peasants specifically for the purpose of enslaving them.

Because of the high cost of entering the slave business, it became the province of an already wealthy elite that, as a social class, became increasingly autocratic, forming commercial alliances with European interests. Coastal African rulers enriched themselves at the expense of their subjects and neighbors. Meanwhile, the poor and rural villagers saw their economic and social lives destroyed as they lived in terror of slave raids. The kingdom of Whydah, for example, imposed a sales tax on slaves, port fees, an obligatory payment to royal officials for moving slaves to the ships, and a special fee for an interpreter to assist in the trade. The kingdom reserved the right to sell select royal slaves before exporters could deal with other local merchants, and assessed a final export tax. The king also required Europeans to use African slave brokers who worked on commission (Klein, 103–29).

During the 17th and 18th centuries, trade affected many aspects of African life. Merchants developed new markets, and new trade routes linked the Atlantic with the interior of the continent. At the same time, African culture retained its traditional values based on family and the authority of elders and spiritual traditions, and these customs shaped the myriad ways according to which Africans approached their economic lives. Unfortunately, in areas affected by the slave trade, the ruthless means by which European and African slavers met each other's demands disrupted much of African life. Unsurprisingly, many Africans began to resist this trade, resulting in the formation of the Suku Kingdom in the south and the revolutions of the 18th century.

~Brian Ulrich

📷 Snapshot

Dutch Trade with Benin

Dutch merchants traded with the people of Benin. On one occasion, the Dutch received
- striped cotton clothes
- blue cloth
- leopard skins
- pepper
- female slaves

    In return, the Benin traders received
- red and silver cloth
- cups
- cotton, velvet, silk, and flannel cloth
- oranges and lemons
- mirrors (Davidson, 104–5)

FOR MORE INFORMATION

Agatucci, C. Central Oregon Community College. *Humanities 211.* 1997. <http://www.cocc.edu/cagatucci/classes/hum211/index.htm>, accessed October 23, 2003.

Austen, R. *African Economic History.* Portsmouth, N.H.: Heinemann, 1987.

BBC World Service. *The Story of Africa.* <http://www.bbc.co.uk/worldservice/focusonafrica/>, accessed October 23, 2003.

Davidson, B. *African Kingdoms.* New York: Time-Life Books, 1966.

Fung, K. *Africa South of the Sahara.* 1994. <http://www-sul.stanford.edu/depts/ssrg/africa/guide.html>, accessed October 23, 2003.

Halsall, P., ed. *Internet African History Sourcebook.* 1996. <http://www.fordham.edu/halsall/africa/africasbook.html>, accessed October 23, 2003.

Klein, H. S. *The Atlantic Slave Trade.* Cambridge, England: Cambridge University Press, 1999.

Ogot, B. A., ed. *General History of Africa.* Vol. 5. *Africa from the Sixteenth Century to the Eighteenth Century.* Paris: United Nations Educational, Scientific, and Cultural Organization, 1992.

THE COLONIAL FRONTIER OF NORTH AMERICA

The significance of the fur trade in British America and New France cannot be underestimated. Initially, there were faint rumblings of discontent among the native populations as the effects of the fur trade altered longstanding traditions and intertribal relations; but Native Americans ultimately became more dependent on European trade goods. As Native Americans increased the volume of their hunting to satisfy the demands of the fur trade, many ritual observances that tied the hunters to the animal world were in danger of being disregarded. The trading posts in particular were thought to be destabilizing to the rhythm of intertribal commerce, a situation that prompted Indians to use unfamiliar and dangerous routes of travel. Nonetheless, as manufactured goods streamed into the wilderness, there were few Native Americans who could not see their usefulness.

European fur traders initially attempted to penetrate the interior of North America by using the same trade routes that the native tribes had used for centuries. The fur trade in New France was established in 1601 under a trading monopoly. The post at Tadoussac was near the mouth of the Saguenay River, where it flowed into the St. Lawrence River. Tadoussac remained a disappointing enterprise, however, because too few furs came into it from the interior. The Indians who visited these posts told of a bounty of furs from the lakes and rivers of the wilderness interior. The most valuable furs were those of beaver, taken in the winter when the coat was most heavy. If the French wanted these at a reasonable price, they would have to travel inland to get them.

Acting on a desire to move into the interior, the French opened a base at Quebec in 1608. Here was the great natural citadel that had been occupied and abandoned by the explorer Jacques Cartier decades before. Montreal, 500 miles farther into the interior, with its forested plains and with its connections to many navigable waterways, would have to wait for almost three decades to become the focus of the fur trade in New France. From these beginnings, the fur trade became the major commercial activity of the frontier colony, with major trading posts and settlements at Quebec, Trois-Rivières, and Montreal.

The English traders, fearing that their native contacts in the New England fur trade would go north to the French, threw themselves into the wilderness in a fur-trading rivalry that would last through the 17th and 18th centuries. Having established the necessary logistics, the English trading posts "leapfrogged" into the interior following the Merrimack, Connecticut, and Hudson Rivers.

Quebec was both the capital of New France and the colony's key settlement. This engraving dates from 1722. Reprinted from Bacqueville de la Potherie, M. de. *Histoire de l'Amérique Septentrionale . . .* 1722. Paris, J.-L. Nion et F. Didot.

After 1748, English traders pushed as far west as the Miami River at Pickawillany. The English advances into the border areas west of Virginia and Pennsylvania were largely a product of commercial interests in the colonies. Within a year, the trading post at Pickawillany had taken on the look of a fort, and a dozen traders were working there. The goods they brought by packhorse over the mountains were much finer and less expensive than those of the French, and they attracted more than 4,000 Indians from all over the Old Northwest, the magnitude of which trade even dwarfed the trade in French Detroit. The French response led to dire consequences. The French began a program of fort building that is considered by most historians of the period a direct cause of the French and Indian War.

European and Native American fur traders differed considerably in the roles that they assumed in the trading process. The Europeans displayed a great division of labor among the traders. Some supplied the capital and political influence to secure a license, others operated the fixed trading posts, and finally some made the face-to-face negotiations with Indian tribes in the wilderness. The colonies of every European nation that was represented in North America at the time acquired a corps of negotiators whose prestige among the Indians enhanced their ability to bargain effectively. On the other hand, the Native Americans who dealt in the fur trade, with the notable exception of the Hurons, usually combined these many roles into a single person. The Native Americans who hunted were most often the same persons who did the trading. They transported the furs themselves and haggled over the bargain with varying degrees of success. A number of tribes attempted to control this aspect of the fur trade by installing themselves as middlemen. Some tribes welcomed their intervention; others decried it. Decades of bloody intertribal conflict, known as the Beaver Wars, were generated by the resulting commercial competition during the 17th century.

📷 Snapshot

Mediums of Exchange in Colonial North America

So far from money economies were the early settlers along North America's frontier that they frequently made use of more accessible mediums of exchange, including
- tobacco in Virginia
- beaver skins in New York
- rice in South Carolina
- specially marked playing cards in New France (Bennett, 140; Langdon, 193)

Wampum was highly valued as a decoration, a medium of exchange, and a device for recording traditions and agreements. For centuries, its manufacture had been limited to coastal tribes that had had access to the shells from which it was made. The importation of red, white, and blue porcelain beads, seemingly as highly valued by the natives as the natural product, greatly enhanced the stockpile of this culturally important item. The most dramatic impact of the fur trade, however, may be that it gave the Indians firearms. But this was not an immediate development, and up until 1640, the trade in firearms was small.

The comprehensive notes of an observer in the mid-18th century provide us with a sense of the diverse trade goods that Englishmen made available to Native American hunters and trappers:

The goods for Indian trade, are guns for hunting; lead, balls, powder; steel for striking fire, gun-flints, gun-screws; knives, hatchets, kettles, beads, men's shirts; cloths of blue and red for blankets and petticoats; vermilion and verdigris; red, yellow, green, and blue ribbons of English weaving, needles, thread, awls, blue, white red rateen for making moccasins, woolen blankets, of three points and a half, three, two, and one and a half of Leon cloth, mirrors framed in wood, hats trimmed fine, and in imitation, with variegated plumes in red, yellow, blue and green, hoods for men and children of fringed rateen, galloons, real and imitation, brandy, tobacco, razor for the head, glass in beads made after the fashion of wampum, black wines, paints, &c.

(Volo and Volo, 171, 173–75, 178–79).

FOR MORE INFORMATION

Bennett, P. W., ed. *Canada: A North American Nation*. Whitby, Ontario: McGraw-Hill, 1989.

Hale, N. C. *Pelts and Palisades: The Story of Fur and the Rivalry for Pelts in Early America*. Richmond, Va.: Dietz Press, 1959.

Langdon, W. C. *Everyday Things in American Life, 1607–1776*. New York: Scribner's Sons, 1946.

Volo, J. M., and D. D. Volo. *Daily Life on the Old Colonial Frontier*. Westport, Conn.: Greenwood Press, 2002.

ENGLAND

To gain access to agricultural and industrial products, consumers in England needed an entire system of bankers, investors, merchants, wholesalers, and retailers. These businessmen created and amassed the capital that entrepreneurs required to start a business, organized world trade ventures, linked producers with shopkeepers, and specialized in the retail sale of a wide assortment of specific goods.

Prior to the 18th century, traveling long distances to conduct business was a daunting prospect. Without a widespread system of banking and credit, travelers had to carry all the funds they needed, in cash, over roads infested with highwaymen. There were few banks and thus few places to save one's money. Surplus funds had to be hidden around the house. More important, capital for entrepreneurial ventures, such as the opening of a store or workshop, had to be obtained from friends or relatives because there was no such thing as a small-business loan.

The insufficient supply of coinage throughout the 18th century encouraged the rise of credit. So scarce were copper and silver coins that many people possessed mint-issued money only rarely. A workman might labor for weeks or months, buying his daily necessities at a petty shop on credit and repaying his debt when his wages were paid or when the harvest came in. Being short of cash, his employer, in turn, might pay not in the coin of the realm but in produce or paper notes payable in the future. Shopkeepers allowed some customers to buy goods on credit and even extended cash loans on occasion. Loans could also be obtained from friends and relatives. Yet these small-time lenders could not supply the range of services, or the size of loans, offered by banks.

Bank interest averaged about 3 percent, and banks offered a somewhat more secure harbor for deposits than did local tradesmen. They also provided mortgages, issued promissory notes or paper money, and dealt in checks and bills. London, which was home to the first banks, remained the financial capital of the nation. Banking was not a new concept there, but the 18th century saw an explosion in the number of

London banks, to nearly 80 by 1800. Even more remarkable was the growth in banking outside London. In 1750, there were 12 banks outside London; in 1797, there were 290.

Investing in stocks was, at least for a spell, a popular way for many 18th-century English to expand their savings. From 1680 to 1720, Londoners invested in a horde of joint-stock companies; from 1698, brokers met at Jonathan's Coffee-House in Change Alley, which in time became the site of the London Stock Exchange. By the second decade of the 18th century, investors had discarded any caution when investing, convinced that if an enterprise issued stocks, those stocks were a sure thing. Eventually, such irresponsible investment practices led to enormous losses and scandal when the enterprise would prove to be worthless.

Trade, although it certainly involved various factors such as the circulation of coins and the ease (or difficulty) of issuing shares of stock, was a visible and concrete part of daily life. Merchants, wholesalers, and retailers formed a complex network of relations that provided 18th-century English consumers with an astonishing assortment of goods. Merchants financed the ships that carried Scandinavian timber, American furs and tobacco, African ivory, Indian tea, and British cloth to and from the British Isles. English merchants also dealt in human cargo.

Despite a widespread belief that slavery was illegal in Britain, ownership of slaves was still perfectly legal elsewhere in the British Empire until 1833. The slave trade made possible in large part the booming economies of Liverpool and Bristol. A half-million slaves came through the port of Bristol between 1698 and 1807, and even more were transported from Liverpool. Slave labor made commodities such as sugar, rum, and cotton cheaply available.

Wholesalers were a far less meaningful presence in 1700 than in 1800. In 1700, much of what people ate consisted of local produce. The actual shopping in 1700 revolved around the weekly and yearly cycles of the market and fair. The market, however, was not destined to thrive. Not every town that needed a market had one. In addition, markets required a direct exchange of cash for goods, and coin was in short supply. Furthermore, most of the poor, and thus perhaps half of the population, could not afford to buy a whole sack of flour at once, or a whole flitch of bacon, and market-stall holders scorned to sell such small quantities. Moreover, the market was held only once a week, but many people preferred or needed to buy their goods each day, sometimes twice a day. By the 1790s, the market as the chief source of food and useful goods was nearly extinct.

What replaced the market was the shop—that is, retailers who themselves depended on and encouraged the growth of wholesalers, the large body of middlemen that included warehousemen, brokers, drovers, and graziers. Once supplied, shops offered convenience for town and village dwellers because they were open on days when the market was not and in places where markets were not held. They offered credit. They would sell small quantities of food, enough for one meal. They also carried items that the markets did not, including tea and sugar. They did not quite replace the market when it came to fresh meat, vegetables, and fruit, but in all other areas, shops triumphed.

Retailers lured customers with the bright, glossy, irresistible appearance of the shops themselves—the candlelit interiors, the bowfront windows, the displays under glass, the gilded decorations, and the sheer variety of merchandise of London's shops. Consumers thus had a wider selection of products at lower cost. More shops meant more competition, which led to advertising and inventive marketing strategies. Better marketing induced even common people to yearn for luxury items such as clocks, watches, and teapots; more competition between shopkeepers meant that buyers could, in theory at least, influence prices and selection with their purchasing power; and the consumer economy was born.

Large towns and cities might add to the basic shops those of clock and watchmakers, booksellers and stationers, confectioners and fruiterers, perfumers, wig makers, opticians, whip makers, carpet and wallpaper sellers, newspaper vendors, print sellers, seedsmen, gunsmiths, glovers, cartographers, florists, fan makers, auctioneers (Sotheby's was founded in 1744, Christie's in 1762), hosiers, and other specialists.

A typical general shop would carry at least the basic necessities of life: wheat and barley flour, bread, tobacco, cheese, bacon, patent medicines such as "Daffy's Elixir" and "Dr. Anderson's True Scots Pills," candles, butter, salt, soap, rice, raisins, currants, figs, pepper, cloves, mustard, and starch. Full-fledged grocers carried a more extensive selection of food. They sold cocoa, hops, fresh meat, wine and liquor, soups and sauces, ginger and cinnamon, quinine, almonds, curries, and dried fruit, oranges, and apples.

Ironically, the rise of shops coincided with a general decline in earning power among the laboring classes. The result was that for many people, even the necessities of life became difficult to afford.

The consumption of merchandise was a complex affair involving many distinct but interrelated business practices. From bankers to retailers, the commercial economy of 18th-century England developed a degree of specialization and customs that gradually satisfied the wants of a portion of consumers (Olsen, 27–29, 137, 188–91, 193–95, 197–98).

To read about trade in Chaucer's England, see the Europe entry in the section "Trade" in chapter 3 ("Economic Life") of volume 2; and for trade in Victorian England, see the section "Trade" in chapter 3 ("Economic Life") of volume 5 of this series.

This advertisement for Pears' Soap implied that those who purchased the product were "comely," "brave," "pretty," and "smart." © Library of Congress.

FOR MORE INFORMATION

Langford, P. A *Polite and Commercial People: England 1727–1783*. Oxford: Oxford University Press, 1992.

Lynch, J. *Eighteenth Century Resources*. <http://newark.rutgers.edu/~jlynch/18th/>, accessed October 10, 2003.

Mui, H., and L. H. Mui. *Shops and Shopkeeping in Eighteenth-Century England*. Montreal: McGill-Queen's University Press, 1989.

Olsen, K. *Daily Life in 18th-Century England*. Westport, Conn.: Greenwood Press, 1999.

FRANCE

Between 1600 and 1800, trade changed the face of consumption in France. Colonial products such as sugar, tobacco, cotton, and coffee became a part of everyday life, so much so that shortages of sugar, a product that had been reserved for medicinal purposes just a hundred years earlier, led to widespread rioting in Paris during the French Revolution. Similarly, tobacco was imported by the shipload, and pipes and snuff became common sights, especially in the growing cities. Perhaps most significant, changing trade patterns and the increased availability of cotton led to a price drop in clothing, so that many people were able to afford underwear for the first time.

This trade revolution began with Spain's and Portugal's domination of Atlantic trade in the 16th and 17th centuries. However, as Spain and Portugal declined in political importance, state-chartered private companies, including the French, Dutch, and British East India Companies, drove European trade. Instead of focusing on the rapidly diminishing returns of silver and gold mines, these companies focused on plantation products such as sugar, tobacco, coffee, and cotton. However, the plantation economy was labor intensive; and as native populations in the New World dwindled, African slavery appeared to be the logical solution to the shortage of workers.

Because of the demand for slaves to work the fields, ships from trading companies traversed the world in what became known as "triangular trade." Western European nations sent ships loaded with silks, cottons, and other manufactured goods to the western coast of Africa, where European traders used the products to buy slaves. Often, the same ships took the slaves from Africa to North and South America and the Caribbean, where the Africans were sold to plantation owners. In the last step of the "triangle," the money gained from selling slaves was used to purchase the raw materials produced by the colonies—materials that not only included the plantation products but also timber, rum, and furs. These products were sent back to western Europe, where they were used to make manufactured goods.

Wealthy plantation owners in the "New World" could and did make staggering amounts of money off the triangular trade. Once in possession of their fortunes, owners often left their plantations in the hands of managers and returned home to France, where they built luxurious homes. Social status in France was closely tied to one's ability to "act" as a noble would, which meant to live a life not marred by "dirty" labor or commerce. After living a life of leisure for years on end, it was possible that these men would be able to purchase titles of nobility for themselves. At the very least, they would eventually enable their sons or grandsons to claim noble status. Trade and money were not the ultimate goals; elevating one's social status was the ultimate plan, and money was only a means to that end.

Worldwide trade generated a number of changes. Wealthy owners returned to France and settled on large estates or expensive city homes. Tea, coffee, calico, and sugar became staples of a population that was wealthier, better fed, and increasing in size. All these changes, in turn, spurred the growth of cities. And the growth in trade generated calls for uniformity in weights and other measures. With such large amounts of money changing hands, and more and more people participating in trade at all levels, a consumer society began to emerge.

One clear indication of the impact of colonial trade was the explosive growth of the coffeehouse or *café*. In France alone, hundreds of cafés opened in the cities and catered to the new consumer. These coffeehouses demonstrate a number of points about the political structure of trade during this period. First and foremost, their very existence demonstrated that international politics had stabilized. During the reign of Louis XIV (1643–1715), the constant warfare between France and other European countries had disrupted trading routes and made the arrival of goods from overseas difficult to ensure. In the 18th century, however, the cafés could count on relatively steady deliveries of the bean that drove their business. Second, the growth of the coffeehouse reveals that the instability characterizing domestic politics a century earlier was all but past. To gather in large numbers and discuss the day's news, literary happenings, or even political ideas was no longer seen as a potentially subversive activity. The café was neither taxed out of existence nor heavily regulated. Monarchs were willing to allow their subjects the freedom of meeting in public places and carrying on discussions of all sorts.

In broad economic and social terms, the coffeehouse trade was equally significant. The fact that hundreds of cafés found willing customers is proof of the consumer revolution that was changing the face of France. Not only were people willing to buy calicos and silks, but they were also willing to spend their growing disposable income on such a transient and frivolous product as coffee (and the socializing that came along with it). However, the gendered nature of the coffeehouse demonstrates that no matter what changes were transforming trading relations, the relationships between men and women remained very similar. Whereas women could drink coffee in the privacy of their own homes, they were welcome in the public coffeehouse neither as drinkers nor as participants in the discussions.

Before the widespread impact of the triangular trade, theologians and philosophers had generally been able to ignore the issue of a person's pursuit of luxurious and frivolous goods or clearly mark it as a sign of sinful conduct. As ever-larger proportions of French society began to participate in this acquisitive behavior, however, philosophical justifications of consumer behavior became more common. The most famous of these treatises, Bernard Mandeville's *Fable of the Bees* (1705), argued for a new perspective on consumption. Rather than condemning the new trends as selfish and vice ridden, Mandeville argued that the economic boom and expansion of wealth to larger segments of society demonstrated that greed was economically productive because the more things people wanted, the harder people would work to obtain their desired objects. As he insisted, society could have "every part . . . full of Vice, Yet the whole mass a Paradise." Ideas such as this demonstrate

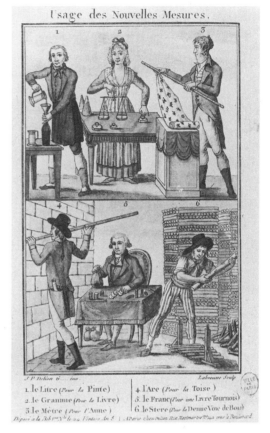

Usage des Nouvelles Mesures, engraving by Labrousse, 1800. In an attempt to create uniformity and increased efficiency, standardized weights and measures were adopted and promoted during the French Revolution and after, benefiting trade, in particular. © Snark/Art Resource, NY.

that the way that we look at our world of capitalism and consumption in the 21st century can be traced back to the economic life of the 17th and 18th centuries.

~*Jennifer J. Popiel*

FOR MORE INFORMATION

Davis, R. *The Rise of the Atlantic Economies.* Ithaca, N.Y.: Cornell University Press, 1973.

Haine, W. S. *World of the Paris Café: Sociability among the French Working Class, 1789–1914.* Baltimore, Md.: Johns Hopkins University Press, 1998.

Lynch, J. *Eighteenth Century Resources.* <http://newark.rutgers.edu/~jlynch/18th/>, accessed October 10, 2003.

Mandeville, B. *The Grumbling Hive: or, Knaves Turn'd Honest.* Edited by J. Lynch. January 30, 1999. <http://newark.rutgers.edu/~jlynch/Texts/hive.html>, (February 20, 2003).

Mintz, S. W. *Sweetness and Power: The Place of Sugar in Modern History.* New York: Viking Press, 1995.

Northrup, D. *Africa's Discovery of Europe 1450–1850.* New York: Oxford University Press, 2002.

Smith, A. K. *Creating a World Economy: Merchant Capital, Colonialism, and World Trade, 1400–1825.* Boulder, Colo.: Westview Press, 1991.

Stein, R. L. *The French Sugar Business in the Eighteenth Century.* Baton Rouge: Louisiana State University Press, 1988.

ECONOMIC LIFE

|

TRADE

|

Africa

The Colonial Frontier
of North America

England

France

Japan

New England

Life at Sea

JAPAN

Trade and commerce covered a wide spectrum of Japanese society during the 18th century. A city such as Ōsaka was the center for commercial transactions in rice, banking practices, government reforms, and the circulation of money in Tokugawa Japan. Wealthy and influential men managed these affairs. Less influential and more numerous, petty merchants also contributed to Japan's world of commerce at this time. Proprietors of small shops of all sorts plied their trade in larger villages and cities throughout the country, making the agricultural and industrial products of Japan available to those who could afford them.

In Ōsaka, perhaps 95 percent of the population of a half-million were merchants and artisans. Perhaps one-quarter were directly involved in rice exchange. Daimyō (feudal warlords) shipped their rice to Osaka, where they exchanged it for money. The city was therefore home to the most commercial-minded people of the country. The city was so self-conscious of its image that it developed a commerce-laced jargon that became a distinct regional language all its own.

By the 18th century, a rice-futures commodity market had developed in Ōsaka. Rice and sake merchants bought tomorrow's rice crops at today's prices, with an eye on selling or trading the actual rice at a profit. The futures market also embraced other commercial crops such as silk, cotton, and flax, and all the other grains and greens typical of Japan.

Because the *bakufu* (national military government) resisted a national currency system, Ōsaka became the center for money exchange. Financial transactions included the exchange of specie (coined money) and paper money for commercial notes backed by rice. Every large rice merchant house in Ōsaka maintained offices in Edo where these notes could be redeemed for goods. All of the Ōsaka merchants honored one another's rice certificates.

Ōsaka's primary rice market was in Dojima. Money, rice futures, vouchers, and other financial instruments of trade were themselves traded in the Dojima market. Many daimyō and even the *bakufu* itself arranged most of their loans there and repaid them with interest. No one could afford to spurn the Dojima bankers. The earthy adage of the era suggested that "when Dojima men fart, even the shōgun smiles and claims it smells sweet."

The *bakufu* by turns tried to stifle, then to encourage, and finally to manage trade throughout the country. Each reform enjoined the society to be frugal. The top *bakufu* bureaucrats sought to set an example for everyone by imposing a 10 percent reduction of their own budget. Everyone was urged to do the same. Eventually, the crisis seemed to pass, and things returned to normal. In reality, nothing had changed since another round of fiscal follies was in the offing.

Much of the confusion can be traced directly to the *bakufu's* obsession with maintaining social segregation based on occupation. Military and administrative power spurned merchants and other businessmen who possessed great, private wealth. The basis for this disdain was neo-Confucian morality, which stipulated that peasants and artisans were productive, bureaucrats were honorable managers and protectors, and merchants were greedy and depraved.

Thus the governing class, which taxed farmers and artisans, believed that to tax the merchants was to collaborate in their nefarious activities. Not that the merchants were clamoring to pay their share of taxes—on the contrary. But because the *bakufu* constantly reviled those involved in trade, many merchants (who could have been the natural allies of the *bakufu*) became wary adversaries of the government.

Ironically, *bakufu* officials made commercial deals with important merchants. After all, a strong economy was in the government's self-interest. Therefore, to ensure supplies and manage prices, the *bakufu* granted official monopolies to wholesale merchants (*ton'ya*). However, any *ton'ya* who prospered more than the financial situation seemed to warrant might find himself the target of *bakufu* hostilities. Also, because the accumulated wealth of merchants endlessly tempted the *bakufu*, the latter might require the former to approve a loan to alleviate government debt.

The Tokugawa monetary system was equally precarious. Officially, the *bakufu* had seized all of the gold, silver, and copper mines in the country and denied anyone else the right to circulate or coin specie. However, Chinese copper coins filtered into the country, and after a time, the Tokugawa turned a blind eye to the unofficial specie.

Worth very little, the coins were round with square holes in the center through which a string was laced. A string of 100 became a unit of currency. Occasionally, strings served as tips, alms, or small gifts for beggars and children.

The *bakufu*, too, coined chunks of gold and silver into a rather complex and cumbersome system of exchange. The largest silver "coin" was actually about the size of a human hand. The *bakufu* preferred that no paper money circulate, but from time to time they would relax this prohibition. If there was anything that remotely resembled a national currency, it was the rice vouchers.

Japan's petty merchants were known as *shonin*. In large part, they went about their business with caution. Within the cities, the *shonin* mostly waited for customers to come to their tiny shops. Most lived in the dank rooms behind the storefronts. Only a very few could afford homes separate from their shops. The *shonin* generally contracted with artisans for a steady supply of manufactured goods and then made occasional trips to these suppliers to buy the finished product.

A few groups plied their products on a national scale. Traders in specialty items such as silk and other textiles, gold, silver, iron products and tools, religious accoutrements, rare spices, sugar, perfumes, and the like had to roam far afield to sell their wares.

Many *shonin* joined guildlike associations (*kobuna-kama*) for mutual protection. These organizations were modeled on the rice guilds and were intended to share costs and risks among many members. These guilds provided members with reliable business contacts and even small-scale banking services but were obliged to pay annual license fees to their city administration.

Greengrocers and fishmongers were required to rise early to buy their supplies at central markets and then hurry home to sell them before the heat of the day wilted or spoiled their wares. Because there was no refrigeration, *chōnin* (city folk) bought their food provisions daily. Restaurants often had them delivered. There were hundreds of other specialty *shonin*—dealers in salt, sake, sugar, charcoal, rice, paper, cooking and lamp oil, soy sauce (shoyu), cutlery, pottery, and tofu, among others. Other dry-goods merchants stocked a profusion of nonperishable necessities of life such as needles, thread, thimbles, flint, fans, umbrellas, candles, pots, and pans, to name but a few.

In short, the urban economies were vibrant and essential during the period. By and large, the society was well served by its merchant class. When left to their own devices, the *shonin* prospered. When harassed and disturbed, they endured.

Transactions involving rice, money, vouchers, and contracts dominated 18th-century Japan's financial and commercial landscape. Less visible, but equally important, were the countless *shonin* who, despite both the inept reforms of government officials and their disdain for merchants, responded to Japanese demands for agricultural and industrial goods (Perez, 150–51, 227–29, 231–37).

FOR MORE INFORMATION

Hanley, S. B., and K. Yamamura. *Economic and Demographic Change in Preindustrial Japan, 1600–1868.* Princeton, N.J.: Princeton University Press, 1977.

Japan Information Network. <http://www.jinjapan.org/index.html>, accessed October 23, 2003.

Leupp, G. P. *Servants, Shophands, and Laborers in the Cities of Tokugawa Japan.* Princeton, N.J.: Princeton University Press, 1992.

Perez, L. G. *Daily Life in Early Modern Japan.* Westport, Conn.: Greenwood Press, 2002.

NEW ENGLAND

At the heart of the establishment of New England colonies was a preoccupation with commerce. To develop a viable community, both the crown and the settlers developed particular trade relations around the globe that enriched a few powerful merchants, often to the overt detriment of Native Americans, slaves, and the settlers themselves.

Native Americans formed an important market for New England trade. They welcomed trade with Europeans, receiving wampum in the form of shells and beads in exchange for hides and skins. Indeed, the first large-scale exports from the colonies were the furs and skins brought in by trappers and traders. In high demand were beaver furs, out of which hats were made. Indians did most of the trapping in the beginning, and traders bartered for hides to be sent to England and Europe.

Often, the Native Americans had no understanding of what it meant to sell land to the settlers because they had little idea of personal ownership of land. Trees, hunting grounds, rivers, and fields were not the private property of any one person. The nearest that any individual came to private ownership of land centered on the family's house and perhaps the patch of land attached to the house. Because villages frequently relocated, ownership of land was not only communal, but also temporary.

Europeans used the Native Americans' naïveté in this regard to acquire huge tracts of land without fully explaining the exclusive rights that they intended to secure for themselves and without fair and proper payment. At first, the Indian tribes believed that "ownership" would not exclude them from using the land. They realized only later that the Europeans were rapidly acquiring exclusive, private use of virtually all the tribal lands in New England.

At the top of the economic hierarchy in colonial New England in 1630 were the nine wealthy merchant-landowners who held the Massachusetts Bay Charter and formed the first Court of Assistants to govern the new colony. Each of them benefited from lucrative holdings of land. Governor Winthrop and his family, for example, were powerful international exporters who controlled more than 3,000 acres of land in the colony, where they raised cattle for sale. His family also maintained huge interests in shipbuilding and iron ore production.

These nine wealthy men assigned monopolies in various areas and put ceilings on the wages of the workmen whom they hired. One of the merchant-landowners' first orders of business in 1630 was to place a ceiling on the wages of much-needed carpenters, joiners, bricklayers, sawyers, and thatchers. The court prohibited servants from selling any commodity without the permission of their masters, and no one could buy land from the Native Americans without permission of the court. In 1631, the court ruled that no one could buy commodities directly from an incoming ship; all had to go through licensed merchants.

The members of the Court of Assistants were continually awarding themselves land and monopolies. One example concerned a member of the original Court of Assistants, William Pyncheon, who controlled most of the fur trading in the first five years of the Massachusetts Bay settlement and who later directed the affairs not

only of the town of Springfield, Massachusetts, but of all the laborers who entered the town, as well.

Early exports included tar and turpentine. As commerce grew in areas such as shipbuilding, fisheries, and fur and metal deportation, more people could find and pay for imported fabric, clothes, china, and silver. Many could also afford commodious, comfortable, well-designed houses.

New England was ill suited agriculturally and economically to the kind of work that slaves performed in the south. Nevertheless, colonial New England played a highly significant and notorious role in the commercial expansion of slavery in the New World. Although there were comparatively few working slaves in New England (New England outlawed slavery in the 18th century), it was New England that introduced and expanded the trade in slaves in the area during the colonial period.

The slave trade began with the Salem-based ship *Desire* in the 1640s. By 1644, New Englanders were bringing in slaves from both the West Indies and Africa. The infamous triangle of trade developed. Slave traders took New World beans, corn, lumber, fish, and other goods to the West Indies in exchange for rum. From the West Indies, the slave traders sailed to Africa, where they exchanged the rum for slaves, and then returned to the West Indies with the slaves, picking up rum, sugar, and molasses to bring back to New England. The healthiest, strongest slaves were always sold in the West Indies to the sugar planters. The comparatively few slaves kept in New England were, on the whole, the weakest physically. An acute shortage of labor in the 18th century prompted the importation of even greater numbers of slaves. By the time of the American Revolution, slave trading was a cornerstone of the New England economy.

The employment of servants constituted another significant commercial feature of colonial America. The term *servant* in colonial New England described men and women who were hired to do various kinds of work on farms, in houses, on ships, or for craftsmen. Sometimes the term described temporary labor, hired during planting and harvesting. A person who voluntarily or involuntarily was legally bound to a master for a considerable period of time, from 2 to 12 years, was called an indentured servant.

The commercial business of providing servants to New England colonists became a lucrative one for some entrepreneurs, and sea captains, English businessmen, and Boston merchants ran an employment service. The economic basis of this form of employment involved commercial agreements and trade that spanned continents.

To get to the New World, some indentured servants sold themselves to a ship's captain to pay for their passage. The captain, in turn, sold their labor to a settler. Usually upon reaching Boston, a settler and the ship's captain would sign a contract whereby the settler agreed to pay the five- or six-pound fare of the servant, furnish him or her with decent food and shelter (though rarely with pay), and at the end of a specified number of years, provide the servant with termination pay. The usual termination pay was 10 pounds or two suits of clothes or, less frequently, a plot of land. Servants bound themselves to their master for 1 to 12 years. In the early days of the settlement, the terms were low, from 1 to 6 years, but as the labor shortage became more acute with the growth of business, the terms lengthened, with a few running to 12 years.

Colonial New England was the site of historically significant commercial activities, several of which (the slave trade, furs) impacted distant cultures and future generations in unforeseen and often violent ways (Johnson, 59–60, 64, 142–43, 148, 160, 199).

FOR MORE INFORMATION

Boorstin, D. J. *The Americans: The Colonial Experience*. New York: Random House, 1958.

Innes, S. *Labor in a New Land*. Princeton, N.J.: Princeton University Press, 1983.

Johnson, C. D. *Daily Life in Colonial New England*. Westport, Conn.: Greenwood Press, 2002.

LIFE AT SEA

The period of European oceanic exploration, including the 18th century, reflected a preoccupation with trading and commercial ventures. Profits were to be made from the bounty of the seas, the slave trade, and trading companies. Portuguese, Spaniards, Dutch, French, and English played major roles, at different times and with different emphases, in the quest for commercial influence and supremacy.

A great deal of maritime trade involved North American goods. The fishing fleets of several European nations set their nets and hooks in the waters off the New England shore. Some set up temporary quarters on the scattered islands to dry and salt their catch. England coveted not only the bounty of the sea but also the timber, shingles, barrel staves, and pine pitch that the forests offered. Other commodities such as furs, potash, turpentine, and distilled rum were equally valued.

Maritime commerce also relied on the slave trade (the "triangular trade"), which involved the three commercial points of the American continents, Africa, and the West Indies (the Caribbean). Molasses, imported from the islands of the West Indies, was distilled in New England into rum. The rum was a valuable commodity that could be used to trade for slaves on the west coast of Africa. The slaves were then traded to the sugar plantation owners on the islands, thereby closing the triangle. The slave trade was outlawed by mutual agreement with Britain in 1808.

The age of sail is particularly noted for the giant monopolies granted to the trading companies of Europe. For centuries, Arab and Persian merchants had transferred trade goods from the Indian Ocean to Europe by an overland route, adding a premium to the price of everything that they handled and raising the value of these commodities in all of Europe. New trading companies established in Europe were cutting out the middlemen and pocketing the profits for their investors.

Thus the small groups of men who were willing to risk their wealth by purchasing the stock of a chartered trading company were given an attentive royal ear when they begged for the privilege of exploiting these potentially profitable new fields of commerce in the name of their country. England, France, Spain, Portugal, and

Holland all had great trading monopolies chiefly in the East and West Indies, while Denmark, Sweden, and Russia chartered smaller or less-extensive enterprises.

Although the various charters differed on specifics, each contained certain essential similarities. In return for sovereignty over the territory in which the company's trading posts and settlements were established, the government gave the company a monopoly over the trade in those areas and over the trade routes established therein. Each company was further given permission to make alliances and contracts with the princes or native peoples of the region; to appoint and to remove civil, military, and judicial officers; to promote the settlement of fertile and uninhabited districts; to defend themselves if trade should be jeopardized; to build, maintain, and man fortresses; to establish and man their own fleet of warships; and to retain all prizes of war.

The major obligation of the ruler to the charter company was to maintain and defend the company's monopoly with both men and ships against the claims of other companies and other rulers. The governments of Europe increased the size of their own navies largely to ensure their ability to intervene successfully in cases such as these.

Activity abounded as the trading ventures of the Virginia Company, Honourable East India Company, and Hudson Bay Company set out for the New World. The Muscovy Company went to Russia, the Turkey Company went to the Levant, and the Africa Company went to the Bight of Benin.

In London, a board of directors oversaw the Honourable East India Company, which was described as "a government owned by businessmen." At its height, the company ruled virtually one-fifth of the world's population and had an army and navy of its own. It was almost as great a military force as it was a commercial one. In the 1820s, the Honourable East India Company maintained an army on foreign shores numbering well over a quarter of a million men—larger than any standing army in Europe at the time.

Maritime commerce included slaves. Here are the sections of a slave ship and the manner in which its human cargo was stored. © Library of Congress.

The Honourable East India Company also maintained a dockyard at Bombay to serve one of the world's largest navies in the form of a giant mercantile fleet. Its naval service patrolled the Indian Ocean and the waters of the East Indies as well as the Persian Gulf. The East Indiamen of the 18th century were of about 500 tons with a crew of 90. Recognized as a discrete category of vessel, they were built specifically for the India trade.

The Portuguese were aided by their position on the Atlantic and their fine blue water port of Lisbon. Lisbon's geographical location and deep harbor allowed large vessels to make their way in and out with little aid or difficulty. Before the end of the 16th century, the Portuguese had expanded their commercial empire along the African coasts and in faraway India. The absorption of Portugal by Spain in 1580 ended the period of Portuguese dominance and made Spain what it had not been before, an important naval power.

Spain's position on the Iberian Peninsula was remarkably favorable, with access to both the Atlantic and Mediterranean coastlines. Voyages to and from the New World were scheduled for either spring or summer in an attempt to avoid the Caribbean storm season. The Spanish entered the 18th century with extensive holdings on the European continent and in the Mediterranean and the Western Hemisphere but were ultimately unable to capitalize on the commercial potential that these regions offered.

The trading nations of northern Europe advanced their sea power at the expense of their southern neighbors by building foundations securely resting on seaborne commerce. The Dutch, who fished their own coast, found that they could exchange an almost-unlimited quantity of salted herring for other products throughout Europe and expanded their trade into the Baltic. Dutch commerce soon dominated northern Europe, and Dutch prosperity came to reside in moving luxuries from all over Europe—cloth made from English wool; wine and olive oil from France, Italy, and Spain; and dried fruit and silks from Greece and far away Persia and Turkey. As much as 75 percent of all goods moving across Europe were carried in Dutch bottoms.

The powerful Dutch East India Company, founded in 1602, built an empire largely by dispossessing the Portuguese in Africa and Asia. Moreover, the Dutch West India Company, founded in 1621, held portions of the coast of Guinea and Brazil, as well as several colonies in North America.

France, cut off from the world by the navies of England and Holland and girdled by enemies on the continent, did not take to the sea with the eagerness of other European nations. The subordination of sea power in this manner must be considered when analyzing French conduct on the world stage throughout the age of sail.

The commercial and trading patterns of the age of sail were truly global. Englishmen drank French wine, Frenchmen used spices from the Dutch East Indies, Dutchmen cooked food in Spanish olive oil, and Spaniards ate salted cod from New England. Sugar moved from the New World to the Old, Asian silks were sold in the markets of Italy, and African slaves were torn from their homes to labor in the Americas (Volo and Volo, 12–13, 21, 31, 33, 35–37, 40–41, 177–80).

FOR MORE INFORMATION

Gardner, B. *The East India Company: A History.* New York: Dorset Press, 1971.

Volo, D. D., and J. M. Volo. *Daily Life in the Age of Sail.* Westport, Conn.: Greenwood Press, 2002.

Professions

Some jobs that do not readily adhere to the categories of agriculture, industry, or commerce fit rather nicely under the term *professions*. In general, professional services during the 17th, 18th, and early 19th centuries ranged in skill but typically required some background education. Professions along the North American colonial frontier, in sub-Saharan Africa, England, Japan, New England, and on the high seas involved the sale of distinctive services, artistic works, or small-scale artisinal activities rather than of anonymous goods.

Many professions required physical dexterity. England's military during the 18th century was active, and common soldiers, as well as their officers, needed physical stamina if they were to perform their duties on the field of battle. Long hours of marching; familiarity with loading, aiming, firing, and reloading muskets; exposure to the enervating effects of cold, wet, hot, and muddy weather; and chronic exposure to disease all contributed to the physicalness of life in the military.

More dexterous still were Japanese firemen, whose acrobatic talents enabled them to dismantle houses that were in the vicinity of an urban fire. The remarkable exploits of these firemen were so visually entertaining that these brave professionals performed their acrobatic moves during celebrations, to the general delight of spectators. The athletic feats of firemen in early modern Japan resembled the talents of many sailors who made their way up and down the rigging, in both calm and stormy weather.

Some professions required a more precise, localized command of the body. Many artisans in ports and on board oceangoing vessels plied their trade on such a small scale that their precise and frequently singular accomplishments distinguished them from larger-scale industrial workers. These men refined their hand-eye coordination and developed certain muscles as they worked with metal (blacksmiths), wood (shipwrights), fiber (rope makers), and canvas (sail makers).

On the North American colonial frontier, two common categories of labor were apprentices and servants. Over time, colonies such as those belonging to New England attracted more skilled professionals including tailors and furniture makers, who met settlers' increasingly refined demands.

The arts, too, were a site of professional economic productivity. Japanese tattoo artists followed a long and rich tradition of inscribing detailed and colorful images on the skin of select customers. The coordination of mental images, visual concentration, and hand movement that professional tattoo artists attained required an impressive exactitude. The actual designs, however, were not universally valued. People with tattoos tended to represent the lowest classes of Japanese society, including outcastes like firemen and tanners, as well as members of the criminal underworld.

Physical movements that depended on the sometimes precise exercise of the human body characterized many professions. Other professions privileged cerebral accomplishments over corporeal ones. As the North American colonies matured, more and more schoolteachers found work, responding to religious and secular demands. Back in England, scholars and tutors earned a pittance instructing young people in language, mathematics, and other fields of inquiry. To supplement their meager incomes, some teachers turned to the written word. Some English writers were able to transform their published interests in literature, economics, translation, and so on into impressive earnings.

Servants throughout the world at this time occupied an intermediate position, vacillating between physical and intellectual responsibilities. Lower-paid servants in England and New England sometimes worked out of sight, performing physical tasks such as sewing and laundry. New England slaves and white female servants were more likely to perform such tasks than were white male servants, who monopolized the coveted positions of valet or butler.

English servants enjoyed advantages to which industrial and agricultural workers did not gain access. These advantages included free lodging, refined clothing (very much a symbol that in today's world readily permits one to discern a "professional" employee from a blue-collar worker), better-quality food, tasteful used furniture, and even social mobility for some male servants, who started their own inns or restaurants.

In Japan, female servants called geisha underwent extensive instruction in makeup, etiquette, poetry, calligraphy, and other pleasing arts to serve their clients. Typically female during the 18th century, these servants sometimes performed sexual services for their clients and yet were especially valued not as prostitutes but as delicate and cultured sources of aesthetic gratification.

All in all, the diverse accomplishments of professionals in the period and cultures covered in this volume suggest an almost chaotic definition of what it means to be a professional. However, all these workers, be they exponents of physical labor or intellectual endeavors, embody a unique economic class by virtue of the unique skills and limited scale of their work.

~*Peter Seelig*

FOR MORE INFORMATION

Burrage, M., and R. Torstendahl. *Professions in Theory and History: Rethinking the Study of the Professions*. London: Sage, 1990.

AFRICA

Many African societies did not have clearly defined occupational classes. The job that one performed was often determined by one's age group and the season. One interesting exception to this was the Mande of the Niger River valley. They believed that certain professions, such as pottery or leather working, were passed down through certain lineages. Blacksmiths, all of whom were men, held the most prestigious occupation. According to tradition, blacksmiths led the *Komo* society, which served as the guardian of tradition and order in Mande society. They also performed

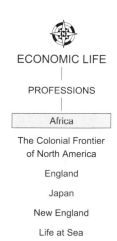

ECONOMIC LIFE

PROFESSIONS

Africa

The Colonial Frontier
of North America

England

Japan

New England

Life at Sea

certain important ceremonies, such as circumcision. According to tradition, the potters represented blacksmiths' female counterparts, and many people believed that potters and blacksmiths always married, although unfortunately we do not have enough information to know how accurate these beliefs were.

This view of skilled and exceptional work derived from the Mande belief that certain professions involved the use of magical powers. The Mande called those who followed these professions *nyamakalaw* (sing. *nyamakala*), and together they formed a separate social class. Although they could not hold political office or become slaves, *nyamakalaw* frequently acted as intermediaries among the political leaders who employed them. Their presence also lent a certain magical sanction to births, naming ceremonies, marriages, and funerals. They were not allowed to marry outside their craft society, and thus the practitioners of this form of magic formed another locus of power and status different from that of the state or religious authorities (Frank, 3).

Another profession that fell squarely into the *nyamakala* category was the *griot*. Griots performed a variety of functions in precolonial Mali. They were best known as bards who recorded the history and traditions of the people. They knew the genealogies of the different lineages and for that reason, were important factors in legal disputes. *Griots* served as tutors to the elite and as witnesses to important events that they might be called upon one day to recount in storylike form. And they, too, witnessed different local ceremonies, such as marriages and naming ceremonies (Hale, 18–58).

The Mande believed that the skill necessary for these professions was only found within the lineages that performed them. Potters claimed that other women lacked the stamina necessary to produce pottery and insisted that no matter how much they studied, the others would never succeed in producing quality work. Practitioners of these crafts were people apart, different from and in some ways superior to other members of the community. The special powers that they possessed made them an important force holding the community together, and they became a special class that helped to preserve and influence daily, as well as ceremonial, customs.

To read about work in Africa in the 20th century, see the Africa entry in the section "Work" in chapter 3 ("Economic Life") of volume 6 of this series.

~*Brian Ulrich*

FOR MORE INFORMATION

Frank, B. *Mande Potters and Leatherworkers: Art and Heritage in West Africa*. Washington, D.C.: Smithsonian Institution Press, 1998.

Fung, K. *Africa South of the Sahara*. 1994. <http://www-sul.stanford.edu/depts/ssrg/africa/guide.html>, accessed October 23, 2003.

Hale, T. A. *Griots and Griottes: Masters of Words and Music*. Bloomington: Indiana University Press, 1998.

Halsall, P., ed. *Internet African History Sourcebook*. 1996. <http://www.fordham.edu/halsall/africa/africasbook.html>, accessed October 23, 2003.

McIntosh, R. J. *The Peoples of the Middle Niger*. Malden, Mass.: Blackwell, 1998.

THE COLONIAL FRONTIER OF NORTH AMERICA

Colonial professions did not necessarily require a formal educational background or indicate wealth and stature. Indeed, any fruitful examination of the daily patterns of professional labor along the North American frontier is perhaps best approached through a survey of two common and revealing forms of labor: indentured servants and apprentices.

Indentured servants provided an early source of labor in the frontier world of North America. Between the 1640s and 1670s, many settlers immigrated to the American colonies as indentured servants. Most were drawn from English agricultural workers. Agents scoured the English countryside making grand promises about the opportunities that awaited them in the colonies. These servants entered into contracts that paid for their transport to the colonies. In return, they agreed to labor for a set number of years. The number of years varied greatly but averaged a little more than four. Contracts could be made directly with the future employer or with other merchants who would sell the contract upon arrival in the colonies. In the earliest settlements, households often put indentured servants to work as servants.

A small percentage of indentured servants were drawn from the English prisons. Former convicts were released from incarceration on the condition that they would migrate to America as servants. Usually, their contracts were for double the usual term of service. While some colonists saw this as good value for their investment, others avoided such labor, uncomfortable at the thought that there could be behavioral difficulties with such a person.

By the 1680s and 1690s, the free-flowing supply of emigrating indentured servants began to subside, and their numbers fell steadily through the remainder of the colonial period. In the Chesapeake region, an average of only two women per year emigrated as indentured servants from 1718 onward. This was in part a result of the improving economy in England, which left fewer individuals willing to leave their home to sell themselves into bondage.

Another source of labor during this period came through the apprentice system. Children who were orphaned or whose families were unable to support them could be apprenticed to learn a skill. Samuel and Elizabeth Edeth bound their 7-year-old son, Zachary, until he was 21 to John Brown to be instructed "in his employment of husbandry." They explained their action, saying that they had "many children and by reason of many wants lying upon them, so as they were not able to bring them up as they desire[d]." In addition to the obvious professions of wheelwright, joyner, blacksmith, or printer, children were also apprenticed to learn farming, reading, and ciphering. A widower with no inclination to remarry might apprentice his daughter and ask that she be taught to read. It is likely that she would be bound to a family that wanted a young girl to help with the household chores. The daughter would learn the skills in which her mother would have instructed her and be taught how to read, as well.

Illustration from the *Book of Trades*. Artisans who made wheels were called wheelwrights and constituted an important industry in England's North American colonies. © Library of Congress.

Financial burdens and single parenthood were not the only reasons for "sending out" children. This custom was particularly popular among Puritans, who often sent their pubescent children to other respectable homes to learn a skill or apprenticed them to a trade. Samuel Sewall sent out his three daughters—Hannah to learn housewifery, Elizabeth to learn needlework, and Mary to learn to read and write. His son, Samuel, was bound as an apprentice. While the parents' intentions were likely in their child's best interest, apprenticeship was sometimes a painful experience. Sewall made the following entry upon Hannah's departure: "[M]uch ado to pacify my dear daughter, she weeping and pleading to go [home] with me."

The contracts, referred to as indentures, legalized the apprenticeship. They specified what duties and behaviors were expected of the servant and what the master or mistress was required to provide the servant in return. It was not unusual for indentures to specify the prohibition of certain social activities. A servant might be required "not [to] play at Unlawful Games nor Contract Matrimony." They might be forbidden to "haunt taverns." The term of service could last for a specific time or until the child reached a certain age. At the satisfactory conclusion of the term, apprentices would receive certain essentials that allowed them to go out on their own. Generally, this transfer involved a provision of clothing and a set of essential tools with which the former apprentices could ply their newly learned trade.

Guardians apprenticed Rebekah Goslee following the death of her father. The 1756 indenture stated that she would "well and faithfully serve [Timothy Hale and his wife Rebecca]. . . . Keep his or their commandments lawfull and honest. . . . Not do hurt nor damage to her . . . master nor his mistress nor consent to be done of others. . . . Not waste the goods of her . . . master nor lend them to any person without his consent . . . not either by day or by night absent herself from her . . . master's or mistress' service, but in all things as a good and faithful servant demene herself."

In return, the Hales were expected to "take reasonable pains to instruct her and also to teach her to read the English tongue." They were also required to supply Rebekah with "sufficient wholesum and complete meat, drinking, washing and clothing and lodging." Rebekah was indentured until she was 18 years old. At the end of her time of service, the Hales had to supply Rebekah with "double apparel," which meant that she would have clothing "to have and to ware as well as on the Lord's Day as on working days." She was to have clothing of both "linen and wool, shoes, stockings and all other." Additionally, Rebekah was to be given "one good cow and one English Bible."

Indentured servants and apprentices were two modes of labor that partially satisfied colonists' demands for professionals, either in the home as servants or in workshops as artisans (Volo and Volo, 133–34, 136–38).

FOR MORE INFORMATION

Innes, S. *Labor in a New Land*. Princeton, N.J.: Princeton University Press, 1983.

Volo, J. M., and D. D. Volo. *Daily Life on the Old Colonial Frontier*. Westport, Conn.: Greenwood Press, 2002.

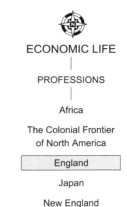

ENGLAND

Although there were many kinds of professional workers who made their services available for purchase in 18th-century England, a few stand out as predominant, including scholars, artists, civil servants (government workers), and lawyers and doctors. Servants, however, were ubiquitous in England's service sector.

Of significant importance, although poorly remunerated, was the household servant. There were an estimated 910,000 servants in England and Wales in 1806. Servants usually gained employment for a yearlong term, beginning and ending at Michaelmas (September 29), and received their pay yearly. They found posts by acquiring referrals and recommendations or, increasingly, by using employment agencies known as "register offices."

Getting a job was half the battle. Keeping it was just as tricky. An employer could dismiss a servant for the slightest cause. Servants, too, often quit, although, for them, the stakes were higher. Finding employment was especially precarious if the servant quit his or her previous job without a good character reference. Nevertheless, turnover was high; the average length of employment in 2- to 10-servant households was from two to four years.

Along with the (low) wages and lodging, domestic service had its perks: in better-off households, servants might wear "livery"—a kind of uniform, cut in fashionable style, which con-

> ### 📷 *Snapshot*
>
> **Servants in 18th-Century England**
>
> In 18th-century England, those with wealth typically employed the services of servants. On January 15, 1798, a Parson Wood-forde noted in his diary that he had distributed the year's wages to his "Farming Man," "Foot Man," "House-Maid," "Cook and Dairy Maid," and to "Barnabas Woodcock . . . Yard-Boy." (Harrison and Wells, 81)

ferred status within the community of servants; servants might be remembered in an employer's will; the housekeeper usually got to keep "broken victuals"—leftover food not desired by the family; and the servants' quarters often inherited chairs with three legs, chipped or scratched dishes, and other damaged, though coveted, goods. About one-third of servants, a disproportionate number of them male, were able to parlay their wages, perks, and experience into social mobility, becoming tradesmen or innkeepers after leaving service.

Another profession was one that involved long hours, miserable conditions, and low pay: military service. The service that military men offered was the promise to fight and to kill in conformity with the orders of the commanding officer. Servicemen in the military varied in number from as few as 30,000 in peacetime to as many as 200,000 during war, not counting the militia. By the end of the 18th century, the militia, founded in 1757, numbered nearly 100,000. The military consisted of common soldiers and officers, considered by many to be two distinct breeds. Indeed, the status of an officer carried with it a certain sheen within the wider context of social distinctions and class. For instance, many officers came not from the rank and file but from the privileged and titled. By 1800, 38 percent of navy officers (and even more army officers) came from the aristocracy and gentry.

There were scholars of various kinds, including tutors and schoolmasters. Some turned to the written word, becoming authors, poets, journalists, or translators. However, the practice of publishers paying authors for the copyright to a work replaced the old system of aristocratic patronage. While plenty of hack writers making very little dotted the literary landscape, a very few writers were quite well paid. Samuel Johnson made 1,575 pounds for his *Dictionary*, Adam Smith 500 pounds for *Wealth of Nations*, Alexander Pope 4,000 pounds each for his translations of the *Iliad* and the *Odyssey*, and Christopher Anstey 2,000 pounds for his *New Bath Guide* (which was so successful that the publisher, as a token of thanks, returned the copyright to Anstey after only five years).

The visual arts, too, offered increasing opportunities for employment. The wealthy required the services of sculptors, silhouettists, enamelists, and painters; a decent painter received between 15 and 20 pounds for a portrait of a face; prominent artists, such as William Hogarth, Thomas Gainsborough, George Romney, John Constable, William Blake, and Sir Joshua Reynolds, received far more for their works. Hogarth made 12,000 pounds from his series *The Harlot's Progress*. The wealthy also employed other professionals: architects, auctioneers, canal engineers, clergy, decorators, and surveyors. Practitioners of law and medicine were increasingly visible in the daily life of 18th-century English.

Government service proved unremunerative for the many and extremely lucrative for the few. Many local offices such as magistrate and constable were technically unpaid. Other jobs, including beadle, watchman, turnkey, and revenue officer, offered low salaries and few, if any, raises. Such minor officials were quite numerous. There were more than 1,500 full-time and part-time customs officers in the Port of London alone in 1718. Jail keepers, or wardens, made varying salaries according to the size and prominence of their institutions. Also, many government workers were independent contractors. Legal clerks and copyists were paid by the page. Some government posts were clearly sinecures, awarded to political cronies or relatives and requiring little if any actual work.

Physicians, if successful, might make thousands of pounds a year. It was the promise of status and income that motivated some to follow the path to the top: years of study at Oxford, Cambridge, or Trinity College in Dublin, followed by a lengthy exam in Latin and membership in the Royal College of Physicians, which entitled one to practice in London.

In reality, however, few physicians followed this course. Oxford and Cambridge were poor places to study medicine. The universities of Edinburgh and Glasgow offered better training. Furthermore, it was possible to evade the university process entirely. Except in a few places with long-established barbers' or physicians' guilds, as in London, no examination was necessary to practice medicine.

Just below the physician on the hierarchy of medical respectability was the surgeon. Descended from the medieval barber-surgeon, who cut hair and flesh alike, the surgeon performed operations and drew blood, neither of which the lofty physician was expected or permitted to do. Medically, the surgeons' training was often even worse than the physicians'.

The lawyer was no more popular then than now. Younger sons of the gentry considered law a good career. It was far more gentlemanly than trade and could lead to high income. Of the thousands of lawyers in England at this time, more than 25 percent lived in London. Almost all lawyers were attorneys, who handled mortgages, civil litigation, wills, and such, and who sometimes provided banking and brokerage services. An act of Parliament passed in the first half of the century required attorneys to be registered and to meet certain minimum qualifications, but this particular class of legal experts was held in perpetually lower esteem than barristers, who argued criminal cases before the courts.

The professions of 18th-century England were a varied lot. There were servants who tended to their master's wishes and military men who trained to kill. Writers and artists furnished society with artistic works while government employees administered state apparatuses. Medical practitioners and lawyers sold their services in the fields of medicine and law, respectively. An increase in these professional occupations swelled the growing middle class (Olsen, 124, 126, 128, 130–31, 138–39, 209, 262–63).

FOR MORE INFORMATION

Corfield, P. J. *Power and the Professions in Britain, 1700–1850*. New York: Routledge, 1995.

Harrison, M., and A. A. M. Wells, eds. *Picture Source Book for Social History, Eighteenth Century*. London: Allen and Unwin, 1955.

Hill, B. *Servants: English Domestics in the Eighteenth Century*. Oxford: Clarendon Press, 1996.

Lynch, J. *Eighteenth Century Resources*. <http://newark.rutgers.edu/~jlynch/18th/>, accessed October 10, 2003.

Olsen, K. *Daily Life in 18th-Century England*. Westport, Conn.: Greenwood Press, 1999.

JAPAN

Some jobs require skills that fail to adhere to the typical categories of agriculture, industry, and trade. Although there were scores of such jobs in 18th-century Japan, three of the more noteworthy professions included urban firemen, tattoo artists, and geisha (female servant-entertainers). All three testify to the mixture of unconventional lifestyles that underlay urban routines.

Firemen were indispensable professionals, as far as Japan's cities were concerned. By the 18th century, each *machi* (city ward) mounted its own fire patrol. The *machi* paid a kind of extortion and insurance fee to professional firemen, who were often *eta* (outcastes). These men (*tobi*) were more dismantlers and house razers than they were firemen. Their chief duty was not to extinguish the blaze but to deprive the fire of fuel. They accomplished this goal by tearing down houses that were burning but more commonly by rapidly dismantling surrounding houses.

Japanese houses were built in sections and usually not permanently nailed but joined into place. Thus the firemen would simply disassemble the house and move it out of harm's way. Residents who had not paid their fees or tipped the *tobi* adequately would see their houses destroyed with the excuse that safety required the professional firemen to save other residences (i.e., those of people who had paid).

The job was very dangerous, which is why individuals belonging only to the lowest level of society would perform it. These men were truly acrobatic in their profession.

Very often, they gave demonstrations at *matsuri* (festivals), scrambling up and down handheld ladders, turning somersaults, and vaulting off roofs for tips. The firemen tattooed their bodies with distinctive designs and maintained their own secret subculture within each community. They attended their own temples and shrines and otherwise maintained separate neighborhoods, usually on the lowest and poorest land, subject to floods and on the periphery of the cities.

Much has been written about the Japanese penchant for inscribing bodies with elaborate and fanciful tattoos (*irezumi*). Indeed, the very first historical document that refers directly and explicitly to Japanese customs mentions tattoos. However, such body decorations by the 18th century were appropriate and common only in a very few instances and social quarters because tattooing had long been used to brand criminals as part of their ostracism.

Many within the criminal underclass, which often mixed freely with the *eta-hinin* (outcastes), were fond of showing their contempt for society by embellishing their tattoos. In the 18th century, almost every fireman, carter, tanner, and carpenter began his apprenticeship with a symbolic tattoo.

The process was as slow and laborious as it was painful, and even dangerous. The principal technique was to inscribe the area with a pattern of tiny surface pinpricks, into which vegetable dyes were daubed. The artists tattooed only small, discrete areas at a time, allowing the transformed skin to heal and then scab over.

Tattoo artists prescribed special secret concoctions, balms, baths, and ointments that helped to speed up the healing process or intensify the color of the tattoo. The tattoo process itself took on mystical and pseudo-religious proportions. Tattoos remained a powerful symbol throughout the era and endured into the 21st century within the ranks of the *yakuza* criminal underworld.

Geisha were not necessarily prostitutes but were indentured servants, sold to geisha masters by their parents. Prior to the early 16th century, geisha had in fact been a male occupation limited to those who had been schooled in the traditional dance and musical forms of the court. Later, more and more women were introduced into the profession, and before very long, they predominated. In the early 18th century, geisha were frequently found in the prostitutes' quarter, where they entertained.

The geisha underwent years of training in makeup, music (dance, singing, and playing instruments), poetry, calligraphy, and most of all, stylish etiquette. Their ultimate goal was to attract men who would sometimes pay huge fees for their services. Geisha were not obligated to have sex with the men who paid for their services, but of course this could and did occur. With the exception of their first coital experience, these sexual encounters were the right and privilege of the geisha themselves. The first vaginal penetration, however, was a commercial arrangement. Customers vied for the opportunity to "deflower the maiden" and paid high fees for the privilege. Thereafter, the geisha arranged and conducted her own affairs, usually with the eventual goals of gaining a wealthy patron to buy out her contract and then perhaps to set her up with her own business.

Geisha were ranked, and their fees corresponded to their ranks. It was seen as socially prestigious to hire geisha to entertain at one's parties, and no self-respecting *chōnin* (city folk) merchant would entertain his friends and customers without them.

Practicing what they had studied, the geisha would sing, dance, recite poetry, and converse with the men, pouring their drinks and lighting their pipes.

The needs and desires of metropolitan existence gave rise to diverse professions, including *tobi*, who dismantled *chōnin* homes with acrobatic skill; tattoo artists, who etched *irezumi* into outcastes, criminals, and even *tobi*; and geisha, whose proficiency in the art of personal entertainment transformed itself into a profitable business. These fascinating professions were not only uniquely urban phenomena but also representative of the danger, social ostracism, and sexual exploitation that featured prominently in 18th-century Japanese daily life (Perez, 28, 154–55, 241–42, 264–65).

To read about work in Japan in the 20th century, see the Japan entry in the section "Work" in chapter 3 ("Economic Life") of volume 6 of this series.

FOR MORE INFORMATION

Dalby, L. *Geisha*. Berkeley: University of California Press, 1998.

Fellman, S. *The Japanese Tattoo*. New York: Abbeville Press, 1986.

Japan Information Network. <http://www.jinjapan.org/index.html>, accessed October 23, 2003.

Leupp, G. P. *Servants, Shophands, and Laborers in the Cities of Tokugawa Japan*. Princeton, N.J.: Princeton University Press, 1992.

Perez, L. G. *Daily Life in Early Modern Japan*. Westport, Conn.: Greenwood Press, 2002.

NEW ENGLAND

Colonial New England began with very few settlers who possessed professional skills. Over the course of the 17th century, more and more immigrants skilled in one profession or another arrived in New England, while colonists who had already made the voyage either learned new skills or made sure that their children acquired useful, vocational knowledge. Slaves, free blacks, and white servants also contributed to New England's growing ranks of professionals. It is important to keep in mind, however, that powerful religious mandates and social prohibitions limited the kinds of professions that a colonist could pursue. One such pressure was termed *secular calling*.

As with other aspects of colonial New England life, religious dogma influenced the character of professional occupations. It was the religious doctrine of secular calling that had reference to vocational life. According to this concept, God called men and women to perform particular tasks or work: Women were invariably called to be housewives and mothers; men were called to specific work as farmers, carpenters, ministers, and so on.

To identify a God-intended profession, believers considered their own talents and inclinations. If a man was powerfully built, had an artistic bent, and was good at working with his hands, he could suspect that he had been called to be a blacksmith. If he excelled in academics and had a way with young people, he could suspect that he had been called to be a teacher. However, inclination and talent were not the only matters to be considered in identifying true secular calling, and here is where the conservatism of the doctrine came into play. Puritan clergy made it clear that the social status into which one was born helped one to identify God's calling.

The magnitude of identifying one's proper work in the world continued to be a solemn business for those who had choices. Nowhere is this more graphic than in the case of diarist Judge Samuel Sewall and his troubled son. In the bitterly cold New England winter of 1696, a matter pressing on Sewall's mind centered on a painful crisis in his son's life. Young Samuel's spiritual distress concerned whether his work as a merchant's apprentice was the calling for which God intended him. On February 10, the elder Sewall prayed, "Give Rest unto my dear Son, and put him into some Calling wherein He will accept of him to Serve Him."

Although women performed many kinds of work, they were largely precluded from any labor outside the house and adjacent land. With few exceptions, a husband's profession defined any professional work that his wife performed. For example, if he were a lawyer, she could assist him in his profession and even carry on the family profession if he died. But the choice always lay with him, not her.

Almost unconsciously, colonists came to think of wealth as the mark both of a good, hard-working person and of God's approval and poverty as the result of shiftlessness. Partly as a consequence of this attitude, few limitations were placed on money making. Sociologist Max Weber argued that the Puritan doctrine of secular calling prepared the way for the rampant unregulated capitalism in post–Civil War America.

In the early and mid-17th century, only in centers of population such as Boston did one encounter a significant degree of professional specialization. A typical street would have taverns, rope makers, a barber, shipmasters, merchants, joiners, shoemakers, blacksmiths, silversmiths, tanners, hatters, and apothecaries (pharmacists). In addition, there were makers of leather goods (called saddle makers) and of barrels (called coopers), dyers, brick makers, glassmakers, paper makers, printers, and makers of alcoholic drinks (called distillers and brewers). One of the famous Boston artisans prominent in American Revolutionary history is Paul Revere, a silversmith and brass smith. Not only does his legend as a famous Revolutionary survive, but his work as an artisan survives as well, for it was he who cast the dome for the Massachusetts State House.

Civilization brought a sufficient abundance of professional services to people of modest means. These people, for example, could use the services of tailors, furniture makers, and stonemasons. On the intellectual front, there were printers of books and newspapers, and better-educated schoolteachers.

Whereas in the south, most slaves who worked outside the house were engaged in the farming of cotton, rice, and tobacco, slaves in New England performed almost every kind of work that white workers did, including skilled, professional labor. Slaves worked for tailors, barbers, bakers, sawyers, and anchor and rope makers. Usually, the master and his one slave worked side by side. A few slaves in New England were apprenticed to physicians, doctors, ministers, and lawyers.

Free blacks often found their economic situation to be harder than that of the slaves, for slaves were able to perform any work that their masters performed. The freed black, however, did not have the sponsorship of any white person and was competing for work with white laborers, who often attempted to bar blacks from certain trades. Most free blacks were limited to domestic service. Colonial records do show that some were able to establish their own businesses as basket makers, shoemakers, barbers, musicians, music teachers, cooks, bakers, grocers, and caterers. Rarely did they expand beyond a small subsistence-level business, however, because they were unable to get credit for expansion.

An acute shortage of labor encouraged the importation of servants from England, Scotland, and Ireland. For an arrived-at price, a colonial family could pay the passage of servants and own their labor for several years. For these "indentured" servants, such employment was a way to have their passage paid to the New World and to be taken care of for a period of time before becoming independent laborers and, in many cases in the 17th century, businessmen or landowners.

The work frequently assigned to indentured servants was domestic housework. Indentured servants also worked in every conceivable job in village businesses. They were in special demand in the building of ships and houses, barbering, cabinetmaking, blacksmithing, and distilling.

Slaves and free blacks, self-employed colonists, and indentured servants all contributed to the growing numbers and types of professions that over the 17th and 18th centuries, generated an increasingly specialized New England economy (Johnson, 55, 57, 65–67, 69–70, 151–52, 155–56, 159–60, 164, 199–200).

FOR MORE INFORMATION

Boorstin, D. J. *The Americans: The Colonial Experience.* New York: Random House, 1958.

Dexter, A. *Colonial Women of Affairs: Women in Business and the Professions in America before 1776.* Boston: Houghton Mifflin, 1931.

Johnson, C. D. *Daily Life in Colonial New England.* Westport, Conn.: Greenwood Press, 2002.

LIFE AT SEA

A host of blacksmiths, shipwrights, rope makers, sail makers, and other skilled marine artisans built up an extensive maritime industry during the 17th and 18th centuries. In addition to these professions must be added the work of seamen, those sailors whose skills and muscle combined to form one of the most intriguing—and typically underpaid—professions of the period.

In ports throughout the world, the water's edge was dotted with many workplaces for the fabrication of metal products. The blacksmith's hammer chimed rhythmically as he beat out the bolts, plates, chains, tools, rudder irons, harpoons, and other nautical ironwork from his waterside shop. Although the blacksmith's shed was usually placed some distance from the highly flammable hemp and flax that could cause a general fire along the waterfront, the smell of burning coal or charcoal still permeated the air when the wind blew from certain quarters.

Shipwrights were more than mere carpenters or woodworkers. Each was expert in a particular trade such as caulking, planking, joinery, and rigging. The shipyards, always near the water's edge, were the workplace of the shipwright and his men.

The slipways were made of massive timbers smoothed on top and laid parallel to the shoreline about 8 to 10 feet apart. These "log beds" might reach 30 or 40 feet inland from the high tide mark. Vessels were constructed on these and were launched from them. Great care was taken that the slipways were constructed at the correct angle and sloped down into the deepest part of the water. Permanent yards were built with stone-filled cribs at the water's edge to shield the slipways from the actions of water, wind, and tide.

Low, narrow buildings several hundred feet long housed the ropewalks. Here long hemp fibers were cleaned and combed through rows of iron spikes. A man called a spinner would coil the fibers around his waist and walk backward, drawing the fiber taut while a boy at a wheel twisted the ends round into yarns. These were then rolled up, tarred, and rewound on bobbins, where they would remain for a year while they seasoned. In time, they would be threaded through the holes of a large metal plate and then pulled and twisted into strands. At this point, combinations of the strands were parted out full length and twisted again into the desired size of rope or cable. As the yarns, strands, ropes and cables were twisted, they necessarily became considerably shorter. The total length of the ropewalk, therefore, dictated the maximum length of rope that could be turned, so that these buildings were sometimes many hundreds of feet long.

Sail makers sat cross-legged in their sail lofts surrounded by canvas bags that were suspended from pegs in order to hold their simple tools. With only a leather palm and needle, countless yards of stiff canvas were fashioned into proper sails, as sail makers sketched patterns on the floors whereupon they laid out the canvas, cut it, and sewed it to size before attaching the bolt rope around the outer edges.

The work required of seamen was physically demanding. Hauling, pulling, furling, and setting were part of the daily routine of shipboard life. A reading of the requirements demanded of ordinary and able seamen attests to the labor required of them. A typical 19th-century mariner's life aboard a ship in port began in the morning, when the seamen stowed their hammocks. Some then began scrubbing the decks and the copper sides of the ship while others cleaned the cannon or scrubbed the smoke funnel, which served as a conduit for the galley fires. Afterward, the crew hoisted boats into the water and guided them to shore for supplies and freshwater reserves. In the afternoon, the seamen prepared the tools needed to lift the freshwater aboard ship and then swept the decks, following which task, the men relaxed, each according to his own tastes, before supper. That evening, the men changed their clothes, went to their appropriate quarters, and slept, in preparation for the next day's tasks.

On the lower decks, a good deal of discontent was always simmering in connection with pay. In the navy, pay was given at a rate determined by the qualities and duties of the individual and by the conditions under which the service was rendered. With regard to the navies of Europe, the pay of the English navy—for which the evidence is probably the best documented—can serve as an example.

At the end of the 17th century, an English merchant seaman could expect an average wage of 50 shillings a month, whereas the naval wage had risen to as little as 24 shillings. In 1697, Daniel Defoe described this dichotomy: "[O]ur seamen lurk and hide and hang back in time of war . . . for who would serve king and country and fight and be knocked on the head at 24 shillings a month, that can have 50 shillings without that hazard?" Nonetheless, the variance in wages continued for centuries. Not only did they receive much less than they would have as merchant sailors (by 1790, merchant seamen could earn 85 shillings while the naval seamen still received only 24 shillings monthly), but all other forms of compensation including working conditions, clothing, and food were dealt with in a haphazard manner.

Equity or a Sailor's Prayer before Battle, by Thomas Tegg. This cartoon lampoons the discrepancy in pay and prize money that favored officers over common seamen. © National Maritime Museum.

Prize, not pay, was the great incentive for the naval life. The value of a captured ship and its cargo in warships of the 18th century were distributed to the captors. However, discrepancies in prize pay benefited those who were already most privileged. One-eighth was reserved for the commander-in-chief, one-quarter to the commander, one-eighth to the master and lieutenants, another to the warrant officers, another to the petty officers, and the remaining quarter to the seamen.

A man could be made richer in an hour of battle than he could ever hope to be after a lifetime of labor ashore. One officer was said to have earned the equivalent of 300 years' pay from his share of a single prize.

Oceanic exploration depended on the skills of professional artisans who forged metal tools; smoothed and joined planking; wound, parted, and twisted rope; and patterned, cut, and sewed sails. And yet, the work of a seaman was no less remarkable, not simply for its exotic setting but for the combination of expertise and raw force that characterized the profession (Volo and Volo, 5–6, 126–28, 134–35).

FOR MORE INFORMATION

Laffin, J. *Jack Tars: The Story of the British Sailor.* London: Cassel, 1969.

Villiers, A. *Men, Ships, and the Sea.* Washington, D.C.: National Geographic, 1973.

Volo, D. D., and J. M. Volo. *Daily Life in the Age of Sail.* Westport, Conn.: Greenwood Press, 2002.

ECONOMIC LIFE: WEB SITES

http://dpls.dacc.wisc.edu/slavedata/
http://www.bell.lib.umn.edu/Products/tob1.html
http://www.heritage.nf.ca/exploration/17fishery.html
http://www.scan.org.uk/exhibitions/anderson.htm
http://www.chs.org/textiles/menswear.htm
http://www.usda.gov/history2/text5.htm

4

INTELLECTUAL LIFE

The human mind is amazing in that it allows people to reflect on ideas so abstract as to be outside the world of sight and touch. Our ideas can be as complex as philosophical considerations of ethics, justice, and even thought itself. The study of ideas is called intellectual history, and it includes science, philosophy, medicine, technology, literature, and even the languages used to record these ideas.

At the basic level, the capacity for abstraction permits people to impose order on (or to see order in) the astonishingly complex universe. As Stone Age people looked at the dark night sky dotted by millions of stars, they organized the view in patterns of constellations that allowed them to map and predict the movement of the heavens. They then echoed the heavenly order in such earthly monuments as Stonehenge in Britain or the Maya pyramids in Mexico. During the 17th and 18th centuries, the study of celestial bodies and events evolved in Western cultures as part of a discipline called astronomy. Through time, this capacity to order things extended from the heavens to the submicroscopic particles that dominate 21st-century physics, as well as to the development of mathematics as the language with which to express these abstractions. An important part of intellectual life throughout history has been the growing evolution of science, but this is only one aspect of the accomplishments of the mind.

Some people have applied their creative capacity for abstract thought to technology, finding ways to make their lives easier. Technological innovations have spread more rapidly throughout the world than even abstract scientific explanations. Horse collars from China, windmills from Persia, and Muslim medical advances transformed medieval western Europe, while the Internet dominates world culture in the 21st century. And during the 17th and 18th centuries, a host of technologies appeared that made, for example, oceanic exploration possible, in turn leading to the establishment of colonies and commercial relations around the world, including in Australia, North America, and sub-Saharan Africa.

What has made these and other escalating advances possible is not an increase in human intelligence. Instead, the ability to record abstract ideas in writing and the tendency to preserve past accomplishments in education have allowed human knowledge to progress. Language and education were central to early-modern Afri-

INTELLECTUAL
LIFE
|
SCIENCE
& TECHNOLOGY

EDUCATION

LANGUAGE
& LITERATURE

HEALTH & MEDICINE

can communities, Tokugawa Japan, North America's colonial frontiers, England, France, and elsewhere. Indeed, the categories of science and technology, education, language and literature, and health and medicine all strongly depend on the formulation and communication of abstract ideas, be they in a scientific treatise, a love poem, a folk tale recounted around a fire, or the blueprint of an intricate instrument.

As a medieval thinker (John of Salisbury) noted, if we can see further than the ancients, it is only because we build on their knowledge. We are as dwarfs on the shoulders of giants, and through our intellectual life, we can look forward to even greater vision.

~*Joyce E. Salisbury and Peter Seelig*

FOR MORE INFORMATION

Tarnas, R. *The Passion of the Western Mind: Understanding the Ideas That Have Shaped Our World View*. New York: Ballentine Books, 1991.

INTELLECTUAL
LIFE
|
SCIENCE
& TECHNOLOGY
|
Colonial Australia

The Colonial Frontier
of North America

England

Japan

New England

Life at Sea

Science and Technology

The period from 1600 to 1800 was a time of considerable changes in European scientific thought. These changes, collectively referred to as the scientific revolution, included radically challenging and mathematically elegant explanations of empirical phenomena. Important scientists, or natural philosophers, included the 16th-century astronomer Nicolas Copernicus, as well as his close and distant successors Galileo Galilei, Johannes Kepler, William Harvey, Robert Boyle, and Isaac Newton. These figures contributed greatly to astronomy, anatomy, chemistry, and physics.

The radical ideas of the period were not always welcome or even readily accessible both in and outside Europe and Britain. Puritan New England's hostile view of contemporary science and the combined influences of Japan's geographical distance and cultural detachment from Western science accounted for two noteworthy exceptions to the scientific advances underway in Europe. Although partially rooted outside Western civilization, the scientific revolution was nonetheless a particularly European occurrence.

Advances in technology accompanied new scientific theories. By the early 19th century, the application in the West of valuable sources of energy to various tools stimulated, and in turn was stimulated by, economic and cultural events in colonial Australia, the colonial frontier of North America, England, New England, and the sphere of oceanic transportation. In particular, scientific theory and utilitarian technology simultaneously influenced people's daily understandings and uses of time, matter, and energy.

Measurement of time with the aid of regularized movement is precisely the function of timekeeping instruments. It was during the 18th century that England first witnessed the widespread use of clocks with two hands. John Harrison's No. 4 chronometer, which enabled navigators aboard oceangoing vessels to determine longitude, demonstrated the usefulness of precise and consistent timepieces.

A select group of scholars in early modern Japan reflected on time. Their goal was to secure an understanding of the nature of time as it related to Japanese history. According to court astrologers, the accession of the first Japanese emperor triggered the beginning of time, which can be fixed, in Western terms, at 669 B.C.E.

In England, governmental decree resulted in a significant shift in the measurement of time. Parliament and the king agreed that the Gregorian calendar must replace the Julian one, resulting in a few comical exclamations and declarations across the Atlantic in England's Anglo-American frontier colonies.

The study of matter included a study of the stars during this time. Unlike Japanese court astrologers, English stargazers often charted the movement of objects in the skies to collect data restricted to those objects. A preoccupation with the skies was a matter of necessity for navigators aboard ship. For instance, attempts to calculate the latitudinal position of a vessel depended on an accurate determination of the sun's location in the heavens. Various tools, including the backstaff and the sextant, facilitated this endeavor in the West.

The investigation of empirically verifiable phenomena concerned not only the distant reaches of the solar system and beyond but also the proximate natural world. In colonial Australia, Lieutenant William Dawes executed meteorological as well as astronomical investigations with the dual goal of contributing to knowledge in the abstract and of facilitating daily life in its hands-on, material manifestations, particularly in relation to agriculture.

In the realm of physics and chemistry, 18th-century English scientists increasingly discarded the long-held belief that the elements of nature were limited to earth, air, water, and fire. Scientific experiments revealed that water, for example, consisted of oxygen and hydrogen and was therefore not simple and irreducible.

New Englanders who followed Calvinistic Puritan doctrine eyed with suspicion and antagonism the recent scientific ideas being popularized in England and elsewhere. Colonists were slow to receive and consider the theories of Copernicus's astronomy and of Newton's physics, which did not extensively circulate among the learned classes until the 18th century.

Ironically, New England would soon benefit from technological breakthroughs, especially those related to engines and the energy used to drive them. Rapid and significant improvements of steam-driven engines back in England occurred at the close of the 18th century. A similar preference for coal, which was replacing charcoal as a source of energy, meant that these engines were now viable tools rather than simply intriguing but impractical curiosities.

As a consequence of 18th-century improvements in the design of engines and the manipulation of power, engine-driven steamships featured prominently in the 19th century, banishing wind-driven ships to a realm of commercial and naval obsolescence.

One can appreciate, by way of example, the comparative emphasis of traditional technology in late 18th-century Japan. To propel a waterwheel that permitted villagers to irrigate their rice paddies, human power drove the ladling machine: villagers incessantly scaled the paddleboat-like mechanism.

The science (theories) and tools (technology) that typified the study and exploitation of nature varied from one century to the next and cross-culturally. For different reasons, colonial Australia, colonial North America (including New England), and Japan did not concurrently undergo the substantial shifts in scientific understanding and investigation that England did. In large part a result of Western oceanic exploration and a growing openness to Western science, these theories of time, matter, and energy eventually extended fully beyond Europe, evolving as they did so. The results have profoundly shaped every conceivable facet of daily life throughout the world.

~Peter Seelig

FOR MORE INFORMATION

MacLeod, R., ed. *Nature and Empire: Science and the Colonial Enterprise*. Chicago: University of Chicago Press, 2000.

COLONIAL AUSTRALIA

The Australian continent was not regarded as a suitable repository of knowledge, and a scientific society was not founded there until 1821. However, the continent was seen as a vast storehouse of natural history to be plundered. Thousands of specimens were sent from Australia to be studied, classified, and exhibited by European scholars and dilettantes. The European thirst for such curiosities generated a vigorous economic trade in Australian scientific specimens of every kind. As explorers pushed farther into Aboriginal land, scientific tools related to 18th-century European cartography, surveying, and engineering surfaced in the local landscape.

The abundance of baffling and exotic animals such as the kangaroo, the koala, and the platypus astounded and delighted colonial observers in Australia. The first scientific description of the platypus was made in 1797, when it was characterized as "an amphibious animal of the mole species" (Robertson and Ward, 33). The first specimen to arrive in London was received with disbelief by English scientists, who thought it was a hoax.

The local fauna was also a popular subject of scientific illustration. No experienced botanist sailed with the First Fleet, but colonial "gentlemen scholars" were imbued with the spirit of the Enlightenment. European museums featured hundreds of botanical specimens for the exposition of global knowledge. One of the earliest illustrations sent to England from Australia was of the waratah, a dramatic and striking native plant that was later adopted as the floral emblem of New South Wales. Botanical knowledge flourished after the arrival in April 1800 of George Caley. Obtaining the sponsorship of the president of the Royal Society, Joseph Banks, who had accompanied Cook on his 1770 voyage to Botany Bay, Caley began a botanical garden in Parramatta and was one of the few colonial scientists to consult Aboriginal people for information.

Robert Brown, another Banks protégé, undertook coastal collecting on the *Investigator* in 1801. His subsequent 1810 publication, *Prodromus Florae Novae Hollandiae et Insulae Van-Diemen,* which includes reference to 3,000 specimens, was a landmark work that radicalized the methods of botanical classification. Austrian scientist Ferdinand Bauer also traveled on the *Investigator* and produced detailed and beautifully executed botanical illustrations.

The Spanish and French also sent expeditions to the region. In 1801, the French explorer Nicholas Baudin and 23 scientists undertook a two-year voyage, making surveys of Australia's southwest coastline. In addition to producing many maps, the specimens that Baudin collected formed a valuable natural history collection for a Paris museum.

Kangaroos are practically synonymous with Australia. Early English explorers on the continent carefully observed these marsupials and wondered at their impressive strength. © The Art Archive/British Museum/The Art Archive.

Navigational investigation was of great importance and was undertaken with vigor. Within a month of arrival in 1788, Captain John Hunter ascertained the latitude and longitude of Sydney, and as the colony's second governor (1795–1800), he encouraged the famous voyages of George Bass and Mathew Flinders. In 1798, Bass and crew explored the south coast to its farthest point at Wilson's Promontory, where they were stranded for almost two weeks. Bass reasoned that the prevailing westerly tides between there and Western Port suggested a strait between the promontory and Van Diemen's Land. Flinders circumnavigated Van Diemen's Land, confirming the separation, which is now known as Bass Strait. In 1801, Flinders began his successful circumnavigation of the continent, which he named Australia.

Lieutenant William Dawes arrived with the First Fleet as a marine. He possessed sufficient skills in the science of astronomy to prompt the astronomer royal to recommend him as colonial astronomer. The Board of Longitude supplied him with instruments, and he was given instructions to erect a small observatory to watch for a comet, erroneously anticipated later in 1788. Dawes also tutored officers' wives in astronomy.

Knowledge of weather patterns was important to the expeditious establishment of productive gardens and crop fields in Australia; Dawes was thus also charged with meteorological observation, and he kept meticulous daily records. He left the colony in 1791 after a disagreement with Governor Phillip and returned to England, taking all the instruments with him, as instructed. No official meteorology was undertaken in the colony until 30 years later, but Dawes's journal has allowed modern scholars to establish early colonial weather patterns with accuracy. Dawes was also a skilled cartographer with knowledge of engineering and surveying, and he contributed much to scientific and intellectual life during colonial Australia's early years.

In the realm of technology, Australia's settlers, who clung to traditional farming techniques, struggled to ensure a water supply. Tanks were cut into the only reliable stream, and individual wells were built. But the settlers lacked knowledge of streams

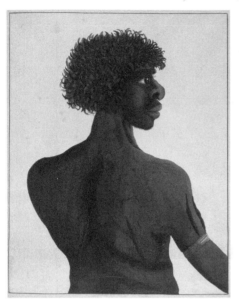

During the early 1800s, a French explorer in Australia sketched this impression of an Aborigine. Port Jackson painter, *Half Length Portrait of Aborigine,* an5600430. National Library of Australia.

that possessed sufficient power to drive mills for pumping water or grinding grain. In 1790, Phillip wrote to Under Secretary Nepean that the manually driven iron mills that were first brought to the colony were "easily rendered useless and destroyed" by dissatisfied or incompetent convicts; and yet, Phillip's continual requests for windmills were ignored (Bladen, vol. 1, 364). Over the subsequent three years, John Baughan experimented with mills that, because of the lack of working animals in the colony, relied instead on manpower. Home Office procrastination and a lack of local milling expertise delayed the first efficient windmill until 1797. By 1809, there were at least nine working mills.

When Governor King first reported to Britain on the excellence of Australian merino wool, he was ordered not to develop it but to send it back to England unprocessed. A viable wool industry did not begin until John and Elizabeth Macarthur, Samuel Marsden, and others successfully experimented with breeding techniques.

Aborigines were subsumed into the category of natural history, and Watkin Tench observed and described their customs, appearance, and body measurements in his journal. Artists such as Sydney Parkinson, Thomas Watling, and the anonymous Port Jackson Painter produced finely detailed illustrations of Aboriginal life and material culture. Aboriginal tools were simple in appearance but highly effective in application, especially flight tools such as the boomerang, the shape of which made use of sophisticated aerodynamic principles.

To read about science among Aboriginal Australians, see the Australian Aboriginals entry in the section "Science" in chapter 4 ("Intellectual Life") of volume 1 of this series.

~*Valda Rigg*

FOR MORE INFORMATION

Australian Academy of Technological Sciences and Engineering. *Technology in Australia, 1788–1988.* Melbourne: Australian Academy of Technological Sciences and Engineering, 1988.

Bladen, F., ed. *Historical Records of New South Wales.* Vol. 1. Sydney: Government Printer, 1892. Facsimilie edition, Marrickville: Southwood Press, 1978.

Fox, L. *Old Sydney Windmills.* Marrickville: Southwood Press, 1978.

Robertson, J., and R. Ward, eds. *Such Was Life, 1788–1850.* Sydney: Ure Smith, 1969.

State Library of New South Wales. *Papers of Sir Joseph Banks.* 1996. <http://www.sl.nsw.gov.au/banks/>, accessed October 23, 2003.

Tench, W. *1788: Comprising A Narrative of the Expedition to Botany Bay [1789] and A Complete Account of the Settlement at Port Jackson [1795].* Edited by Tim Flannery. Melbourne: Text Publishing, 1996.

THE COLONIAL FRONTIER OF NORTH AMERICA

Neither scientific investigation nor the application of the resulting knowledge to technological advancements and inventions played a significant role in colonial

America. Adapting to the wilderness consumed the settlers' time and energy, leaving few occasions for abstract investigations or laboratory experiments. Only after settlers had solidly established a material and civil foundation for their society did science and technology attract greater interest. Despite the general absence of these areas of research, the colonies were not void of enlightened thought, as the following discussions of agronomy and astronomy reveal. Furthermore, colonial technology presented itself as a necessary, if unsophisticated, pursuit, as the discussion of frontier lighting clearly exemplifies.

Scientific agriculturalists in England, such as Jethro Tull, believed that active cultivation of the soil was the secret of its fertility. Deep plowing was his answer to diminished crop yields, as this helped to dry out wet land and allowed the soil to better profit from rainfall. Jared Elliot, a minister and doctor from Connecticut, correctly believed that the fertility of the soil was associated with the organic matter that it contained. He showed that the addition of swamp mud to the soil increased the yield and improved the crops, and he was one of the first to note that certain crops rebuilt the soil. Ultimately, he was able to show that animal manures, cover crops of red clover and timothy, and a year's rest between plantings could significantly improve agricultural production. Later experiments showed that root crops such as turnips and carrots helped the soil. Moreover, turnips could be used as winter feed for livestock.

Astronomy was another field of inquiry that influenced (though quite indirectly and inertly) daily colonial practices along the frontier. On May 22, 1752, King George II approved a bill that reformed the calendar then in use and eliminated 11 days from the year. The bill, passed by Parliament, proposed that all of Great Britain and its colonies switch from the Julian calendar, which had been used for centuries in one form or another, to the Gregorian system, which had been implemented throughout much of the Catholic world in 1582. The act stipulated that the day following Wednesday, September 2, 1752, would be Thursday, September 14, 1752. Moreover, New Year's Day in England would move from March 25 to January 1.

Scholars in general, and astronomers in particular, had long and widely recognized that the old calendar imprecisely accounted for the actual length of the year. The Julian cycle was more than 11 minutes short, causing the start of the astronomical "New Year" to drift through the calendar as the missing minutes, hours, and days accumulated over the centuries. Hipparchus of Alexandria had noticed the difference in the second century C.E. by taking careful astronomical observations of Earth's relative position with the stars. In the centuries that followed, Arab astronomers and others had established that the old calendar was simply wrong.

In Anglo-America, much less notice was taken of the reform, and those colonists who paused to examine the change sometimes graced their comments with a dose of wit. Benjamin Franklin noted in *Poor Richard's Almanac* that colonial America could learn to appreciate the bill's unintended benefits.

Be not astonished, nor look with scorn, dear reader, at such a deduction of days, nor regret as for the loss of so much time, but take this for your consolation, that your expenses will appear lighter and your mind be more at ease. And what an indulgence is here, for those who love their pillow to lie down in peace on the second of the month and not perhaps awake till the morning of the fourteenth.

Whichever calendar the colonists followed, they could hardly read or mark it at night without proper lighting, which was poor in the rough and impermanent homes dotting the colonial frontier. Small windows let in limited amounts of light, and once the sun set, the fireplace was the greatest source of illumination. The simplest lighting technology was the pine knot, or what settlers called candlewood. Reverend Higginson described these candles as "the wood of the pine tree, cloven in two little slices, something thin, which are so full of moysture of turpentine and pitch that they burne cleere as a torch." They were often held in an iron holder, which had a pincer-like end that held the wood securely. Because they "droppeth a pitchy kind of substance," a flat stone was often placed beneath them to catch the tar that they secreted.

Grease or fat lamps were also used. These lamps were small, shallow containers, commonly iron, in which tallow, grease, or oil was placed. The wick was held in a projecting spout. These lamps commonly had a hook and chain link that permitted them to be hung from a nail in the wall or from the back of a chair.

The simplest candles were rushlights. One made them by stripping away the outer layer of common rushes, leaving the pith. This would then be soaked in tallow or grease and allowed to harden. Rushlights were placed in holders similar to those that held the candlewood.

Colonial settlers were fortunate to discover that the waxy berries from the bayberry bush made very pleasant candles. Swedish naturalist Peter Kalm wrote about them in 1748 after a trip to America: "There is a plant here from which they make a kind of wax. . . . Candles of this do not easily bend, nor melt in summer as common candles do; they burn better and slower, nor do they cause any smoke, but yield rather an agreeable smell when they are extinguished."

As indicators of vibrant intellectual investigations, the areas of science and technology failed to attract much attention along North America's colonial frontiers. Nevertheless, interest in agronomy, astronomy, and lighting technology expanded people's understanding of natural phenomena while contributing to the settlers' practical needs (Volo and Volo, 113–14, 116, 147–48).

FOR MORE INFORMATION

Chaplin, J. E. *Subject Matter: Technology, the Body, and Science on the Anglo-American Frontier, 1500–1676.* Cambridge, Mass.: Harvard University Press, 2001.

Duncan, D. E. *Calendar: Humanity's Epic Struggle to Determine a True and Accurate Year.* New York: Avon Books, 1998.

Volo, J. M., and D. D. Volo. *Daily Life on the Old Colonial Frontier.* Westport, Conn.: Greenwood Press, 2002.

ENGLAND

By 1800 in England, an interest in science had spread widely among not only professional scientists but also hobbyists and informal experimenters. Indeed, many

of the 18th century's scientists made their living by other means. Joseph Priestley was a Nonconformist clergyman, and James Watt was an industrial entrepreneur. New theories in physics and chemistry, the collection of data in astronomy, and vigorous debate in the earth sciences accompanied a number of significant developments in technology, including advanced watches and steam-driven engines. Often complementing each other, advances in science and technology reshaped the needs, wants, and possibilities of people's daily existence in 18th-century England.

The most significant developments of the 18th century were in the study of electricity. Priestley, for example, worked with the attraction and repulsion of electrical charges. Scientists, including physicists and chemists, had for centuries believed that the four basic irreducible elements were earth, air, fire, and water. At the beginning of the 18th century, they also believed that a substance called phlogiston was found in flammable bodies. Materials would burn until all their phlogiston was gone or until the surrounding air was too saturated with phlogiston to absorb any more.

These beliefs were largely eradicated by century's end. Air, for example, was discovered to be composed of several different kinds of gases. Soon, other scientists began to isolate and describe different kinds of gases. Scottish chemistry professor Joseph Black discovered carbon dioxide (CO_2); Priestley discovered that plants not only thrived in the presence of CO_2 but also required sunlight. Priestley used this information to construct a theory of photosynthesis. And Priestley's observation that oxygen and hydrogen, ignited with an electric spark, yielded water discredited the traditional belief that water was a nonreducible element.

At about the same time, the phlogiston theory was coming under attack. The idea that phlogiston was contained in all flammable bodies was plausible only if burned materials *lost* weight as the supposed phlogiston was released into the air. In the 1770s, it was established that roasted metals actually *gained* weight. Discounting phlogiston meant that substances such as iron and silver could be considered elements.

Astronomy struggled against a basic lack of precision. Astronomers began the century with telescopes, although not particularly large ones. The greatest sky charters of the century were William Herschel and his sister, Caroline. Caroline discovered eight comets, and William cataloged 848 double stars and 2,500 nebulae and discovered a sixth planet—Uranus—in 1781. He also built large telescopes, including a massive 40-foot reflector with a 48-inch mirror that weighed half a ton.

Later in the century, popular interest shifted from physics, chemistry, and astronomy to earth sciences, such as botany and zoology. Earlier, Sweden's Karl Linnaeus had revised the taxonomy of these sciences, and Captain James Cook's voyages to Brazil, Tahiti, Bora-Bora, New Zealand, Australia, Jakarta, and South Africa, with the wealth of species that they brought to British attention, spurred enthusiasts to collect and classify specimens.

A chemical laboratory. By the 18th century, the English performed scientific experiments in labs like the one pictured here. © CORBIS.

Naturalist Sir Joseph Banks, who accompanied Cook's first voyage, returned with about 30,000 plant and animal specimens, discovered about 2,400 new plant and animal species, and became one of the most famous people in Britain.

In geology, the chief controversy centered on competing theories that explained the formation of mountains. It had been observed that mountains were often composed of a granite core, covered with sedimentary layers of increasing thickness toward the base. Neptunists claimed that the granite was older than the sedimentary layers, which had been deposited by the primeval flood as it receded. Plutonists claimed that the granite was newer, thrust up from below the sedimentary layers by volcanic activity, with the upper sedimentary layers being eroded to reveal the granite core at the summit.

Changes in the world of science often accompanied transformations in the tools used in everyday life. For example, pocket watches and household clocks provided a more rigorous numerical and geometrical conception of time. Until the late 17th century, most clocks had only one hand—an hour hand. The 18th century was the first to be dominated by two-handed clocks. A preoccupation with the precise time became possible, and this was, after all, the century in which the adage "time is money" was coined in Britain's American colonies. But each parish church set its clock to local time, often by means of a sundial. When it was noon in London, for instance, it was about 12:11 in Bristol and 12:04 in Reading. Only in the 19th century, with the development of railroads, would nationwide synchronization of clocks become necessary.

Around 1800, power sources were limited. People relied for energy on horsepower, windmills, or waterwheels, each of which had its drawbacks. The iron industry alone annually used 300,000 loads of timber, mostly oak, which was first laboriously converted into charcoal and then burned in order to smelt iron from ore. With England's timber resources in serious jeopardy, the Darby family of Coalbrookdale developed a technique for smelting iron using coal (coke) instead of charcoal. Coal became more popular, and it was the dominant blast-furnace fuel by 1800.

But there was a problem. Coal mines could be dug only so deep before they filled with water, and the pumping systems available early in the century were inadequate to the task. Fortunately, several inventors developed steam-driven engines capable of driving air and water pumps. Thomas Newcomen built a five-horsepower engine in 1712. Although not tremendously efficient, Newcomen's engine made shafts as deep as 100 fathoms possible. More coal enabled more smelting at higher temperatures, yielding better metal, and thus more and better parts for more and better engines. Mining, smelting, and engine design thus drove each other; each improvement in one area led to greater efficiency in the others. By the end of the century, there were more than 2,000 steam engines in Great Britain, most of them being used to perform industrial tasks.

Scientists such as Joseph Priestley and William Herschel provided the intellectual insight and emotional perseverance required for the shifts in scientific understanding that took place in England (and elsewhere) during the 18th century. Inventors such as James Watt applied these same human characteristics of imagination and resolve to the mechanization of industrial machines. The impact that these and other changes in theory and practice had on daily life was considerable. After all, the possibility of both the manipulation of electricity and the substitution of large-scale factories for traditional cottage industries constitutes but two of the more prominent transformations to which England of the 18th century contributed its resources (Olsen, 111, 294–99, 300–301).

To read about science in Chaucer's England, see the Europe entry in the section "Science" in chapter 4 ("Intellectual Life") of volume 2; for Elizabethan England, see the England entry in the section "Health and Science" in chapter 4 ("Intellectual Life") of volume 3; and for Victorian England, see the Victorian England entry in the section "Science" in chapter 4 ("Intellectual Life") of volume 5 of this series.

FOR MORE INFORMATION

Lynch, J. *Eighteenth Century Resources.* <http://newark.rutgers.edu/~jlynch/18th/>, accessed October 10, 2003.

Olsen, K. *Daily Life in 18th-Century England.* Westport, Conn.: Greenwood Press, 1999.

Wolf, A. *A History of Science, Technology, and Philosophy in the Eighteenth Century.* London: Allen and Unwin, 1952.

JAPAN

According to Japanese cosmology written in the *Kojiki*, time had begun with the accession of the first emperor, Jimmu, to the imperial throne in 660 B.C.E. If they had been counting from that fanciful date, then the first year of Kyowa (1801) might have been listed as 2461. Scarcely anyone except a few imperial court astrologers had any such idea. The people in the countryside cared more about how many days it was until harvest or until the ancestors returned (*Obon*) to the village.

In the realm of agricultural technology, most villages had large communal grindstones. They were basically two wheels of coarse granite or other abrasive stone. One wheel was mounted horizontally as the base with a pole anchored in the center. The other smaller wheel would then be mounted on a horizontal axis attached to the base wheel's upright pole. The upper grindstone wheel would roll on the base, turning in a tight circle, grinding the grain between itself and the other wheel. A horse or buffalo provided the energy needed to set the grindstone in motion.

Another major agrarian tool was the waterwheel. The basic principle is that of a paddleboat propeller. The wheel was constructed of a dozen or so spokes radiating from the center. Concave scoops were mounted at the ends of the spokes. People would then turn the wheel by "climbing" it endlessly. The scoops would ladle up the water, carry it to the top of the wheel as it turned, and then deposit it with a splash on the other side of the wheel. In this manner, a continual stream of water could be pumped from a ditch onto a higher paddy field.

Although largely disengaged from Western shifts in scientific and technological knowledge, Japan of the 18th century contained within its well-guarded borders a culture of abstract and practical customs that evinced its own rigorous traditions in science and technology (Perez, 63, 180–81).

To read about science in Japan in the 20th century, see the Japan entry in the section "Science" in chapter 4 ("Intellectual Life") of volume 6 of this series.

FOR MORE INFORMATION

Japan Information Network. <http://www.jinjapan.org/index.html>, accessed October 23, 2003.

Perez, L. G. *Daily Life in Early Modern Japan*. Westport, Conn.: Greenwood Press, 2002.

INTELLECTUAL
LIFE

SCIENCE
& TECHNOLOGY

Colonial Australia

The Colonial Frontier
of North America

England

Japan

New England

Life at Sea

NEW ENGLAND

Colonial New England did not establish itself as a site of scientific and technological experimentation. Perhaps this absence of empirical pursuits related to the stultifying effects of Puritan dogma. On the other hand, the New England Puritans adopted the doctrine of secular calling with fervent commitment. Thus, although it is true that Puritans taught that the religious (spiritual) calling to please God always superseded secular (worldly) pursuits, their actions usually remunerated and shed great praise on worldly success. The rewards of material endeavors and the congregation's gradual exposure to other ideas of the time, such as natural philosophy and Deism, both of which stressed observable fact in the visible world, cut away the very spiritual bedrock of Puritanism.

The Puritans in the 17th century knew full well that the new philosophies and sciences would be dangerous for their church. For decades, they had assiduously kept these ideas from their communities as best they could, not even allowing them into the Harvard curriculum. Newtonian physics, for example, which appeared in 1687 and was introduced to America in 1708, was not seriously considered in New England until Cotton Mather explained it in 1721, more than 30 years after its appearance. In 1714, Mather was also the first learned man of influence in New England to support the Copernican theory of the universe—some 178 years after Copernicus offered his theory that the earth moved around the sun rather than the theory that the sun moved around the earth.

The history of a young Bostonian named Benjamin Franklin illustrates the impact that new ideas in philosophy and science were having in America in the 18th century. Franklin's ancestors had been religious dissenters whose leaders in America had, for 70 years, censored and burned books that challenged Puritan belief. However, in 1718, Franklin was 12 years old and able to read without fear Xenophon's *The Memorable Things of Socrates* and books by such freethinkers as John Locke, the earl of Shaftesbury, and the Deist Anthony Collins. In his teens, Franklin came strongly under the influence of Deism; that is, he did not believe that the Bible was the revealed word of God and was early on convinced that works were much more important than faith. Thus Franklin did not belong to or attend church services, declaring that sermons left him unedified—this, despite his claim to have no animosity toward the church.

Many of the intellectual men who would soon found the United States of America shared Franklin's notions. Thomas Jefferson described himself as a Christian Deist; and Thomas Paine, who explained his Deist philosophy in *The Age of Reason*, was a strident critic of both organized religion and its clerical spokesmen.

Although it is true that the masses of New Englanders, still Calvinistic in their beliefs, were in vehement disagreement with these philosophical radicals, the new ideas had a share in weakening the Old World Puritan view and had a profound impact on American life, especially in the formation of the rights and liberties of the nation that was yet to be born (Johnson, 204–5).

FOR MORE INFORMATION

Conkin, P. *Puritans and Pragmatists: Eight Eminent American Thinkers.* New York: Dodd, Mead, 1968.

Johnson, C. D. *Daily Life in Colonial New England.* Westport, Conn.: Greenwood Press, 2002.

LIFE AT SEA

The sailors who navigated vessels from one place to another relied on the accumulated scientific understanding of direction, position, and speed. The technological application of these concepts resulted in the production of longitude-measuring tools, precise clocks, compasses, and maps. Ultimately, technological and scientific advances led the way to steam power as a substitute for wind power. By the mid–19th century, wind ships with wooden hulls were ceding to steam ships constructed largely from metal.

In determining direction, a series of well-known landmarks acted as absolute starting points and signposts along the way. Among these were the island groups in the Atlantic. For example, navigators knew that if they sailed due east from the Canary Islands, they ultimately reached the west coast of Africa. If they sailed due west, they came to the Bahamas in America. This method of navigating the oceans came to be known as dead reckoning. The term derives from the habit of recording a "deduced" estimation of position as "de'd." in the logbook. Dead reckoning remained the most commonly used form of navigation into the 20th century.

When actually navigating a ship, the master needed to know not only where he was at the beginning of the trip but also at the end of each day's journey. Tides, currents, and the sailing qualities of the vessel were among several factors other than the direction of the wind that conspired to make the determination of the distance and the direction traveled by a vessel very difficult even for a single day.

A sailor moored in the harbor at Portsmouth, England, knew his absolute position; but once out of sight of land, he "saw nothing but sky and water and realized the omnipotence of God." Mariners needed to approximate position based on the estimated speed and direction of a vessel and without the aid of accurate calculations, which were frustrated by changeable and erratic winds, unknown and complex currents, and the inconsistent performance of the vessel.

Sailors developed several methods for approximating the speed of a vessel through the water. Mariners tied small knots at definite intervals in a rope, called a *log*, which was dropped from the stern of the moving vessel. A 30-second sand glass was used to determine the time. The number of knots pulled from the reel in the time that the sand took to fall was a reasonable estimate of the speed of the vessel. A vessel that pulled six knots from the reel was doing six nautical miles per hour.

The position on the earth north or south of the equator is called latitude, and the position around the globe east or west is called longitude. Both latitude and longitude are used today, and they seem to us an inseparable pair. Although the precise determination of longitude eluded mariners and inventors for centuries, a number of instruments were devised for measuring latitude, including the cross-staff, the backstaff, and the sextant. Each of these allowed the mariner to determine the angle between the sun at noon and the horizon.

Longitude has been precisely measured on land since the invention of the pendulum clock, but its determination at sea was difficult to accomplish. Changing temperature and humidity combined with the rolling of the vessel so as to render otherwise accurate pendulum clocks all but useless. In 1714, the British government offered a reward of 20,000 pounds for the invention of any timekeeping mechanism that was precise enough to permit the determination of a ship's longitude within 30 nautical miles at the end of a six-week voyage.

In 1729, John Harrison invented an imprecise timekeeping mechanism that could fulfill this requirement. Over the next three decades, Harrison improved his mechanism four times, ultimately devising the No. 4 Timekeeper (or chronometer).

The chronometer was essentially a well-made watch that suspended in a box from a set of two bearings. These bearings allowed the mechanism to remain horizontal whatever the inclination of the ship. Moreover, a careful use of different metals in the construction allowed the timepiece to self-compensate for expansion and contraction from the effects of heat and cold. Chronometers exhibiting these features proved to be capable of keeping time for six months with less than one second of error per day.

The magnetic compass was a great boon to navigation. With the magnetic compass, setting a course in a particular direction seems easy. Point the compass so that north lines up with the magnetic needle (which itself lined up with the magnetic poles of the planet) and choose your direction from among the points of the compass. Sixteen of these were named, including four principal points (north, east, south, and west), the major position between these (such as northeast), and the positions between the lesser point (such as east north east). Because the earth is a giant magnet, a compass needle, which is also magnetized, will always lie in a north-south line with the earth. Unfortunately, the geographical poles of the earth are not in the same place as the magnetic poles. A compass pointing at the magnetic north perhaps points—or perhaps not—to the geographic north.

The difference between the observed compass reading of north and the actual location of the geographic North Pole is called magnetic declination. Magnetic declination varies with the magnetic field of the earth, the position of the compass, and the position of the magnetic pole, which wanders with time. In 1580, magnetic north was 11 degrees east of the geographic pole. In 1820, it was 20 degrees west, and in 1970, it was 7 degrees west.

The magnetic pole was not the only thing that had changed. The wooden wind-ship design that epitomized the era of sailing vessels on the high seas during the 17th and 18th centuries had reached its practical engineering limits by the 1850s. Wind ships could make hundreds of miles in a day, and the American clipper ship *Challenger* reached a record 400 nautical miles in 24 hours. Under these conditions, it seemed unlikely that steam would ever compete economically with sail.

Nevertheless, after the 1850s, metal-hulled, steam-powered marine technology advanced, and the traditional technology of the wooden-hulled sailing vessel grew relatively stagnant. Steamers began driving the wind ships of all nations off the most profitable routes (Volo and Volo, 51–55, 57–58, 299–301).

FOR MORE INFORMATION

Macintyre, D. *The Adventure of Sail, 1520–1914*. London: Elek, 1970.

Volo, D. D., and J. M. Volo. *Daily Life in the Age of Sail*. Westport, Conn.: Greenwood Press, 2002.

Education

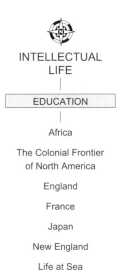

INTELLECTUAL
LIFE
|
EDUCATION
|
Africa

The Colonial Frontier
of North America

England

France

Japan

New England

Life at Sea

From the early 17th to the early 19th century, people in Africa, North America's frontier colonies, England, France, Japan, and New England received education and applied their learning to the exigencies of everyday life. Seamen and officers sailing the oceans also underwent specific training that sometimes resembled formal schooling and, at other times, was equivalent to on-site training.

Many officers-in-training aboard British warships spent years learning firsthand the skills that could someday garner them command of their own vessel. Navigators, in particular, greatly benefited from a practical application of their knowledge of algebra, geometry, and trigonometry. And some men profited from their free time, teaching themselves the principles of navigation or how to read and write.

African education was very regularly a mixture of formal and informal cultural traditions. Elders and storytellers relayed a sense of duty and moral obligation to boys and girls, who imitated the patterns of behavior around them, thus learning through absorption about their communities and about their respective roles within these communities. Such informal education contributed significantly to the behavioral and intellectual development of Japanese and New England families, as well. Instruction throughout 17th-century colonial New England was chiefly the responsibility of families, not of academic institutions. Along the colonial frontiers, informal education focused on practical matters. For instance, daughters learned from their mothers the skills of cleaning, budgeting, sewing, cooking, and so on.

Nevertheless, formal schooling was present in each of the cultures discussed here. Some were religious, and others were secular. Religious schooling featured prominently in Christian and especially Muslim communities. Christian missionaries launched schools in the places where they were established. Coptic monasteries in northeastern Africa represented one outpost of Christendom on the continent.

More numerous still were Muslim schools in Africa. The study of Islamic law and theology took place in the Funj. Children studied the Qur'an, suras, and Arabic (reading and writing), even though Arabic might not be their native tongue.

Although rural Japanese schools adopted a largely secular curriculum, the learning itself took place in Buddhist temples, for it was here that people who were qualified to teach reading and writing—monks and village elders—could assemble the locals for class. Larger temples and monasteries produced acolytes and monks who possessed a more rigorous religious instruction.

Religious instruction was of considerable importance in colonial New England, and no more so than among those people who professed to be Puritans. Churches offered classes, focusing on English and a thorough familiarity with religious beliefs. Although such instruction was narrow, it did broaden itself over time to include secular studies. Along the North American colonial frontier, Christian-centered religious instruction was also important.

New England also featured more secular, vocational schools in which students learned the principles of navigation, surveying, ship design, accounting, and other practical skills. Higher education at Harvard and other colleges rested on a comparatively secular study based on a combination of religious, humanistic, mathematical, and scientific studies.

In France, reforms in education resulted in a more secularized academic setting in which not only the curriculum changed but so did the methods of teaching and learning, as well. Whereas classical languages and theology had reigned in many French schools, contemporary languages and the natural and social sciences took on greater significance in the decades preceding the French Revolution. In addition, methods of teaching and learning that reflected both a prioritization of affirmative instruction and a hands-on familiarization with ideas rapidly gained prominence over disciplinary lectures that featured an emphasis on the recitation and memorization of statements.

In England, students attending poor schools learned about proper behavior and the value of social conformity. Boarding schools such as Eton instructed children of the well-to-do, with an emphasis on useful knowledge such as reading, writing, geography, accounting, and law. The English universities of Oxford and Cambridge stressed Latin, Greek, and related humanistic studies.

Not everyone received the same education as his or her peers. Boys were typically privileged over girls. Islamic instruction in Africa frequently deterred females from acquiring the same rigorous instruction that was available to males. Girls in England, Japan, and New England complied with the cultural injunction to learn the "womanly arts," which almost invariably concerned some combination of sewing, cooking, playing musical instruments, and on the whole, being graceful and pleasing.

Compared with the masses, members of wealthy families could expect to have access to better-quality institutions. This access meant not only that the wealthy received a more solid education than the majority but that they could count on the likelihood of obtaining a materially and socially comfortable position in the community, as well. By 1800, a majority of those who attended England's boarding schools and universities later became peers. Good birth and breeding were formidable determinants in the selection of candidates for the instructive post of midshipman and for a seat at the Royal Naval Academy. African rulers sought to bolster their power by identifying themselves with the wider, deeply rooted tradition of Islamic scholarship, and African trading families tended to have at least one scholar in the family.

Education was not a straight and simple fact among Africans, English, French, Japanese, North American colonists, and shipboard sailors and officers. To varying degrees, a number of contrasts exemplified the educational landscape: formality and informality, religion and secularism, males and females, wealth and poverty, authority and powerlessness. These contrasts are interesting not just for the tensions that they reveal in societies of the time but also for the tensions that are pertinent in today's world.

~Peter Seelig

FOR MORE INFORMATION

Gwynne-Thomas, E. H. *A Concise History of Education to 1900 A.D.* Washington, D.C.: University Press of America, 1981.

AFRICA

In Africa, young people absorbed the traditions and customs of their cultures as part of the routine of daily life. Education was thus as much a social process as it was a separate sphere of daily life, since both the stories people told in the evenings and the chores they performed during the day facilitated young people's identification of their roles in life and their places in the world. However, many people also belonged to a more formal educational tradition, most notably the Muslims, who pursued learning as a religious obligation.

By imitating their elders, African children learned the basics of their trades and of customary participation in village life. As they grew older, they received more and more sophisticated tasks in the daily work of the family and so gradually learned the routine of the parent of the same sex. At the same time, the religious and historical traditions of the people were passed down in oral stories told in the evenings for entertainment, sometimes by professional storytellers and at other times by village elders who had a talent for entertainment. In this way, young people learned the basics of their culture simply in the course of growing up.

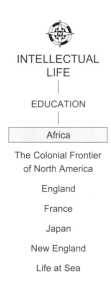

INTELLECTUAL
LIFE
|
EDUCATION
|

More formal education related to initiation into adulthood. Age and lineage most often served to organize African societies. When the time came for a certain age group to enter into adulthood, men went to a special ritual location where elders introduced them to the responsibilities of men in the community. Some areas had similar groups for women. In the south, a chief convoked an initiation school when one of his sons reached puberty. The son became the leader of his peers, who were expected to be his companions and supporters. The group remained apart from society for several months, during which time the young men learned the group's customs, performed physical feats, and underwent circumcision. Following this series of customs, the men were officially considered adults, took adult names, and could marry (Curtin et al., 249).

In Kano, sons went to Qur'an school once they had learned to count to 10.

Where literate societies existed, Africans developed more formal educational systems to process the learning of the wider societies to which religions connected them. Christian missionaries from Europe founded schools based on Western patterns of instruction, and a few chiefs even sent their sons overseas to study. During the 18th century, European schools existed at Cape Coast, El Mina, and Accra along the lower Guinea coast. Missionaries had to teach prospective converts to read the gospels. Education was also seen as a way of promoting European ways of life in African society, which Europeans saw as uncivilized. Even before the 17th century, Coptic monks from northeastern Africa received higher education, and Coptic monasteries became important centers of artistic and literary production not only in religion but in the history of the religious community, as well (Ogot, 427).

The most extensive African educational system, however, was found in the Islamic world. In Islam, learning the Qur'an, Islamic law, and other subjects associated with religion has been a religious duty. Muhammad himself is reported to have said, "Seek ye learning though it be in China," while Ali, an early caliph, is credited with declaring, "I am the slave of him who has taught me even one letter." Al-Azhar University in Cairo was the world's leading center for Islamic learning, while Fez in Morocco and Timbuktu in Mali were also important. During the 18th century, the Omani colonization of the Swahili coast led to numerous scholarly connections between those two regions. Such scholarship was a duty for both men and women, although in many areas, some people discouraged female participation (Hitti, 393, 409).

Rulers patronized Islamic scholarship as a means of showing their dedication to Islam. In the kingdom of Bornu, around Lake Chad, rulers partook of religious scholarship and held debates over controversial points of law and theology. N'Gazargamu became a key stop on the road to knowledge for African Muslims during the 18th century. *Ulama,* the Arabic term for a religious scholar, received stipends to support their work. Students who had developed specific interests traveled widely, seeking teachers who were experts in these areas; hence, supporting a scholar meant also creating a study circle.

At the same time, some religious scholars refused to associate themselves with political power and, in rural areas, set up isolated religious communities called *mal-*

lamati. Heavily influenced by Sufism, these *mallamati* communities gathered around a particular leader who was believed to have *baraka,* or divine blessing. Leadership in them was hereditary, partially because of the belief that *baraka* was hereditary and partially because the endowment grant that helped provide the community with its financial base was passed down within the families of the founding *ulama.* In five stages, students in these communities learned not only how to recite the Qur'an but also how to write it from memory.

Another type of Islamic community was found in the Funj of what is now Sudan. Here, rulers played host to Sufis and religious scholars who founded schools of Islamic law and theology. These schools were usually attached to a Sufi lodge and often grew into towns, with the descendants of the founder maintaining the authority of the lineage. In the western Sahara, nomadic schools became the rule, and teachers and students traveled much, as did the merchants and herders.

In Kano, sons went to Qur'an school once they had learned to count to 10. According to descriptions from the 19th century, their first task was to learn the opening and final surahs, and then how to read and write the Arabic script. After that, they proceeded through the Qur'an one-sixtieth at a time, starting from the back. Every time a student made it through one-sixth of the Qur'an, there was a celebration. Graduations were marked with feasting and the slaughter of a bull, while the graduating students wore a turban and recited the first part of the Qur'an before their teacher, other scholars, classmates, and relatives (Reichmuth, 424).

Qur'anic education continued to bear many of the attributes of other African educational systems in that, in many areas, family members became important teachers. Many West African trading families always included several religious scholars whose first teachers would be their relatives, although most sought outside teachers to increase their prestige. Perhaps one in three religious scholars in Timbuktu had a family member as one of their instructors. In addition, those who entered religious training still learned the work expected of them in the lineage, and when seeking outside teachers, they performed those same services for those teachers (Saad, 60–74).

African education thus depended in large part on religion, whether either a formal confessional community, such as Christianity and Islam offer, or the all-encompassing traditional religious practices found throughout the continent. Family was an important component of religion; even in Islam, the teacher was regarded as a stand-in for the father. Education enabled people to find their place in the world, whether as a member of a local community with its own ways and relationships with the world or in a broader civilization that spanned continents. In this way, Africans were linked with one another and with the world. Religion generated an awareness of and the ability to advance their many cultures.

To read about education in Africa in the 20th century, see the Africa entry in the section "Education" in chapter 4 ("Intellectual Life") of volume 6 of this series.
~Brian Ulrich

FOR MORE INFORMATION

Curtin, P., S. Feierman, L. Thompson, and J. Vansina. *African History.* London: Longman, 1995.

Davenport, T. R. H., M. F. Katzen, L. Thompson, and M. Wilson. *A History of South Africa to 1870*. Edited by M. Wilson and L. Thompson. Cape Town and Johannesburg: David Philip, 1982.

Halsall, P., ed. *Internet African History Sourcebook*. 1996. <http://www.fordham.edu/halsall/africa/africasbook.html>, accessed October 23, 2003.

Hitti, P. K. *The History of the Arabs: From Earliest Times to the Present*. 7th ed. London: Macmillan, 1961.

Ifemesia, C. *Traditional Humane Living among the Igbo: An Historical Perspective*. Enugu, Nigeria: Fourth Dimension, 1979.

Ogot, B. A., ed. *General History of Africa*. Vol. 5. *Africa from the Sixteenth Century to the Eighteenth Century*. Paris: United Nations Educational, Scientific, and Cultural Organization, 1992.

Reichmuth, S. "Islamic Education and Scholarship in Sub-Saharan Africa." In *The History of Islam in Africa*, edited by N. Levtzion and R. L. Pouwels, 419–40. Athens: Ohio University Press, 2000.

Saad, E. N. *Social History of Timbuktu: The Role of Muslim Notables and Scholars 1400–1900*. Cambridge: Cambridge University Press, 1983.

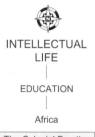

INTELLECTUAL
LIFE
|
EDUCATION
|
Africa

The Colonial Frontier
of North America

England

France

Japan

New England

Life at Sea

THE COLONIAL FRONTIER OF NORTH AMERICA

Almost all education on the colonial frontier of North America was provided informally on the fringes. Parents had the responsibility to educate their children in the manners and morals of their community. Where settlements were more established, an organized effort was made to provide more formal instruction. Some children were sent to dame schools as early as three years old, where they were introduced to the "three Rs." These classes were extremely basic and held in the house of the schoolmistress to enable her to attend to her household chores, as well as to her students. Once the children reached an age at which they were needed at home or in the fields, their education usually ceased. Reading received the greatest emphasis.

Female literacy in the rural areas remained stagnant at about 33 percent for the entire period. The education of young women was viewed as less essential when compared with that of young men. A period newspaper quoted an anonymous father advising his wife on how to educate their daughter:

Teach her what's useful, how to shun deluding;
To roast, to toast, to boil and mix a pudding;
To knit, to spin, to sew, to make or mend;
To scrub, to rub, to earn & not to spend.

While parents surely loved their children, their demonstrations of affection in some ways differed from those of today. Some frontier Puritans believed that children were born empty of knowledge and goodness and full of will. Children were lectured about the sudden deaths of other children and were required to read intimidating verses from the Bible. They were taught never to be confident of their salvation. Samuel Sewall recorded his daughter's breakdown while reading from scripture:

"Betty can hardly read her chapter for weeping; tells me that she is afraid she is gone back, does not taste that sweetness in reading the Word which she once did; fear that was once upon her is worn off. I said what I could to her, and in the evening pray'd with her alone."

Women were often taught to read because they needed to read the Bible to themselves and to their children. Sometimes female indentures, children when their contracts were signed, were promised reading lessons during their tenure. However, it seems that many of the women who were readers were not taught to write because society saw no need for them to do so. For instance, while the burden of rearing a family greatly added to a woman's responsibilities, fathers were responsible for the education of their children, in which they were the ultimate authority. Issac Norris wrote of his two daughters, "They are a constant care as well as great amusement and diversion to me to direct their education aright and enjoy them truly in the virtuous improvement of their tender minds."

The Quaker attitude toward children's education was quite different. Households were child centered. It was believed that young children should be protected from the world and nurtured within a controlled environment. Parents preferred rewards to punishments, and as children grew older, adults appealed to their reason rather than to their fears. William Penn advised parents to love their children "with wisdom, correct them with affection: never strike in passion, and suit the correction to their age as well as fault. Convince them of their error before you chastise them."

Children of Dutch North American settlers enjoyed a more carefree and emotionally encouraging form of education. Perhaps encouragement in the classroom derived from Dutch parenting in general. Such parents were open in their displays of affection for their youngsters. Anne Grant, traveling in colonial New York, reported: "You never entered a house without meeting children. Maidens, bachelors, and childless married people all adopted orphans and all treated them as if they were their own." She described picnics, parties, and other fun activities for children that took place regularly. She noted that the Dutch colony's educational practices were quite distinct from New England's: "Indeed, it was on the females that the task of religious instruction generally devolved. . . . [T]he training of children . . . was the female province."

Settlers and their peers in England and on the European continent often considered the intellect and emotional mind-set of Native Americans parallel to those of children. Consequently, reform-minded educators from among the settlers' ranks hoped, through a narrowly conceived education program, to "improve" the minds of Native Americans. After the French and Indian War, in 1769, Reverend Eleazer Wheelock opened a school in Hanover, New Hampshire, for Native Americans recruited from St. Francis and elsewhere, as well as for colonists and others. This is considered the founding of Dartmouth College. Nonetheless, the Iroquois clearly rejected Wheelock's request to educate their youth. Mary Jemison, who lived among the Iroquois for 60 years, observed, "I have seen . . . the effects of education upon some of our Indians, who were taken when young from their families, and placed at school before they had had an opportunity to contract many Indian habits, and there kept till they arrive to manhood; but I have never seen one of those but what was an Indian in every respect after he returned."

Education in the North American frontier colonies was basic at best. Ranging from informal instruction along the sparsely populated borders to more formal settings in established communities, frontier education also gave rise to varying methods of instruction, including the Puritanical approach, which curiously indulged in fear and self-loathing, to the more affirmative practices of Dutch and Quaker settlers. Females, who typically received a less-extensive formation than males, and Native Americans, whom various settlers targeted for a Western, Christian schooling, occupied the margins of North America's colonial instruction (Volo and Volo, 68, 101, 127–30).

FOR MORE INFORMATION

Cremin, L. *American Education: The Colonial Experience.* New York: Harper and Row, 1970.

Volo, J. M., and D. D. Volo. *Daily Life on the Old Colonial Frontier.* Westport, Conn.: Greenwood Press, 2002.

ENGLAND

The debate in England over what should be taught in school and, indeed, who should go to school at all, was an energetic one, particularly in the middle and later parts of the 18th century. In the absence of a universal, government-financed system of education, a diverse assemblage of personal initiatives and informal institutions materialized. Besides the endeavors of individuals and families toward self-improvement, there were tutors, charitable schools for the poor and disadvantaged, grammar schools and "dame" schools for the sons and daughters of middle-class families, boarding schools for the privileged, and two illustrious universities for England's elite.

Throughout the period, all education relied for its existence on private industry or the support of private subscriptions or endowments. The government felt no responsibility to educate any, much less all, of its future citizens. As a result, many children never went to school. Whatever learning they did acquire came from lectures by itinerant scientists, almanacs, parental tutelage, nursery rhymes, church sermons and decorations, instruction by trade masters or journeymen, and advice from neighbors and relatives. Those who could afford a more organized approach to education often hired tutors for their children. Freed slave Olaudah Equiano, a working man, hired tutors to teach him hairdressing, mathematics, and music.

Schools for the poor were almost always charitable ventures, founded to train pious servants and workers who would stay sober, and opposed by those who feared that literacy would make the rabble "fractious and refractory." Some employers insisted on Saturday or Sunday school for their child laborers. There was even a school to teach poor blind children to support themselves by weaving baskets. There was also no standardization of curriculum from one school to the next. The focus might be on Anglican doctrine, accounting, or Greek poetry. To call the curriculum of such schools unambitious is being overly kind. Instructors and administrators spread their academic focus wide and thin.

At the top of the social scale, the curriculum was entirely different. At expensive boarding schools such as Rugby, Winchester, Eton, Westminster, and Harrow, pupils learned Greek, Latin, grammar, composition, the works of John Milton and other English authors, oratory, and history. Boarding schools placed a lesser emphasis on geography, mathematics, fine arts, fencing, and modern foreign languages such as French and Italian. There were also, as critics of these "public schools" pointed out, gambling, drinking, homosexual dabbling, and ruthless cruelty. Teachers joined in the torture; beatings were the primary method of discipline in a large majority of schools. Nonetheless, wealthy parents sent their sons to such schools in increasing numbers, mostly because of the social connections that one could make during youth and exploit later in life. By 1800, 70 percent of English peers had attended Eton, Westminster, Winchester, or Harrow.

Between the handful of elite public schools and the vast numbers of charity schools lay a middle ground, chiefly home to miscellaneous grammar and "dame" schools, which the children of tradesmen and artisans attended. Or-dained ministers and unemployed intellectuals tended to run gram-mar schools; women oversaw most dame schools. They taught whatever would bring in the most pupils: a little religious doctrine, a little Latin, and plenty of comparatively useful knowledge—read-ing, writing, geography, accounting, shorthand, science, law, business correspondence, French, navigation, and drafting. Pupils would study for a few years and then leave to seek an apprenticeship or to take over the family business.

In this picture, a school bully outside an English school torments two younger children, forcing them to fight each other tied up. © Hulton Archive/ Getty Images.

England had only two universities—Oxford and Cambridge—the students of which, being drawn largely from public-school rolls, ei-ther were men of leisure seeking polish and companionship or were future clergymen on scholarships. All were Anglican. Both Oxford and Cambridge boasted some formidable intellects among their fac-ulty and students, but enrollment remained fairly low (not quite 200 new students per year at mid-18th-century Oxford). The instruction was of little practical use, consisting usually of Latin and Greek, with some philos-ophy and a smattering of science. Neither university had written exams until the end of the century. They were, for the most part, comfortable clubs based on pa-tronage and privilege. Not a little emphasis on social standing and political power inserted itself into university attendance: whereas less than 35 percent of English peers had attended Oxford or Cambridge in 1701, more than 60 percent of English peers had attended Oxford or Cambridge by 1799.

The best universities in Britain—and arguably, in the world—were in Scotland, where the medical training in particular was superior. In any case, after leaving a university, it was customary for a young man of wealth to go abroad on a Grand Tour, spending thousands of pounds for up to three years of travel in France, Ger-many, Italy, and elsewhere.

Although there was no substantial reform of the educational system in the 18th century, there was expansion. Schools multiplied and literacy rose, albeit slowly. At midcentury, about two-thirds of men and one-third of women could sign their names, a basic indicator of writing (though not reading) skills. Because people usually master reading more easily than they do writing, it seems fair to guess that somewhat more than those proportions of men and women could read at least a little. Literacy rates rose with income; male literacy was nearly universal in the middle class and above. Education, if no better in 1800 than in 1700, was both more common and more necessary for survival and success.

From the individual efforts of those hungry for an education to the cultural institutions of Oxford and Cambridge, 18th-century England relied on a hodgepodge of customs and institutions, largely unreformed, to keep itself literate and learned. Although the system was inadequate to the task, literacy and learning survived and, at times, flourished (Olsen, 222–25, 227–29).

To read about education in Chaucer's England, see the Europe entry in the section "Education" in chapter 4 ("Intellectual Life") of volume 2; for Elizabethan England, see the England entry in the section "Education" in chapter 4 ("Intellectual Life") of volume 3; and for Victorian England, see the Victorian England entry in the section "Education" in chapter 4 ("Intellectual Life") of volume 5 of this series.

FOR MORE INFORMATION

Jewell, H. M. *Education in Early Modern England.* New York: St. Martin's Press, 1998.
Lynch, J. *Eighteenth Century Resources.* <http://newark.rutgers.edu/~jlynch/18th/>, accessed October 10, 2003.
Neuburg, V. *Popular Education in Eighteenth Century England.* London: Woburn Press, 1971.
Olsen, K. *Daily Life in 18th-Century England.* Westport, Conn.: Greenwood Press, 1999.

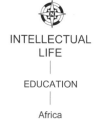

INTELLECTUAL
LIFE
|
EDUCATION
|
Africa

The Colonial Frontier
of North America

England

France

Japan

New England

Life at Sea

FRANCE

To early modern French thinkers, or *philosophes*, education seemed an ideal means by which to perfect society and to create "enlightenment" insofar as education seemed to make people rational, freeing them from superstition. The logic behind these arguments was that if an improper or incomplete education was the source of public ills, a proper education could help fix those problems. If, as philosophes believed, evil in the world came from men's ignorance, then educational reform was key to social progress.

Although the idea that the child was the key to the future was not entirely original, new areas of inquiry, especially within psychology and the social sciences, seemed to create a level of intellectual certainty that had not existed before. In this context, educational reform became especially prominent as a topic for philosophical debate after the mid-18th century. The year 1762 saw the publication of Rousseau's educational treatise *Emile*, which inspired both imitation and hostile response across the continent. During the next decade, the pope formally disbanded the order of the Jesuits (the Society of Jesus), the leading educators in continental Europe. The dual influence of the possibilities inspired by the vacuum in the secondary schools formerly controlled by the Society of Jesus and the ferment surrounding educational philosophy led to an outpouring of thought on the function and method of education.

Pedagogues argued that the old forms of education were misguided in their intent to prepare men primarily to serve God and the Church. The writings of pedagogue and attorney Louis-René Caradeuc de la Chalotais exemplify this position. His *Essay on National Education or Plan of Study for Youth* (1763) advised replacing religious education with a secular and state-run education intended to prepare students for national citizenship rather than for membership in a church or life in a religious order. He de-emphasized doctrine, along with the Latin in which it had been taught, and entirely replaced dogma with a general moral education. Natural history, contemporary history, and modern languages, as well as technical skills useful for life in the modern world, were to be the focus of the new education.

Etching by Jean-Jacques de Boissieu, 1804. This illustration depicts an idealized French class in botany. Notice the hands-on teaching method and the relaxed learning atmosphere. © Library of Congress.

Changes in method were also needed. Because the student was to arrive at a rational understanding of the world instead of memorizing dogma, rote memorization and drilling gave way to more innovative techniques that would appeal to the student's natural abilities and inclinations. In the end, this education intended to produce a society in which all citizens used their productive capacities to their highest potential.

Despite the fact that Enlightenment rhetoric about rationality seemed to be universally applicable, intellectuals often and actively opposed the expansion of elementary schooling. In the 17th century, La Salle's Christian Brothers had begun to use the method of simultaneous or mutual instruction to teach more students at reduced costs. Teaching a large number of students, however, remained controversial and even subversive within a social order that had not yet subscribed to the value of popular education.

It is not difficult to see why "popular" culture could pose an especially troubling problem for Enlightenment society. According to the new scientific thinkers, the masses were irrational and ignorant. Freeing "the people" from their ignorance could undermine the structures of obedience that, by preserving the lowly economic position of laboring classes, had contributed to French economic growth during the 18th century. It was for this reason, for example, that Voltaire, in his correspondence with la Chalotais, agreed with the policy of keeping the children of peasants illiterate.

However, when economic and social circumstances were less favorable, questions of educating the masses tended to force themselves to the fore. As France's economic and social conditions declined over the course of the 1770s and 1780s, reformers began to believe that education was one way to solve the potential political problems posed by the less fortunate. Educational theorists began to look for answers to the pedagogical questions that were most applicable to the lower classes, such as what subjects should be taught and how these topics might respond to the need for occupational training, in addition to superceding popular "superstition" without diminishing respect for authority.

In terms of specific recommendations, these programs tended to focus on practical matters, emphasizing physical education, moral training, and practical instruction. A more hardy worker meant more productivity, and women who nursed and cared for their own children would in turn raise generations of farmers and artisans who could spend more time laboring. Moral training would help promote an understanding of social obligations and encourage obedience to the ruling classes, while a better grasp of practical matters relating to math and accounting (both for the business and the household) would encourage frugality and financial independence. For this reason, the teaching of basic arithmetic and practical geometry received a great deal of praise.

Literacy, on the other hand, was often viewed with suspicion in France. A worker did not have excess hours to fritter away on reading and would not have enough understanding to choose edifying material even if he could find the time. Additionally, imperfect philosophical or theological knowledge could only be dangerous, tempting members of the populace into their own "incorrect" interpretations. While pedagogues began to argue that not only math but also basic reading and writing would contribute to the improvement of the lower classes and social stability, it was generally only to a degree that would allow the lower classes to manage more easily their personal and work affairs. Immediate need, not distant philosophical concerns, determined the topics recommended for inclusion in the curriculum.

Thus, while enlightened views on educational reform shared a common set of assumptions about civic duty, secular education, and the need to plan for a productive society, one ought not to conclude that philosophers wished to set up a plan of education that would "enlighten" the masses. The agenda that is most typical of Enlightenment philosophers did not involve an extension of learning to all people through a system of universal education, even if they wished to use the new ideas and forms of education to create a more progressive society.

~Jennifer J. Popiel

FOR MORE INFORMATION

Chisick, H. *The Limits of Reform in the Enlightenment: Attitudes toward the Education of the Lower Classes in Eighteenth-Century France.* Princeton, N.J.: Princeton University Press, 1981.

Fontainerie, F. de la. *French Liberalism and Education in the Eighteenth Century: The Writings of La Chalotais, Turgot, Diderot, Condorcet on National Education.* New York: Burt Franklin, 1932.

Furet, F., and J. Ozouf. *Reading and Writing: Literacy in France from Calvin to Jules Ferry.* Cambridge, England: Cambridge University Press, 1982.

Leith, J. "Modernization, Mass Education, and Social Mobility in French Thought, 1750–1789." In *Studies in the Eighteenth Century*, edited by Robert Francis Brissenden. Vol. 2. Canberra: Australian National University Press, 1973.

Lynch, J. *Eighteenth Century Resources.* <http://newark.rutgers.edu/~jlynch/18th/>, accessed October 10, 2003.

Maynes, M. J. *Schooling in Western Europe: A Social History.* Albany: State University of New York Press, 1985.

Munck, T. *The Enlightenment: A Comparative Social History, 1721–1794.* New York: Oxford University Press, 2000.

Palmer, Robert Roswell. *The Improvement of Humanity: Education and the French Revolution.* Princeton, N.J.: Princeton University Press, 1985.

Rousseau, Jean-Jacques. *Emile, or On Education.* Edited by Peter D. Jimack. Translated by Barbara Foxley. London: Everyman, 1993.

JAPAN

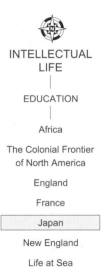

Education in 18th-century Japan occurred in establishments that prominent village leaders, samurai (warrior-administrators), and Buddhist priests maintained. These establishments existed in rural areas as well as in cities. Typically secular in character, the education that one received in early modern Japan varied according to one's sex, profession, and class. In addition to schools, literate Japanese taught themselves many complex techniques of all sorts, including procedures for agriculture, with the help of published texts.

The temple was still at the heart of Japan's spiritual life. Rural education took place in temples, and the institutions were called "parish schools" (*terakoya*) if only because, frequently, the temple was the only public building in the area. Also, in rural Japan at least, monks were virtually the only literate people.

Practically every samurai was literate, having been schooled in the literary as well as the martial arts. In fact, samurai children spent more time in school learning to read and write than they did on fencing, riding, or archery practice. By the 18th century, after all, the samurai were really more bureaucrats than warriors. Less than 5 percent of them (policemen generally) used their martial training to any great extent.

The residents of most *chōnin* (city folk) *machi* (wards) established and maintained at least one informal school. In the countryside, these *terakoya* were located in the local Buddhist temple, usually the only public building in the village. It has been suggested that upward of 80,000 *terakoya* existed throughout the country by the middle of the 19th century. Estimates of literacy are notoriously inaccurate, but some scholars claim that male literacy approached 25 percent at the end of the 18th century. Female literacy, which was not encouraged by the government, was probably a fifth of that.

Literate monks or the occasional educated *gonō* (village headman) peasant staffed the *terakoya*. These teachers nurtured cultural literacy for the community. Although the schools themselves were called parish schools, the education inculcated there was primarily a secular and rudimentary type rather than religious. Buddhist priests were also cultural custodians of the past, since Japan's extensive literature reposed in temple storehouses.

In the cities, the teachers were often lower-ranking samurai who taught in order to supplement their paltry stipends. The curricula were primarily of a neo-Confucian perspective, using moral treatises as primers. Many *chōnin* schools employed shop clerks to teach the use of the abacus (*soroban*) and other rudimentary forms of mathematics and bookkeeping. Every daimyō (feudal warlord) maintained a *han* (district) school for the education of his samurai.

Many *chōnin* girls were integral to their family's commercial enterprises, particularly because many young wives ran the business while the husband was away. Not surprisingly, then, many young girls attended their own segregated classes, where they absorbed the basics of mathematics, drilled in the writing system *kana* (the symbols of which represent the sounds of spoken syllables) and learned to read the few kanji (written characters) necessary for the business (the kanji for "rice," "gold," "silver," "paid," and so on). Of course, most girls also received some kind of training in what their families considered to be the "womanly arts," whether that meant to sew and cook or to play musical instruments, dance, or sing. They usually did so at the feet of their older sisters, mother, or other female relatives. Young married women learned the craft, trade, or social graces of the family into which they had married.

For religious acolytes and monks, most larger temples and monasteries conducted religious education, but very few commoners ever matriculated; one had to become a monk to take advantage of such specialized training. Virtually all monks were literate in Japanese, a few in Chinese, and a very few in Sanskrit.

Samurai children enjoyed a very short childhood. At about age seven or eight, the males began to attend school and were expected to behave like samurai. Girls received an appropriate education to prepare them to be good samurai wives and mothers. As harsh as this custom may seem, European visitors likened the treatment of children very favorably to comparable treatment in Europe at the time. The Jesuit Francis Caron noted in 1637:

The parents educate their children with great care. They are not forever bawling in their ears, and they never use them roughly. When [the children] cry [the parents] show a wonderful patience in quieting them, knowing well that young children are not of an age to profit by reprimands. This method succeeds so well, that Japanese children ten or twelve years old, behave with all the discretion and propriety of grown people. They are not sent to school till they are seven or eight years old, and they are not forced to study things for which they have no inclination.

Although the written language was difficult to master, virtually the entire male samurai class was literate. In addition to administrative tasks, samurai needed to become literate to take on the role of the moral sage in society. Philosophers preached the need for a balance of the literary and military arts (*bun-bu*) within the ruling class, and education facilitated the transformation of the samurai warrior into a samurai bureaucrat. Thus, samurai learned that the moral sage was to value the literary (*bun*), as well as the military (*bu*), arts. Aphorisms abounded to reinforce the dictate that henceforth, samurai were to wield the writing brush as adroitly as the sword.

A number of educational manuals were written on virtually every subject, including business methods, food preparation, calligraphy, painting, flower arrangement, tea ceremony, home and garden decoration, clothing (making and repair), and even special books for young women on home economics topics. One title, *Higher Learning for Women (Onna Daigaku)*, was first published in 1715 and enjoyed several publication runs throughout the century and into the next.

One of the more popular educational literary genres in the countryside was the agricultural manual (*nōsho*), which depicted the latest advances in planting, irrigation, animal husbandry, hybrid seeds, new fertilizers, forestry, and even new recipes.

Going to school was not unheard of in 18th-century Japan. While the curricula were primarily secular in nature, they were also functional, with schools teaching social morality and vocational skills above all else (Perez, 47, 159–60, 286, 288).

To read about education in Japan in the 20th century, see the Japan entry in the section "Education" in chapter 4 ("Intellectual Life") of volume 6 of this series.

FOR MORE INFORMATION

Dore, R. P. *Education in Tokugawa Japan.* Berkeley: University of California Press, 1965.

Japan Information Network. <http://www.jinjapan.org/index.html>, accessed October 23, 2003.

Perez, L. G. *Daily Life in Early Modern Japan.* Westport, Conn.: Greenwood Press, 2002.

NEW ENGLAND

During the 17th and 18th centuries, colonial New England developed a structurally complex, though intellectually narrow, education system. Despite a good deal of overlap, one can distinguish three basic divisions within this system: religious instruction, with its curricula rooted almost exclusively in Puritanism; vocational education, including apprenticeships and instruction for girls, slaves, and servants; and finally, secular education, which, although deeply reflective of Puritan values (and likely a result of them), inspired the development of elementary and secondary (grammar) schools, as well as colleges. Even a concern for the souls of Native Americans prompted colonists to emphasize the need for Godly lessons outside their frontier settlements.

New England settlers believed that it was in the best interests of both Native Americans and settlers to give natives religious instruction. Ironically, Native Americans taught the English settlers far more than the English taught them. The Native Americans had their own religion, their own culture, and their own values, and they resisted the negation of their own beliefs that the assuming of English beliefs entailed. Conversely, Native Americans possessed the kind of knowledge that the

English needed to survive. The information that they so generously conveyed to the settlers transformed the everyday life of colonial New England.

New England education fell under the forceful influence of Christianity, particularly the Puritan brand of Protestantism. The tendency in the 17th century was to place the responsibility for religious instruction in the family first and only secondarily with the clergy; but by the end of the 17th century and throughout the 18th century, religious instruction of students was the responsibility of schoolmasters or ministers. These church groups often consisted of as many as 200 students, who ranged from 7 to 31 years of age. Girls and boys were instructed separately on different days of the week, and while boys received instruction until they were well into their thirties, girls were dismissed at age 16.

A large part of any religious education was learning to read the English language to read Scripture. The other half of religious education was what was called *catechism*, or a body of religious beliefs that the students first memorized and the teacher then explained.

Vocational education was also important. Most boys were expected to learn the trade of their fathers. However, some fathers were able to contract with artisans and placed their seven- or eight-year-old children in apprenticeships. As apprentices, the boys trained by working side by side with a skilled craftsman. The apprenticeship system never flourished in New England, and yet there was a pressing need for skilled labor of all sorts. To train young men for New England industry, vocational schools taught them such subjects as navigation, seafaring, surveying, shipbuilding, mathematics, accounting, and business.

Young women from comfortably situated families went to schools that taught the "female arts," as they were called: piano, voice, French, and sometimes dancing, needlework, and painting. Girls learned to spin, weave, and sew. Women were not welcomed into trade or professional schools, but they received on-the-job training when they worked beside their husbands.

New Englanders did not forbid or limit the education of their slaves as southerners did. Rather, masters and clergymen encouraged their slaves to become literate, well read, and well trained. For many slaves who took on the same work as their masters, education and training were vocationally necessary. Slaves often received an elementary education in language and mathematics, sometimes followed by industrial training.

By the time that legislation required communities to set up schools, New Englanders in some areas had already done so. For example, Boston had a school in 1635, Newport in 1640, Hartford in 1642, and Windsor, Connecticut, in 1644. The Old Deluder Satan Law of 1647 specified that every town of 50 householders was to pay someone to teach reading and writing to the community's youth. These communities paid for these first schools by assessing parents, by taxing residents, or by a combination of revenue sources.

The teaching of reading was the primary aim of these elementary schools. Writing was considered a distinct skill to be developed after reading had been mastered. To learn how to read, students used *The New England Primer*, learning the letters of the alphabet, two-letter combinations, words of increasing syllables, and then sentences, which often taught a biblical or a moral truth. The "A" sentence was, "In Adam's Fall We sinned all." The "P" sentence was, "Peter denies His Lord and cries."

The Old Deluder Satan Law of 1647 also made provision for grammar schools in towns of 100 families. Grammar schools (variously called writing schools, Latin schools, and secondary schools) originally instructed students who were planning to go to college and furnished them with a seven-year education based on the rote memorization of Latin grammar, arithmetic, and the classics. To enter a grammar school, a student, around seven or eight years of age, had to read a passage from the Bible or from the Psalter.

Only the wealthy could send their sons to a grammar school and then on to Harvard. The most famous of these schools was the Boston Latin School, founded in 1636, which received public support but never had more than 100 students during the 17th century.

Girls were not at first allowed to enter the grammar schools. In the mid–18th century, some of the grammar schools were opened to both girls and boys, who were taught not the traditional Latin curriculum but only the three Rs.

Higher education came to New England in 1636 with the founding of Harvard College. Other colleges opened in New England before the American Revolution—Yale in 1701, Brown in 1764, and Dartmouth in 1769, for instance—but for most of the colonial period, Harvard set the standard and dominated the field.

Harvard enjoyed a solid curriculum and adequate faculty. A four-year degree was established in the English tradition, and graduate study was available in theology. The curriculum consisted of grammar, logic, rhetoric, arithmetic, geometry, astronomy, metaphysics, ethics, natural science, Greek, Hebrew, and ancient history. It was not intended to be practical in any way but to provide a knowledge of God. Latin, which students had mastered in grammar school, was the language of instruction.

The first Harvard students ranged in age from 10 to 30, although most were around 15. As in the elementary and grammar schools, discipline at Harvard College was severe. Students under the age of 18 who misbehaved were whipped or had their ears boxed. Older students were fined or publicly admonished.

In colonial New England, there was education, but the end result was possibly more narrowing than broadening. Nevertheless, that colonial New England tended toward—and sometimes even insisted on—education and

Established in 1636 by the Massachusetts Bay Colony government, Harvard College (pictured here in 1720) initially served as a training ground for Puritan ministers in New England. © North Wind/North Wind Picture Archives.

literacy for all children is of immense importance. The three overlapping categories of religious instruction, vocational education, and (partially) secular education provided New England colonists with a system of education that proved itself adaptable over the coming centuries (Johnson, 153–54, 172, 174–78).

FOR MORE INFORMATION

Cremin, L. *American Education: The Colonial Experience.* New York: Harper and Row, 1970.
Johnson, C. D. *Daily Life in Colonial New England.* Westport, Conn.: Greenwood Press, 2002.

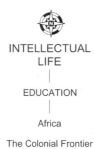

LIFE AT SEA

The education of navigators, seamen, and officers was as diverse as the skills being learned. Navigators benefited from, but did not require, a working knowledge of mathematics and the natural sciences of the day. Ordinary seamen also learned their tasks, although the preference was understandably for practical training as opposed to bookish studies. The selection of officers depended on a combination of formal and informal education, social pressure, and monetary influence.

The Portuguese first established a school for navigators in the 15th century, and Spain set up a similar institution a century later. Italian navigators dominated the discovery of the New World but faded thereafter as prominent figures in the development of transoceanic trade. The French were quick to produce up-to-date nautical treatises, instruments, and sea charts, and the Dutch were among the first to make transoceanic shipping a business. Strangely, the English, who would exit the era as the dominant ocean-trading nation, were particularly backward in accepting the new nautical sciences. As late as 1570, there were no schools for navigators in England comparable with those on the continent. Not until the Armada fight in 1588 did the English take navigation seriously.

Although most professional navigators learned the mathematics of their trade in the formal atmosphere of a class, a good deal of their practical training was accomplished at sea under the watchful eye of a master instructor. Plain sailing was a simplified method of determining a course by assuming that the earth was a flat surface crisscrossed with imaginary lines of longitude and latitude like a checkerboard.

Of course, even the crudest of sailors understood that the earth was not flat. A flat earth was simply more convenient as an intellectual model than a curved one. The methods of plain sailing were remarkably accurate for short distances in the tropical and temperate zones of the earth, but they were much less precise as vessels approached the polar extremes of navigation. Here, the lines of longitude took on a pronounced curve, and the absolute distances between the lines of longitude in terms of miles decreased radically.

Nonetheless, well into the 18th century, it was rare to find a good navigator capable of moving with confidence across the open ocean. Precise navigation required an educated knowledge of several specific variables that could interact in various ways. Among these were position, speed, direction, and time. Some simple instruments for measuring each existed, but few were accurate and dependable in all circumstances. Truly accomplished navigators mastered many difficult concepts found in modern algebra, geometry, trigonometry, geography, astronomy, meteorology, vector analysis, and physics. In the absence of accurate maps and charts, precise instruments for determining speed and position, and accurate clocks capable of keeping time at sea, it is a wonder that seamen were able to navigate a vessel at all. In fact, one of every seven ships that left port before the modern era was never heard from again.

The education of ordinary seamen depended a good deal upon the availability of green hands, or boys, among the crew. If there were sufficient green hands, the ordinary seamen would be given preference over them in the light work and occasionally in the work to be done on the rigging. By this means, green hands could extend their knowledge and progress toward the position of able seamen.

Sometimes, when there were plenty of men, boys were never asked to do any but the simplest tasks. Nonetheless, in an ordinary day's work, boys were taught a number of skills—somewhat like apprentices, although no formal system existed. These skills included work with knots on ropes and yarns, simple ropework, and the loosing and furling of light sails. Boys stood a watch as did every other seaman and went aloft when working sails. When first aboard, they were immediately sent aloft to accustom themselves to the motion of the vessel and to moving about the rigging, but in work, they were rarely above the tops or to the ends of the yards. They were allowed to take the wheel in light winds and gradually become competent helmsmen.

A ship's crew required a sailor learned in navigation technology. Consequently, navigation schools were instituted. © National Maritime Museum.

Some sailors took advantage of the long shipboard hours to improve their minds. Robert Ferguson recorded that he gave lessons to two shipmates. Of one, Frank Gomez, he wrote, "He is very anxious to learn to read and write. To offset the lessons, he does little odd jobs for me." Some men had gone to sea so early in life that their formal education was quite limited. It is reported that John Scott DuBois, captain of the *Ann Alexander*, was just such a man and that he paid shipmates to instruct him in spelling, writing, and reading. Others saw the opportunity to expand their knowledge into other fields. Ferguson reported that he had borrowed a book on navigation from the captain and was "studying navigation the best I could without a teacher."

In between ordinary seamen and higher officers were sailors skilled in narrow and demanding fields. The gunner needed "quite a few exceptional qualifications, including being expert in higher mathematics, an excellent chemist, and a past master at logistical calculations."

As for the education of naval officers, interested youths of good birth and breeding who had been carefully selected went to sea under royal patronage "to learn the ropes." The popular concept of midshipmen as young boys is not always accurate. Certainly, some lads who were 12 to 14 years old were aboard ships as midshipmen, but the majority were young men in their late teens and twenties. For four years, midshipmen learned the skills of ordinary and able seamen and served as petty officers (or master's mate) at sea for two years more. It was also possible to attend the Royal Naval Academy for three years, join a ship, and serve for three more years of sea duty. In either case, six years of preparation made even the youngest midshipman a more mature individual. Thereafter, they stood for an examination of their skills and knowledge in an attempt to receive a commission. Regardless of birth or fortune, only by passing a difficult and comprehensive examination could a midshipman receive his lieutenancy.

Education was requisite to the needs of a crew on the open seas. Navigators, seamen, and officers alike relied on numerous traditions of learning, both formal and informal, so as to facilitate the successful completion of a voyage (Volo and Volo, viii, 49–50, 102, 105, 107, 148).

FOR MORE INFORMATION

Thrower, W. R. *Life at Sea in the Age of Sail*. London: Phillmore, 1972.
Volo, D. D., and J. M. Volo. *Daily Life in the Age of Sail*. Westport, Conn.: Greenwood Press, 2002.

INTELLECTUAL
LIFE
|
LANGUAGE
& LITERATURE
|
Africa

The Colonial Frontier
of North America

England

France

Japan

New England

Life at Sea

Language and Literature

During the 17th and 18th centuries, language and literature were central to people in sub-Saharan Africa, North America's colonial frontiers, England, France, Japan, and New England, as well as to passengers, sailors, and officers aboard oceangoing vessels. These civilizations represent many language families, in both their spoken and written modes. Whatever the mode, the content of linguistic communication often zeroed in on an objective. Sometimes this objective was encouragement of socially accepted morality. Other times, the objective amounted to open criticism of existing social, cultural, political, or even literary standards. Despite attempts at censorship, the blossoming of literary genres resulted in a curious blend of diversity and uniformity.

Africans, of course, did not speak or write in the same languages in which Europeans or Asians spoke and wrote. Indeed, Africa revealed an enormous range of languages spoken throughout the continent. Four language families accounted for 2,000 languages spoken in Africa. Only one, the Afro-Asiatic language family, which included Hausa, Arabic, and Hebrew, had native speakers outside the continent.

Along the North American frontier, native languages differed widely and included Muskhogean, Algonquian, Iroquoian, Siounan, and Caddo. Settlers brought European languages—most notably English and French—to their New World settlements.

The islands that made up Britain and Japan also contained a remarkable assortment of languages and dialects. In Britain, English shared company with Cornish, Welsh, and Gaelic. And although the standardization of the Japanese language made significant headway during the 18th century, people from different regions and cities continued to speak a dizzying array of dialects.

Language was spoken, written, and very occasionally acted out (as in communication between ships, where sailors holding colored flags communicated brief instructions). Because literacy varied, the spoken language was the most common, as it is today. Throughout Africa, the spoken word was more venerated than the written word. In fact, the spoken word was the preferred mode of storytelling. Ethiopia's epic *Kebra Nagast*, which concerns the Queen of Sheba and her relationship with Solomon, received articulation in frequent performances, even though the tale existed in written form.

At times, the words chosen were colorful, indeed. The English idiom included many familiar swear words, as well as some surprising ones. During the 18th century, for example, the word *belly* was considered improper, whereas the word *stomach* was wholly acceptable. In polite company, the blasphemous expression "Who the devil . . . ?" evolved into the harmless "Who the deuce . . . ?"

These attempts at censorship were not restricted to England. Japanese society, being extremely status conscious, developed "honorific speech," which specific segments of society could expect to hear when addressed by their inferiors. In 17th-century New England and along parts of America's colonial frontier, censorship became a way of life, as Puritans and Quakers alike made sweeping denunciations of poetry and fiction while joining with the government in targeting any specific work that suggested frivolity or irreverence.

Nevertheless, critics of censorship found ways to articulate their ideas. The Yoruba in Africa were fond of traveling poets, who would tell tales to eager listeners. Sometimes, these listeners included kings. Traveling poets who enjoyed the opportunity to perform before a king also enjoyed legal protection from an angered king. In case the poet criticized the powerful ruler, the king was legally bound to refrain from censoring or punishing the audacious bard.

In France, scandalous details of a sexual nature appeared in widely read (and often concealed) works such as Madame de Riccoboni's *Letters of Mistress Fanny Butlerd* and Denis Diderot's *Memoirs of a Nun*. In England, social and political commentary was commonplace. John Gay's celebrated *Beggar's Opera* ridiculed the prime minister of England. Controversy was, in itself, an advertisement. Novels in which the themes of romance and immoderate expressions of passion featured prominently garnered a reputation for ruining perfectly proper ladies by, among other things, exaggerating the pleasures to be had in the company of men.

Literary genres abounded. The homesickness of long voyages prompted many whale men to compose poignant letters to family and other loved ones. On the high seas, letter writing took its place alongside other categories of literature that included memoirs, administrative documents, bills, receipts, logbooks, and diaries.

In 17th-century New England, the most popular (and approved) literary genres were Puritan treatises and sermons published for the religious edification of the reader. Religious tracts were also popular in 18th-century England, as were Gothic tales of villainy and passion, daily newspapers, periodicals that delivered light fare to subscribers, and other diversionary works ranging from poetry to pornography. France became famous for its *Encyclopedia*, a cultural production that mirrored much of that era's popularization of rationalism and empiricism.

Japanese readers in both rural and urban settings bought and rented books in the thousands. News printings, romances, fantasy tales, diaries, erotica, comedies, and wills hint at the range and popularity of Nipponese reading material.

Language and literature, thus, covered a great deal of linguistic diversity during the 17th and 18th centuries. Different language families corresponded to different cultures. Whether written or spoken, the many genres of articulation reflected every value, concern, and aspiration that people throughout the world experienced in their daily lives.

~*Peter Seelig*

FOR MORE INFORMATION

Fischer, S. R. *A History of Language*. London: Reaktion Books, 1999.

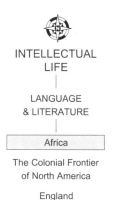

AFRICA

According to an old Yoruba folktale, the spider god Anansi once decided he wanted to keep all the wisdom in the world for himself. And so he gathered all he could find and placed it into a large gourd that he then decided to secrete in the forest. Once in the forest, Anansi hung the gourd around his neck and climbed a tall palm tree atop which the spider god hoped to place the gourd; but as he tried to climb the tree, the gourd kept getting in his way. His son, who was watching all this, suggested that he sling the gourd over his shoulder instead. Anansi thought this wise but, noting that he would not have considered this strategy alone, decided it was better for many—and not one—individuals to have wisdom, and so he scattered the wisdom all around (Miller, O'Neal, and McDonnell, 12).

In Africa, wisdom was passed down in literature. Often, this took the form of proverbs but it also included riddles, stories, and longer poems that depicted the virtues of some great hero. In addition, Africans used the epic poem genre to serve as a record of their history and explain why certain dynasties ruled. Minstrels and storytellers, who were found throughout the continent, visited courts and villages, depending on their skill and reputation, and enchanted all with stirring performances of their culture's literary tradition. Africans valued the spoken word more than the written. In the words of a minstrel, "Other peoples use writing to record the past, but this invention has killed the faculty of memory among them. They do not feel the past any more, for writing lacks the warmth of the human voice" (cited in Niane, 41).

Africans spoke more than 2,000 different languages. Of these, most belonged to the Niger-Congo family, which stretched from Wolof and Yoruba in the west to Swahili along the east coast and to Shona in the south. Much smaller was the Khoisan family, found in the Kalahari Desert and featuring clicking noises represented in modern writing by an exclamation point. In the northeast was the Nilote-Saharan, which included Nubian and Songhay. The fourth African-language family was Afro-Asiatic, which included Hausa, Arabic, and Hebrew and was the only family to have native speakers outside Africa.

Of these, the Afro-Asiatic languages had the oldest written literature, as well as a tradition of literacy passed down through religious scholarship. In Ethiopia, literature included the *Kebra Nagast*, with which Ethiopian kings justified both their rule and expansion of the empire. It told of the Queen of Sheba, believed to be in Ethiopia, and her journey to Jerusalem to learn the wisdom of Solomon. With him, she had a son named Menelik, who was born after her return and became Ethiopia's first king. Menelik later went to visit his father and brought back the Ark of the Covenant. At the end of the work, the world is divided between Rome and Ethiopia, which together will spread the gospel. Although it existed in written form, the *Kebra Nagast* was still performed as an oral epic throughout the 17th and 18th centuries.

In Islamic Africa, an important epic was the *Sundiata*, named for the first king of Mali. It tells of his mother, the buffalo woman, whom two hunters gave to the Malinke ruler. Later, the Malinke ruler became Sundiata's father. Sundiata found himself exiled by his brother, who had inherited the throne, and their sister was sent on a mission to destroy Soumaoro, the sorcerer king. She was taken prisoner but learned that the source of Soumaoro's power was his fowl, and she escaped to tell Sundiata, who used the knowledge to destroy him. On the strength of this victory, Sundiata united the 23 kingdoms of the Niger Bend and ruled with wisdom.

Poetry was almost always written for some royal patron; among the Swahili, the oldest extant poem today is the *Epic of Tambuka* written in 1728 for the Sultan of Pate.

African storytelling was as much about performance as it was about recall. Among the Hausa, people would gather around a fire at night, and the person telling the story would begin with the words, "Here she is, here she is," to which the audience replied, "Let her come so that we can hear." The narrator's story would feature many different tones of voice to excite emotion in the audience. One stock character of Hausa folklore was the cunning and resourceful spider. In addition, Hausa literature featured the lion, as king of the animals, and the wise jackal, called "Learned One of the Bush," as well as *jinn* (spirits), sorcerers, and witches. Many historical tales focused on Kanta, the king who had won independence from Songhay in the 16th century. At the end of a tale, the narrator uttered some standard phrase to indicate its fictional nature, such as, "Let it fall upon the rat's head" or "Were it not for the spider I would tell as many lies as I could." There were also important Hausa poets, one of whom, Ibn as-Sabbagh, composed an ode commemorating a victory won by the king of Bornu. He and other scholar-poets came to be folk heroes in their own right, and people made pilgrimages to their tombs (Andrzejewski, Pilaszewicz, and Tyloch, 191–95).

Among the Yoruba lived professional poets and storytellers who performed at different celebrations and told stories in the villages. They were allowed to criticize even the king; it was against the law for the king to take offense when a poet criticized him. At the village level, when people gathered to hear stories, the teller began with riddles to keep the audience members alert. Then he said, "Here is a tale," to which the audience replied, "Let's have the tale." The narrator followed by initiating the actual story with the words, "The lot for my chosen tale has fallen on the head of . . . " followed by the name of the main character, and a phrase such as, "When human beings had eyes on their kneecaps" or "When there was ample leisure for everybody"—statements that were equivalent to "Once upon a time" (Andrzejewski, Pilaszewicz, and Tyloch, 157–62).

Africans looked to literature to explain their world and how to live in it, as well as for entertainment. When relaxing at the end of the day, they went to listen to the stories that they would remember all their lives. Through stories such as that of Anansi or the jackal, Africans expressed the values of their societies, and through epics such as that of *Sundiata*, they preserved a sense of their past and their heroic ideals. In many ways, story lay at the center of African culture, and the masters of the stories helped to maintain the unity of society by encouraging people to remember who they were and whence they came.

~*Brian Ulrich*

FOR MORE INFORMATION

Agatucci, C. Central Oregon Community College. *Humanities 211*. 1997. <http://www.cocc.edu/cagatucci/classes/hum211/index.htm>, accessed October 23, 2003.

Andrzejewski, B. W., S. Pilaszewicz, and W. Tyloch, eds. *Literatures in African Languages*. Warsaw: Wiedza Powszechna State Publishing House, 1985.

Fung, K. *Africa South of the Sahara*. 1994. <http://www-sul.stanford.edu/depts/ssrg/africa/guide.html>, accessed October 23, 2003.

Halsall, P., ed. *Internet African History Sourcebook*. 1996. <http://www.fordham.edu/halsall/africa/africasbook.html>, accessed October 23, 2003.

Miller, J. E., R. O'Neal, and H. M. McDonnell, eds. *Literature of Africa*. Lincolnwood, Ill.: National Textbook, 1999.

Niane, D. T. *Sundiata: An Epic of Old Mali*. Translated by G. D. Pickett. London: Longman Group, 1965.

Okpewho, I. *The Epic in Africa*. New York: Columbia University Press, 1975.

THE COLONIAL FRONTIER OF NORTH AMERICA

No single set of material characteristics has been found to unite the diverse nations that made up the Native Americans into a single people. Ethnologists have therefore settled on the commonality of language as a gauge to determine lineal relationships among the tribes. There were two great linguistic stocks of native peoples in the northeastern quadrant of North America. One of these was Algonquian; the other was Iroquoian. Because these Native Americans left no written records of their own, much of what is known about them derives from Jesuit missionaries and white captives, neither of whom can be considered unbiased and objective. It is important, therefore, for students of the colonial period to recognize the conjectural nature of much of what was written about the life and appearance of native peoples.

As many as five different languages were spoken among the native peoples of the southeastern woodlands. Besides Algonquian, the most common language was the

Muskhogean tongue, which was spoken by the Creek, Choctaw, Chickasaw, Timuca, Natchez, and Seminole nations, among others. The Siounan language, most commonly spoken by the Winnebago and Sioux on the Western Plains, was also the language of the Tutelo, Catawba, and Yuchi in the southeast. Caddo was spoken by the peoples of Arkansas, Louisiana, and parts of east Texas, while the Cherokee and Tuscarora of Tennessee, northern Georgia, and the Carolinas spoke an Iroquoian tongue that marked them as recent invaders.

It is generally accepted that the New England Puritans who came to America could read the Bible, as the reading of the Holy Scripture by the individual was a foundation stone of their religious belief. Many anecdotes from the period, however, have survived about the level of illiteracy among frontier settlers. Well-meaning, but otherwise misguided, scholars and antiquarians have kept a number of these anecdotes alive; and some unwary historians have been led to believe that the literacy of the frontiersmen was uniformly low and that their speech patterns and written word were of inferior quality. Careful research suggests that this was not the case.

In the 17th century, men on the frontier seem to have had a literacy rate of approximately 50 percent. This figure improved to 65 percent by the early 18th century. The standard used for defining literacy in these cases was the ability to sign one's name, a skill that runs parallel to, although slightly below, reading proficiency and likewise runs parallel to, although slightly above, the ability to write.

As would be expected, literacy varied greatly according to wealth and social class, but it also varied from one ethnic group to another. Based on the examination of wills, deeds, and other public documents, German Protestants and French Huguenots were possibly 90 percent literate, while the Scotch-Irish were likely much less so. Nonetheless, fewer than 30 percent of lowland Scots used a "mark" rather than a signature on surviving documents from the mid-18th century, suggesting that as many as 70 percent could write. Ironically, literacy rates in the coastal settlements seem to have been higher in the early colonial period than they were later, and higher among the gentry and craftsmen than among laborers. These patterns in America mirror similar findings for Britain during parallel periods of time.

The availability of books and other reading material can be used as a good indicator of literacy. A few exceptional families owned large collections of books in the backcountry. A 40- or 50-volume library was considered vast, even in the late 18th century, but a lack of books in the frontier communities does not necessarily account for widespread illiteracy among settlers. Some causes of illiteracy were rather a matter of the poor availability of books in general and the priority given to moving tools, provisions, livestock, and firearms through the wilderness on poorly constructed roads. In most frontier estates that reached probate, at least a few books were included in the inventories. These were generally primers, prayer books, practical handbooks on farming, and treatises on medicine. An unusual number of books on mathematics and surveying exist, denoting not only literacy but mathematical acumen. Nonetheless, the most common book to be found on the frontier was the Bible.

Perhaps the most famous literary genre among colonists was the captivity narrative, the exemplar of which is Captain John Smith's *General Historie* (1624). One of the earliest accounts, this book was written for a European audience. As with similar works, it offered its readers firsthand, though somewhat distorted, information about the native peoples in the New World. It is probably best read to gain insight into the European mind and perspective of the New World rather than to secure knowledge of the culture of the Native Americans.

More significant in a literary sense were the numerous accounts of captivity that were written mainly by or about pious Christian women, a subgenre that persisted well into the first quarter of the 18th century. These writings were as much spiritual autobiographies as descriptions of extraordinary events experienced by ordinary people. They became journeys of salvation through suffering and despair, with the authors declaring how nothing more than their religious faith saved them.

As did other narratives of the time, Elizabeth Hanson's Quaker narrative *God's Mercy Surmounting Man's Cruelty, Exemplified in the Captivity and Redemption of Elizabeth Hanson* (1728) seemed to be a spiritual allegory of divine favor. Widely read, these accounts epitomized the spiritual trial and redemption theme, which reinforced certain religious beliefs of those seeking signs of Providence at work in the world.

By the mid-18th century, captivity narratives had become more secular. The stories became more a recounting of an extraordinary experience. They also at times became a vehicle for spreading propaganda against the Indians, the French, or the English, depending on which group was perceived as the enemy at the time. At the same time, obscurity and extinction threatened Native American languages (Volo and Volo, 19, 22, 99–100, 250–51).

FOR MORE INFORMATION

Archiving Early America. *Early America.* <http://earlyamerica.com/>, accessed October 23, 2003.

Elliott, E. *The Cambridge Introduction to Early American Literature.* Cambridge, England: Cambridge University Press, 2002.

Volo, J. M., and D. D. Volo. *Daily Life on the Old Colonial Frontier.* Westport, Conn.: Greenwood Press, 2002.

INTELLECTUAL
LIFE
|
LANGUAGE
& LITERATURE
|
Africa

The Colonial Frontier
of North America

England

France

Japan

New England

Life at Sea

ENGLAND

Britain, which was home to several languages other than English, possessed a vast store of linguistic and literary imagination. In the 18th century, common speech—particularly vulgar speech—was a vital and entertaining means of expression. For the adept, writing and reading offered several forms of amusement. Even lending libraries were on hand to promote the consumption of the various genres of fiction, which not infrequently stirred controversy and passions alike. Finally, advancements in mail delivery made letter writing less problematic and transformed the reading of periodicals such as newspapers and magazines into a nationwide phenomenon.

Britain was host to a multitude of accents, dialects, and even languages. Cornish was still spoken in parts of the far southwest until about 1780, and Welsh and Gaelic were still in common use in areas outside England. Most residents of the Isle of Man spoke their own language, Manx, as well. However, it was English that dominated spoken and written speech.

The 18th century's gloriously varied swearing was a widely practiced art that moral tracts condemned, acts of Parliament outlawed, reforming societies combated, and the *Spectator* chastised as "foolish" and "unnecessary." Only in the 1770s did those who used coarser terms such as *bitch, big with child, belly, breeches,* and *smock* replace them with softer terms such as *she-dog, pregnant, stomach, small-clothes,* and *chemise.*

For most of the century, however, people of all ranks swore heartily. Many of the terms they used were sexual in nature: son of a bitch, son of a whore, you bitch's baby, son of a whore of Babylon, bastard, hussy, and slut (although slut usually specified a woman who was messy or dirty rather than sexually overaccessible). Many of these terms were rendered incompletely in print to spare the delicate: w—e, b—h, and the ever-popular f**k or f—k. Variations on the term included f—k-finger and f—k-fist, applied to female and male masturbators respectively.

Terms for body parts and functions were also popular: piss and fart (which only became vulgar from about midcentury), bloody (which meant only either "sanguinary" or "exceedingly" till midcentury and gained increasing vulgarity over the next hundred years), cack, shit, and ass or arse. A typical usage of the last is in a 1793 handbill, which attacks a well-paid peer "for setting his Arse in the House of Lords and doing nothing."

Other popular curses involved religious or quasi-religious themes: Lord, Jesus, God damn it, damn me, by Jupiter, Devil hang you, damn my eyes, damn ye, by the Lord, Hell and the devil, by Christ, by Heaven, God's flesh, God's fish, good God, my God, what the devil, the devil take me, and be damned to you. Many religious oaths were made milder by deliberate mispronunciation or substitution. Thus, God, God's wounds, and similar oaths became odds fish, odds bob, egad, odds bodikins, by gad, who the deuce (instead of devil), and gadzooks.

In the absence of televisions, computers, movies, and stereos, people found different ways to amuse themselves, and one way involved language. Those who could wrote in their diaries or scribbled poetry or autobiographies, activities not confined to the wealthy. Literacy was high enough generally to create a fair number of working-class authors. Literate people could also read to themselves or to their families and friends, and the 18th century witnessed an unprecedented consumption of reading material: histories, biographies, magazines, scandal sheets, newspapers, pornography, political tracts, sermons, collections of folklore and ballads, and poetry.

Novels could be purchased (for fairly considerable sums) or borrowed. For-profit circulating libraries, usually run by booksellers, aided the consumption of written material. There were 390 such libraries by 1800. Even though they stocked mostly nonfiction, they did their biggest trade in current fiction and plays. It was the fiction that made libraries controversial, for it was widely believed that ephemeral romances were ruining young women by raising their expectations of marriage, encouraging premarital sex, and wasting their time.

Some fiction appealed to readers for their comical social commentary. John Gay's *Beggar's Opera* satirized Prime Minister Robert Walpole as *"Robin of Bagshot, alias Gorgon, alias Bluff Bob, alias Carbuncle, alias Bob Booty."*

Published in 1740, the hugely popular novel *Pamela* by Samuel Richardson relates the story of a lady's maid whose determined chastity wins her the heart and hand of her squire employer. Henry Fielding's parody *Shamela* turns Richardson's virtuous servant Pamela into a greedy, calculating trollop. Other significant categories of reading included children's books, created by publisher John Newbery, and reference texts: the *Encyclopaedia Britannica* was published in 1773.

For correspondence by mail within Britain, turnpikes had a profound effect. For most of the 18th century, the delivery of mail was slow and haphazard. London had a penny post, but it was alone in this advance until 1765, when the Post Office Act was passed. Before 1765, sending a letter halfway across the country was prohibitively expensive for most consumers.

Title page of *Gentleman's Magazine,* January 1780. The table of contents appears on this title page of a popular English publication of the period. © Library of Congress.

A better method was found in 1784 with the first special mail coach, which made the Bath-to-London run in 16 hours at an average speed of about seven miles per hour. The red, maroon, and black mail coaches carried a coachman, a guard, four inside passengers, and no more than one outside passenger. The passengers' fees kept down the cost of mail while increasing revenue, a strategy that could not have worked without improved road conditions.

The mail-coach system had several effects, one of which was the rapid appearance of newspapers and magazines. London's first daily newspaper, the *Daily Courant,* was founded in 1702. A host of others followed. Papers broadcast matrimonial scandals, political news, reports of crimes, lists of stolen property, advertisements for products and jobs, and the prices of goods at market. Only a few thousand people might actually buy a successful provincial paper, but they would share the paper with others or read it aloud to coworkers and friends.

A new type of periodical, the magazine, was also enjoying its first real success. About 250 of them were published during the century. There were magazines for men's issues, women's issues, fashion, pornography, politics, and religion. The *Gentleman's Magazine* in the 1730s could sell 10,000 copies. The reading public also consumed a host of annual periodicals and ephemeral publications: almanacs, political ballads, handbills, cartoons, and pamphlets such as those by radical Tom Paine.

Spoken and written English amused, angered, informed, ridiculed, and titillated the century's English people. Language exemplified their interests and concerns in a host of forms, many of which have since expanded their impact on public and private knowledge (Olsen, 8, 72, 151, 160–61, 169, 182–84, 250).

To read about language and literature in Chaucer's England, see the Europe entry in the section "Language and Literature" in chapter 4 ("Intellectual Life") of volume 2; for Elizabethan England, see the England entries in the sections "Language and Writing Systems" and "Literature" in chapter 4 ("Intellectual Life") of volume 3;

and for Victorian England, see the Victorian England entry in the section "Literature" in chapter 4 ("Intellectual Life") of volume 5 of this series.

FOR MORE INFORMATION

Lynch, J. *Eighteenth Century Resources*. <http://newark.rutgers.edu/~jlynch/18th/>, accessed October 10, 2003.

Montagu, A. *The Anatomy of Swearing*. New York: Macmillan, 1967.

Olsen, K. *Daily Life in 18th-Century England*. Westport, Conn.: Greenwood Press, 1999.

Rogers, P. *Literature and Popular Culture in Eighteenth Century England*. Totowa, N.J.: Barnes and Noble, 1985.

FRANCE

Although, today, novels and encyclopedias seem to have little in common with each other, the 17th and 18th centuries saw the simultaneous rise of both literary genres. And despite the rather divergent intents of their authors (novels to entertain, encyclopedias to educate), these two genres of print became increasingly popular for similar reasons. The rising middle class began to acquire more leisure time, which generated more education and therefore more people who knew how—and who had time—to read. Their recreational literature often betrayed the concerns of the middle class: promoting rationalism, exploring the nature of human relationships and moral codes, and above all, depicting life as it ought to be. It then should be no surprise that the *Encyclopedia, or a Systematic Dictionary of Science, Arts, and the Trades* (1751–77), which was an attempt to gather together and present all human knowledge, is as much a part of the canon of 18th-century literature as are famous works of fiction from the same period.

In French, the word for novel, *roman*, is closely linked to *romance*, which was a common feature in novels of the period, just as it is today. What is often referred to as the first modern French novel, *The Princess of Clèves*, by Madame Lafayette (1678), was a historical romance that attempts to analyze human emotions and the social expectations surrounding marriage, using characters from the 16th century. Lafayette's characters promote what was then a new middle-class idea of marriage based on companionship and romantic love, not a cold and loveless arranged marriage founded on wealth and title. Although Lafayette's readers were often shocked at the abandonment of accepted aristocratic norms for marriage even as they were drawn to the depiction of this new ideal, her novel only paved the way for more radical changes.

Hundreds of novels were published in the first half of the 18th century, and most of their plots no longer used historical events or fables, the authors instead dismissing these genres as belonging to the past. Novels now tended to focus on relatively ordinary individual people, their psychology, and descriptions of their social environment and influences. Because the characters and plots in these novels depicted the wide range of possible human action, including immoral behavior such as se-

duction, even more people condemned the 18th-century novel as immoral, useless, and detrimental to decent behavior. After all, not only did the novel destroy the "real" literary forms such as the epic or tragedy, but it also seemed to provide a blueprint for leading women astray. Did men want to learn how to entice women into bed or trick them into losing their virtue? Novels such as Madame de Ricco-boni's *Letters of Mistress Fanny Butlerd* or Denis Diderot's *Memoirs of a Nun* seemed to provide a crash course in such subjects, as the heroines were deceived or betrayed by men (and women) who had claimed to love them.

📷 *Snapshot*

Memoirs of a Nun

Denis Diderot was a French intellectual who provided French readers with a notably scandalous bit of literature, *Memoirs of a Nun*. In it, a superior punishes any nun guilty of the slightest infraction, forcing her to undress in preparation for a whipping and duly noting the victim's physiognomy: "What a charming white skin! How deliciously plump you are! What a lovely neck! What fine hair! Sister Saint-Augusta, you are ridiculous to be so shy. Let down your underclothing! I am a woman and your Superior. What a splendid bosom! How firm it is!" (Diderot, *Memoirs of a Nun*, 137)

This concern over the indecency of the novel was heightened by the prominence of women in novels: as characters, authors, and above all, as readers. Lending libraries in bookstores meant that even women who had little money could participate in this new form. A small subscription fee guaranteed that women of relatively modest means could read the latest novels, either in serial form in periodicals or by borrowing a copy from a bookseller. If Madame de Riccoboni could write such scandalous material, what end would there be to the bad influence that pierced the souls of women who read of Fanny Butlerd's seduction or the lesbian experiences of Diderot's nun? When philosopher Jean-Jacques Rousseau wrote his autobiographical *Confessions* in 1782, he devoted a great deal of space to the novel, decrying the impact that novels and other literary "trash" had not only on the female mind but even on his own, presumably more immune, male psyche.

Rousseau's protest perhaps seems strange, given that his novel *Julie, or the New Eloise* (1761) was one of the 18th century's best-sellers. However, his novel, in its attempt to depict women engaged in proper behavior, was not simply an attempt to recast the morals of his society but an easy reconciliation with the same impulse that led philosophes of status to attempt to compile all knowledge in an encyclopedia. Far from providing fodder for the whims of women, Rousseau's novel described life as it ought to be, in the most "perfect" sense. Rousseau intended to educate his women readers, in the most rational sense.

By the end of the 18th century, the values, goals, and social critique that had been found in novels surfaced in newspapers and became codified in one of the most important French works ever, the *Encyclopedia*. Whereas many popular French novels were decried for their threat to morality, the *Encyclopedia* attracted a great deal more attention from royal censors, who revoked their permissions for printing shortly after the first volumes appeared and who tried to suppress its publication on more than one occasion. Despite the numerous articles that dealt primarily with facts belonging to geography, mathematics, or grammar, many articles on the arts, sciences, and trades were logically viewed as subversive. Among the *Encyclopedia*'s 32 volumes of text and illustrations the articles on "Transubstantiation," "Miracle," and "Father" used rationalism to mock the doctrines of the Roman Catholic Church even as articles on "King" and "Lordship" questioned the hierarchical construction of society.

Equally threatening were the engravings that accompanied the volumes of text. Processes that ranged from glass blowing and ironwork to salt production or purse making were outlined in a series of illustrations. These illustrations intended to convey both the practical importance of mechanical processes and the ways of working. In theory, the plates were so detailed that any rational person could replicate the process, eliminating the monopoly of knowledge that the guilds had held.

Ultimately, the *Encyclopedia* communicated to literate people what only guild masters, kings, and priests were supposed to know and suggested that all truth was subject to individual rational inquiry. Just as the novel had opened up social codes and brought middle-class ideals to a popular form, so too did the *Encyclopedia* open up access to knowledge and bring rationalism to interested readers.

~*Jennifer J. Popiel*

The Newspapers, engraving by Louis-Léopold Boilly (1795?). By the later 18th century, literate French had become avid readers of all sorts of informational publications. Note that the women are off to the right and back, appearing less enthusiastic than the men. Bibliothèque Nationale/Paris/France. © Giraudon/Art Resource, NY.

FOR MORE INFORMATION

Chartier, R. *The Cultural Uses of Print in Early Modern France*. Princeton, N.J.: Princeton University Press, 1987.

D'Alembert, J. Le Rond. *Preliminary Discourse to the Encyclopedia of Diderot*. Translated by R. N. Schwab. Chicago: University of Chicago Press, 1995.

Dejean, J. E. *Tender Geographies: Women and the Origins of the Novel in France*. New York: Columbia University Press, 1993.

Diderot, D. *The Encyclopedia: Selections*. Edited and translated by S. J. Gendzier. New York: Harper and Row, 1967.

———. *Memoirs of a Nun*. Translated by Francis Birrell. London: Routledge, 1928.

Goodman, D., and J. Popiel. *The Encyclopedia of Diderot and D'Alembert: A Collaborative Translation Website*. February 2003. <www.hti.umich.edu/d/did/index.html>, (February 27, 2003).

Lafayette, Madame de. *Princess of Clèves*. Translated by Nancy Mitford. New York: New Directions, 1994.

Lynch, J. *Eighteenth Century Resources*. <http://newark.rutgers.edu/~jlynch/18th/>, accessed October 10, 2003.

Rousseau, J.-J. *Julie, or the New Eloise*. Translated by J. McDowell. University Park, Penn.: Penn State Press, 1987.

Society for French Historical Studies. *H-France*, Newsletter about French Culture and History. 2001. <http://www3.uakron.edu/hfrance/>, accessed October 23, 2003.

JAPAN

The Japanese spoken language is a rich and complex one. It is laced with words representing the natural environment, particularly the forests and ocean. Its structure is related to language groupings of Central Asia, which include Mongolian, Manchu, and Korean. There are also many words borrowed from Polynesia and the other South Pacific archipelagoes. Japanese who wrote books in the many genres of popular literature during the 18th century first had to familiarize themselves with the grammar, sounds, writing system, and vocabulary of the language.

Japanese sentence structure typically contains nouns that have no inflections for gender or plurality, but context and word "markers" can connote those meanings. Verbs and adjectives can conjugate for tense and can acquire conditional and negative fragments. Adjectives and adverbs, although somewhat different than in English, generally modify and precede nouns and verbs.

In Japanese, animate subjects are differentiated from inanimate, and human from nonhuman, and different verbs are used for each. Numbering usually requires "counting markers" to differentiate whether one is counting people, animals, flat objects, long objects, or round objects, among others.

When spoken, each syllable receives almost equal stress. Unlike Chinese, which is tonal, Japanese is rapid-fire, with each syllable and word pronounced in a rather metronomic manner. The five vowels (a, e, i, o, u) can stand alone to form one syllable or combine with consonants (ka, ni, so, mu, and so on). Platal consonant combinations can occur (kyu, byo, ryu, and so on), and double consonants create an accented pause (kok-kai, shup-pan). Verbs come at the end of sentences, but sometimes question markers (*ka? no? wa?*) or conjunctions such as "so," "therefore," and "however" (*wake, desu ga, soro soro*) appear.

The Japanese language is very status conscious, there being nouns, verbs, and even sentence structures that change according to the person to whom one is speaking. A distinct style known as "honorific speech" (*keigo*) indicates that the person to whom one is speaking is a social superior.

Apparently, significant oral traditions existed from one region to the next. It has been suggested that the people of Kyōto did not speak the same dialect as the people of Edo. However, the political pretensions of the Tokugawa *bakufu* (national military government) helped to standardize both spoken and written language systems. The *bakufu* issued a plethora of edicts, admonishments, and commentaries to the various feudal warlords (daimyō), who after a time learned to mimic the *bakufu* style of writing. Similarly, the thousands of samurai (warrior-administrators) who accompanied their daimyō to Edo as part of *sankin-kotai* gradually mimicked the spoken dialects of the capital.

To be sure, regional dialects continued to flourish in remote areas, but scholars agree that by the end of the 18th century, the standard Edo dialect had become the common language of the nation.

Japan did not have a writing system prior to the seventh century, when it began to adapt the Chinese system of writing to spoken Japanese. This in itself was a tremendous accomplishment, since spoken Chinese and Japanese are about as different from each other as Navaho is from Italian.

Chinese written characters (kanji) are symbols, each of which represents a word (and thus an idea), whereas the characters in the English alphabet are letters that always represent sounds, never exclusively words. In the 18th century, Japanese used kanji sometimes to stand for words (and thus ideas) and sometimes to represent sounds.

Written literature had a long, rich tradition in Japan. But the height of common popular literature awaited the late 17th century and the whole of the 18th century, when woodblock became the predominant method of printing texts.

Within the cities, literacy was the norm rather than the exception. By about 1700, there were 493 publishers in Edo. By 1800, there were 917. In 1692, a government survey reported the existence of more than 7,300 titles of books in print. Estimates suggest that in 1808, Edo accommodated 656 bookstores and more than a hundred libraries.

Because books were expensive to publish, many bookstores rented books by the week. The common fee was 10 percent of the cost of the book for a five-day rental. A common publishing run from one set of woodblocks was about 300, but some titles sold up to 4,000 copies. In addition to books, a number of smaller pieces were published. *Kawaraban* (tile prints) announced news of fires, earthquakes, and other calamities but also informed the public about politics, gossip, and even some foreign news.

The early part of the 18th century witnessed an explosion of popular literature within the large cities of Japan. A form of literary narrative called "diversionary stories" (*otogi-zōshi*) became popular in the first quarter of the century. These short stories, fables, fairy tales, and romantic episodes were descendants of those told by wandering minstrels, itinerant priests, and beggars.

A related genre was the *ukiyo-zōshi* (tales of the floating world). These books were full of comedy and sex (including homosexuality) and were increasingly written in the simple writing system, *kana*, which was better suited to the semiliterate.

The *ukiyo-zōshi* genre was further divided into types of writing that included comedy, erotic tales, and "tales of human affection." Pornographic picture books, theatrical playbooks, and collections of poetry all sold thousands of copies among the lowly *chōnin* (city folk).

Scarcely a barbershop, teahouse, café, or brothel could be found without stacks of cheap booklets with which customers could while away the hours. If the wills and estate lists of rural village leaders are an accurate indication, the rural areas of Japan enjoyed the popular literature as well.

Other literary conventions were popular, including *shunga* (pictures of spring)—books that were little more than pornography, although they might be considered marriage manuals because they featured cartoonlike depictions of sundry sex acts with genitalia exaggerated in size lest the viewer mistake what was being depicted.

There can be little doubt that the 18th century saw the birth of reading as a popular pastime for even the common people. Diaries and wills attest to the pop-

---

 Snapshot

Japanese Humor

Japanese discourse has had a long tradition of ribald humor. The following joke, one of many adapted from traditional texts, mirrors not just a little the contours and content of contemporary humor.

> A pale languid man shuffled into the doctor's office. "I need a prescription that will reduce sexual drive."
>
> The doctor looked at him dubiously. "You really don't seem to need it."
>
> "You're right, but it's for my wife." (as cited in Dykstra, 2)

---

ularity of books, as long lists survive that indicate that virtually every household had a small or modest library.

Despite the complexity of Japanese grammar, pronunciation, writing, and reading, the 18th century witnessed a surge in popular literature. These literary genres were popular both in cities and in villages, a fact that suggests relatively widespread literacy (Perez, 55–59, 285–88).

To read about Japanese literature in the 20th century, see the Japan entry in the section "Literature" in chapter 6 ("Intellectual Life") of volume 6 of this series.

FOR MORE INFORMATION

Dykstra, A. H., ed. *Sexy Laughing Stories of Old Japan*. Tokyo and San Francisco: Japan Publications, 1974.

Japan Information Network. <http://www.jinjapan.org/index.html>, accessed October 23, 2003.

Keene, D. *The Pleasures of Japanese Literature*. New York: Columbia University Press, 1988.

Perez, L. G. *Daily Life in Early Modern Japan*. Westport, Conn.: Greenwood Press, 2002.

INTELLECTUAL
LIFE
|
LANGUAGE
& LITERATURE
|
Africa

The Colonial Frontier
of North America

England

France

Japan

New England

Life at Sea

NEW ENGLAND

In colonial New England, the literary arts were submitted to frequent and extensive prohibitions deriving in large part from Puritan dogma and from those who enforced it. Although the Bible and religious texts including the Psalms and sermons were popular, other genres of writing appeared, although not always in public forums.

A large committee of Puritan clergy translated the Psalms from the Hebrew into everyday English in *The Bay Psalm Book* (1640), principally for use in the service. The committee members' aim was not only to have an accurate translation but also to avoid that which, in their minds, constituted devilishly or popishly seductive singsong verses. Hence, clergymen attempted to eliminate the lyrical poetry of both the Hebrew sources and the English King James Bible. Whether they succeeded is debatable.

The powerful Puritan and Quaker clergy denounced literary arts such as poetry and fiction. Although printers operated in New England cities, especially Boston, the clergy and the magistrates kept a close eye on the materials that were published, halting the production of texts deemed irreverent, irreligious, or treasonous and denouncing anything that promoted frivolity, immorality, or idleness. In 1726, Cotton Mather, in *Manuductio Ad Ministerium*, had this to say of literary and dramatic art of all kinds:

How much do I wish that such Pestilences, and indeed all those worse than EGYPTIAN TOADS . . . might never crawl into your Chamber! The UNCLEAN SPIRITS that COME LIKE FROGS OUT OF THE MOUTH OF THE DRAGON, AND OF THE BEAST; which GO FORTH unto the young People of THE EARTH, and expose them to be dealt withal as the Enemies of GOD.

One of the most popular works written in New England, "Day of Doom," by Michael Wigglesworth, was a long, nightmarish poem. Several New England writers who did not gain fame until later—Anne Bradstreet, Edward Taylor, and Phillis Wheatley—are now celebrated for their exceptional poetry. However, these authors seem to have been exceptions—their cases proof of the widespread discouragement of poetry in general.

Wigglesworth's poem, for example, was tolerated and admired because it met the criterion for the little poetry that was sanctioned: it served a permitted religious purpose. Wigglesworth's poem, which was important enough to be memorized by New England schoolchildren, was a fire-and-brimstone dramatization of Puritan doctrine, with each damned soul arguing with the Judge about why he or she should be saved. The Judge's responses are expositions on such things as innate depravity, the Fall, predestination, and infant damnation.

The poems of Anne Bradstreet, daughter of lieutenant governor (and later governor) Thomas Dudley, and those of Edward Taylor, Harvard College–educated minister in Westfield, Massachusetts, were little known in their lifetimes. Both poets seemed to realize not only that their chosen genre was questionable but also that what they had to say as poets would be unpopular and misunderstood.

In one of her poems, Bradstreet writes, "I am obnoxious to each carping tongue / Who says my hand a needle better fits." Her poetry also makes what would have been considered the unfitting, irreligious comparison of her husband to Jesus Christ.

Edward Taylor's poetry was never published in his lifetime, nor was it his intention that his poetry ever appear in the light of day, even after he died. Unlike Bradstreet's subject matter, Taylor's was almost wholly religious, but he certainly sensed that many of his sentiments were potential sources of controversy in his community.

With the diminishing absolute power of the clergy in the 18th century came more open tolerance for poetry. Yet, even here, the enduring verse had a sermon or message to deliver. Phillis Wheatley, an African slave living in 18th-century Boston, used poetry as a medium for expressing herself on religious subjects and on the deaths of famous men. In one of her poems, "On Being Brought from Africa to America," composed in 1773, she defies those in her community who argued that the conversion of black people to Christianity was useless. Wheatley's defense of black people juxtaposed with her ardent support of Christianity, the religion of her master and of New England slaveholders, is curious.

'Twas mercy brought me from my *Pagan land,*
Taught my benighted soul to understand
That there's a God, that there's a *Savior too:*
Once I redemption neither sought nor knew.
Some view our sable race with scornful eye,
"Their colour is a diabolic die."
Remember, *Christians, Negros,* black as *Cain,*
May be refin'd, and join th' angelic train.

The one literary genre that flourished in colonial New England was the treatise or sermon. This was the form that inspired early publishers in New England. Printing houses formed to publish sermons, and sermons became the publishers' mainstays, addresses of particular eloquence often appearing within weeks of their first oral delivery in the meetinghouse. In 1741, Jonathan Edwards delivered his famous sermon "Sinners in the Hands of an Angry God" to parishioners in Enfield, Connecticut. Edwards's successful representation of hell generated such groaning and loud weeping in the audience that he had to ask attendees to quiet down so that he could complete his sermon.

Popular publications included practical works and those religious works of a character acceptable to Calvinist dogma. Joining "Day of Doom" on the colonial New England best-seller lists were the Bible, *The Bay Psalm Book*, the almanac, and the *New England Primer*. There were many books of catechism (religious recitations, especially for children), but by far the most widely used were John Cotton's *Spiritual Milk for Boston Babes* and the *Westminster Assembly's Shorter Catechism*, which were later appended to the primary textbook the *New England Primer*. These presented a series of questions and answers on fundamental religious principles.

Alongside popular and clergy-approved religious texts such as Michael Wigglesworth's "Day of Doom" developed an impressive, though often concealed, body of New England colonial literature, including the representative efforts of Anne Bradstreet, Edward Taylor, and Phillis Wheatley (Johnson, 22, 120–22, 155, 172).

FOR MORE INFORMATION

Archiving Early America. *Early America.* <http://earlyamerica.com/>, accessed October 23, 2003.

Johnson, C. D. *Daily Life in Colonial New England.* Westport, Conn.: Greenwood Press, 2002.

Murdock, K. B. *Literature and Theology in Colonial New England.* Westport, Conn.: Greenwood Press, 1970.

LIFE AT SEA

Ordinary seamen put few of their thoughts on paper. As educated men, officers tended to write about contemporary events in journals and letters and to produce memoirs in their retirement, as did Captain Samuel Samuels and admirals Thomas Hardy and Cuthbert Collingwood. Naval administrators and heads of state have also left a wealth of material. Admiralty Secretary Samuel Pepys, for instance, left more than 15,000 letters written at the end of the 17th century for historians to consider.

The hundreds of surviving documents, bills of lading, customs receipts, and logs of most merchant vessels are abysmally dull and are composed of largely repetitive details. A few other entries are quite exciting, as shown in the following excerpt.

Piped all hands to quarters and cleared for action. 1/4 before 4 the enemy got under weigh [*sic*] to engage us. At 4 P.M. being within good gunshot commenced a brisk connonade on the starboard side which the enemy returned. 10 minutes past 4 P.M. she wore ship and struck her colors. Gave three cheers.

Seamen did produce a fair amount of artwork in their logbooks, journals, and charts. Officers illustrated their logbooks with unique landmarks, vessels sighted, or unusual scenes encountered during a voyage. Charts were embellished with sketches of dolphins, birds, and islands.

The journals kept by crewmembers were less common. Some extant examples contain excellent illustrations portraying shipboard life and documenting the villages and people of exotic ports. Virtually all of these works were done in simple pen and black ink, although some used different colors of ink.

Whale men in particular were prolific letter writers. Letter writing provided a place for them to air their deepest feelings and most private thoughts. "Here we are 8 days from home. It seems to me more like 8 months. . . . I am more homesick than ever before," wrote Captain DuBois to his wife. In a separate letter he confided, "I think that I will take a barth [*sic*] this evening [but] I have no towels, that is something I have foregotten [*sic*]."

Mail delivery from sea was neither swift nor easy; yet the desire to maintain ties with loved ones drove seamen to devise numerous methods of overcoming the vast gulf of oceanic distances and the separation of unremitting time. Wives sent letters addressed as simply as "Capt. Nathan Jernegan, Ship *Splendid*, Pacific Ocean." Letters were mailed at embassies, at missions, and even in barrels nailed to trees on lonely islands. Outward-bound ships would drop off letters, while ships that were concluding their voyage would pick up letters to be carried back home. Charles Island in the Galapagos became known as Post Office Bay. Its large box, covered with a giant tortoise shell and nailed to a post, was a popular drop-off and pick-up point for whalers. Ships that "gammed" (met at sea or at anchorage) would exchange mail as well as newspapers and news.

Most officers, as educated men, kept personal journals or diaries. Naval commanders were also under some obligation to send out detailed dispatches to their superiors. These were sometimes simple compilations of day-to-day activities, but they often took the form of long, graphic narratives, especially after a particularly successful engagement. These dispatches were a chance for commanders to praise their subordinates and revel in their own success. In this regard, the last paragraph of British admiral Cuthbert Collingwood's dispatch written the day after the Battle of Trafalgar (1805) serves as an example:

After such a victory, it may appear unnecessary to enter into encomiums on the particular parts taken by the several commanders; the conclusion says more on the subject than I have the language to express; the spirit which animated all was the same: when all exert themselves zealously in their country's service, all deserve that their high merits should stand recorded; and never was high merit more conspicuous than in the battle I have described.

Historians and maritime scholars know much about the nature of British naval tactics because, from an early date, they were formalized into a written body of signals and maneuvers called the *Sailing and Fighting Instructions*.

In fleet engagements comprising many ships on each side, the admiral needed to command the actions of his subordinates and of individual vessels while witnessing the overall conflict develop. Because there were only rudimentary means of communication by sight, speaking trumpet, or messenger boat, a series of prearranged visual signals were instituted, each with its own meaning. These signals were the basis for the *Instructions*.

The admiral's pennant, a long narrow flag colored to suit his rank, was flown from the masthead of his flagship, locating him in the center squadron. Sailors made signals by raising colored flags and pennants in different positions on the admiral's flagship. These were repeated on all the ships throughout the fleet. The signals were severely limited in scope, most being sailing instructions that pertained to the movements of the fleet at sea. However, some signals were deemed fighting instructions in that they were used in combat.

The language and literature of seamen and officers ranged from diaries, journals, and personal correspondence to logbooks, bills, receipts, and even flag signals. Interestingly, no period has generated such a huge catalog of historical fiction as that of the age of sail. Pirates and buried riches came to life in Robert Louis Stevenson's *Treasure Island* and Rafael Sabatini's *Captain Blood*. Herman Melville's *Moby Dick* and *Billy Budd* brought the daily life of seamen to the public. However, C. S. Forester remains the dean of maritime novelists. A 20th-century author, Forester serialized the British Navy's exploits dating from the Anglo-French wars of the late 18th century and became, thanks to his combination of realistic and fanciful depictions of characters and events, one of the most popular authors of his time. Forester's first naval adventure, *Beat to Quarters*, was published in 1937 (Volo and Volo, ix, x, 148, 150–51, 210).

FOR MORE INFORMATION

Edwards, P. *The Story of the Voyage: Sea-Narratives in Eighteenth-Century England.* Cambridge, England: Cambridge University Press, 1994.

Rogers, J. G. *Origin of Sea Terms.* Mystic, Conn.: Mystic Seaport Museum, 1985.

Volo, D. D., and J. M. Volo. *Daily Life in the Age of Sail.* Westport, Conn.: Greenwood Press, 2002.

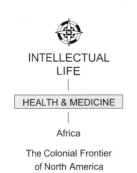

INTELLECTUAL
LIFE
|
HEALTH & MEDICINE
|
Africa

The Colonial Frontier
of North America

England

France

Japan

New England

Life at Sea

Health and Medicine

Physical and mental well-being is of great value, especially to those who are suffering from some manner of ailment. During the 17th and 18th centuries, people in sub-Saharan Africa, North America's frontier communities, France, England, Japan, New England, and aboard European and American sailing vessels frequently had occasion to ponder the importance of a sound body and mind, as well as the competence of established medical practices in their respective societies. Insofar as the status of health and medicine in these societies possessed certain points in common, the themes of health, hygiene, medical professionals, remedies, and mental illness merit a brief and integrated examination.

Medical knowledge throughout the societies discussed in this volume was slight compared with that of the contemporary world. Beyond this foreseeable bit of truth lie less-obvious realities. For example, Native Americans in colonial North America's frontier and coastal regions tended to be healthy peoples, free from many of the harmful diseases that plagued Europeans. To treat those illnesses that did occur, many Indians used tobacco smoke, ritual mask ceremonies, and herbs. However, the relative health of Indians came to an end with the arrival of European settlers and their diseases.

At the same time, colonial New Englanders established a relatively healthy community. They lived longer and heartier lives than, among others, colonists in the south. Historians have variously attributed this good fortune to the presence of trained doctors, to a colder climate that limited the baneful consequences of malaria and typhoid, and even to the bountiful share of apples that colonists ate.

Whereas sailors and officers aboard ship were prey to a host of maladies (often associated with poor diet), Japanese had comparatively fewer reasons to visit the doctor. In particular, their good health is attributed to a religious emphasis on hygiene.

Hygiene, or cleanliness, varied from one culture to the next. In Japan, relaxing at public baths (sento) and hot springs (onsen) was a popular tradition that contributed mightily to the health of the islands' peoples. This distinctively Japanese concern for cleanliness and an aversion toward "pollution" resulted in widespread attempts to sanitize food, drink, and natural waterways, as well.

Hygiene in England, New England, and aboard ships was fairly terrible. Although mineral spas were popular among English ladies and gentlemen, their general hygiene reflected an ignorance of and disregard for the foul fumes, litter, and effluence that was a daily part of city and rural life. Sailors worked hard to keep the vessels on which they sailed clean, but the close quarters, lack of refrigeration, and other impediments inevitably created an environment ripe for infectious and dietary illnesses. As for New Englanders and frontier colonists, they rarely bathed, brushed their teeth, or sanitized clothing and food. On the other hand, Native Americans in the region routinely took sweat baths in straw and stone sheds, in which water was thrown on heated stone floors to create sweltering vapors.

Medical professionals were present in each of the societies discussed here. English physicians, surgeons, dentists, nurses, and midwives all betrayed a basic ignorance of illnesses, their causes, and their cures. The same was true for surgeons and surgeons' mates aboard British warships, as well as New England and Japanese doctors.

Quack prescriptions were notable across cultures during this period. French doctors prescribed animal dung to ailing patients. Medical prescriptions in England included a combination of eggshells and snails to reduce the painful symptoms of some long-since-forgotten complaint. Japanese pharmacists recommended that their patients take sweat, semen, and excrement as directed. And it was not uncommon for New England doctors to prescribe with great confidence various curative concoctions, including one that blended sow bugs with white wine.

Not all cures of the time sound quite so bizarre today. Japanese acupuncture, massage, and *moxa* (the burning of medicine onto the skin) were accepted treatments for countless ailments and are still practiced in Japan, other parts of Asia, and increasingly, throughout the world. And people aboard oceangoing vessels benefited from what came to be required portions of certain foods (sauerkraut) and drinks (fruit wine, spruce beer) that contain vitamin C, a valuable nutrient that prevents the hideous and often fatal effects of scurvy from developing.

Finally, mental or spiritual health was not a neglected theme in these various societies. New England Native Americans entrusted spiritual healing to special male doctors. Colonial New Englanders, particularly 17th-century Puritans, were apt to interpret cases of depression, hallucination, and the like as convincing proof of evil afoot; that is, people suffering from what we often diagnose as mental illness were, according to Puritans, possessed by the devil's spawn. Finally, many Japanese believed that the impeded flow of unseen energies known as *chi* resulted in poor health, both physical and mental, a conception that is popular today in Eastern and non-Eastern societies.

~*Peter Seelig*

FOR MORE INFORMATION

Williams, G. R. *The Age of Agony: The Art of Healing, c. 1700–1800.* Chicago: Academy Chicago Publishers, 1986.

INTELLECTUAL
LIFE
|
HEALTH & MEDICINE
|
Africa

The Colonial Frontier
of North America

England

France

Japan

New England

Life at Sea

AFRICA

Prior to the introduction of European medicine during the colonial period, Africans had their own ideas of disease and models of health maintenance. The African view of disease frequently drew on religious beliefs regarding spirits and ancestors, which played a role in people's everyday lives. For that reason, disease often represented a community affair and was dealt with by religious rituals. Even in areas that had access to Islamic medical learning, many people relied on charms and other sorts of magic to cure their ailments. However, systems for comprehensive health maintenance often evolved into important social institutions that empowered many individuals while preserving the well-being of the community.

During the 17th and 18th centuries, Africa experienced many significant epidemics, one cause of which resulted from the expansion of settled regions into new areas where people did not possess immunity to all the possible disease-causing bacteria. In central Africa, the clearing of land for new food crops led to the spread of mosquitoes, malaria, and yellow fever. Disease also spread when different cultures came into contact with one another, including the Europeans. In addition, the introduction of new means of managing environmental resources sometimes upset existing balances between humans, animals, and disease-causing organisms, resulting in the additional spread of disease. This process continued well into the colonial period (Ogot, 531).

In many sub-Saharan African societies, people believed that certain forces such as deceased ancestors and other spirits or minor divinities caused illness. Thus, African concepts of health included not only biological maladies but also other phenomena attributed to spirit possession, such as insanity, emotional disturbances, and socially objectionable behavior. All were treatable by ritual means because of their common origin and were frequently considered a communal affair.

One common way of dealing with such illnesses was through a cult of healing, such as the *lemba* cult in Kongo. Following the association of an illness or other problem with a certain type of spirit, people would go to a local *lemba* healer and through rituals usually involving song, drumming, and dance, would have their problem diagnosed and treated. During this process, they learned to assert power over their affliction while bonding with their fellow cult members. Chickens and pigs were also sacrificed at appropriate points during the course of treatment, both for atonement and for the unity of the group at a communal meal.

The ultimate goal was to transform weakness and suffering into empowerment and total wellness, as illustrated in this *lemba* song: "That which was the sickness, has become the path to the priesthood." After vanquishing their malady, many *lemba* initiates went on to become healers themselves, helping others to overcome the problems from which they themselves had once suffered. For other types of illnesses, diagnosis and therapy fell to members of the sufferer's lineage because illness was held to be a matter affecting them all (Janzen, 87–107).

The Hausa of West Africa also took a comprehensive view of health, with the Hausa word *lafiya* referring not only to physical maladies but to all problems in the general social order. The Hausa also saw the communal effects of illness. When a man was weak, not only was he lacking in *lafiya* but his entire compound suffered, as well, because of his inability to fulfill his social role (Wall, 170–71).

The Hausa divided illnesses into two types. Most minor ailments they considered *Ciwon Allah*, or illnesses of God. God had seen fit to make discomfort a part of human existence, and hence people could become ill through such things as cold weather, bad food, or wetness. Other illnesses, however, came about through malevolent spiritual powers and were called *Ciwon Miyagu*, or illnesses of evil. People believed witches could capture and destroy a person's soul or cause some other serious medical problem. Sometimes the souls of the deceased would attack their friends and relatives, leading to a period during which the victims lost interest in their everyday lives (Wall, 183–203).

Illnesses were treated with herbs, the knowledge of which was often handed down within families. Moreover, traveling medicine sellers participated in medicinal treatments. And Muslim leaders sought to cure illnesses using what was called "the medicine of the Prophet." This involved such practices as drinking ink that had been used to write verses of the Qur'an (Wall, 214–15, 236).

African medical practices thus focused not just on bodily illness but on all problems and behaviors that caused disruption to the general social order. Ritual cults of different kinds represented one of the chief methods of treatment, as did the use of herbs, amulets, and other magical charms. Although the effectiveness of some of these cures is perhaps questionable, the worldview to which they point reveals a concern for community values and the complete individual—a worldview that served as a useful basis for healing on a communal level.

To read about health and medicine in Africa in the 20th century, see the Africa entry in the section "Health and Medicine" in chapter 6 ("Intellectual Life") of volume 6 of this series.

~Brian Ulrich

FOR MORE INFORMATION

Feierman, S., and J. M. Janzen, eds. *The Social Basis of Health and Healing in Africa.* Berkeley: University of California Press, 1992.

Ford, J. *The Role of the Trypanosomiases in African Ecology: A Study of the Tsetse Fly Problem.* Oxford: Clarendon Press, 1971.

Halsall, P., ed. *Internet African History Sourcebook.* 1996. <http://www.fordham.edu/halsall/africa/africasbook.html>, accessed October 23, 2003.

Janzen, J. M. *Ngoma: Discourses of Healing in Central and Southern Africa.* Berkeley: University of California Press, 1992.

Ogot, B. A., ed. *General History of Africa.* Vol. 5. *Africa from the Sixteenth Century to the Eighteenth Century.* Paris: United Nations Educational, Scientific, and Cultural Organization, 1992.

Wall, L. Lewis. *Hausa Medicine: Illness and Well-Being in a West African Culture.* Durham, N.C.: Duke University Press, 1988.

THE COLONIAL FRONTIER OF NORTH AMERICA

The inhabitants along the North American colonial frontier recognized two types of health care: that of the American Indians and that of the settlers. However, it was not unusual for the settlers to adopt the medicinal practices of the native populations and apply them to colonial health concerns.

Native American mask societies were a notable element of woodland religion. The False Faces were a "medicine" society in terms of health care. A carved wooden mask, usually of grotesque portions and details, represented when worn a mythological being invoked by the wearer to aid humankind in the elimination of disease. Society members might blow tobacco smoke through the mouth of a mask on the sick to heal them. Another mask society was the Corn Husk Faces, the members of which wore masks during the midwinter rituals connected with farming. Almost all of the woodland nations gathered annually for the Green Corn, midwinter, and harvest rituals, where the activities of the mask societies were prominent.

On the frontier, herbs served both the spice rack and the medicine chest. The tradition of using plants as "physicks" for healing, as well as seasoning for food, accompanied the settlers from Europe. Garden herbs were likely to be the only medicines available. Hyssop was mixed with honey to make a cough syrup, yarrow was placed on wounds to stop bleeding, and savory was used to treat colic.

Many herbs, such as marjoram, had a variety of uses for an assortment of complaints. Tea from marjoram leaves was recommended to patients for the relief of spasms, colic, and indigestion. When chewed, it eased toothaches. Mixed with honey, the leaves lessened bruising. With information from the Indians, colonists expanded their knowledge of the medicinal properties of native plants. Indians introduced settlers to bee balm, which was brewed into "Oswego tea" that provided the ailing with relief from colic, fever, or colds. Some herbs were used as pesticides to deter flies, fleas, and moths. Herbs also provided dyes. Tansey shoots produced a green grey, yarrow blossoms gave yellow, and the stems and leaves of sweet cicely yielded an olive color.

For the colonists, the loss of a child was a frequent occurrence. One in 10 infants did not survive the first year of life, and 4 out of 10 children died before age six. Common diseases that stole away these infants included measles, diphtheria, whooping cough, mumps, and chicken pox. Hannah and Samuel Sewall had 14 children and 1 child stillborn. Seven of the children died within 25 months of birth. Anne Lake Cotton gave birth to nine children in 20 years. She lost her first child two months before the birth of her second child. The next four survived infancy, but the last three died at or shortly after delivery. Mary Holyoke gave birth to 12 children in 22 years. Only four survived infancy.

Accidents claimed children, too. Frontier households were bustling, cluttered places that were not always child safe. Open fires, kettles of hot water, privy holes, unfenced ponds, and open wells were daily dangers to a toddler or a small child. Busy adults and older children could easily lose sight of one of the smaller children in a crowded household. Alice Walton returned from visiting her husband in the field to find her toddler missing. She questioned an older child, who responded, "It was here just now presently." The child was found drowned in an unfenced water hole.

Nicholas Gilman's cousin "narrowly escaped drowning being fallen into a kettle of Suds." Fortunately, the mishap was seen, and the child was "pulled out by his heels" in time. Hannah Palmer's daughter was not so fortunate. While Hannah was still recovering from giving birth and grieving the loss of twin daughters who died five days prior, her older daughter fell into a kettle of scalding water and died the following day.

It would be an error to accept the unsupported claim that the life expectancy of colonials was much shorter than that of modern Americans. The average age at which people died was driven down by very high rates of infant mortality, death from disease and accident among the young, and death among young women in childbirth. Those who survived adolescence seem to have had a life expectancy well into their seventies. Indeed, it should be noted that military service was demanded of men up to the age of 60 in almost all of the colonies. This would suggest that men of this age were still expected to be vigorous and healthy. Perhaps the settlers' willingness to experiment with native approaches to health contributed to this physical resilience (Volo and Volo, 45–46, 99, 126–27, 152–53).

FOR MORE INFORMATION

Boorstin, D. J. *The Americans: The Colonial Experience.* New York: Random House, 1958.
Volo, J. M., and D. D. Volo. *Daily Life on the Old Colonial Frontier.* Westport, Conn.: Greenwood Press, 2002.

ENGLAND

Medical practitioners and medical institutions in 18th-century England dealt with a wide range of diseases. Physicians, surgeons, apothecaries, and midwives treated ailing patients. Hospitals and dispensaries also existed and proved with occasional humor (and occasional horror) their limited usefulness. Common vermin such as lice and maladies, ranging in severity from aches and pains to bladder stones and cancer, created discomfort, pain, and fear among many people and often prompted attempts at self-medication.

In the 18th century, "all that could be done" in medicine was very little. Physicians had some understanding of anatomy but only a few effective treatments, including quinine and, later, inoculation. Physicians could diagnose few diseases with accuracy; that which was not plague or smallpox was likely to be classified loosely as a "fever." These doctors of medicine were ignorant of the role played in disease by parasites such as lice and fleas.

Because it was expensive to call in a doctor, most people waited until they had exhausted every other resource. Doctors therefore often saw only the most desperate cases. As a result, most people believed that doctors were as likely to kill their patients as to heal them. Needing to do something dramatic, or because they really believed it would work, doctors resorted to visible but useless or even harmful measures—bleeding, dosing with dangerous drugs, raising blisters on the skin, and inducing vomiting. Except in a few places such as London, no examination was necessary to practice medicine.

Surgeons, unlike physicians, performed operations and drew blood. Medically, their training was often even worse than physicians'. Rudimentary education was only one of the obstacles to successful surgery. Because there were no reliable anesthetics, surgical patients were usually given alcohol or opium beforehand. Furthermore, little was known about infection. Medical practitioners rarely washed their hands, even when they had come directly from another patient.

Surgery was exceedingly rare, and the actual number of surgical procedures (other than bleeding) was small, limited to trepanation (drilling a hole in the skull to relieve pressure against the brain), tonsillectomy, lithotomy (the removal of bladder stones), the excision of skin and breast cancers, and amputation. All surgeons strove to minimize the time that an incision lay open. A bladder-stone removal by the reigning expert, William Cheselden, could take 30 seconds to one minute; the amputation of a leg by an expert took two to four minutes. Nevertheless, because of the prevalence of infection, almost one in five of Cheselden's lithotomy patients died.

Below the surgeon in status was the apothecary, who dispensed drugs. Middle- and working-class people who could not afford physicians consulted apothecaries instead. Well below the apothecaries were the midwives and nurses, who were overwhelmingly female. Drawn chiefly from the working class, nurses were often accused of thievery, drunkenness, and licentiousness and were domestic servants as much as medical staff.

Hospitals, founded by wealthy subscribers, served orphans, women in labor, and the indigent and working-class ill. In terms of reducing the patients' mortality, these institutions accomplished little. All hospitals were home to vermin, especially lice, which clung to walls, beds, patients, and doctors' coats. At Chelsea and Greenwich Hospitals, patients captured their lice and pitted them against one another in races.

About 1793, a medical practitioner amputates the agonized patient's right leg, while a group of medical students watches and learns. © The Art Archive/ British Museum/Eileen Tweedy.

The "undeserving" or unreferred poor used dispensaries, which became increasingly popular as the 18th century passed. Dispensary staff saw patients, diagnosed ailments, dispensed drugs, and sent the patients on their way. By 1800, 50,000 people a year were being treated at such institutions.

Illness thrived in part because personal cleanliness was not a priority. Frequent, full-body washing was rare; most people preferred just to rinse their hands and faces. Soap was expensive and often heavily taxed. Washing clothes was difficult early in the century, before cheap and washable cotton replaced wool as the dominant fabric. Shirts were typically changed once a week.

Dental care was part of the morning ritual for some at least. The well-off chewed cinnamon, cloves, honey, orange peel, and other substances to sweeten the breath, and many people used tooth powder or abrasive sticks to clean the teeth, or they used a new invention—the toothbrush. Nonetheless, yellow or black teeth, crooked teeth, and foul breath remained commonplace.

Specialized care was little better. Eyeglasses existed for those who could afford them. Lost eyes could be replaced with glass ones. If something went wrong with one's teeth, dentists hand-drilled cavities—as always, with no anesthetic but alcohol—and filled the resulting holes with molten tin, lead, or gold.

Few remedies or palliatives existed for contagious illness. For venereal or "foul" diseases, a common treatment was "salivation," devotees of which stipulated that the patient be dosed for days or even weeks with toxic quantities of mercury in either ointment or pill form. The treatment caused drooling (sometimes as much as three pints per day), swollen gums, and loosening of the teeth.

Diseases of malnutrition were also rife. Starvation was rare, but so was a healthy, balanced diet. Lack of vitamin C caused scurvy, which involved exhaustion, swellings, spots, trembling, and a delay or reversal in the healing of wounds. Vitamin D or calcium deficiency caused rickets, the sufferers of which, principally children, developed enlarged livers and heads and bent, crippled spines and limbs. A host of other perils awaited people of all classes: industrial accidents, farm accidents, gout, poisoning as a result of toxic cosmetics, cancer, dropsy, rheumatism, ulcers, itches, infected feet, and the inevitable amputations and maimings of wartime service.

Sufferers from various diseases sought remedy or relief at one of England's numerous mineral spas or seaside retreats, such as Bath. There, the seekers of health relaxed in the spa, where they got perhaps their only full-body bath that year, in water on which floated filth, skin flakes, and urine. Other people, perhaps most, treated their ailments at home. Some chose commercial remedies: perhaps Dr. Bateman's Pectoral Drops, Dr. Hooper's Female Pills, or some other curiously named concoction made of ingredients that included egg shells and snails.

Some invested in home health manuals; others relied on folk remedies or blind instinct. They touched hanged men to cure goiter and swollen glands, drank hawthorn tea or asses' milk, made charms of babies' amniotic sacs, and ate eye of pike for toothaches, pigeons' blood for apoplexy, cockroach tea for kidney ailments, and spiders for fever. Not all home remedies were useless, however. Quinine, dung poultices, foxglove (digitalis) for heart problems, and cod-liver oil had medical benefits.

The limitations of 18th-century English medicine meant that people who suffered from ailments, identifiable or not, continued to suffer, even until death. These same limitations made medical practitioners and institutions suspect in the eyes of would-be patients. It would take considerable advances in science and technology before the practice of medicine could enjoy more success (Olsen, 262–65, 267–68, 270–73).

To read about health and medicine in Chaucer's England, see the Europe entry in the section "Health and Medicine" in chapter 4 ("Intellectual Life") of volume 2; for Elizabethan England, see the England entry in the section "Health and Science" in chapter 4 ("Intellectual Life") of volume 3; and for Victorian England, see the Victorian England entry in the section "Health and Medicine" in chapter 4 ("Intellectual Life") of volume 5 of this series.

FOR MORE INFORMATION

Lynch, J. *Eighteenth Century Resources.* <http://newark.rutgers.edu/~jlynch/18th/>, accessed October 10, 2003.

Olsen, K. *Daily Life in 18th-Century England.* Westport, Conn.: Greenwood Press, 1999.

Porter, D. *Patient's Progress: Doctors and Doctoring in Eighteenth-Century England.* Stanford, Calif.: Stanford University Press, 1989.

FRANCE

The most well known epidemic disease of the medieval and early modern eras, the bubonic plague, or Black Death, began to disappear from France in the 17th century. This rapid killer had first surfaced among Europeans in the 14th century, when it disfigured its victims with swollen and weeping pustules that were closely followed by death's arrival. In the face of this disease, doctors could do very little except "leave early, go far, and come back late." Even if doctors had remained in plague-stricken areas, the priests who administered last rites were far more likely to be useful at the bedside than were doctors. However, the plague began to decline in virulence around 1660 and disappeared from France altogether in the 18th century, paving the way for doctors to participate more fully in the diagnosis and treatment of individuals who, despite being sick, had a good chance of recovery (Brockliss and Jones, 40).

The fact that medical practice became more important after the near disappearance of the bubonic plague did not immediately correspond to the development of a "modern" medical corps, as most medical science in France was still heavily influenced by medieval medical principles and practices. Physicians, surgeons, and apothecaries generally relied on religious doctrine, astrology, and medieval philosophy for the diagnosis and treatment of diseases. Alchemy, or the art of turning base metals into gold, quite possibly seems only distantly related to the art of healing. Certainly by the 19th and 20th centuries, research related to alchemic science or other forms of "magic" had been thoroughly discredited and separated out from medical science. However, until the rise of clinical and experimental medicine, physicians were as likely to turn to alchemic or astrological ideas as to experimental science. At the end of the 18th century, as France headed toward the political crisis of 1789, science finally experienced its own revolution, with medical treatment moving out of the hands of common practitioners such as midwives, priests, and local practitioners and into the hands of doctors who had received training at universities.

Before this period, however, the most common medical treatments were based on accepted medical science as outlined by the second-century physician Galen. Galenic science taught the importance of maintaining balance within the body's natural fluids or "humors." These humors were divided into four categories: yellow bile (urine), black bile (feces), phlegm, and blood. Each humor corresponded to personality traits and to the four "elements" of the universe: fire, earth, water, and air. Yellow bile had a relationship to anger and correspondingly to fever; black bile represented depression; phlegm caused sluggish behavior; and blood was associated with passion or inflammation. An excess of any humor would throw the body out of its natural balance, causing the symptoms that a patient would exhibit.

In this context, the physician's job was to restore balance between the humors through a prescribed manipulation of diet, medicine, or other treatments. An excess of blood could be remedied in several ways. A lancet could be used to make a small incision in a vein, or leeches could be applied to suck blood slowly from the human body, a practice that would slow the pulse and reduce irritation in the patient, thereby balancing the humors. If an excess of yellow bile was determined to be the cause of a patient's symptoms, emetics, which caused the patient to vomit, were recommended. Similarly, cathartics and purgatives could also be used to restore a necessary balance to the body.

By current or even 19th-century medical standards, physicians and other healers knew remarkably little. Germs, bacteria, and viruses were all unknown concepts, and scientists' understanding of human physiology was weak. However, in the context of early-modern French science, these treatments made sense. Physicians and patients knew that a medicine was "working" by its "effects" on the human body. Whether or not an emetic cured a patient, it would clear out the stomach, and the patient's vomiting demonstrated that the emetic was operating as it should. Cathartics acted as laxatives, emptying the bowels and demonstrating yet another "successful" treatment. "Cupping," or applying heated cup-shaped objects to the skin to draw blood to the surface of the skin, also demonstrated an "effective" treatment insofar as the desired result was not necessarily a cure but an external process that could counteract the internal inflammation.

Modern medical science tells us that some treatments, such as the ingestion of animal dung (an obviously revolting practice), were also very unlikely to benefit the patient. Some treatments, such as mercury and aloe, prescribed for internal ingestion, could even be fatal. Many, however, were likely beneficial, such as the application of aloe to a burn or the prescription of opium (in measured amounts) to dull pain. Calamine eased itching, and chalk could absorb stomach acid. Regardless of whether these treatments actually cured patients, however, the patient's own perspective on the healing was often as important as the doctor's. The patient would expect results from the medicine, and laxatives, emetics, and bloodletting certainly demonstrated results.

Of course, physicians were not the only medical personnel to whom patients could turn, and indeed, physicians often complained that people in need of assistance only turned to medical practitioners as a last resort—that is, when priests and apothecaries had already botched the job and it was too late to save the patient. Despite that claim, midwives often successfully treated "female problems" and delivered babies, and herbalists and apothecaries were generally those who mixed the potions, teas, and medicinal treatments described previously. However, as the practice of medicine came to encompass a more professional and university-trained corps of practitioners, popular medicine (frequently practiced by women) became removed from what was "real" medicine, and a professional corps of surgeons and physicians determined the medical course of the 19th and 20th centuries. In the new medical world, dissection and experimentation led to the acceptance of proper anatomical principles as developed by Vesalius, not Galen, and doctors also came to accept the new studies on circulation, infection, and disease.

~*Jennifer J. Popiel*

FOR MORE INFORMATION

Brockliss, L. W. B., and C. Jones. *The Medical World of Early Modern France.* New York: Clarendon Press, 1997.

Foucault, M. *The Birth of the Clinic: An Archeology of Medical Perception.* New York: Pantheon, 1973.

Gelfand, T. *Professionalizing Modern Medicine: Paris Surgeons and Medical Science and Institutions in the 18th Century.* Westport, Conn.: Greenwood Press, 1980.

Lynch, J. *Eighteenth Century Resources.* <http://newark.rutgers.edu/~jlynch/18th/>, accessed October 10, 2003.

Marland, H. *The Art of Midwifery: Early Modern Midwives in Europe.* New York: Routledge, 1993.

Newman, W. R., and Anthony Grafton. *Secrets of Nature: Astrology and Alchemy in Early Modern Europe.* Cambridge, Mass.: MIT Press, 2001.

Ramsey, M. *Professional and Popular Medicine in France, 1770–1830: The Social World of Medical Practice.* New York: Cambridge University Press, 1988.

JAPAN

The care of those afflicted by disease and ailments in 18th-century Japan generally involved several forms of prevention and treatment unique to that country's culture. A ritual obsession with cleanliness, exterior remedies (acupuncture, massage, and *moxa*), and pharmaceutical concoctions were part of Japan's attempts to maintain health and reduce suffering.

The relative lack of disease in 18th-century Japan reflected in part the country's preoccupation with ritual cleaning within the Shintō religion. That is, Japanese early on adopted much more stringent personal hygienic practices, such as hand washing, mouth rinsing, and bathing.

Bathing at hot springs (*onsen*) was a popular medicinal regimen that became common in terms of pilgrimages and therefore tourism. Japan's numerous geothermal vents produced thousands of natural *onsen* that were convenient to virtually everyone in the country. Sulfurous springs were particularly popular because the belching sulfur was deemed to be medicinal. Extended stays in *onsen* were believed to treat hundreds of ailments and discomforts. Of course, only the wealthy could afford extended stays, although some of the mutual-aid societies intended the funds to be used for *onsen*.

Sento (public baths) in large cities sometimes included deep hot baths (*ōfuro*), but bathing was usually done communally. Descriptions of traditional *ōfuro* abound in the travel literature of the 18th and 19th centuries. More common were steam baths that needed very little water and little fuel to heat them if used in confined spaces. The steam would open the pores and loosen the accumulated dirt on the surface of the skin. Strategically placed sloshes of water or judicious use of a damp towel then wiped the dirt away.

Also, Japanese only ate their vegetables cooked or pickled, they maintained individual sets of eating utensils that were not shared, and they commonly drank water only after it had been boiled, usually in tea.

The very concept of purity in Shintō and the collective responsibility caused by population pressures kept Japanese from polluting their running streams of water, as well.

The basic philosophical foundations of medicine in Japan involved the idea that the body was matter influenced by cosmic and natural energies called *chi*. *Chi* flowed through everything, including all of nature. The natural channels of *chi* currents kept the body animated and nourished. When these channels were blocked, *chi* energy was pent up and denied to portions of the body. One could unblock the flow through the use of finger pressure, massage, ointment, and heat, as well as through the application of other stimuli such as needles inserted into the skin topically.

Acupuncture (*hariryōyi*), massage, and *moxa* (*moe-kusa*; the burning of medicine topically on the skin) were the most common exterior remedies for sickness and injury. For acupuncture, medical practitioners inserted hairlike iron, silver, copper, and more rarely, gold needles into specific points along the axial avenues or channels that freed up the movement of *chi*. Medical practitioners similarly used deep and sometimes painful massages to stimulate the movement of *chi*. Practitioners of *moxa* burned small herbal concoctions directly on the skin to dilate the interior channel. The German-born scholar and doctor Engelbert Kaempfer was a man who spent much of his life traveling throughout Asia and, during the early 1690s, visited Japan and its people, about whom he recorded the following observation: "I found the backs of the Japanese . . . of both sexes so full of scars and marks of former exulcerations, that one would imagine they had undergone a most severe whipping."

This *moxabustion* or *moxacautery* could also involve "cupping," whereby glass globules could be cupped to the skin. This procedure involved burning a tiny bit of desiccated herb on the skin and then immediately covering it with a glass cup. The combustion of the *moxa* created a vacuum as the oxygen was consumed within the cup, causing the skin to pucker. It was believed that the cup also sucked up internal impediments that had blocked the channels of *chi*.

In 18th-century Japan, most medicine worthy of the name was practiced rather than administered. "Doctors" in Japan were really just practitioners and purveyors. In many cases, the "craft" was an inherited one, much in the manner of any other artisanal skill.

Pharmacists and healers gathered thousands of herbs, grasses, roots, and animal parts (especially blood, sweat, semen, urine, excrement, and venom). The pharmacists then processed these raw materials into secret formulas, using desiccation, distillation, grinding, cooking, brewing, pickling, and virtually every other method of combination. Most were little more than quack nostrums, but not a few apparently were effective when used for particular symptoms.

Scores of pharmaceutical manuals were printed during the period, and many more almanacs contained medical advice, as well. In the early 18th century, the *bakufu* (national military government) relaxed their ban on Western medical journals. Particularly popular were books on surgery.

Commoners in Japan, however, patronized native medical practitioners. Some people had recourse to shamans, and it must be said that both seemed equally efficacious (or ineffective). Hospitals were almost unknown, and the few that did exist were more in the realm of leper hostels.

Midwifery was not as highly developed an art as in the West. Most women could aid younger women during delivery, but the practice commonly remained securely within the extended family, without recourse to village specialists. As in the rest of the world, birth was still accomplished with the help of gravity. Medical science had not "progressed" to the point where women were laid on their backs for the convenience of the doctor, but to the detriment of the mother. The woman in labor perched or squatted on a low stool, while another woman supported her from behind until the baby's head appeared. Mothers remained seated after birth to help with the delivery of the placenta and were only allowed to lie down after they had suckled the baby for the first time.

Cleanliness, external cures, indigenous and imported medicines, and (for the wealthy) baths in natural hot springs constituted some of the more widespread medical practices in Japan during this time (Perez, 221, 245–47).

To read about health and medicine in Japan in the 20th century, see the Japan entry in the section "Health and Medicine" in chapter 4 ("Intellectual Life") of volume 6 of this series.

FOR MORE INFORMATION

Dunn, C. J. *Everyday Life in Traditional Japan.* Tokyo: Tuttle, 1969.

Jannetta, A. B. *Epidemics and Mortality in Early Modern Japan.* Princeton, N.J.: Princeton University Press, 1987.

Japan Information Network. <http://www.jinjapan.org/index.html>, accessed October 23, 2003.

Perez, L. G. *Daily Life in Early Modern Japan.* Westport, Conn.: Greenwood Press, 2002.

Red Beard. Toho Co., Ltd. Directed by Akira Kurosawa. Videocassette, 1985.

NEW ENGLAND

Native Americans suffered from a set of ailments that, nevertheless, failed to detract from their relatively solid health. However, with the arrival of Europeans and European diseases against which the native populations had not developed resistance, Native Americans began dying in drastically higher numbers. Colonists, themselves, proved to be healthier than their English counterparts. That the often-bizarre treatments that many colonial physicians prescribed for their patients contributed to this effect is doubtful. However, the interpretive diagnoses that Puritan clergymen attributed to illnesses and signs of poor health provided New Englanders with a sense of comprehension regarding the link between maladies and God's wrath.

Native Americans suffered from few diseases while benefiting from good teeth, healthy childbearing, a low death rate, few deformities, and an effective natural medical system. They often lived to be 60, many to 80, and some to 100. The ailments with which they did have to contend included arthritis, rheumatism, neuralgia, chills, fever and pleurisy, infections from injuries and wounds, eye trouble (probably caused by smoke-filled wigwams), and ear complaints. European settlers, however, carried diseases against which the immune systems of Native Americans could not effectively resist. As a result, many died.

Among native medical practitioners, witch doctors, who were men, oversaw psychological and spiritual changes and ailments, whereas women ministered to the body with natural medicines, salves, spas, and casts for broken bones. These women also had effective ways to treat frozen limbs, for example, and used a process involving bark and cement for setting broken bones.

New England Indians used the sweat bath, akin to a sauna, as a cleanser of body and soul. This structure, tall enough to stand in, was built of stones and straw near some body of water. A stone floor was heated thoroughly by a fire before throwing water on the floor to produce steam. Sometimes a whole family would remain in the

sweat bath, singing and chatting for about an hour, and then exit the structure to submerge themselves in the nearby pond or stream before applying oil to their bodies.

In New England, the life expectancy for colonists who lived to be 20 years old was about 65, much higher than in other parts of the country. Some have attributed the better health of New England colonists to a colder climate, where malaria and typhoid (although they did exist) were less likely to be the constant plagues that they became in more southerly, swamp-infested climates.

Medical care may have been better in New England than elsewhere. A physician named Samuel Fuller came to Plymouth on the *Mayflower*, and the Massachusetts Bay Company arranged in 1629 for a physician named Abraham Pratt and a surgeon named Robert Morley to join the company in the Salem and Boston areas. The ministers who were attracted to the New World were usually trained in both theology and medicine at Cambridge University. Some clergymen in small communities, such as Edward Taylor, the poet, who lived in Westfield, Massachusetts, doubled as physicians.

The better health of New Englanders could scarcely be attributed to better hygiene, however. Sanitation, disinfection, proper drainage of sewage, toothbrushes, bathtubs, and indoor bathing were almost nonexistent among colonists in the 17th century.

Although the same physician who treated the master's family attended sick slaves, and white midwives delivered the children of slaves, the health of black slaves was not as good as that of whites. They seemed to be especially subject to death from smallpox, measles, respiratory disorders, rheumatism, and mumps. Many were injured at their work, as was the case with white workers, as well; but in New England records, we do not find the evidence of disfiguring beatings and mutilation that were described in wanted posters for runaways in the south—although whites in New England certainly administered beatings to both black slaves and white servants.

Traditionally, there were four professionals who practiced three distinct branches of medicine: the trained physician; the surgeon, who was qualified to pull teeth, do bleedings, and lance infections; the apothecary, who prescribed various medicines; and the midwife. By the 18th century, the first three positions had become one, and students of medicine now received their training by reading medicine with an individual doctor.

The chief cures were bleeding, applications of poultices (herbs wrapped in cloth and applied to the skin), and medicines taken by mouth. Inoculations for smallpox were known. Settlers medicated themselves with either substances that they ordered from the apothecary or herbs that they gathered themselves, often on the advice of native peoples, or that they bought from itinerant medicine men.

The cures prescribed by Dr. John Perkins, one of Boston's leading physicians, illustrate the state of colonial medicine in the 18th century. For scrofula (a form of tuberculosis that attacks the glands), he recommended sow bugs soaked in white wine. For palsy (involuntary shaking), he recommended bathing in a hot bath of urine and absinthe. For nervous weakness of the eyes, he recommended shaving the

An Hiftorical

ACCOUNT

OF THE

SMALL-POX

INOCULATED

IN

NEW ENGLAND,

Upon all Sorts of Perfons, *Whites, Blacks,* and of all Ages and Conftitutions.

With fome Account of the Nature of the Infeƈtion in the NATURAL and INOCULATED Way, and their different Effeƈts on HUMAN BODIES.

With fome fhort DIRECTIONS to the UNEXPERIENCED in this Method of Praƈtice.

·Humbly dedicated to her Royal Highnefs the Princefs of WALES, by *Zabdiel Boylfton,* Phyfician.

LONDON:

Printed for S. CHANDLER, *at the* Crofs-Keys *in the* Poultry. M. DCC. XXVI.

New England combated smallpox with, among other things, this 1730 pamphlet about inoculations. © Getty Images/Hulton Archive.

head. Perkins also noted the causes of death of some of his patients. Widow Alcock, he wrote, died of a hot bread supper.

Puritan religious doctrine played an integral part in the psychological and physical state of New England settlers and their attitudes toward illness. All psychological ills were ordinarily attributed to possession by demons and witches. Modern physicians have speculated that a repressive and frightening theology that stressed individual and collective guilt, graphic descriptions of the horrors of hell, and a lively demonic supernatural probably contributed to psychological problems. A typical example can be found in Samuel Sewall's diary as he worried about his daughter's anxiety, fainting spells, and physical debilitation brought on by her fear of hell.

The clergy invariably attributed illnesses to both individual and collective sin. At the funerals of children who had died of natural causes, ministers attributed the deaths to the sins of the parents. Ministers were also convinced that epidemics of disease, and especially the deaths of Puritan leaders, were proof of God's anger toward a sinful community, which had brought disaster on itself.

The relative health of New England colonists contrasted sharply with the declining health of entire native populations. When colonists did fall ill, they might seek the advice of a physician, among whose prescribed recipes were not a few peculiar antidotes. Puritan clergymen strongly believed, however, that greater adherence to God's dictates could restore the health of the ailing (Johnson, 103–5, 139–40, 153).

FOR MORE INFORMATION

Boorstin, D. J. *The Americans: The Colonial Experience.* New York: Random House, 1958.
Johnson, C. D. *Daily Life in Colonial New England.* Westport, Conn.: Greenwood Press, 2002.

LIFE AT SEA

Surgeons who traveled aboard ship were responsible for the health of their crew. The most notorious malady that befell mariners was scurvy. Over time, experiments with diet indicated that certain foods (those high in vitamin C) could diminish or even eliminate the effects of this debilitating illness.

One surgeon was appointed to each British warship. They were not necessarily doctors but were examined as to their medical knowledge by a panel of three fleet surgeons before receiving their warrants. A subsidiary of the admiralty's Navy Board, the Hurt and Sick Board, examined surgeons for certification, provided most medical supplies, and administered the hospitals.

Usually, surgeons had previously served for some time as surgeons mates (one to three per vessel). The surgeon and his mates would establish a medical station on the orlop deck or in the cockpit. In battle, they generally worked on the orlop deck below the waterline. Seamen who helped the surgeon and his mates were called loblolly boys. Surgeons were paid a stipend per month and a fee per man on the vessels in which they served. Yet the operators of oceangoing vessels always faced a

shortage of surgeons, ultimately requiring that the former pay a substantial bounty, proportioned for service in first to sixth rate warships, to attract the latter. Naval surgeons ranked as equals with army surgeons and could carry a plain officer's sword.

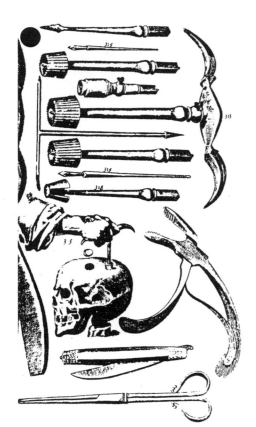
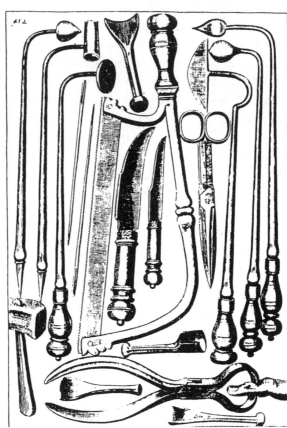

During battle, women were known to assist the surgeon and his mates in attending to and comforting the wounded. Seaman Charles M'Pherson recorded his observations after a battle: "Nine of the petty officers had wives aboard who were occupied with the doctor and his mates in the cockpit, assisting in dressing the wounds of the men as they were brought down, or in serving such as were thirsty with a drink of clean water. . . . Two of the number, I think it but justice to mention, acted with the greatest calmness and self possession."

From *The Surgeon's Mate*, by John Woodall, 1617. The tools of a shipboard surgeon included an instrument with which to bore a hole into the top of a patient's skull. © Library of Congress.

The need to provide foodstuffs that would keep for long periods of time in an age without refrigeration led to the drying or salting of a great deal of the food given to seamen. An undifferentiated diet of such foodstuffs ultimately led to serious physical difficulties. Scurvy, the most prevalent of the diseases found among seamen, was thought to originate from people's exposure to highly salted provisions and bad water. In fact, the main cause of scurvy was a deficiency of vitamin C, for which people could compensate by adding fresh vegetables and fruits to their diet.

Scurvy was a terribly disabling affliction. If neglected, it could, and did, cause death. William Hutchinson experienced the ravages of the disease in 1739 and lived to write about it in great detail only because his ship reached a port where fresh provisions could be bought in time. His troubles began after breakfast, when he experienced chest pains. He, as well as many others, was relegated to his hammock. As Hutchinson put it, "my armpits and hams grew black . . . and I pined away to a weak, helpless condition, with my teeth all loose, and my upper and lower gums swelled and clotted together like a jelly, and they bled to that degree, that I was obliged to lie with my mouth hanging over the side of my hammock, to let the blood run out, and to keep it from [choking] me." He later attributed his survival to the acquisition of fresh supplies and herbal remedies.

In 1747, James Lind experimented with a dozen scurvy victims by giving pairs of men different remedies in an attempt to discover a cure. He reported his findings to the admiralty in 1753:

The most sudden and good effects were perceived from the use of the oranges and lemons; one of those who had taken them . . . became quite healthy. . . . The other [man given oranges and lemons] was the best recovered of any in his condition.

Based in part on these discoveries, the admiralty began to issue bushels of malt in hogsheads, portable soup, and some lemons to vessels proceeding on long voyages. In 1768, Captain James Cook made a report of the efficacy of these remedies:

The ship's company had in general been very healthy owing in great measure to sour krout [sic], portable soup and malt. . . . By this means, and the care and vigilance of . . . the surgeon, this disease was prevented from getting a footing in the ship.

In 1775, Admiral Samuel Graves noted that "the seamen always continue healthy and active when drinking spruce beer; but in a few days after New England Rum is served, . . . the hospital is crowded with sick."

 Snapshot

Deaths at Sea during the Revolutionary and Napoleonic Wars

During the period between 1793 and 1815, Europe was at war, and naval fleets sailed the seas searching for prey. Yet 80 percent of the 100,000 deaths aboard ship resulted from disease or accident. That is to say, 80,000 sailors succumbed to noncombat hazards. Only 7 percent of deaths were due to actual fighting. (Lavery, 201)

The efforts made by mariners to solve the problem of scurvy should not be minimized. The true cause of the disease was unknown at the time, and the sciences of nutrition and medicine, as we know them, were in their most formative stages. Using a method of trial and error, seamen found a series of remedies that exhibited a wide spectrum of efficacy in the prevention of scurvy. Only those high in vitamin C—a nutrient that was unknown at the time—could produce a cure. Fresh vegetables, potatoes, oranges, lemons, vinegar (in the sauerkraut), mashes made from grains, fruit wines, and small beers made from the young buds of spruce trees provided this essential vitamin. With time, lemon juice and the more palatable lime juice became the focus of those whose responsibility it was to maintain the health of crews at sea (Volo and Volo, 104, 106–7, 124–26, 156).

FOR MORE INFORMATION

Carpenter, K. J. *The History of Scurvy and Vitamin C.* Cambridge, England: Cambridge University Press, 1986.

Lavery, B. *The Arming and Fitting of English Ships of War, 1600–1815.* London: Conway Maritime Press, 1987.

Volo, D. D., and J. M. Volo. *Daily Life in the Age of Sail.* Westport, Conn.: Greenwood Press, 2002.

INTELLECTUAL LIFE: WEB SITES

http://library.upenn.edu/exhibits/rbm/kislak/colonial/colonial/.htm
http://web.uvic.ca/shakespeare/
http://www.hyperhistory.com/online_n2/History_n2/a.html
http://www.art-and-archaeology.com/timelines/japan/edo.html
http://www.columbia.edu/cu/lweb/indiv/africa/cuvl/SciTech.html
http://www.clas.ufl.edu/users/gthursby/taoism/iching.htm

5

MATERIAL LIFE

Material life describes all the things we use, from the houses that give us shelter to the food and drink that sustain us, from the clothes that protect us to the vehicles that transport us from one location to another. Even cities fall under the category of material life insofar as they are physical objects that we use, albeit on a large scale. At the same time, studying material life is fascinating in its details. We learn that handkerchiefs were a luxury in 16th-century Europe, designed to set the wealthy apart from the peasant who used a hat or sleeve, or that underwear was only widely adopted in Europe in the 18th century.

In this volume, which roughly covers the years from 1600 to 1800, the material lives of Africans south of the Sahara, the inhabitants of colonial Australia, natives and settlers of North America's colonies (including New England), English, French, Japanese, and sailors on the open seas are treated according to their variations, points of intersection, and curious parallels. One can discover the main seasonings that colonists in New France and on British America's frontiers used or learn about the different types of oceangoing vessels that plied the high seas during the 17th and 18th centuries. One can compare and contrast the styles of clothing that men and women, as well as boys and girls, wore in New England with those worn by people on the outlying frontier settlements.

Aside from the delicious details like these that bring the past to life, the study of material life reveals much about society as a whole. For example, cultures that rely on rice as a major staple have to invest a great deal of labor into its cultivation, whereas societies that thrive on corn (maize), which is not labor intensive, have ample spare time. This distinction, which is evident from the entries on food in Africa, Japan, and North America, reflects the extent to which material concerns such as food carry over into economic concerns such as agriculture. People who had access to raw materials, such as iron ore, developed in ways different from those that did not, and groups that possessed domesticated animals or large plows relied on organizing principles that were different from other peoples'. If we know what a culture uses in its material life and even in its cities, then we know a great deal about those people's lives in other categories of existence.

As we study material life, it is also important to remember that humans want much more than the bare necessities of life. Indeed, we are creatures of desire rather than need, and this longing has fueled much of the progress in the world. We want spices to flavor our food, not just nourishment; we want gold to adorn us as much as we want clothing to cover us. Cultures (as in the West) in which people have acquired a taste for change in fashion transform themselves (not necessarily for the better) in all areas much more rapidly than those (as in Asia) in which people have preferred a more conservative approach to clothing. All in all, the details of our daily life matter. From the Stone Age, when humans adorned themselves with cowrie shells as they wielded stone tools, to the modern world shaped by high technology, humans have been defined by the things that we have used. Our material life reveals and shapes who we are.

~*Joyce E. Salisbury and Peter Seelig*

FOR MORE INFORMATION

Braudel, F. *The Structures of Everyday Life*. New York: Harper and Row, 1979.
Diamond, J. *Guns, Germs, and Steel*. New York: Norton, 1997.

MATERIAL LIFE
|
FOOD
|
Africa

Colonial Australia

The Colonial Frontier
of North America

England

Japan

New England

Life at Sea

Food

Any casual reference to food typically brings to mind a means whereby people find satisfaction or contentment; that is, one who eats does so in an attempt to experience the pleasures that a meal can offer—tastes, textures, colors, and the whole ritual of eating, itself. A preoccupation with food as a source of pleasure held true in the 17th and 18th centuries in various cultures around the globe. However, the availability of sufficient amounts of food was by no means assured in places such as sub-Saharan Africa, colonial Australia, North America's colonial frontiers, England, Japan, and New England, as well as aboard ships. Nor was good-tasting food to be expected. Still, a great variety of ingredients and cooking styles combined with social customs to form a wide range of fare that would satisfy most anybody's tastes.

Nowhere else did meals during this period display their variety than in their ingredients. Meats, vegetables, fruits, grains, seasonings, and sweeteners were prepared in various combinations and proportions. People ate meat in every culture discussed in this volume, although the Buddhist proscription against the eating of animals diminished the Japanese consumption of meat, which nevertheless included insects and worms. The Shona in the south of Africa ate beef, caterpillars, and ants; 18th-century English took pride in their love of beef but were also known to dine on all kinds of meat, including turtle and pigeon. Turkeys, goats, cows, and pigs furnished North American settlers with a source of protein, as did fish and seafood. Early colonists in Australia were, at times, forced to consume kangaroo, although they often would have preferred more traditional meats.

Vegetables and fruits were as diverse as they were important to the diets of many societies. Yams constituted the staple food in the diet of West Africans. Sweet potatoes played a key role in the lives of Japanese peasants; bananas in the African

Great Lakes region; plums, cherries, and apples for colonial New Englanders; and raisins and figs for English puddings and cakes. All these ingredients helped to diversify the taste and nutritional value of meals.

Grains were of immense importance. Polished (white) rice accompanied the meals of city folks and the well-off in Japan, whereas peasants and poorer people consumed wheat, barley, and millet. The same distinction held true in England, where the wealthy preferred white bread to whole wheat, rye, barley, oats, and mixed grains. A certain social stigma restricted these coarser and more nutritious grains to the masses. An unappetizing mixture of flour, salt, and water—baked until as hard as a brick—constituted the chief food for European and American sailors aboard ship.

Seasonings and sweeteners were common in Africa. In West Africa, palm oil lent a distinctive taste to vegetables and meats. The Maasai considered honey to be one of the five food groups (the other four being meat, milk, tree bark, and blood). For the English of the 18th century, trade and colonial ventures resulted in a medley of fragrant, mouthwatering spices and herbs, among which can be counted ginger, nutmeg, cinnamon, and teas. Also, cane sugar and honey pleased many a sweet tooth throughout the island. During their voyages, sailors received fixed portions of molasses, which was a relatively cheap sweetener that settlers in North America also used alongside the native supply of maple syrup. Japanese were extremely experimental when it came to seasoning dishes, adding to them flakes of dried fish; herbs such as fennel, dill, and anise; and vegetables. Australian colonists seasoned their dishes with foods such as parsley, celery, and sarsaparilla, which were native to the region.

The preparation of foods involved cooking styles, fermentation, and preservation. Everywhere, cooks variously boiled, baked, roasted, fried, and steamed foods. Fermentation, in particular, was common in Africa (yams and bananas), England and colonial New England (baked breads), and Japan (the bean paste called *miso*). Finally, food preservation was exceptionally important for cultures that did not have access to nature's bounties year-round. Ships' crews ate salted beef and pork. Colonists in North America, before smoking the meat of wild game, steeped it in brine. Native Americans dried and salted meat, fish, roots, and corn for the winter months, a process also common in early modern Japan.

Both the number and types of meals available differed from culture to culture and also from one class to the next within a given culture. Sailors ate breakfast at 8:00 A.M., dinner (lunch) at noon, and supper at 5:00 P.M. An approximate sequence held true in England and in colonial New England, where dinner, which was sometimes served in the afternoon, was the large, significant meal of the day. In England, the wealthier that one was, the later that one dined. In Japan, peasants traditionally ate two meals per day, whereas urbanites and those of means ate three. Clearly, the culture of food was central to daily life in all these regions.

~Peter Seelig

FOR MORE INFORMATION

Fernández-Armesto, F. *Near a Thousand Tables: A History of Food.* New York: Free Press, 2002.

AFRICA

Food is a basic human need, but in Africa, it can be much more. Eating and drinking form an important part of life's daily rituals, whether these involve talking to friends or showing courtesy to guests. Food was not merely sustenance but also a means by which people formed and maintained relationships. Grain, fruits, and vegetables were staples; meats sometimes a luxury. Most Africans grew their food locally; however, kola nuts became an important item in long-distance trade. To the south, the San peoples had an economy based on hunting and gathering, supplemented in some areas by exchange with farmers. When food became scarce, as it did in East Africa during the early 17th century, it could alter the entire social structure.

In the forests of West Africa, yams formed the cornerstone of people's diet, although its lack of proteins, vitamins, and minerals meant that it needed supplementing with meat and leafy vegetables. The harvested yams were soaked in a pot, ground into paste, and then collected into bags in which they were left to ferment under the sun for one full day. The fermented yams were then boiled and strained before becoming a family's morning porridge. The same batch of yams reappeared throughout the day as stew. Yams that were kneaded into dough and rolled into balls were placed in a seasoned mixture of palm oil, seeds, and green vegetables (July, 113–14).

Africans used the palm not only to season food but for drink as well. Two types of palm trees grew in the forests of Africa: a raffia palm in the swampy areas, which flowered once after 7 to 10 years and then died, and an oil palm in drier regions. Palm wine came from the sap and was acquired by cutting off a tree's inflorescence and inserting a draining tube that emptied into a gourd below. The Lele of Congo drank palm wine from a special double-headed cup that allowed the wine to pass between the two heads. At the end of the day, the men would gather together on the outskirts of a village to discuss events, each toting his own cup tied to his loincloth through the handle (Mack, 159).

The kola nut was an important food item that was also an important trade good. Gathered along the Guinea coast, they were used throughout much of the continent as an addictive stimulant, being very rich in caffeine. Workers chewed on kola nuts to keep up their energy. In West Africa, the nuts also held important social significance as an offering to invited guests or as a pledge of political allegiance. When people entertained, the guests were first given water, followed by kola nuts. The nuts were also distributed to all guests present at a birth celebration or funeral.

In the southern part of the continent, the San found food by hunting and gathering. They traveled in kinship bands of not more than 100 people within a given area and collected roots, plants, insects, game, and fish. In areas where they had contact with farmers, the San made deals in which the farmers gave them milk, grain, and pots in exchange for meat. The San were also known to carry water in ostrich eggshells, each of which held one liter. Women prepared these by drilling a hole in the shell, shaking out the inside of the egg, rinsing and deodorizing the shell with aromatic herbs, and making a small grass stopper. Sometimes these eggs were buried in areas of little water and then dug up when needed (Mack, 180).

The food that came from hunting was an important cultural symbol throughout Africa, and many African folktales have a hunter as a hero. In East Africa, oral traditions of the kingdom of Shambaa tell of a hunter named Mbegha who came from far away and killed wild pigs that were uprooting the crops. He then gave the meat to the people, who made him their king. This tale reveals how the ritual importance of eating in African culture functioned to bind people together. Ritual meals also formed a vital part of many traditional festivals, with presentations of food to symbolize social obligations. Eating rituals also involved ancestors, as in Madagascar, where people kept spoons in the northeast corner of their houses along with other ritual objects. The Malagasy used special spoons for eating at rituals that involved links between the living and their ancestors, such as the building of a new house or grave.

The Maasai, also from East Africa, ate five different things: meat, milk, blood, tree bark, and honey. Specialties of Zanzibar included curry, fish, octopus, and sugar juice. In the Great Lakes region, the diet revolved around bananas, which were used to make everything from starchy pastes to beer. In the south, Shona meals consisted of beef, caterpillars, ants, fruit, mushrooms, and grain, among other things. Methods of food preparation included boiling, grilling over a fire, and cooking on stones near a fire. The Shona also used grain to make beer. Some areas of Africa brewed beer from corn or sorghum, as well.

Despite the continent's plenty, famine remained a danger for many parts of Africa. During the 16th and 17th centuries, the Great Lakes and East Africa experienced severe food shortages, including the Great Famine of 1617–21, at the end of which the Nile reached its lowest peak since records were first kept in 622 c.e. That famine also saw a disease that completely destroyed the cattle herds. People in northern Uganda called this period *Nyarubanga*, or "sent by God," because it was the worst disaster in their history. Because of this catastrophe, the early 17th century became an era of migrations and is regarded as the starting point for the oral traditions of the peoples that were formed from those migrations. The Niger Bend area also experienced a severe famine from 1738 until 1796. In the south, the Shona fought famine through a process called *mukomondera*, wherein someone borrowed grain and repaid it without interest during the next good harvest. The Shona also sometimes traded daughters for food (Ogot, 781–89).

Africans ate a few staple crops, which differed throughout the continent, and used these crops in a variety of ways to make food. In addition, eating formed an important part of the rituals of everyday life. Most food was acquired by farming, but hunting and gathering were also common. Africans used the resources of their environment to improve the production and storage of their food, often in innovative ways. Most important, they adapted to their circumstances in times of food shortage, leading to new traditions and ways of living.

~Brian Ulrich

FOR MORE INFORMATION

Halsall, P., ed. *Internet African History Sourcebook.* 1996. <http://www.fordham.edu/halsall/africa/africasbook.html>, accessed October 23, 2003.

July, R. W. *A History of the African People.* 5th ed. Prospect Heights, Ill.: Waveland Press, 1998.

Mack, J., ed. *Africa: Arts and Cultures.* New York: Oxford University Press, 2000.

Ogot, B. A., ed. *General History of Africa.* Vol. 5. *Africa from the Sixteenth Century to the Eighteenth Century.* Paris: United Nations Educational, Scientific, and Cultural Organization, 1992.

COLONIAL AUSTRALIA

In May 1788, British marine captain Watkin Tench, who sailed to Australia, wrote in his journal that "fresh provisions were becoming scarcer than in a blockaded town" (Tench, 65). In effect, the European newcomers to Australia were blockaded—by water on one side and mountains on the other—and the quest for nourishment was a continuing dilemma during the colony's foundation years.

The settlers ignored the indigenous diet in favor of their frequently futile attempts to grow familiar English food. Aborigines were hunter-gatherers who nourished themselves with fish and animals, which were supplemented with native fruits, seeds, and roots. Consequently, the newcomers assumed that because the Aborigines did not cultivate land, they could teach Europeans little about sustenance.

On the outward voyage, pease pudding, which was a mash of split peas that were soaked and boiled, was a staple, but it lacked sufficient nutrition. In the absence of fresh vegetables, many early settlers quickly succumbed to the debilitating effects of scurvy and dysentery. It was at this point that the colonists discovered the nutritional and medicinal value of native plants such as parsley, celery, and the sarsaparilla leaf.

Although the First Fleet arrived in January 1788 with livestock and poultry, many of the animals either perished on the meager grass feed or soon strayed beyond reach. In June, a convict herdsman allowed the cattle to escape, ruining the colonists' chances of a meat and manure supply. The cattle were not found, nor was there any replacement stock for four years. Tench rated the chances of the colony's capacity to raise cattle for meat as "chimerical and absurd" (Tench, 80).

When the first crops in Farm Cove failed, orders were given for everyone to establish vegetable plots and to seek fresh meat from local birds and animals, although few of the mostly former urban dwellers possessed hunting skills. Maize (Indian corn) was preferred to flour, and being easier to grow, it was used for bread.

The first (weekly) ration for adult males was meat and bread, seven pounds each; peas, three pints; butter, six ounces; and rice or flour, one-half pound. Women received two-thirds of a man's ration, and children received one-third. Because of the precarious nature of supply, colonial leaders intermittently rationed food and reduced working hours to preserve energy. Even the fortunate few who were invited to dine with Governor Phillip were asked to bring their own bread.

When faced with the real and grim prospect of starvation, colonial leaders became increasingly severe in their punishments of food theft. In September 1789, the supply ship *Guardian* hit an iceberg en route from England, losing its cargo, and famine loomed by February of the following year. Another 200 settlers were sent to Norfolk Island. After the wreck of *Sirius* there in March, the possibility of starvation again arose. The settlers survived on petrel birds, hunting them to near extinction. In Port Jackson, rations were again reduced "without distinction" to "four pounds of flour, two pounds and a half of salt pork, and one pound and a half of rice, per week" (Tench, 121). Only a few months' supplies remained, so all boats were pressed into fishing. The number of kangaroo hunts mounted, although its meat was not favored by the colonial palate. Those in Van Diemen's Land (established 1803; now Tasmania) fared better due to their willingness to consume kangaroo and emu.

The colony hovered on the brink of starvation until the arrival of the Second Fleet in June 1790. Unfortunately, although it brought provisions, it also brought more than 700 new mouths to feed. By November, the colony was again facing hunger and further rationing. In December 1791, Tench expressed anxieties over news of war between England and Spain, dreading the capture of supplies destined for Sydney. He also wrote of some soldiers copying the Aboriginal practice of pulling a ligature tightly around one's belly in order to inhibit the effects of hunger. As a result of a limited turn of fortunes, those on Norfolk Island could during the following year enjoy potatoes, cabbages, bananas, pears, apples, oranges, and strawberries while those in Port Jackson still went hungry.

Despite the colony's food difficulties, successful farming was eventually established, and with regular and reliable imported provisions, a new arrival to the settlement could, in 1810, boast of dining on "all the luxury and elegance of the finest tables" (Symons, 20).

To read about food among Aboriginal Australians, see the Australian Aboriginals entry in the section "Food" in chapter 5 ("Material Life") of volume 1 of this series.

~*Valda Rigg*

FOR MORE INFORMATION

Gollan, A. *Tradition of Australian Cooking*. Canberra: Australian National University Press, 1978.

Historic Houses Trust of New South Wales. *Colonial Food and Drink 1788–1901*. Exhibition Catalogue. Sydney: Craft Wentworth, 1985.

Pearn, J., and C. O'Carrigan. *Australia's Quest for Colonial Health*. Brisbane, Queensland: Department of Child Health, Royal Children's Hospital, 1983.

Symons, M. *One Continuous Picnic: A History of Eating in Australia*. Adelaide, South Australia: Duck Press, 1982.

Tench, W. *1788: Comprising A Narrative of the Expedition to Botany Bay [1789] and A Complete Account of the Settlement at Port Jackson [1795]*. Edited by Tim Flannery. Melbourne: Text Publishing, 1996.

THE COLONIAL FRONTIER OF NORTH AMERICA

The earliest colonists ate the same food in much the same manner as the Indians who taught them, but as time went on, the settlers learned to adapt the natural foods of the area to their traditional ways of cooking.

The settlers' average diet consisted of boiled, stewed, or steamed meats and fish, peas, cornmeal cakes and puddings, and wild berries. Peas were boiled or baked, eaten hot or cold, and could be expected at any meal including breakfast. Settlers learned to cultivate native crops, especially pumpkins, squash, and melons. They eventually planted fruit trees and cultivated vegetable gardens of a wider variety. The gardens were close to the house and commonly planted in raised beds.

Settlers learned to appreciate the bounty that was theirs for the gathering. Watercress, wild leeks, milkweed shoots, and dandelions were boiled with wild game, as were chestnuts, hickories, butternuts, walnuts, and acorns. Sugar maples yielded sap, which was made into sugar, candy, and syrup. The bounteous amounts of grapes, gooseberries, cranberries, currants, blueberries, strawberries, raspberries, and blackberries were enjoyed fresh in season and made into tarts.

A typical breakfast included toasted bread, cheese, and any leftover meat or vegetables from the previous day. In summer, milk often accompanied the meal. Dinner (lunch) was the main meal of the day, and it would have made the most of the season's offerings. A heavy pudding stuffed into a cloth bag would steam over vegetables and meat, or meat with fresh or dried vegetables would be boiled in water. Supper, too, was a simple affair.

Menus reflected the season's bounty. While spring brought reassurance of nature's renewal and promised the bounty of the harvest, it was the least generous of all the seasons. Spring provided little in the way of fresh produce, and stores put away in the fall were greatly depleted by this time. In summer, a family could dine on leek soup and garden greens. For a fall dinner, they sometimes feasted on recently slaughtered pig or goose meat with apples. In winter, sauces and produce that had been preserved from the harvest rendered standard fare such as boiled meats more appealing.

What was available to a family in the winter and spring depended on a wife's careful preservation of their excess harvest. Food was stockpiled in a variety of ways. Vegetables such as beets, cabbage, carrots, onions, parsnips, potatoes, radishes, turnips, and winter squash were stored in root cellars where the climate allowed. Other vegetables such as corn, beans, and peas were dried and used in cooking. Colonists preserved green corn by turning back the husk (leaving only the last, very thin layer) and then hanging it in the sun or a warm room to dry. When it was needed for cooking, it was parboiled and cut from the cob. String beans, squash, apples, and pumpkin were strung on thread and hung to dry. Cabbage was made into sauerkraut. Colonists could also preserve vegetables and fruits by making them into pureed sauces.

Fall was the time for slaughtering. While the men typically dispatched the larger animals, housewives often slaughtered smaller pigs, which were easier to keep than other livestock because they could be fed on most anything. Pork could be easily preserved in a number of ways, such as pickling, salting, and smoking. Much of the pork would have been jarred in a solution of brine and stored in the dairy, where the temperature was generally cooler. Some of the pork was also preserved as bacon. The slabs would be salted in tubs for several weeks in early winter before being hung in the chimney for smoking.

Baking became an important skill and was traditionally done one day a week. Some homes had exterior, freestanding bake ovens that were protected by a small wooden roof and open-sided structure. Other homes had ovens built into the fireplace. If a house had no oven, baking was done in iron kettles.

A housewife planted a variety of herbs in her garden. Herbs were among the first things planted. Parsley, skirret, and sorrel were harvested for "sallets." Cooked and served hot or cold, with an oil and vinegar dressing, they accompanied many dishes. Herbs also had tremendous value as seasonings for meats that had been heavily salted. Early records and seed lists provide insight into what colonists considered to be essential herbs. In 1631, John Winthrop, Jr., ordered seeds for angelica, basil, burnet, dill, fennel, hyssop, marjoram, parsley, rosemary, savory, thyme, and tansy.

Both Native American cuisine and the foods that were native to North America heavily influenced the cooking habits of settlers. Necessity and a genuine appreciation for these foods shaped the seasonal preservation, preparation, and consumption of all manner of vegetables, meats, breads, and seasonings (Volo and Volo, 149–52).

FOR MORE INFORMATION

Kavasch, E. B. *Native Harvest: Recipes and Botanicals of the American Indian*. New York: Random House, 1979.

Root, W. L. *Eating in America: A History*. New York: Morrow, 1976.

Volo, J. M., and D. D. Volo. *Daily Life on the Old Colonial Frontier*. Westport, Conn.: Greenwood Press, 2002.

ENGLAND

Roast beef, simply prepared, and in great quantities, was indeed the quintessential British dish. However, if one were blessed with sufficient wealth, one could take pleasure in a wide assortment of ingredients and dishes. Cooking, too, became easier thanks to the useful guidance of step-by-step recipes found in cookbooks. Still, food was, for most English in the 18th century, the largest portion of the budget, absorbing (along with drink) about two-thirds of the family income. In hard times, those who were struggling would neglect meat and vegetables in favor of more bread. It is therefore not surprising that the character of one's diet depended on one's economic status. Eating habits varied greatly in relation to one's class, work, and location.

The English were devoted to beef eating. A club was established to this national pastime in 1735, and songs were written about the glories of beef. Yet beef, while often consumed, was by no means a universal part of the English diet. Expanding trade brought new items to the table or reduced the price of old ones: pineapples, curries, ginger, molasses, cinnamon, macaroni, figs, pistachio nuts, rum, cocoa, rice, tea, coffee, pepper, sugar, olives, anchovies, Parmesan cheese, almonds, and peacocks. There were plenty of homegrown ingredients, as well. One of the century's most popular cookbooks, Hannah Glasse's *The Art of Cookery Made Plain and Easy*, lists more than 160 different ingredients organized according to the months in which they are in season.

The first chapter of Glasse's cookbook, on shopping, brings to life a world in which adulterated bread and milk, spoiled meat, and vegetables contaminated by "night soil" (human waste) were commonplace. Her admonitions to shoppers make it clear that butchers often substituted one animal for another, cheap cuts for expensive ones, and spoiled meat for fresh.

The preparation of food was also more hands-on. Glasse's instructions for roasting a pig begin with how to kill it: "Stick your pig just above the breast-bone, run your knife to the heart." They continue with how to clean, de-hair, gut, and dry the carcass. Because few prepared foods were available, cookbooks included information on pickling, preserving, brewing, and fermenting.

Cookbook instructions were rather imprecise. Ingredients are often given in vague terms—"a handful," "a little," "a lump." Other differences are more startling. The limitations of the kitchen fire made broiling and boiling far easier than baking; a recipe for "Pigeons Transmogrified," therefore, calls for the birds to be seasoned with salt and pepper, wrapped in puff pastry, then in cloth, and boiled for an hour and a half. Glasse gives nine animal-head recipes, including the particularly ominous-sounding "calf's head surprize."

People of both great and small means treated themselves to special foods. Street and fair vendors sold gingerbread, cheesecakes, nuts, oysters, shrimp oranges, and pig-shaped pastries with currant-filled bellies and currants for eyes. Children were fond of raisins, cakes, sugarplums, figs, and pudding. An 18th-century pudding was not what modern Americans would call pudding; it was instead a conglomeration of suet, flour, dried fruit, and spices, all wrapped in a cloth and boiled.

Most of the laboring diet was bread. All classes preferred white bread, but those people who could not afford white flour grudgingly ate bread of whole wheat, rye, barley, or maslin (a mixture of grains). In Scotland and the northern English counties, such as Lancashire and Yorkshire, oatmeal often replaced bread. Other staples of the laboring diet were cheese, treacle (molasses, used as a cheap alternative to sugar), greens from the garden or market, potatoes, dumplings, broths, and stews. Laborers rarely consumed eggs and milk. Although there was very little actual famine in England, especially compared with continental Europe, hunger and poor nutrition were certainly common enough.

Artisans, merchants, shopkeepers, prosperous farmers, and members of the professions, who could expect more variety and bounty in their diet, would have eaten all the foods found in poorer households, plus oatcakes and mutton. A middle-class breakfast, eaten at about 8:00 a.m., would have included tea with sugar, coffee, hot chocolate, and buttered bread toasted over the fire.

Dinner, served at about 2:00 or 3:00 P.M., was the principal meal and might last several hours on festive occasions. It featured several dishes, including a choice of meats, meat pies, soups, vegetables, fish, salad, jellies, and in more affluent households, fruit. On March 6, 1795, Parson Woodforde ate "for Dinner a Couple of boiled Chicken and Pigs Face, very good Peas Soup, a boiled Rump of Beef very fine, a prodigious fine, large and very fat Cock-Turkey roasted, Maccaroni, [and] Batter Custard Pudding." All who could afford to do so ate voraciously. After dinner, in genteel households, the women retired from the room, while the men remained in the dining room to smoke pipes and drink heavily.

Late in the afternoon, people stopped to take tea, a practice that, in the 20th century, developed into a separate meal. It consisted chiefly of tea and hot rolls or muffins. Supper, eaten shortly before retiring, was a light meal of cold meats, boiled eggs, salad, or other simple fare.

The rich ate all their meals at later hours, and they ate more food, better cuts of meat, and sometimes more complex, French-influenced dishes. An upper-class dinner could feature venison, ham, turkey, cod, pigeons, lobster, sweetbreads, crab, pheasant, turtle, turbot, duck, or salmon, as well as the ubiquitous chicken and beef. There might also be root vegetables, asparagus, tarts, jellies, fruit pies, cheesecakes, out-of-season fruit, cream, sweetmeats, truffles, and copious and varied alcoholic beverages. The rich could also afford more spices, and they began to hire French or French-influenced cooks to create showy dishes.

Some people, chiefly travelers and unmarried men, chose to eat away from home at pubs, inns, taverns, coffeehouses, shops, tea gardens, and full-fledged restaurants, including Dolly's Beefsteak House. Travelers at coaching inns could not expect anything fancy—cold meats, salads, cheese, wine, punch, and eggs were standard fare. City taverns and coffeehouses were the resort of single men, professionals conducting business, club members, and literary types such as Sir Richard Steele, who wrote to his wife from a tavern that he would join her "within half a bottle of wine."

Glasse's cookbook gives an interesting, but limited, view of English eating habits in the 18th century. Sumptuous meals consisting of varied and exotic ingredients were by no means a universal staple of the English diet. Poverty and scarcity not only prevented many people from eating well but also kept them periodically or even perpetually malnourished. Food and diet were a reliable indicator of economic status (Olsen, 199, 231–37).

To read about food in Chaucer's England, see the Europe entry in the section "Food" in chapter 5 ("Material Life") of volume 2; for Elizabethan England, see the England entry in the section "Food and Drink" in chapter 5 ("Material Life") of volume 3; and for Victorian England, see the Victorian England entry in the section "Food" in chapter 5 ("Material Life") of volume 5 of this series.

FOR MORE INFORMATION

Lynch, J. *Eighteenth Century Resources*. <http://newark.rutgers.edu/~jlynch/18th/>, accessed October 10, 2003.

Olsen, K. *Daily Life in 18th-Century England*. Westport, Conn.: Greenwood Press, 1999.

Wilson, C. A. *Food and Drink in Britain: From the Stone Age to Recent Times*. New York: Barnes and Noble, 1974.

JAPAN

Japan developed as distinctive a cuisine as can be found anywhere in the world. Tastes and culinary conventions would, with the second coming of the West, change rapidly after the mid-19th century; so, 18th-century tastes are arguably said to be the most "natively" and distinctively Japanese. Profiting from culinary imagination, Japanese integrated a number of grains, herbs, fish, roots, beans, oils, and preserved foodstuff into aesthetically pleasing cooking styles.

Traditionally, Japanese did not eat much meat. Most historians argue that the traditional Buddhist proscription against killing and eating animals is responsible for this lack of animal protein in the Japanese diet.

Nevertheless, in the 18th century, Japanese ate an astounding variety of foods. Virtually every specimen of flora and fauna had been tried and every method of preparation considered, not withstanding grasshoppers, crickets, grubs, worms, and other insects.

Given Japan's obsession with rice, one might be surprised to find that in the 18th century, it was not a food staple for more than half of the population. Most peasants could not afford to eat it, at least not in its most costly form: "polished" sticky white rice. The Tokugawa *bakufu* (national military government) enjoined peasants to eat the "lesser" grains of wheat, millet, and barley and thus to reserve the rice for their social betters.

When it was available, rice was steamed and consumed. Rice was also ground into flour, which could be used to make all manner of things including rice crackers, grilled hard bread, steamed or boiled dumplings, and noodles. Pounded rice cakes (*mochi*) were a great treat, particularly in soups and as a snack at *matsuri* (festivals).

Most peasants cooked wheat, barley, and millet in one-pot gruels and porridges, spicing them up with herbs, vegetables, dried fish, and whatever else was available and seemed tasty. Many fruits, berries, nuts, beans, edible grasses, tubers, and legumes were also popular, as were herbs and spices such as fennel, dill, anise, parsley, cayenne pepper, ginger, marjoram, and sage.

Probably the most miraculous vegetable was the sweet potato. The tuber root was very high in carbohydrates and could be stored for very long periods without serious spoilage. The judicious use of sweet potato gruels mixed with straw, grass, bark, roots, and virtually every vegetable kept peasants alive.

Japanese did wonderful things with beans and other legumes. "Green" legumes such as peas, snap beans, sugar pods, snow peas, and the like were cooked and eaten right along with their pods and husks. Others were shucked, dried, and cooked later.

To prepare tofu, Japanese boiled beans and skimmed off the froth, which was then allowed to congeal. The amorphous rubbery substance was cut into slabs and eaten plain, in soups, or with sauces, vegetables, and spices added.

For miso, cooks boiled beans for several hours, mixed them with salt and wheat malt, and then allowed the combination to ferment in wooden vats for months. The decomposed grit could be formed into a thick paste, which was then diluted in small amounts with water into the salty, cloudy soup that is familiar to most diners in Japanese restaurants today.

Japanese extracted a number of vegetable oils that they used to good effect. Sesame, safflower, rapeseed, and various nuts produced an ample supply of cooking oil, much of which could be used to fuel lamps, as well. Peasants did not use much oil to cook; most things were roasted or boiled. In the cities, sautés and grilling employed considerably more oil.

As a rule, most peasants ate only two meals a day. Most *chōnin* (city folk), who presumably worked at home, could therefore eat lunch. Samurai (warrior-administrators) were said to eat two meals daily, like peasants, but from the evidence, they routinely ate three when traveling. The typical meal was said to be *ichiju-issai*—one soup, one vegetable—but this in fact referred to the side dishes accompanying rice or the other main course. The soup was ordinarily clear broth or miso. A few flecks of dried bonito (a type of fish) shavings, a piece of tofu, a shard of seaweed, a swirl of egg, or other flavoring might swim in the soup, but even then it was 99 percent water. The vegetable might very well be a freshly cooked beet, carrot, sweet potato, or one of Japan's myriad "greens," but more likely, it was a pickled vegetable.

Food for the *chōnin* and lower samurai classes was not altogether different than for their peasant cousins, except that there was a great deal more available for the city folk. Because the *bakufu* and daimyō (feudal warlords) feared that their armed samurai might rise in rebellion if deprived of food, most cities fared rather better than the countryside in times of want and famine. Demographers suggest that *chōnin* and samurai probably consumed half again as many daily calories as the peasants. City folk also ate dramatically more protein.

Pickling, salting, or desiccating in Japan preserved virtually every foodstuff. The intent was to save the food for a time when the product would be otherwise unavailable. All sorts of vegetable matter were chopped and sliced into bite-size pieces and then steeped in brine or vinegar for months. Various spices, herbs, and seasonings enhanced the flavor of the pickles (*tsukemono*). Every 18th-century farmhouse contained a *tsukemono* barrel. A few pickles accompanied virtually every meal, and it was this food that constituted the vegetable in the traditional *ichiju-issai* meal.

Many foods were preserved in salt also. Most of these were marine products, but there were nuts and vegetables as well. Fish were packed in salt or desiccated. The most common was bonito, which, when dried, would flake into bits to flavor soup and stews. In addition, scores of seaweed, kelp, and other ocean "grasses" were dried. Virtually everyone is familiar with the sheets of seaweed (*nori*) used to wrap a type of sushi (*nori-maki*), but a more common use was to cut it into strips for soup flavoring.

Most Japanese ate their meals at home. However, by the 18th century, there were literally hundreds of restaurants. It is estimated that one-quarter of the male population in Edo ate their daily lunch at noodle stands and shops, and many more dined out at least once a week on the way to the theater or brothel.

There were a number of specific cooking styles (*ryori*) that took on almost philosophical pretensions. The Buddhist vegetarian *shojin ryori* style, which was especially inventive in creating nutritious, savory dishes, probably was the most important method used throughout the country. Special delicacies like mochi, raw fish with vinegared rice (sushi and sashimi), and various stews, dumplings, and flavored sake (rice wine) were specific to annual celebrations.

Chopsticks (*hashi*) were the most basic and most important tool for eating. Very easy to make and to use, Japanese *hashi* were much shorter than Chinese chopsticks. Certain rules of etiquette governed a person's use of *hashi*. One was never to leave them stuck in a bowl of rice. One was never to gesture with or point the chopsticks at other people. Simple courtesy prevented people from dipping into a common dish without turning the *hashi* around to use the butt ends to fish out something.

All in all, Japanese in the 18th century had an astonishing number of flavorful foods available to them that helped to brighten up their otherwise drab diets. Most peasants rarely tasted fancy dishes except at *matsuri*. Rich peasants, travelers, and people who lived in the larger cities had thousands of such dishes to choose from (Perez, 71–75, 77–80, 82, 85, 195).

To read about food in Japan in the 20th century, see the Japan entry in the section "Food" in chapter 5 ("Material Life") of volume 6 of this series.

FOR MORE INFORMATION

Hanley, S. B. *Everyday Things in Premodern Japan: The Hidden Legacy of Material Culture.* Berkeley: University of California Press, 1997.

Ishige, N. *The History and Culture of Japanese Food.* London: Kegan Paul, 2001.

Japan Information Network. <http://www.jinjapan.org/index.html>, accessed October 23, 2003.

Perez, L. G. *Daily Life in Early Modern Japan.* Westport, Conn.: Greenwood Press, 2002.

NEW ENGLAND

Colonists had to abandon many of their favorite English and European dishes when they arrived in the New World. Local ingredients replaced traditional English ones, and the recipes of New Englanders, partially reflecting the cooking habits of Native Americans, took on a unique character of their own.

A Native American mother would begin the day by boiling water into which were placed the game she had skinned and dressed, as well as nuts, dried squash, or pumpkin from her storage baskets and bags. The family ate the morning soup using clamshells as scoops. Portions of this soup were available throughout the day, as family members felt hungry.

To preserve foods, Native Americans dried and salted wild meats, fish, pumpkin, and corn. These provisions were contained in baskets and bags and stored in the wigwam or buried underground for use in winter.

Vegetables were usually boiled in a large clay pot over a fire inside or outside the wigwam. Meats were boiled, broiled, or roasted over a fire. Breads and cakes, of which there was a large variety, were baked on the hearth or on fireproof green birch bark or clay containers suspended over open fires. Corn and wild rice were boiled.

Native women contrived seasonings and spices from roots and leaves gathered near the village. Salt was not a long-standing element in their diets, but sugar from the maple tree was widely used. The dishes that were original with the Native Americans included baked and boiled beans, pumpkin, and squash, succotash, bean soup, corn chowder, hominy, and corn on the cob. They also introduced berry cake and breads, chiefly of corn: cornbread, corn fritters, and johnnycake. But they also made breads from nuts, squash, and pumpkins.

Food played a critical role in the immediate survival of the European colonists who settled New England. In the case of the Plymouth Plantation, they arrived at Massachusetts in November, disembarking at Plymouth in December, when natural vegetation had already disappeared beneath the frost and when it was too late to plant. In addition, most of the supplies of the two-month voyage had spoiled.

Although New Englanders were obviously strongly habituated to the eating habits of England, the scarcity of all kinds of foods in New England forced the settlers to experiment with different ingredients that were native to the New World or that could be grown and processed there.

The colonists' situation on the Atlantic coast led them to a dependence on food from the sea. When they first landed, eels were a popular food because they were easily caught. Then cod became the mainstay. Settlers gradually added herring, bass, sturgeon, alewives, shad (a despised fish), and mackerel to their diets, as well as mussels, clams, and lobsters.

There was an abundance of wild game in the New World, including rabbit, venison, squirrels, bears, and raccoons. Wild birds, especially turkeys (some reportedly weighing 40 pounds), pigeons, and geese graced their tables as well. The game was skinned, gutted, soaked in brine for several weeks, smoked, and then hung in the attic for the winter.

Goats provided settlers with cheese and milk. Milk that was not immediately consumed was made into butter and cheese. Properly stored in a cool place, both could last for months without spoiling. Cheese quickly became a main part of the diet.

The ordinary settlers had to wait far too long to have the fine-textured wheat bread they cherished in England. So, bread was of necessity made of hardier grains such as corn, rye, and oats. Indian corn continued to be a chief source of grain. It was eaten fresh in season and dried, with some of it ground for use as a cereal or bread throughout the year.

In the New World, settlers found a plenitude of wild berries and other fruits and easily grew other varieties from imported seeds. Apples, pears, cherries, plums, and quinces were in good supply and complemented the winter diet, thanks to drying. Nuts grew wild and were a valuable food source. Vegetables such as turnips, parsnips, beans, pumpkins, and squash were frequent ingredients in colonial meals. And New Englanders had no shortage of sweeteners. The main sources were native, such as honey. Moreover, Native Americans instructed settlers in the art of tapping maple trees.

Many seasonings, including wild sage and dill, were available in the wild for adventuresome cooks, who learned from Native Americans how to use them. In port towns, those who were of means imported pepper, capers, cloves, cinnamon, other spices, ginger, olives, tea, and currants from England and the West Indies.

Meals were cooked in a large walk-in fireplace. Often, several fires were going in a single fireplace, for each dish had to have a different fire with which to cook the ingredients properly. The popularity of one-dish meals derived in part from the need for only one fire in the fireplace. Biscuits were cooked in a frying pan or placed directly on the hearth and covered by an upside-down pan buried under hot coals.

Breakfast came at a busy time of day in the New England household. The women were usually occupied with milking and other chores, so it was not convenient to prepare a cooked breakfast. This meal therefore consisted of foods that could be eaten without much preparation. A large breakfast included leftovers (such as meat from the previous day), bread, and cheese. The usual meager everyday breakfast was corn mush and milk.

Dinner came in early afternoon and was the most substantial meal of the day. The New England dinner was exclusively a one-pot dish: a leek soup, an eel pie, or a stew of pork and apples, for example. More often it was made of spoon-size pieces of boiled meat with a sauce of vegetables such as beans or peas. (Only in upper-class households were meat and vegetables cooked separately.) New Englanders had a great love for sweets, so the meal usually ended with a fruit pie. Supper was usually cornmeal mush and the juice from the day's dinner.

The settlers ate from what were called trenchers—carved wooden (usually poplar) bowls. Poor families usually ate from the same trencher. The only utensils were spoons and occasionally, knives. Forks did not make their way to New England until the late 17th century. As conditions and economics improved, settlers began to possess tableware made of pewter, horn, or silver. China became available in the 18th century.

Slaves' food differed little from that of the white master's family. Slaves ate very well in New England. Both slaves and servants in New England not only ate the same food provided for the master's table but also typically ate at the same table as the master, a custom so widespread as to cause comment on the part of travelers to New England who were unused to seeing servants eating with their betters.

From the establishment of Plymouth plantation, New England colonists developed a unique diet based on a mixture of Native American practices, European traditions, and the offerings of the New England environment. Fish and seafood, wild game, dairy products (particularly from goats), grain (often from corn), and indigenous fruits, vegetables, sweeteners (maple syrup and honey), and seasonings comprised the mainstay of breakfasts, dinners, and suppers for Native Americans, whites, and blacks in colonial New England (Johnson, 95, 98–102, 139, 141, 153).

FOR MORE INFORMATION

Johnson, C. D. *Daily Life in Colonial New England.* Westport, Conn.: Greenwood Press, 2002.

Kavasch, E. B. *Native Harvest: Recipes and Botanicals of the American Indian*. New York: Random House, 1979.

Root, W. L. *Eating in America: A History*. New York: Morrow, 1976.

LIFE AT SEA

Meals aboard ship varied in quality according to one's status. The provisioning of a vessel was of great importance. Sailors sometimes had a selection of foods to eat during mess, but the sea biscuit was the mainstay of meals. Still, food could serve the purposes of entertaining, especially among officers, their wives, and any guests. The success of these banquets, however, depended a good deal on the expertise of the cook.

When fitting a ship for sea, the captain (or master) was continually engaged in one business matter or another. One of the most important tasks was the purchase and storage of provisions for his crew for an extended voyage. The basic requirement was for food that, although not spoiling or otherwise losing its nutritive value, would yet provide the crew with sufficient calories and a balance of vitamins.

A mess consisted of six to eight men. The mess cook actually did no cooking, but he received the uncooked provisions, delivered them to the ship's cook, and retrieved them for his messmates.

The staple food for seamen throughout the Western Hemisphere was sea biscuit, or ship's bread, which was notorious for being virtually indestructible and resembling neither biscuit nor bread. Made with flour, a little salt, and just enough water to make a stiff dough, sea biscuit was baked into a four-by-four-inch rock-solid square about a half-inch thick. Sailors had to soak it to make it edible or nibble it about the edges. When the biscuit was poor, it was either too hard or moldy and wet. It was noted for being filled with weevils and maggots. One could evict these creatures by toasting the cracker or breaking it up into a mug of liquid and then skimming off the pests. Sea biscuit provided a good-quality ration when combined with other foods, and a man could exist on as few as three crackers a day.

When exiting a port, a ship could serve fresh meat and vegetables, a state of affairs that would last for two days. At this point, the seamen would consume sea rations, which typically consisted of fixed servings of biscuit (the equivalent of about nine crackers), four weekly servings of beef, three of pork, three of beans, two of rice, two of molasses and vinegar, and butter and cheese. With few exceptions, European navies maintained a dietary regimen similar to this throughout the period.

The provisions required for an extended voyage can be exemplified by those needed to prepare the *Bounty* for a solo 18-month voyage to the Pacific. The *Bounty*

While officers often dined in the captain's quarters, common seamen ate alongside the cannons where they worked all day. This mess table hangs from the ceiling, and the plates are securely stored in a wall cabinet. © National Maritime Museum.

was a ship-rigged, lightly armed transport of 230 tons. The captain, Lieutenant William Bligh, thought the ship was oversparred and too small for its crew of 46 men. The foodstuffs consisted largely of sea biscuit. Also brought aboard were casks of salt pork and salt beef, dried peas, malt, barley, wheat, oatmeal, and sauerkraut. Finally, some fancy foodstuffs were taken aboard for the officers. The carpenters built several small cages for livestock, such as a dozen chickens, a few pigs, and a half dozen sheep. Hard cheeses were brought aboard. Provisions were replaced at stops made during the voyage.

One of the more common diversions among sea officers was entertaining. Dinner at the captain's table offered an opportunity for the officers to share with their colleagues an appreciation for the good taste that each diner attempted to display in the sharing of food, wine, and friendly conversation.

Wives joined their husbands and their messmates for meals. A mess consisted of 6 to 8 men who ate from a common pot, but the addition of wives brought the number to 12 to 16. Food was ordinarily plentiful if monotonous, consisting of boiled salt meat, hard biscuits, and dried peas. Breakfast was at 8:00 A.M., dinner was at noon, and supper was at 5:00 P.M.

Women were not provided rations of food. Husbands had to share their apportionments with their wives and any child they had. This treatment was unique to the navy; the wife who traveled with her soldier husband in the army received a two-thirds ration, and their children received a half-ration each in their own right. This allotment was continued even when families of soldiers were being transported by ship, creating the gross inequity of soldiers' families being granted sustenance on the very vessel where the families of the seamen were formally denied any additional rations.

The wives of officers of wardroom rank ate with the commissioned officers and enjoyed the benefits of a varied diet of fresh meats, delicacies, and wine. Wives of the boatswain, carpenter, and gunner ate separately from both the commissioned officers and the seamen but also had the benefit of being able to supplement their victuals with fresh meat, wine, coffee, and tea. As much as commissioned officers were likely to loathe the women of the lower deck, these men were even likelier to enjoy the company of ladies of quality who sometimes traveled on naval ships. Lady passengers were sheltered in the officers' quarters and entertained at dinners that sometimes rivaled those given ashore.

One institution belonging to the British Admiralty, which oversaw the general management of the navy, was the Victualing Board. This institution appointed pursers and supplied the navy with food and drink. It had its own breweries for making beer, bakeries for ship's bread, and slaughterhouses for salt pork and beef. Of course, cooks, not administrators, prepared the food.

📷 *Snapshot*

Cockroaches aboard Ship

Cockroaches aboard ship joined sailors and officers at mealtime but were evident in other settings, as well. Even to the 17th-century Western mind-set, the presence of these pests was intolerable, as the following firsthand account indicates: "Every kind of food, when exposed for only a few minutes, was covered with these noxious insects [cockroaches], and pierced so full of holes that it resembled a honeycomb. They were fond of ink and ate out the writing labels; books, however, were secured from their ravages by the closeness of the binding, which prevented them from getting in between the leaves." (as cited in Thrower, 100)

Cooks were never considered seamen, and no seamanship was required of them. It was not uncommon for the cook to be an older seaman infirmed by age or the loss of a limb. The cook spent most of his time tending the fires in the galley, where he cooked for both the officers in the cabin and the men in the forecastle. If passengers were on board, he also cooked for them and was sometimes assigned a helper in the galley in the form of a boy. The need to maintain the galley, boilers, pans, and utensils occupied most of his day. He was able to sleep at night and, on some vessels, had a bunk in the galley. Often, a good deal of friendly familiarity existed between the cook and the men. A bad cook was a misery on a good voyage, whereas a good cook made a bad voyage all the more bearable.

Food was an essential provision aboard any oceangoing vessel. The quality and quantity of servings affected the mood and energy of all on board (Volo and Volo, 97–98, 104, 121–22, 151, 157–58).

FOR MORE INFORMATION

Lavery, B. *The Arming and Fitting of English Ships of War, 1600–1815*. London: Conway Maritime Press, 1987.

Thrower, W. R. *Life at Sea in the Age of Sail*. London: Phillimore, 1972.

Volo, D. D., and J. M. Volo. *Daily Life in the Age of Sail*. Westport, Conn.: Greenwood Press, 2002.

Drink

Beverages are of considerable importance in today's world, whether as part of a meal or not. Perhaps surprising is the central relevance that beverages of all sorts exerted within the contexts of colonial Australia, the North American colonial frontier, England, Japan, New England, and Western oceangoing cultures between 1600 and 1800. The historical relevance of alcoholic and nonalcoholic beverages in these regions comes into focus when considering their governmental and economic effects during this period.

People drank liquids that either contained or did not contain alcohol. Those drinks that did not contain alcohol were most often water or tea. In early modern Japan, hot water was an important beverage because it was both affordable and healthy. Boiled water killed off dangerous bacteria, and when cooked with rice, it assumed significant nutritional value.

Potable water was also of chief importance to the colonists in New England, particularly to those who were the first to arrive to the area's shores. With water supplies dangerously low aboard ship, the first settlers based the location of their settlements in large measure according to the presence and sustainability of springs and ponds. Similarly, the first Australian settlers selected their settlement based chiefly on the sustainability of a naturally occurring water supply.

Of course, those who sailed across oceans during the 17th and 18th centuries depended on fresh water supplies to last for the duration of the voyage. Ships' captains fixed and enforced daily allowances of water. Some ships took special care to top off their water reserves by capturing rainfall in canvas sails and immediately diverting it to the stores below.

As for tea, England's consumption of this popular drink expanded throughout the 18th century and benefited from a variety of types that suited many tastes and incomes. Green teas and black teas, strong or weak, were available for purchase. Some were expensive while others were cheap. Tea consumption in England even obeyed the intense, but transitory, influence of trends, which would popularize certain blends over others. Interestingly, the relatively high price of coffee was one factor that boosted the popularity of tea in England.

Tea was also popular among New England colonists, who at first used the leaves and stems of native plants and shrubbery to flavor heated water. The essence of raspberry and blackberry was especially common. The same approach to the local production of tea characterized Japan's peasantry, which mixed (the more affordable) stems and lower leaves of tea plants with water. Citrus juice or blades of grass were familiar and zesty additions to Japanese teas, which were served either hot or lukewarm.

For those who wanted to "sweeten" their tea, so to speak, many a beverage containing alcohol could be obtained without much effort. Sailors and their shipboard betters regularly received provisions that included beer, wine, and grog (honeyed rum diluted with hot water).

By far, sake was the most popular drink among 18th-century Japanese. Reverence accompanied the production and consumption of sake, a rice-distilled wine that possessed important links to religious tradition, most notably to Shintō ritual.

In England, alcohol played a central role in daily life. Indeed, the general population seemed to carry on with their daily habits in varying states of intoxication, thanks to the ease of access that exemplified all types of beer, ale, wine, liquor, and drink, in general. As with England, colonial New England displayed a widespread affection for alcohol, to the point that beer was as likely a candidate for a breakfast beverage as milk.

The economic impact of beverage consumption should not be overlooked in any of these cultures. The slave trade that developed among Europe, Africa, the West Indies, and the Americas depended on rum, which Western slave traders, in exchange for slaves, gave African slave traders.

Along North America's frontiers, settlers with alcohol exchanged it for furs that Native Americans had trapped. By the 18th century, the distillation of rum from molasses had become an enormous industry in New England. No different was Japan's sake industry, in which urban-centered production was large-scale and highly complex. And the demand for tea in England generated the vast network of trading institutions that comprised the considerably powerful East India Company, which found itself in competition with tea smugglers trying to undersell the official tea enterprise. Colonial Australians relied on alcohol not merely as a means of relaxation but as a mechanism by which to order society. Colonial officials there established grain monopolies, licensed the use of intoxicating drink, and made purchases of goods and services with spirits that were on hand.

The social and economic influence of beverages prompted many governments during this period to exercise their authority in various directions and manners. The "Rum Rebellion" erupted in colonial Australia when the governor attempted to put an end to some of the alcohol-related practices that had profited the officers there. In England, Parliament attempted to control the consumption of gin by repeatedly increasing taxes on the popular drink, and not without some success. In New England, pressures from England to reduce the colonies' rum industry accompanied internal efforts to cope with drunkenness. These efforts typically involved arrests and fines for public intoxication. And Japan's government continually forbade its peasantry from partaking in the manufacture and consumption of sake.

~Peter Seelig

FOR MORE INFORMATION

Edwards, G. *Alcohol: The World's Favorite Drug*. New York: Thomas Dunne Books, 2002.

COLONIAL AUSTRALIA

Water was a constant problem for the first Australian colonists, and at first, their only reliable supply was a fresh water stream, known (because of the practice of carving "tanks" into the stone to collect rain) as the Tank Stream. For the first few years, it remained a good source of water; but wasteful practices and droughts reduced its utility so much that by 1791, Watkin Tench referred to it as a "drain of morass" (Tench, 179). With regard to water, settlements established around the Hawkesbury River fared better.

Tea was an avidly consumed beverage, and its regular import was quickly established, but the most sought after beverages, for both consumption and trade, were alcoholic. At various times, the colonial government prohibited the trading of food rations for spirits, but some settlers who successfully evaded this ban (especially officers of the New South Wales Corps) made themselves wealthy with monopolies. The colony gave wine production a try when Governor Phillip planted vine cuttings in Farm Cove. Although the grapes were described as possessing a "flavor high and delicious," successful viticulture was not established until the 1820s (Tench, 179).

Beginning in 1793, officers were entitled to land grants, resulting in a significant increase in wheat fields. Some of these officers established grain monopolies and effectively diverted grain from foodstuffs to the distillation of spirits. In order to settle alcohol debts, smaller landholders sold their grain to monopolists.

Despite the stringency of the penal settlement, convivial drinking was a constant of life that often bordered on the excessive. Governor Hunter granted two retail liquor licenses in 1792 and 1796 but had to grant more because of the use of "every little hut [as] a settling house for retailing spirits." Hunter claimed to have prevented "much intoxication" by his liberality (Hunter, 593). Although liquor was used as a "small reward" for industrious workers, the authorities persistently evinced anxiety over alcohol and its effects on the colony. At times, drinking hours were regulated and convicts banned from visiting alehouses. However, problems induced by alcohol related as much to its use as currency as to its intoxicating effects. Illicit stills making "sly grog" flourished, and private drinking continued unabated.

Possibly the most serious threat to the rule of law was the so-called Rum Rebellion against Governor Bligh, notorious for the mutiny against him on the *Bounty* in 1789. Bligh arrived in Australia in 1806 with orders to suppress the trade in liquor, to the chagrin of officers and others who had prospered from it. In addition, his attempts to introduce order to the Sydney townscape alienated some leaseholders. In February 1807, Bligh outlawed the use of rum as currency, and in December, he had Macarthur, one of the profiteers, arrested. The military, in turn, arrested Bligh and installed George Johnston as administrator. After his usurpation, Bligh was illegally held under house arrest for more than a year because he would not agree to return to England. In 1809, the 73rd Regiment of Foot, commanded by Governor Lachlan Macquarie, replaced the New South Wales Corps, and a less-turbulent decade began. Alcohol, however, remained one of the continent's favorite forms of entertainment.

~*Valda Rigg*

FOR MORE INFORMATION

Gollan, A. *Tradition of Australian Cooking.* Canberra: Australian National University Press, 1978.

Historic Houses Trust of New South Wales. *Colonial Food and Drink 1788–1901.* Exhibition Catalogue. Sydney: Craft Wentworth, 1985.

Hunter. *Historical Records of Australia*, series 1, vol. 1. The Library Committee of the Commonwealth Parliament, 1914.

Pearn, J., and C. O'Carrigan. *Australia's Quest for Colonial Health.* Brisbane, Queensland: Department of Child Health, Royal Children's Hospital, 1983.

Symons, M. *One Continuous Picnic: A History of Eating in Australia.* Adelaide, South Australia: Duck Press, 1982.

Tench, W. *1788: Comprising A Narrative of the Expedition to Botany Bay [1789] and A Complete Account of the Settlement at Port Jackson [1795].* Edited by Tim Flannery. Melbourne: Text Publishing, 1996.

MATERIAL LIFE
|
DRINK
|
Colonial Australia

The Colonial Frontier
of North America

England

Japan

New England

Life at Sea

THE COLONIAL FRONTIER OF NORTH AMERICA

European settlers introduced alcoholic beverages to the Native American populations inhabiting the colonial frontier. The results were devastating for the Native Americans; however, settlers continued to trade their rum, brandy, beer, and ale for fur from the interior, thus contributing to the pernicious effects of alcoholism within a population that had previously had little or no contact with fermented drink. Settlers themselves imbibed heavily, typically serving some form of alcohol with every meal. Watering holes coupled entertainment with drink and contributed to an atmosphere of casual and widespread alcohol consumption.

Alcohol was considered a necessary part of the fur trade. Every canoe of trade goods that was sent into the interior had at least some liquor on board. The Jesuits, who detested the practice of trading alcohol to the Indians, considered it the most potent weapon of the devil. Its introduction at the missions was thought to lead to the immediate degradation of the Indians. The Indians were at first fascinated by alcohol's hallucinatory effect, but the novelty quickly wore off and was replaced by an almost-universal craving. "The introduction of alcohol into [their] hallucinatory world of dreams, demonology, and fractionalized emotions and spiritual beliefs could not have been anything but devastating. With a few drinks of brandy an Indian could release his soul from his body . . . as though they had been looking on from a point of vantage entirely outside themselves."

Although many native peoples made a weak sort of beer from maple syrup or spruce buds, none of the western or northern tribes had discovered the process of fermentation. They therefore had developed no tolerance for strong drink. Moreover, there are theories held by some historians that a physiological cause related to the sugar content of their blood could explain the almost-immediate reaction that many Native Americans had when exposed to strong drink. Regardless of the cause, they exhibited an extraordinary susceptibility to the effects of alcohol consumption, a susceptibility that most fur traders exploited to the detriment of the Indian population.

Whether physiological, spiritual, or cultural, the effect of alcohol on Native American behavior was reported by contemporaries as pathological and devastating, as noted in the following pronouncement: "The liquor made them more than quarrelsome; it literally drove them mad." There seemed to be no limit to the senseless violence to which a drunken Native American might resort, and the women were equally affected. "Their habitual modesty evaporated," and they were capable of violent acts that they would not have considered in a sober state. Robert Juet, a sailor on the Dutch vessel *Half Moon,* noted in 1609 that "there is scarcely a savage, small or great, even among the girls and women, who does not enjoy this intoxication, and who does not take these beverages when they can be had, purely and simply for the sake of being drunk." While the Indians quickly learned what alcohol would do to them, they seemed powerless to resist it, and it is certain that many individuals experienced a physical addiction.

The alcohol used in the fur trade was not rum or brandy as such but a watered-down version of strong spirits known to the Canadian *habitants* (inhabitants) as "whiskey blanc." It was made in three strengths. The weakest, 1 part spirits diluted in 36 parts water, was for tribes new to alcohol; the intermediate strength, for tribes familiar with liquor, was reduced by only one-sixth; and the strongest blend was cut by one-fourth. A barrel of brandy or rum, brought into the wilderness with a great expenditure of effort, could be made to provide many times its volume as a trade good. The sometimes lethal effects of even these diluted alcoholic beverages serve to emphasize the utter vulnerability of the Native Americans to the unscrupulous methods of many European fur traders.

Settlers served beer or cider with most meals. "Strong" beer was brewed annually in October and in most cases was made by those with expertise in the craft. "Small" beer was a milder beverage that any housewife could concoct. It was brewed every week or so and consumed shortly thereafter. Frontier farmer J. Hector St. John de Crèvecoeur reported, "Some families excel in the method of brewing beer with a strange variety of ingredients. Here we commonly make it with pine chips, pine buds, hemlock, fir leaves, roasted corn, dried apple-skins, sassafras roots, and bran." Cider was an excellent way to preserve the apple harvest. The liquid from the pressed fruit was allowed to ferment naturally in the cellar until it was mildly alcoholic. Cider that was served in taverns had a slightly higher alcoholic content from the sugar that was added during the fermentation process.

Before the temperance movement gained popularity in the middle of the 19th century, taverns and alehouses were in many cases considered respectable men's clubs and served as public centers for political gatherings, assemblies of merchants and local farmers, and fertile fields for the recruiting of soldiers. These establishments typically provided entertainment in the form of card games, bowling, shuffleboard, music, and singing for travelers.

Men and even boys as young as 12 were allowed to buy whatever alcoholic beverages they wanted. Popular drinks in cold weather were hot buttered rum and a concoction called "flip." The common variety of flip was a mixture of rum, beer, and brown sugar into which a hot poker was plunged. The heat warmed the mixture without seriously diminishing its alcohol content. Warm-weather drinks included many kinds of beer, ale, porter, cider, wine, and a long list of liquors. If ice was not readily available (and it usually was not), then one could chill a drink by placing the bottle on a rope or in a water bucket and hanging it in the cool water of a well. The temperature of the water in a well is rarely higher than 45 degrees even on the warmest day.

A formidable and dangerous component of daily life on the frontier, alcohol was the drink of choice among settlers. Among Native Americans, it came to be an extraordinarily addictive and destructive European import (Volo and Volo, 15–16, 150, 177–78).

FOR MORE INFORMATION

Mancall, P. *Deadly Medicine: Indians and Alcohol in Early America*. Ithaca, N.Y.: Cornell University Press, 1995.

Volo, J. M., and D. D. Volo. *Daily Life on the Old Colonial Frontier*. Westport, Conn.: Greenwood Press, 2002.

MATERIAL LIFE
|
DRINK
|
Colonial Australia

The Colonial Frontier of North America

England

Japan

New England

Life at Sea

ENGLAND

Tea and alcohol formed the core of English beverages in the 18th century. Fruit juice was too expensive, milk was often adulterated, and water was usually unsafe to drink, especially in London. Coffee was expensive—the poor drank a substitute made of horse chestnuts—and according to continental visitors, poorly made; one critic called English coffee an "atrocious mess of brown water." The virtual exclusion of coffee as an acceptable beverage left tea, drunk without milk, and alcoholic beverages. The public obsession with beer, ale, gin, wine, port, rum, and whiskey generated calls for reform and regulative legislation. Little could be done, however, to put a dent in alcohol consumption, which, along with tea, typified English beverages.

All social classes drank tea, from dukes to the simplest dairymaids, the latter of whom bought used tea leaves from rich people's cooks and used and reused the leaves. Enterprising souls even sold tea by the cup to haymakers during harvest.

Because tea had little nutritive value, and because it was expensive, many opposed its use by workers. Opponents' arguments, however, were ignored. Tea consumption rose dramatically during the century. The East India Company imported 67,000 pounds in 1701 and about 8 million by 1801. Smugglers brought in even more, perhaps twice as much.

Teas were either green or black, and they came in many varieties and levels of quality. Strong types, like green "gunpowder tea" or black pekoe, were blended with hyson or "bloom tea," which was generally weaker. Congou was the most popular type; bohea, the cheapest and least fashionable, was drunk on its own mostly early in the century when prices were high. Later in the century, it was more commonly mixed with congou to form an intermediate blend called "congou kind."

Those who were not drinking tea drank alcohol, usually to excess. Porters, carriage drivers, nurses, hospital patients, and prisoners were routinely drunk; indeed, some of the smaller jails were actually located in alehouses.

Yearly gin consumption ran into the millions of gallons, perhaps as many as six gallons per person per year. Known as "strip me naked," "Hollands" (because the English learned to use essence of juniper from Dutch distillers), or "geneva" (after the French word for juniper, *genèvre*), gin was attractive principally because it was strong and cheap. Accordingly, the shops sometimes advertised that one could get "drunk for a penny" and "dead drunk" for twopence.

Gin was controlled for most of the century by legislation, but the distilling industry was a powerful one, and in 1750 it absorbed about half the output of the nation's wheat fields, which pleased the farmers. Nonetheless, in 1729, Parliament put a five-shilling-per-gallon tax on home-distilled spirits, tightened licensing requirements for alehouses, and imposed a license fee of 20 pounds to sell gin. It was unenforceable and encouraged the sale of new liquors not specifically covered under the law. In 1733, the law was repealed. The consequence was a huge increase in the sale and consumption of gin. In 1736, Parliament tried again, placing a sales tax on gin and on all other spirits and reimposing a retail license fee.

The Ravages of Strong Drink, by James Gillray. England was very much taken with "punch" and other alcoholic beverages, often at the expense of good health. © Library of Congress.

Like the 1729 act, the one of 1736 was largely useless and was repealed in 1743. Further acts of 1743 and 1751 restricted sales by distillers and shopkeepers, and these controls, combined with naturally rising grain prices, gradually reduced spirit consumption. The gin problem became less urgent in the second half of the century, although drunkenness remained widespread.

As part of a general conservative trend, attitudes toward drink became slightly more negative toward the end of the century. Women encouraged the substitution of tea for alcohol as an evening beverage. Even the hospitals, long the home of drunken patients and drunken staff, began to reform.

Drinkers had ample choices available to them. There was, of course, beer; the inmates of Marshalsea Prison drank 600 pots of it on one day alone in 1775. Greenwich Hospital allotted 14 quarts a week to each patient. There was a great variety of beers. In addition to large-scale producers, a multitude of small brewers and home brewers manufactured beer. Early in the century, the pub goer had a choice of ale, beer, or twopenny (a cheap beer that sold for twopence a quart); half-and-half, meaning half beer and half twopenny; or three-thread, meaning a mixture of ale, beer, and twopenny. Three-thread was eventually premixed and sold in one cask as "entire," later called "porter" from its popularity with London porters. Especially rich, strong porters were known as "stouts." Sometimes beer was served heated. Cider was ever popular but was dangerous even in smaller amounts because brewers made it in lead containers.

Wine was the drink of the upper and upwardly mobile middle classes. They drank champagne, claret (red wine, usually from France), port (cheaper than claret, because import duties were lighter for Portuguese than for French products), sack (white wine from Spain or the Canary Islands, often quite sweet, and increasingly replaced by port), brandy, burgundy, cherry brandy, and other types, including Sheraaz, Zante, Lissa, and Calcevella. "Burnt" wine, with some of the alcoholic content removed by fire, was popular, as was burnt champagne, an archetypal drink for a society lady's evening at Vauxhall. The type of wine drunk in a particular household varied according to income but also according to politics; Jacobites drank French wines as a statement of support for France, which harbored the Pretenders, whereas Whigs, to express the opposite sentiment, drank port. Some preferred their wine mixed with other substances. Punch, a popular beverage, was brandy mixed with citrus fruit and sugar.

Alcohol, in whatever form, was certainly England's drug of choice. There was some use of laudanum, a little recreational ether sniffing, and a great deal of consumption of pipe tobacco and snuff. But it was beer, rum, gin, whisky, brandy, punch, and wine that accompanied meals, sometimes replaced meals, and gave a significant number of Britons a daily dose of inebriation.

The stereotypical view of English drink in this era—tea, ale, port, and hard liquor—is not far from the mark. The uninterrupted drunkenness of many imbibers led some to condemn drink. Both the numerous kinds of intoxicating beverages available and seemingly unending occasions during which to enjoy a sip kept alcohol as typically English a beverage as tea (Olsen, 238–42).

To read about drink in Chaucer's England, see the Europe entry in the section "Drink" in chapter 5 ("Material Life") of volume 2; and for Elizabethan England, see the England entry in the section "Food and Drink" in chapter 5 ("Material Life") of volume 3 of this series.

FOR MORE INFORMATION

Jennings, P. *Inns, Ales, and Drinking Customs of Old England*. London: Bracken Books, 1985.

Lynch, J. *Eighteenth Century Resources*. <http://newark.rutgers.edu/~jlynch/18th/>, accessed October 10, 2003.

Olsen, K. *Daily Life in 18th-Century England*. Westport, Conn.: Greenwood Press, 1999.

JAPAN

Leaves boiled in water, together with fermented grains, furnished 18th-century Japanese with their staple beverages: alcohol and tea. The preparation of soy sauce, perhaps surprisingly, resembled that of Japanese alcohol. However, it was potable hot water that was most accessible to commoners.

The poorer folk often could not afford tea, let alone sake, so it was common for them to drink hot water with meals. Experience taught the rural masses that with the exception of the high mountain streams, cold water often made people sick because of pollutants from farming communities. There were several superstitions regarding drinking cold water, as well. A popular variant was to drink the water used to wash and "start" the cooking of rice. When the rice water began to boil, some would be decanted to allow the rice to steam uncovered. The peasants were right that this water was healthy. The boiling killed most of the bacteria, and the powder that had been rinsed off the rice retained some of the nutrients left from polishing off the bran.

By this time, poor-quality tea was relatively inexpensive. Peasant tea often comprised stems and lower leaves and required a considerably longer time to steep than the premium teas. It was common to toss a pinch of tea into a pot of water and let it boil for several minutes. It was less bitter that way, and the principal properties of tea (caffeine and tannic acid) steeped into the water anyway. A cheap alternative was boiled wheat tea (*mugi-cha*), which, during the hot summer months, was allowed to cool as much as possible. Herbs, citrus peel, and various grasses could add flavor and zest to hot water, and many possessed medicinal qualities as a bonus.

Those who could afford good-quality tea rarely drank anything else. Introduced into Japan by Chinese Buddhist priests, it was chiefly the drink of drowsy monks who would drink a bowl of the bitter liquid to ward off sleep during late-night meditations. The Zen tea ritual (*chanoyu*) had popularized the drink in the medieval period, and by the 17th century, it had become popular with the common folk as well.

The other major drink in Japan was of course sake. Older than written history, sake had attained a prime status in the society and in the native Shintō religion. The beverage's preparation had been refined over perhaps two millennia. Japanese did not grow grapes for wine, distill grain mash for whiskey, or brew beer. Virtually the only alcohol was brewed sake. It is called "rice wine" by some because the brewing and fermenting were similar to grape wine production. A rice mash was brewed with small amounts of wheat or millet; yeast was introduced, and the mash was allowed to ferment. The sake was strained, decanted, and cleared at various steps, and the final clear liquid was stored in wooden casks. By the 18th century, it was produced in huge quantities, primarily in the larger cities. There was perhaps a score of grades and common rankings, depending on their intoxicating properties, taste, clearness, and even smell. It was used as a social lubricant, of course, but also in various Shintō rituals.

The *bakufu* (national military government) issued an almost-annual proscription against sake's manufacture and consumption among the peasantry, and it often advised the *chōnin* (city folk) to avoid it, as well. The fact that the proscription had to be issued so often and so regularly suggests that someone was not taking the rules very much to heart.

Virtually any peasant with enough common sense to follow a recipe could prepare a preliminary liquor called "cloudy sake" (*shochu*), and some could make pretty good sake. *Shochu* was particularly popular among rural brewers. It was brewed from rice and wheat and fermented with potato juice. The alcohol content varied wildly from one batch to another to the point that it was occasionally poisonous. Few peasants could afford to buy sake from a proper brewer, but sake production was an excellent way to hide surplus rice, and it could turn a tidy profit or garner social prestige if it was donated to the local *matsuri* (festivals).

Within the Licensed Quarters, tea and sake shops sprang up as places of assignation. Originally, not much in the way of food was purveyed there, but an enterprising shop owner could always make a few salty snacks available to patrons to encourage them to drink more sake or tea. For that reason, Japan developed an inordinate number of steamed, grilled, salted, and pickled tidbits to whet one's thirst. Japan's touted, late night, bar culture probably originated in late 18th-century Edo.

Another form of brewing was not for alcohol but for shoyu, which is known in the West as soy sauce. This concoction had come to Japan from China, although rather later than sake. It was something of a minor by-product of tofu and miso paste production, which derive from the soya bean.

Shoyu is actually as much wheat as it is soy in content. Soybeans are boiled until soft and then blended with an equal amount of wheat grist. The mixture is cooked and fermented for a day. An equal amount of salt is added and then diluted with enough water to equal two-and-a-half times the original volume of the mixture. The admixture is stirred several times a day for two weeks or so and then allowed to sit covered for two to three months. At this point, the shoyu producer decants and strains the mixture. The resulting dark liquid was used full strength or diluted as a cooking, marinating, and dipping sauce. Until the late 18th century, no regular method to control the quality of shoyu existed. At that time, the major brewer, Kikkoman, discovered "quality-control" methods, and shoyu became quite popular, even among the poor peasants.

The brewing of alcoholic beverages such as sake (and cooking sauces such as shoyu) produced delicacies that the average Japanese living in the 18th century could not afford to drink. Instead, teas of varying quality and boiled water constituted the staple drinks for most people during this period (Perez, 76–77, 80, 194–96).

FOR MORE INFORMATION

Ishige, N. *The History and Culture of Japanese Food*. London: Kegan Paul, 2001.

Japan Information Network. <http://www.jinjapan.org/index.html>, accessed October 23, 2003.

Perez, L. G. *Daily Life in Early Modern Japan*. Westport, Conn.: Greenwood Press, 2002.

NEW ENGLAND

New England colonists drank water, tea, milk, beer, cider, and harder beverages such as rum. The consumption of alcohol eventually created certain problems with which the English government, as well as individual colonists, grappled. Not so obvious, perhaps, is the importance that fresh water played in the decisions of New England's earliest European settlers concerning the location of their settlements and even the survival of their communities.

For the people who came to New England as part of the Plymouth Plantation in 1620, a problem more immediately pressing than food was the need for potable water. However, one of the first exploration parties that left the ship found sufficient springs and ponds for drinking water.

An identical need surfaced for the settlers under John Winthrop, who arrived in Salem in 1630. The goal was to locate fresh, drinkable water in the Charlestown-Boston area, which was the site of Winthrop's settlement after he and his followers had quit Salem. The Charles River, which emptied into the Atlantic Ocean, was a relatively short, saline body of water. They did discover a plentiful spring of fresh water, but it was on the shoreline and completely under seawater except at low tide. This need for fresh water, more than anything else, led them westward—to Cambridge (then called Newtown), Watertown, and other points.

The settlers came to know the value of drinking lots of fresh water, a habit they did not bring with them from England. Tea was made from raspberry and blackberry leaves, sage, and goldenrod. Milk and beer were often drunk at breakfast.

They also made beer and cider. Apple orchards were established fairly quickly, and the main drink of the settlers came to be cider, a drink with low alcohol content, fermented with some form of sweetener. The biggest job in the fall was the addition of sugar to apples for the great quantities of cider—from 10 to 30 barrels—that the colonies' inhabitants required throughout the year. The concoction was left in the cellars to ferment along with any beer that the householders had made from barley. Of all the colonists throughout the New World, the New Englanders were undoubtedly the healthiest. Some writers have theorized that they enjoyed physical vigor because they ate many apples and consumed fair amounts of cider.

Despite New England's trouble with alcohol abuse and the frequent and brutal measures taken to curb drunkenness, New Englanders began (early in the history of their settlement) the business of distilling rum from molasses imported from the West Indies. Brewers and distillers quickly became key elements in the economy because they required both large amounts of capital and many workers, supported other industries such as barrel making, and saw an endless demand for their products.

The attempt by England in 1733 to slow New England production by interfering with its importation of molasses for breweries and distilleries contributed to Anglo-America's growing unhappiness with the mother country. By some accounts, the distillation of rum was New England's greatest manufacturing industry at the middle of the 18th century. There were 30 distilleries in Rhode Island and 63 in Massachusetts, which produced 2.7 million gallons of rum in 1774. Rum, which was aged with apples, was distilled in New England and was regularly dispensed to workers, who drank the liquid from tankards made of wooden staves.

Drinking alcoholic beverages was an accepted part of the colonial New Englander's socializing and relaxation, whether at home or in public houses. Both private residences and taverns were stocked with hard cider, rum, ale, wine, and other alcoholic drinks, which were freely imbibed not only by ordinary citizens but also by the clergy and religious magistrates. One of Reverend Phillips's allotments in 1630, for example, included a hogshead of malt. Importers of liquor, brewers, distillers, and tavern keepers were licensed to ply their trades in New England. Men met in taverns to drink while they listened to speeches or considered matters of public importance. The religiously educated jurist Samuel Sewall is a good example. Sewall often mentioned having a bottle of wine with his meals at home, serving his guests expensive wines, and being served wines and liquors at the houses of his friends or in taverns. He pointed out that state business involving other members of the court and the governor routinely took place in taverns such as the Patten in Boston. On July 15, 1712, Sewall and his wife took a 10-quart jug of Madeira to a barn raising.

It is no surprise that with the heavy drinking in New England came problems of public drunkenness. Nevertheless, drunkenness was not tolerated, and there were more arrests for disturbances resulting from drunkenness than for any other crime. The punishments were occasionally limited to fines but often involved being placed in the stocks and beaten "severely" or "sharply."

Tired or hungover workers frequently did not get up to begin work on time and performed poorly at their labors. Servants who partied without or within their master's property reflected negatively on and shamed the family, and masters often complained of sexual misconduct on the part of servants. To discourage drinking and gambling, the two favorite leisure-time activities of servants, local courts passed laws forbidding tavern keepers and sailors aboard ship from entertaining servants.

Beverages, be they fresh water, mild tea, or heartening cider and rum, figured prominently in the daily lives of New England colonists. In fact, drink figured in the colonists' worsening relations with the British. The tariff on tea resulted in the rebellious dumping of tea into Boston Harbor in 1773. Tariffs affecting beverage imports and exports were serious contributors to the advent of the American Revolution (Johnson, 65–66, 95–96, 98, 100, 102, 128, 166).

FOR MORE INFORMATION

Brown, S. C. *Wines and Beers of Old New England*. Hanover, N.H.: University Press of New England, 1978.

Johnson, C. D. *Daily Life in Colonial New England.* Westport, Conn.: Greenwood Press, 2002.

LIFE AT SEA

The image of seamen, pirates, buccaneers, and mariners, in general, would not be complete without some alcoholic beverage nearby. But rum and ale were not the only drinks important to sailors. Drinkable water was an essential provision aboard any vessel.

The most common sign found along the waterfront of a seaport was probably the silhouette of a mug of ale or a bottle of rum. Sandwiched between buildings were the sailors' taverns, which dotted the entire harbor area. Sign boards bearing dolphins, anchors, capstans, and mermaids beckoned the sailor to groggeries with descriptive names such as the Jolly Tar, Crow's Nest, Spyglass, Admiral's Cabin, Flags of All Nations, or Spouter Inn. The interiors of these haunts ranged from dives with long wooden benches beneath low-beamed ceilings from which ships lanterns hung to plush, gilt halls festooned with velvet drapes.

Taverns and alehouses served a definite social purpose, providing both food and drink. Most did not provide rooms or overnight accommodations, however. These were left to the inns and ordinaries, a distinction in service well understood by 17th- and 18th-century patrons. Men, and even boys as young as 12, were allowed to buy whatever alcoholic beverages they wanted. Popular drinks in cold weather included hot buttered rum and a concoction called flip. The common variety of flip was a mixture of rum, beer, and brown sugar into which a hot poker was plunged. The heat warmed the mixture without seriously diminishing its alcohol content. Warm-weather drinks included many kinds of beer, ale, porter, cider, and wine, as well as a long list of liquors. If ice was not readily available (and it usually was not), then one could chill a drink by placing the bottle on a rope or in a water bucket and hanging it in the cool water of a well. The temperature of the water in a well is rarely higher than 45 degrees even on the warmest day.

Fresh water was essential aboard ship, but it was all but undrinkable under normal circumstances. Beer and grog were considered more healthful, and wine was thought the best drink for maintaining the health of the crew in the tropics. The daily allowance of water was left to the discretion of the captain, but the custom was to allow a gallon per man per day. Every officer received a gallon for his own use, and an additional pint for washing was drawn by the steward for each officer. The men received three pints directly (minus that used in the grog), and a pint for cooking was drawn by the cook for each man in a mess. The sick were allotted a small additional amount during their illnesses, and the livestock were given enough to keep them alive. An account of the use of water was carefully kept in the log even to the point that the amount boiled off in heating was recorded.

The *Bounty* took on 42 tons of drinking water in its tanks for the first leg of its journey from England to the Canary Islands. Although the ship suffered from no shortage of water, like any good captain, Bligh ordered awnings to be spread to catch

A captain often dined with the officers under his command. However, it is likely that, in such settings, alcohol was imbibed to the extent depicted in this picture only on rare occasions. © National Maritime Museum, London.

the rain. Rather than mix it with the stagnant water in the ship's tanks, he filled many hogsheads with fresh water. A 42-gun frigate with a crew of almost 200 was recorded to have taken aboard 102 tons of water that, with careful and disciplined husbanding, lasted almost 12 weeks.

When a ship entered port, the task of bringing aboard water was of great importance. Large boats, often held in the center of the ship, would travel to shore, towing large, empty casks through the water. Then, the seamen would fill the casks with drinkable water, seal them tightly, and roll them back to the shore. To get the full casks from the shore to the awaiting ship, the seamen would next bind the casks into a makeshift raft and tow it out to their thirsty crewmates.

Not all beverages served the needs of sailors. Much of New England traded cod with the Caribbean for molasses, with which to make rum. The average American drank almost four gallons annually, but slavers used much of the rum to trade for African slaves. This three-way traffic—molasses, rum, and slaves—was actually fueled by the fisheries of the Grand Banks. The triangular trade, as it is known, was extremely lucrative. Thus, although drink, be it alcohol or water, was a vital concern for the captain of any vessel, some beverages supported oceanic travel in entirely indirect ways (Volo and Volo, 3–4, 124, 267).

FOR MORE INFORMATION

Lavery, B. *The Arming and Fitting of English Ships of War, 1600–1815.* London: Conway Maritime Press, 1987.

Volo, D. D., and J. M. Volo. *Daily Life in the Age of Sail.* Westport, Conn.: Greenwood Press, 2002.

Housing and Furnishings

In our daily existences, homes are where we come from and go to. They serve as a base of operations, one that physically distances us from the wider society. Homes played no less a role during the 17th and 18th centuries, and instances of this truth apply to sub-Saharan Africa, North America's colonial frontiers, England, Japan, and New England, as well as to merchantmen, ratings, and officers aboard ships. Beyond this general reality, however, lie many fascinating variations related to the shapes, materials, and furnishings that characterized homes in each of these cultural regions. Indeed, within a given society, factors such as wealth and birth were key in determining the kind of home in which one lived.

The shapes of houses differed from one another according to cultural standards. Among the families of officers, oceanside homes with flat roofs were typical, affording the home's occupants an elevated view of the horizon. In 18th-century England, many homes were multistoried, being a series of additions and renovations that resulted in precariously tilted rectangular edifices that blocked the sun's light from the streets below. Japanese homes were often one story with clearly defined angles, while African residences were far more varied; some, for example, were shaped like cones and others like bells.

Materials used in the construction of homes also varied. Woven straw and bamboo, in addition to paper screens, were the chosen materials for walls in early modern Japanese homes. Stone, brick, and wood were typical of homes in Western ports, England, and colonial New England. In the British colonies of North America, Indians applied bark to the walls of their wigwams, whereas settlers of different cultural backgrounds preferred different materials. The Dutch, for example, opted for bricks whereas the Germans and Scotch-Irish specialized in log cabins. Africans made use of many different materials: skin tents among the Tuaregs; mud walls and grass roofs throughout West Africa; coral along the eastern coast of Swahili; and clay-covered wooden stakes among the Shona.

Home furnishings included, among other things, carpets, books, lighting (candles, oil lamps), religious altars, artistic objects, and beds. The first European settlers in New England slept on bedrolls or layered straw covered with cloth. Sailors in the Royal Navy slept on hammocks scattered throughout the gun decks. Among the Shona, men and women slept on elevated beds on both sides of the door to their home. Japanese slept on earthen floors, straw mats, and futon mattresses.

Homes needed fires for cooking and heating purposes. Fireplaces occupied the center of wigwams in New England, necessitating a constant effort to ventilate the smoky interior. The Shona also situated fireplaces in the middle of their homes. Homes in colonial New England featured fireplaces and brick chimneys. In early modern Japan, people cooked and warmed themselves with fireplaces and stoves, increasingly switching to the latter over the course of the 18th century.

Social customs strongly influenced the type of home in which one lived. The residences of Japanese peasants were far less ornate and crafted than those of prominent Japanese businessmen; and in Japanese cities, one-story tenements housed masses of workers and their families. In England, the poor lived in crowded rooms with earthen floors, while the middle class could expect to own a carpet, a few books, and a few prints with which to decorate their interior walls. Persian rugs, Chinese wallpaper, and vast libraries characterized the residences of England's top tier. In some parts of British North America, oiled paper was a common substitute for glass panes in colonists' windows.

Social distinctions were perhaps most prominent on oceangoing vessels. In the Royal Navy, ratings serving on a warship were allotted 14 inches of space, not nearly enough for even a trunk, which a half dozen men typically shared. In contrast, an admiral's quarters seem extravagant: a day cabin, where he worked; a dining cabin, where meals were served and company entertained; and a sleeping cabin, to which he and any family retired at the close of the day.

The shapes, materials, and furnishings of a residence did not simply result from homogeneous cultural dictates but were, and remain, potent indicators of social and economic divisions within each society, a fact that holds no less true today than it did during the 17th and 18th centuries.

~*Peter Seelig*

FOR MORE INFORMATION

Schoenauer, N. *6000 Years of Housing.* New York: Garland STPM Press, 1981.

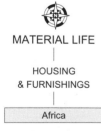

MATERIAL LIFE
|
HOUSING
& FURNISHINGS
|

AFRICA

It is impossible to generalize about housing in Africa, which varied with the climate, resources, and lifestyles particular to different areas. Ranging from the simple tents of nomadic herders in the Sahara Desert to the multistory dwellings along the Swahili coast, urban Africans lived in a variety of conditions adapted to their individual cultures. In all areas, people lived in a group, be it a nomadic clan, city, or farming village. Frequently, house construction and maintenance involved the whole community. Housing also represented the social structure, with people living in family groups as part of a common compound, or in large, highly decorated houses that served as a sign of wealth or status.

In the Sahara, pastoralists lived simply, as their way of life required mobility more than comfort. The Berber group known as the Tuareg, for example, lived in skin tents supported by posts and surrounded with mat sidings. At the start of a day, people could easily fold this edifice up and take it to their next stopping place. In the eastern Sahara, the Teda lived in homes of interlaced pilings covered with plants or antelope hides. The Teda traveled only with the coverings, leaving the main structure in place under the assumption that they would eventually return to that location. Similarly, the Khoisan of southern Africa used semipermanent housing that could be packed up and moved to a new location (July, 49).

In the farming villages of West Africa, houses were also simple, although not as portable. West Africans generally lived in mud dwellings with palm or grass roofs and a veranda surrounding an interior court. To build a house, workers puddled together mud and water in a hole and then laid the resulting mixture around the floor plan of the building. Shelves were built directly into the walls. Because heavy rains could damage a mud building, the acquisition of fresh sand from rivers represented one common chore for children. Among the Yoruba, four ridgepole houses with verandas would surround the courtyard. This courtyard often contained pots to collect the rainfall, while special drains carried away the excess water (Willett, 127–32).

This Khoisan family is preparing its home. Note that the man in the background is erecting the framework for a hut. © Stapleton Collection/CORBIS.

The Fon of West Africa lived in compounds under the control of the man who was head of the household.   of his wives and her child or children occupied a separate hut within the compound. People in the Kongo kingdom also lived in villages composed of numerous compounds that individually sheltered a household (Thornton, 29).

More sophisticated were the dwellings of the Swahili in the east coast city-states. In Gedi, along the coast of modern Kenya, flat-roofed houses made of coral or mortar had a single story and consisted of a bedroom, living room, storeroom, bath, and kitchen. Many also sported a courtyard in front. The ruler's palace was, of course, more ornate and featured rooms for state functions, the harem, and special salesrooms (July, 84).

Upper-class residents throughout the Swahili coast lived in houses of one or two stories with porches and benches that faced out onto the street. Wall niches in these houses held luxury items for all to see and admire. People entered these homes through a courtyard, and the rooms were set back in rows parallel to the front. Along the lower coast, the lower classes lived in simple mud or thatch houses, usually on the periphery of towns or in fishing villages (Horton and Middleton, 116–19).

The Shona, who lived in what is now Zimbabwe, inhabited circular huts supported by walls of wooden stakes plastered with clay. For a roof, they used tight thatch that formed a cone directly above the central fireplace, the smoke from which helped discourage insects from making the construction their home. People slept on raised beds of clay, with the man on one side of the door and the woman on the other. When children reached a certain age, they were given smaller huts apart from the main one to help to conserve space and preserve decency (Beach, 48–49).

A basic cone-on-cylinder model was common throughout Africa. In the extreme south of the continent, people lived in small, beehive-shaped dwellings in which two sets of semicircular arches crossed at right angles. Scattered peoples also resided in bell-shaped houses made of straw. In East Africa, the palaces of Bungara and Bunyoro also exhibited a conical shape and were made of reeds (Hull, 50–51).

African housing was constructed from local materials and adapted itself to the occupants' lifestyle. The homes of Swahili merchants helped provide a place for their business and enhanced their social status, whereas the tents of the Tuareg were portable enough to move from one place to another as the people migrated with their herds in search of pasture. Africans south of the Sahara lived simply, with minimal comforts, much as peasants do the world over. Most housing was simple and easy to construct on short notice. Yet these dwellings formed an adequate physical setting for their daily lives.

~Brian Ulrich

FOR MORE INFORMATION

Beach, D. *The Shona and Their Neighbors*. Cambridge, Mass.: Blackwell, 1984.

Halsall, P., ed. *Internet African History Sourcebook*. 1996. <http://www.fordham.edu/halsall/africa/africasbook.html>, accessed October 23, 2003.

Horton, M., and J. Middleton. *The Swahili: The Social Landscape of a Mercantile Society*. Malden, Mass.: Blackwell, 2000.

Hull, R. W. *African Cities and Towns before the European Conquest*. New York: Norton, 1976.

July, R. W. *A History of the African People*. 5th ed. Prospect Heights, Ill.: Waveland Press, 1998.

Thornton, J. K. *The Kingdom of Kongo: Civil War and Transition, 1641–1718*. Madison: University of Wisconsin Press, 1983.

Willett, F. *African Art: An Introduction*. New York: Thames and Hudson, 1993.

THE COLONIAL FRONTIER OF NORTH AMERICA

Homes on the colonial frontier varied with the means and needs of the families who built them. Often, initial construction was limited, and additions to enlarge the structure were attached as time and situation permitted. In certain areas, houses commonly followed one of three plans: the one-room plan, the two-room plan, and the lean-to plan. Swedish, German, Scotch-Irish, and Dutch variations on housing included log cabins and brick homes. Belonging to the overall structure of a home were specific elements such as windows, entrances, fireplaces, and chimneys. Furnishings completed the simple and functional colonial home.

The one-room plan was the most basic pattern and the earliest type of house constructed in the colonies. Well into the 18th century, this type continued to be common for frontier dwellings, as well as for small and poorer dwellings throughout the colonies. The front door of such a structure typically opened into a small vestibule, which contained a steep, narrow staircase that traversed the width of the entry. To one side of the vestibule was a doorway leading into the main room. Known as the "hall," it served as a combination kitchen, dining area, living area, and in some cases, a bedroom. It had a low ceiling and a double layer of boards on the floor.

As the century closed, molded pieces were attached to form the earliest paneled walls. The most prominent feature in the room was the large fireplace. The depth of the fireplace extended into the area behind the staircase. The upstairs consisted of a large sleeping area that featured a sloping roof in a one-and-a-half-story house and a roof of full height in a two-story house.

Aside from the addition of a second room to the other side of the chimney and porch, the two-room house followed the plan of the one-room house. The addition was called the "parlor." Upstairs were two rooms known as the "hall chamber" and the "parlor chamber." On occasion, another room projected over the porch and was consequently known as the "porch chamber." Prior to the 19th century, rooms were basically multipurpose. Furniture in first-floor rooms was often placed against the walls when not in use and moved into position as needed.

The lean-to plan was the two-room plan with the addition of a room at the rear of the house. This room served as a separate kitchen and workspace for other domestic chores but could also function as a bedroom. Above the lean-to was a loft that may have been used for additional sleeping, as necessity dictated. A cooking fireplace was also added at the back of the central chimney mass. A common lean-to house had as many as five fireplaces built into a single chimneystack.

In the middle and southern colonies, frontier homes were often built of squared or rounded logs. Although the Swedish are often given credit for introducing this construction to the colonies, German and Scotch-Irish settlers embraced the log cabin, doing much to popularize it. Early log cabins were frequently only one room with both front and rear doors. Next to the large interior chimney was a ladder or steep stair that led to a loft. The rooms seldom exceeded 24 feet in length because it was difficult to find suitable timber of greater size.

The Dutch were some of the most skilled bricklayers in Europe. Quite naturally, they preferred to continue to use brick in the construction of their homes in America. The brick was laid in a variety of patterns, some of which were quite striking. When brick was unavailable, the Dutch used whatever materials were at hand. Many houses along the lower Hudson River and in New Jersey were built of stone.

Windows, which were few in 17th-century New England homes, were even rarer in frontier homes. In place of glass, some colonial homes featured oiled paper or sliding board shutters. Letters to England urged emigrants to bring glass for windows, which during this period were diamond-shaped panes arranged in a lattice pattern. By 1650, glazed windows were commonplace in prosperous New England homes but not along the colonial frontier.

Entrance to the home was made through a heavy door constructed from two layers of boards, the outer of which ran vertically and the inner horizontally. Driven through both boards were hand-forged nails that appeared as studs and clenched on the inside. The door was supported by hinges. The earliest hinges were made of wood. Later hinges were made of wrought iron. At night, a heavy wooden bar, placed across the inside doors, further secured the abode.

Inside the frontier home, the fireplace was the center of activity. A fire would burn every day of the year. The central fire warmed the house and provided a means for cooking. While sustaining life with light, heat, and means of cooking, the fireplace also presented a potential danger; an out-of-control fire could quickly burn an entire house to the ground.

Generally, frontier furniture was simple, solid, and painted. It would be an error to believe that frontier homes were decorated with tree stumps and crude tables made of saplings. Much of the furniture consisted rather of backless benches and stools. Chairs, especially those with arms, were a luxury, and their use was reserved for the head of the household. Meals were served from a board table made from two or three long planks that rested on a pair of trestles. The most valued piece of furniture was usually the bedstead. The term *bed* originally referred to the mattress only, which was simply thrown on the floor for sleeping and rolled up out of the way during the day. Mattresses were stuffed with corn husks, straw, bits of felt or wool, or any other soft material that could be spared. All in all, the housing of settlers on the North American colonial frontier progressively expanded the size, materials, and soundness of their dwellings (Volo and Volo, 141–43, 145–47).

FOR MORE INFORMATION

Morrison, H. *Early American Architecture: From the First Colonial Settlements to the National Period.* New York: Dover, 1987.

Volo, J. M., and D. D. Volo. *Daily Life on the Old Colonial Frontier.* Westport, Conn.: Greenwood Press, 2002.

MATERIAL LIFE

|

HOUSING
& FURNISHINGS

|

Africa

The Colonial Frontier
of North America

England

Japan

New England

Life at Sea

ENGLAND

English homes and their furnishings in the 18th century differed from one another with regard to the passage of trendy architectural styles and to the disposal of wealth available to the proprietor. The homes of the poor and laboring classes satisfied a need for shelter from the elements, while the middle class, who imitated the luxuries found in the homes of the affluent, embraced imported lacquerwork, Persian carpets, mahogany fixtures, and indoor plumbing. Even a pet or two added a gilded finish to a privileged English residence.

At the bottom of the socioeconomic scale, homes were not ornamental but were functional shelters, pure and simple. There were slums in the city and cottages in the country. To judge by contemporary accounts, the English poor lived better than those in other countries, but they were still crowded together, often in a single room that measured little more than 100 square feet, sometimes in a single bed, sometimes in a simple pile of shavings or straw or matted wool on the floor. Floors were made of flagstones or packed earth. In the cities, the crowding was pitiful, with as many as 10 people living in one room. Some lived in shacks or cellars.

The belongings of the poor were limited. They possibly had a few family heirlooms, some pots and pans, wooden platters and cups, and perhaps a few pewter dishes or mugs. The rural poor heated their cottages with scavenged sticks and, if possible, warmed their beds with hot bricks wrapped in flannel. Lighting, as was the case with heating, indicated an auspicious turn in fortune because candles were expensive. Some people made their own with a rush wick and hoarded animal fat.

Houses of artisans, merchants, shopkeepers, and professionals varied in size, cost, and style. Some people lived in town houses—fresh new terraces with shared walls, or top-heavy survivors. Others built "country boxes" and commuted to the city. A few generalizations can be made. The rich and the middle class had some rooms for guests—a drawing room, for example, or a parlor, or a guest ("state") bedroom—and some that were just for family and servants.

Isaac Ware described the layout of a typical town house at midcentury "for the reception of a family of two or three people, with three or four servants." The house typically had five floors, each possessing approximately two rooms and a closet (smaller room). In the front of the basement was the kitchen and, nearby, a cistern containing the water used for cooking and cleaning. The ground floor usually comprised a fancy front parlor, a slightly less formal back parlor, and a passage linking the two. On the second floor, the dining room occupied the front area, and a bedroom and closet made up the back area. Two bedrooms made up the third floor, above which was the garret. Here, a series of smaller rooms provided living quarters for the household servants. Two staircases—one ornate, the other less so—facilitated passage from one floor to another.

The "closets" were not used to store clothing. An 18th-century closet, or cabinet, was a small private office, used to store personal papers, diaries, books, and memorabilia. Other furnishings in a typical, middle-class home would probably have included a clock, a candelabra filled with candles, oil lamps filled with coal or whale oil, carpets, books, a mirror, "china figures," screens, curtains, brass door locks, fireplace tools, and a few sentimental or satirical prints on the walls.

The kitchen had a large open fireplace, fueled by coal, lit with phosphorus matches or a tinder box, and fitted with a turnspit that could accommodate skewers of various sizes. Women, employers, and servants alike gathered there to sew by the fire and to do the laundry. The clothes had to be boiled first, necessitating the hauling of plenty of water. Then they were wrung in a mangle, a device with weighted rollers. Laundry was hung out on ropes to dry.

Furniture, which had formerly been made of oak or of walnut veneer over another wood, such as beech, was now of expensive mahogany, as was the wainscoting on the walls. Gilded mirrors, hand-painted Chinese wallpaper, and carpets from Persia decorated the upper-class homes, the libraries of which often displayed thousands of volumes. The dining table was set with porcelain, silver, and high-quality blown glassware. The chimney pieces and staircases might be made of marble.

Indoor plumbing was rare, and relieving oneself was a clumsy process at any social level. The rich, in their country or town houses, used chamber pots, which were then carried by servants to a cesspool. In the city, the cesspool was often in the garden or basement and was emptied periodically by a night-soil man, who would load the contents into a cart to be carried away to the country. The traditional after-dinner departure of the ladies in fashionable households, leaving the men alone in the dining room for further conversation and drink, was at least in part a toilet issue. The women, upon leaving, would head for "close stools" where they could relieve themselves privately, while the men could open a sideboard or a sliding wall-panel to retrieve a chamber pot. Then they urinated, often without interrupting their toasts and arguments. In the country were chamber pots or "jordans" for nighttime emergencies and a "necessary house" for all other times.

Toilet paper, as a purposely designed product, lay in the future. In the meantime, most used scrap paper; Lord Chesterfield described a man who routinely tore a few pages from a book of Horace, read them while defecating to illuminate his mind and then used them to clean his backside. Not until the last quarter of the century would a reliable water closet be constructed, and even then it remained a luxury item.

The homes of the middle class and the prosperous distinctly contrasted with the homes of the poor and laboring. A preoccupation with aesthetically satisfying rooms, furnishings (imported and domestic), and pets was not possible for the vast majority of English. Such homes did, however, represent the ideals of English living during the 18th century (Olsen, 84–86, 89, 92–93, 268–69).

To read about housing in Chaucer's England, see the Europe entry in the section "Housing" in chapter 5 ("Material Life") of volume 2; for houses and furniture in Elizabethan England, see the England entry in the section "Houses and Furniture" in chapter 5 ("Material Life") of volume 3; and for housing in Victorian England, see the Victorian England entry in the section "Housing" in chapter 5 ("Material Life") of volume 5 of this series.

FOR MORE INFORMATION

Byrne, A. *London's Georgian Houses*. London: Georgian Press, 1986.

Girouard, M. *Life in the English Country House*. New Haven, Conn.: Yale University Press, 1978.

Lynch, J. *Eighteenth Century Resources*. <http://newark.rutgers.edu/~jlynch/18th/>, accessed October 10, 2003.

Olsen, K. *Daily Life in 18th-Century England*. Westport, Conn.: Greenwood Press, 1999.

Ross, D. *The Georgian Period*. 2001. <http://www.britainexpress.com/History/Georgian_index.htm>, accessed October 23, 2003.

MATERIAL LIFE

|

HOUSING
& FURNISHINGS

|

Africa

The Colonial Frontier
of North America

England

Japan

New England

Life at Sea

JAPAN

The type of home in which a Japanese family lived depended on the class and wealth of the household. Peasants lived in small, unadorned and crudely built—but durable—houses. Well-off merchants enjoyed a more delicate, open home. The wealthiest simply expanded on this latter style, while petty merchants, lower-class samurai (warrior-administrators), and many other urban dwellers lived in cramped apartment complexes and barracks.

Japanese employed a method of foundation that depended on the very weight of the roof to stabilize the rest of the house. Upright log columns were mounted directly onto flat boulders, which were imbedded in the earth. The heavy weight of the thatched roof was transferred down the uprights.

This type of construction absorbed the destructive earthquakes to which Japan was prone. Similarly, the Japanese house could sway and adjust to the heavy monsoon and even typhoon winds that periodically hit the country.

Few wooden dowels (and virtually no iron nails) were used to fasten the house together. Uprights were often lashed to the roof joists, or an intricate post-and-lintel system joined the two with wooden locks. A single ridgepole and a few planks provided a frame for a thatched roof of thick sedge.

Almost no houses were made of brick or stone. Even stone buildings and walls were not mortared. Stones were hewn to fit together closely. The exterior walls were often formed by weaving split bamboo between the uprights or by fastening thick sedge mats in place. Sometimes a plaster of sticky mud was daubed over the mats, which dried into something resembling stucco.

Most houses were relatively small, scarcely 20 feet on a side, without any dividing interior wall. The floor was smoothed earth, although in more prosperous families, rough wooden planks could provide some dryness. Almost all homes had a large, flat rock embedded into the entryway, where people would remove and leave their sodden straw sandals or muddy *geta* (platform shoes) before entering the house. Most doors were little more than curtains, although some peasants fashioned reed mats fixed to bamboo frames to provide a more substantial door. There were no windows.

In most *minka* (peasant homes), a fireplace was sunken into the common floor of the one-room cottage, sometimes surrounded with an adobe-like hearth. By the 18th century, many *minka* had enclosed earthen stoves (*kamadō*) instead of fireplaces, but in most villages, these were simply an expensive luxury. The major attraction of these stoves was that two or often even three or four different pots could be heated simultaneously.

The sleeping quarters were little more than a dry corner along a side of the house. The whole family huddled together to share body warmth because only the rarest family could afford to burn a fire through the entire night. Also, it was very dangerous to do so unless the fire was tended throughout the night. People slept in their clothes and covered themselves with straw mats. By the 18th century, most farmers could afford cotton futon quilts stuffed with cheap batting. Many could also afford a thicker futon mattress as well.

By the 18th century, perhaps half of the peasants had graduated to more sophisticated housing, a type more familiar to readers who imagine a "typical" Japanese house.

The open-sided or *Shoin* style raised the floor of the house two to three feet above the ground and employed movable and interchangeable sections of the walls and floor. The exterior walls were actually standard-size screens mounted on rectangular wooden frames. These screens slid on recessed runners mounted in the floor and the overhead lintel. The outer-wall screens were usually thicker and more substantial than the inner screens.

Rush woven mats (tatami) were mounted on wooden frames and stuffed with tightly packed layers of straw. The mats were springy and plush enough to serve not only as carpeting but also as mattresses.

Ordinarily, one room (the one closest to the garden) was designated as a formal reception area. In that room, one exterior wall was permanent rather than movable.

In Japan, floor mats were popular and relatively simple to make, consisting of rice straw, smoothly woven reeds, and cloth binding. © Michael Maslan Historic Photographs/ CORBIS.

Sets of recessed shelves were built into the wall, and a recessed nook (tokonoma) was created to become the focus of the room. The tokonoma served as a sleeping place and was built up several inches above the surrounding tatami.

Other furniture included oil lamps, candlestands, colored paper lanterns, and polished, bronze mirrors, as well as horizontal, split bamboo screens and folding screens (byōbu) of two or three hinged panels that served as decorative room dividers. On the whole, however, Japanese did not use much furniture, conveying a Zen-like simplicity of the interior space with but a few subtle framing decorations.

The garden in Japan was seen as extended living space. It was carefully constructed to give the feeling of a rustic countryside. Special rocks, trees, flowers, and bushes were situated in precise patterns, as were stone lanterns and tiny, humped Chinese bridges. Artfully laid flagstones created footpaths that seemed to lead off into nearby forests but usually led only to the adjoining privy. Wells and cisterns were constructed so as to contribute to the impression of rusticity.

The privy has a very special place in Japanese architecture. It was much more than a necessary but noxious area where one rid oneself of malodorous body wastes. Indeed, most Japanese incorporated the rustic style of their home into the privy building. Often, a latticework enclosure overgrown with plants hid the doorway to the privy, and the stone path seemed to disappear into a rustic hedge.

Kitchens in *Shoin*-style houses retained much of the squalor of the rural farmhouse. This area was never covered with tatami; often, it was floored with duckboards that allowed water to fall beneath the house. Some even retained the packed earth doma of the farmhouse for kitchens, laundry areas, and bathrooms. Many houses retained open-hearth fireplaces for cooking, but most people could afford *kamadō*. Water had to be hauled into the kitchen. Many rural homes had their own wells, and the homes in the cities had common cisterns.

In most cities, the majority of residents lived in long blockhouses (*nagaya*). These were one-story tenements that were divided into individual apartments. They shared a common roof, and contiguous apartments shared interior walls with their neighbors. Each family had its own private doorway but frequently shared kitchens and always shared wells, cisterns, and privies.

The actual construction of the buildings was more like that of the rural *minka* than of the *Shoin*. Mud-wattled walls and thatched roofs were the norm in the beginning of the 18th century. By the end of the era, most *chōnin* (city folk) blockhouses had substantial doors and walls, as well as tiled roofs, and many even had a few tatami in the living quarters.

In most castle towns (*jokamachi*), samurai families lived in *chōnin-style* blockhouses. In Edo, most of the common samurai were unaccompanied by their families, so they lived in barracks or occasionally in tiny cell-like apartments, if their rank warranted the privacy.

The very few wealthy among the *chōnin* and samurai lived in mansions that incorporated the finest of the *Shoin* amenities: larger estates, gardens, several tatami rooms, and servants who managed the entire place. Those places were more like museums than homes.

In sum, there were a number of household styles. The *Shoin*-style, or open-sided, home was usually the residence of substantial people. In villages, only wealthy village headmen could afford the *Shoin* house; the other villagers generally lived in the dank, cramped *minka*. In more urban settings, ordinary *chōnin*—like their peasant counterparts—could ill afford the luxury of a *Shoin* house and, more often than not, lived in tenemant-like communal buildings (Perez, 101–14, 193, 207).

To read about housing in Japan in the 20th century, see the Japan entry in the section "Housing" in chapter 5 ("Material Life") of volume 6 of this series.

FOR MORE INFORMATION

Hanley, S. B. *Everyday Things in Premodern Japan: The Hidden Legacy of Material Culture.* Berkeley: University of California Press, 1997.

Japan Information Network. <http://www.jinjapan.org/index.html>, accessed October 23, 2003.

Koizumi, K. *Traditional Japanese Furniture.* Tokyo: Kodansha International, 1986.

Morse, E. S. *Japanese Homes and Their Surroundings.* New York: Dover, 1961.

Perez, L. G. *Daily Life in Early Modern Japan.* Westport, Conn.: Greenwood Press, 2002.

NEW ENGLAND

The buildings that Native Americans and European settlers constructed in the New England area served as important family and religious sites. These constructions also reflected the intermittent material scarcity and abundance to which settlers adapted themselves throughout the 17th and 18th centuries.

Tribes in different parts of New England built structures called wigwams, all of which had tight and complex frames. The outside of the wigwam was covered with tree bark sewed with both needles made of bone and thread made of the roots of evergreen trees. Bark and hides sometimes covered the inside walls, which were frequently decorated. The result was a waterproof shelter.

The edifice featured one or more doorways, covered with a flap of heavy hides that could allow access to the wigwam without letting snow inside. The flap, when pulled back, allowed smoke out of the wigwam. Several flapped windows or doors assisted in the process of ventilation.

Inside the wigwam were several platforms, each used for a different activity. The family slept on one platform, worked on another, ate on another, and so on. These were covered with sealskins, deerskins, and grass mats. Skins also functioned as coverings for sleeping. In the center of the wigwam was the fireplace.

New England colonists, unlike Native Americans, were newcomers to North America, and their housing reflected this fact. Indeed, it is interesting to envision exactly how one would survive upon disembarking a ship thousands of miles from home and then encountering a land untouched by the kind of civilization to which one had become accustomed, especially in a climate that would prove brutally cold in winter.

One of the quickest ways to improvise a shelter involved using crude hoes and spades to dig caves into the sides of hills. Some settlers covered the small opening of their caves with a dried animal skin abandoned by a Native American. A few other settlers found discarded teepees made of skins. Typically, the wealthy gentry had brought tents over with them on the ship for use as immediate shelter.

Most of the gentry of the Massachusetts Bay Colony were able to begin construction of spacious, comfortable houses immediately because these future homeowners had the money not only to bring the necessary tools and materials with them but also to hire laborers to begin construction. They planned for an entryway and staircase, three or four great rooms on the ground floor with a kitchen in the back, and three or four bedrooms upstairs. Two or three fireplaces and chimneys provided heat for both downstairs and upstairs rooms.

Slowly, common men living in caves who worked all day building other people's houses began constructing more substantial, although still temporary, structures of daub (clay) and wattle (woven sticks) in order to get through the winter. These low-ceilinged, one-room structures of about 10 by 12 feet consisted of stakes planted upright in the ground and of leafy branches interwoven with the stakes. Mud and clay covered these walls.

In the spring, with enough money to secure land and purchase some imported tools, the settlers were ready to build more livable quarters. They began by digging a 6-by-7-foot-deep excavation about 20-by-20-feet wide. They covered their log walls with different materials, including hides, cloth, sod (that is, dirt to which grass and other hardy vegetation was still attached), or bark. They made a roof of logs covered with bark and heavily daubed with clay to keep water out. The clay-daubed fireplace proved to be an obvious fire hazard. These flimsy huts, which lasted for four years at the most, soon began to rot from the New England rain and snow and required daily repairs.

By the end of their second year, settlers often built a more stable house, which began with the excavation of a cellar about 20-by-20 feet and, above it, one huge room. The builder drove heavy logs into the ground every few feet to form a solid skeletal structure. A sawmill in the area sawed planks from logs. The builder then fitted these planks in an overlapping pattern, both inside and outside the skeletal structure. Sod, thatch, or wood and bark shingles covered roofs.

Windows were little more than two slits covered with oiled paper protected by wooden shutters. To impede the entrance of an intruder or animal, doorways were low and small, so that even a short woman was forced to bend double to enter. Chimneys were made of brick, which a local brick maker had formed of clay and had fired in his oven. The single great room or hall served as a kitchen, dining room, living room, bedroom, and workroom. The children slept in the loft, which also served as storage space.

Homeowners typically improved on their log house, adding a kitchen, a storage shed, and a second enclosed room inside the great room, which functioned primarily as a private master bedroom. Over time, a staircase might replace a crude ladder, and the upstairs could contain several bedrooms. If a farmer owned the home, he might build a barn and a larger storage building.

Early settlers slept on bedrolls brought from England or on straw beds covered with cloth brought from England. At first, their only chairs were blocks of wood axed from the forest. Later, homeowners or local artisans used oak, pine, hickory, and maple to craft chairs, bureaus, tables, bedsteads, buffets, and cupboards. Kitchen and tableware were made of wood, iron, and eventually, pewter. Girls and women wove flax yarn to create an extensive store of table and bed linen. For light, settlers used fireplaces, candlewood (smoky pine logs cut in half and lit), and occasionally, candles.

By the 18th century, the colonial houses of many residents had three full floors, multiple fireplaces, an elegant entryway decorated with leaded glass, a mansard roof with as many as seven or eight gables, 30 or 40 shuttered glass windows, and well-manicured grounds.

A typical kitchen in colonial New England. Boston: Society for the Preservation of New England Antiquities, 1935.

The quarters of servants and slaves in colonial New England were decent on the whole. In most instances, in both rural and urban areas, slaves lived in the house with the master's family, and their accommodations differed little in quality. Some slave families occupied the entire second floor of the house. In smaller houses, they could be found sleeping in the same room with their master and his family. Occasionally in Rhode Island and parts of Connecticut, where the acreage was larger and the slaves more numerous, they occupied separate cabins, as they did in the south.

The edifices in which people in New England ate, slept, entertained themselves, worked, and worshiped reflected the character not only of the surrounding environment but also of the particular culture in which the edifices were designed and constructed. Wigwams and settlers' homes, be they caves, huts, log cabins, the quarters of slaves and servants, or the mansions of the gentry, predominated the New England landscape wherever Native Americans or colonists resided (Johnson, 73–81, 86–87, 137, 153, 167).

FOR MORE INFORMATION

Earle, A. M. *Customs and Fashions in Old New England.* Williamson, Mass.: Corner House, 1969.

Johnson, C. D. *Daily Life in Colonial New England*. Westport, Conn.: Greenwood Press, 2002.
Morrison, H. *Early American Architecture: From the First Colonial Settlements to the National Period*. New York: Dover, 1987.

LIFE AT SEA

Sailors made their homes on land and on sea. The level of comfort in both locations typically varied according to one's status aboard ship. Officers enjoyed greater comforts, while seamen made do with very little.

The buildings that lined the waterfront varied both in their construction and in their purpose. Made of stone, brick, or wood, the buildings also varied greatly from place to place. Many were done in gray and white stucco; others were simply in gray wooden siding, pink marble, or red sandstone. Small single-story sheds occupied positions next to clapboard houses and multileveled edifices.

Seaports had their sheds, shanties, and shacks, but they also had their mansion rows, which were built by wealthy shipowners and captains. The first big houses were generally built right beside the water, where they faced the wharves and counting houses of their owners. Away from the immediate noise of the wharves, but close enough to oversee the activity, newer homes surrounded themselves with lawns, flower gardens, and fine trees.

One distinguishing characteristic of many of these homes was a flat, roof-top platform with ornamented rails. This structure afforded a grand view of the harbor and provided an early opportunity to see the masts of arriving ships as they broke the horizon. When a husband's ship was expected, the wife of the ship's master could often be seen pacing the platform hoping to catch that first glimpse of her beloved's returning ship. The sight of the lonely woman pacing the lofty perch long after the ship had been expected earned them the designation of "widow's walks."

Inside the homes of the "first families," spacious rooms were filled with delicate porcelains, carved soapstone, exquisite embroidered silks, and handsome teakwood furniture brought back from voyages to the Orient. Highly prized Canton ware graced the dining-room tables. Returning sea captains also brought back exotic produce such as pineapples. It became a custom to place a pineapple on the front gate or door to alert visitors of the captain's return. From this practice, the pineapple came to be a symbol of hospitality, a tradition that survives today.

Standing in sharp contrast to the more idyllic residences was the maze of alleys and by-ways meandering around the dockside or crisscrossing through the warehouse area. Sometimes called a "Fiddler's Green," this urban neighborhood was a cluster of the port's poorer residences, shacks, and more disreputable taverns and shops.

Boardinghouses made up a large portion of any Fiddler's Green. Former seamen, retired from the rigors of the life at sea, ran the most respectable ones. They offered the sailor what he needed most: a decent bed, fair victuals, and a few good drinks.

The living environment aboard any ship alternated between cold and damp or hot and humid. The orlop and hold had no direct ventilation. All ships were regularly fumigated by burning sulfur, and the below decks were periodically washed down with vinegar. This added to the smell of wet canvass, tar, stagnant seawater, and rotting wood. Life was made even less tolerable by the constant motion of a vessel either wallowing in ocean swells or plunging through rough seas.

The conditions under which naval personnel lived varied according to both rank and type of ship. Admirals and captains always fared best, and small vessels obviously offered far fewer places in which cabins and berths could be provided than did large ships. In the case of a 74-gun ship, the captain had a day cabin that was under the poop deck and that opened onto the stern gallery. The cabin featured two quarter galleries, one of which was fitted as a lavatory. Forward of the day cabin was the captain's sleeping cabin and a dining cabin known as the coach. Moving forward along the quarter deck were cabins for the captain's clerk and for the master. The commissioned officers slept in very small cabins, with room for only a sea chest and a cot or a hammock. The surgeon and the purser usually berthed on the orlop deck. The other inferior officers berthed on the main deck in cabins under the forecastle.

In merchantmen, the crew was usually crowded into the forecastle or found space on the open well deck on which to curl up in a blanket. In warships, even small ones, the crew had the dubious luxury of berthing in the between decks and were encumbered only by the guns.

Ratings commonly hung their hammocks among the guns while sleeping. Each man was given a hammock number, and no more than 14 inches of space was allotted to each man. Few ordinary seamen had individual sea chests, but the men of a mess might share one. Each mess of six to eight men ate, if they were below deck, from a common pot at a table suspended from the rafters in the space between the guns, or, if they were allowed on deck, on a square of oil cloth. The men usually sat on their sea chests or on a pair of benches at the table.

The wardroom was fitted with two lavatories for the officers in the quarter galleries. Forward of the forecastle on a platform over the bowsprit were the crew's lavatories, called the head. There were also two semicircular roundhouses that served as lavatories for the warrant officers and sometimes for the petty officers. All the lavatories aboard were simple holes cut in plank seats that discharged directly into the sea. Those facilities in the quarter galleries, being like a small closet, offered some privacy, but the lavatories in the fore of the ship were largely open to the wind, weather, and sea spray.

Sailors made their home where they could. Captains could spend their time surrounded by the comforts of either a flat-roof house or day cabin. Seamen, on the other hand, typically found themselves either relegated to the Fiddler's Green or crowed between decks (Volo and Volo, 2, 8–10, 119–21).

FOR MORE INFORMATION

Lavery, B. *The Arming and Fitting of English Ships of War, 1600–1815.* London: Conway Maritime Press, 1987.

Volo, D. D., and J. M. Volo. *Daily Life in the Age of Sail.* Westport, Conn.: Greenwood Press, 2002.

Male Clothing

Exhibiting remarkable diversity, 17th- and 18th-century clothing for boys and men simultaneously reflected and reinforced important values along the frontiers of colonial North America and in colonial Australia, England, France, Japan, New England, and Western oceanic travel. Clothing was so distinctive that one could identify not only the culture and era represented in the costume but also the wearer's social status.

Many materials went into the clothes that people wore. Sailors' clothing was made of linen, felt, straw, canvass, wool, and leather, to name only the most important materials. Native Americans in colonial New England put together clothes from the skins and furs of bear, deer, and moose, making sure that the fur of the hide faced inside. New England colonists produced pants, jackets, and shirts from linen and wool, while relying on leather for shoes. People in early modern Japan produced clothing from cotton, hemp, and straw, although tailors often formed specialized attire from more luxurious fabrics such as silk. Silk, along with fine cotton, was the preferred material among France's elite, whereas the masses made do with wool and rough linen.

Infants and boys sometimes dressed differently than their adult counterparts. In England, parents wrapped their baby sons in cloth, a tradition known as swaddling, and one that effectively prevented the baby from moving. For much of the 17th and 18th centuries, the dress of French boys was similar to that of girls. In France, once a boy grew too big and active for swaddling, he wore frocks identical to those worn by girls. Finally, he likely received a pair of long pants (pantaloons). Japanese boys wore long robes called *kosode,* which, while resembling adult male *kosode,* were proportionally smaller.

Garments covered a person's legs, torso, feet, and head according to the dictates of climate, money, material, and class. Sailors typically wore white trousers, whereas their officers dressed in stockings and breeches, both white. Below the waist, Japanese men wore underwear in the form of a loincloth. In hot weather, a lower-class man did not need to wear anything over this garment. However, *kosode* were common, and samurai (warrior-administrators) sometimes dressed in silk trousers. Men in England wore many different types of pants. Before longer pants became fashionable, toward the end of the 18th century, breeches were popular. Ending below the ankle, they were fixed at the center-top with buttons, sometimes attaching a flap that served as a kind of fly. A string or fashionable buttons fastened the bottom of the breeches to the leg.

Around the torso, officers in the British and French navies were something of a spectacle, taking great pains to project a lofty image of rank and reputation. Coats were blue or red, single breasted or double breasted, and outfitted with stylized collars, buttons, cuffs, lapels, lace, and pocket flaps. In England, gentlemen wore ruffled shirts and turned-back cuffs, but workers usually managed without the cuffs. Vests were also popular.

The English wore shoes over their stocking-covered feet, and over the course of the 18th century, buckles came to replace shoelaces. Sailors, when on shore or aloft, wore black leather shoes, as did colonial New Englanders, but boots were common among workers. Native Americans wore moccasins made from leather and fur. Indeed, French and English settlers along North America's colonial frontier adopted Indian leggings for their high functionality. Japanese specialized in sandals and other footwear fashioned from straw.

The three-cornered cocked hat epitomized male headwear in England and New England, as well as among naval officers in the West. Other headwear included wigs in England and New England. Often powdered and pampered, wigs were, within certain circles, a symbol of fashion excess. Those who were disposed to Puritan notions of decency made a supreme effort to convince wayward New Englanders of the irreligious nature of wig wearing. In place of wigs, Japanese men tied their long hair into ponytails. Samurai wore knots of hair atop their head, although disgraced samurai had to forego this privilege and revert to ponytails or loosely worn long hair. Colonial Australian settlers wore hats, woolen caps, "cabbage tree" hats, and if a person's income permitted, powdered wigs and beaver hats.

Men also wore accessories. In England, going out in public meant that a man, if desiring to convey good breeding and discriminating taste to passers-by, sported gloves, a handkerchief, and a cane. In a similar vein, samurai complemented their refined attire with a few objects symbolic of their honored position in society. Silk strings attached tobacco pouches to the sashes of samurais' *kosode*, in the sleeve pockets of which one would likely find handkerchiefs containing amulets or some other personal item of significance.

Despite the great variation of male clothing that these cultures exhibited, they shared several basic concerns. First was an effort to distinguish men's clothing from boy's clothing. A second concern related to a division of the male body into legs, torso, feet, and head, with an eye toward relatively unimpeded movement. Third was a preoccupation with "making a statement," typically involving the use of refined clothing and accessories with which to project an aura of personal sophistication.

~Peter Seelig

FOR MORE INFORMATION

De Marly, D. *Fashion for Men: An Illustrated History*. London: Batsford, 1989.
Hollander, A. *Sex and Suits*. New York: Knopf, Random House, 1994.

COLONIAL AUSTRALIA

On their arrival in Australia, male convicts were to receive clothing from the government, but this formal promise rarely occurred, for want of a reliable supply. Thus boys and men who were new to Australia generally wore whatever they arrived in. The first official 1788 issue for males was as follows:

Two jackets
One waistcoat
One pair of breeches
Two shirts
One hat
One woolen cap
Two pair of shoes
Two pair of stockings

Clothing was for utility and protection, but in such a small and divided society, it also denoted status. Although convicts were not uniformed, clothing distinctions were immediately obvious not only between convicts and the free but also among members of the military, some of whose uniforms were striking and opulent and all of whose uniforms looked positively refined alongside the shabby convict garb.

Shortages of clothing and shoes occurred as frequently as food shortages. In 1790, Watkin Tench wrote that the convicts' clothing was in such a state that patching could barely "preserve the remains of decency" (Tench, 124). He added that even soldiers were turning out without shoes. The first boot-making factory in colonial Australia did not begin manufacture until 1809. Within a few years, illegal trading began in new and used clothing among the marines and other speculators, who made huge profits. Clothing, like spirits, became another form of unofficial currency.

Men generally wore their hair short, with sideburns but no chin hair. The occasional application of rouge denoted good health. Early officials wore wigs and dressed their hair with powder.

Wealthier males wore high beaver hats with narrow brims; others adopted the "cabbage tree" hat, a local millinery development at the end of the 1790s. Woven from the palm fronds of the cabbage tree, its wider brim offered men protection from the harsh Australian sun.

By the turn of the 18th century, the general transfer of supplies from far-off locations to Australia improved. Costume historian Marion Fletcher has noted that at this time, a fashionable gentlemen's outfit consisted of waistcoat, ruffled shirt, and a high-stand frock coat. This was worn over tight breeches to suggest an elegant leg line with a cut-away coat to flatter the line below the waist. He was shod in buckled pumps or elegant midcalf boots. Even the ill-tempered Governor Bligh was willing to spend up to one thousand pounds on his outfit to maintain his status and authority through personal appearance.

Australia's first British military presence consisted of the English marines, who were in New South Wales from 1788 to 1791. Their most obvious and distinguishing feature was the long, tapered, red double-breasted jacket. Ratings wore a black bicorn hat, pale breeches, and brown knee-high gaiters. Officers distinguished themselves from their inferiors with buckled pumps, knee-high hosiery, an epaulette at one shoulder denoting rank, a pink sash at the waist, and a sword. All had shiny buttons featuring a rope and anchor at both the openings and cuffs, and all presented a figure of force and authority.

In 1792, the New South Corps replaced the marines, and although differing in small details, the uniform retained the distinctive red jacket while cutting a more elegant, but still authoritative, figure. Men of the various loyal associations (civilian militia) adapted a modified version of the military uniforms, including the striking red coat.

A fashion consciousness also permeated the lower echelons of society. Jane Elliott's study of contemporary account books reveals that many males purchased much of their partners' clothing. Items similar to those preferred by the gentry were acquired, and they did not scrimp on their own clothing. In his free time, a resourceful male convict could dress in a frilled shirt, waistcoat, and well-tailored coat.

Although male laboring attire was rough and rudimentary, men needed to make statements about their changing status in colonial Australian society. They could do that by dress and personal appearance that emulated their "betters."

To read about the clothing of Aboriginal Australians, see the Australian Aboriginal entry in the section "Clothing" in chapter 5 ("Material Life") of volume 1 of this series.

~Valda Rigg

FOR MORE INFORMATION

Elliott, J. 1995. "Was There a Convict Dandy? Convict Consumer Interests in Sydney, 1788–1815." *Australian Historical Studies* 26, no. 104 (1995): 373–92.

Fletcher, M. *Costume in Australia, 1788–1901.* Melbourne: Oxford University Press, 1984.

Flower, C. *Duck and Cabbage Tree: A Pictorial History of Clothes in Australia, 1788–1914.* Sydney: Angus and Robertson, 1968.

Scandrett, E. *Breeches and Bustles: An Illustrated History of Clothes Worn in Australia, 1788–1914.* Lilydale, Australia: Pioneer Design Studios, 1978.

Stanley, P. *The Remote Garrison: The British Army in Australia, 1788–1870.* Kenthurst, Australia: Kangaroo Press, 1986.

Tench, W. *1788: Comprising A Narrative of the Expedition to Botany Bay [1789] and A Complete Account of the Settlement at Port Jackson [1795].* Edited by Tim Flannery. Melbourne: Text Publishing, 1996.

THE COLONIAL FRONTIER OF NORTH AMERICA

In terms of dress, the eastern tribe people who occupied North America were not all that different in appearance from those of other woodland Indians, making it unnecessary and redundant to describe each nation separately. Many of the items of clothing worn by these nations were generic and designed around the same set of available materials, which were chosen largely for their practicality. Individual and tribal differences surfaced largely in the decoration of these items.

Early descriptions tell of painted deerskin robes, brass ornaments, and copper pipes. The surviving clothing artifacts that serve as examples of these nations have remarkable refinements in cut and exhibit sophistication in assembly. The long period of contact between the eastern woodland nations and white settlers resulted in a fusion of European and Native American artistic and technological practices, and the multitribal reorganizations that followed the native dispersions of the 17th century perhaps accurately explain the hybridized appearance of many native objects now in museums.

Indian men wrapped a piece of cloth about six feet square around themselves by way of outerwear. Europeans sometimes described this article of clothing in terms of the Roman toga. According to Peter Kalm, who traveled the area in the mid-18th century, the Hurons used "a shaggy piece of cloth, which is either blue or white, with a blue or red stripe below. This they always carry over their shoulders, or let it hang down, in which case they wrap it around their middle." And Pierre Pouchot noted in his memoirs on the Anglo-French wars in North America that in inclement weather, Indian men would "fasten their blanket below with their belts, and make them pass over the head like a monk's hood, arranging them so well that they expose only their nose and hands." Otherwise, the men threw their blanket loosely over one shoulder, and even in the hottest weather, they might be seen strutting about their villages.

Once the tribes came in contact with the Europeans and sold them furs for trade items, individual Indians readily adopted cloth shirts made of linen, blankets, loin-cloths, and leggings made of coarse wool. One contemporary explained that the men of every nation differ in their dress very little from each other, except those who trade with the Europeans. A great number of the male Indians also began to dress in jackets and vests mixed with the aforementioned loincloths, Indian leggings, and footwear.

Kalm wrote that most Indian men could not be persuaded to use trousers because "they thought these were a great hindrance in walking." They wore instead a slip of cloth or dressed skin known as a breechclout, which was about a half-meter wide and a meter-and-a-half long. This they put between their legs and tied around their waists with a conveniently broad belt or cord. A French soldier noted, "The two ends of the loincloth are folded over in front and in back, with the end in front longer than the one in the back."

Men, as well as women, seem to have favored the European style of shirts, but Captain Jonathan Carver, who traveled in the area during the latter half of the 1760s, remarked that they left the collars and cuffs open because fastening them "would be a most insufferable confinement to them." The consumption of shirts among Indians was very great. A plain men's shirt could be bought for a large beaver pelt or deerskin. With ruffles, the price doubled; and for children, a smaller pelt or skin was charged. Shirts were sometimes decorated with vermilion mixed with grease.

Several styles of moccasin construction have been identified as belonging to the Algonquian, Iroquoian, and other tribal styles. The leather skins were sometimes dressed in the European manner; at other times, they were left with the fur on them. It was also noted that Native Americans frequently went without moccasins but usually wore their leggings even when barefoot. They also had shoes for winter wear that were similar to lace-up boots.

Male Indians wore leg coverings. Nicholas Cresswell, who traveled widely through the backcountry, considered leggings an essential item: "These are pieces of coarse woolen cloth wrapped round the leg and tied below the knee with a string to prevent the snakes biting you." Woolen and leather leggings of the Native American style were adopted by most frontiersmen and rangers. Many French and English troops serving on the frontiers would appear in traditional uniform coat, waistcoat, and shirt—only to be clothed from the waist down in moccasins and breeches topped with Indian leggings.

A center hair roach was most common on the head of male Indians, but some tribes allowed the hair to grow to great length. William Bartram, who traveled among the Muskhogeans, reported that the men shaved their heads, leaving only a narrow crest or comb that began at the crown of the head, where it was about two inches broad and about the same height. The hair was "frizzed upright," but as the crest moved farther to the back of the head, it gradually widened to cover the "hinder part of the head and back of the neck" in a lank of hair terminating in a tail or tassel, the length of which was ornamented in various ways. Male Indians had no patience for facial hair and plucked it at the root with clamshell twisters.

Young men distinguished themselves by creating giant loops in their earlobes. The young men could not extend their ears in this manner unless they had been tested as warriors. The ear loops were reported to have reached a diameter of four inches. Indian trader James Adair observed that "the young heroes cut a hole round almost the extremity of both their ears, which till healed, they stretch out with a large tuft of buffalo wool mixt with bear's oil. They then twist as much small wire round as will keep them extended in that hideous form."

> *Male Indians had no patience for facial hair and plucked it at the root with clamshell twisters.*

Colonial frontiersmen wore long, loose-fitting shirts with wide sleeves. Their breeches, made of wool or linen, came just below the knee and were held closed about the leg with either buttons or buckles. The lower leg was encased in a woolen thread stocking. In the 17th century, the outer garment worn by men on special occasions was a close-fitting item known as a doublet, but the average laborer or farmer wore a simple pullover garment much like a woolen shirt or jacket. In the 18th century, waistcoats and long-tailed coats became fashionable, but the day-to-day work clothes remained essentially the same. By the mid-18th century, long-legged trousers became more common than breeches for work. Few adjustments in the weight of fabric were made for seasonal variations in temperature.

Over the course of the 17th and 18th centuries, Native American clothing styles absorbed European styles, striking a unique balance between the two. Men, in particular, wore traditional breechclouts and moccasins, along with collars, cuffs, and linen shirts. Traditional hairstyles and body decorations contributed to the Native American male's striking appearance, wholly distinguishing him from his European counterpart (Volo and Volo, 22–25, 27, 30, 32, 36, 155).

FOR MORE INFORMATION

Copeland, P. *Working Dress in Colonial and Revolutionary America.* Westport, Conn.: Greenwood Press, 1977.

Earle, A. M. *Costume in Colonial Times.* New York: Scribner's Sons, 1911.

Volo, J. M., and D. D. Volo. *Daily Life on the Old Colonial Frontier*. Westport, Conn.: Greenwood Press, 2002.

ENGLAND

After a brief time wrapped snuggly in blankets (known as "swaddling"), boys became accustomed to a uniquely masculine style of dress. In adulthood, men wore shirts, vests, jackets, and (over their drawers) a pair of pants. Shoes and stockings were standard features, as were the wig and the tricornered cocked hat, the latter two being representative of male attire in 18th-century England. Perhaps less apparent were the powders, perfumes, cleansers, and rouge that men of means occasionally applied to their wigs and their bodies.

A parent or caretaker would often dress a boy infant in a shirt, wrap him in a square cloth, and then wrap him round and round with a three-inch-wide woolen strip called a roller. His arms remained bound to his body, and the whole package was covered with an additional blanket. At about four months or so, the arms were freed from the swaddling, but the lower extremities were still swaddled for a few months. Swaddling, although still widely practiced in 1740, was almost universally abandoned by the end of the century.

At about age four, boys were "breeched," or put into distinctively masculine clothes for the first time. Early in the 18th century, young boys wore tight knee breeches, which evolved into looser, longer trousers (or tight pantaloons) by the late 1770s. Typically, a boy's costume from the ages of four to eight was a "skeleton suit," a pair of loose trousers buttoned to the jacket.

Men's suits had three essential pieces: vest, jacket, and pants (then called waistcoat, coat, and breeches). When a man got dressed, he put on a shirt, often with ruffled sleeves and, at the throat, a jabot (frilled neck opening) or cravat (something between a tie and a scarf). The richer he was, the more glorious his ruffles and the cleaner his shirt. He also put on a pair of drawers, or linen underwear, tied at the waist and knees.

Over the shirt, he put on a waistcoat, which at the beginning of the century looked more like a coat than like the modern vest. Waistcoats had long, tight sleeves, often with one wrist button left undone to display the shirt ruffles. Waistcoats also had a small standing collar or no collar at all, fit the body closely to the waist, and proceeded to flare out over the hips in flaps. Usually, the waistcoat was only buttoned at the waist. The waistcoat underwent a transformation between the 1720s and 1760s, losing its sleeves, increasing the height of the collar, and gradually exposing more of the thighs. Coats, which were worn over waistcoats, followed similar trends.

South of all these coats and waistcoats and over his linen drawers, a man wore breeches. Until about 1730, they were closed in front by buttons without a fly; after that, the closure was usually a "fall," a central flap buttoned on both sides near the waistband. The breeches ended either just above or just below the knee; working-class breeches were tied there; better breeches had a slit and buttons and then a buckle at the bottom. In the second half of the century, as waistcoats and coats were cut to reveal more of the breeches, men's legs became a focus of sexual attention. Consequently, breeches got tighter. Long pants of any kind did not become fashionable until the 1790s, when some began to wear pantaloons—ankle-length tights that a wearer buttoned from ankle to calf along the outside.

Men wore shoes and stockings. A garter was wrapped twice around the stocking top and buckled or tied in place. Shoes were made of black leather and featured red or black heels and buckles that fastened the shoe over the tongue. From the 1780s, men gradually began to forgo buckles in favor of shoelaces. Brightly colored slippers were sometimes worn indoors, and boots of all kinds were worn for riding, hunting, traveling, and soldiering. Farmers, laborers, and some servants wore "high-lows" (short lace-up boots).

Most men wore their hair close cropped, almost shaved, and covered their heads with wigs available at a wide range of prices. Wigs were usually made of human hair or horsehair. Human hair was best and most expensive; horsehair was cheaper. A gentleman dressing in the morning would wear a powdering jacket to protect his clothes and a mask to protect his clean-shaven face, while a barber greased the wig with pomatum and then applied powder, usually white or gray, with a bellows or puff. Artisans often removed the wig in order to work.

Wigs were long at the beginning of the 18th century, when Thomas D'Urfey described beaus "in wigs that hang down to their bums." Later, wigs displayed a more modest length. At the end of the century, they went out of fashion for good (except in the law courts) when powder taxes and sympathy for French revolutionaries made short, natural hair the rage.

Drawn and etched by Deighton in 1800. On the left is an English gentleman wearing clothing that was fashionable around 1700. On the right is an English gentleman's outfit 100 years later. Notice that the wig and sword cede to a natural hairstyle and a walking stick, respectively. © Hulton Archive/Getty Images.

The hat worn atop these wigs was the three-cornered cocked hat—a brim of varying width, which was turned up in one or more "cocks." The cocked hat was usually made of black beaver-fur felt and was often trimmed with a button or jewels and loop, a feather, lace, braid, or a feather fringe.

Poorer countrymen wore round, uncocked straw hats. For riding, stylish young men adopted, late in the century, the jockey cap, a rounded cap with a flattened peak in the front, sometimes adorned by a buckled band. They also began to wear a round, flat-topped hat with an uncocked brim for riding and driving—the antecedent of the top hat. Artisans also sometimes wore the nightcap in lieu of a wig while working or playing.

An array of cosmetics and accessories completed the appearance of the well-dressed man. In addition to perfumed wig powder, gentlemen used scents and cleansers. They might rouge their cheeks and lips and darken their eyebrows, perfume their linen, or use wrinkle or acne creams.

The general trend in 18th-century male costume leaned toward simplicity—plainer fabrics, duller hues, slimmer lines, tighter fit, and less ornamentation. Indeed, the basic set of garments—underwear, shirt, pants, and jacket—remains fundamental to Western formal and informal dress. Admittedly departed are the tricornered hats and the powdered wigs, but hair care and headwear continue to occupy the attention of many men (Olsen, 102–5, 107–8).

To read about clothing and fabrics in Chaucer's England, see the Europe entries in the sections "Clothing" and "Fabrics" in chapter 5 ("Material Life") of volume 2; for clothing in Elizabethan England, see the England entry in the section "Clothing and Personal Appearance" in chapter 5 ("Material Life") of volume 3; and for fashion in Victorian England, see the Victorian England entry in the section "Fashion" in chapter 5 ("Material Life") of volume 5 of this series.

FOR MORE INFORMATION

Buck, A. *Dress in Eighteenth-Century England*. New York: Holmes and Meier, 1979.

Lynch, J. *Eighteenth Century Resources*. <http://newark.rutgers.edu/~jlynch/18th/>, accessed October 10, 2003.

Olsen, K. *Daily Life in 18th-Century England*. Westport, Conn.: Greenwood Press, 1999.

FRANCE

In the 17th and 18th centuries, France was the acknowledged fashion leader of Europe. French prominence was especially notable in the luxury trades, with Austrian, German, and Russian seamstresses often modeling their clothes after Parisian fashions that were sent abroad in the form of dolls sporting the current clothing in miniature.

During the reign of Louis XIV (1643–1715), dolls exhibiting miniature fashions for men frequently included bodices that fit tightly at the chest and waist, as well as ample sleeves, decorated with a trimmed, lacey layer of silk in a contrasting color. Men's coats, although not nearly as long as women's skirts, tended to require a great deal of material and presented a flowing outline. Over the course of the 18th century, male clothing fashions changed. Men witnessed their tightly fitted waistcoats evolve into a more loosely fitted robe.

Of course, although French silks, frills, and lacey things were world renowned and high fashion trends in continental Europe followed Parisian styles, "fashion" in clothing did not always indicate extravagant costuming. Members of guilds and trades, ranging from bakers, butchers, and masons to lawyers, all had their own costumes, specific to their occupation. Butchers, for example, wore long aprons to protect their clothing from spattering blood, and blacksmiths donned hats while working to protect their hair from hot cinders and ash. Workingmen in all trades were likely to wear long trousers and rough clothing made of wool or linen, whereas noblemen would wear knee breeches and clothing made of silk or fine cotton. Lawyers marked a middle ground between the casual attire of the worker and the opulence of the noble; they wore long black robes, much like the robes that judges wear today.

The styles of poorer men were also often driven more by necessity than fashion consciousness. "Matching" stripes in the lower classes meant ensuring that the stripes on clothing all ran the same direction on the garment, so that vertical stripes decorating an article of clothing on a man's torso would generally mean that the stripes on the sleeves would run in circles around the arms. This was not a fashion decision, but a decision driven by finances; sleeves could be taken from a leftover edge of fabric instead of from a larger, unused piece that was needed elsewhere. However, even this styling was reserved for men with some degree of wealth. Those who possessed little money for cloth might purchase scraps and make their shirts out of multiple types of fabric, with sleeves from one fabric and another fabric for the front or back.

Boys' clothing often appeared even more mismatched or tattered. Until the later 18th century, no clothing was designed specifically for children. From the time that they left swaddling clothes as infants, even children of relatively wealthy parents would have had garments that had been cut to size and passed down either from older siblings or from a mother. In other words, boys who had not yet reached the age of six did not wear pants but dressed in outfits that looked a great deal like their mothers' outfits.

As was the case with girls, young boys wore corsets, petticoats, and dresses or long skirts with bodices that were differentiated from the adult woman only by a large and wide collar. The primary differences between the outfit of a young boy and that of a girl could be seen in the hair; although both boys and girls not infrequently had their hair styled in ringlets, girls would be more likely to have a simple cap whereas their brothers went bareheaded. For all children, however, clothing sizes were often rough.

As the 18th century progressed and as more and more parents found themselves with disposable income, clothing designers opened up a new market by creating and fitting outfits specifically promoted for children. These fashions still tended to mirror the fashions of the mother, but they were often made of washable material that allowed the boys to run and play with less fear of ruining their clothing. Women's fashion magazines began to picture fashionable little sons in sailor suits. Thus, as trends in men's fashions changed over the years, boys living in 1800 France came to enjoy a great deal more physical freedom than their counterparts in 1600 France.

~Jennifer J. Popiel

FOR MORE INFORMATION

Berg, M., and H. Clifford. *Consumers and Luxury: Consumer Culture in Europe, 1650–1850.* Manchester: Manchester University Press, 1999.

Blum, S. *Eighteenth-Century French Fashion Plates in Full Color: 64 Engravings from the "Galerie des Modes," 1778–1787.* New York: Dover, 1982.

Cumming, V., and A. Ribeiro. *The Visual History of Costume*. London: Batsford, 1989.

Ewing, E. *Everyday Dress, 1650–1900*. London: Batsford, 1984.

———. *History of Children's Costume*. London: Anchor Press, 1977.

Kipar, N. "L'Age d'or and Kirke's Lambs Civilian and Military Living History." February 2003. <www.kipar.org/index.html>, (February 22, 2003).

Lynch, J. *Eighteenth Century Resources*. <http://newark.rutgers.edu/~jlynch/18th/>, accessed October 10, 2003.

Maeder, E., ed. *An Elegant Art: Fashion and Fantasy in the Eighteenth Century*. Los Angeles: Los Angeles County Museum of Art, 1983.

Starobinski, J., K. Tsukamoto, P. Duboy, A. Fukai, J. I. Kanai, T. Horii, J. Arnold, and M. Kamer. *Revolution in Fashion: European Clothing, 1715–1815*. New York: Abbeville Press, 1989.

Stibbert, F., and A. Lensi. *Civil and Military Clothing in Europe from the First to the Eighteenth Century*. New York: Blom, 1968.

Dangerous Liaisons. Warner Bros., Inc. Directed by Stephen Frears. Videocasette, 1989.

JAPAN

By the 18th century, Japanese clothing was fairly well standardized; a basic adult size was made for each sex and another for all children. While boys' and girls' clothing were quite similar, men's clothing acquired unique features, often according to profession and social rank.

Although virtually every man and woman wore a *kosode*, the pattern and length of the cloth of this loose robe differed according to the sex of the wearer. In general, the *kosode* was cut from a single simple loomed piece of cloth 12 yards long by 14 inches wide and sectioned into eight rectangular pieces. Men wore the robe somewhat loosely, with the front left panel folding over the right (to do the opposite was to tempt fate; only a corpse was dressed right over left) to a comfortable snugness. A simple sash tied at the waist traditionally held the robe together. A boy's *kosode* was cut to about two-thirds size and could accommodate him from about age 6 to about age 13, when he would symbolically receive his first adult *kosode*.

When boys reached some appropriate age (it varied greatly by class, profession, and region), they would receive a symbolic set of adult clothes. Among samurai (warrior-administrator) boys, the age was approximately 15, at which time the boy would be allowed his first set of *hakama* (silk trousers). At the coming-of-age ceremony (*genpuku*), his head would be shaved in the *chonmage* (topknot) style, and he would be called by his new adult name.

Among commoners, males wore *fundoshi*, which were similar to the samurai loincloth (*shita-obi*). In warm weather, men who were peasants or common workers in the city wore little else but could wear a cotton *kosode*, often tied with a length of straw rope or a cheap cotton rag. Almost all men carried a two-foot-long rectangular towel-scarf that could be tied around the forehead as a sweatband. It could also be worn around the neck like a scarf, at the belt to be used to wipe sweat from the brow or armpits, bunched on the head like a turban, or used as a washcloth.

A fortunate peasant or commoner might own a padded overcoat (*kappo*) to be worn over the *kosode*. In the countryside, straw raincoats (*mino*) could serve as snow coats, as well. Rice straw was simply bunched and basted to a scrap of cloth that could be fastened around the neck. Together with a sedge hat, this outfit could keep someone remarkably dry and warm.

Cotton or hemp mittens (*tekko*) were common in the frostier northern climes. In the cities, most *chōnin* (city folk) could afford a sedge hat and a cheap oiled paper (*kasa*) umbrella. *Chōnin* store clerks usually dressed in short *kosode*-like livery coats that were worn open. When they sported a symbol on the back, they were called "advertising cloaks." The distinctive colors of these coats designated the rank of the wearer in the shop. Higher clerks also tied a portable ink and brush set to their *obi* (sash) to take orders quickly.

A short *kosode* robe (*yutaka*) was commonly worn when one came out of the bath, and there were many nightclothes, including one type that was like a sleeping bag with sleeves and a neck.

Men from the ranks of commoners rarely spent much time, energy, or treasure in dressing their hair. Once or twice during the warm months, someone in the village would round up several males and trim their hair down to the scalp. Otherwise, men would simply gather up loose strands of hair during the winter and tie them together into something like a ponytail.

The samurai wore the most elaborate and specialized costumes, but by the 18th century, they had simplified their dress unless they were formally attired in the presence of their daimyō (feudal warlords) or other high officials. Males wore a *shita-obi* (the previously mentioned loincloth), which was a simple cotton rectangle about eight inches wide and five feet long. It was wound twice around the waist and once between the legs as a primitive jockstrap. A short, open *kosode*-like shirt covered the torso. In cold weather, one could top this with a padded underjacket. Next came the *kosode*, which was tied with a simple sash.

A samurai was fully dressed when he donned a pair of cotton split-toed socks under ordinary split-toed straw sandals (*zori*). If he had to be prepared to run (as in battle), he might wear *waraji*, straw sandals that were like *zori* except that they fastened around the ankles with straw cords.

On formal occasions, a samurai could don several other pieces of uniform. The daimyō and other very high officers

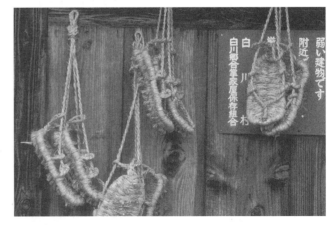

Rice straw, which was plentiful in Japan, served as the central material for Japanese slippers, called *zori*. © Craig Lovell/CORBIS.

might wear padded robes that were often made of silk and might be embroidered as well. They might also wear silk underwear instead of the *shita-obi*. An outfit of silk trousers and coat was more common for ceremonial purposes. *Hakama* were curious garments that had their own *obi*-like sash sewn into the waist piece. The bottoms of the *hakama* often tied around the calf. The *haori* was a sleeveless coat that tucked into the top of the *hakama*. It was made of a very stiff material that extended the shoulders like epaulets.

Most samurai carried a tobacco pouch (*tabako-ire*) anchored by a silk cord and fob to the *obi*. Some carried their own pipes and a piece of flint with which to light a fire. Frequently, they carried a case in which they might keep their personal seal (*hanko*), medicine, and small amulets, talismans, copper coins, and the like. More often than not, such small items could also be wrapped in a handkerchief and dropped into the pouchlike corners of the *kosode* sleeve.

Samurai men had hairdressers too. Upon coming of age, the forelock was shaved, and the long back hair was gathered up with a plaited string (*motoyui*) into a cascading topknot. The hair was gathered into the *chonmage* so that war helmets fit the head better and did not slip around, as would have been the case if the head was closely shorn. The hairstyle continued long beyond the time samurai actually had to wear helmets. The hair was washed about once a week, carefully combed, and set into the immobile *chonmage*. Disgraced samurai were shorn of their topknot, and the *rōnin* (masterless or literally, wave men) who had lost their positions as samurai showed their status by wearing the hair long and loose or in a ponytail.

Japanese boys, teenagers, and men wore distinct clothing. Peasants wore the simplest attire out of necessity, whereas *chōnin* dressed in more varied and colorful outfits, often related to their professions. The samurai, however, benefited the most from comfortable, stylish, and rather elaborate costumes, hairstyles, and accessories (Perez, 89–95, 99).

FOR MORE INFORMATION

Hanley, S. B. *Everyday Things in Premodern Japan: The Hidden Legacy of Material Culture.* Berkeley: University of California Press, 1997.

Hildreth, R. *Japan: As It Was and Is.* Willmington, Del.: Scholarly Resources, 1973.

Japan Information Network. <http://www.jinjapan.org/index.html>, accessed October 23, 2003.

Perez, L. G. *Daily Life in Early Modern Japan.* Westport, Conn.: Greenwood Press, 2002.

NEW ENGLAND

The clothing, accessories, and hairstyles of Native American men differed significantly from those of colonial men. In particular, New England settlers, often of the Puritan faith, wore dark and relatively drab clothing to church. However, some colonists, in addition to their church and work clothing, had the financial means to dress in decidedly more elegant attire, a cultural phenomenon that led to grave concerns throughout New England concerning the religious propriety of extravagance.

The clothing of the New England Native Americans was made of skins and furs. The men wore loose, armless shirts made of a single bear, deer, or moose hide, with the fur side inside. Smaller hides, usually raccoon, were attached to the shirt at the shoulder to hang over the upper arm. Trousers and moccasins were also constructed of hides. Native American children went naked in summer until they reached their teens.

Men in different tribes had special traditions for dressing their hair. One 1724 account by a Jesuit priest, the Reverend Joseph Lafitau, includes a description of the Iroquois. On one side of the head, the hair was cut short; on the other, it was grown to full length and tied into two or three topknots.

We know something of the clothing worn in colonial New England from a number of sources. The body of laws of the Massachusetts Bay Colony indicates something of the attitude toward apparel and its connection to class distinctions. Also in existence are colonial inventories of the clothing worn by Salem men, inventories of possessions left in wills, communications sent to England ordering clothing, and portraits, chiefly of families of the gentry.

Descriptions that survive in inventories and orders for clothing discredit the enduring stereotype of Puritan settlers dressed only in black, white, and gray. It is true that for church meetings and other ceremonial occasions, men (and women) favored black to denote the seriousness of the affair, much as a person from the 21st century might wear black to a funeral. But the record shows that everyday dress, especially coats, caps, and gowns, were very colorful, usually in soft shades of green, yellow, red, russet, orange, purple, and blue, all colored from native dyes.

Clothing in colonial New England was made of both native and imported materials. Men's shirts, jackets, and pants were made primarily of linen and wool and were usually home produced after 1640. Shoes could also be produced at home from leather. Men also wore work clothes of tanned leather, usually in the form of buckskin breeches and jackets. Masters provided their servants with decent clothes.

Inventories indicate the items of clothes worn by men. One such source is a list of clothes worn by laboring men who arrived in Salem in June 1629. Included in the list are four pairs of shoes and stockings, garters, shirts, doublets (or short jackets), breeches, a leather-lined wool suit, a cape, and various belts, caps, and gloves. On an ordinary workday, a man would wear a fairly snug doublet, a long shirt, breeches that came below his knees, long stockings, sometimes protective canvas stockings (called boot hoses) worn over these, and leather boots. On Sunday, he might change his cap for a felt hat and his boots for black shoes.

Research has shown that New England boys, from the time they could walk, wore the same kinds of clothing as did their fathers.

One of the most controversial matters of fashion and attire in New England concerned the wearing of powdered wigs. Male citizens found the vogue of wig wearing to be very seductive, especially in the last decades of the 17th century and in the 18th century. Devout members of the community, especially the clergy, were appalled at what they considered to be ungodly and unnatural foppery. One illustration comes from the diary of Samuel Sewall, a lay minister and Puritan judge who visited and admonished wig-wearing men. On Friday, November 6, 1685, he made a note of such a visit and the bizarre justification of the wig wearer:

Having occasion this day to go to Mr. Hayward the Publick Notary's House, I speak to him about his cutting off his Hair, and wearing a Perriwig of contrary colour: mention the words of our Savior, Can ye not make one Hair white or black: and Mrs. Alsop's sermon. He alleges, the Doctor advised him to do it.

On June 10, 1701, Sewall called on another wig wearer, this time a young man who put up a determined argument:

Having last night heard that Josiah Willard had cut off his hair (a very full head of hair) and put on a Wig, I went to him this morning. Told his Mother what I came about and she call'd him. I. . . . Told him that it was condemn'd by a Meeting of Ministers at Northampton in Mr. Stoddards house.

Gentlemen adopted not only wigs but took to wearing large silver buckles on their shoes, ruffled shirts, and heavy brocade dressing gowns. These gowns were so expensive and impressive that when a man in possession of such clothing had his portrait painted, he made a point of wearing such clothing.

In the 18th century, however, both the primitive conditions in the New World and the Puritan displeasure with extravagance left an indelible impression on American attire and Europe's vision of Americans. Benjamin Franklin, while he presided over Philadelphia culture, indulged himself by wearing a wig or a ruffled shirt; but when he made the trip to France to represent America and Americans, he left his fancy European clothes at home and appeared in drab homespun clothes, with only his own hair and a coonskin cap on his American head.

Colonial American fashions for men revealed the tension between clothing that functioned from a purely practical standpoint and clothing that possessed a certain extravagant receptivity to fashion. Native American men also took time to prepare themselves according to a particular visual mode of style (Johnson, 87, 89, 90–93, 138, 166).

FOR MORE INFORMATION

Copeland, P. *Working Dress in Colonial and Revolutionary America.* Westport, Conn.: Greenwood Press, 1977.

Earle, A. M. *Costume in Colonial Times.* New York: Scribner's Sons, 1911.

Johnson, C. D. *Daily Life in Colonial New England.* Westport, Conn.: Greenwood Press, 2002.

LIFE AT SEA

With regard to clothing, the styles of most cultures divide along lines of sex. The clothing of men follows certain fixed patterns, distinct from those that characterize women's clothing. During the 17th and 18th centuries, females occupied a very minor space on boats and ships. Hence, status rather than sex constituted the crucial line of division by which clothing was evaluated. Common seamen wore certain fashions, loosely systematized and cut with an eye to function more than to form. Officers' uniforms were another story. Subtle variations of color, accessories, number, and so on could either enhance or detract from an officer's attire.

Neither the merchant marine nor the navy issued clothing to sailors prior to the 19th century. Most merchant seamen brought a small bag of serviceable clothing with them when they signed on. "A sailor, in the usual striped trousers and short jacket, often carried all his worldly goods wrapped in a kerchief." Replacement items came from the slops chest. This was a supply of personal goods purchased by the master or his agent, kept for sale to the seamen, and charged against their wages.

The navies of the world eschewed uniforms for ratings (common seamen) prior to the middle of the 19th century. The American and French revolutionaries had no uniform dress for seamen, who used their own clothes, which sported many regional variations and personal preferences.

Nonetheless, mariners tended toward certain characteristic articles of clothing that identified them as seamen. Sailors favored long, loose trousers, either white or striped. A *coatee*, which is a coat with short tails, was replaced with time by a short practical jacket without tails, usually dark blue. These were worn with a waistcoat and a white, checked, or striped shirt. Black leather shoes were worn ashore and when going aloft. Round hats were popular. They could be made of felt, straw, or canvass, and they were often tarred or painted to make them waterproof and to give them body. A low crowned hat with a narrow brim (much like a civilian top hat) was common in Admiral Nelson's navy. This hat probably derived from a tricorn hat with the brim trimmed. The pirate-like bandanna topped with a tricorn hat was less common than Hollywood movies would lead one to suppose and would not have been tolerated in either the merchant or the naval service.

When working, sailors often resorted to woolen caps or stocking caps. Petticoat breeches of white or natural linen, with skirtlike wide legs to midcalf, were worn without stockings or shoes for dirty work. This garment, an ancient one sometimes called a pair of slops, continued to be worn until 1820 and was worn over better clothes with a canvass apron for protection.

In cold weather, sailors put on woolen pea jackets and frocks; in warm weather, jackets and pullover frocks of cotton or linen duck were preferred. In tropical climates, sailors might be found barefoot in shirts and slops. Linen canvass coats impregnated with boiled linseed oil were used as slickers (raincoats) in foul weather, but these were used to keep out the wind more than the cold as a sailor's clothing was almost always wet. There were few places on a ship where clothing would dry once wetted.

In the American and most European services, the connotation of rank through clothing was based on the cut and style, as well as the number and arrangement of buttons and braiding. In the merchant service, officers rated a better set of clothing than seamen, but this privilege varied in accordance with the personal preferences and pocketbooks of the individual. The clothing of many merchant officers imitated that of naval officers. There was no standard, but it can be assumed that masters and mates dressed better than seamen. Idlers probably had one set of shore clothing and another set of work clothes that were characteristic of their fellow tradesmen. Petty officers dressed as ordinary seamen.

Naval clothing for officers was dictated by the regulations of the admiralty, and they changed slowly with time. Because they were made by tailors rather than issued by the navy, even uniforms sometimes lacked uniformity. At the beginning of the 19th century, the British Admiralty had the most comprehensive clothing regulations of any European service. These regulations branched into dress and undress uniforms. The small clothes—waistcoat (vest), shirt, stockings, and breeches—for all officers were white, as was the lining of all officers' coats. Three buttons appeared on the cuffs and pockets of uniforms that had them.

The regulations of 1795 stipulated that epaulets be worn nowhere but on dress uniforms. Senior captains wore epaulets on both shoulders; junior captains wore them only on the right shoulder; and officers below the rank of captain were prohibited from wearing them. There is evidence that epaulets appeared unofficially on uniforms as early as 1783. The adoption of the epaulet quite possibly forced itself on the Royal Navy, as other nations generally acknowledged them as a symbol of authority. They were not universally popular with British officers, who regarded them as a "French Ornament."

Tricorn hats for officers were replaced with bicorns, worn "fore and aft" about 1800. Hats usually sported a large cockade. Buckled shoes were worn with all uniforms. Lieutenants favored Hessian boots when on duty. All officers above midshipman were allowed swords. Light, "small swords" were carried on formal occasions, whereas fighting swords were used at sea.

Both seamen and officers had their customary attire. However, the former enjoyed far greater discretion regarding their particular "style." Officers, whether of the French or English persuasion, followed rigid and respected guidelines that no warrant officer would dare to disregard and that no admiral would pause to question (Volo and Volo, 112–16).

FOR MORE INFORMATION

Laffin, J. *Jack Tars: The Story of the British Sailor*. London: Cassel, 1969.

Thrower, W. R. *Life at Sea in the Age of Sail*. London: Phillimore, 1972.

Villiers, A. *Men, Ships, and the Sea*. Washington, D.C.: National Geographic, 1973.

Volo, D. D., and J. M. Volo. *Daily Life in the Age of Sail*. Westport, Conn.: Greenwood Press, 2002.

MATERIAL LIFE

Female Clothing

Although any sweeping generalization regarding female clothing is likely to be fraught with exceptions, it is not inaccurate to assert that between 1600 and 1800, some cultures evinced a strong tendency to equate immobility with feminine dress and ease of movement with undistinguished dress. Hence, women hoping to evoke an aura of prestige, elegance, and ladylike qualities adhered to modes of fashion that favored cumbersome attire over conveniently fitting garments. On the other hand, women who labored in the fields or in urban settings sacrificed grace and style to benefit from practical outfits, which did not interfere in their work. Of course, within the generality of this framework existed important variations that derived from the unique features of dress in colonial Australia, the North American colonial frontier, England, France, Japan, New England, and Western maritime culture.

From infancy to the beginning of adolescence, girls did not often dress differently from boys. In Japan, girls wore *kosode*—long, layered robes—as did boys. The attire of New England girls during the colonial period apparently agreed in both cut and material with that of their mothers and female elders. Although on the wane, swaddling in 18th-century England applied equally to girls as to boys, whose parents and caretakers outfitted the babies with shirts, wrapped them in cloth and blankets, and fitted their heads with caps.

Distinctions between male and female clothing became more prominent as girls reached adolescence. In England, after wearing a unisex frock for years, young women started donning linen shirts and corsets. Japanese girls, upon reaching the age of 13 or so, had their eyebrows shaved, replacing them with false ones. At this point, girls would dress in a *kosode*, the style of which represented not only adulthood but also femininity.

Ladies in colonial Australia hoping to convey their elegance relied on costumes made of cotton imported from India, calico, and muslin, as well as on feathers, ribbons, and other accessories. Native American women rendered feminine attire elegant by gracing it with buffalo hair; bark; ox, deer, and elk skins; ribbons; colored porcupine quills; and crafted glass beads and copper bells. English women who dressed in the hope of conveying a sense of feminine charm contended with a slew of passing fashions and unwieldy and heavy styles. Particularly noteworthy is the emphasis on creating false rumps and hips: hoop petticoats, pocket hoops, cork rumps, and other large, rigid contraptions kept both suitors at an appropriate distance from the ladies and the mobility of the women wearing such contrivances relatively impaired. Ladies in France went through a number of fashion phases, ranging from very wide, immobile skirts to simple dresses.

Japanese ladies demonstrated their elevated status by dressing in multiple layers of very stylish *kosode* that covered silk panties and that displayed detailed prints, patterns, and hand-painted designs. In contrast, ordinary Japanese women who wished to wear a *kosode* wore only one.

Women whose work obliged them to dress practically tended to prefer functional dresses that, while permitting adequate movement, continued to establish the wearer's basic femininity. For example, women working indoors in England wore aprons that neither displayed the cuffs, flounces, ruffles, and embroidery of lacy petticoats nor abandoned the general cut of a woman's garment. The same practical clothes characterized 17th-century colonial New England. Here, a woman doing household chores would wear colorful but basic garments, beginning with an ankle-length shift, an underskirt and chemise, a skirt and bodice, and finally, an apron. The layers kept the wearer warm without significantly prejudicing her capacity to work. Female laborers in colonial Australia manufactured "Parramatta dress," known for its rough look and feel.

On the wide-open stretches of ocean that greeted wives of sailors and officers who accompanied their husbands out to sea, the frequently inclement climate and unrefined surroundings quickly convinced women of the need to dress in clothing that did not add to their woes. One telling instance concerns the frequent use of pattens, sturdy platform overshoes that women wore to avoid getting their feet wet on deck. Gaiters, which protected their ankles, were also popular. The fabric of their clothes was robust, cheap, and of a color that was slow to reveal blemishes.

Japanese women living in the countryside participated in farming and under the blazing sun, wore sedge hats or turbans, a pinafore (a shirt that fastens from the back), and breeches or flared trousers. Such practical clothing was unlike that of the wives of samurai (warrior-administrators), who could not participate in replanting seedlings or harvesting, even if they wanted to, for fear of misplacing their tortoiseshell hair jewelry, lacquered combs, mirrors, amulets, tweezers, combs, and handkerchiefs.

Puritan New England had to contend with an increasing desire on the part of women to imitate the latest fashions on the other side of the Atlantic. During the late 17th century and throughout the 18th century, the ability to acquire and enjoy luxuries, including stylish apparel, burdened the religious doctrines associated with the first Puritan settlers, who continued to control the government in Massachusetts. In 1634, the Court of Assistants passed a law requiring women to desist from dressing in any clothing that was decorated with lace or fancy thread. The continued proliferation of fashionable women's clothing, such as high-heeled shoes, ornamented bonnets, brocade, silk, ribbons, and lace, as well as hoop petticoats, attests to a wider failure to control the often-debilitating effects of female fashion.

~Peter Seelig

FOR MORE INFORMATION

Squire, G. *Dress, Art, and Society, 1560–1970.* New York: Viking Press, 1974.

COLONIAL AUSTRALIA

Most of Australia's first female convicts arrived in the colony destitute and in threadbare rags, and because threads and needles were difficult to obtain, that is how they remained in the early years. The first official 1788 issue for females was as follows:

one jacket
two petticoats
two shifts
two pair of stockings
two pair of shoes
two caps
one each neck and handkerchief
one hat

Shortages of clothing and shoes occurred as frequently as food shortages. In 1790, Watkin Tench wrote that the convicts' clothing was in such a state that patching could barely "preserve the remains of decency" (Tench, 124).

Clothing was for utility and protection, but in such a small and divided society, it also denoted status. Although convicts were not uniformed, clothing distinctions were immediately obvious between the convicted and the free, as well as between, on the one hand, daughters and wives of the privileged and, on the other hand, those girls and women who were of humble means.

Such was the dire need for clothing that at many times, women convicts were assigned to work exclusively on making male "slops" (basic work attire), which the colonial administration issued on a temporary basis, to be returned to stores at the end of the week's work. From 1803, when the "Female Factory" was instituted at Parramatta, confined women were put to work weaving woolen cloth for government-issue clothing. The manufactured results of these women's efforts became widely known as "Parramatta cloth," carrying with it connotations of socially inferior dress.

Wives who accompanied public officials could pack better clothing in anticipation of their new colonial home, and from 1803, ladies could scour the pages of the *Sydney Gazette* in search of fabrics and frippery to enhance their appearance. Their Indian cotton, calico, and muslin dresses, worn without corsets underneath, displayed simply cut flowing lines.

Hats of well-to-do women featured feathers and ribbons, whereas poorer women wore mop caps. By 1804, the colony could support a hatter who advertised in the *Sydney Gazette* that he could provide for "every branch of the Business."

Although female laboring attire was rough and rudimentary, it made powerful statements about the changing social status of settlers in colonial Australia. Girls and women could use dress and personal appearance that emulated their "betters" to make such statements.

To read about the clothing of Aboriginal Australians, see the Australian Aboriginals entry in the section "Clothing" in chapter 5 ("Material Life") of volume 1 of this series.

~*Valda Rigg*

FOR MORE INFORMATION

Elliott, J. 1995. "Was There a Convict Dandy? Convict Consumer Interests in Sydney, 1788–1815." *Australian Historical Studies* 26, no. 104 (1995): 373–92.

Fletcher, M. *Costume in Australia, 1788–1901.* Melbourne: Oxford University Press, 1984.

Flower, C. *Duck and Cabbage Tree: A Pictorial History of Clothes in Australia, 1788–1914.* Sydney: Angus and Robertson, 1968.

Scandrett, E. *Breeches and Bustles: An Illustrated History of Clothes Worn in Australia, 1788–1914.* Lilydale, Australia: Pioneer Design Studios, 1978.

Stanley, P. *The Remote Garrison: The British Army in Australia, 1788–1870.* Kenthurst: Kangaroo Press, 1986.

Tench, W. *1788: Comprising A Narrative of the Expedition to Botany Bay [1789] and A Complete Account of the Settlement at Port Jackson [1795].* Edited by Tim Flannery. Melbourne: Text Publishing, 1996.

THE COLONIAL FRONTIER OF NORTH AMERICA

The female clothing of the settlers united to a limited but notable extent with Native American patterns of female dress. Women's and girls' garments, leggings, footwear, hairstyles, headwear, and ear loops remained predominantly traditional, but European clothing—especially ruffled and lace shirts—proved acceptable and even desirable to some Native American women. At the same time, female settlers in North America continued to dress in the same basic fashions that their peers both in New England and across the Atlantic followed.

Upon contact with Europeans, Native American women were not so quick to give up their traditional clothing styles, but they readily replaced skins and woven grass with colored broadcloth. Women wore European shirts, and one contemporary noted that "the women are fond of wearing ruffles bordered with lace. They never take them off, except to sleep, until they are used up for time, and finally they become black from use."

There is no evidence that Native American women wore loincloths. Instead, they wore a skirt of deerskin or cloth. They took a square piece of cloth similar to that used as an outer wrap and placed it around their waists as a "sort of loose petticoat" that reached only to the middle of the leg. The skirts were reportedly covered with "brass runners and buckles" by way of ornamentation, and the edge was sometimes bordered with red or other colored strips of material.

The leather that was used to make the basic native shift was reportedly deerskin, wild ox, or elk. The garment covered the shoulders and the bosom. A strap that passed over the shoulders and gathered about the waist by a belt kept the entire piece of clothing close to the body. Waist belts seem to have been made of leather, twisted bark fiber, a wide strip of broadcloth, or woven yarn and functioned to tuck either shirts or shifts in about the waist. One observer also noted that "the Indian females continually wear a beaded string round their legs [hips], made of buffalo-hair, . . . [which] they reckon a great ornament as well as a preservative against miscarriages, hard labor, and other evils." In general, each woman had one basic body garment that was worn as long as it would last and was then thrown away, "without any attempt at cleanliness" being made in the interim.

Until they were age four or five, Native American children went entirely naked in good weather, and they were provided with a little blanket in which to wrap themselves in bad weather. Thereafter, children seem to have worn the same styles and designs as their parents, with the exception of size. Girls were noted to wear shifts that were much shorter than the matrons'.

Both males and females wore leg coverings. Called leggings, leather stockings, *mitasses,* or Indian gaiters, all were essentially the same item of clothing. They were worn for protection against thorns or brush and quite possibly helped in avoiding snakebites. Leggings were usually made of leather or coarse cloth—scarlet wool was reported to have been a favorite among the Great Lakes tribes.

Almost every schoolchild knows that Indians wore leather moccasins on their feet. A one-piece construction, "an ancient form," seems to have been favored by the tribes of the southeast. An appliqué of woven porcupine quills or decorated woolen cloth covered this moccasin's front seam and side flaps. In the eastern areas of Canada, a separate top, or vamp, covered the instep and was sewn to the body of the shoe with a thick puckered seam. In the Great Lakes region, both styles seem to have been popular. A more complicated design, requiring three pieces and often attributed to the Iroquoian peoples, had a separate sole of tough leather to which the sides of the moccasin were stitched with deer sinew. A seam was visible along the top of the foot and at the heel. This style also had flaps that turned down over the ankle. The folded edges as well as the fronts and backs could be decorated with ribbons, dyed porcupine quills, glass beads, and tiny copper bells. Reported to be quite efficient, Indian lace-up boots, worn during the winter months, were very warm and relatively dry.

The women made the footwear for the men, as well as for themselves, using deer sinew or a thread from the bark of a linden tree that the French called *bois blanc*. After acquiring the bark, the moccasin maker boiled it in water for a time and then pounded the material with a wooden club until it became soft and fibrous. She then sat twisting the fibers into a thread by rolling it on her thighs. The bark thread, thus manufactured, was the equal of "a fine hemp cord."

The women generally wore their straight, black hair long with beads, wampum, or feathers for decoration—"so long that it generally reaches to the middle of their legs and sometimes to the ground." They sometimes wore a small cap or coronet of either brass or copper on their heads and bored small holes in their earlobes through which they passed earrings and pendants, much as women do today.

Although fashions changed from the 17th to the 18th century, the basic clothing of the frontier woman consisted of the same essential European-inspired items. The basic undergarment was known as a shift. Over this, a woman wore her stays and usually several petticoats. The outermost layer consisted of a waistcoat or short gown and skirt. An apron was generally worn to protect the skirt. Adult women wore a coif or cap to contain their hair. Most frontier families had only one set of "best" clothes, which were saved for Sundays and special occasions. For inclement weather, colonial women wore cloaks. It was these European-inspired clothing styles that eventually replaced the traditional, female clothing of Native Americans (Volo and Volo, 24, 27–30, 32, 36, 154–55).

FOR MORE INFORMATION

Boucher, F. *20,000 Years of Fashion: The History of Costume and Personal Adornment*. New York: H. N. Abrams, 1967.

Volo, J. M., and D. D. Volo. *Daily Life on the Old Colonial Frontier*. Westport, Conn.: Greenwood Press, 2002.

ENGLAND

In 18th-century England, a girl, while still a newborn infant, would be swaddled. The parent or caretaker would dress her in a shirt and then wrap her in cloth from

chest to feet, her arms straight against the body. At this point, a blanket would cover the whole bundle, and caps would fit snugly over the head. It was believed that this confinement made the body grow straight. Swaddling, although still widely practiced in 1740, was almost universally abandoned by the end of the century.

When the swaddling was removed, girls dressed in frocks: simple dresses with fastenings in the back. When girls matured into young women, dressing became more complicated. First came the undergarments. When a woman dressed in the 18th century, she first put on a chemise: a linen shirt that hung to just below the knees. Then she tied a string around her waist. Over the chemise, she wore a set of "stays"—a corset, stiffened by metal or whalebone strips often supplemented in front by a stomacher (a decorative triangular piece), which was widest at the top.

Stays were all but gone by the end of the 18th century, but for most of the century, it was believed necessary for good posture to put children of both sexes into stays at an early age.

> *Women's hair grew tall, small, big, bigger, and small again by turns.*

For the first decade of the century, a petticoat and overskirt—suspended over a "false rump" usually made of cork—covered a woman's legs and overskirt; but in 1709, the hoop petticoat entered the world of fashion and rapidly gained popularity. In its early form, it was round and dome shaped, consisting of seven or eight cane or whalebone hoops strung together with fabric tapes. The whole contraption was tied around the waist with a drawstring. From the 1740s to 1760s, the hoop became almost rectangular and very wide and then began to disappear except at court. For "undress" (casual dress), women still continued to wear small, separate side hoops, called "pocket hoops" or "false hips." In the 1770s, the "cork rump" made a reappearance, and padding shifted from the sides to the back, growing smaller and smaller with the late-century emphasis on natural, classical dress.

After addressing the undergarments, a woman next put on a dress. A woman's dress consisted of three pieces—bodice, overskirt, and petticoat. Two of them, the bodice and overskirt, were often joined. Sleeves were usually just above or below elbow length and might have turned-up cuffs, flounces, or ruffles at the ends.

For the first half of the century, one popular dress style was the mantua, an open robe. From 1735 to the 1750s, women also wore "wrapping gowns," closed robes with tight bodices and round necklines; one side crossed over the other in front and was fastened with brooches, ribbons, or girdles. The low necklines of the 1750s attracted the attention of libertines and moralists alike.

The 1770s and 1780s favored open gowns with fourreau backs, tight bodices, and bosoms puffed out. A riding habit, consisting of a skirt, masculine-style waistcoat, cravat, and frock coat, became popular for riding, walking, and traveling, despite a fierce outcry that it was unfeminine.

In the 1780s, a daring fashion was introduced: the chemise dress, often a simple cylinder of white muslin gathered at the neck by a drawstring and at the waist by a wide sash. In the mid-1790s, the sash grew narrower and the waist ever higher, rising to just beneath the breasts. Influenced by Classical antiquity and French Revolutionary simplicity, the chemise dress featured long skirts, little or no false rump, few underclothes, a long petticoat that matched the dress, long sleeves, and a high neckline.

Women's hair grew tall, small, big, bigger, and small again by turns. For the first decade of the century, it was worn in a "tower" above the forehead. Curls hung at the temples, and the back hair was gathered into a bun. Working women, and even fashionable women from 1720 to the 1750s, wore the "simple coiffure," with curls or waves around the face and a bun at the upper back of the head. From the 1730s to 1750s, some women wore the Dutch coiffure, with the back bun replaced by ringlets hanging to the nape of the neck.

From the late 1760s to the late 1780s, peaking about 1778, there was an era of big hair that has yet to be exceeded. These "towers of powdered hair" were supported by wads of false hair, elaborately styled, greased with lard, and powdered at least once a day.

On their heads, most women wore the "chip" or straw hat, usually flat crowned and with a wide brim. Often worn tilted, it was typically tied onto the head. On their legs, women wore white or black stockings, sometimes with lace or colored triangular decorations called clocks. Most women wore worsted stockings at least part of the time, but better-off women often wore silk or cotton. Women's shoes were often high-heeled, with pointed toes and straps that either buckled or tied over the instep.

Women carried items with them: pocket handkerchiefs, fans, long straight canes, parasols for the sun, umbrellas for the rain, muffs to warm the hands in cold weather, and snuffboxes, to name a few. Those who could afford to do so made liberal use of cosmetics. A rich woman's dressing table likely displayed wart remover, rouge, paint for whitening the face, a depilatory (such as vinegar, walnut oil, quicklime, or cat's dung), sticks or powder for cleaning the teeth, "a never-failing remedy for offensive breaths, a famous essence to correct the ill scent of the arm-pits," perfume, and a curling iron.

Although girls' clothing would be relatively plain until adolescence, the multitude of component pieces to a young woman's attire, as well as their ever-changing styles, more than compensated for this early simplicity (Olsen, 95–100, 107–8).

To read about clothing and fabrics in Chaucer's England, see the Europe entries in the sections "Clothing" and "Fabrics" in chapter 5 ("Material Life") of volume 2; for clothing in Elizabethan England, see the England entry in the section "Clothing and Personal Appearance" in chapter 5 ("Material Life") of volume 3; and for fashion in Victorian England, see the Victorian England entry in the section "Fashion" in chapter 5 ("Material Life") of volume 5 of this series.

FOR MORE INFORMATION

Buck, A. *Dress in Eighteenth-Century England.* New York: Holmes and Meier, 1979.

Lynch, J. *Eighteenth Century Resources.* <http://newark.rutgers.edu/~jlynch/18th/>, accessed October 10, 2003.

Olsen, K. *Daily Life in 18th-Century England.* Westport, Conn.: Greenwood Press, 1999.

FRANCE

In the 17th and 18th centuries, France was the acknowledged fashion leader of Europe. French prominence was especially notable in the luxury trades for women, with Austrian, German, and Russian seamstresses often modeling girls' and women's attire after Parisian fashions that were sent abroad in the form of dolls sporting the current clothing in miniature.

Under the reign of Louis XIV (1643–1715), dolls with patterns for fashionable women and men would have had similar silhouettes. Outfits for either sex usually had bodices that fit tightly at the chest and waist. These outfits also displayed voluminous sleeves that were both slashed to reveal a layer of silk in a contrasting color and trimmed with a great deal of lace. The end result amounted to a great deal of material that presented a flowing outline. Women's skirts reached the floor, whereas men's coats did not.

Adult female fashions changed in shape as the 18th century progressed. Women's shapes widened dramatically with the addition of panniers, or very large bustles at the hips that expanded the width of the gown. At their most extreme, the panniers' undergowns made it look as though women were placing large baskets on either hip under their skirts. Women's dresses became so large that doors in the royal courts had to be expanded to allow women to fit through them, although a collapsible bustle was eventually developed that rendered the task of squeezing through passageways appreciably easier. Women's mobility was still remarkably limited, however, because the hairstyles and headdresses that accompanied this clothing were overpowering; styles that towered as many as six or seven feet above the head of particularly stylish aristocratic women forced them, when traveling from one place to another, to take a seat on the carriage's floor.

The extremes of these styles soon gave way to a desire for more simplicity. Simple cotton dresses replaced embroidered silks and brocades, petticoats disappeared, and corsets were loosened or abandoned altogether. The empire-style dress of the Napoleonic era is especially representative. With its high waist and simple lines, it emphasized the natural lines of a woman's figure. Some considered these dresses more scandalous than the ornate dresses of ages past, for many of the new dresses were made of muslin that, when soaked or dampened with water, displayed more than just the shape of the woman inside the dress.

Of course, although French silks, brocades, and jewelry were world-renowned and high fashion trends in continental Europe followed Parisian styles, "fashion" in clothing did not always indicate extravagant costuming. The styles of poorer women were often driven more by necessity than by fashion consciousness. "Matching" stripes in the lower classes meant ensuring that the stripes on clothing all ran the same direction on the garment; hence, a vertical stripe on the bodice of a dress would generally mean that the stripes on the sleeves would run in circles around the arms. This was not a fashion decision, but a decision driven by finances: sleeves could be taken from a leftover edge of fabric instead of carefully cut from a piece that could be used elsewhere. Even this styling was reserved for women with some degree of wealth, however. Those who had little money for cloth might purchase scraps and make their shirts out of multiple types of fabric, with one fabric for sleeves and another fabric for the front or back. Women's skirts were also made of multiple fabrics sewn together to provide enough cloth for the voluminous skirts that were generally the style.

Girls' clothing could look even more mismatched or tattered, given that, until the later 18th century, no clothing was designed specifically for children. From the time that they left swaddling clothes as infants, even girls of relatively wealthy parents would have had garments that had been cut to size and passed down, either from older siblings or from a mother.

Girls of all ages wore corsets, petticoats, and dresses or long skirts with bodices that were differentiated from the adult woman only by a large and wide collar. Interestingly, young boys also wore such outfits. The primary differences between the outfit of a young boy and that of a girl could be seen in the hair: although both children could have long hair in ringlets, girls would be more likely to have a simple cap while their brothers went bareheaded. For all children, clothing sizes were often rough. Girls would get a dress that was very long and wear it until it became knee-length, with adjustments in the bodice where necessary, so that, over the lifetime of the garment, it would probably range in fit from very loose to overly tight.

As the 18th century progressed, more and more parents had disposable income. Savvy trendsetters in the clothing industry responded to and encouraged this emerging market by creating and fitting outfits specifically designed for girls. These fashions still tended to mirror the fashions of the mother, but they were often made of washable material that allowed the girls to run and play with less fear of ruining their clothing. Women's fashion magazines began to picture fashionable little children in their own styles of clothing, which included short dresses with pantalettes for girls (to maintain their modesty when they ran and played). Girls, as with their mothers, enjoyed a great deal more physical freedom in 1800 than they had in 1600.

~Jennifer J. Popiel

These six plates depict the evolution of French fashion for women from the year 1796 to 1804. Of particular note is the steady decline of headgear. In all six, however, there is a belt, sash, or close-fitting part that extends around the torso right below the breasts. © Perry Casteneda Library.

FOR MORE INFORMATION

Berg, M., and H. Clifford. *Consumers and Luxury: Consumer Culture in Europe, 1650–1850.* Manchester: Manchester University Press, 1999.

Blum, S. *Eighteenth-Century French Fashion Plates in Full Color: 64 Engravings from the "Galerie des Modes," 1778–1787.* New York: Dover, 1982.

Cumming, V., and A. Ribeiro. *The Visual History of Costume.* London: Batsford, 1989.

Dangerous Liaisons. Warner Bros., Inc. Directed by Stephen Frears. Videocasette, 1989.

Ewing, E. *Everyday Dress, 1650–1900.* London: Batsford, 1984.

———. *History of Children's Costume.* London: Anchor Press, 1977.

Kipar, N. "L'Age d'or and Kirke's Lambs Civilian and Military Living History." February 2003. <www.kipar.org/index.html>, (February 22, 2003).

Lynch, J. *Eighteenth Century Resources.* <http://newark.rutgers.edu/~jlynch/18th/>, accessed October 10, 2003.

Maeder, E., ed. *An Elegant Art: Fashion and Fantasy in the Eighteenth Century.* Los Angeles: Los Angeles County Museum of Art, 1983.

Starobinski, J., K. Tsukamoto, P. Duboy, A. Fukai, J. I. Kanai, T. Horii, J. Arnold, and M. Kamer. *Revolution in Fashion: European Clothing, 1715–1815.* New York: Abbeville Press, 1989.

Stibbert, F., and A. Lensi. *Civil and Military Clothing in Europe from the First to the Eighteenth Century.* New York: Blom, 1968.

MATERIAL LIFE

FEMALE CLOTHING

Colonial Australia

The Colonial Frontier
of North America

England

France

Japan

New England

Life at Sea

JAPAN

By the 18th century in Japan, a standard adult size of clothing was available for each sex, and another for all children. Adjustments could be made with a few tucks here and a few stitches there. The kimono for women of this period varied significantly depending on one's social status. For instance, the dress of samurai women was much more colorful and involved than was the attire of peasant and simple *chōnin* (city folk) women. However, the summit of ornate dress, hairstyle, and accessories belonged to geisha (female servant-entertainers) and other distinguished female entertainers.

Fundamental to virtually every costume was the *kosode.* This loose robe was simplicity itself. It was cut from a single simple loomed piece of cloth 12 yards long by 14 inches wide and was sectioned into eight rectangular pieces. The type of *kosode* that women wore differed in style from that of men. Girls and boys dressed alike, wearing a *kosode* that was cut to about two-thirds size. Girls and boys wore this *kosode* until their early teens, when they symbolically acquired their first adult *kosode.*

Among samurai girls, the age of transition from children's clothing to adult clothing took place at the age of 13 or so, when they experienced their first menses. The girl had her eyebrows ceremoniously shaved (*mayuharai*) and false ones drawn higher on the forehead.

Samurai women dressed most fancifully and elaborately. Wealthy women might wear silk panties and several layers of colored silk *kosode* to emulate the heroines of the famous Japanese novel *The Tale of Genji,* but most wore one simple *kosode* and *obi* (sash) over their silken drawers. There were hundreds of dyes and dying methods, so the samurai women's *kosode* were often very colorful and otherwise elaborately decorated. Prints, patterns, and even painting directly on the cloth were all very common.

Samurai women were more likely to wear jewelry than were men. Rings were practically unheard of, although we can sometimes see them on the fingers of famous prostitutes and geisha in *ukiyo-e* (woodblock) prints. Earrings were also extremely rare—virtually unknown, in fact. The chief adornment was worn in the hair. Tortoiseshell and lacquered wooden combs were common, and geisha sported elaborately jeweled hairdressings, as well. Flowers were also sometimes worn in the hair, often as much for their pleasant aroma as for their decorative qualities.

Wealthy women often carried parasols in their rare ventures into the sun. Most carried a fair number of accoutrements in their sleeves, including fans, handkerchiefs, combs, tweezers, makeup, mirrors, amulets, and sometimes a diminutive tobacco set.

Commoner women usually wore some kind of undergarment, usually a short *kosode*, or a hip sash. Over the *kosode*, they wore hip aprons and pinafores, which were like backwards shirts, open at the back. They often wore tight breeches or flared trousers that gathered and tied at the calf when they worked in the fields, particularly when stooping to transplant rice seedlings.

Women's footwear differed little from men's. Rain clogs (*geta*) consisted of a plain eight-inch plank of wood with two grooves cut into one side. Two pieces of wood were hammered into the grooves perpendicularly, and then a hole was drilled into the plank at one end. Two short lengths of straw rope were knotted together at one end and the loose ends threaded through the hole in the wood. The loose ends were then looped and the ends fastened to the side of the plank, one on either side. A *geta* was kept on the foot by threading the ropes between the big and second toe. The two pieces of wood elevated the wearer above the mud or snow, and the foot was kept relatively dry.

Peasant women often affected a decorative bun worn at the nape. Some wore a comb or ribbon at *matsuri* (festivals), but during the rest of the year, they wore their hair plain or tied with a straw cord. When working out in the sun, women wore sedge hats or fashioned their hand towels into a bandana or turban. *Chōnin* women were more apt to decorate and dress their hair, but many tied their hair up with a cloth. Wealthy *chōnin* women emulated the hairstyles of samurai women.

Except for *onna gata* (female impersonators), geisha, and prostitutes, only samurai women wore the most elaborate and decorative hairstyles. The basis of most styles was the chignon bun, but there were hundreds of variations. There were distinct styles for little girls and young virgins, for young wives, for various stages of early, middle, and late matronage, and for "retired" (old) women. Because very few women dyed their hair (and then only to cover approaching gray), decorations worn in the hair were the only colorful variations. As in most societies, the brighter colors of ribbons, combs, or pins were appropriate only to the very young. Older women had to make do with more somber patterned ribbons.

Female entertainers were expected to invent new, fanciful, and elaborate styles virtually every week. Most geisha and high-class prostitutes went regularly to professional hairdressers. Their hair was washed, combed, oiled, and then decorated with a host of combs, mirrors, and pins. Samurai and wealthy *chōnin* women often bustled off to their hairdressers immediately after seeing a new style, taking along a woodblock *ukiyo-e* print as an example.

In ancient times, noble women shaved their natural eyebrows and, using lamp soot, drew in decorative black brows that were an inch higher on the forehead. Not many Japanese women in the 18th century continued this curious decoration, but some did. Some also continued to blacken their teeth with rust-iron dust mixed with gallnut and lacquer. The effect was quite shocking to most Westerners but was supposed to ensure that women did not look like "grinning skeletons" when they smiled or laughed. Some women painted their lips and rouged their cheeks. Most, at least, dusted their faces and necks with a white powder mixture of white clay and rice flour.

During the 18th century, prominent contrasts in female attire in Japan depended on class and profession. Peasant women dressed in simple, functional clothing, whereas women belonging to samurai and wealthier merchant classes could afford to dress more fancifully. However, it was geisha, celebrated prostitutes, and *onna gata* who set trends in clothing design, hairstyle, and accessories (Perez, 89–90, 94–95, 97, 176–77).

FOR MORE INFORMATION

Dalby, L. C. *Kimono: Fashioning Culture*. New Haven, Conn.: Yale University Press, 1993.

Hanley, S. B. *Everyday Things in Premodern Japan: The Hidden Legacy of Material Culture*. Berkeley: University of California Press, 1997.

Hildreth, R. *Japan: As It Was and Is*. Willmington, Del.: Scholarly Resources, 1973.

Japan Information Network. <http://www.jinjapan.org/index.html>, accessed October 23, 2003.

Perez, L. G. *Daily Life in Early Modern Japan*. Westport, Conn.: Greenwood Press, 2002.

NEW ENGLAND

Female clothing for Native American women reflected the materials that the surrounding environment furnished in abundance. Colonial women dressed much as did their English counterparts but developed certain unique qualities, including those related to church clothing. Moreover, female settlers during the 17th century displayed a tendency to avoid elaborate clothing, which many Puritans considered to be excessively immodest and in violation of appropriate religious behavior.

The clothing of Native Americans in New England was made of skins and furs. Women wore dresses or skirts that came to their knees, as well as cloaks, leggings, and moccasins, all made of skins. In southern New England, some of the women made cloth of plant fiber, which they used as summer clothing. Girls went naked in summer until they reached their teens.

The appearance of Puritans in New England was distinctive and sometimes parodied. The excessively plain, drab dress seemed to match the gloomy, judgmental faces of community leaders who disapproved of ornamentation and extravagance; but the stereotype (going back to the early 17th century in England) of a people wearing only black, white, and gray is a false one. The everyday dress of women—especially coats, caps, and gowns—were very colorful, usually in soft shades of green, yellow, red, russet, orange, purple, and blue, all colored from native dyes.

Women usually wore caps and shawls of linen or wool. Indeed, women's clothing was primarily made of linen and wool and was usually home produced after 1640. As plentiful as furs were and as cold as the climate was, colonial women did not appear to wear fur coats and hats as men sometimes did.

A colonial woman would wear a three-piece gown consisting of a skirt, bodice, and sleeves. Over this, she wore an apron. Under the gown, she wore an underskirt of linen or a petticoat or both, as well as a chemise. Her underwear was a shift (an ankle-length, elbow-length piece of linen clothing). Often a woman wore almost five layers of clothing. She also wore a kerchief, kept her hair under a cap, and wore stockings, leather shoes, and overshoes. New England women, unlike English women, did not wear billowing skirts, headdresses, or jewelry, without even the exception of wedding rings. Research has shown that New England girls, from the time they could walk, dressed as their mothers did.

In the last decades of the 17th century and throughout the 18th century, the influence exerted by the British presence in New England intensified, particularly with regard to fashion and especially among those who lived in the cities and had money. No longer were homespun and simplicity the rules of the day. For women, the adoption of fashionable wear meant stiffer, more cumbersome, and more restrictive clothes. They adopted hoop petticoats, for example, which caused their skirts to make a wide circle on the floor. They wore whalebone stays in their undergarments to pinch in their waists. They adopted high-heeled shoes, elaborate bonnets, and velvet, brocade, and silk gowns trimmed with ribbons and lace. Fashion-conscious women also highly prized jewelry.

The governing bodies of Massachusetts Bay and local communities passed regulatory laws concerning clothing. The nature of these laws arose from material scarcity, religious dogma, and class references. For example, in the New World, the necessity to remain frugal to survive buttressed the Puritans' bias against extravagance in clothing. Four years after the founding of the Massachusetts Bay Colony, on September 3, 1634, the Puritan Court of Assistants found it expedient to publish a law against the buying of extravagant clothing and targeted specific women's clothing. The court prohibited colonists, including women, from making or buying "immodest fashions" including "any apparel, either woolen, silk, or linen, with any lace on it, gold, silk, or thread, under the penalty of forfeiture of such clothes."

For church meetings and other ceremonial occasions, women—like men—favored black to denote the seriousness of the affair, much as a person from the 21st century might wear black to a funeral. With the backing of the clergy, the Court of Assistants in the New England colonies strongly legislated clothing with an eye on class distinctions. Law forbade those whose incomes fell within fixed limits from dressing in certain kinds of garments. To emphasize the class determination with regard to apparel, the magistrates instructed the officers of townships to be on the alert for any persons of low status who wore

Typical 18th-century dress of New England women and girls. Boston: Society for the Preservation of New England Antiquities, 1935.

clothing that they were forbidden to wear. However, such officers were to be aware of important exceptions to this law, including, but not limited to, officials' "Wives and Children, who are left to their discretion in wearing of Apparel."

While the clothing of Native American females did not seem to inspire the disciplinary hostility of religious and class-conscious authority figures, female attire in the Puritan-dominated New England settlements of the 17th century did just that (Johnson, 87, 89, 90–92, 138).

FOR MORE INFORMATION

Copeland, P. *Working Dress in Colonial and Revolutionary America.* Westport, Conn.: Greenwood Press, 1977.

Earle, A. M. *Costume in Colonial Times.* New York: Scribner's Sons, 1911.

Johnson, C. D. *Daily Life in Colonial New England.* Westport, Conn.: Greenwood Press, 2002.

LIFE AT SEA

Although women were relatively absent from the Western vessels that trekked across the seas and oceans of the world during this period, they did occasionally accompany crews as family members or visitors. Because the adaptation of clothing to a specific context is rarely a matter of chance, it can be expected that women aboard ship modified their dress to the needs of the situation.

The demands of the sea become all the more rigorous for women when clothing was factored into the equation. Nineteenth-century fashion did not conform to living aboard ship. Although captains' wives were quite probably, when at home, among the most fashionably dressed ladies in England, ship's planking and salt spray would have played havoc with the long skirts of taffeta and silk common to the day. Most women found it more practical to adopt a version of what would have been heavy work dress for chores ashore such as laundry. The fabric of such clothing was sturdy, inexpensive, and of a color that would not show dirt.

Skirts were kept at, or altered to, ankle length. The wrapper was a loose robe that buttoned down the front and was generally used as a dressing gown. Once shortened, it would have made for very comfortable attire for a woman. American women also put their "Yankee ingenuity" to work when it came to footwear. Wave-swept decks certainly proved to be a challenge. Some women wore pattens, which were metal or wooden platforms that slipped over the shoe to raise the wearer above mud or water. Others wore gaiters to protect their ankles or made protective wear of their own design. Thus, although women were infrequent voyagers aboard sailing vessels, their occasional presence there resulted in considerable modifications to female attire (Volo and Volo, 165–66).

FOR MORE INFORMATION

Volo, D. D., and J. M. Volo. *Daily Life in the Age of Sail.* Westport, Conn.: Greenwood Press, 2002.

Transportation

Between 1600 and 1800, people were generally less dependent on vehicles as a means of transportation than we are today. In the 21st century, the importance of automobiles, subways, trains, and aircraft has never been greater or more widespread. With the exception of people who devoted their lives to oceanic travel, life did not hinge on the absence or presence of systems of transportation, nor was the quality of life as severely interrupted when existing transportation collapsed as it is today during such technological catastrophes. Still, transportation was central to the character of daily life along North America's colonial frontiers and in England, in Japan, and most important, in Western oceanic travel.

Transportation during this period in history was, for practical purposes, limited to land and water. Aside from rare balloon rides, air travel was an impossibility. Those who traveled on water navigated rivers, canals, lakes, seas, and oceans. The most significant culture associated with this mode of transportation in the 17th and 18th centuries centered on the merchant ships and navies of the West. Experts who are familiar with the many types of wind-driven vessels that plied the waters of the Atlantic and Pacific Oceans distinguish between boats and ships, a boat being any vessel that fit aboard another vessel and a ship having to possess at least three masts. In general, the identification of a type of vessel involved rigging for merchant vessels and the number of guns and decks for naval vessels.

North America's colonial frontiers, New England, and England were substantially invested in oceangoing travel. In contrast, early modern Japan displayed such a great hostility toward external cultures that during the 18th century, the government prohibited the Japanese people from traveling outside Japan proper. Officials imposed and enforced severe restrictions on shipbuilding and fishermen, insisting that no vessel leave sight of the shore, for fear that the far-off crew might consort with foreigners.

England, Japan, and North America's frontier settlements also had to deal with transportation across internal bodies of water. Japan and England were islands, the rivers of which furnished as many advantages as they did drawbacks. On the one hand, river transport in England was cheaper than land routes. On the other hand, the existence of floods, ice, obstructions, and tolls slowed or even brought to a standstill travel along rivers. Similarly, Japan's many streams and rivers, while useful to villagers who relied on the water for sustenance and farming, impeded travel and transport. Thanks to the construction of wood and rope bridges, rope ferries, horses, and brave people on foot, this impediment did not prove ruinous. Indians and settlers along North America's colonial frontier relied extensively on river (the St. Lawrence and Hudson-Mohawk) systems, as well as on the Great Lakes.

On land, people traveled by foot and by vehicle on many types of roads. England's road system was in poor shape. The ravages of weather and a near-total lack of upkeep translated into roads that were difficult to distinguish from the surrounding countryside. Variously muddy or dusty, overland routes suffered from a deficiency in distance

markers and road signs, as well as from the significant hazard posed by criminals. In Japan, fear of social disturbances led the government to impose restrictions on cross-country transportation, which, while not as severe as those limiting travel outside Japan, were significant. Native American trails and portages served the settlers well if and when the latter had access to these traditional paths.

By the end of the 18th century, efforts to improve roads and vehicles in England were noticeable. The institutionalization of turnpikes (toll roads) led to increased funds for maintenance and consistency, thus enhancing the quality of overland transportation. Early modern Japan, however, already possessed an impressive network of roads consisting of five central highways, which served the needs of regional warlords traveling to and from the capital, Edo. Posts and inns along the way maintained the reliability and relative comfort of these vast thoroughfares. Roads even surfaced along North America's frontiers.

Finally, a number of types of land-based vehicles existed in far-flung regions. In Japan, horse-drawn vehicles existed chiefly for the transportation needs of well-off urban residents, even though warlords visiting rural areas were known to make use of carriages. In colonial North America, canoes and horse-drawn wagons were popular for people who were traveling long distances and who were capable of finding rivers and paths that lent themselves to such vehicles.

Carts, wagons, and carriages appeared in England. In London, coaches served the community much as taxis do in today's metropolises. Different types, including the rapid post chaise and the slower stagecoach, could be heard, as well as seen, bouncing along unpaved streets and roads. Even privately owned four-wheeled and two-wheeled carriages driven by the passenger existed, predating by more than a century modern society's obsession with automobiles, an obsession that has developed into a necessity of sorts. The fact that most 17th- and 18th-century people moved from point A to point B with only the aid of their feet and perhaps a walking stick reveals the incredible transformation that transportation and daily life have undergone together.

~Peter Seelig

FOR MORE INFORMATION

Ridley, A. *An Illustrated History of Transport.* London: Heinemann, 1969.

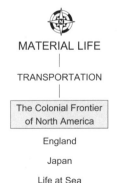

MATERIAL LIFE

|

TRANSPORTATION

|

The Colonial Frontier
of North America

England

Japan

Life at Sea

THE COLONIAL FRONTIER OF NORTH AMERICA

Rather than being a trackless wasteland, the colonial frontier was actually a network of well-established and interlaced water routes. Just as surely as the Appalachian Mountains stood as a barrier to easy entry into the interior of North America from the English colonies on the Atlantic coast, the St. Lawrence River served the French of Canada as a convenient water route to both the Great Lakes and the whole center of the continent. Historians often cite French control of this vital waterway as a key to human interaction with the continent. Although a simple survey of a map would suggest that the French had a geographical advantage over the Anglo-Americans, the available water routes to the interior that the French and the English actually used were nonetheless approximately equivalent.

On the St. Lawrence River, medium-size ships could sail a considerable distance inland to the limits of navigation. One of the most important obstacles to navigation was at the narrows between Montreal and Lake Ontario. The Hudson-Mohawk river system served the English in somewhat the same manner as the St. Lawrence served the French. The limit of navigation by sailing vessels on the Hudson was at the falls near Albany. Thereafter, goods and passengers were transferred by hand to canoes capable of being operated by human power on the Mohawk or on the streams and lakes of the Adirondack region. Both systems led to the Great Lakes.

The geography of North America was hidden from early explorers and missionaries. No maps at all existed for most of the continental interior. It would take Europeans hundreds of years to record the actual contours of the continent on maps, while Native Americans simply carried the interlocking pattern of streams, rivers, and lakes in their minds. Besides the Hudson River, the major rivers of the northeastern Atlantic Seaboard in this region have been the Delaware and the Susquehanna. For almost their entire length, the Hudson, Delaware, and Susquehanna Rivers were navigable by canoes, with only a few small falls and rapids interrupting the journey.

Without either the native watercraft known as the canoe or the larger bateau, most travel in North America would have been impractical. Nonetheless, the canoe did not guarantee unimpeded passage during all seasons of the year. Streams swollen by meltwater and heavy rains were just as impassable as those that turned into a long wet puddle of boulders in the dry seasons. Travelers often had to exit their vessels and drag them through shallow water and across bars of gravel and sand.

The key to the inland waterways of North America proved to be a pattern of short land bridges, known as portages, where goods and boats could be manhandled overland from one water route to another. The Native Americans had discovered these interconnections through centuries of travel. East of the Mississippi River, the important portages could be divided into three distinct systems. Those that went east-west along the St. Lawrence River Valley and through the Great Lakes region gave access to the furs of the Western Plains. Others gave a north-south passage from Hudson's Bay through the Great Lakes to the Mississippi River and its tributaries such as the Ohio and Tennessee Rivers. Finally, a series of portages led northward from the Hudson River Valley through the Lake George–Lake Champlain Valley and the Richelieu River to the St. Lawrence River.

For the French, the major stumbling block to the easy movement of trade goods to the west was the great falls in the Niagara River as it flowed between Lake Erie and Lake Ontario. The portage around the falls required a tortuous route along the Niagara River gorge of more than 12 miles. Niagara Falls, taken together with the numerous rapids in the St. Lawrence, made French navigation into the interior more difficult than it seemed at first glance.

For the English, the major difficulty in moving west lay in the four- to five-mile distance between the headwaters of the Mohawk River and the westward-flowing Wood Creek near present-day Rome, New York. This almost-flat land bridge between watercourses was called the Great Carrying Place. The current of Wood Creek swept travelers first to Oneida Lake, then to the Oswego River, and finally into Lake Ontario. Once in Lake Ontario, the English faced the same difficulty that the French did in relation to Niagara Falls—the difficulty of moving farther west.

Frontier exploration and settlement were greatly influenced, and somewhat eased, by the existence of a relatively well-articulated network of Indian trails and paths. Many Indian routes were well-beaten paths, two to three feet wide, worn into the ground by centuries of use, and easily located. These provided ready access to the major river valleys, stream crossings, portages, and mountain passes of the region. Indian trails rendered the heavily forested areas less of a barrier than they would have otherwise been.

Although the Native Americans, lacking wheeled vehicles, did not develop wide roads, settlers found that the Indian trails and paths were passable for men and packhorses. Consequently, packhorse trains of 10 to 12 horses were initially the main carriers of trade goods. Drovers and their helpers often walked along these trails, driving sheep, pigs, or cattle to market with the help of dogs. Some roads, however, were built to support wagons, carts, and artillery. In Pennsylvania, large wagons, known as Conestogas, were developed to take advantage of these roads. Capable of carrying tens of tons of goods, these wagons required six horses to pull them at even a slow pace. The Conestoga cargo wagon was the principal means of transport to the interior Appalachians. Beyond the reach of the military roads, two-wheeled carts pulled by horses or by oxen outnumbered the larger wagons. Elegant carriages, two-wheeled chairs, and chaises were used in the cities but were not seen on the frontier.

Transportation along the colonial frontier relied on natural systems such as rivers (the St. Lawrence River and the Hudson-Mohawk system) and lakes (the Great Lakes) to transport people and material from the coastal regions to the interior and back again. Paths were discovered or developed, including portages, Indian trails, and roads, all of which served to link to one another the crisscross of waterways so vital to both Native Americans and settlers. Finally, vehicles including horses, canoes, and wagons proved useful when available and adaptable to the surroundings (Volo and Volo, 7–8, 10–14).

FOR MORE INFORMATION

Rouse, P. *The Great Wagon Road, from Philadelphia to the South.* New York: McGraw-Hill, 1973.

Volo, J. M., and D. D. Volo. *Daily Life on the Old Colonial Frontier.* Westport, Conn.: Greenwood Press, 2002.

ENGLAND

The basic means of transport in 18th-century England were as they had been for centuries: ship, foot, and horse. Because England was an island nation, ships carried much of its cargo to other parts of Great Britain and to colonies and foreign lands. British merchant ships—8,000 of them at the time of the Seven Years' War—

imported and exported goods ranging from spices and flax to beer and nails and enabled sailors to catch seals for oil and pelts.

Some of the most profitable traffic was in passengers, willing or unwilling: land-owners sailed to the West Indies, slaves were transported from Africa, indentured servants headed from Britain to America, and convicted felons were conveyed to America and later to Australia.

Within England, much of the country was accessible to river transport. It was slow, but cheaper than hauling goods overland. Rivers, however, had their own problems: flooding, ice, drought, erosion, obstructions caused by garbage and mills, and tolls charged by local landowners. The solution to this horde of problems was canals. During the 1760s and 1770s, canal development boomed. By 1790, navigable waterways had been extended to 2,223 miles. Canal and river hauling were incredibly cheap.

Unlike canals and rivers, roads were everywhere, but in a terrible state. They were potholed, narrow, rutted, dusty in summer, impassably muddy in winter, and indistinguishable in places from the surrounding countryside, often unmarked by signs, poorly drained, and the resort of highwaymen. Nevertheless, merchants had to convey goods to buyers, and travelers had to get from one place to the next.

Only the poorest people walked such roads. Even in London, where walking might seem justified, the rich preferred to avoid the smells and filth of the streets. Therefore, they hired others—sedan chairmen—to do their walking for them. The sedan chair was a box mounted on rails, lined with cloth inside, and opened by means of a hinged top and doors. A footman would summon it with the call, "Chair! Chair!" and then wait for competing chairmen to come running. The passenger sat inside while two men, one in front and one behind, carried the chair by holding the horizontal rails. An advantage of the sedan chair was that, unlike a coach, it could be brought directly into the house, allowing the passenger to disembark in private.

The sedan chair was impractical for long distances, and in such cases, horsepower replaced manpower. Packhorses, laden and led by a man afoot, moved many goods and were especially useful in mountainous places or in other regions where the roads were bad.

Horses could drag even more when harnessed together and hitched to a wagon or cart with its load sheltered by a collapsible canvas cover. Despite having a top speed of about two to three miles per hour, a six-horse wagon could legally haul six tons of goods, making it approximately five times more efficient than six packhorses.

Just as no one who could afford to ride would walk, no one who could afford to ride in a coach would ride in a wagon. There were various coaches for hire: the thousand or so hackney coaches that served London as taxis; the post chaise; and the stagecoach. The post chaise, having no seat for a driver, required a postboy (often a 50- or 60-year-old man in a red or yellow jacket) who sat on one of the horses and piloted the vehicle. It traveled almost universally at a gallop, creating a furious clatter of hooves and wheels and a terrifying, jolting experience for anyone inside. The stagecoach was cheaper because it was slower—about four miles per hour—and more crowded. Four to six passengers sat inside; additional riders sat on top of the carriage. There would be periodic stops to exchange tired horses for fresh ones and to allow the passengers to eat and sleep.

The rich invested in vehicles that they could drive themselves: the four-wheeled phaeton, which featured a seat perched above wheels four to five feet in diameter and was pulled by two to six horses, and a variety of two-wheeled carriages. The cost of a new coach, as well as a pair of matched horses, restricted such transportation to the well off. By midcentury, there were 7,250 private coaches and carriages in London alone. The number doubled by 1765. Used coaches could be had at a reduced price, and some people made use of "contract hire," in which a service provided the coach for a fixed period of time.

Picture by Hogarth, ca. 1750. As a coach prepares for its trip, passengers and onlookers bid their farewells. Note the woman on the left announcing the departure with a yell and a bell. © Hulton/Getty.

The factor that contributed most to the coaching boom was the gradual improvement of the roads. At the beginning of the 18th century, roads were the sole responsibility of the parish through which they ran, but it became clear that reliance on local taxes and statute labor was insufficient. The answer was the turnpike, or toll road, which forced users to contribute money for the maintenance of the roads. After 1714, the government awarded private trusts with the responsibility of turnpikes.

England was part of an island that during the 18th century, also maintained an extensive empire. Thus, English transportation encompassed oceangoing vessels alongside smaller boats that navigated the nation's rivers and canals. The extent of England's merchant fleet, however, did not undo a general reliance on roads, although walking was far less preferable to horse-drawn (or, in the case of the sedan, human-drawn) overland vehicles. Improvements in England's roads and road-care system enhanced the attractiveness of post chaises, stagecoaches, two-wheeled carriages, and the four-wheeled phaeton. This fascination with wheels was an 18th-century precursor to our contemporary obsession with automobiles (Olsen, 172, 174–80).

FOR MORE INFORMATION

Lynch, J. *Eighteenth Century Resources.* <http://newark.rutgers.edu/~jlynch/18th/>, accessed October 10, 2003.

Olsen, K. *Daily Life in 18th-Century England.* Westport, Conn.: Greenwood Press, 1999.

Pawson, E. *Transport and Economy: The Turnpike Roads of Eighteenth Century Britain.* London: Academic Press, 1977.

Ross, D. *The Georgian Period.* 2001. <http://www.britainexpress.com/History/Georgian_index.htm>, accessed October 23, 2003.

MATERIAL LIFE

TRANSPORTATION

The Colonial Frontier
of North America

England

Japan

Life at Sea

JAPAN

Transportation across Japan's difficult rocky and hilly terrain required a number of aids, including carriages, bridges, ferries, and horses. Trips outside Japan, however, were prohibited. Even within Japan's borders, the government rigorously enforced bans on travel. Nevertheless, provincial warlords and their samurai warrior-administrators had to make trips at the behest of the military government located in Edo, a requirement that resulted in a network of roads, inns, and other accommodations.

Carriages were primarily urban conveniences. Two-man palanquins were common on the major highways, but no one used them in the rural areas unless a daimyō (regional warlord) was visiting.

These palanquins were of two main types. The *kago* was a basketlike contraption that was suspended from a pole carried by two or more porters. The multicarrier types had two poles. If there were more than two carriers, one or more could compensate for the weight by shifting to the back when going uphill or to the front when going down. The rider sat cross-legged at the bottom of the basket, which could be quite uncomfortable on long trips.

The other type, the *norimono*, was more like a small cage and had a solid, flat floor on which to sit. These were mounted on top of a packhorse, or rather on top of the bags and other luggage strapped on the horse. Almost no wheeled carriages plied the rural roads because, although the roadbed was hard-packed and generally well maintained, the rains would quickly turn the dirt into mire. Two-wheel oxcarts had been used in previous eras but had almost disappeared except in Kyōto.

By the 18th century, the country had been at peace for nearly a century, so probably more people rode in *kago* (palanquins) than astride a horse. Even when they did ride, they mounted from the right side of the horse and then sat in a cross-legged position while the real horseman walked ahead, leading the animal by the reins.

With regard to stream and river transportation, there were three types in the countryside. The first type, bridges, facilitated (rather than constituted) transportation. Japanese constructed a variety of bridges across narrow streams. Trees were sometimes felled or dragged across a small stream and then trimmed of branches and bark in order to construct balance beams. Grappling ladder ropes could be suspended over deeper and longer spaces, and trestle bridges were constructed from time to time.

The second type of fording transportation was the rope ferry. These appeared to be simplicity itself because they required only two working parts. One needed some kind of float, such as a boat or a raft on (or in) which to place the cargo. By stretching across the water a stout rope that was anchored to firm objects on either side, the ferryman could simply pull the ferry across to the other side. To do so over a swift-running stream (which most of Japan's rivers were) was trickier than first imagined. A man would have to be very strong to keep a boat, even one that was firmly tethered to the rope, moving across the strong current.

The third fording method was the use of sure-footed horses or men to carry goods and people across water. This approach could only be accomplished in shallow, wide, flooded areas and not in swift-running deep rivers. A final method was to wait until the flood had receded and then cross on one's own power.

Despite an abundance of laws that made it difficult, Japanese in the 18th century did a great deal of traveling. In order to "freeze" the status quo in the early 17th century, the *bakufu* (national military government) forbade the permanent movement of people. The reasoning was that there would be many fewer of the wrenching social disturbances that had plagued Japan in the 16th century if everyone could be forced to stay where he or she was. Peasants who had to travel even short distances were required to show signed permission slips from the village headman to anyone who challenged them.

Added to those political constraints, Japan's physical topography made travel difficult and even dangerous. The country was formed by tremendous geological uplift from volcanic activity, which had created craggy coastlines and steep mountains. The streams were narrow, short, and very rapid. Therefore, not many Japanese rivers were suited to boat traffic, and many had gouged deep canyons that made normal crossings perilous.

In addition to strict laws against travel abroad, to disappear from view of those on land made sea travelers liable to execution upon return. The *bakufu* had severely limited the construction of oceangoing vessels. Large, deep-draft, sternpost rudder ships were forbidden in order to assure the government that Japanese would not be able to sneak away and rendezvous with any European ships.

Yet, the *bakufu* in effect sabotaged its own restrictions against travel by way of its "alternate attendance" (*sankin-kotai*) hostage system. To control the powerful warlords, the *bakufu* required that their immediate families remain as hostages in Edo, a stipulation that transformed these families into guarantors of the daimyō's good behavior. Every daimyō was also required to spend half of his time in his *han* (province) capital and the other half in attendance of the shōgun (military overlord) in Edo.

The *bakufu* developed an elaborate and extensive post station system to deal with the sudden increase in the number of travelers. Five officially designated highways served the needs of *sankin-kotai*, the most famous being the Tokaidō, which went through Kyōto and Nagoya on the way to Edo. No fewer than 53 post stations were established on the Tokaidō, itself passing through perhaps 60 percent of Japan's urban population.

In addition, a number of postal and message systems facilitated the rapid transmission of letters throughout the region. Normal messages were conveyed on the thrice-monthly express, which took about a week from Kyōto to Edo; by the end of the 18th century, the common time of delivery did not exceed three-and-a-half days. More urgent messages could reach Edo in only a day, riders stopping only to change horses along the way.

This simple picture depicts several types of transportation along the Tokaidō in Japan. © Cabinet Library Collection.

Because the *sankin-kotai* entourages of the major daimyō were quite large, they were scheduled two or three days apart to allow the inns and post stations time to recover from one before the next one came along. Signboards along the roads informed the traveler which groups were scheduled.

Licensed hostlers were allowed to establish official inns at post stations. By the 18th century, the inns were quite plush and accommodating. Virtually every inn could provide an escalating level of service commensurate with one's ability to pay.

Transportation in 18th-century Japan could be dangerous indeed, given the *bakufu* restrictions on travel. However, those who did travel (and who had to travel, given the *sankin-kotai* obligations) used carriages, horses, bridges, ferries, and if all else failed, their own feet (Perez, 181, 184, 214, 301–4).

FOR MORE INFORMATION

Dunn, C. J. *Everyday Life in Traditional Japan*. Tokyo: Tuttle, 1969.

Japan Information Network. <http://www.jinjapan.org/index.html>, accessed October 23, 2003.

Perez, L. G. *Daily Life in Early Modern Japan*. Westport, Conn.: Greenwood Press, 2002.

LIFE AT SEA

What are sea-lanes? How did hulls of ships keep from leaking? Where is the spar deck in relation to the main deck? What is the difference between a ship and a boat? How did sails, masts, and rope rigging combine to propel a vessel through water? This entry, devoted to the transportation of oceangoing vessels, provides answers to these and other related questions.

The sea initially presents itself as a great, common highway over which ships may pass in any direction, yet the majority of travelers and traders during the era of wind ships were determined to use certain paths across the sea to the exclusion of others. These paths have come to be known as the sea-lanes. Encounters with helpful or contrary winds, adverse tides, helpful currents, dangerous obstacles, and reassuring landmarks dictated the most commonly used sea routes. By the 18th century, the established sea-lanes connected natural resources, suppliers, seaports, cities, and markets to one another over remarkably wide expanses of ocean.

The vessels that followed these sea-lanes were of many different types. Merchant vessels were categorized by their rigging (as in a ship, bark, or sloop), while reference to naval vessels largely relied on the number of gun decks and the available armament on board (as in a 100-gun three-decker, a 74-gun third rate, or a 44-gun frigate). Interestingly, there is no universally accepted system for recording this information. The vocabulary introduced in this entry is based on American and British terminology, which is different from that used in other countries and sometimes at variance within itself.

The foundation of the vessel, the watertight container that carried the crew and cargo, was the hull. The planning of a merchantman's hull provided primarily for buoyancy and cargo space; on a warship, for protection and the ability to mount and

MATERIAL LIFE

TRANSPORTATION

The Colonial Frontier
of North America

England

Japan

Life at Sea

to sustain the stress of large guns; and on a smuggler or privateer, for speed. In any case, the safety of the crew and passengers was of prime importance.

From early times, hulls were made with overlapping planks attached to a skeleton of flexible ribs. This style, known as lapstrake, was very flexible, but wanting in strength.

From the 16th century, oceangoing vessels were built with a new type of hull—carvel built—having planks that met flush at their edges and providing a smooth, solid surface above and in the water. A fibrous mixture of caulking and tar filled the spaces between the planks, and the entirety received a coating of paint. In the last quarter of the 18th century, the bottom was commonly sheathed in copper.

The carvel-built hull was supported by a framework of stout ribs attached to a heavy beam known as the keel. The wood most preferred for the keel was elm or oak because they best resisted rotting, which resulted from continuous immersion in sea water.

When the timbers for the construction of a vessel arrived at the shipyard, they were stored in open-air sheds for about a year, allowing the green wood to "season"—that is, to reach its own natural form before shipbuilders shaped the wood into a finished component. Timbers were sometimes boiled or steamed to enable the shipwrights to bend them.

The timbers were fastened together by the use of joints, held fast by oak trunnels, or treenails, which varied from one to two inches in diameter and stretched up to three feet in length. Holes were drilled through each joint, and the trunnels were driven through the holes to act as large wooden pins.

With the keel laid and the ribs and skeleton in place, the vessel was left for another season before the planking was added. Merchant vessels, more lightly ribbed than warships, usually had a single layer of planking. A warship—stoutly ribbed to withstand the pounding of an opponent's guns and the weight and stress of its own—had two layers of planking attached to the frame, one on the inside and one on the outside. This often gave the hull a thickness of more than a foot.

The size of the hull was determined by its cargo capacity. Small coasting vessels might have a capacity of 60 to 70 tons, while warships might range from 300 to 800 tons. Really large vessels were over 1,000 tons.

Whereas warships used the deck space to hold fighting men and weapons, merchant vessels used almost all of their deck space for cargo. Although warships held hundreds of men, they were a good deal more comfortable than merchant vessels, on which every empty square foot represented a loss of profit.

The decks of a ship can be regarded as so many floors. On the upper or spar deck, the space between the bows and the foremast was called the forecastle. The space between the foremast and the mainmast was the waist, and that from the mainmast to the stern was the quarter deck. Behind the mizzen mast was the poop deck, a raised deck beneath which was the captain's day cabin. All around the upper deck were bulwarks. Attached to these were square casings called hammock nettings in which the seamen and midshipmen deposited their hammocks.

Most men-of-war did not carry a full tier of guns on the spar deck, the waist being open to the sky with gangways on each side. The deck below the spar deck was the main deck. This and the one below, called the lower gun deck or berth deck, had full tiers of gunports and guns. Between and among these guns, the men ate and slept. Next, below the lower gun deck, was the orlop deck, the first without gun ports cut in the hull. The aftermost part of the orlop had an enormous space for storing dry provisions. Below the orlop was the hold. Forward and aft in the hold were the powder magazines. The rest of the hold was used to store wet provisions (in barrels), chains and cables, and the shot locker, which held the cannonballs. In the aft-most part of the hold was the spirits room, holding the rum and liquor and guarded day and night by a sentry. Set between the beams that supported the tiers of the hold were the water tanks from which the water for daily consumption was pumped.

Many nautical experts point out that not all the vessels that plied the seas were ships; but neither were they all boats. A ship was a large vessel with at least three masts and a particular arrangement of rigging and sails. A boat was a smaller craft capable of being carried on another vessel.

Between and among these guns, the men ate and slept.

Most boats, although equipped with oars and a rudder, had V-shaped bottoms. Others were flat bottomed or round bottomed and relied on oars to permit sailing. Boats were often used to ferry passengers, members of the crew, and supplies back and forth from the shore or between other vessels. Boats were sometimes used to explore rivers and inlets and to send forces ashore in amphibious landings. Large vessels carried a complement of craft variously described as longboats, jolly boats, and cutters.

The jolly boat was a small boat (16 feet), usually hoisted and carried at the stern of merchantmen. The term *cutter* also referred to a small boat (18 to 20 feet), and it should not be confused with the much larger sloop of the same name. The longboat, later called a launch (20 to 24 feet) on a merchantman, was usually carried between the fore and main masts. Warships carried their boats on the spars stored over the well deck but towed them or cast them free when going into battle.

Boats' seaworthiness was often remarkable. A pinnace was a boat somewhere in size between that of the longboat and that of the cutter. Captain William Bligh, in a remarkable feat of seamanship, traveled 3,000 miles in a 23-foot launch overloaded with 19 men after the crew of the *Bounty* mutinied.

There were two basic types of sails: square and fore-and-aft. Square sails perpendicular with the center line of the ship rested on wooden poles known as spars. Most of the sails on 17th- and 18th-century merchant ships and warships were square sails. Although efficient, the square sail was labor intensive. Fore-and-aft sails generally required fewer hands.

The general name for all the timbers (horizontal and vertical) used in setting up the rigging and sails was *spar*. Each spar was a huge piece of wood. The term *mast* was applied to those vertical timbers from which were swiveled horizontal timbers such as yards, booms, or gaffs used to support the sails. The three masts were named (from bow to stern) the fore, the main, and the mizzen.

Added to the vertical spars that served as masts was the bowsprit, a nearly horizontal timber protruding from the front of the vessel. Attached to the bowsprit, which was often 3 feet in diameter and 25 yards long on larger vessels, were long triangular sails called jibs.

A vessel was considered seaworthy if it could sail "by and large." The term *by the wind* meant that the wind was blowing from the front of the vessel. Sailing "large" meant that the wind was from behind the mast. No sail can propel a vessel directly into the wind. By the 18th century, four-sided sails could be set fore and aft for sailing into the wind and swung out to the side to take better advantage of a following wind than could triangular sails.

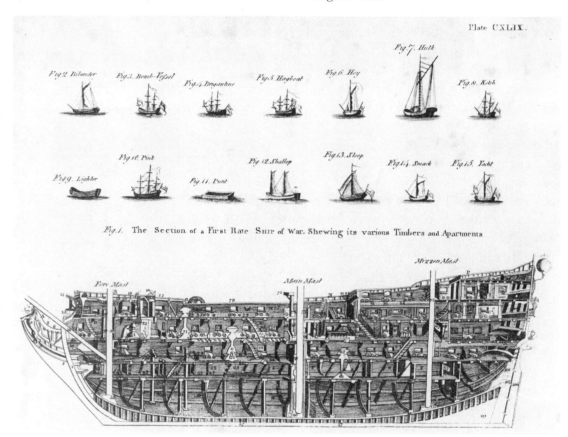

A diagram of the interior of a first-rate ship.

The identification of a vessel as a particular type was largely judged by the rigging aloft. A ship was a vessel with a fore, main, and mizzen mast, all of which were fitted with square sails. A bark was a three-masted vessel with square sails on the fore and main masts and fore-and-aft sails on the mizzen mast.

Smaller two-masted vessels included the brig (both masts fitted with square sails); the brigantine (fore mast square, main mast fore and aft, with a square main topsail); schooners (vessels equipped with two or more masts rigged with fore-and-aft sails only); and sloops (single-masted vessels similarly rigged).

The galleon class combined the lines of a large row galley with the strength of a ship and the firepower of a fortress with the seaworthiness of an oceangoing privateer. While most closely associated with the Spanish treasure fleets, the galleon was any large ornate ship from the 16th through 18th centuries that had a high poop deck, a high forecastle, and a pronounced bow. The galleon dominated ocean traffic for almost 200 years.

Large sailing vessels were equipped with an amazing quantity of rope. All rope rigging was divided into two general types: standing rigging and running rigging. Standing rigging supported the masts and yards. Running rigging was passed through blocks and pulleys to adjust the position of the sails relative to the wind. Hemp fiber was the most common material used to make rope rigging throughout the period.

The main components of the standing rigging were the stays and shrouds, which supported the masts vertically. The stays were strong cables running along the central line of the vessel that helped to hold the masts in place. Shrouds held each mast laterally and were attached to the sides of the vessel by chains. Smaller ropes called ratlines, which formed the distinctive ropelike ladder up which sailors scrambled to attain the tops, crossed the shrouds.

Clew lines were the final major piece of running rigging. The purpose of the clew lines was to bring the sail up for furling. The sail when furled was lashed firmly to its yard.

Transportation relies on vehicles and paths upon which these vehicles tread. In the case of 18th-century oceanic travel, ships and boats were the vehicles, and the sea-lanes furnished the paths (Volo and Volo, 30, 63–64, 66–69, 72–73, 75, 77, 79–81, 83, 87).

FOR MORE INFORMATION

Ireland, B. *Naval Warfare in the Age of Sail*. New York: Norton, 2000.

Lavery, B. *The Arming and Fitting of English Ships of War, 1600–1815*. London: Conway Maritime Press, 1987.

McCracken, P. *Maritime History on the Internet*. 1995. <http://ils.unc.edu/maritime/home.shtml>, accessed October 23, 2003.

United Kingdom Royal Navy. *Royal Navy History*. <http://www.royal-navy.mod.uk/static/content/211.html>, accessed October 23, 2003.

Volo, D. D., and J. M. Volo. *Daily Life in the Age of Sail*. Westport, Conn.: Greenwood Press, 2002.

City Life

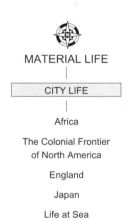

Cities dating from the 17th and 18th centuries were smaller, less populated, and less impressive from a technological perspective than are today's cities. Nevertheless, they occupied important and exciting places in the material lives of sub-Saharan Africans, colonial North Americans, English, and Japanese. Even in the world of oceanic transportation, cities—in the form of ports—performed an essential service. Across the divergent cultures discussed in this section, certain thematic parallels concerning the various material functions of cities and their infrastructure surface again and again.

Much as cities do today, cities dating back several hundred years attracted diverse populations. Attempts to arrange residences for these peoples involved different organizing principles. In particular, the division of cities into identifiable zones fell along occupational and ethnic lines. Some African cities, however, developed neighborhoods of sorts, featuring closely bunched homes, all of which served the needs of a particular kinship group.

In Nagasaki, non-Japanese denizens lived in carefully demarcated wards, so that the Chinese, Korean, and Dutch inhabitants of the city did not reside in the same neighborhoods. Likewise, in England, urban settings boasted communities arranged along ethnic characteristics. Welsh, Cornish, Irish, German, Swiss, and Jewish communities contributed to a diverse, and sometimes tense, urban atmosphere in London. For instance, most of London's Jews lived in Whitechapel.

The city of Kano in Hausaland divided its wards so as to separate its Yoruba population from Ghadames, and both of these from the city's Arab community. Ports in North America and throughout the world served as international commercial hubs that could remind one of modern-day airports, teeming with people from all over the world. In North America, the walls of forts and of fortified villages were more than symbolic delineations of boundaries between Indians and settlers.

When ethnicity did not dictate the division of an area's residential wards, occupational affiliations made up the gap. The neighborhoods of 18th-century England's cities often belonged squarely to one particular economic class of people. Working-class, middle-class, well-to-do, and fashionably radical neighborhoods were clearly outlined in people's minds. Similarly, 18th-century Edo's residential districts, though less segregated than before, continued to feature wards for fishmongers, blacksmiths, metalsmiths, and hereditary outcastes. And in the city of Benin, where one ethnic group predominated, the division of wards was based not surprisingly on occupation.

Cities as a whole functioned in a variety of ways. Frontier "cities" that North American settlers constructed functioned primarily as defensive demarcations. At the same time that stockades, blockhouses, and garrison houses served to repulse the enemy (be they Anglo-Americans, French, or Native Americans), these fortifications established—in a very material way—the inroads that settlers were making along the frontiers.

In early modern Japan, which was highly urbanized, many cities acted as economic centers of activity. Thanks to its location on the Inland Sea, Ōsaka became a center of trade. London, with its access to the Thames, enjoyed a similar role during the 18th century. In fact, ports around the world served the commercial requirements of Western oceangoing vessels. Boston, Amsterdam, Seville, Havana, Capetown, and Fort St. James at the mouth of the Gambia River all made use of their access to important waterways.

Cities were not simply economic centers. Edo, London, Boston, and Gondar were political centers, as well. Edo's whole existence depended in large part on the political obligation of warlords to pay regular and extended visits to the capital. Families of warlords remained in Edo, requiring the services of all kinds of merchants, retailers, artisans, cooks, and maids. Of course, the government employed no small percentage of Edo's population.

Gondar, in particular, exemplifies the multifaceted nature of urban settings during this period. In addition to being the imperial capital, Gondar was a militarily defensive site, a crossroads where three trading routes met, an open market, and a major concentration of religious activity. With so much variety in the air, it is not surprising that some of its inhabitants adopted elite views of themselves, equating urban culture with cultural excellence, a trend common among Swahili city dwellers, just to cite one example.

Cities were not nearly as equipped to manage the material needs of large populations as are many of today's cities. However, infrastructure existed that was impressive, if only for the limited technological know-how on which it rested. Supplying water to a city is one of the most important aspects of any city's infrastructure. North American colonists founded villages and fortifications at sites where fresh water was readily available, and Native Americans such as the Iroquoian- and Algonquian-speaking peoples erected semipermanent and permanent communities where a river or pond could provide the community with fresh water. Japanese cities made use of open trenches to supply city folk with water. Later, conduits constructed from wood, bamboo, and clay came to the fore. In the same way, London delivered water to neighborhoods and even to individual homes in pipes that were at first made from wood, but that later graduated to iron.

The material existence of cities underlaid the formal and informal patterns of daily life for urban inhabitants throughout the 17th and 18th centuries. From—and into—these material foundations flowed the ethnic, economic, and political attributes of each city's host culture.

~Peter Seelig

FOR MORE INFORMATION

Hall, P. G. *Cities in Civilization*. New York: Pantheon Books, 1998.
Mumford, L. *The Culture of Cities*. San Diego: Harcourt Brace, 1996.

AFRICA

African cities often reflect many trends of the cultures of which they are a part. Some, such as Timbuktu in the Niger valley, became important centers of international commerce and culture. Aksum in Ethiopia and Ife in the Yoruba country of West Africa had religious significance and represented the heartland of their respective cultures. Most of these cities were agrarian in nature, with over two-thirds of the male population working on outlying farms. The layout of these urban areas reflected kinship ties among the residents, with members of a common lineage living in a given ward or quarter. Although cities could arise based on anything from location along a trade route to a formally established political center, once they existed, they tended to become places with at least some degree of culture and diversity (Hull, xiv).

African cities featured clusters of individual dwellings belonging to members of the same lineage or other kinship group. Each of these clusters represented a subdivision of the city, often under the control of its own leaders. In this respect, urban organization paralleled that of many of the surrounding rural areas. In more cosmopolitan cities, such as Kano in Hausaland, wards represented the territory of a

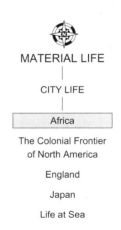

given ethnic group: Yoruba lived in Ayagi, Ghadames and Arabs from Tripoli in Dandalin Turawa, and Nupe in Tudun Nufawa. An official with the title *Magajin Gari*, or "Mayor of the Town," governed most Hausa cities and answered directly to the emir. The city of Benin, on the other hand, consisted almost entirely of Edo and had wards based on occupation (Hull, 77–78).

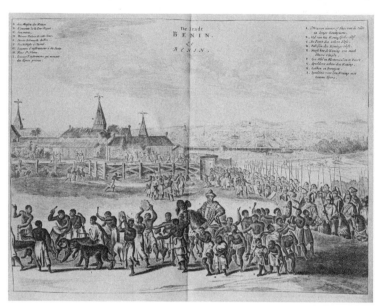

In the 17th century, a Dutch artist rendered this portrait of Benin. © The Art Archive/Navy Historical Service Vincennes France/Dagi Orti.

Along the east coast, the Swahili developed a civilization based off the concept of urbanism. They claimed that city dwellers possessed *utamaduni*, a word that, although difficult to translate, essentially refers to characteristics such as refinement and reputable ancestry to which civilized people have access. Those outside the city were *washenzi*, or barbarians. At the center of Swahili cities lay an open area for diverse community activities, such as marriages and funerals, poetry competitions, and meetings. The mosque represented the most important feature. In fact, the construction of the central mosque represented the founding of the city, regardless of any settlement that had previously occupied the site.

In the Swahili language, members of a common kin group were "of the same gate," which referred originally to gates opening onto the central enclosure and later to gates belonging to the outside walls of the city. The central street divided the city in half, and the residents of the two halves engaged in competition with each other, especially during celebration of a new year. An area of mud and thatch housing surrounded a Swahili city and served as home to those whose ancestors were ex-slaves and to others unable to gain patrician status (Horton and Middleton, 115–31).

Such differences in social status became a common feature that marked sub-Saharan Africa's urban landscape. For example, in Abomey, capital of the West African kingdom of Dahomey, it was forbidden to build houses of more than four tiers of mud swish, and only the king could have a two-story dwelling. The palace compounds of the Yoruba rulers featured especially large verandas for public receptions. Also, in Yorubaland, distance from the ruler's palace became an important mark of one's place in the government hierarchy. Throughout many areas of Africa, people practiced segregation on the basis of religion or ethnic origin. Sometimes rulers pursued segregation as an actual policy, whereas in other places, newcomers simply moved into neighborhoods that hosted people like them (Hull, 86–90).

Many regions boasted ancient cities that served as traditional political and religious centers. For example, Aksum, connected to ancient Ethiopia and to the legends of the Queen of Sheba, continued to serve as the coronation site for that kingdom's rulers for centuries. However, the true center of political power had often moved elsewhere in accordance with wider-scale political and social changes. Thus, in 1636, Emperor Fasiladas established a capital at Gondar with a giant stone-and-mortar crenellated castle called Fasil Gemb. This and the palaces of the next two rulers came to represent a special imperial quarter of the city, eventually surrounded by its own defensive wall. Because of its location along three major caravan routes, Gondar also developed a large open market near the palaces.

Most merchants there professed Islam and lived in a settlement just southwest of the city proper called the Eslam Bet. Jews also lived in this area and inhabited a settlement of their own west of the Muslims. Most Jewish women became potters. Gondar also featured several dozen churches and the residence of the metropolitan, who was typically an Egyptian appointed for Ethiopia by the Coptic Patriarch of Alexandria. In the northwest lived people called the Qemants, who engaged mainly in providing the city with wood (Pankhurst, 109–17).

Europeans also founded cities in Africa during the 17th and 18th centuries. These often began as fortified trading posts, such as the French Saint-Louis across from the mouth of the Senegal River or the Fort St. James at the mouth of the Gambia River. The purpose of these trading posts was to protect a particular European nation's sphere of influence from its European rivals, as well as to draw the trade of the region toward the coast, where it would come under the control of European merchants. Over time, these trading posts also became important entrepôts in the slave trade. The Dutch founded Capetown in South Africa as a midway station connecting the Atlantic and Indian Oceans to each other (Ogot, 268–70).

African cities were thus founded in a variety of different ways and served a number of different functions based on their history and geography. However, many had key elements of social organization in common, such as the voluntary or involuntary segregation of different population groups based on such factors as kinship, religion, and nationality and the reflection of differences in social status that architecture and other elements of the urban landscape reflected. All cities, however, could serve as meeting places for people and ideas from across the continent and around the world.

~*Brian Ulrich*

FOR MORE INFORMATION

Halsall, P., ed. *Internet African History Sourcebook*. 1996. <http://www.fordham.edu/halsall/africa/africasbook.html>, accessed October 23, 2003.

Horton, M., and J. Middleton. *The Swahili: The Social Landscape of a Mercantile Society*. Malden, Mass.: Blackwell, 2000.

Hull, R. W. *African Cities and Towns before the European Conquest*. New York: Norton, 1976.

Ogot, B. A., ed. *General History of Africa*. Vol. 5. *Africa from the Sixteenth Century to the Eighteenth Century*. Paris: United Nations Educational, Scientific, and Cultural Organization, 1992.

Pankhurst, R. *The Ethiopians*. Malden, Mass.: Blackwell, 1998.

THE COLONIAL FRONTIER OF NORTH AMERICA

Any discussion of city life on North America's colonial frontier must take into account the general absence of large, bustling cities. And yet, a looser and more

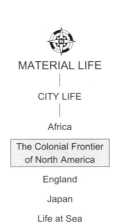

embracing conception of what constitutes a city permits a revealing survey of community life among both the native peoples and their colonial neighbors. Most notable is the universal emphasis there on militarily defensive structures either surrounding a frontier "city" or standing nearby. The constant danger of attack from a tribe bent on retaliation or from settlers hoping to expand their settlement's territory convinced all frontier inhabitants that fortified villages, stockades, blockhouses, garrison houses, and forts were indispensable.

The Iroquoian-speaking peoples lived in permanent fortified villages that were home to substantial populations. Iroquoian villages were usually built near a lake or riverside but were set back to prevent surprise attack by canoe-borne raiders. Villages were always located near a source of fresh spring water. They were surrounded by as many as four concentric rows of palisades (fences of stakes) topped with a scaffold from which the walls could be defended.

The Algonquian peoples were still roaming in extended family groups of about 20 persons during the period and did not establish permanent cities or large-scale villages with extensive stockades. Nonetheless, 50 to 100 dwellings, or wigwams, could be scattered about a semipermanent town with rudimentary fortifications.

The coastal Algonquian-speaking peoples had smaller villages of 10 to 20 dwellings. The northeastern coastal nations had semipermanent dwellings much like those of the north-central peoples, but the midcoastal tribes and the nations of the southeastern woodlands seem to have favored a more permanent scaled-down longhouse between 25 and 50 feet in length with straight sides and a dome-capped roof. The longhouses were arranged in orderly rows on a central plaza with extensive gardens all around. If the village was stockaded, the longhouses were more tightly bunched together.

Community life on the frontier was by no means secure. Indians were present on the fringes of even the largest settlements along the seacoast. As early as 1607, the English settlers of Jamestown, Virginia, understood the need to create a fortified village for protection against possible attack. These local safe havens became known as blockhouses, garrison houses, and sometimes (euphemistically) forts.

The term *blockhouse* designated a square structure of strongly laid-up logs or timbers with a second floor overhanging the first. The door, if located on the first floor, was heavily barred; if on the second floor, it was accessed by a ladder. Walls built of timber, with gates securely bolted and barred at night, usually surrounded blockhouses; families whose homes were not considered defensible slept in blockhouses in times of crisis. Blockhouses were also incorporated into military strong points within or near a fort.

In each settlement enclave, one or two stoutly built houses, known as garrison houses, were chosen as sites for refuge and local defense. Most of these were private residences given over to the public defense in times of crisis. Garrison houses were commonly built of thick wood (either in the form of round logs or squared timbers) and wood shingles. The attic floor was constructed of strong timbers covered with a thick layer of sand or ashes, an ingenious strategy that allowed the attic to act as a firestop for the rest of the building if the roof was set on fire. Garrison houses could be of one or two stories, and it was not uncommon for the second floor to overhang the first. This allowed the defender to shoot down along the wall of the first floor or to pour water on brushfires laid up against the sides of the building.

One necessary characteristic of a good garrison house was a well or large cistern inside the house, or one that was easily accessible by the defenders if outside. Because Native Americans lacked artillery and relied on fire as their primary means of reducing defensive structures, such an arrangement almost certainly allowed the defenders to outwait all but the most determined siege.

Forts on the frontiers were constructed of masonry, timber, earthworks, or a combination of these materials. The choice of a particular material was largely a matter of availability, with timber being the most commonly used material for new or temporary structures. When formal construction projects were undertaken, the initial stages of the work were done in wood and earth, but the colonial government provided the money for the finished fort to be built of stone.

Accessible from within the fort, its bastion could feature a water supply, powder room, storeroom, or hospital. Behind the curtain walls or beneath the ramparts, fortified rooms called casemates were erected. Barracks, storerooms, offices, and stables could be found herein. The casemates were accessed from the parade and often had firing loops or firing slits that faced outward toward the enemy's position. These loops and slits often looked out into a great ditch or dry moat, through which the enemy troops were forced to pass.

The entryway to most North American forts in the 18th century was either through the ditch or over a narrow bridge that crossed the ditch. A fort's defenders could lift this bridge during an emergency. Some forts had wet ditches or ditches that could be suddenly flooded. Wet ditches better served the purpose of preventing undermining of the walls but were particularly unpopular in the colonies because of the health hazard associated with damp air and stagnant water. They also inhibited the defenders' ability to counterattack.

The constant threat of attack from unfriendly combatants, be they Native Americans or settlers, quite directly justified the many defensive features that epitomized the largest (and smallest) municipal conglomerations along North America's colonial frontier (Volo and Volo, 36–38, 215, 219–22, 255, 260–61).

FOR MORE INFORMATION

Volo, J. M., and D. D. Volo. *Daily Life on the Old Colonial Frontier*. Westport, Conn.: Greenwood Press, 2002.

Wilson, S. *Colonial Fortifications and Military Architecture in the Mississippi Valley*. Urbana: University of Illinois Press, 1965.

ENGLAND

London, "the supreme city," was home to about a half-million people in 1700, to 900,000 in 1801, and to a bit more than 10 percent of England's population as a whole. By 18th-century standards, it was a giant. Its closest English competitor in

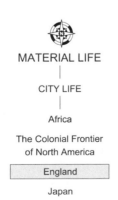

1801 was Liverpool, with only 78,000 residents. Although London remained the center of England's political, economic, and cultural life, other cities of rapidly expanding dimensions and importance, including Birmingham, Manchester, and Liverpool, played no small part in England's evolving character.

London dazzled the visitor with its sheer size and variety. There were glass-fronted shops packed with merchandise, bustling docks forested with towering ships' masts, hospitals, coffee houses, taverns, alehouses and brandy shops, three synagogues, and 300 churches. There were dozens of markets for fish, coals, vegetables, meat, leather, livestock, grain, meal, and a host of other goods. Then there were the people: servants running errands, pickpockets, footpads, prostitutes, beggars, ballad sellers, rioters, and country squires in town on business, along with communities of Welsh, Cornish, Irish, black, Huguenot, German, Swiss, and Jewish Londoners.

Rain or smog (or both) almost perpetually filled London's skies. Sunny days were rare enough to create a holiday spirit. The streets, atrocious in the first half of the century, improved in the 1760s to merely bad. Streetlights in London, which was better lit than most European cities, helped to prevent accidents and robberies. A company under contract maintained oil lamps and reflectors till about midnight; in 1736, the period of lighting was extended to sunrise.

The delivery of water was an important feature in London. Water was pumped from the Thames through wood (later iron) pipes about six inches in diameter that led to public pumps or to the lead plumbing of private houses. Houses paid a yearly fee for this optional service, even though the water ran only three times a week. The system was imperfect. The wooden mains lasted only a few years and leaked vigorously under the best conditions.

Through London wound the Thames, London's great waterway, running from the western countryside all the way to the sea in the east. The Thames was the greatest roadway of the town and hosted slave ships, small fishing boats, passenger ships, and cargo ships bearing ivory, oil, wine, tobacco, rice, indigo, cotton, grain, furs, hemp, tallow, coal, iron, and lumber. For the first half of the century, London Bridge was the only bridge across the river. Those who chose not to take the bridge were forced to take a horse ferry (which moved horses, coaches, and people, alike) or to hire one of the nearly 40,000 watermen who rowed passengers up, down, and across the river.

The system as it stood could not last. Boats were too numerous and hopelessly impractical. Change came when Westminster Bridge, begun in 1739, opened for traffic in 1750 and put the old horse ferry out of business. The structures atop London Bridge were removed, and in 1769, Blackfriars Bridge opened just west of the city, about midway between the other two bridges.

London was home to many notable structures and neighborhoods. On Ludgate Street was the brand-new St. Paul's Cathedral. The tallest building in London, its restoration successfully concluded in 1710. At the southeastern corner of the city, right on the Thames, stood the Tower of London, which housed the crown jewels, the Mint, and the occasional execution. The tower, open for tours to the paying public, was already militarily obsolete.

Working-class suburbs expanded north and were, all in all, unfashionable. However, things only got worse, from a snob's perspective, as one headed east. The East End held narrow lanes, slums, shops, foreigners, and the unsightly industries that helped make London productive. Whitechapel was home to most of London's 20,000 Jews.

It was London's West End that saw the most prodigious growth in the 18th century. This growth was the culmination of a series of factors, including partnerships between developers and aristocratic landlords, the West End's proximity to parks and Parliament, and the perception that the best and most fashionable people already lived there. However, the area as a whole grew increasingly seedy late in the century, and the fashionable fled west—to Bloomsbury's Soho, for example, which, although intended to attract the rich and titled, appealed to the merely well off, as well as radicals, intellectuals, and artists.

To the northwest, Marylebone began to follow the Bloomsbury example, and cheap houses for the middle class began to multiply. South of Marylebone, it was another story altogether. Mayfair and St. James's, the gems of the West End, attracted those with taste, connections, and money. Splendid townhouses and wide streets fronted the squares.

St. James's Square had the advantage of being situated right next to a royal palace and park. Surrounded by St. James's Street in the west, Piccadilly in the north, the Haymarket in the east, and Pall Mall in the south, St. James's housed dukes, as well as lesser nobility. Prime ministers and members of Parliament lived nearby. Even the businesses were high end.

Provincial towns sprouted civilizing institutions that mimicked London's: pleasure gardens, libraries, theaters, bookstores, coffeehouses, hospitals, and scientific societies. Nevertheless, regional idiosyncrasies remained. In the English Midlands, Birmingham—a mere village in 1700—grew to about 37,000 in the early 1770s and became the first provincial city to exceed 50,000 about 1780. Buoyed by its manufacture of toys, buttons, shoes, buckles, guns, clock parts, knives, and other metalwork, Birmingham acquired a library (1779), a hospital (1766), a respected scientific club called the Lunar Society, and a lively theatrical tradition.

The streets, atrocious in the first half of the century, improved in the 1760s to merely bad.

Directly north of the Midlands lay the county of Lancashire, home to two rapidly growing cities, Liverpool and Manchester. Liverpool owed its existence in part to the slave trade, launching 107 slave ships in 1771 alone, compared with London's 58. The city acquired a library, a hospital, a new lunatic asylum, and a new jail. Manchester, too, grew quickly. The advent of steam power overcame the city's paucity of waterpower to run mills, and Manchester came into possession of a theater, Literary and Philosophical Society, street lighting, a police force, and a hospital, making Lancashire one of the few counties in England with more than one hospital.

The image of London in the 18th century, so alive in so many respects, tends to overshadow the dramatic growth that other English towns and cities were simultaneously undergoing. Still, it was London, the center of a nation's government, the locus of its financial dealings, and a place of so much movement and diversity, that inspired the imagination with wonder (Olsen, 57–67, 71–72, 76, 78).

To read about urban life in Chaucer's England, see the Europe entries in the sections "Urban Economic Life" and "Great Cities" (London) in chapter 3 ("Economic Life") of volume 2; for Elizabethan England, see the England entry in the section "City Life" in chapter 3 ("Economic Life") of volume 3; and for Victorian England, see the Victorian England entry in the section "Urban and Rural Environments" in chapter 3 ("Economic Life") of volume 5 of this series.

FOR MORE INFORMATION

Lynch, J. *Eighteenth Century Resources.* <http://newark.rutgers.edu/~jlynch/18th/>, accessed October 10, 2003.

Olsen, K. *Daily Life in 18th-Century England.* Westport, Conn.: Greenwood Press, 1999.

Schwartz, R. *Daily Life in Johnson's London.* Madison: University of Wisconsin Press, 1983.

MATERIAL LIFE

|

CITY LIFE

|

Africa

The Colonial Frontier
of North America

England

Japan

Life at Sea

JAPAN

Familiarity with Japan's major cities (especially Edo) and with urban lifestyles among the various classes during the 18th century will facilitate an appreciation of Japan's metropolitan world as it existed during the early modern period.

Japan was among the world's most urbanized countries in the 18th century. The population stabilized at about 30 million for the entire 18th century. City residents constituted about 10 percent of that number. No country in Europe had an urban population greater than 2 percent. Put in another way, 18th-century Japan accounted for only 3 percent of the world's total population but boasted 8 percent of the world's total urban population.

In 1750, Japan had three of the world's five largest cities. Edo had a semipermanent population of more than one million, and Ōsaka and Kyōto each had populations of about 500,000, the same as Paris and London. Five of Japan's cities had populations over 100,000, while there were only 14 cities of that size in all of Europe.

The primary reason Japan had so many large cities concerned political expediency. In the first decades of the 17th century, the Tokugawa *bakufu* (national military government) had forced all of their vassals to concentrate their armies into one castle per district (*han*). Every castle engendered a surrounding town (*jokamachi*), some of which expanded into large cities.

In 1800, Edo was not only Japan's largest *jokamachi* but the world's largest city. Sitting at the head of Uraga, a large protected natural harbor in the distant east of the country, Edo had became the capital of the newly established Tokugawa *bakufu* around 1600 and is today known as Tokyo.

The *bakufu* had mandated a system called "alternate attendance" whereby daimyō (feudal warlords) were required to spend half of their time in the presence of the shōgun (the emperor's military assistant) in Edo and the other half in their home castle town. Daimyō families were required to remain in Edo as hostages.

Each daimyō was required to bring an appropriate entourage of samurai (warrior-administrators) and servants. Most daimyō brought at least 500 samurai. Many brought more than 1,000. By 1700, the population of Edo had soared to more than one million. About half the population lived there permanently; the other half was constantly being rotated.

Some 100,000 people were Tokugawa family members or their closest retainers. Another 400,000 samurai and their families were "part-time" (but often actually permanent) residents. Still, only about half of the population was samurai; the other half consisted of *chōnin* (city folk) who served them.

Rapid urbanization created tremendous problems in the area of water supply. An early system employed open trenches that tapped into a nearby spring and that relied on gravity for movement. Later, the mains were improved into water conduits of squared wooden sluices, hollowed bamboo, and eventually even some fired clay tiles. Four more water systems were eventually built. All accounts agree that the amount of fresh water was sufficient for the needs of the one million inhabitants.

At Edo's center was the shōgun's towering castle, surrounded by concentric circles of samurai barracks. Within the castle walls, the *bakufu* conducted both family business and the national offices of the shōgun, whose most trusted hereditary vassals (the *hatamoto*) saw to important governmental tasks.

In the lower reaches of Edo, *chōnin* of every type resided in their own neighborhood wards (*machi*), of which there were over 1,700 during the period. The designation of *machi* had often reflected the vocation of those living in the district. For example, the *Kome-cho* (rice ward) and the *Kamiya-cho* (paper dealers' ward) had traditionally housed rice dealers and paper dealers, respectively.

By the 18th century, however, the *machi* had absorbed all kinds of artisans and merchant houses. Only fishmongers, blacksmiths, and metalsmiths, in addition to the hereditary outcaste *eta* (ritually polluted because of their involvement with death—butchery, tanning, mortuary, and so on), remained in their own distinct *machi*.

The *machi* were subdivided into even smaller sections according to familial and commercial relations. These smaller units were usually bunched around a common tutelary Shintō shrine, and denizens often referred to the areas as *mura* (neighborhood). Many of the shrines contained their own cemeteries, thus creating a common ancestral home within the city.

Kyōto, the home of the powerless emperor and the center of many important Buddhist temples, continued to be a very large city. It was strategically placed not only between the eastern and western portions of the country but also at the southern end of Japan's largest lake, Biwa. Kyōto served as the headquarters for most of the major Buddhist sects in Japan. The city was dotted with some 7,000 to 8,000 temples.

Ōsaka was scarcely a day's journey away from Kyōto. Its position on the Inland Sea made it Japan's largest trading center. Although its harbor was unsuitable as a deepwater port, hundreds of small trading ships plied its harbor.

Nagasaki was Japan's most cosmopolitan city during the 18th century. The resident aliens were of three nationalities: Chinese (by far the greatest in number), Koreans, and Dutch. They all resided in their own carefully monitored enclaves and submitted to annual ritual testing (*fumi-e*) to ensure the government that they were not Roman Catholic Christian.

In 1700, about 25 cities had populations of more than 30,000, and perhaps another 1,500 marketing or temple towns had populations in excess of 10,000. Of these urban conglomerations, many had sprung up to provide food and lodging for the hundreds of thousands of samurai who, because of the "alternate attendance" (*sankin-kotai*) hostage system, traveled the road to and from Edo. Not surprisingly, those towns that were situated at crossroads, river crossings, harbors, and other such convenient places burgeoned most of all.

The types of dwellings that characterized Japanese cities of the period evoke the more particular—and thus the more familiar—aspects of urban daily life. Most *chōnin* lived in individual apartments in blockhouses (*nagaya*) built by urban landlords. The apartments each had their own entrances but often shared common facilities such as wells, reception rooms, gardens, kitchens, storage, and toilets. Whereas a few wealthy merchants could afford separate houses, many common *chōnin* lived in the rear of their modest shops.

Because houses were made of wood and paper, entire sections of Japanese cities burned down about every 20 years. The fabled Meireki fire of 1657 killed over 100,000 people in Edo and destroyed more than half the city. Another huge fire in 1772 burned almost half the city, and another in 1788 is said to have destroyed 357,000 homes, rendering 80 percent of the city homeless. In 1720, the *bakufu* stipulated that all newly constructed houses be built with ceramic tile roofs and mud plaster walls.

The material foundations of Japan's 18th-century urban population reflected the society's complex family, economic, intellectual, and religious cultures. The most urbanized country in the world, host to the world's largest city (Edo), Japan was clearly more advanced in its material conceptions of cities than a focus on agriculture and village life would lead one to believe (Perez, 112–13, 143–45, 147–49, 151–53, 155, 220).

FOR MORE INFORMATION

Japan Information Network. <http://www.jinjapan.org/index.html>, accessed October 23, 2003.

Leupp, G. P. *Servants, Shophands, and Laborers in the Cities of Tokugawa Japan.* Princeton, N.J.: Princeton University Press, 1992.

Nishiyama, M. *Edo Culture: Daily Life and Diversions in Urban Japan, 1600–1868.* Honolulu: University of Hawaii Press, 1997.

Perez, L. G. *Daily Life in Early Modern Japan.* Westport, Conn.: Greenwood Press, 2002.

Yazaki, T. *Social Change and the City in Japan: From the Earliest Times through the Industrial Revolution.* New York: Japan Publications, 1968.

LIFE AT SEA

The visitor to a thriving seaport town during the 17th and 18th centuries was beset with a fusion of sights, smells, and sounds. The typical seaport town was set

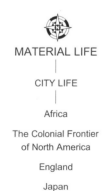

against a forest of spars, masts, and rigging amid an almost-incomprehensible web of ropes, cables, and lines. Warehouses lining the wharves opened their arms to the ships heavy with coveted cargoes. Wagons, carts, and wheelbarrows rumbled and clanged their iron-rimmed wheels across the cobblestone streets. Each breeze bathed the waterfront with a diverse mixture of odors—the pleasant fragrances of spices, oils, and salt air offsetting the less-inviting smells of tar, wet canvas, and rotting fish.

In the Americas and particularly in New England, where wood was plentiful, most wharves and docks were made of wood. In Europe, where wood was valued at a premium, and in the Caribbean, where the weather and temperature combined to shorten wood's useful life, the building material of wharves and docks typically consisted of stone, brick, or accumulated rubble. Solid rows of warehouses, ropewalks, and sail lofts lined the seaport's center, and heavy cargo cranes adorned its edges.

Besides the essential workplaces, taverns, banks, marine insurers, and residences for the population, there were many shops stocking a variety of common consumer goods, such as carpeting, window glass, pewter ware, boots and shoes, firearms, wines, and spices. Many shops dealt in fine fabrics, sewing notions, jewelry, tailoring, wigs, tobacco products, and leather-bound books. The majority of the waterfront shops served the needs of the mariners, offering ironwork, sails, hooks, lines, nails, coarse cloth for sailors' clothing, lead shot and gunpowder in kegs, axes, knives, swords, and even cannon and ball.

Of all the early European nations that colonized the New World, Spain was most favored in the natural excellence of so many of its ports. San Juan and Havana became important ports, inside which ships could undergo repairs, resupply themselves with victuals and naval stores, and take on their cargo. Throughout the 18th century, Havana ranked among the very best shipyards of the world, easily outdistancing its American rivals. The Spanish warships built in Havana's four slipways enjoyed a reputation for resilience and were the envy of the Spanish shipyards in Europe.

Until the 1760s, the town of Newport, Rhode Island, was the leading port in New England. This apparent success was largely attributable to the triangular trade; the slave trade with the islands of the West Indies, and the west coast of Africa. The slave trade was outlawed by mutual agreement with Britain in 1808, and Newport came to rely on other New England towns for commodities to export.

Boston and New York were rival ports. Three times as many vessels began their passage from New York than from Boston Harbor. Yet the heart of maritime New England remained Boston. The city came to dominate the region's commerce. By 1807, Boston's total commercial shipping surpassed that of the next three New England ports combined: Portland, Salem, and Newburyport.

In 1614, a group of Dutch shipowners formed the New Netherlands Company (Dutch West India Company), a successful fur-trading monopoly. The small outpost of New Amsterdam was founded at the southern tip of Manhattan and grew slowly, but by 1640, the Dutch had built a fort there and were maintaining a garrison. Notwithstanding the town's apparent readiness, a squadron of five English ships entered the harbor in 1664 and took possession of the town without a fight. Dutch

New Amsterdam quickly changed to English New York (named for the duke of York, later James II).

European ports were quite different from those of 18th-century America. Rather than a series of mostly brick docks and piers extending directly from the seashore, the ports of Europe generally consisted of long narrow wharves clinging to the banks of rivers that led into the sea.

The Thames River, London's waterway to the deep seas, had stone steps or stairways leading down from stone-lined riverbanks to the water's edge. Although shipping from London had, by 1660, declined almost to the point of stagnation in the face of French, Dutch, German, and Scandinavian competition, prosperity returned by the 18th century.

Endless trains of barges and a forest of masts could be seen lining the quays of all the port cities of the Dutch Republic. Amsterdam was a port of antiquity. In the 17th century, it was the largest port in the world. Built on a series of 90 islands joined by approximately 200 bridges, Amsterdam featured many impressive buildings that stood not on solid ground but on piers. Its warehouses, adorned with ornate gables, were known for their singular beauty. Amsterdam never developed the sleazy wharf culture of other seaport towns. A sea dike built on the north side of the city and dikes on either side of the Amstel River protected the city from floodwaters and provided it with its first three streets. The broad dam built across the river gave the town its name. Besides Amsterdam, other Dutch ports such as Texel, Hague, Flushing, and Antwerp became great centers of trade.

A seaworthy vessel is launched from the French shipyard at Rochefort in October 1751. Ports were an integral part of life on the high seas. © The Art Archive/Bibliothèque des Arts Décoratifs Paris/Dagi Orti.

The grand Spanish port of Seville was actually a series of ports stretching up the Guadalquivir River from Cadiz to Seville. Seville's inland position necessitated a laborious and time-consuming journey downriver, but it "provided protection against the assaults of all those who were tempted by the gleaming precious metals and other riches of the Indies." The Calle de la Mar, or "Street of the Sea," was the hub of activity for mariners. Sailors hoping to join a crew waited there to attract the attention of ships' masters.

The French had a number of good and moderately good ports, including Rochefort, Toulon, Cherbourg, Nantes, Boulogne, and LeHavre. However, only one port, Brest, was outstanding as a French naval base. The harbor at Brest, where as many as 500 ships could be moored, was one of the best in all of Europe, with an entrance two miles wide. The port had a complete dockyard and shipbuilding facility.

Cities in the form of seaports were an integral part of oceanic travel during the 17th and 18th centuries. They offered a unique, vibrant, and sometimes unsavory range of experiences. In the Americas, ports such as San Juan, Havana, Newport, Providence, Boston, and New York acquired strong economies and favorable reputations. In Europe, the older seaports of London, Amsterdam, Seville, and Brest each possessed unique features that in the coming decades, would develop or recede in accordance with the ebb and flow of history (Volo and Volo, 1–3, 11–13, 16–17, 21–23).

FOR MORE INFORMATION

Bourne, R. *The View from Front Street: Travels through New England's Historic Fishing Communities.* New York: Norton, 1989.

Hugill, S. *Sailortown.* New York: Dutton, 1967.

Volo, D. D., and J. M. Volo. *Daily Life in the Age of Sail.* Westport, Conn.: Greenwood Press, 2002.

MATERIAL LIFE: WEB SITES

http://www.utexas.edu/cola/depts/ams/online/smith/projects/bradstreet/marriage.html
http://www.ilt.columbia.edu/pedagogies/rousseau/contents2.html
http://www.cuisinenet.com/glossary/newengl.html
http://www.japanesekimono.com/
http://www.kyohaku.go.jp/tokuten/otya/tyaindexe.htm
http://www.uiowa.edu/~africart/toc/history/giblinstate.html

6

POLITICAL LIFE

The ancient Greek philosopher Aristotle (384–322 B.C.E.) claimed that humans are by definition political animals. By this he meant that an essential part of human life involves interacting in the public sphere with people who do not belong to our intimate families. It is these relationships—along with their complex negotiations—that permit the development of cities, kingdoms, nations, and civilization itself. Throughout history, different cultures have developed different political systems with which to organize their lives, and all political systems are in constant states of change as they accommodate to the changing needs and interests of the populace. Political life involves two different spheres of influence: organizing the relationship among those within a political unit and negotiating the relations between different political entities (countries or tribes or kingdoms). However, at its basic level, politics is about power—finding out who has it and who does not.

People create a political system, first of all, to assure themselves of internal peace and security. As the 17th-century political theorist Thomas Hobbes noted, without a strong authority, people's incessant struggle for power would result in a life that is "nasty, brutish, and short." This is why we want our power structures to be clear. Our political systems also clarify and solidify our loyalties and allegiances—nationalism has served as a sentiment that can unify people with diverse interests and backgrounds.

As people interact in ever-widening circles, our political life must negotiate the often-difficult relations with other kingdoms, countries, or empires. Diplomacy is the tool of our political life that functions to smooth these interactions, and war is the breakdown of these negotiations. In war—which has unfortunately dominated so much of human history—we can often see the noblest and worst expressions of our human spirit. In war, we can also definitively see the struggle for power that marks our political life.

Taken together, these general characteristics of politics apply to all the societies covered in this volume. During the 17th and 18th centuries, the societies of sub-Saharan Africa, colonial Australia, the North American colonial frontier, England, France, Japan, New England, and Western maritime travel all developed or maintained formal political institutions that met two basic requirements: domestic order

POLITICAL LIFE
|
GOVERNMENT

SOCIAL STRUCTURE

LAW, CRIME,
& PUNISHMENT

WARFARE

and external security. The mechanisms wherein the strains of these cultures' political lives found a voice included government; social structure; law, crime, and punishment; and warfare.

Governments tended to dominate the creation of laws. The actual implementation of laws (and related punishments) usually involved separate practices, although not always separate bodies. The same was true for warfare. Certainly, governments played a role in determining relations with neighbors, but the development of proven strategies, weapons, and military leaders was, again, constitutive of another category of political life.

Finally, it is extremely important to recognize the potency of informal, less-visible political structures. The ordering of society into separate classes was more than a set of laws or governmental pronouncements. It involved a deeply rooted acknowledgment on the part of most individuals regarding the truth, or at least the imperative authority, of such laws and pronouncements. The individuals of this period recognized and usually accepted the social differences that they had learned from birth. No less influential than governments in the governing of society have been social structures that interacted with and often reinforced existing governments, laws, and military institutions. Ultimately, however, it was another variable—power—that determined the political landscape.

~*Joyce E. Salisbury and Peter Seelig*

FOR MORE INFORMATION

Van Evera, S. *Causes of War: Power and the Roots of Conflict.* Ithaca, N.Y.: Cornell University Press, 1999.

POLITICAL LIFE
|

Government

The diverse societies that are treated in this volume all possessed governing bodies that differed significantly from one another. Whereas the following entries stress the unique characteristics of governments in sub-Saharan Africa, North America's frontier settlements, England, France, Japan, New England, and the world of Western maritime travel, a survey of the governments belonging to these various societies of the 17th and 18th centuries reveals a good many commonalities that, although hardly identical, are nonetheless identifiable, possessing deep, perhaps even interconnected, roots.

Religion was an important factor in the structure of several of these governments. In colonial North America, Catholic French settlers opposed Protestant Anglo-American settlers. Some Anglo-American settlers were Catholic, creating an uproar among their Protestant peers. The establishment of colonial New England in the early 17th century found its main impetus in Puritan doctrine, and the government that controlled the Massachusetts Bay Colony for most of the century went to great pains to establish and maintain a strong association with religious institutions.

In Africa, religion also contributed to the character of governments. The ruling family in Christian Ethiopia traced its lineage to Solomon and Sheba, whereas the Bornu monarch around Lake Chad patronized Muslim leaders to enhance his own prestige. Traditional religions advanced the authority of African rulers, as well. The Mutapa emperor benefited from a general consensus that he possessed special bonds with a spiritual realm, thus enabling him to rule better than a less-privileged individual. The French Bourbons were Protestants but ascended to the French throne thanks in part to their willingness to convert to Catholicism.

Formal government structures formed another cross-cultural pattern during this period. The British Royal Navy provides an excellent example of multileveled, multifaceted governing institutions, which attended to the varied organizational and administrative needs of Britain's navy. The admiralty, consisting first and foremost of a Board of Admiralty, itself chaired by the first lord of the admiralty, conducted the demanding business of governing the many aspects of building, maintaining, and improving a navy. Various subsidiary boards handled a host of concerns, including weaponry, medicine, and ship construction. The pattern of government aboard a naval vessel was no less strict, comprising a hierarchy of rigorously delineated duties and chains of command related to warrant officers, midshipmen, commissioned officers, captains, admirals, commodores, and ratings.

In early modern Japan, the formalization of government resulted in many operating levels. From an abstract perspective, the lucid outline of these levels, starting with the emperor and his military assistant, the shōgun, followed by regional warlords, samurai warrior-administrators, and finally, village elders, seems to be as formalized a government as could be found anywhere during this period. In reality, however, Japanese government operated in accordance with many informal rules, alongside its more ceremonial patterns.

In addition to religion and formalization, a third common feature of government during this period concerns the tension between centralization and local self-rule. In New England, the influence that both the Massachusetts Bay Colony's governor and the Court of Assistants exercised over society seemed overweening to many colonists, especially to those living outside Boston proper. As a result, local efforts to found town governments at the expense of Boston's regime occurred repeatedly and with success. Other New England communities outside Boston's range of influence fiercely defended their autonomy. Along North America's colonial frontier, alliances between Indians (the Iroquois Confederacy) and settlers (Anglo-Americans) proved useful in the struggle against New France (French Canada).

Eighteenth-century Japan's central government was, in reality, one factor among several that amounted to a complex system of competing interests and customs. On the one hand, the shōgun demanded that regional warlords spend a good part of each year in Edo, the country's capital. Despite this not-so-subtle attempt to augment the power of the central government, regional warlords and, especially, villages continued to exercise a substantial amount of autonomy with regard to the daily affairs of local government.

A similar contrast characterized 18th-century England, where cities, parishes, counties, and boroughs continued to preserve varying degrees of local independence at a time when Parliament was busy extending its prerogatives to the detriment of monarchical authority. In France, local autonomy ceded a great deal of its existence to the rise of absolute monarchy during Louis XIV's reign.

Finally, protest and change were not unfamiliar to governments during this period. For instance, shifts in power were proceeding, as mentioned, in England, where the influence of the monarchy was ceding to that of Parliament. Across the channel, the French began the period covered in this volume with an unsuccessful rebellion against the monarchy (the Fronde) and ended the period with a far more effective one (the French Revolution).

As previously mentioned, 17th-century New England's Massachusetts Bay government, with its heavy-handed, Puritanical approach to governing, inspired protest and ultimately its own decline. Protest was most notable among disgruntled Puritans such as Roger Williams, who parted ways with the Boston leaders and then established a colony in Rhode Island. Late in the century, the English crown revoked the Massachusetts Bay Colony's charter, effectively ending the Puritan government's monopolization of rule.

An even more radical shift in governmental power took place in Senegambia, where ruling African warlords relinquished considerable power to members of the lower class. Nasir ad-Din exemplified the concerns and drama of this power shift. Likewise, the focus of government in Allada suffered from intense dissent among the Aja people. This dissent eventually ended in the fragmentation of the old Aja confederation and the founding of a new kingdom, Dahomey.

All in all, the diverse patterns of government among these societies frequently evinced some basic similarities, not the least of which included the influence of religion, attempts at formalization, tensions between centralization and local autonomy, and protest that led to change.

~*Peter Seelig*

FOR MORE INFORMATION

Lynch, J. *Eighteenth Century Resources*. <http://newark.rutgers.edu/~jlynch/18th/>, accessed October 10, 2003.

Finer, S. E. *The History of Government from the Earliest Times*. Oxford: Oxford University Press, 1997.

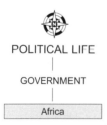

POLITICAL LIFE

|

GOVERNMENT

|

AFRICA

During the 17th and 18th centuries, Africans organized their societies in a number of different ways. Some states had a religious basis, such as Christianity, Islam, or a traditional African religion. Other peoples organized their societies around the family, either by perceiving the state as a giant family based on an articulated set of foundational traditions or by forming actual family connections among the state's different leaders. In some parts of Africa, people lived without states, and custom upheld by tribal elders regulated society. In all these systems, a person tended to view religion and tradition as related models on which to determine his or her actions.

Christian Ethiopia had perhaps the longest continuous governing tradition in Africa and was ruled by kings who claimed descent from Solomon and the Queen of Sheba through their son Menelik. Farther west, the kings of Bornu around Lake Chad patronized the Muslim religious leaders, who in turn supported their government. Along the Mediterranean coast, Turkish military men ruled in the name of the Ottoman Empire.

Oyo was the largest of the Yoruba states of West Africa and, as with Kongo, had a form of elected monarchy. Its ruler, the Alafin, had to commit suicide following a vote of no confidence by a council of elders. Along the Atlantic coast south of Yoruba country, the Aja peoples underwent change during this period. Traditionally, they had lived in a confederation based on the idea that the state was like an extended family. Allada, the most prestigious Aja realm, represented the father kingdom, while other kingdoms were the brothers of that high father-king. The king of Allada approved the elections of the other kingdoms. In return, they owed him the obedience due a father in an Aja family. The Yoruba actually had a similar structure under the Alafin (Akinjogbin, 15).

The coming of Europeans, however, changed the balance of power, and the brother kingdoms began to challenge the central authority. Because of this, many people left their homes to found a new kingdom called Dahomey. They argued that the state was not a family but a "pot riddled with holes," a situation requiring each citizen to help "plug the holes" and thus to maintain a sound existence for the overall system.

The slave trade affected African politics during the 17th and 18th centuries, particularly in Senegambia. At the beginning of the 17th century, *ceddo* warlords, traditional African leaders who competed over the European commerce, dominated the Senegambian slave trade while governing society with increasingly arbitrary force. Large numbers of the lower classes began turning to Islam, which provided a program for a divinely ordained, just society. During the late 17th century, a leader named Nasir ad-Din encouraged a popular uprising known as the Marabout Wars, after the marabout class of African Muslim leaders. Nasir ad-Din and his followers sought to reform society through the application of strict versions of Islamic law to society under the leadership of Muslim religious leaders. His chief rallying cry was against slavery: "God does not ever allow kings to pillage, kill, or enslave their people; rather they must keep and protect them from their enemies, the people not being made for the kings, but the kings for the people" (cited in Ogot, 274).

African Muslims viewed this struggle as jihad, or striving to promote Islam, in this case by waging war against its enemies. Initially, the movement succeeded in deposing the old aristocracies of the Senegambian kingdoms, but then French intervention restored them and drove the Muslims inland. However, the conflict continued, and during the 18th century, the region was the site of a series of popular revolutions inspired by the Marabout Wars, revolutions that resulted in the overthrow of despotic governments. Unfortunately, the new theocracies soon turned to the slave trade themselves, although with certain limitations based on Islamic law.

Kings of Kongo also ruled from a religious base, a mixture of Christianity and traditional African traditions. These kings, who married numerous wives and whose powers included control over rainfall, were considered sacred and were addressed as *Nzambi mpungu*, or "supreme creator." The royal family formed the nobility and governed different villages and territories. Power passed down through the mother, except in the case of the monarchy, which a council of eight men and four women were responsible for electing (Ogot, 550–55).

This illustration from the 1686 book *Description de l'Afrique* shows a group of Kongo noblemen displaying their clothing and accessories in a series of poses. Reprinted from Leo Africanus. 1686. *Description de l'Afrique*. Paris, E. Leroux.

In the south, lineage states ruled the grasslands. Two of these, Luba and Lunda, occupied the territory between the Zambezi and Kwango Rivers. Luba villages were made of households linked together by perceived family ties, as were the villages themselves at the regional level. Each province of the kingdom had its own chief who ruled by his connections to a local spirit. The king was considered to belong simultaneously to all clans and to none, having connections with the local lineage of his mother even as he had no separate clan of his own. Dead kings continued to exercise power by speaking through women who tended their shrines (Ogot, 595).

The Lunda kingdom was believed to exist under a single family, that of the Mwant Yav, or "lord of the viper." New territories became part of the kingdom as their chiefs married into the family, often after a war. Thus all the officials and provincial leaders were related, and their family obligations formed the glue that held the state together. In addition, when a new official took an office, he was supposed to all but become his predecessor, taking on his name, wives, and relatives. The king also had *takwata*, special officials who collected the tribute.

South of the Zambezi River, the Mutapa Empire used ritual means to control its territory. The emperor kept in touch with the spirit world on behalf of all his people, while his own ancestors spoke through spirit mediums. In addition, a ceremonial fire at the imperial court obligated all territorial leaders to make an annual journey there so that they could personally rekindle the flames as a symbol of imperial loyalty. The emperor also played an important role in rain making. He was not an absolute monarch, however, having to rely on the spirit mediums before making important decisions (Ogot, 644–46).

Many people in Africa also lived in what are called "stateless societies," in which the customs of both local elders and religious leaders existed independently of a central government. The Luo of the Great Lakes area grouped various organizations according to age, and the members of each organization exerted authority over those who were younger. There were also religious groups made of multiple clans. Clan chiefs were sometimes hereditary, but at other times they were elected by a council of elders. Some groups of the West African forests possessed a similar organization. Yet these groups, too, began to form more centralized states during this period.

In African government, one can see both tradition and change in the 17th and 18th centuries. Traditional and innovative attitudes unique to sub-Saharan Africa, combined with the effects of Europeans who infused Africa with both Western ideas and a demand for slaves, meant that political traditions underwent constant revision in response to new situations.

~Brian Ulrich

FOR MORE INFORMATION

Agatucci, C. Central Oregon Community College. *Humanities 211.* 1997. <http://www.cocc.edu/cagatucci/classes/hum211/index.htm>, accessed October 23, 2003.

Akinjogbin, I. A. *Dahomey and Its Neighbors, 1708–1818.* Cambridge, England: Cambridge University Press, 1967.

BBC World Service. *The Story of Africa.* <http://www.bbc.co.uk/worldservice/africa/features/storyofafrica/>, accessed October 23, 2003.

Fung, K. *Africa South of the Sahara.* 1994. <http://www-sul.stanford.edu/depts/ssrg/africa/guide.html>, accessed October 23, 2003.

Halsall, P., ed. *Internet African History Sourcebook.* 1996. <http://www.fordham.edu/halsall/africa/africasbook.html>, accessed October 23, 2003.

July, R. W. *A History of the African People.* 5th ed. Prospect Heights, Ill.: Waveland Press, 1998.

Ogot, B. A., ed. *General History of Africa.* Vol. 5. *Africa from the Sixteenth Century to the Eighteenth Century.* Paris: United Nations Educational, Scientific, and Cultural Organization, 1992.

THE COLONIAL FRONTIER OF NORTH AMERICA

Native Americans, the English, and the French practiced and developed widely divergent governmental institutions along North America's colonial frontier. The function of these governments often depended on interclan, intertribal, and international preoccupations, as well as on preexisting governmental structures, such as the limited monarchy and splintered politics of England and the powerful monarchy and centralizing tendencies in France.

Many tribes and confederations lived along the frontier regions. The Algonquian-speaking peoples were active and transient in present-day Canada and the Great Lakes. The Iroquoian-speaking peoples encompassed not only the Iroquois, who inhabited present-day New York State, the southeastern Atlantic seaboard, and parts of present-day Canada, but also the Hurons, who settled in the present-day province of Ontario. Both were organized around established political organizations. The history of the Iroquois Confederacy of the Five Nations (later Six) is particularly well documented because of its close alliance with the English in the final struggle with the French for empire.

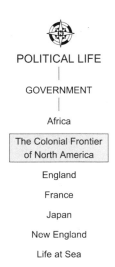

A social unit with governmental functions, the clan was, at least among the Iroquois, matrilineal, a situation that is far removed from a matriarchy, in which the women actually rule the tribe. However, the more settled tribes designated greater political power to females. Some Algonquian peoples separated their clan-based tribal government along "sky" and "earth" divisions known as moieties. The sky clans were named for birds and were dedicated to the pursuits of peace, the adjudication of blood feuds, and the promotion of harmony, whereas the earth clans were devoted to preparations for war, defense, and policing the tribe. The political leaders of the tribe were chosen from sky clans, and the war chiefs were chosen from the earth clans. This dual division of power among the clans manifested itself in diverse forms in many Algonquian communities.

Social relations between colonists and natives were very complex and volatile. The Creek chief Tomo-Chi-Chi, here with his nephew, sold land to the frontier settlers of Georgia and, in doing so, angered many members of his tribe. © National Anthropological Archives, Smithsonian Museum.

The English practice of designating different portions of their colonies with separate names (unlike the French practice of referring to their entire colony as New France) mirrored the political allegiances of the English colonial settlements in North America. The earliest English colonists called their New World home Virginia in honor of the unmarried Elizabeth I, the Virgin Queen. The Pilgrims referred to their settlements as New England. The Royalists in the southern colonies called them the Carolinas in honor of King Charles I. The Catholics called their home Maryland. Parts of New Netherlands were renamed New York and New Jersey when the English took them from the Dutch; and Pennsylvania was named for its founder. Finally, Georgia was dedicated to the reigning English monarch at the time of its establishment.

Almost as confusing as all these politically charged names in the English colonies were their many types of government. Some colonies were virtually self-governing while others obeyed governors who answered to the Crown. Still others were under the jurisdiction of proprietors or trustees. No two were alike in their governance, and it should be remembered that no two were settled by a single distinct and homogeneous population of immigrants.

Unlike the French in North America, most of the English colonies were virtually independent in their formative years. When James II became king of England, he attempted to cancel many of the royal charters under which the colonies had been formed. He succeeded in placing the entire Atlantic coast from Maine to Delaware under a royal governor, calling it the Dominion of New England. But William III, who replaced the deposed James II, reissued many of the original charters in a modified form. Nonetheless, Massachusetts was partitioned, and both it and the new colony of New Hampshire became royal colonies. Meanwhile, Rhode Island retained its right to elect its own government, and Connecticut retained its original charter by refusing to yield it up, opting instead to hide it in an oak tree.

The royal colonies of New York and New Jersey were particularly unfortunate in their court-appointed governors, many of whom proved to be arrogant, dishonest, or incompetent. The proprietary colonies of Pennsylvania and Maryland were somewhat more fortunate in their governance. Pennsylvania was converted into a royal colony for a brief time, but the proprietorship was reinstated by the beginning of the 18th century. Maryland underwent a political and military upheaval in 1688 because its founder, George Calvert, the first Lord Baltimore, had been a Catholic. It was thought that the Catholics in Maryland might support the deposed king instead of the stalwartly Protestant William III. It was therefore not surprising that William answered a petition of the colony's Protestant settlers by appointing a Protestant royal governor.

The two southern colonies known as the Carolinas began as a single entity, but by 1710, a separate governor was appointed to each. This date marks the separation of North and South Carolina. The tract of land that became Georgia in 1732 was given to a set of eight trustees under a limited charter. At its expiration, the colony reverted to the king, with Lord Granville being the sole remaining trustee with any interest in the colony.

Delaware remains an enigma in the colonial period, and it is almost certain that Lord De la Warr never discovered that the colony bore his name. The Swedes founded Delaware, which the Dutch and, later, the English seized as prize territory. Thereafter, both Maryland and Pennsylvania competed early on with each other over their respective claims to the region. Throughout most of the 18th century, Delaware's identity merged with Maryland's. It was not considered an independent colony until the eve of the American Revolution. Similarly, Maine was part of Massachusetts, and Vermont part of New York, until after the War of Independence.

In 1633, a group of entrepreneurs known as the Company of One Hundred Associates acquired a large grant of land in New France. In return for the right to trade for furs and appoint a governor in New France, the Hundred Associates promised to settle the French territory with 4,000 colonists within 10 years, protect them, and support the Catholic missions, which sought to convert the native population. The governors of French Canada ruled the civil government in cooperation with the Council of Quebec, a group made up of representatives from three municipal districts (Quebec, Trois-Rivières, and Montreal), the administrator of Montreal, and the father superior of the Jesuits. The representative members obtained their nominations from the powerful fur trade interests that made up the Hundred Associates. The nominees gained approval from the king and appointment from the governor-general of all Canada.

The Crown overhauled the system for governing New France in 1664. The Hundred Associates no longer appointed the governor. Instead, the Ministry of Marine back in France nominated a governor, whom the French king could then appoint if he so chose. Also, an intendant of justice, police, and finances was appointed to act as a business manager for the king. Able to exercise power without consulting the council, the intendant acted as a barrier between the civil government and the bishop so that the Church could no longer interfere in purely civil matters.

Clans served the Algonquian and Iroquoian peoples as useful governmental institutions through which political tendencies could be exercised. Fragmented by religious and political traumas, the English colonies were simply mirroring England's concurrent, but far more dramatic, upheavals of the 17th century. During this same period and well into the 18th century, France stood as Europe's preeminent absolute monarchy, imparting its emphasis on centralization to its North American colony, New France (Volo and Volo, 19–21, 39, 56, 59–60, 95–97).

FOR MORE INFORMATION

Archiving Early America. *Early America.* <http://earlyamerica.com/>, accessed October 23, 2003.

Neylan, S. *Canadian History on the Web.* 1996. <http://members.rogers.com/dneylan/>, accessed October 23, 2003.

Ubbelohde, C. *The American Colonies and the British Empire, 1607–1763.* New York: Crowell, 1968.

Volo, J. M., and D. D. Volo. *Daily Life on the Old Colonial Frontier.* Westport, Conn.: Greenwood Press, 2002.

Zoltvany, Y. F. *The Government of New France: Royal, Clerical, or Class Rule?* Scarborough, Ontario: Prentice-Hall of Canada, 1971.

POLITICAL LIFE
|
GOVERNMENT
|
Africa

The Colonial Frontier
of North America

England

France

Japan

New England

Life at Sea

ENGLAND

Eighteenth-century England possessed a limited monarchy and an active legislature, Parliament. While the governmental duties of the Crown were ever more ceremonial, members of Parliament enjoyed extensive influence on the Privy Council and in the Cabinet, including the position of prime minister. However, corruption and secrecy plagued the national government. A multitude of local officials administered to local affairs, including elections, but even elections (which involved only a small percentage of the adult population) led to grief and scandal resulting from the electoral system's obviously discriminatory standards. Britons voiced their grievances in more than a few ways, including riots.

There were two political parties in England, the Whigs and the Tories. Tories associated with the Church of England and the rural gentry, tended to be religiously orthodox, and had little sympathy for religious Dissenters. Whigs, on the other hand, being more sympathetic toward religious minorities, often belonged to Dissenting sects, themselves. They were typically businessmen, financiers, civil servants, naval officers, and urbanites.

King George I and King George II sided with the Whigs, who consequently ran England between 1715 and 1760, after which time the Tories began to reclaim some positions as magistrates, members of Parliament (MPs), and ministers.

Britain's monarchs were becoming less important just as Britain was becoming more important. At the beginning of the 18th century, monarchs theoretically retained a good deal of power, although not as much as their continental counterparts. They headed the executive and judicial branches of the government, as well as the Church of England. Moreover, they could veto legislation, declare war, make peace treaties, prorogue (dissolve) Parliament, appoint cabinet ministers, nominate judges, and award all titles.

In practice, however, these powers were limited. The Crown was heavily dependent on Parliament, which approved the royal budget, known as the Civil List. Still more significant, the monarchs were perpetually in need of funds for wars, building projects, and patronage.

Even in the monarch's sphere, Parliament played a role. The Privy Council, a body of dozens of advisers to the ruler, was composed chiefly of past and present Parliamentarians. The Cabinet, a subset of the Privy Council, was a more powerful advisory body. It always included the prime minister and the secretaries of state, who were members of Parliament, as well. These men served as advisers to the Crown, but they answered indirectly to Parliament, which could impeach them or (more commonly) announce that it would no longer support their plans. Once such a failure of confidence in the ministry occurred, the prime minister usually resigned and a new government would form.

Little by little, royal power receded. By 1800, monarchs no longer vetoed legislation, attended Cabinet meetings on a regular basis, or dismissed judges. What remained was ceremonial function and influence: pressuring government employees to vote for a particular parliamentary candidate, or killing a bill in the House of Lords by threatening to withdraw "royal favor" from those who voted for it. The overall decline in royal influence created a vacuum of unclaimed power, which Parliament easily assumed.

Parliament, this "gang of notorious robbers," had two divisions: the House of Commons and the House of Lords. The 558 members of the Commons were usually wealthy landowners and were elected to their posts. The House of Lords was composed of Englishmen, Welsh peers, and Scottish peers, along with Anglican bishops. The peers were referred to as lords temporal, and the bishops as lords spiritual. All members of Parliament, in both houses, were Protestant; it was illegal for Catholics to hold office or to vote.

Parliament was the most powerful legislature in Europe, but by modern standards, it was an unrepresentative and often unprofessional body. It met in Westminster in a room that was cramped and poorly designed. Moreover, Parliament did very little, especially early in the 18th century. It approved the budget and levied taxes, directed foreign policy, and exercised some control over executive and judicial appointments.

Parliament also passed private acts sponsored by individuals or private organizations, usually to get divorces, enclose land, gain citizenship, or build improvements such as lighting, turnpikes, and canals. To get a private act through Parliament could take as long as eight years. Even including private bills, Parliament passed only about 50 acts a year in the early decades of the century and about 200 a year in the 1780s. Absenteeism was high in the second half of the century, with more than half the members in attendance only rarely. On the whole, the national government left important issues such as education, welfare, health care, and law enforcement to local government or private enterprise.

Local officials included sheriffs, who administered elections for each county and for the city of London; churchwardens; laymen, who helped to administer parish church property; parish poor law overseers; town mayors; aldermen; city councilors and members of town corporations; burgesses, 12 of whom governed the city of Westminster; constables; and magistrates, or justices of the peace, who served as local lawmakers, administrators, and judges.

The electorate for both local and national office was extremely small. Women and Catholics were barred from voting. Of Protestant adult males, only a minority could vote, even at the local level. The number of eligible voters actually dropped during the course of the 18th century, to about 3 percent of the total population and about 7 percent of the adult male population. The percentage of adult males who could vote was both absolutely and proportionately larger in England than it was in Scotland, where fewer than 3,000 men had the franchise.

Elections depended on the two types of seats in the Commons: county and borough, the latter meaning that the constituency was a particular town. In counties, the ownership of land with a minimum value typically bestowed on the proprietor the right to vote. In "freeman boroughs," one could vote by being a "freeman," which is to say, by possessing the right to carry on one's trade within its walls. Not all boroughs, however, were freemen boroughs; in some, only the members of the town council held the franchise. In 1761, 201 boroughs had fewer than 500 eligible voters. The town of Bath had just 32. Yet there was little outrage.

According to the terms of the Septennial Act (1716), it was necessary to hold a general election at least once every seven years (although the monarch could prorogue a particular Parliament earlier and thus call for an early election). In an election year, some seats would not be contested at all, as in "pocket boroughs" or "rotten boroughs." Pocket boroughs were so called because all, or almost all, of their votes were dependent in some way upon a wealthy individual or family and tended to vote "as directed." They were thus "in the pocket" of someone. Rotten boroughs were towns that, despite having a diminished voting population, continued to enjoy as much political representation as expanding towns and cities.

Royal and legislative doings were recorded, discussed, and satirized in political magazines and newspapers, cheap pamphlets, ballads, riddles, handbills, graffiti, and scatological cartoons. Organized political clubs and impromptu gatherings met at coffeehouses and pubs, and crowds gathered outside the Houses of Parliament on days of important debate. As early as the 1720s, the British liked to call themselves a "nation of politicians" or a "nation of prime ministers."

The failure of the Stuarts and their supporters, the Jacobites, to regain monarchical power in England exposed the weakness of the English monarchy as a governing institution. A legislature (Parliament) and not a king or queen exercised more and more control over the very affairs of state that had previously been the unique concern of the monarchy. Yet the contrast between a people interested in politics and a government afraid of openness resulted far less in a revolutionary impulse to transform the current system of government than in a periodic—and curiously conservative—disdain for the politicians of the day (Olsen, 1–7, 9, 11).

To read about government in Elizabethan England, see the England entry in the section "Government" in chapter 6 ("Political Life") of volume 3; and for Victorian England, see the Victorian England entry in the section "Government and Politics" in chapter 6 ("Political Life") of volume 5 of this series.

FOR MORE INFORMATION

The Colombia Encyclopedia, 6th ed. "Great Britain." 2001. <http://www.bartleby.com/65/gr/GreatBri.html>, accessed October 23, 2003.

Hill, B. W. *The Early Parties and Politics in Britain, 1688–1832.* New York: St. Martin's Press, 1996.

Lynch, J. *Eighteenth Century Resources.* <http://newark.rutgers.edu/~jlynch/18th/>, accessed October 10, 2003.

Olsen, K. *Daily Life in 18th-Century England.* Westport, Conn.: Greenwood Press, 1999.

Ross, D. *The Georgian Period.* 2001. <http://www.britainexpress.com/History/Georgian_index.htm>, accessed October 23, 2003.

Schama, S. *A History of Britain.* British Broadcasting Corporation, The History Channel. Video series, 8. Videocassette, 2000, 2002.

FRANCE

Before 1600, few people would have been able to predict that the dynasty that produced kings for Austria and Spain, the Habsburg family, would have to cede political prominence to the French Bourbons over the course of the next 100 years. There were two reasons that a powerful France, ruled by the Bourbon family, seemed unlikely. First, the Protestant Bourbon family was not France's dynastic family; the Catholic Valois ruled France. More important, religious division within the French nobility contributed to the warfare and bloodshed that had torn 16th-century France in two, limiting the effective power of the monarch.

During the Wars of Religion, the Catholic Valois kings had been caught between the Guises and Bourbons, two militant noble families that lined up on opposite sides of the Catholic-Protestant divide. As French Protestants, the Bourbons resisted what they claimed was the illegitimate rule of an idol-worshiping tyrant (as they held the Catholic king to be). The Guise family added fuel to the fire by massacring Protestants. It looked as though France would degenerate into civil war.

The strife was brought to a halt when Henry of Navarre, a Bourbon, came to the throne after the Valois failed to produce an heir. To establish control over the country, Henry IV publicly submitted to a religious conversion in 1593, embracing Catholicism, allegedly explaining his decision with the phrase, "Paris is worth a Mass." Mindful of the Huguenot minority, however, he also granted a large degree of religious toleration in the Edict of Nantes of 1598. This political decision gave priority to the development of a strong and durable state and allowed the government to begin to solve the problems that the French state faced.

To reassert control of the independent nobility and strengthen state power, Henry IV needed to establish an unquestionable authority for the monarchy. To accomplish this end, as well as to limit the power of the nobility, he developed a new bureaucracy and sold prestigious offices to the highest bidder. Both of these policies meant that the hereditary nobility retained less and less local power and influence over governmental decisions. Despite Henry IV's assassination in 1610, the stage was set on which a strong monarch would develop France into a great power.

Louis XIII and his prime minister, Cardinal Richelieu, took full advantage of the precedent set by Henry IV. In another move that placed political influence and stability over religious adherence, Louis XIII joined with Protestant Sweden against

Catholic Spain during the Thirty Years' War. By the time that the peace treaties ending war between the Catholic powers were signed, France had become ascendant over Spain, and the monarchy had crushed popular and noble resistance to policies at home.

Louis XIV, known as the Sun King, also used his reign (of 72 years) to fulfill the promise of Henry IV's plans. Louis XIV was only five years old when he ascended to the throne. Not surprisingly, nobles who had lost power in the state growth and bureaucratic expansions under both Henry IV and Louis XIII seized on the regency as a prime opportunity to reassert their own influence in politics. The ensuing revolt, called the Fronde, posed a serious threat to the power of the French crown.

In the end, the monarchy survived this challenge to its authority, but when Louis XIV came into his own as a ruler, he vowed to make sure that nothing like the Fronde could ever happen again. To accomplish his goal of ruling securely and absolutely, Louis XIV continued the policies of his predecessors but also began to use cultural, political, and economic influence in new ways so that he might maintain his ascendancy over the aristocracy.

Louis XIV glorified his image to a degree never before seen in France. Nobles who wished to receive pensions or positions of influence had to come to Versailles to wait upon the king, and they would compete for favors such as the right to hold a candle by his bedside or hand him his pants as he got out of bed in the morning. Those nobles who declined to participate would soon discover that the king's largesse was not available to them. The palace of Versailles provides perhaps the clearest example of the Sun King in all his glory. At court, Louis XIV depicted himself as the Greek god Apollo, god of the sun. This image was projected in paintings and statues in the various rooms as well as statues and fountains on the grounds of the chateau; the magnificence of the buildings and gardens made the power of the monarch abundantly clear.

Un petit souper a la Parisienne—or—A Family of Sans-Culottes Refreshing after the Fatigues of the Day, etching by James Gillray, 1792. The sans-culottes participated in the Terror during the French Revolution. This British depiction of them creates an impression of total savagery, associating this notion with the urban working class. Above the fireplace, the notions of liberty (*liberté*) and equality (*égalité*) are mocked. © Trustees of the British Museum.

Abroad, the message of the king's domination found its bloodiest voice in incessant warfare and increased territorial control. In his wars, Louis XIV seized land from the Spanish Habsburgs and princes of the Holy Roman Empire. These wars were expensive and required a great deal of material and men, which furthered the demands for increased taxes and bureaucratic control. Jean-Louis Baptiste Colbert, Louis XIV's finance minister, gained fame and fortune as he managed the economy. Despite lavish spending on armies, wars, and castles, Colbert managed to balance the budget.

All of these components made it easy to believe and understand claims that the monarch was "absolute," that is, ordained by God to rule and maintain order in society, answerable to no one on earth for his policies. Philosophers such as Jean

Domat and Bishop Bossuet even earned lifelong pensions for their treatises, explaining and defending the theoretical and practical bases of divine-right monarchy.

Although Louis XIV may have had a generally free hand in waging war and building monuments, this type of government took a toll on the country. Supporting the king's constant wars and large armies became progressively more difficult, especially after the death of the brilliant finance minister. Additionally, the rulers that followed Louis XIV were neither as politically savvy nor as personally charismatic. Soon enough, the reign of Louis XVI would turn into the French Revolution, and the "divine-right" king would answer to the mob and end up losing his head in 1793.

~*Jennifer J. Popiel*

FOR MORE INFORMATION

Beik, W. *Absolutism and Society in Seventeenth-Century France: State Power and Provincial Aristocracy in Languedoc*. New York: Cambridge University Press, 1985.

———. *Louis XIV and Absolutism: A Brief Study with Documents*. Boston, Mass.: Bedford/St. Martin's, 2000.

Burke, P. *The Fabrication of Louis XIV*. New Haven, Conn.: Yale University Press, 1992.

Church, W. F. *The Impact of Absolutism in France: National Experience under Richelieu, Mazarin, and Louis XIV*. New York: Wiley, 1969.

Collins, J. B. *The State in Early Modern France*. New York: Cambridge University Press, 1995.

Hacken, R. *The History of France, Primary Documents*. 1996. <http://www.lib.byu.edu/~rdh/eurodocs/france.html>, accessed October 23, 2003.

Lynch, J. *Eighteenth Century Resources*. <http://newark.rutgers.edu/~jlynch/18th/>, accessed October 10, 2003.

Ranum, O. *The Fronde: A French Revolution, 1648–1652*. New York: Norton, 1993.

Society for French Historical Studies. *H-France, Newsletter about French Culture and History*. 2001. <http://www3.uakron.edu/hfrance/>, accessed October 23, 2003.

JAPAN

During the 18th century, Japan exhibited an interesting and dynamic system of checks and balances that preserved peace throughout the century. However, Japan was also a country characterized by a simmering conflict between nationalizing tendencies and an entrenched need for local and regional autonomy.

The so-called *baku-han* was a combination of the *bakufu* (national military government) and the *han* (regional governments). According to this governmental system of checks and balances, a *Seii-tai-shōgun* (barbarian-subduing generalissimo) acted as a military deputy for the Japanese emperor, who, in theory, was the most powerful man in Japan. The shōgun required regional warlords (daimyō) to swear loyalty to the emperor but allowed them to maintain almost complete autonomy in their 270 semi-autonomous *han*, where daimyō maintained an army of warrior-administrators (samurai), who also served the shōgun.

In the 18th century, the shōgun and his *bakufu* resided in the *jokamachi* (city) of Edo (which would eventually become Tokyo).

By 1700, the Tokugawa regime occupied the *bakufu* and had been in power for nearly a century. Indeed, the Tokugawa *bakufu* would remain in power for nearly another century and a half.

By the time of the third shōgun, the *baku-han* system was in fairly good working order and most of the major aspects of governance were in place. Able men selected from among the Tokugawa entourage (*hatamoto*) administered the *bakufu*. The *bakufu* made a point of selecting the most able men regardless of their social ranks. A board of senior councillors (*rōjū*) handled foreign, religious, imperial, financial, and daimyō affairs. In short, the board handled all of the issues concerning the management of the country as a whole.

Fudai daimyō (daimyō who were traditional allies of the shōgun) who handled the affairs of the Tokugawa family received the designation "junior councillors" (*wakadoshiyori*). Their tasks included managing the judicial, political, social, and financial affairs of the extensive private Tokugawa estates, which amounted to nearly one-third of all the arable land in the country. In addition, they oversaw the administration of all the gold, silver, copper, coal, and iron mines in the country. The councillors appointed ministers (*bugyō*) to administer the five large cities in the country: Edo, Kyōto, Ōsaka, Nagasaki, and Sendai. *Fudai* daimyō performed these tasks in addition to managing their own *han*.

An extraordinary aspect to the *baku-han* system of government concerned the policy of "alternate attendance" (*sankin-kotai*). According to *sankin-kotai*, each daimyō was required to maintain a residence in his *han* and another in the capital, Edo. Daimyō spent at least half of their lives there. Furthermore, *sankin-kotai* required that the family of each daimyō remain as hostages in Edo and that each daimyō maintain a samurai entourage appropriate to the administrative needs of his *han*. This was designed to sap the daimyō's finances but also to create an aura of pomp and circumstance in Edo. Daimyō could not adopt, marry, or make other social alliances without permission from the shōgun, who also required them to tear down all "superfluous" castles in accordance with a costly national public works project; most daimyō were entitled to only one such castle per *han*.

To ensure the shōgun that the daimyō were obeying his rules, an elaborate system of spies came into existence, incorporating the younger siblings or jealous concubines of the daimyō, as well as wandering monks, minstrels, nuns, blind masseurs, and anyone else who could insinuate him- or herself into the daimyō courts.

Another important aspect of the *baku-han* system was the codified seclusion of the country after 1640, which not only barred almost all foreigners from Japan but also prohibited Japanese from traveling outside (and often within) Japan. Chinese, Korean, and Dutch traders were restricted to Nagasaki. Until the 19th century, Japan would remain relatively isolated from the rest of the world.

The Tokugawa *bakufu* did not actually govern the entire country. By no stretch of the imagination can the *bakufu* be said to have been a national government in the modern sense. Although daimyō could be removed from office if they mismanaged their *han*, they were almost autonomous within their individual domains. Given that the system endured in relative peace for more than two-and-a-half centuries, one must concede that it worked tolerably well.

Just as *bakufu* administrators delegated most of the actual governance of *han* to the daimyō's samurai, these samurai left the administration of Japan's approximately 63,000 rural villages (*mura*) to local hereditary headmen (*gonō*).

Even though the samurai did interfere in the lives of the peasants, the laws and official notices that the samurai circulated to every village were all in the abstract and not the particular. It was much preferable to issue orders and depend on the *gonō* to enforce the strictures.

In many villages, however, a council of village elders (*otona* or *toshiyori*) met from time to time to manage village affairs. These men were commonly the heads of the important families in the village. They served as a council to determine tax assessments for the entire village. In some villages, these councils were almost democratic in nature because the heads of virtually every household sat on the council. All in all, peasant villages were self-sufficient, self-governing, and self-perpetuating.

Japanese government during the 18th century essentially amounted to a balance between centralization and regional autonomy. From the powerless emperor and his powerful military assistant, the shōgun, down to the regional daimyō, the pervasive samurai administrator-warriors, and the village *gonō*, Japan was a complex web of powerful exhortations and constraints that resulted in a great deal of autonomy for both daimyō and the villages in their domains (Perez, xii, 22–24, 26, 131–32, 144).

To read about government in Japan in the 20th century, see the Japan entry in the section "Government" in chapter 6 ("Political Life") of volume 6 of this series.

FOR MORE INFORMATION

Japan Information Network. <http://www.jinjapan.org/index.html>, accessed October 23, 2003.

Perez, L. G. *Daily Life in Early Modern Japan.* Westport, Conn.: Greenwood Press, 2002.

Totman, C. D. *Politics in the Tokugawa Bakufu, 1600–1843.* Cambridge, Mass.: Harvard University Press, 1967.

NEW ENGLAND

Native American government emphasized consensus over fixed laws. The New England colonists, on the other hand, acquired their settlements from legal documents called charters, which established trading companies and which acquired monarchical approval. The most powerful trading company was the Massachusetts Bay Company, which established itself in New England, with its capital in Boston. Here, a governor and a Court of Assistants lorded over a General Court and, later, over both an oppositional body of legislators and a host of local representatives. Nevertheless, the Crown soon grew weary of both the governor and the Court of Assistants, revoking the colony's charter and instituting greater oversight from London.

Native peoples who inhabited New England were organized into numerous tribal societies, which were in turn divided into villages. Some of the more prominent New England tribes were the Pawtucket of Cape Ann; the Wampanoag of Cape

Cod; the Massachusetts of the Boston area; the Pequot, Paugussetts, and Mohegan of Connecticut; the Narragansett of Rhode Island; the Algonquian of Holyoke, Massachusetts; the Pocumtuck of Deerfield, Massachusetts; the Mohawk on the western frontier of Massachusetts, New Hampshire, and Vermont; and the Penobscot and the Abenaki of Maine.

A leader called a great sachem presided over each of the tribes. The means of choosing the sachem and the extent of his power varied from tribe to tribe. In southern New England, the sachem was a hereditary post passed down through the female line. In northern New England, the post of chief sachem was awarded to the man who demonstrated the greatest ability to lead. In the southern area, the great sachem held absolute power; in the north, his was an advisory post. On rare occasions, the chief sachem was a woman. Within the tribe were numerous villages over which subsachems, sometimes called sagamores, presided.

New England tribes had no body of laws. Instead, tribes received guidance from the council, tribal custom, and public opinion. Within the council, which usually included both women and men, the elderly commanded great respect. Depending on the matter at hand, consideration might go on for hours or days, and a decision seldom went forward without a unanimous recommendation from the great sachem and the council.

The main colonial New England settlements were at Plymouth, Salem, and Boston, Massachusetts; Hartford and New Haven; Providence, Rhode Island; and smaller scattered communities throughout New Hampshire and Maine. The people in each of these settlements developed governments unique to their situations.

The most formidable, far-reaching, and influential government in colonial New England was the Massachusetts Bay Colony, with its capital in Boston. On March 19, 1629, King Charles I of England signed a charter granting the Massachusetts Bay Company the right to establish a settlement in New England. The charter became, of necessity, the constitution for everyone living in the Massachusetts Bay Colony, eventually including all of what is now Massachusetts, most of Connecticut, and most of Maine and New Hampshire.

📷 *Snapshot*

Communication in Colonial New England

Communication between localities was relatively lacking in the early years of colonial New England. In 1631, Governor Endicott refused to travel from Salem to Boston because he lacked the strength to "wade across the fords." (Earle, 329)

Before the group left England, it was decreed that the business of the colony would be conducted at four meetings a year of the "Great and General Court," consisting of the 12 members of the company plus the governor.

In addition to a "Great and General Court," government of the colony was the task of a governor, a deputy governor, and a court of 18 assistants to be elected annually by the company. John Winthrop, one of 12 members of the company, was elected governor, and Thomas Dudley was elected deputy governor. These men would constitute the first legislature. At the time of settlement, the 11 or so other members of the company were the only settlers designated as freemen—those who could vote.

Once in New England, the Massachusetts Bay Company filled all the places on the General Court and all the places on the Court of Assistants with the same 10 or so members of the company. After four years, there were only 2 new assistants named beyond the original 10, and one of those was the son of Governor Winthrop. For 50 years, the number of assistants remained about half the number specified in the charter.

The Puritan church was unquestionably the center of life for any New England community. Only church members could vote and hold office, despite the facts that church members were in a decided minority and that securing church membership was an arduous process. None of the women or indentured servants could vote.

As the years passed, the number of freemen grew, and more people were needed to conduct the everyday business of the colony. Moreover, some bold individuals voiced their suspicions that the government was denying them representation. These publicly aired complaints led to the organization of a second legislative body in May of 1634. The Court of Assistants would constitute an upper house, and representatives from each township were elected to serve as members of a lower house. In addition, town government was formalized in Massachusetts in 1636 with the establishment of the Town Act, granting freemen the power to allocate lands and to take care of local business.

Despite the addition of a lower legislative body of representatives from villages and the right to participate in town meetings, the vote at colony level was still restricted to the comparatively few men who had been admitted to church membership, although there were strong voices of protest against the policy, including most notably that of Roger Williams, who found his way to what is now known as Rhode Island. There, he founded a colony where church and state were entirely separate, the franchise having nothing to do with church membership and all settlers being free to worship, or not worship, as they pleased.

For most of those first decades, colonial New England was governed without serious interference from England, without the slightest regard for the various kings of England, and without regard for the directives written into the charter that made English settlement in the New World possible. However, as early as the mid-1670s, England's displeasure with the New England colonies was beginning to take on an ominous tone that the settlers could not ignore. Finally, on July 21, 1684, Charles II revoked the charter of the Massachusetts Bay Colony and simultaneously negated the practice of requiring church membership of voters.

A royal governor and council appointed by the Crown now occupied the executive and judicial branches of the government. Property ownership rather than church membership became the standard for the franchise, and villages benefited from a restoration of local self-government. Nevertheless, the Congregational or Puritan Church continued to exert control over the government of Massachusetts Bay until 1812 (Johnson, 25, 33–37, 39, 41–42, 133–34).

FOR MORE INFORMATION

Archiving Early America. *Early America.* <http://earlyamerica.com/>, accessed October 23, 2003.

Earle, A. M. *Home Life in Colonial Days*. New York: Macmillan, 1928.

Haskins, G. L. *Law and Authority in Early Massachusetts: A Study in Tradition and Design*. New York: Macmillan, 1960.

Johnson, C. D. *Daily Life in Colonial New England*. Westport, Conn.: Greenwood Press, 2002.

LIFE AT SEA

For the European nations taking part in the economic expansion of the 16th through the early 19th centuries (1588–1815), sea power was the fundamental principle that could determine whether empires would rise or fall. Overwhelming sea power, and the quest to maintain or regain it, proved a decisive factor in the history of all of Europe during the period. England, in particular, furnishes an excellent example of the institutions and regulations that governed oceanic transportation during the period. These bodies of tradition and legislation fall rather neatly into two categories: merchant vessels and the Royal Navy. Regarding merchant vessels, the formal system of government passed from the owner of the ship to its master and from there, to the master's mates, the idlers, and seamen (able, ordinary, and green hands). The official administrative bodies governing the Royal Navy were even more formal in their arrangement. The British Admiralty, with its First Lord, Board, Navy Board, and numerous subsidiary boards, saw to the needs of the navy. Aboard ship, officers (ranging from admirals down), and ratings (naval seamen), as well as marines, constituted the official hierarchy along which official channels of authority passed.

The owners of merchant ships typically provided a vessel to a master, supplied it through his agents, and gave the master varying instructions as to the manner in which he was to get a crew. Thus the person with overall responsibility and power on board a merchant vessel was the shipmaster, or simply the master. He was sometimes called the captain, a term of rank in the naval service not correctly applied to the master in the merchant service.

The master had absolute power aboard ship. The entire working of the ship lay under his responsibility, yet he never went aloft or did any work with his hands. He was always addressed as "captain" and answered as "sir."

It was usual for the master to call all hands aft for a talk about the nature of the voyage and his personal expectations with regard to their duties. He was sure not only to stress his authority and that of his officers but also to make the rules of conduct perfectly clear to the crew. Thereafter, the master rarely dealt directly with the crew, choosing rather to act through the influence of his officers.

The master relied heavily on his supervising officers, who were called mates. The first and second mates were always addressed as "mister" and answered as "sir."

The first mate never did work with his hands. He received his orders directly from the master and transmitted them to the crew. On deck, the first mate, whom the owner of the ship hired, often appeared to be the only officer in command of the vessel, but he would not attempt to exercise any unusual power, such as punishing a man. He needed to be an energetic and vigilant man who was well acquainted with all aspects of a seaman's work. Maritime law commonly made the first mate the immediate successor of the master should the latter die or become unable to perform his duties.

The second mate was the commander of the starboard watch. He was usually chosen by the master and did not automatically replace the first mate should the latter become incapable of performing his duties. His duties included the maintenance and care of all the spare rigging, blocks, and sails, as well as of the tools used to work on the rigging. Unlike the first mate, the second mate, when he was about the decks and aloft, was expected to do the same jobs as the common seamen.

Almost every merchant vessel of a large size carried aboard a number of specialized workmen known as idlers. Idlers commonly included the carpenter, the sail maker, and the cook. Very large vessels might also have a cooper, steward, armorer, and other professionals.

Idlers had no authority aboard ship, not even over the youngest boy. The crew properly addressed idlers as "mister," but they were never answered as "sir." Any order from the mates to the idlers would "come somewhat in the form of a request."

Neither the master nor his mates ever took the wheel or tiller. Steering the vessel was left to the men. Every seaman aboard was expected to stand as helmsman at some point in the voyage.

Mariners were generally divided into three classes: able seamen, ordinary seamen, and boys or green hands. All green hands were classified as boys regardless of their age or size. Both in the merchant service and in the navy, each man rated himself when he signed aboard. There were few abuses of this system, as every man knew that if found incompetent to perform the duties for which he signed, his wages would be reduced.

A "competent knowledge of steering, reefing, furling, and the like" was taken for granted even of an ordinary seaman, but an able seaman also had to replace worn, chaffed, and split rigging.

An ordinary seaman was one who, from lack of experience or strength, could not quite perform the duties of the able seamen. He could maintain a course under normal circumstances and could usually do the simpler parts of rigging such as making common knots.

Some ordinary seamen had great difficulty working in the rigging but were hired for their strength in pulling and hauling. These "sheet-anchor men" worked on the forecastle, where they handled the anchors and jibs. Several decks below were the "holders," who worked among the casks and provisions.

If an officer wished for someone to loose a light sail, take a broom and sweep the decks, hold a log reel, coil a rope, slush or scrub a mast, touch up a bit of tar, or help in the galley, he would call on one of the boys or green hands. It was within this class that political power was almost invariably from without.

The experience, professionalism, training, and morale of the British Royal Navy produced a service superior to that of any other maritime nation during the age of sail. The personnel and officers of the 18th century made the Royal Navy, which formed England's first and most important line of defense, the ideal to which all other European navies aspired. For these reasons, the men of the Royal Navy have come to represent the naval personnel in this period.

The Board of Admiralty controlled the Royal Navy's administration. This board was composed of seven commissioners headed by the first lord of the admiralty, who was usually a political appointee rather than a senior naval officer. There were, among the commissioners, experienced and distinguished sailors. The commissioners met every day, including holidays, and took decisions collectively.

> *The gunner needed "an almost total disregard for personal safety."*

The admiralty itself was responsible for the building and repair of ships, the commissioning of officers, the supervision of the Royal Marines, the operation of the Impress Service, and the management of the Navy Board. The admiralty had an experienced and diligent staff of 60 bureaucrats and clerks who enjoyed good pay and working conditions. As a consequence, the admiralty as a whole was a very efficient bureaucracy.

The Navy Board, a subsidiary of the admiralty, designed, built, and supplied the ships, ran the dockyards, appointed the warrant officers, and purchased or manufactured all the navy's stores and equipment except cannon. The Navy Board was further divided into appropriately named boards dealing with the transport of troops and military supplies, the provision of food and drink for the crews, and the care of the hurt and sick. The Ordnance Board tested, developed, and supplied cannon to both the army and the navy.

The Navy Board examined and appointed men as warrant officers on naval vessels. Ordinary and able seamen comprised the bulk of a vessel's crew but could progress to the rank of petty officer. Warrant officers included the purser, boatswain, and gunner.

The purser was a warrant officer in charge of the ship's nonmilitary stores and was financially responsible for food and drink if the wastage at the end of a voyage was greater than one-eighth. Many pursers gave short weight and measure when dealing out rations to avoid this penalty.

The boatswain's main duties were to supervise all the deck activity and to encourage the men in their work. If friendly persuasion or the force of their personality did not work, they, or the boatswain's mates, might use a rope's end or a cane as a starter.

The aspiring gunner served at least four years, one of which was as a petty officer. The gunner cared for the cannon, prepared the cartridges for them, and ensured the proper flow of powder and projectile to the gun decks during battle. The gunner needed "an almost total disregard for personal safety." His domain was the magazine in which the powder was stored. Herein, with his feet clad in felt slippers and with copper tools to prevent static discharge, he and his assistants made up the ammunition for the guns.

The rank of midshipman was an intermediate one between that of warrant officer and commissioned officer. In part by virtue of their upward mobility, midshipmen were superior to warrant officers and, after years of practical learning and testing, could receive command of a naval vessel.

Any commissioned officer in command of a naval vessel was its "captain." A lieutenant was allowed to command only "unrated" vessels—generally, sloops of war with fewer than 20 guns. A captain who was granted the temporary title of commodore could be placed in charge of more than one vessel in a squadron. Admirals commanded whole fleets or parts of fleets.

There were three grades of admiral: rear admiral, vice admiral, and admiral. Admirals accompanied the fleet on the flagship. The ship was usually chosen from among the larger warships of the fleet or because of the admiral's admiration for its captain.

Able seamen, who were not officers, might be promoted to the lowly rank of petty officer if they possessed or developed particular skills. Coopers, trumpeters, cooks, and sail makers were ranked as petty officers.

Whereas many officers had some permanent connection with the navy, the seamen, sometimes called ratings, were not considered members of the naval service. Rather, they were part of a ship's company. Mariners did not join the navy but joined or were pressed (forced) into the employment of a particular vessel and remained a part of that vessel's crew until killed, wounded beyond service, or paid off when the vessel ended its voyage or was put out of commission. Thereafter, seamen moved with relative ease from one vessel to another as their own preferences dictated. The first lieutenant granted a rate to every seaman who joined a ship. From this rate came the man's pay and duties. A captain could promote or demote a seaman from this initial rate at any time.

Most naval ratings were volunteers. They joined the navy for many reasons. Initially, they could expect a bounty when signing on, in addition to a couple of months advance in wages. Thereafter, they earned their monthly wage, which, although irregularly paid, accumulated as long as the ship was in commission. Their wages included food, and no deductions were made, apart from the costs of slop, clothing, or tobacco. Other seamen were pressed into service.

Marines were not seamen and were not used to labor aboard ship except to help with unskilled work. Marines had their own officers who messed in the wardroom. Their training was as infantry, and their purpose aboard ship was twofold. They made up the bulk of any boarding or landing parties should the situation avail itself; and they were a ready force, separate from the seamen, that the sea officers could use to enforce discipline and prevent mutiny among the crew. Marines provided the sentries at the captain's door, the magazines, the spirits room, and the stores. In battle, they took station in the tops where they served as sharpshooters, using standard sea service muskets to fire at the enemy decks below.

England's merchant vessels and Royal Navy represent the two basic categories according to which prescribed rules of conduct manifested themselves throughout the period. Although looser in structure than the Royal Navy, merchant vessels nevertheless maintained a strict and fairly constant system of official authority. The Royal Navy, with its rigid designation of authority along a fixed chain of command, was comparatively the best-governed navy during the 18th century (Volo and Volo, 93–97, 99, 101–9).

FOR MORE INFORMATION

Gardiner, L. *The British Admiralty*. Edinburgh: Blackwood, 1968.

McCracken, P. *Maritime History on the Internet*. 1995. <http://ils.unc.edu/maritime/home. shtml>, accessed October 23, 2003.

United Kingdom Royal Navy. *Royal Navy History*. <http://www.royal-navy.mod.uk/static/ content/211.html>, accessed October 23, 2003.

Volo, D. D., and J. M. Volo. *Daily Life in the Age of Sail*. Westport, Conn.: Greenwood Press, 2002.

Social Structure

Not all patterns of organization in a given society reflect visible and overt institutions such as governments, schools, police, and the like. The organization of communities can be informal and implicit, as much as formal and explicit. Indeed, the power of subtle, almost intangible, social norms can produce effects that shape a community's social structure far more effectively than the prescriptions of a law or the threat of police force. During the 17th and 18th centuries, communities associated with sub-Saharan Africa, the North American colonial frontier, England, Japan, New England, and Western oceanic exploration corroborated the considerable impact that social norms had on social structure.

Birth was a common factor in determining one's place in a given social structure. According to neo-Confucian principles in Japan, social classes were hereditary. If one had farming parents, then one was meant to be a farmer, and not a warrior, artisan, or merchant. In fact, the role of birth in determining one's status expanded significantly in Japan, as the notion of households replaced the broader, more inclusive notion of families.

Among English families, any child born into the nobility was ensured many of the privileges of those "born to the manor." In the same way and in general, poor parents gave birth to poor children who grew up to be poor adults, and middle-class parents gave birth to middle-class children who grew up to be middle-class adults, with the possibility of social mobility limited to opportune marriages or to infrequent acknowledgments of talent.

Throughout Africa, birth indicated kinship, which in turn indicated one's obligations within the community. Entire villages and states could trace their lineage to a single ancestor, either through matrilineal or patrilineal lines. Some African societies placed an equal emphasis on a mother's and father's influence over lineage. Similarly, some Native Americans along the colonial frontier organized society according to matrilineal principles: the husband in a marriage would go to live with his wife's family.

The measure of wealth was another factor that helped to situate a person in a social structure. In early modern Japan, the privileges of individuals who commanded great wealth did not necessarily translate into respect. Successful businessmen could not expect their wealth to purchase the reverence of those around them. According to neo-Confucian beliefs, merchants were an inferior class and, on the social scale, were superior only to "nonhumans," or "nonpeople."

Wealth in colonial New England was extremely important in determining one's social status. For instance, those who contributed relatively modest sums of money to the Puritan religious establishment could expect to occupy an equally modest seat far from the pulpit. On the other hand, the men who contributed handsomely to the religious establishment earned front-row accommodations for their wives, as well as for themselves.

In Ethiopia, the development of private property promoted the establishment of a landed gentry there, while the spread of Islam in West Africa resulted in the propagation of rules of property ownership associated with Muslim beliefs.

Ethnicity, much like birth and wealth, played host to a dizzying array of labels that, when assigned to a distinct group of people, positioned them within the wider social context and identified them according to a series of detailed, although largely arbitrary, social functions. On many American sailing vessels, nonwhites such as Chinese and Africans from the West Indies performed the same tasks as other sailors, while foreigners in the British Royal Navy included Americans, West Indians, and Russians.

Within the mind-set of many colonial New Englanders, Native Americans increasingly occupied the role of heathen inferiors. Hence, colonists came to view Native Americans, regardless of their intentions or behavior, as a menace to the constructive functioning of colonial society. Blacks living in colonial New England generally occupied another identifiable role: quite simply, that of the slave. Here, the goal was not to eradicate a group of people but to harness the physical labor of a supposedly intellectually mediocre so-called race in order, among other things, to facilitate economic growth.

Along North America's colonial frontier, Iroquois disputed with their not-too-distant ethnic neighbors, the Hurons. Throughout the colonial settlements, communities of Germans, Scotch-Irish, Dutch, French Protestants, and English, being only marginally integrated, tended to comprise distinct ethnic enclaves.

Finally, societies conceptualized the male sex apart from the female sex, assigning different meanings and values to each one. In Japan, women learned how to bow to the men around them. In colonial New England, a married woman's status often depended directly and wholly on her husband's status. This same relationship held true aboard naval vessels, where a captain's wife went to great pains to distance herself from most individuals whose social standing was below that of her husband. Although she could discuss certain prescribed topics with the steward, conversation with a seaman would have constituted a significant breach of etiquette.

Although by no means exhaustive, the preceding survey of common themes characterizing the social structures of a handful of cultures during this period sheds light on the importance that birth, wealth, ethnicity, and sex had in determining, according to sociopolitical dictates, one's collective and individual identity.

~Peter Seelig

FOR MORE INFORMATION

Althusser, L. *Essays on Ideology.* London: Verso, 1984.

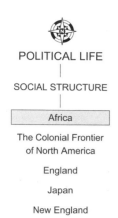

AFRICA

In most of sub-Saharan Africa during the 17th and 18th centuries, the most important sources of status were perhaps kinship groups, which served as the main principle of organization for social and economic activities. Religion also played an important role, as priests or religious scholars could exert their influence throughout society and quite independently of their status within a kinship group. Many societies divided themselves into age groups in which the older members ranked above the younger ones, regardless of lineage. Finally, special conditions such as states and slavery created people of differing status, although custom, rather than force, ideally regulated relationships among different status groups. During this period, however, the introduction of hierarchical ideas from Europe contributed to the breakdown of traditional social structures, leading to new patterns of power and authority in many areas of the continent.

Kinship systems are not unique to Africa; they have also existed and continue to exist in the Middle East, Central Asia, Oceania, and many other areas of the world. In 17th- and 18th-century Africa, however, kinship generally formed the entire basis of the social structure. Many states were portrayed as families, founded by a common ancestor, with the local regions representing different branches of the same family. In the Shambaa kingdom of East Africa, oral traditions portrayed all the regional chiefs as children of the royal line. Usually, all the families in a village would claim a common ancestor, as would pastoral groups that wished to share resources or form an alliance. Essentially, kinship groups defined one's sphere of mutual obligation in times of war, famine, or other crisis and set out the manner according to which people shared resources and leaders exercised political authority.

The basic unit of a kinship group was not the nuclear family but the lineage: an extended family usually reckoned back five or six generations. The manner in which lineages were determined depended on the culture. In patrilineal societies, people reckoned their descent through male ancestors; that is, children became part of the father's lineage. In matrilineal societies, on the other hand, people looked to their female ancestors, with children belonging to their mother's lineage. Matrilineal systems did not entail that women were in charge but only that they were more important in determining identity. The Bemba of Central Africa were matrilineal, whereas Arab tribes in North Africa were patrilineal. A third type of lineage structure, cognatic, manifested itself among some Swahili groups. In these areas, children belonged equally to both their mother's and their father's lineages. In some hunting-and-gathering societies, children themselves chose whether to join their mother's or father's clan. The choice, however, was permanent.

One important point that must be made about lineages is that they often did not represent authentic blood ties. For example, if two clans wished to form an alliance or share resources, they would "discover" a common ancestor so that the alliance would fit into the lineage system. Such an alliance was possible because most people were only vaguely aware of exactly how they descended from the common ancestor anyway. Similarly, different types of fictive kinship occurred when a lineage would adopt someone, usually to absorb that person's services or talents into the lineage.

A unique manifestation of fictive kinship occurred at Swahili weddings. Individuals who were called Inviters "invited" people to contribute to the organization of wedding festivities, and this event defined the social group for that occasion. Another unique Swahili relationship was *utani,* or "joking relationship." In this bond, people who were thinking about forming a fictive kin relationship, such as marriage, would joke with and tease each other in lieu of more formal commitments.

In all African kinship groups, status derived from seniority. The cities and villages that were believed descended from the oldest offspring of the common ancestor possessed more prestige than others, as in the Yoruba city of Ife, believed to be their earliest city. At the same time, authority within a lineage usually lay with its oldest male member in a patrilineal system, or sometimes with the brother of the oldest female in matrilineal societies. Sometimes, family groups would break off from the wider group and form a new lineage in order to seek better pasture or farmland. These new lineages, however, remained connected with their old kinship groups. In much of Africa, members of different lineages even worshiped different gods and spirits that were important to their respective families.

As important as it was, kinship was only one of the ways in which African societies were structured during this period. One other important structure, which cut across lineages, was the age set. These age sets were determined by either the time at which someone was born—as among the Igbo—or the time at which a person entered adulthood—as among the Kikuyu. The age set determined people's roles in the life of the village as a whole. The usual range of a given group was two or three years, although sometimes it could be as high as six. Sometimes, these groups had special initiation rites. Among the Igbo, a group of individuals reaching puberty would select a leader, a patron, and a name. Names for the age sets represented either the characteristics of its members or the age at which they reached puberty or were born.

Among the Igbo, the different age sets passed through age grades that determined the type of work that they performed in the village. Children, for example, performed simple tasks and learned the basics of such things as the chase and the meaning of ceremonial masks. Teenagers would collect contributions for community projects, as well as clean the village. In addition to working on large building projects, men in their late twenties to their late forties went to war and guarded property. Those in their fifties and sixties exercised a limited authority over the workers. Finally, the oldest men of the village made decisions for the community, whether the matter concerned an internal dispute or dealings with outsiders (Ifemesia, 82–84).

At all age grade levels, age sets had to answer to the next oldest age set. At the same time, an age set could form groups advocating particular policies within the community, and the fact that age sets cut across lineage lines made them an important glue holding communities together. Age sets also disciplined their own members, so that the energies of all were ideally channeled to the good of society. Each age set had its own pride and reputation, and many community projects evolved into competitions among the different age sets to determine which set was most proficient at a given task or form of entertainment. Age sets also represented an important means of integrating outsiders, as members of an age set treated one another as equals.

Class also became an important element in some African social structures. Certain lineages were more prestigious than others, and these prestigious lineages sometimes formed a social elite in a given community. Among the Swahili, lineages that traced a usually fictitious genealogy back to the Middle East possessed more prestige than those with African origins. The sharifs, or descendants of Muhammed, were the most prestigious of all. In practice, the key to achieving a high social standing among the Swahili corresponded to the accumulation of wealth through successful trading, especially in the Indian Ocean trade. Academic prestige was also of importance in establishing class distinctions. Both Swahili and Hausa families gained in status when they produced prominent religious scholars.

Concepts of social class underwent change during this period as groups and individuals began to acquire control over private property. Prior to this widespread transformation, most of Africa followed a *lamana* system, or one in which people produced goods and services for consumption without control over the means of production. In Ethiopia, for example, the early modern period witnessed the creation of a landed gentry that began to concentrate economic resources and political power in its own hands. As the kingdom expanded, these elites created new estates and converted the former populations into laborers. Along the Mediterranean coast, the Ottoman Empire granted landed estates to Turkish elites or local favorites who worked the land in the same way. Even in the Great Lakes region, farmers began seeking the protection and resources of pastoralists in exchange for labor. The 18th-century Islamic revolutions in West Africa also led to the adoption in those areas of Middle Eastern ideas of property ownership outlined in Islamic law (Ogot, 26–30).

This era saw the rise of the *prazo* system in the Shona country of southern Zambezia. The Shona had earlier possessed a ruling oligarchy; however, in late precolonial Africa, Portuguese adventurers called *prazeros* began to establish estates and presented themselves as a new noble class superior to the local chiefs. These chiefs consequently passed on to the *prazeros* a portion of the estate's production, while the *prazeros* became middlemen in the trade between southern Africa and the rest of the world, especially Europe and the Americas. In addition, the Portuguese newcomers adopted many African customs and functioned as overchiefs in the territories that they controlled. They also developed a special labor force drawn from the surrounding regions called the Chikunda, which some have characterized as a "slave army" (Ogot, 652).

New types of slavery also became prominent in parts of Africa at this time. Slavery in Africa had long existed; people who were captured in war, for example, became the slaves of the victors. With the development of capitalism, however, slavery became an important part of many people's daily lives, perhaps best exemplified by the frequent raiding for slaves who would, if they survived the voyage there, labor in the Americas. At the same time, slaves became a more significant part of African societies.

Not all African slaves received the same harsh treatment as did the plantation slaves of the Americas. Along the Lower Guinea coast, for example, slaves could marry nonslaves, hold independent jobs, and often inherit the property of their masters. Most slaves in Africa, however, were not so fortunate. In the Lulonga valley, slaves worked the fields until a chance to sell them overseas presented itself to the slaves' owner. Among the Tio, there were so many slaves from among the Boma that the word used for Boma came to mean a stupid or low person in general, a result of the cruel stereotype that people had of those whom they owned. In the Congo River valley, the Bobangi slave traders referred to their slaves as "dogs" when discussing their sale (Ogot, 539–40).

In Senegambia, slavery intersected with another important element of the social structure—the religious community—because Islamic law forbade the enslavement of Muslims. After the revolutions that brought the Islamic governments to power in regions such as Futa Djallon, the new rulers found that Europeans would only accept slaves in exchange for their own goods. Hence, the jihad, which Muslims originally used to oppose slavery, gradually became an excuse to hunt for slaves among the non-Muslim populations. These slaves were sold to Europeans or kept in slave villages called *runde*, where they performed agricultural labor to support the state (Ogot, 193).

The themes outlined here represent simply a few principles for the organization of African societies. Each of sub-Saharan Africa's many cultures had its own distinctive features, which may have mirrored some, none, or all of these principles. In addition, other factors affected African societies of this period, such as religion, which, while often related to kinship groups, could give people an additional tie to the wider world; economics, which created commercial ties among people in widely ranging areas; and political offices, which, in regions dominated by states, could create special

> *Under capitalism, slavery became an important part of many people's daily lives.*

kinds of social classes above the rest of society. Kin, age, and status groups, however, remained the backbone of most of Africa south of the Sahara throughout the 17th and 18th centuries, acting both as a graph by which people came to understand their place in the world and as a mechanism of support and cooperation that ensured the smooth functioning of daily life.

~Brian Ulrich

FOR MORE INFORMATION

BBC World Service. *The Story of Africa.* <http://bbc.co.uk/worldservice/africa/features/storyofafrica>, accessed October 23, 2003.

Halsall, P., ed. *Internet African History Sourcebook.* 1996. <http://www.fordham.edu/halsall/africa/africasbook.html>, accessed October 23, 2003.

Horton, M., and J. Middleton. *The Swahili: The Social Landscape of a Mercantile Society.* Malden, Mass.: Blackwell, 2000.

Ifemesia, C. *Traditional Humane Living among the Igbo.* Enugu, Nigeria: Fourth Dimension, 1979.

McIntosh, R. J. *The Peoples of the Middle Niger.* Malden, Mass.: Blackwell, 1998.

Ogot, B. A., ed. *General History of Africa.* Vol. 5. *Africa from the Sixteenth Century to the Eighteenth Century.* Paris: United Nations Educational, Scientific, and Cultural Organization, 1992.

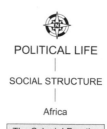

THE COLONIAL FRONTIER OF NORTH AMERICA

During colonial times, native peoples lived in close proximity both to the French community in present-day Canada and to a hotpot of English, Scotch-Irish, Dutch, Flemish Walloons, French Huguenots, Quakers, and German Protestants in Anglo-America. The settlers' increasing demand for labor in the English colonies created a market for African slaves, for whom the old colonial frontier represented bigotry, repression, unremunerated work, and mortal danger.

The Algonquian-speaking peoples were active and transient in the precontact period in present-day Canada and the Great Lakes, hunting and foraging in small bands that came together annually for fishing, summer encampments, and religious ceremonies. More settled in their lifestyle than the Algonquians, the Iroquoian-speaking peoples generally comprised the Iroquois and their relations known as Hurons. Their culture was usually organized around established political organizations, an annual agricultural cycle, and permanent, fortified villages. The Iroquois Confederacy of the Five Nations (later Six) was closely allied with the English but not with the Hurons, whom the Iroquois dispersed in 1649.

Smaller than a confederacy or a tribe, the clan offered a structure to aboriginal society that was organized around common female ancestors. When a man married, he moved in with his wife and her relatives. These matrilineal relatives would join to build a large clan-oriented longhouse, to clear and tend the outlying fields, and to care for and educate the young. The clans took names from among a number of animals, birds, plants, and even mythical beings; but wolves, bears, foxes, elk, deer, hawks, and eagles predominated. All the clan's material wealth—including the fields, dwellings, and the village itself—belonged to the women.

In 1633, the French Company of One Hundred Associates took possession of New France from Florida to the Arctic Circle, and from Newfoundland to the source of the St. Lawrence River and its tributaries. It was understood that the Hundred Associates would have a fur trade monopoly and the right to govern the colony as they saw fit as long as they brought 4,000 colonists to settle the area within 10 years.

The colonists of French North America were the *habitants* (inhabitants); yet for many decades after the founding of the colony, they were few in number. *Habitants* were considered the permanent residents of New France. Their recruitment was typically the task of men of rank, merchants, or even the French king. Living on farmsteads cut out of the forests along the rivers and streams of Canada, *habitants* found little difficulty in making a living on the rich, virgin soil. Provided that they obtained the proper licenses and followed the colony's regulations, individual settlers could find the fur trade quite lucrative.

The earliest English colonists settled at Jamestown in Virginia in 1607; Plymouth, Massachusetts, in 1620 (the Pilgrims); and the Massachusetts Bay Colony, chiefly between 1629 and 1640 (the Puritans of New England). The second wave was composed of a small Royalist elite and a larger number of indentured servants from the south of England who settled in Virginia from approximately 1642 to 1725. The third movement was composed of persons from the northern Midlands of England

and Wales who came to the Delaware River Valley from 1675 to 1725. Although all three waves shared a common language and adherence to the Protestant faith, they spoke different dialects, built their houses differently, held diverse views on business and farming, and had different conceptions of public order, power, and freedom.

Beginning in the first decade of the 18th century, the Scotch-Irish (also called Ulster Scots) began to arrive at the port of Philadelphia. They were predominantly Presbyterians. Having pushed the Irish Catholic population out of Ulster, these Scots not only formed a hatred for the English, who attempted to force Anglicanism upon them, but also despised the tolerant Quakers for their pacifism. On the frontier, the tough-minded Scotch-Irish unabashedly believed that they were foreordained by Scripture to take their land from the Indians, by force if necessary. The peak periods of Scotch-Irish emigration thereafter were in 1741, 1755, and 1767.

The Calvinist Dutch and their religious brethren, the Flemish Walloons and French Huguenots, had a significant influence on frontier life. Walloons were French-speaking Calvinists from the southernmost provinces of the Spanish Netherlands. The Huguenots were Protestant refugees from within France. Both the Walloons and Huguenots were targets of the relentless persecution of the Catholic regimes of Spain and France, respectively. Their greatest concentration was to be found on the island of Manhattan in the settlement of New Amsterdam and at Fort Orange on the Hudson River at Albany. The flood of Dutch emigration to New Netherlands survived the change to English governance. Indeed, Dutch emigration to America remained significant until about 1735, and the Dutch penetrated the frontier along Indian trails, rivers, and their tributaries.

Quakers, or Friends, made extraordinary efforts to develop the Delaware River valley and southeastern Pennsylvania, and their influence contributed strongly to the formulation of a uniquely characteristic colonial frontiersman and settler. For generations, Quaker farmers combined their religion and farming experience into a spiritual framework that effectively confronted the challenging conditions of the frontier. By the beginning of the 18th century, their efforts had created the most successful of all the English colonies as measured by contemporary standards.

VISIT OF OGLETHORPE TO THE HIGHLAND COLONY.

Not all settlers in the British colonies were English. In this picture, James Oglethorpe, founder of the Georgia colony, greets settlers from the Scottish Highlands. © CORBIS.

Noted for their somber clothing and sparse households, the German settlers in America were generally Lutherans and came nearly destitute to the frontiers. German-speaking settlements developed throughout the 18th century, and the pace of this immigration did not falter until the advent of the American Revolution. By 1750, they had penetrated into the far northwestern portion of New Jersey and west into Pennsylvania. They tended to separate themselves from other groups, a process aided by their unfamiliarity with the English language.

The African presence on the frontier was significant. Almost all the Africans who came to America came as slaves. Ethnologists have determined that most African Americans can be traced by lineage to one or the other of only 13 tribes that inhabited the western part of the African continent. These tribal societies were largely agricultural ones. The Africans who came to America as slaves, therefore, were already experts in farming methodologies and animal husbandry.

Some blacks of African heritage came to America as freemen and wage earners, and many of these moved to the frontier to escape white prejudice in the coastal communities. It should be remembered that race-based slavery was a legally recognized institution throughout the English colonies, north and south.

The black frontier experience was otherwise little different than that of white settlers. Native Americans were no more tolerant of blacks invading their lands than they were of whites. Black families were just as likely to be attacked and slain as were white families. A significant exception to this indiscriminate violence was the case of the Florida wilderness, where Indians and escaped black slaves seem to have formed an alliance to resist European colonialism (Volo and Volo, 19–21, 39, 97, 105–8, 110, 112–13, 159–62).

FOR MORE INFORMATION

Fischer, D. H. *Albion's Seed: Four British Folkways in America*. New York: Oxford University Press, 1989.

Nash, G. B. *Red, White, and Black: The Peoples of Early America*. Englewood Cliffs, N.J.: Prentice-Hall, 1982.

Volo, J. M., and D. D. Volo. *Daily Life on the Old Colonial Frontier*. Westport, Conn.: Greenwood Press, 2002.

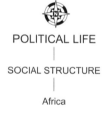

ENGLAND

For 18th-century men and women, class determined almost everything—diet, dress, times of waking and sleeping, occupation, education, and even sometimes cause of death and means of burial. Those English who held titles were England's nobility. Peers, in particular, were protective of their status and recognized that their titles conferred upon them great privilege and prestige. The overwhelming majority of English held no title but still accepted or even helped to preserve a rigid class system. At the top of this group were the untitled wealthy (the gentry); below them, a conglomeration of not rich but not poor citizens; and below them, a vast number of poor and struggling laborers and their families.

The number of actual titleholders was extremely small. They made up less than 0.02 percent of the population at the end of the 18th century. From 1784 on, peerages (any title above baronet) were created at a faster rate. For such a small group, peers owned a great deal, controlling about 20 percent of England's land value.

In addition to those with titles, there were those whose wealth alone raised them to the upper class. The great magnates were, like peers, very rare, belonging to perhaps a hundred families. However, there were thousands of other families with fewer holdings whose land rents still enabled them to live lives of leisure. These were the gentry, whose ranks most middle-class Britons yearned to join. The gentry were composed chiefly of those who owned land but who did not till it themselves.

Some gentry also owned land in and around London and augmented their fortunes by developing upscale housing projects. Others invested in stocks, turnpikes, mining ventures, and trading companies.

Below the gentry—petty squires, military officers, bishops, parsons, and members of Parliament—stretched the vast, ill-defined territory of the "middling sort." This group included merchants and shopkeepers, bankers, prosperous small farmers, clerks, attorneys, apothecaries, schoolmasters, industrialists, innkeepers, architects, curates, and engineers. These were the people who typically had an education, business acumen, or a special craft skill that recommended them. Not always defined by income, the middle class included wealthy businessmen who, because of their dependence on trade rather than on land or titles, found themselves belonging to the middle—not the upper—class. Depending on where the line is drawn, the "middling sort" possibly included anywhere from about 16 to 42 percent of all families.

Those who had little but their bodies to offer or whose crafts paid poorly formed the lower class. These were the wage laborers in field and factory, miners, peddlers, seamstresses, prostitutes, canal bargemen, domestic servants, knife grinders, ostlers, cattle drivers, fishmongers, paupers, and common soldiers and sailors. There were a great many of them—more than 600,000 domestic servants alone. The poor certainly made up over half the population. The minimum income for survival was about 20 pounds a year, and there were a good many people making well below that sum. More than 20 percent of all families required charitable assistance.

It is uncertain how much social mobility actually existed in 18th-century England. Many successful tradesmen and manufacturers came from humble origins, although the men who rose far and fast in their business usually had, somewhere along the line, profited from a stroke of good fortune—marriage to an heiress, an inheritance, or the influence of "friends" (not one's intimate companions but people in a position to help one's career). Usually, a woman could enhance her social status only by marrying.

True rank and its privileges remained closely guarded. For one thing, it was extremely rare for a man still active in trade, however successful, to rise to membership in Parliament or to win a bride from a prominent landed family. Second, entry into the peerage on one's own merits was nearly impossible. Although a number of peerages were created during the century, most were promotions of lesser peers or replacements of lines that had died out. Third, although a man might invest his mercantile profits in land, thus moving into the gentry, this difficult practice was particularly uncommon. Huge country estates rarely became available for purchase.

The classes were vastly unequal; yet no revolution either shook or toppled the social structure. Most people, even the poor, believed in the system in its ideal form. The upper class had the most to lose from a massive upheaval. The middle class had enough upward mobility to keep it reasonably content. The lower class believed in the rich's feudal responsibility to the poor; the disenfranchised masses, even when they resented the gentry, expected it to fulfill its obligations to those in need.

Failure to provide a suitable example and to care properly for their subordinates were the most common complaints against the rich, who were widely seen as preoccupied with duels, London, adultery, foreign fashions, fox hunts, and gambling.

The poor, in turn, were taken to task for insubordination, drunkenness, criminality, ignorance, improvidence, self-indulgence, and laziness. In the eyes of their betters, rural laborers were "perverse, stupid and illiterate," urban workers were "debauched, ill-mannered," and all were "swinish." Partly as a consequence of these attitudes, elements of the privileged classes subjected the poor to countless lectures and sermons on good work habits, meek religiosity, and the virtue of starving quietly. The poor were advised to frequent church constantly while avoiding bad company, swearwords, and gin shops. To be fair, the rich and titled shouldered their share of social duties, including the avoidance of soups made from gravy, the collection of skim milk and its distribution to the poor, and church attendance in the presence of servants.

England was not entirely a country of whites. Estimates of the total black population of Britain vary widely, but it seems likely that of the 15,000 to 20,000 black residents of London, fewer than half were slaves. The others, whether they had ever been enslaved or not, met with a limited tolerance. They belonged mostly to the lower class, and the vast majority were servants. Many blacks in England married whites, and spousal arrangements appear to have caused little alarm as long as no class boundaries were crossed. A few blacks were quite well off, such as Soubise, the protégé of the duchess of Queensberry, or Dido (Elizabeth) Lindsay, grandniece of Lord Mansfield.

Despite England's rigid class system during this period, a number of factors contributed to the progressive homogeneity of British, and especially English, culture. Newspapers and novels were one such factor. Common sources of entertainment, morality, and excitement generated common conceptions of how life should be lived. Physical mobility blurred regional differences, as landed gentry migrated between their country estates, London, and holiday spots such as Bath and Brighton. Workers, too, moved in search of jobs. Servants of the rich might travel with them. Men joined the army, navy, or militia. All of these trends only intensified in the coming centuries, helping, although only in part, to offset the boundaries of class (Olsen, 14–15, 17, 19–22, 29).

To read about social structure in Chaucer's England, see the Europe entries in the sections "Social Structure," "Aristocracy," "Peasants, Serfs, and Slaves," and "Urban Social Structure" in chapter 6 ("Political Life") of volume 2; for Elizabethan England, see the England entry in the section "Hierarchy" in chapter 6 ("Political Life") of volume 3; and for Victorian England, see the Victorian England entry in the section "Class and Caste Experience" in chapter 3 ("Economic Life") of volume 5 of this series.

FOR MORE INFORMATION

Lynch, J. *Eighteenth Century Resources*. <http://newark.rutgers.edu/~jlynch/18th/>, accessed October 10, 2003.

Olsen, K. *Daily Life in 18th-Century England*. Westport, Conn.: Greenwood Press, 1999.

Porter, R. *English Society in the Eighteenth Century*. New York: Penguin Books, 1990.

JAPAN

The structure of Japanese society during the 18th century lends itself to several perspectives. One can study the number of Japanese and their distribution between rural and urban areas, or one can examine social classes and their interrelations. An inspection of family structure can also be informative. This section uses all of these approaches to facilitate knowledge of Japanese social structure during this period.

It is estimated that the population in 1600 Japan stood at about 17 million. By 1721, it had increased to about 30 million but then remained basically static for the next century. The lower classes constituted perhaps 95 percent of the population; yet we know very little of the lives of peasants, artisans, and petty merchants except from what the elites tell us about them.

Throughout the 18th century, the structure of Japanese society rested on the neo-Confucian beliefs of the 12th-century Chinese philosopher Chu Hsi. The basic premise of neo-Confucianism was that human society reflected natural cosmic laws and that people were separated into four hereditary social classes, all of which were complementary and mutually exclusive.

By 1700, the samurai, or warriors, had become civil bureaucrats and administrators. They therefore remained at the top of the social scale by virtue of their administrative contributions to society. The farmers ranked next because they contributed food—the staff of life—to Japan. Residing in small villages close to their ancestral farms, peasants largely governed their daily lives. Beneath them were the craftspeople or artisans who produced utilitarian items for all of society. Most were city folk who produced their crafts to be sold elsewhere by other people. The final and lowest stratum on the social hierarchy was that of the merchants, who were considered to be a parasitic class that served society only by moving goods from places of production to areas of consumption. Most merchants resided in cities.

Far beneath these four classes were people considered to be nonessential, often called *hinin* or "nonhuman": beggars, thieves, musicians, actors, prostitutes, and surprisingly, priests and other religious persons.

Nearly 90 percent of the population lived in the rural countryside and therefore rarely, if ever, encountered the samurai. The *chōnin*, or city folk, merely served the samurai as merchants, artisans, servants, and purveyors of every sort.

To govern the samurai, daimyō (regional warlords) passed laws on their *han* (daimyō domains) modeled after *bakufu* (national military government) codes. Like all other mem-

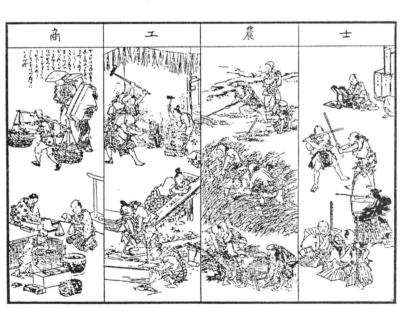

The four traditional classes in Japan during the 18th century were businessmen (traders), the artisans (manufacturers), the peasants (farmers), and the warriors (samurai). © Cabinet Library Collection.

bers of society, samurai were to behave as neo-Confucianism dictated, a duty that required samurai to obey their superiors and to manage their inferiors wisely.

The everyday lives of the common folk were not idyllic. Peasants worked hard in order to pay high taxes in an already-precarious environment. Yet most peasants were fairly well nourished and comfortable. Among the peasantry, many farmers practiced nonagricultural tasks. Among those who raised agricultural crops, some were wage laborers, and many more were tenant farmers, working the fields of a landlord class.

By and large, the peasant population of Japan lived in small- to medium-sized rural villages. The neo-Confucian ideal of rural, agricultural, self-sufficient villages hinged on the principle of "three generations under one roof." It is possible that many homes in the villages did indeed contain a small extended family of a farmer, his wife, one or two children, and perhaps one or both of his parents.

The obvious aliens to the village included the samurai and daimyō but also extended to any other nonmembers, among whom one could count itinerant peddlers, seasonal workers, hired hands from other villages, troubadours, actors, wandering monks, and the like. These members of the social structure were particularly susceptible to the effects of social ostracism, which was more horrible than anything that the daimyō or samurai, or even the *bakufu* itself, could inflict upon a person.

All things considered, then, the ideal small village probably comprised 100 peasant families with a total population of around 400 people. Village headmen were certainly to act as moral models and advisors. Within each peasant family, fathers were to rule their households and nurture their children in the moral ways of the ancestors; children were to be dutiful to their parents; wives were to obey their husbands.

The city commoners were even better situated in their lives than their peasant brethren. Most lived in cities, which were infinitely cleaner and safer than anywhere else in the world. They enjoyed a varied and nutritious diet, clean water, safe streets, sewage and trash removal, and even efficient local government. They benefited from a high degree of literacy, access to cheap entertainment, and inexpensive, good-quality medical care.

In the city, the laws also reflected neo-Confucian social ethics. Like the peasants in their villages, the *chōnin* were enjoined to be frugal, industrious, and honest in their professional and personal activities. The government periodically and routinely issued sumptuary laws that forbade *chōnin* from wearing particular types of clothing (especially silk) and from eating, drinking, and generally behaving in a manner "above their station." Fathers were instructed to protect and educate their sons in the ways of the merchant; wives were to obey their husbands; children were to love and obey their parents and provide for them in their old age; and everyone was enjoined to obey their samurai masters.

Outcastes, called *eta* (literally, abundant pollution) or *hinin*, were probably descendents of prisoners-of-war (usually Koreans) but were often also convicts, fugitives, or criminals, as well as the deformed or leprous. Most Japanese considered them to be ritually unclean, morally base, and probably damned by their karma. Therefore, *eta* and *hinin* found themselves restricted to undesirable vocations, including those of morticians, executioners, leather workers, and nightsoil collectors.

The definition of families rested on the idea of the household, or *ie*. To facilitate control over social structures, the government recognized the existence only of the *ie*. The head of the *ie* spoke for the household. People could enter the *ie* by birth, marriage, or adoption. They could leave it by death, disinheritance, and marriage outside the *ie*. The *ie* continued until no one remained to inherit either property or title.

The social structure that governed the lives of 18th-century Japanese encompassed a great number of relations in society, including class, age, sex, urban, rural, religious, and governmental relations, to name the most important (Perez, xiii, 13, 15, 73, 129, 137, 154, 159, 164, 213, 251–52).

FOR MORE INFORMATION

Dunn, C. J. *Everyday Life in Traditional Japan*. Tokyo: Tuttle, 1969.

Japan Information Network. <http://www.jinjapan.org/index.html>, accessed October 23, 2003.

Perez, L. G. *Daily Life in Early Modern Japan*. Westport, Conn.: Greenwood Press, 2002.

NEW ENGLAND

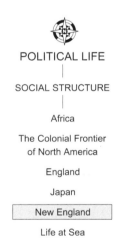

Social stratification was widespread throughout the New England colonies. Churches, colleges, and the role of labor all exhibited rigid and complex hierarchical patterns that divided along lines of age, gender, race, vocation, religion, wealth, and marital status. Slaves (of native and African descent) and white servants represented two important classes of colonial New Englanders.

In 1620, the native peoples who had inhabited New England for thousands of years numbered about 75,000, far more than the European settlers in the 1620s and early 1630s. For many Puritans, the Native Americans were subfiends in the service of the devil, whose domain included any untamed land in the New World.

In colonial New England, social stratification was everywhere very much apparent and perhaps no more so than in Puritan meetinghouses, which represented every category of New England inhabitant. The pews of the wealthy were usually large and decorated with columns. Pews for the poor were often no more than rough plank benches. Seating rules dictated that black worshipers occupy an elevated pew in one corner of the meetinghouse. (The segregation of black worshipers continued in Boston churches well into the 19th century.) Women generally sat on one side of the church and men on the other. A section of the church was also devoted to young boys.

The larger churches recognized as many as 15 ranks determining church seating. The first seats around a table were for the trustees of the church, the judges, and those who contributed 40 shillings to the church. The first six pews were reserved for males who contributed substantial amounts for their seats, the first one costing

30 shillings and the sixth 9 shillings. The seventh pew was for young men. The eighth was for boys. The ninth was for ministers' wives and widows and for women whose husbands were 40-shilling contributors. The next three pews were for women whose husbands were lesser contributors. The 14th rank and pew were for girls. And the 15th was for anyone.

Alongside churches, New England's institutions of higher education also exhibited the colonies' intense social stratification. Although the occasional poor, deserving college student received a scholarship and although some students paid their way with farm produce, most students were from families with money and position. Going to Harvard was extremely expensive, costing the equivalent of an average laborer's entire two-year income. One-half of 1 percent of the men of New England went to college. Fewer than 500 students graduated from college in the entire 17th century in New England.

The rigidity of the colonial social structure also emerged in the realm of work. It was blasphemy to assume a calling or work outside the social level to which one was born. A person born into a peasant family was not to try to follow work unsuitable for someone of this humble social station. Ministers, legislators, and merchants did not typically come from the lower classes.

The leaders in the Massachusetts Bay Colony were wealthy Englishmen. Reasoning from the doctrine that success in business was a sign of God's supreme approval, successful businessmen felt entirely justified in keeping political power exclusively for themselves and in passing legislation that served to benefit themselves. With legislative tools at its disposal to manage the colony's commerce, the court set about forming monopolies and restrictions on labor.

Very few black people made their homes in New England during the colonial period. By 1715, the time of the first reliable census of race, there were 158,000 whites living in New England and 4,150 blacks. By 1776, the number of blacks had increased to 16,034. Most of the black slaves in New England were concentrated in the hands of very few families. Less than one-eighth of New England families owned slaves. The term *slave* was rarely used, however. Owners preferred the less-onerous term *servant* or the euphemistic *perpetual servant*.

In colonial New England society, slave traders assumed political, economic, and social positions of leadership. Four of the most prominent traders were judges, and several were colonial governors and lieutenant governors. John Hancock, famous signer of the Declaration of Independence, was a partner of James Rowe, a slave trader. The founders of Brown University in Rhode Island made their fortunes as slave traders.

The topography, climate, and soil of New England made slavery an impractical arrangement on the region's small farms, quite unlike the vast spreads of single, "cash" crops on southern plantations, where slavery flourished. Moreover, the fervor of New England Puritans and other religious dissidents placed troubling doubts and a decided distaste for slavery in the minds of the majority of the New England population, despite the unfettered exploitation of slaves by a comparatively few wealthy merchants and land holders. Because of these factors, by 1790, slavery had been outlawed in all of New England.

The first mention of free black people in New England occurred in 1646 when New Haven's governor, Theophilis Eaton, freed his two slaves and built them a house; but no accurate record of the actual numbers of free blacks exists. Subsequent to 1646, there were increasing numbers of free blacks in New England. Despite their legal status, free blacks were considered the social inferiors of whites and basically lived with most of the same limitations and discrimination that burdened slaves.

In New England, another category of labor was more widely used: voluntary "indentured" Caucasian servants. Indentured servants were typically Europeans who wanted to settle in North America but could not afford the cost of the Atlantic passage. Therefore, they signed a contract, agreeing to work as a servant for a settled colonial family in exchange for passage across the Atlantic. One essential characteristic distinguished a white servant from a black slave. Unlike black slaves, white servants were not in servitude for life—their contracts were for a few years—nor were their children automatically slaves.

In the 1630s, indentured servants arriving in New England on ships from the mother country made up about 21 percent of the passengers. Upon the ship's arrival at a port city, little care was given to these passengers of servants, especially to the old and sick, who would bring the least money as servants. Many were quarantined indefinitely. In a number of cases, buyers and sellers separated a servant family when it served the formers' best interests.

For the poor, criminals, debtors, and even prisoners of war, indentureship in New England was one way to begin life anew. Although life in service could be hard and even unjust, New England servants could often look forward to eventual land and business ownership and thus to an economic independence and well-being that the same individuals could never hope to achieve in England.

A study of the social structure of colonial New England reveals a society that was deeply and elaborately partitioned. Churches, colleges, and the workforce were three of the most prominent sites wherein social stratification manifested itself. Slaves and indentured servants represented two social classes that occupied the margins of power (Johnson, 21–22, 55–57, 133, 147, 149, 150, 155–57, 159, 163, 168, 179).

FOR MORE INFORMATION

Johnson, C. D. *Daily Life in Colonial New England*. Westport, Conn.: Greenwood Press, 2002.
Pestana, C. G., and S. V. Salinger, eds. *Inequality in Early America*. Hanover, N.H.: University Press of New England, 1999.

LIFE AT SEA

The crews of vessels making their way across the vastness of the sea-lanes understood the formal systems of government that regulated their professional conduct. However, the existence of less-formal, unofficial values and norms—social struc-

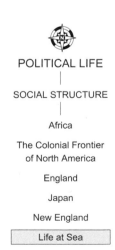

tures—created a separate, although closely related, field of understanding to which officers and sailors of all ranks and ratings cautiously conformed.

In the late 17th century, officers first began to seek a lifelong career in the navy, and the social structure among the complex ranking of officers reflected rigid class structures, as a whole. Especially in the British Royal Navy, the selection of officers depended largely on wealth, status, or family connections. Frequently, one could obtain the officer's post of midshipman, which promised advancement and perhaps command of a naval vessel, solely by virtue of family influence or outright purchase.

The formal rules regulating the informal selection and interaction among officers were intricate and often inflexible. A frigate of the period supplies a case in point. Aboard a frigate were more than a dozen officers: captain, first lieutenant, up to six junior lieutenants, at least two marine officers, and a couple of "passed midshipman" (later called ensigns). These men ate together in the wardroom. Also of "wardroom quality" were the warrant officers: surgeon, chaplain, sailing master, and purser. After the wardroom officers came the lesser warrant officers such as the boatswain, chief gunner, and carpenter. Ranking below the midshipmen who had not yet passed their examinations were the petty officers. These were the last to be separated from the seamen by rank.

Far from comprising a homogeneous class, these officers splintered into distinct groupings. Each grade among the officers jealously guarded its own rights and prerogatives and as it is noted in Samuel W. Bryant's *The Sea and the States*, men of rank "would have jumped overboard before they would have sanctioned the slightest change in the organization of ship-board life."

In relation to officers, seamen came from a particular class of society with a distinctive lifestyle. They generally resided along the coasts in sections of town peculiar to themselves. Like other laborers, seamen shared attitudes, language, and a common store of knowledge characteristic of their trade. The available evidence from the 18th century suggests that crews of warships were overwhelmingly composed of young men, typically in their mid-twenties, who were able seamen. By comparison, the typical seamen who worked in the merchant service were in their early thirties and were divided between able and ordinary seamen.

A considerable number of foreigners served in the Royal Navy, as they did in most of the navies of the world. These included Americans, Frenchmen, West Indians, and Russians. The number of Americans was remarkable; one of the complaints made by the United States that led to the War of 1812 concerned the impressment of American nationals at sea. Also, many of the men serving in the navy were nonwhite. This trend was especially evident in the Royal Navy, which, with its far-flung possessions, recruited its sailors from around the world.

The more effective an officer's sway over his men was, the more successful the vessel's overall performance would be. The seamen understood that able officers would reward the deserving few with advancement, possibly to the rank of petty officer—no mean ambition for a seaman. Ultimately, the conditions under which they served were largely based on the good will of the ship's officers. Some naval personnel were treated as little more than slaves.

Any suggestion of drafting men away from a happy ship and well-respected officers aroused instant protest from the crew. When captains changed ships, they hoped to take with them as many reliable men from their former crew as possible. One officer of the period wrote, "I have taken great pains to discipline and make them a tolerable ship's company, which was very bad when I had them first. . . . It would be a little hard . . . losing my people."

An officer or seaman who lost favor with the crew could find himself the brunt of subtle but biting persecution. One such technique required the skills of a chantyman, who would make up his own lines as he sang to the crew. Chanties might poke fun at the cook or recall a sailor's misadventures in port. The well-known "Drunken Sailor" served as a warning to the crew member who let his workload fall to his shipmates when he was unfit for duty after a celebratory night in port. Chanties could also give voice to displeasure with the captain or officers. If outspoken, any instigator of such chanties, as well as his accomplices, would likely bring upon themselves stinging punishment. These delicate circumstances obviously required that the chantyman be particularly attuned to each officer's tolerance of the subject of a song.

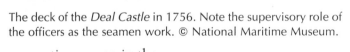

The deck of the *Deal Castle* in 1756. Note the supervisory role of the officers as the seamen work. © National Maritime Museum.

Dining was deeply rooted in the formalities surrounding the concept of hospitality, but the need to maintain the prestige of each man's rank could make dinners stiff and awkward. By custom, only the captain could start a conversation—even in the presence of passengers—and he was under some obligation to set the tone and pick the topics of discussion for the dinner.

The captain could use an invitation to eat at his table as a sign of approbation for his junior officers, but he needed to avoid inadvertently offending or unconsciously ostracizing any of them. Nor could he show too much zeal for his subordinates, which would be bad for the overall discipline and ordering of the ship.

Among the seamen, class fragmentation was sometimes less rigid than it was among the officers. Different messes on the same ship might invite others from outside their normal group to dine with them, and dinner guests from outside the ship, if available, were commonly made welcome. Of course, seamen did not eat with officers and gentlemen.

The physical and economic nature of the seaport was such that everybody, in addition to knowing everybody else, knew his or her specific niche in the life of the community. Nevertheless, few people formed very warm relationships outside their trade. The sailor, who could not speak to the shipmaster aboard ship, did not expect a warm collegiality when they met on the streets of town. A hierarchy developed wherein the deep-water captains, shipbuilders, bankers, underwriters, ministers, and other professionals became a sort of aristocracy.

Merchant and naval crews, be they on land or water, submitted to countless, unofficial imperatives. These social structures were inextricably bound to other categories of society having to do with class, attire, ethnicity, music, food, and gender (Volo and Volo, 8, 104–6, 109–10, 145, 151–52).

FOR MORE INFORMATION

Bryant, S. W. *The Sea and the States: A Maritime History of the American People*. New York: Crowell, 1967.

Thrower, W. R. *Life at Sea in the Age of Sail*. London: Phillimore, 1972.

Volo, D. D., and J. M. Volo. *Daily Life in the Age of Sail*. Westport, Conn.: Greenwood Press, 2002.

POLITICAL LIFE
|
LAW, CRIME,
& PUNISHMENT
|
Colonial Australia

The Colonial Frontier
of North America

England

Japan

New England

Life at Sea

Law, Crime, and Punishment

From approximately 1600 to 1800, legal traditions and institutions, along with the people who actually enforced them, involved more than the arrest, prosecution, conviction, and sentencing of possible transgressors. They helped to distinguish what was criminal from what was not criminal and then elucidated what constituted a capital crime, as opposed to a noncapital crime. Colonial Australia, the North American colonial frontier, England, Japan, New England, and sailors, officers, and pirates on the high seas all had to contend with the powerful menace of crime and punishment through the interpretive lens of legal doctrine.

Each society had a set of legal traditions and institutions that over the long term, provided individuals with relatively stable rules of behavior. In Japan, the central government interrupted the relative autonomy of villages and peasants to delineate a few crucial rules to which those living in rural areas were expected to conform. Most important were the obligations to obey the government and to pay taxes.

Colonial New England's founding legal institution was the Massachusetts Bay Company's charter, which contained no mention of citizens' rights. In 1648, a legalized code compensated for this initial lack of concern for civil liberties. In colonial Australia, the basic rules of conduct were represented in the General Standing Orders, which benefited from no legislative input simply because no legislative body existed in colonial Australia. In the Articles of War, the British Royal Navy instituted a set of rules that dictated the correct behavior and punishment of officers and sailors.

Throughout the eighteenth century, England continued the trend of emphasizing common (state) law over canon (church) law, which partly contributed to the island nation's growing tradition of progressive legal procedures, including trial by jury and no imprisonment without trial. Nevertheless, the deeply uneven distribution of wealth and privilege throughout English society translated into equally irregular legal practices, which discriminated against the poor and marginalized.

During this period, law enforcement was nowhere as organized as in today's societies. However, courts and police-like institutions did exist. In Japanese cities, wards had their own night watchmen, who performed several useful tasks. Samurai rarely performed police duties. In England, justices of the peace issued arrest warrants, made arrests, judged suspects, and mediated disputes. Also on hand were lawyers, constables, Charlies (paid watchmen), and beadles. Colonial Australia's governor had to rely on convicts for a police force because the local marines were unwilling to perform constabulary duties. A similarly informal police force existed along the colonial frontier in North America where settlers organized themselves into militias.

In all of these cultures, it was commonly recognized that capital offenses differed from noncapital ones. In colonial Australia, noncapital offenses would be punished with fines, secondary transportation (to an island), months on the battery gang, rationing, extra work, and flogging.

In England and Japan, conviction for counterfeiting brought with it a possible death sentence. Other common offenses that were punishable by death included theft, rape, and murder. In New England, those found guilty of behavior that was ruled blasphemous, idolatrous, or fundamentally impious ran the risk of parting with their lives. The Salem witch trials and the execution of four Quakers in a Puritan-dominated region demonstrate exactly how seriously the threat of death accompanied perceived impiety.

Capital crimes in the British Royal Navy centered on mutiny or sedition. Because discipline aboard naval vessels was imperative for the smooth running of England's greatest military and economic asset, officers brooked no threat of insubordination among the crew members. In the world of merchant ships, masters who suspected officers of misconduct could not punish them aboard ship but could only remove them from their duties and confine them to their quarters until a court of inquiry could investigate the allegations and consider a court martial.

Punishment was often violent and public, meaning that those who handed out sentences often considered imprisonment and jails to be of secondary importance. Indians along North America's colonial frontier frequently engaged in the kidnapping of settlers, submitting many of them to scenes of humiliation, torture, and death. When European settlers kidnapped Indians, murder and enslavement of the prisoners typically ensued. In New England, convictions for noncapital offenses such as fornication (heterosexual sex between unmarried adults) carried with them whippings, brandings, and the cutting off of ears. Some judges sentenced convicts to a term of involuntary servitude.

On the high seas, masters and captains punished sailors by cutting their allowance of food and drink, ordering them to perform hard work, or flogging them, often in front of the crew. English also preferred public shaming and encouraged large crowds to witness a convict being pilloried or flogged. Those who received death sentences were commonly escorted along the road from Newgate to Tyburn before meeting the noose. Japanese, too, practiced capital punishment, roasting, burning, crucifying, and cutting the unlucky to death. Not much luckier were those Japanese who survived the effects of public floggings.

Legal traditions (long-standing practices) and institutions (courts) guided a good many legal practices during the 17th and 18th centuries. Actual law enforcement was still a mixture of formal and informal mechanisms. Very much established, however, was the distinction between capital and noncapital offense, as was the identification of which crimes belonged in which category and which punishments appropriately corresponded to which crimes.

~Peter Seelig

FOR MORE INFORMATION

Black, D. J., ed. *The Social Organization of Law*. New York: Seminar Press, 1973.

POLITICAL LIFE
|
LAW, CRIME,
& PUNISHMENT
|
Colonial Australia

The Colonial Frontier
of North America

England

Japan

New England

Life at Sea

COLONIAL AUSTRALIA

Australian convicts in the 18th century were relatively freer than in later periods, when the reforming zeal of mid-19th century authorities regulated life more closely and when authorities applied punishments more strictly.

The legal framework of the law comprised the Court of Civil Jurisdiction, the Court of Criminal Jurisdiction, and a Vice Admiralty Court to deal with piracy. As Governor Phillip was a retired naval officer, his legal authority shifted from a military tradition to a civil one in an effort to overcome the anomaly of convicts being tried under military law. A judge advocate, David Collins, assisted the governor, although neither he nor his successor during the period, Richard Atkins, had legal training. Colonial Australia hosted no professional judge until 1810.

Governor Phillip was empowered to pardon convicts, to conscript men for military service, to impose martial law, and to grant land, although there was no negotiation with the Aboriginal owners. The first orders were made against stealing and the killing of stock. Those who refused to work would not be fed, and male trespassers in the women's tent would be fired upon. As the marines refused to undertake policing duties, Governor Phillip established a night watch of 12 compliant convicts to patrol the township, as well as a Row Boat Guard for the harbor and foreshores.

Magistrates ruled on minor offences and could order arbitrary punishment, whereas criminal cases were subject to court hearings. In place of juries was the judge advocate, and case decisions were the responsibility of six military officers. A majority, rather than a unanimous verdict, was sufficient in criminal cases, except for those involving a death sentence. These latter cases required a majority of five, or four if sanctioned by the Home Office.

Without a legislature in the colony, governors formulated laws and promulgated them as general standing orders. David Neal's work shows that colonists generally respected the rule of law and the courts. All segments of society used courts to seek justice and, in some cases, to settle grievances and grudges. Convicts' rights were not inviolate, and inevitable abuses of process took place. Power, patronage, cliques, expertise, experience, and the character of officeholders all influenced the application of the law. Although most governors declared that punishments would apply equally for offences against Aboriginal people (who were ostensibly British subjects since their dispossession in 1788), the colonial legal system often flouted the rule of law in such cases.

Convicts were regarded as dead in British law, but in New South Wales, they had some rights and were not legally slaves. Two married convicts successfully launched Australia's first civil action, against their ship's master for loss of their baggage; and the first criminal court convened on February 2, 1788, to hear charges against two officers for assault and stealing.

The Court of Criminal Jurisdiction protected capital and corporal punishment. However, local punishments evolved, including both secondary transportation to Norfolk Island or Newcastle and banishment to small remote islands. Some offenders were placed in the

A print of Australia's first Government House, Melbourne 1919, Sir William Johnson, *First Government House*, an7675243. National Library of Australia.

pillory. Although sexual abuse of women pervaded the colony, there were cases of capital punishment for rape, especially when it involved children.

During times of serious food shortages, the theft of food brought swift retribution on the gallows. In 1788, six marines were convicted of pilfering from the public store and were executed. In 1804, a convict was hanged for stealing a bag of sugar. Selling clothing brought six months on the battery gang for convicts. A free person would be fined three times the value of the article and forbidden to receive clothing from the store.

Governors had almost autocratic powers, but they were often pragmatic in their application of the law. Some laws evolved without stringent regard for legality (Kercher, 29). The Ticket of Leave system, a form of parole, was an example. Other forms of local punishment included reduction of rations, fines, and extra work, which the convict sometimes performed in iron collars or leg irons, and instances exist of shaving women's heads to humiliate them.

Punishments on Norfolk Island were generally fewer and less severe than elsewhere. After the loss of the store ship *Sirius* in 1790, the commandant Major Ross declared martial law. As on the mainland, a person who was caught stealing from the public store faced capital punishment. Breaches in the military's rigid code of honor also attracted punishment. Under Ross's regime, a soldier who had lied to a superior officer received 400 lashes for "unsoldier-like behavior" (Fidlon and Ryan, 220).

Punishable offences included theft, neglect of duty, selling government-issue clothing (often for liquor), absences from work or malingering, breaking curfew, insolence, and seditious language. Fear of sedition was heightened after periods of dissent abroad. In 1802, Governor King reminded the colony that seditious association and activity would bring secondary transportation and a thousand lashes. Flogging was an expected and largely accepted form of discipline in the military and penal systems. It was not always completed in one session, so that the offender would be capable of continuing work, and remission of the balance was sometimes granted.

England spared the lives of hundreds of convicted criminals, sending them to Australia instead of to the gallows. Thomas Rowlandson, *Convicts Embarking for Botany Bay,* an5601547. Rex Nan Kivell Collection, National Library of Australia.

During the colonial period, several serious insurrections resulted in martial law and summary executions. In 1804, a group of mostly Irish Catholics rebelled, and two convict insurrections took place on Norfolk Island. Possibly the most serious threat to the rule of law was the so-called Rum Rebellion against Governor Bligh, who was notorious for the mutiny against him on the *Bounty* in 1789. Bligh arrived in Australia in 1806 with orders to suppress the trade in liquor, to the chagrin of officers and others who had prospered from it. In addition, his attempts to introduce order to the Sydney townscape alienated some leaseholders. In February 1807, Bligh outlawed the use of rum as currency, and in December, he had Macarthur, one of the profiteers, arrested. The military, in turn, arrested Bligh and installed George Johnston as administrator. After his usurpation, Bligh was illegally held under house arrest for more than a year because he would not agree to return to England. In 1809, the 73rd Regiment of Foot, commanded by Governor Lachlan Macquarie, replaced the New South Wales Corps, and a less-turbulent decade began.

~Valda Rigg

FOR MORE INFORMATION

Fidlon, P. G., and R. J. Ryan, eds. *The Journal and Letters of Lt Ralph Clark, 1787–1792.* Sydney: Library of Australian History, 1981.

Frost, A. *Arthur Phillip, 1738–1814: His Voyaging.* Melbourne: Oxford University Press, 1987.

Government of New South Wales. *Index to Bench of Magistrates Cases, 1788–1820.* <www.records.nsw.gov.au/indexes/benchofmag/introduction.htm>, accessed October 23, 2003.

Kercher, B. *An Unruly Child: A History of Law in Australia.* St. Leonards, Australia: Allen and Unwin, 1995.

King, P. *New South Wales General Standing Orders: Selected from the General Orders Issued by Former Governors, from the 16 February 1791 to the 6 September 1800.* Sydney: Government Printer, 1802.

National Library of Australia. *Australian History on the Internet.* <http://www.nla.gov.au/oz/histsite.html>, accessed October 23, 2003.

Neal, D. *The Rule of Law in a Penal Colony: Law and Power in Early New South Wales.* Sydney: Cambridge University Press, 1991.

State Library of New South Wales. *Papers of Sir Joseph Banks.* 1996. <http://www.sl.nsw. gov.au/banks/>, accessed October 23, 2003.

THE COLONIAL FRONTIER OF NORTH AMERICA

Unaccustomed to their frontier surroundings, settlers perceived North America's borderland as savage and perilous. Law and order thus amounted to a kind of un-regulated cycle of attack and reprisal between colonists and Native Americans, who were reeling from the upheaval that resulted from, as they came to see it, the intolerable actions of the European colonies. The taking of captives and other transgressions were common to both sides of the conflict. However, the threat of such offenses frequently came from within a native or colonial population, as Nathaniel Bacon's violent challenge to Virginia's legal and political authorities exemplifies.

The system of clans among Native Americans provided a basis for the concept of blood revenge. Revenge fueled much of the intertribal raiding and counter-raiding among the region's Native Americans. Small groups of related warriors would slip off into the wilderness to seek out and kill the members of other tribes with whom they had a grudge, usually based on the death or mistreatment of one of their own clan members. In this regard, "Jolicoeur" Charles Bonin, a French soldier in New France who was familiar with indigenous customs in the region, noted "When . . . injured, he is capable of going [600 miles] or more to surprise his enemy and satisfy his revenge with blood." Blood revenge caused hostilities to drag on for long periods.

The difficulties of living on the colonial frontier were numerous indeed. Carving a homestead from the woodlands required hard and persistent work. The greatest challenge, however, was perhaps surviving the intense strain created by fear of Indian attack. Stories of "outrages on lives and property" kept the settlers in an increasing state of anxiety.

Attacks were not always simply impromptu events brought about by the accidental crossing of settlers' and raiders' paths. At times, the raiders entered an area and studied the inhabitants prior to staging their onslaught, or they implemented strategies to draw unsuspecting residents into ambush. Furthermore, Indians commonly took captives in enemy raids. Like scalps, they were trophies of their conquest. Revenge was a motive for some abductions. The unfortunates chosen for this purpose—usually men—were subjected to abject humiliation, ritualistic torture, and cruel death. Captives who were weak, who posed a danger to the raiders, or who proved overly troublesome in the least respect were likely to be dispatched, typically with a blow to the head by a tomahawk-wielding warrior.

The Indians who raided the frontier areas between New France and the Anglo-American colonies tended to take captives for ransom. Captives were frequently ransomed in exchange for valuables, for pledges of peace, or for other prisoners. Funding for redemptions came from both private and public sources, although obtaining the release of public funding was not always easy. From time to time, colonial legislatures tried to forbid the use of public money for such purposes. In a 1710 letter, Joseph Dudley, governor of Massachusetts, expressed sympathy for the lot of the captives but repeated his steadfast resolution: "never to buy a prisoner of an Indian, lest we make a market for our poor women and children in the frontiers."

Europeans also understood the value of captives. Indian abductees could ensure the safety of those in enemy hands, provide bargaining power for political concessions, and assist the colonial governments as instruments of diplomacy, as interpreters, and as intermediaries. The total number of colonists seized during the colonial period is greatly eclipsed by the number of Indians whom Europeans abducted and then enslaved or exhibited. Europeans captured Indians and used them in all of these capacities, as well as in slavery. Unfortunately, the words and thoughts of these captives were not preserved for us to study. Following the attack upon the Pequot Indians, the settlers enslaved the women and children and, fearing the warriors, sold the surviving men and boys into slavery in the West Indies.

Some Native American prisoners made the most of their circumstances and were powerful allies to their captors because of their willingness to flourish in their new situations. Many others resisted being made instruments of conquest and escaped through suicide. Still others used the knowledge they gained while in captivity against their former captors.

Bacon's Rebellion in Virginia in 1676 exemplifies the dangers that the existence of large bodies of unregulated militia presented to effective colonial governance. By the age of 26, Nathaniel Bacon maintained a successful plantation on the James River and had enough wealth and influence to sit on the council of the elderly royal governor, William Berkeley. By 1670, the settlers' expansion of plantations into the interior had intensified friction with the Native Americans. In the summer of 1675, the local militia from Virginia crossed into Maryland and slaughtered almost two dozen Doeg and Susquehannock Indians in a feud over some missing hogs. The Indians retaliated, and the settlers demanded further retribution.

The governor rejected the more aggressive course favored by the colonists and ordered an end to any vigilante action. He also ordered the establishment of a series of weakly garrisoned stronghouses in the border areas secured by a ranging force of 125 cavalrymen. The frontier planters scoffed at Berkeley's design, as it would raise the level of taxation to a point that the planters could not bear.

Nathaniel Bacon and his followers called for a thousand volunteers to raid the Indian settlements. This action was successful in suppressing the Indian attacks, but Bacon refused to disband his army. Before long, Bacon's followers began to call for sweeping changes in the colonial government. They elected a new House of Burgesses, with Bacon as one of its members.

As friction between Berkeley and Bacon increased, Virginia became split into increasingly belligerent factions, and active warfare broke out between the two. Contemporaries considered the ensuing rebellion a spontaneous uprising against the tyranny of an obstinate royal governor. Ultimately, the governor fled and abandoned

On the colonial frontier, Native Americans were often depicted as savage, as this illustration from the book *Indian Barbarities* indicates. © Library of Congress.

the seat of government at Jamestown to Bacon's followers, who burned the town. Almost immediately thereafter, Bacon contracted a fever and died.

The rebel army simply melted away, and the governor returned with nothing but vengeance on his mind. He captured and summarily hanged all the members of the rebellion whom he could identify. Their property was confiscated, and their families were turned out of their homes. Word of Berkeley's program of revenge was reported to King Charles II in London, who, shocked at the governor's lack of restraint, presently recalled and replaced him. Royal troops were sent to the Virginia colony, and thereafter the upheaval slowly died down.

On the frontier, the concept and practice of law was less tangible than in other, more established areas. The traditions of the native populations regulating the punishment of misdeeds were increasingly put to the test while an unknown variable, colonial settlers, imposed itself onto the hitherto accepted practice of blood revenge. Instead of renouncing conflict, both sides engaged in assaults, murder, rape, impressments, torture, and imprisonment, often against each other but also within their proper communities (Volo and Volo, 40, 191–93, 231–33, 236–38, 240, 248–50).

FOR MORE INFORMATION

Axtell, J. *The European and the Indian: Essays in the Ethnohistory of Colonial America*. New York: Oxford University Press, 1981.

Boorstin, D. J. *The Americans: The Colonial Experience*. New York: Random House, 1958.

Volo, J. M., and D. D. Volo. *Daily Life on the Old Colonial Frontier*. Westport, Conn.: Greenwood Press, 2002.

ENGLAND

English law was unusual in that it stressed the rights of the accused while openly favoring the wealthy and titled. With this paradox as a starting point, one can see that the assortment of competing types of law and law courts only complicated matters. A further irony concerns an apparent distrust, on the part of the English, of law enforcement and the simultaneous pleasure that ordinary English derived from the torture and execution of prisoners at the hands of their captors.

In some respects, the 18th-century English justice system was highly advanced. It afforded the accused strong protections, including strict evidentiary rules, jury trials, and the revered principle of habeas corpus, which banned imprisonment without trial. In other respects, the system was haphazard and chaotic. Patchwork jurisdictions, judicial improvisation, uneven enforcement, widespread corruption, and an almost complete lack of police protection plagued participants and observers alike. And lawsuits required money for court and attorneys' fees and for bribing, transporting, or locating witnesses; increasingly, the poor simply could not afford it.

Two principal types of law were practiced—canon (church) law and common (state) law—in two distinct types of courts. Common law, which by 1736 commanded supremacy over canon law, concerned itself with debt, credit, and criminal

POLITICAL LIFE

LAW, CRIME,
& PUNISHMENT

Colonial Australia

The Colonial Frontier
of North America

England

Japan

New England

Life at Sea

violations. Trifling cases might receive handling on the spot from the local magistrate; more serious cases awaited trial at the county's quarter sessions or the twice-yearly arrival of the circuit court justices for the assizes. Appeals and high-level cases could go to one of several common law higher courts.

Justices of the peace had a long list of duties that only grew with time. These law enforcement officials issued arrest warrants, made arrests themselves, took statements, and interrogated suspects. They also acted as judges without juries, mediating petty disputes. This staggering array of largely unremunerative duties made the job of justice of the peace seem thankless, demanding, irritating, and undesirable. On the other hand, it offered unparalleled power over one's community.

Another authority figure was the lawyer. Younger sons of the gentry considered the law to be far more gentlemanly than trade, and it could lead to high income. Over 25 percent of the thousands of lawyers in England at this time lived in London. Lawyers dealt with mortgages, wills, and civil litigation and occasionally worked in finance. Barristers, who argued criminal cases before the courts, looked down on such attorneys, and an act of Parliament passed in the first half of the century required them to be registered and to meet certain minimum qualifications—not a sign of absolute confidence.

Like prosecution, the duties of patrol and arrest were largely left to public service and private enterprise. Each parish had a constable or two—Westminster as a whole had 80; metropolitan London as a whole, about 1,000—to serve for one year without pay. They were expected to maintain their regular trade and perform their constabulary duties in their spare time. In practice, virtually no one of means ever served, choosing instead to hire a substitute from a force of paid professional constables.

London had paid watchmen, called "Charlies." They cried the hours, woke people who needed to rise early, helped drunks home for a small fee, and got drunk themselves. Westminster had about 300 Charlies; metropolitan London, about 2,000. The parish beadle also had limited law enforcement responsibilities, mostly in the form of rousting vagrants. It is important to note, however, that even law-abiding citizens vigorously resisted the idea of a professional police force, seeing in it the first step toward tyranny.

Despite inadequate or nonexistent police protection, criminals were arrested in substantial numbers for both minor and major offenses. In the former category were such crimes as embezzlement, minor vandalism, forgery, manslaughter, attempted murder, perjury, breach of promise, swearing, trading on Sunday, keeping unlicensed alehouses, homosexuality, very minor thefts, failing to support one's family, and performing abortions. Capital crimes, which rose in number from 50 in 1689 to about 200 in 1800, included poaching, counterfeiting, forgery, sheep stealing, killing a cow, looting, theft or robbery of even small items, associating with gypsies, entering land with intent to kill rabbits, chipping stone from Westminster Bridge, bigamy, and major vandalism.

Outfitted with lanterns and staves, watchmen like these three often patrolled urban neighborhoods in 18th-century England. © Library of Congress.

Plenty of punishments were available for noncapital crimes, but jail was not among the preferred options. Few people, except debtors, were jailed for years at a time. Only toward the end of the 18th century did reformers turn to long jail terms in state-of-the-art prisons with solitary-confinement cells.

Wardens and jailers operated on a free-enterprise system, seeking to squeeze the largest possible fees from their inmates. Shipment to America, chiefly to the southern colonies as cheap labor on tobacco plantations, awaited those whose crimes were too serious for a few months in jail but not serious enough to merit execution. This punishment, called transportation, was sometimes for a limited time, such as seven years, and sometimes for life. In the 1770s, the American colonies rebelled, ending transportations there for good. Late in the 1780s, transportation began again, but this time the destination was Australia.

Even for minor crimes, judges were reluctant to impose jail sentences. Instead, they preferred to impose public pain, shame, or discomfort. Sometimes this meant the pillory, a wooden frame that locked the head and hands in place. Those not pilloried were sometimes branded. Another common punishment was public flogging, and it was a holiday of sorts when women, particularly prostitutes, were flogged. Crowds would gather to see these women stripped to the waist and beaten.

The number of executions was significant—about 1,200 Londoners over the course of the century and as many as about 200 a year in England and Wales together. In London, the procession began every six weeks at Newgate, where the condemned boarded an open cart that was accompanied by their coffins. They made their slow way westward to Tyburn, where the triangular gallows awaited them. On the way, they stopped at taverns, drinking heavily and promising to pay the bill "when they came back."

At Tyburn, tens of thousands gathered for the express purpose of seeing death, suffering, bravado, and cowardice. The condemned made final speeches, hoped for a last-minute reprieve, and listened to prayers from the chaplain; nooses were placed around the doomed necks, and then "away goes the Cart, and there swing my Gentlemen kicking in the Air."

As common law gained precedence over canon law, and as justices of the peace, magistrates, Charlies, beadles, constables, and police informers struggled to enforce the law, criminals committed crimes. Those who were lucky escaped undetected; those who were unlucky received a prison term, a sentence of transportation, or a public flogging; and those who had no luck at all received a death sentence and no commutation or reprieve. Through all this business, English law remained an example of enlightened justice, where the rights of the accused were worth preserving (Olsen, 17, 205–6, 208–9, 211–18).

To read about law in Chaucer's England, see the Europe entry in the section "Law" in chapter 6 ("Political Life") of volume 2; for Elizabethan England, see the England entry in the section "Justice and Legal Systems" in chapter 6 ("Political Life") of volume 3; and for Victorian England, see the Victorian England entry in the section "Law and Crime" in chapter 6 ("Political Life") of volume 5 of this series.

FOR MORE INFORMATION

Hay, D. *Albion's Fatal Tree: Crime and Society in Eighteenth-Century England*. New York: Pantheon Books, 1975.

Lynch, J. *Eighteenth Century Resources*. <http://newark.rutgers.edu/~jlynch/18th/>, accessed October 10, 2003.

Olsen, K. *Daily Life in 18th-Century England*. Westport, Conn.: Greenwood Press, 1999.

POLITICAL LIFE

|

LAW, CRIME,
& PUNISHMENT

|

Colonial Australia

The Colonial Frontier
of North America

England

Japan

New England

Life at Sea

JAPAN

Enforcing behavior in Japan's countryside and cities was the business of several assemblages of Japanese. Those who meted out punishments did so with the goal of peace in mind. All segments of society lived under certain distinct sets of obligations, and during the 18th century, warlords and warriors were not immune to chastisement or even worse.

The 32-article law code known as the Keian Proclamation, issued in 1649, demanded that peasants obey all *bakufu* (national military government) law and pay their taxes promptly. They were to devote themselves to their fields by day and engage in making items necessary for their lives at night. They were to live simply and frugally and avoid drinking sake or tea. They were not to eat rice, because it was destined for tax payment, but were to subsist on the "simple grains" of barley, wheat, millet, and sorghum. It should be noted that most 18th-century villages lived up to the *bakufu* ideal.

Villages were required to maintain a message board where new laws, wanted posters, and other messages were posted. The villages were also required to maintain three separate official village registers. One listed the regular members of the village by age, sex, and relationship to the head of household. Births, deaths, and changes in headship or marital status had to be noted carefully. Another register listed servants working in the village at any given time, giving information on their age, sex, and previous residence. The third register was of anyone who visited the village. Traveling merchants, entertainers, artisans, priests, and the like had to be accounted for.

As much as possible, disputes were settled internally. The behavior of everyone was monitored and controlled, usually within the *gonin-gumi* (five-person village administration) but ultimately throughout the entire village. Punishments were meted out communally. Restitution was the order of the day for crimes of property, although apparently these were very rare because no one had very much and a thief would have found it nearly impossible to hide stolen articles because everyone knew who had what. More serious crimes of violence and passion seem to have also been quite rare. Physical injury and loss of property required the adjudication of the entire village. Apparently, the most severe punishment was ostracism and banishment, being tantamount to a death penalty.

The some 63,000 individual villages of Japan occasionally responded to perceived injustice from their samurai (warrior-administrator) overlords with collective violence aimed at redress. These uprisings, called *ikki*, which means something like "united action," varied in size, scope, and ultimate goal, but all were carefully considered responses to injustice. Villagers did not enter into them rashly.

Usually, an increase in taxes, a refusal to defer taxes after a natural calamity, or a new regulation judged to be discriminatory or ruinous to a village sparked resentment among peasants. Because the villages had no real representative voice in the samurai administration, village leaders often wrote letters of protest or sent petitions to whichever government ruled over them. These letters were dangerous. People who signed their names were often punished for their temerity.

Because the samurai harshly and haughtily refused many petitions, the next step of *ikki* often seemed more palatable to the village leaders.

In all of these uprisings, the peasants firmly believed that morality and justice were on their side. After all, the wealthy were to behave benevolently toward the less fortunate. The discontented participants in *ikki* therefore were very careful to issue manifestoes and petitions beforehand, explaining their actions in neo-Confucian social terms.

Scarcely any daimyō (regional warlord) could afford to appear to be incompetent in the eyes of the *bakufu*. Positive proof of corruption or incompetence was to have one's peasants in rebellion. Virtually every *ikki* came to the attention of the *bakufu*, which questioned the daimyō about such disturbances.

Law enforcement in cities began with male residents of the *machi* (city wards) who acted as night watchmen. In addition to policing the area to keep out burglars and strangers, the watchmen sounded out the hour, using a complex system of signals that included conch horns, drums, bells, and gongs.

Unless *chōnin* (city folk) had committed a very serious crime, the samurai did not usually become involved in their punishment, preferring to let the *chōnin* handle their own justice. In the case of samurai, however, formal courts commonly existed for their adjudication. Samurai were expected to behave wisely, and often their punishments were harsher than for *chōnin*, the rationale being that the former should have known better.

The general objective in legal cases was to keep and to restore the peace. Public flogging and exposure to the taunts of the crowd usually sufficed to create a sense of real dread in most miscreants.

For more serious crimes, death came slowly as executioners roasted, burned, crucified, or drew apart (with oxen) the convicted criminal. The dreaded "death of a thousand cuts" took days, as prisoners were stripped naked and then wrapped tightly in fishnets. Executioners would by turns slice off bits of skin that protruded through the net and then cauterize the wound with sake or with hot metal, only to repeat the process endlessly until the person died of shock.

Compared with these punishments, meted out for murder, tax pilfering, currency counterfeiting, rape, or arson, minor crimes such as gossiping, brawling, theft, gambling, and petty violence accorded less severe punishments.

The *Buke shohatto* (regulations for military houses) dealt mostly with rules for marriage, adoption, succession, and "proper behavior." Separate laws were issued regarding the administration and control of religious institutions. Virtually every daimyō copied the *bakufu* laws.

Theoretically, samurai enjoyed the right of *kirisute-gomen* (cut and continue), which meant that, brandishing their swords, they could cut down any commoners who offended them without penalty. In reality, it was most inconvenient for a samurai to practice *kirisute-gomen,* for any samurai who did so would be hard-pressed to find any *chōnin* who would serve, cater, provision, or lend to him. Therefore, daimyō forbade samurai to practice such arrogant punishments and exacted "apology money" from those who did as indemnity to the family of the deceased or injured man.

Villages and cities regulated their legal affairs with a degree of autonomy but did so under the legislative eye of the *bakufu,* which issued edicts, directives, and council to all layers of society (Perez, 29–34, 139–40, 154, 158).

To read about law and crime in Japan in the 20th century, see the Japan entry in the section "Law and Crime" in chapter 6 ("Political Life") of volume 6 of this series.

FOR MORE INFORMATION

Japan Information Network. <http://www.jinjapan.org/index.html>, accessed October 23, 2003.

Perez, L. G. *Daily Life in Early Modern Japan.* Westport, Conn.: Greenwood Press, 2002.

Steenstrup, C. A *History of Law in Japan until 1868.* New York: Brill, 1991.

Wigmore, J. H., ed. *Law and Justice in Tokugawa Japan.* Tokyo: Kokusai Bunka Shinkokai, 1969.

NEW ENGLAND

With the exception of Rhode Island, the most important generalization that can be made about law in colonial New England—especially the Massachusetts Bay Colony—as it affected the daily lives of its citizens concerns the influence of Puritan clergy and Puritan religious principles on colonial law. The law to which the colonial magistrates turned first and the one that was most important to them was biblical law, specifically, the Ten Commandments; and their constant advisers were not legal scholars but clergyman with little or no legal training. The most infamous case of religious intolerance by Massachusetts Puritans involved Anne Hutchinson.

Anne Hutchinson was a highly educated, religious young woman who gave enormously popular instruction to adults in the Massachusetts Bay. Such instruction was, however, to be solely a male prerogative. When ordered to cease her meetings, she refused. Hutchinson was brought to trial twice—in 1637 and 1638—on charges of treason. Found guilty, she fled the Massachusetts Bay Colony for Rhode Island and later for New York.

Exile was not the only mode of punishment. Seventeen crimes could result in the death penalty, and all but the crimes of rape and nonappearance in a capital trial invoked specific scriptural authority from five Old Testament books. The crimes also included idolatry, blasphemy, murder, bestiality, sodomy, adultery, kidnapping, and cursing a parent. In most cases of capital crimes, the ultimate penalty of death was rarely carried out, although the language in most cases reads that the miscreants "shall surely be put to death." A significant use of the death penalty involved religious intolerance when Massachusetts's officials had Quakers executed.

The most notorious cases in which nonviolent "offenders" suffered the death penalty involved the "witches" in Salem and elsewhere. The first stage of these cases began with accusations of witchcraft throughout New England and ended with wholesale arrests in Salem in 1692. By October, 20 people had been executed for witchcraft. Hundreds had been held in prison; some had died there. Dozens had to flee; hundreds more who survived the ordeal had their land and possessions confiscated; and untold numbers had seen families, friends, and communities irrevocably broken apart.

Crimes that did not carry the death penalty but were nevertheless considered sufficiently serious to warrant grave consequences included lying, burglary, fornication, battery, Sabbath violations, lewd behavior, swearing, and vilifying authorities. Nuisance crimes of lesser importance included galloping through the streets, gambling, dancing, drinking toasts, smoking near buildings that could catch fire, disturbing the peace with loud noises, and celebrating Christmas.

The most frequent crime brought into colonial New England courts was fornication—sex between men and women who were not married to each other, including betrothed couples who married shortly thereafter. In almost every year and in every colony, arrests for fornication exceeded arrests for petty thefts, which included stealing apples from orchards. The chief punishments for fornication were whippings, along with fines. Indeed, the most frequently used punishment was public whipping.

Between 1659 and 1661, officials in Massachusetts had four Quakers put to death, including Mary Dyer. Today, this statue occupies the grounds of the Massachusetts State House in remembrance of the effects of religious intolerance. © Library of Congress.

Branding people on the forehead was another popular form of punishment not considered barbarous or cruel. The brand identified the miscreant for life: *B* for burglary, *T* for theft, *F* for forgery, *AD* for adultery, *V* for lewdness, *D* for drunkenness, or *I* for incest (which usually meant marrying the widow of a brother).

Evidently, the Puritans did not consider mutilation excessively cruel. Phillip Ratliffe of Salem in 1631 had both of his ears cut off for criticizing the government. Indeed, the authorities chopped off the ears of individuals convicted for a variety of crimes, including that of being a Quaker. The piercing of the tongue with a red-hot iron was a form of punishment applied to those who used their tongues to malign authorities or to express heretical opinions. In 1631, for example, the court sentenced the blasphemous Joseph Gatchell to "have his tongue drawn forth out of his mouth and pierced through with a red hot iron."

Involuntary servitude was another category of punishment. The courts ordered certain people to be bound over for a period of years so that these individuals could work for masters whom the magistrates had deemed responsible family men. Working-class people who were judged to be immoral were placed in indentured positions where a strong master could oversee their behavior. Criminals and debtors often found themselves ordered into temporary "slavery" by the courts, which also specified the time of the service. The case of John Kempe shows the court's personal manner of dealing with a criminal: "John Kempe, for filthy, unclean attempts with three young girls, was censured to be whipped both here, at Roxberry, and at Salem, very severely, and was committed as a slave to Leift Davenport."

The misdemeanors for which servants were most often punished fell into the categories of running away, getting drunk, sexual looseness, impudence, idleness, and theft. Between 1620 and 1750, officials recorded 700 instances of runaways in the Massachusetts Bay Colony. Running away was considered one of the most heinous of crimes because the master lost a valuable investment. The punishment for running away always involved whippings. Nevertheless, the courts seriously considered servants' complaints about insufficient care and on occasion ordered employers to dress a servant better or to see to his or her health.

As for the legal status of slavery, *The Body of Liberties of 1641*, a poorly written, ambiguous law, legalized slavery in New England. In one or more, but not all, New England communities, laws existed such that blacks were not allowed to leave their villages without a pass, to be on the streets during church, to hold social gatherings out of doors, or to keep domestic livestock. Other discrepancies in the legal treatment of blacks were prevalent. Free blacks were not allowed to entertain black or mixed-race slaves or Native Americans in their houses. Laws did not treat blacks as full citizens. Blacks had to pay taxes but could not vote. They were excluded from the peacetime militia yet subject to the draft in time of war. They were socially ostracized and segregated in harborside ghettos. Black children were forbidden from attending public schools.

During the 17th century, much of New England's legislative process derived not from the Massachusetts Bay Colony's charter but from individual laws passed by the Court of Assistants. Under the extensive influence of Puritan clergy, legal bodies that saw to the implementation of laws dealt harshly with religious minorities, religious dissenters such as Anne Hutchinson, and innocent defendants, such as those accused of witchcraft during the Salem witch trials. Penalties included, but were not limited to, capital and corporal punishment, forced servitude, public humiliation, and exile. Servants and blacks were the objects of severe legal prohibitions (Johnson, 19, 23–24, 46–47, 49–52, 149, 156, 162, 164, 187–89, 192–93).

FOR MORE INFORMATION

Haskins, G. L. *Law and Authority in Early Massachusetts: A Study in Tradition and Design.* New York: Macmillan, 1960.

Johnson, C. D. *Daily Life in Colonial New England.* Westport, Conn.: Greenwood Press, 2002.

Salem Witch Museum. 1996. <http://www.salemwitchmuseum.com/>, accessed October 23, 2003.

LIFE AT SEA

Navies and merchant crews depended on, and sometimes suffered from, legislation that regulated oceanic travel and that combated criminal activity. At times, the laws seemed to encourage criminal activity, as was the case with gangs of government-organized gangs that forced seamen into naval service. At other times, laws clarified the nature of the acceptable response to a given transgression, and no transgression was more despised than piracy.

Historians are divided over what proportion of seamen were volunteers and what proportion were pressed or conscripted into the navy. The "press" seems to have originated in the 13th century, but its most infamous incarnation dates from the Quota Act of 1795. This legislation compelled every county in Britain to provide a number of recruits (based on the county's population) who were to fill the need for sailors, a need that was a direct consequence of the wars following the French Revolution. Civic authorities offered bounties and remitted the sentences of criminals and debtors to fill the quota, but forcible impressment still proved necessary.

The Impress Service was naturally unpopular, and the press gang, composed of a group of seamen armed with cudgels and commanded by a naval lieutenant, was both feared and physically resisted in performing its duties. These gangs forcibly abducted men between the ages of 18 and 55 who were "not apprentices or gentlemen." Merchant seamen were their preferred targets. Press gangs pressed some men who had just entered port in merchant vessels that had not yet come to anchor.

The impressment system was largely arbitrary, harsh, and unsympathetic to the men whom it conscripted, but it did satisfy the manning needs of the navy. Seamen in the Royal Navy had no right to shore leave, making desertion difficult. In any case, the entire crew, both volunteers and pressed men, were paid off at some point and discharged at the end of a ship's commission so that service in the navy was for only a limited period.

A master of a merchant vessel, or a captain in the naval service, could punish a seaman for "sufficient cause," but the correction could not be disproportionate to the offense. Officers, however, were immune from punishment because their status protected them. They could only be removed from duty or be confined to their cabins until a court of inquiry or court martial could be convened. Of course, an indignant but imaginative captain could, without violating the regulations, chastise an unrepentant officer. Captains could order such officers to serve in the masthead for junior officers, stand watch for more senior men, or perform other disagreeable duties.

In the merchant service, no law or regulation defined a master's modes or instruments of punishment, but the master was enjoined to behave in a temperate and decent manner in all cases. The mode of correction might involve a personal rebuke or imprisonment aboard ship. The master might not withhold food and drink from—nor might he beat or wound—a seaman. Flogging and other criminal punishments in the merchant service, once common, became almost nonexistent in the 19th century as legislation in many countries made the master answerable for what occurred aboard his ship.

With regard to discipline and punishment, most navies had regulations that were commonly referred to as the Articles of War. The British articles, dating from 1731, applied in war or peace, and any breech of them brought specific punishments or discipline. Nineteen of the articles carried the death penalty.

The definition of capital crimes could be quite broad. A seaman's complaints, even if justified, needed to be couched in the most careful of terms because crimes such as "mutinous assembly" and "sedition" were largely open to the determination of the ship's officers.

A naval captain had wide discretion in inflicting punishment. He could admonish the offender, stop his grog (honeyed rum diluted with hot water), water his grog, disrate him, put him to work at the pumps (a physically challenging labor), cause him to run the gauntlet, keel-haul him, or flog him. By 1790, running the gauntlet and keel-hauling—dragging the bound man underwater along the length or width of the vessel—had fallen into disuse, but flogging remained a favorite corporal punishment into the 19th century.

Until 1806, the British Admiralty allowed any number of lashes to be administered. Thereafter, only 12 lashes for an offense were permitted, but a particularly cruel officer could sidestep this regulation by making multiple charges against the offender.

So that neither the embarrassment to the offender nor the deterrent effect on his shipmates would be squandered because of a lack of showmanship, the captain had all hands that were not needed to operate the vessel summoned to "witness punishment." Under the supervision of the surgeon, who could stop the ceremony on medical grounds, the boatswain or his mates stripped the offender to the waist, tied him to a grating or the capstan, and administered the lashes. Known as the "cat-o'-nine-tails," this instrument of torture featured a lash with nine thin pieces of line, each with a knot in its length. The "cat" not only raised welts but also cut and permanently scarred the skin. It was said that the "cat" was kept in a red bag to hide the blood that it drew.

Courts of inquiry were compulsory when a vessel was lost and when capital offenses, imprisonment, or heavy flogging were imposed. Officers who were found guilty of an offense could be dismissed from service, broken in rank or seniority, or shot. Seamen who were found guilty of capital offenses were usually hanged from the fore yardarm of their ship. This mode of punishment usually failed to break a man's neck and caused him to languish for a long period, kicking and struggling as he slowly strangled.

Because piracy was a capital crime, pirates went to extraordinary lengths to cover their tracks. In many cases, pirates killed every person aboard a victimized vessel in order to conceal their deeds. They changed the names of their own vessels, adopted aliases, and shifted their operations from their original vessels to prizes better suited to their trade. The only dependable records about pirates seem to have come from the government agencies and naval squadrons assigned to suppress them.

Pirates and press gangs, each occupying opposing extremities along the legal spectrum, reflected the unusual working of criminal activity and legislated directives. Still, if a mariner were found guilty of a serious offence, the resulting punishment aboard ship or back in port was frequently brutal and protracted, be it corporal or capital (Volo and Volo, 111–12, 130–33, 218).

FOR MORE INFORMATION

Mutiny on the Bounty. 1935. MGM, directed by Frank Lloyd. Videocassette.

Thrower, W. R. *Life at Sea in the Age of Sail.* London: Phillimore, 1972.

Volo, D. D., and J. M. Volo. *Daily Life in the Age of Sail.* Westport, Conn.: Greenwood Press, 2002.

Warfare

POLITICAL LIFE
|
WARFARE
|
Africa

The Colonial Frontier
of North America

England

Japan

New England

Life at Sea

Each of the cultures discussed in this section was no stranger to warfare, and during the 17th and 18th centuries, they all maintained armed forces. England and its colonies in North America were in and out of armed conflicts, typically with the French and with Native Americans. Warfare on the high seas was pivotal to these conflicts, acting as an extension of conflicts on either side of the Atlantic. In sub-Saharan Africa, warfare was at times endemic, and the victors in a conflict could enslave the conquered populations and either keep them for slave labor or sell them to buyers. Japan stands out as the one culture discussed here that did not enter into any significant military conflict during the 18th century, a fact that perhaps reflects the island culture's self-imposed isolation. Thus Japan and its long tradition of martial ventures acquired during this century a symbolic, rather than a practical, attraction. Samurai warrior-administrators carried swords for status more than for protection.

The elements of warfare can be broken down into three categories: armies, their weapons, and their strategies. The armies of England were of two types: one was a standing or permanent mass of soldiers, and the other was a militia characterized by greater flexibility into and out of uniform. Military life was miserable for regular troops, who suffered poor pay, exhausting physical routines, tasteless and meager rations, and the threat of instant death or grave injury. Officers benefited quite significantly from better pay, food, and respect.

Africans, too, found that standing armies were effective. Such professional armies were foreign, however, to North America's colonies in both British America and New France. Here, militias protected individual settlements, and sometimes all able-bodied men had an obligation to serve. Only after the establishment of these settlements did regular troops from England and France engage in the defense of their respective colonies. The act of "pressing," or forcing, an individual into service was most closely associated with British naval practices.

Types of weapons varied in sophistication. On one end of the spectrum were the simple knives, tomahawks, and bows and arrows of Native Americans along the North American colonial frontier. Most Africans also resorted to spears, shields, and daggers. As was the case with Native Americans, Africans quickly made room for European firearms in their arsenal of weapons. On the other end of the spectrum were Europeans and Japanese, who had developed relatively advanced uses of gunpowder and firearms. Japanese, however, voluntarily refrained from the mass production and provision of guns to its samurais, instead relying on the even more traditional swords, longbows, and leather-and-iron uniforms so often associated with this breed of warrior. Colonists in North America, on the other hand, made frequent use of muskets and pistols. Of course, on their decks, warships carried powerful cannons, the number of which could intimidate the bravest foe. The ships themselves were also weapons, ranging from cutters, schooners, corvettes, and frigates to enormous men-of-war.

Different military strategies reflected different traditions and needs. On the colonial frontier in North America, Indians attacked small, isolated targets late at night or early in the morning. The settlers reacted to these threats by combining traditional methods of warfare with those of the native population. The Songhay and other West African societies used cavalry to overwhelm their enemies. English armies traversed fields and fjords in huge masses, and on open battlefields they formed geometric lines across from their opponents. On the high seas, the great European navies adopted different strategies in an effort to undermine their foe's strengths by challenging its weaknesses. The British Royal Navy, being larger and more successful than the French fleets, practiced a seek-and-destroy approach to annihilate the French. Sensing the precariousness of their situation, the French hoped to keep the British nervous and fatigued and thus responded to the English threat with a resist-and-threaten strategy.

Warfare was a crucial element of everyday life during the 17th and 18th centuries. Whereas 18th-century Japan benefited from an absence of large-scale conflict between professional armies, rulers and administrators in sub-Saharan Africa, Europe, and North America assembled armed forces of varying competence and size and, guided by a number of strategies and tactics, led them into battle.

~Peter Seelig

FOR MORE INFORMATION

Van Evera, S. *Causes of War: Power and the Roots of Conflict.* Ithaca, N.Y.: Cornell University Press, 1999.

POLITICAL LIFE

|

WARFARE

|

Africa

The Colonial Frontier
of North America

England

Japan

New England

Life at Sea

AFRICA

From one culture to the next, war and peace followed similar patterns throughout the African continent south of the Sahara. The events of each armed conflict depended on the current power of states and of other political groups in relation to one another and on their access to resources. When conflict arose, people settled it either diplomatically or militarily according to the customs of a given region. Warfare could be either little more than a skirmish or long and destructive, with noncombatants usually suffering the most. During the 17th and 18th centuries, the introduction of gunpowder from Europe changed the weapons of war. The presence of

European powers significantly altered the diplomatic landscape, integrating Africa into global politics and particularly into the Atlantic economy.

In stateless societies, all men would at some point have an opinion concerning relations with other clans, villages, or cultures, while in organized states, such matters remained the purview of the ruler and his advisors. To keep in contact with other states, Africans used diplomats who carried messages and negotiated either alone or in small groups. During the 17th century, many rulers began keeping permanent representatives in areas of importance. When groups proved unable to resolve an issue through such means, however, war ensued.

The usual causes of African wars included territorial expansion, control of natural resources, the acquisition of wealth through booty or tribute, and control of trade routes. On rare occasions, religion or ideology also played a role. In many societies, all adult males provided military service, while in others, the rulers kept a standing army that defended the country, conquered new territory, and kept order at home. Some conflicts degenerated into major wars lasting for years and with thousands of casualties; others lasted for only a single small battle.

Before hostilities commenced, one side issued a declaration of war so that the other could prepare its defenses and send women and children to safety. The Fante of West Africa, for example, sent a herald to their enemies to tell them a war had begun and to open talks concerning when and where it should take place. Among the Gannawarri of northern Nigeria, it was customary to wait three days between the dispute and the beginning of the war, a period called the "knife-sharpening time." The Ibo and their neighbors notified their enemies of declarations of war by leaving plantain leaves and piles of powder on the paths.

In the savanna areas of West Africa, cavalry played an important role. Found in places such as Songhay and Futa Toro, cavalry represented an elite unit, while com-moners served only as foot soldiers, who, in these so-cieties, carried a shield, dagger, and light thrusting weapons such as javelins and spears. Forts and fortified villages featured significantly in defensive strategies. In addition, fleets of war canoes carrying as many as 100 warriors each plied the waters of the large rivers and Lake Chad. Depending on the society, military command fell to clan and territorial elders, the one most skilled in battle leadership, or designated war chiefs.

Illustration from H. Barth's *Travels and Discoveries in Northern and Central Africa,* 1857. A fortified Songhay village.

Special ceremonies often marked the end of wars, as well. Conflicts between the Kikuyu and Maasai peoples in modern Kenya ended with the slaughter of an ewe and a pledge that if one side ever harmed the other, the aggressors would be slaughtered just like the ewe. Defeated populations were either killed or captured. Along the Gold Coast, the kings theoretically enjoyed the rights to all captives, but the chiefs often received many of them as rewards for their service. In some areas, Islamic law dictated the treatment of prisoners and in particular stipulated that slaves receive good treatment and that families remain together. As the slave trade with Europeans became more profitable, the acquisition of slaves specifically for sale became an important motive for war in its own right. Moreover, some people who escaped execution were drafted into victorious armies or held hostage (Muriuki, 84).

The introduction of gunpowder during the 17th and 18th centuries did not significantly alter many aspects of African warfare. Acquiring such weapons certainly became an important goal of many states, but the armies frequently failed to use them effectively. Some peoples, such as the Ashanti, used them to overpower their neighbors; yet Oyo prevailed in a war against Dahomey even though only the latter had guns. In the Lake Malawi area, firearms did allow the Makua to begin resisting Portuguese colonialism (Ogot, 830).

African warfare thus resembled warfare in many other parts of the world and functioned as a tool of community policy. Usually observed by all parties, a set of formal and informal regulations governed warfare. As in most places, people fought wars for land, resources, and ambition. All adult males could participate in war, although in more centralized societies, men played different roles based on status and training. In the end, warfare probably hurt noncombatants more than it did the actual warriors.

~*Brian Ulrich*

FOR MORE INFORMATION

BBC World Service. *The Story of Africa.* <http://bbc.co.uk/worldservice/africa/features/storyofafrica>, accessed October 23, 2003.

Halsall, P., ed. *Internet African History Sourcebook.* 1996. <http://www.fordham.edu/halsall/africa/africasbook.html>, accessed October 23, 2003.

Muriuki, G. *A History of the Kikuyu, 1500–1900.* New York: Oxford University Press, 1974.

Ogot, B. A., ed. *General History of Africa.* Vol. 5. *Africa from the Sixteenth Century to the Eighteenth Century.* Paris: United Nations Educational, Scientific, and Cultural Organization, 1992.

Smith, R. S. *Warfare and Diplomacy in Pre-Colonial West Africa.* New York: Methuen, 1976.

THE COLONIAL FRONTIER OF NORTH AMERICA

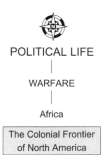

POLITICAL LIFE
|
WARFARE
|
Africa

The Colonial Frontier
of North America

England

Japan

New England

Life at Sea

The struggle for control of North America was also a contest over which methods and rules of warfare would be used. For centuries, the Native Americans had fought among themselves using knives, clubs, and tomahawks made of wood and stone. The bow and arrow of the eastern woodland tribes of North America were unsophisticated and technologically inferior not only to those developed by European and Asian cultures but also to those found in South and Central America. Native Americans shifted from traditional weapons to firearms as quickly as they became available, but it has been pointed out that they "never really mastered the white man's weapon." Nonetheless, native war practices in terms of tactics, prisoners, and personal behavior on the field of battle changed little even with the introduction of firearms.

The tactics employed by Native American warriors against colonists, as well as against other Native Americans, were simple and effective. They generally struck first without a formal declaration of war, using the basic offensive tactic of surprise. They commonly attacked isolated cabins and remote villages, often at dawn. Most attacks, however, took the form of ambushes made in forested regions. These attacks were especially effective against nonmilitary targets such as small parties of settlers or fur traders. Colonial militias periodically organized punitive expeditions into the frontier regions. Because the Indians rarely chose to stand and fight, colonials learned to threaten and burn their crops and villages. The Indians were thus forced into an active defense that trained soldiers could break.

One undeniable characteristic unified all colonial forces. Lacking large standing armies, colonials relied heavily on provincial forces or local militias for protection against attack or for prosecuting war against others. Not until the final struggle for control of the continent did armies from Europe join the fray.

At first, the French in New France eschewed any form of military force in their dealings with the Indians. The French monarchy ordered that those who arranged any commercial or religious ventures in New France provide their own garrisons. These scanty garrisons of private mercenaries found it nearly impossible to mount an effective resistance to the unfriendly Iroquois. In 1664, the French government made a commitment of royal troops to New France for the first time.

The French government relied on professional troops, the "independent companies," to police New France and raised the inhabitants of Canada (the militia) only in the most severe emergencies. From 1684 to 1760, the independent companies took part in almost every engagement against the enemy in North America. Although suffering setbacks, they successfully withstood English and Iroquois attacks.

Beginning in 1746, regular army units from France augmented the independent companies. However, in the unconventional style of frontier warfare, the independent companies—often serving with militia and Indian allies—were simply more successful than regular troops.

Their regulation armament included a sword and a flintlock musket with bayonet. Being lighter and more reliable than English military arms of the period, French firearms were generally of superior quality. A powder horn was slung over the shoulder on a thin leather belt to provide priming powder.

For almost a century and a half after the founding of the first English colony, no formal establishment of regular army troops was used in America for defense. In part, this was because of the character of the colonists—religious dissenters or political outsiders who tended to distrust professional military forces. Instead, each English colony designed its own systems of defense, generally fashioned around a militia formed of its male citizens. These organizations were remarkably similar when one considers the number of individual colonial governments involved in militia formation. Differences among militia are more easily ascribed to regional characteristics rather than to any genuine inconsistency.

The settlers in New France and in the British colonies waged war against each other and sought useful alliances with native tribes. Here, the famous French explorer Samuel de Champlain and two fellow travelers fire on the Iroquois, in effect siding with the Algonquians. The Iroquois eventually became useful and adept allies of the British. Reprinted from Samuel de Champlain, *Voyages* . . . Paris, Chez lean Berjon, Avec privilege du Roy, 1613.

Officials instituted periodic training days and formed a cadre of elected or appointed officers. Militias also obtained a local stockpile of gunpowder and a few artillery pieces, along with armor, pikes, and other items not commonly available to the early settlers. These improvements became characteristic of most militia systems. Local company strength ranged from 65 to 200 men but often fell below 65, at which time units from neighboring communities might combine with one another. Local command was loosely invested in a captain, subalterns, and sergeants. Early on, every able-bodied man was a potential soldier and had a legal obligation to serve, although magistrates, ministers, slaves, and those who suffered from physical and mental impediments or extreme old age were generally exempt from military duty.

Evidence suggests that there was little uniformity of dress, each man wearing what he thought best for his own comfort and circumstance. In most colonies, each militiaman was required to bring his own musket (or rifle), one pound of lead balls, powder in proper proportion to the ball, a one-quart canteen or water bottle, and a hatchet, tomahawk, or hunting knife. However, the range and accuracy of the firearms were unimpressive.

Only after 1754 were large numbers of regular officers sent to the English colonies. Without exception, British regular officers seem to have been knowledgeable in the tactics of irregular warfare. These men were thoroughly acquainted with the concepts of skirmishers, flankers, and advanced parties of scouts, all of which concepts were included in technical literature and training manuals. The British record with regard to irregular warfare was exemplary.

During the 17th and 18th centuries, warfare along the colonial frontier pitted Native American warriors against colonial troops and French and English armies against each other. In New France, informally trained militias joined with the independent companies, the members of which learned about irregular military strategy and tactics from actual experience, and the two surpassed in skill the regular French troops, whose presence in present-day Canada came late in the colony's history. In the English colonies, militias were distinctly less regulated than their counterparts in the British army; however, the latter constituted an effective fighting force along the frontier (Volo and Volo, 180–81, 183–86, 189–90, 197–99, 201–5, 209).

FOR MORE INFORMATION

Archiving Early America. *Early America*. <http://earlyamerica.com/>, accessed October 23, 2003.

Ferling, J. *Struggle for a Continent: The Wars of Early America*. Arlington Heights, Ill.: Harlan Davidson, 1993.

Last of the Mohicans. Twentieth Century Fox Film. Directed by Michael Mann. Videocassette, 1992.

Leckie, R. *A Few Acres of Snow: The Saga of the French and Indian Wars*. New York: Wiley, 1999.

Volo, J. M., and D. D. Volo. *Daily Life on the Old Colonial Frontier*. Westport, Conn.: Greenwood Press, 2002.

ENGLAND

The 18th century saw England engaged in wars fought on both land and sea throughout the globe. A good many Englishmen served in the army and navy in a variety of positions. Common soldiers and sailors and high-ranking officers all had stories to tell, and their stories relate a difficult, mostly unpleasant life for the common soldier or sailor and a slightly more agreeable one for the officers.

Military service involved long hours, miserable conditions, and low pay. The size of the military varied from as few as 30,000 in peacetime to as many as 200,000 in war, not counting the militia. By the end of the century, the militia, founded in 1757, numbered nearly 100,000. The government assembled wartime forces in various ways: by holding recruiting drives, by offering bonuses for enlistees, and by using press gangs to force layabouts into the army and navy.

Ordinary seamen, soldiers, and militiamen were overwhelmingly poor. Officers, on the other hand, were frequently wealthy and well connected. By 1800, 38 percent of naval officers and an even higher percentage of army officers came from titled or landed families. Wealth was a prerequisite because commissions had to be purchased. A lieutenant colonelcy cost about 3,500 pounds.

At times, the army enjoyed widespread admiration. Officers lived well, and officers and men alike had the reputation of being dashing lovers. Yet the army was the least popular branch of the service. Its infantry, in particular, gained a reputation for nuisance. Army units on the move were a mass of carts carrying baggage for officers, plus provisions and ammunition. Herds of cattle, packhorses, cooks, laundresses, carpenters, smiths, hospital attendants and supplies, servants, traders, prostitutes, and soldiers' families accompanied the fighting men along their ponderous journey.

The men, dressed in heavy red wool uniforms, carried their packs, food, water, tent equipment, blankets, weapons, and 60 rounds of ammunition. Their arms were flintlock muskets, clumsy weapons with a reliable range of about a hundred yards. The average soldier could load and fire his gun only two or three times a minute, juggling powder, cartridge, ball, and rod; with the bayonet fixed, loading was almost impossible, and firing was highly inaccurate.

Soldiers received notoriously poor pay, from which there were deductions for food, clothing, weapons repairs, and the veterans' hospital. In addition, they faced lice, death from sunstroke or disease, and brutal discipline, both in peacetime and in war. Death and dismemberment in battle were all too common. Common soldiers begged if disabled and often stole if healthy; crime rates usually went up when soldiers came home from war.

The navy was much more popular. During war, crews shared in the loot. Captains and admirals received the lion's share, but the seamen, cooks, and stewards shared 25 percent. Sailors did not have to carry heavy packs or wear thick uniforms; they dressed lightly in caps, loose trousers, and shirts.

Despite a preference for the navy, military duty on the high seas could be brutal. As did soldiers, sailors faced disease, death, and injury at worst and hard work, stench, and cramped quarters at best. The food—salted meat, oatmeal, peas, butter, cheese, beer, and biscuits—was often rotten or filled with weevils and maggots.

Soldiers and sailors risked a high degree of discomfort both during peacetime and during war. Whether these men were on board their fighting vessel or on the land marching to battle, the horrors of service were not necessarily limited to the horrors of combat. Exhausting physical exertion, harsh discipline, low pay, inedible food, and miserable living conditions were the potential lot of any common fighting man in the army or navy (Olsen, 130–33).

To read about warfare in Chaucer's England, see the Europe entry in the section "Warfare and Weapons" in chapter 6 ("Political Life") of volume 2; and for Victorian England, see the Victorian England entry in the section "War and Military" in chapter 6 ("Political Life") of volume 5 of this series.

FOR MORE INFORMATION

Lynch, J. *Eighteenth Century Resources.* <http://newark.rutgers.edu/~jlynch/18th/>, accessed October 10, 2003.

Olsen, K. *Daily Life in 18th-Century England.* Westport, Conn.: Greenwood Press, 1999.

Rogers, H. C. B. *The British Army of the Eighteenth Century.* London: George Allen and Unwin, 1977.

JAPAN

Although Japan had an active and intense history of warfare, the 18th century was a time of peace. Nevertheless, Japan preserved its military heritage in the form of castles, weapons, uniforms, and martial arts. Interestingly, the samurai, once Japan's warrior class, was by now principally an administrative class. However, they too safeguarded their military traditions in a variety of ways.

Castle construction had long historical roots in Japan. Imposing stone walls, rammed earth, and deep moats surrounded the castle keep and were topped with castle towers, parapets, and firing stations. A concentric ring of walls and moats created a secondary line of defense. A daimyō (regional warlord) and his most trusted vassals had their residences there. The samurai elite lived secure within these imposing fortifications, whereas lesser warriors were housed in barracks nearby.

In the samurai residences, streets were built with an eye toward military defense rather than convenience. Gates commonly stood at either end of castle streets, which were constructed at zigzag angles to impede the way of invaders. Stone steps were constructed at odd angles, depths, and heights to frustrate anyone who might try to run up them. Stone walls usually curled upward toward the right to take advantage of the fact that most warriors wielded swords in their right hands. That is to say, invaders were hampered as they went upward because the walls were always on their right. Defenders had clear lines to slash because the walls were on their left as they faced downward.

Despite being at peace since about 1640, artisans in Japan continued to produce military products. Most impressive of all was the sword, which represented the "soul" of the samurai. Japanese ironworkers experimented with all sorts of metal alloys and smithing techniques to improve the Japanese curved blade (*katana*).

The "double-back" method, although time consuming, tedious, and highly labor-intensive, produced a superior product. Sword makers heated the metal until it was white hot, folded it back on itself, and fused the halves together by pounding them with a heavy maul hammer. After the metal cooled in water, successive heatings and poundings over several months eliminated more and more impurities from the metal, transforming the iron into steel. The entire process took on a religious aspect. Shintō priests were called in at critical junctures of the production to purify the blade ritually.

At this point, artisans painted the blade with a secret concoction of clay and ashes, spread thicker on the back of the blade and thinner along the single cutting edge. Artisans then polished and honed the blade for months. Commissioned swords were tested before they were delivered to their new owners. The best way to test the new sword, of course, was on the human body. Obviously, not many individuals volunteered for this task, so sword testers obtained the bodies of condemned prisoners. The rank of a sword corresponded to the proficiency with which it sliced through limbs, torsos, and even groups of torsos. The blade would feature an engraving of these results, a gruesome advertisement.

In the 18th century, the killing power of the *katana* was no longer as essential as it had been a century or two before. In fact, it had become a social symbol, and few samurai could afford to commission a superior new blade. The cost of a new top-line blade ran as high as the equivalent of three years of an average samurai's annual income.

Extremely flexible and light, Japanese armor was not made in sheets of metal. Instead, it was constructed of small pieces of iron and of lacquered leather that were sewn together with silk. The tightly sewn segments were nearly impervious to sword cuts, spear thrusts, or arrows. Huge epaulets and wide-brimmed sloping helmets served as additional protection for the dangerously unarmored neck and face. In defense of a flight of arrows, a samurai typically hunched his shoulders and scrunched his head down much like a turtle, making him nearly impervious. The entire suit weighed perhaps 30 pounds (compared with the European suit, which weighed up to four times more). By the 18th century, however, samurai were bureaucrats more than warriors and therefore wore their armor only for ceremonial purposes.

Japanese longbows were justly famous for their strength and accuracy. These killing machines were seven to nine feet long and made of laminated wood. The bow was held not in the middle, as is common everywhere else in the world, but farther down so as to enable the samurai to take advantage of the severe arch.

Curiously, Japanese had stopped production of most firearms by the early 18th century. Historians disagree as to why this was so. Perhaps it was a conscious attempt to stop the proliferation of military technology and return the samurai to the rustic ideal of *bushido* (the way of the warrior). Perhaps it was to concentrate the few cannons and harquebuses, still closely guarded in locked armories, in the hands of the *bakufu* (national military government). Whatever the reasons, armories became museums rather than manufacturers of firearms.

The martial arts incorporated many diverse practices and styles. The samurai developed *kendo*, the art of fencing with bamboo (*shinai*) or wooden swords (*bokken*). Because fencing with actual *katana* blades was very dangerous, the *bakufu* declared the practice illegal. Most *kendo* schools developed their own training exercises (*kata*) and, by the end the 18th century, staged interschool tournaments.

Unarmed *ashigaru* (non-samurai foot soldiers) and warrior monks developed the so-called empty-hand techniques. Because Buddhist monks were forbidden to continue the warlike ways that they had followed in the 15th and 16th centuries, they needed to develop self-defense methods to protect themselves, methods that are today known as the martial arts. The origins of karate, jujitsu, judo, aikido, *sojutsu, nagewaza, atewaza, hapkido,* and the other martial arts are clouded in secrecy and myth, but by the mid–18th century, more than 100 schools flourished.

Many samurai practiced the art of "sword pulling" (*tachikaki*). The idea was to draw the sword from the scabbard and simultaneously deal a lethal blow in one swift, smooth motion. Archery on foot (as opposed to the *yabusame* mounted variety), horsemanship, horse racing, harquebus gunnery, and foot racing through obstacle courses were similarly martial in origins.

Japanese military structures consisted of castles, weapons, uniforms, and martial arts. However, the 18th-century Japanese samurai class, resting on a tradition of active military ventures, was more like a museum devoted to its military heritage than an active fighting force (Perez, 122–25, 196–200, 278, 281).

To read about war in Japan in the 20th century, see the Japan entry in the section "War" in chapter 6 ("Political Life") of volume 6 of this series.

FOR MORE INFORMATION

Japan Information Network. <http://www.jinjapan.org/index.html>, accessed October 23, 2003.

Perez, L. G. *Daily Life in Early Modern Japan.* Westport, Conn.: Greenwood Press, 2002.

Perrin, N. *Giving Up the Gun: Japan's Reversion to the Sword, 1543–1879.* Boulder, Colo.: Shambhala, 1980.

NEW ENGLAND

Military conflict during colonial New England's history centered on the struggles both between settlers and Native Americans and between the English and the French.

Some native peoples, such as the Massachusetts tribes, enthusiastically welcomed European settlers to their shores up to the third decade of the 17th century. Their motives were mixed. Many believed that the armed Europeans would protect them from their more powerful native enemies. Some tribes also welcomed trade with Europeans and exchanged skins and hides with them for wampum (small beads).

Ten years following the 1630 arrival of John Winthrop and his party, the Native Americans' welcome of the settlers had worn out. The settlers had appeared on the scene with two objectives regarding Indians: secure their land and convert them to Christianity. Indeed, the English assigned their own rules to native peoples, who quickly came to view the mechanism of trade as the settlers' means of exploitation.

The native tribes of New England had both harmonious and discordant relationships with one another. Many tribes were on friendly terms, trading not for necessities but for decorative elements such as beads and shells, copper, and tobacco pipes. Different tribes congregated to trade, socialize, and plan cooperative efforts. For example, some tribes joined to form a united front to discourage hostile actions from unfriendly peoples.

New England tribes were not free of territorial disputes and other conflicts. Certain tribes were more aggressive than others and were not above raids on their neighbors' provisions or attempts at appropriating the territory of other tribes. The Pequot and Abenaki tribes, for instance, took advantage of weakened tribes and stole their crops. Sometimes defensive stances were taken against other tribes, especially those with different languages. Smaller, unarmed native communities naturally feared the large and powerful Iroquois tribe, which had invaded New England and secured firearms from the Dutch. When armed conflicts did occur, the fighting and torture of captives were brutal. The victors in any sustained conflict slaughtered their male enemies and took the women and children of their enemies into their own tribes.

There were many conflicts between settlers and natives throughout the colonial period. One of the first major conflicts occurred in 1637. Word reached Boston in July that Pequot Indians had killed an English trader named John Oldham. The New England colonies raised a militia and waged war against the Pequot for a solid year. On June 5, 1637, a militia destroyed a large Pequot village at Stonington, Connecticut. Pequot men and boys who were eventually captured were sold into slavery in the West Indies. The women and girls became slaves to white settlers in New England. The few survivors in this tribe left for the west.

Although no open warfare erupted between settlers and native peoples for 40 years after this incident, relations between them were hardly cordial. Individuals from both camps were guilty of murders and thefts, and the English continued to take over land. Moreover, the Narraganset in Rhode Island quarreled with Massachusetts Bay businessmen under the Atherton Company when the latter began commandeering immense amounts of Narraganset land. In this case, the European settlers of Rhode Island sided with the native tribes against the settlers of Massachusetts Bay and Connecticut. Immediate disaster was averted when the king of England, Charles II, intervened at Rhode Island's request to side with the Narraganset and voided the claims of the Atherton Company.

The reason for the continued disintegration of relations between colonists and Native Americans was simple. The colonists were determined to secure key Indian land as part of their expansion into the Connecticut Valley, and the Indians were determined that this would not happen.

The Wampanoag chief, King Philip, had historically been friendly with the settlers, but suspicions mounted, rumors raged on, and the English demanded that various tribes surrender their weapons. For years, King Philip and other sachems inwardly seethed over such humiliation. Finally, in June 1675, after the Plymouth

Colony executed three of King Philip's men for the murder of an informant, the Indian chief began his raids on settlements in a yearlong war in which many native tribes sided with the settlers. Some 50 towns along the frontier were burned. By 1676, the war had resulted in the deaths of about 2,000 English and about 4,000 Native Americans.

With the decisive defeat of King Philip's forces in 1676 (King Philip himself was killed, drawn and quartered, and his head brought to Boston for display) came the virtual end of the native tribes in New England. There was no longer a question of negotiating for land. All Indian land was up for confiscation now that the settlers had appropriated Indian land as the spoils of war, dictated the terms for takeovers, and executed scores of prisoners of war. However, New England businessmen realized the cash value of the prisoners; thus many more were sold into slavery and shipped to the West Indies, Spain, and the Mediterranean. Those Indians deemed less dangerous became bound servants in the colonies in order to alleviate the perpetual labor shortage there. In the 1620s, the Native Americans in the area had numbered around 75,000 people. Their people had lived in New England for thousands of years. By the 1680s, decimated by disease, alcohol, and wars with the settlers, their numbers had dropped to 20,000, only half the number of the new European settlers.

King Philip—also known as Metacomet—waged war against the settlers of New England during the mid-1670s. King Philip and his Indian alliance suffered defeat, and by 1678, the interior of New England no longer posed a significant threat to the European settlers. © North Wind/North Wind Picture Archives.

One further notorious clash between Native Americans and settlers during the colonial period occurred on February 29, 1704, at a time when many tribes had sided with the French in the fight between French and English over the domination of northern New England. A company of 28 Frenchmen and 200 Native Americans launched an attack on Deerfield, Massachusetts, a town of 300 residents. Forty-eight Deerfield residents were killed and 111 were taken hostage.

The French and Indian War was the most important North American conflict between European powers during the colonial period. This conflict, waged primarily in the Ohio Valley, began on May 28, 1754, and pitted the French against the British; it also included important alliances between the European powers and native tribes. In 1755, the French were turned away from the New England colonies, but war raged on in nearby New York State. Not until February 1763 did the French and Indian War end with English victories in Canada.

With the defeat of many of their Indian and French rivals in and around New England, the English believed the region to be a secure component within the British Empire. The Revolutionary War (1775–83) would dispel this mistaken belief (Johnson, xix, 141–45).

FOR MORE INFORMATION

Archiving Early America. *Early America.* <http://earlyamerica.com/>, accessed October 23, 2003.

Johnson, C. D. *Daily Life in Colonial New England.* Westport, Conn.: Greenwood Press, 2002.

Leach, D. E. *Flintlock and Tomahawk.* New York: Macmillan, 1998.

Roux, L. *The French and Indian War Home Page.* <http://web.syr.edu/~laroux/>, accessed October 23, 2003.

LIFE AT SEA

Warfare and sea power were among the chief concerns of many rulers and military strategists throughout the 17th and 18th centuries. Although England, being an island nation, is most representative of this trend during this period, other European nations and their colonies similarly concerned themselves with the outfitting of navies and the development of strategies and tactics for dealing with potential or actual adversaries.

The British developed the best-known system for classifying warships. A "rate" was a classification system for warships that expressed the number of long guns (cannons) officially carried aboard.

Designated as line-of-battle ships, warships having more than 50 guns were either first, second, or third rates. First and second rates had three gun decks. Third rates had two. First rates carried in excess of 100 guns, second rates 90 to 98, and third rates 80, 74, or 64. The third rate "74" was the most common battle warship in 18th-century European navies. These and larger warships were often called men-of-war.

Fourth rates were 50-gun vessels with either one or two decks. In the early 18th century, fourth rates would have been intimidating adversaries but later became undergunned and too small to serve in the line.

Fifth and sixth rates and unrated vessels included sloops-of-war, cutters, and schooners. These vessels were less powerful than men-of-war but were very seaworthy and swift, providing solid combat service while satisfying communication and supply needs.

Finally, there were privateers. As with mercenary armies hired to fight on land, privateering was a form of private enterprise in which governments commissioned vessels to raid the enemy on the high seas during wartime. The privateer's commission allowed the seizure, capture, or destruction of the vessels and cargo of only a specified enemy (or enemies). More important, privateers insisted that they be allowed to pocket the proceeds from the sale of the captured ship and cargo—and to do so without being exposed to a charge of piracy.

Strategy and tactics are related, but they are not equivalent. Heads of state or commanders of military forces strategize with maps in a planning room, whereas the on-site commanders at the point of contact apply tactics to the enemy. English and French naval strategies can serve as classic examples of different attitudes toward sea power in the age of fighting sail.

The primary strategy of the British Royal Navy of the 18th century was to bring the enemy fleet to battle and destroy it, thereby preventing a possible armed invasion

of Britain, Scotland, or Ireland. To attain this objective, the English needed to maintain an overwhelming strength at sea. In the 1740s, for example, the British had 90 ships-of-the-line and 84 frigates, numbers that increased during the next decade. By comparison, the French had 45 ships-of-the-line and 76 frigates, and the numbers of French vessels fell as those of the British increased during the Seven Years' War.

The disparity in fleet size is best explained in terms of French naval strategy. The French objective in maintaining a fleet was to protect France's trading establishments, island outposts, and colonies. Therefore, the French required only enough ships either to resist scattered incursions of their empire or to threaten British interests.

The British Royal Navy employed fleet tactics that can be categorized into several groups. Historically, the earliest fleet tactic was the melee—characteristic of the great fleets of the 16th century in which individual vessels became entangled. The line abreast and the line ahead were also tactics. The line abreast, with friendly ships sailing one beside the next using the guns in their bow against the enemy, was quickly abandoned, as the firepower of the ship came to reside along its sides. The line ahead, which maximized the number of guns that could be brought to bear upon the enemy fleet at one time, came to dominate fleet tactics in the age of sail and was not to be displaced until the widespread deployment of the gun turret after the American Civil War.

A late 17th-century cannon and its accessories are displayed in this useful illustration from the 1691 book *Sea Gunner's Companion*. © National Maritime Museum.

French naval tactics are much simpler to summarize. The French fleet fought in a line ahead almost without exception throughout the 18th century. Moreover, French commanders rarely expended their resources in "slugging matches" that were meant to sink or capture enemy vessels and instead, were happy to break off an engagement after dismasting, diverting, or otherwise slowing the enemy fleet.

A meeting at sea usually brought increased exertions on the part of each commander, who hoped to ascertain the actual characteristics of an approaching vessel before irrevocably committing himself to an encounter. A lightly armed merchantman or a slaver would immediately run. Privateers or pirates might try to run along a parallel course before abandoning a possible prize. The warship, however, was under some obligation to stand and make a fight.

The period between first sighting an unfriendly sail and closing with the enemy in battle was always one of considerable activity, as the crew readied their vessel for combat. The maximum range of naval guns could be well over a mile. However, the practical range of cannons in the 18th century was usually no more than about 200 yards, and fighting ranges were perhaps as close as a "pistol shot" (under 50 yards). As the distance between lone contestants (as opposed to fleets) closed, each commander would attempt to maneuver his vessel so as to bring the greatest possible number of guns to bear upon his opponent while simultaneously avoiding those of the enemy. Attempts to grapple the enemy vessel, entangle the rigging, or ram the opposing vessels into a conglomerate mass were all based on the hope that a boarding party might successfully decide the issue.

When not formed as part of the boarding party, marines were generally sent with their muskets to the fighting tops, from where they could fire down on the deck below or drop hand grenades into the open hatches of the enemy.

Whether rated or unrated, warships adhered to a complex classificatory system, especially in the British Royal Navy. Strategy and tactics, which varied both over time and from one country to another, dictated the number, type, and use of these warships in relation to wider diplomatic, economic, and military concerns (Volo and Volo, 69, 197–99, 201, 209, 220–21).

FOR MORE INFORMATION

Creswell, J. *British Admirals of the Eighteenth Century: Tactics in Battle.* London: Allen and Unwin, 1972.

Mahan, A. T. *The Influence of Sea Power upon History, 1660–1783.* New York: Dover, 1987.

Marcus, G. J. *The Formative Centuries: A Naval History of England.* Boston, Mass.: Little, Brown, 1961.

McCracken, P. *Maritime History on the Internet.* 1995. <http://ils.unc.edu/maritime/home. shtml>, accessed October 23, 2003.

United Kingdom Royal Navy. *Royal Navy History.* <http://www.royal-navy.mod.uk/static/ content/211.html>, accessed October 23, 2003.

Volo, D. D., and J. M. Volo. *Daily Life in the Age of Sail.* Westport, Conn.: Greenwood Press, 2002.

POLITICAL LIFE: WEB SITES

http://mars.acnet.wnec.edu/~grempel/courses/wc2/lectures/peasantsaristos.html
http://www.rekihakh.ac.jp/e_gallery/edozu/index.html
http://sun.menloschool.org/~sportman/westernstudies/first/1718/2000/eblock/tokugawa/ analysis.html
http://www.bbc.co.uk/worldservice/africa/features/storyofafrica/index.shtml
http://www.hyperhistory.com/online_n2/History_n2/a.html
http://www.koryubooks.com/library/wwj1.html
http://www.westerncape.gov.za/history.asp
http://www.wsu.edu/~dee/TOKJAPAN/SHOGUN.htm

7

RECREATIONAL LIFE

Play is serious business. All mammals play, but humans have cultivated recreation to the level of high art. After family and work, most of our energies and time are devoted to recreational activities, and as any modern sports enthusiast knows, we can play with as much passion as we work. What are recreational activities? In this volume, recreation corresponds to three distinct categories: games, holidays, and arts and hobbies. Nevertheless, there are several characteristics that all play shares. First, it is voluntary—one cannot be forced to play. As such, it is in fact the very essence of freedom, and even slaves and prisoners have treated themselves to games or music or dance for the sheer voluntary quality of the activities. During the 17th and 18th centuries, those belonging to the least-privileged classes played games, celebrated holidays, and amused themselves with arts and hobbies. Instances of recreation during this period include Japanese peasants who flew kites, seamen who decorated whalebone, Native Americans who refined the art of tattooing, French neoclassical painters who combined stoic restraint with vivid images of courage, Christian Kongolese who celebrated Halloween, colonial Australians who participated in horse match races, and black slaves in colonial New England who celebrated the election of black "governors."

Second, recreation operates, to a large extent, outside the scope of "real" life and is limited in time, duration, and space. Thus playtime almost defines "work" time; recess at school not only offers a break from study but significantly marks the serious times when one is to learn, as well. In 18th-century England, for example, the workweek did not include Sunday, a day of rest that frequently extended to Monday.

Third, recreation has its own rules, which are more rigorous and predictable than anything we can find in our more complex "real lives." At the end of the game— and there is a definitive end—there is a winner and loser, and the rules are clear. Of course, cheating is always a possibility (archaeologists have even found loaded dice in Anglo-Saxon settlements), but even unsportsmanlike conduct is recognizable. It is quite likely that we love games precisely for the clarity of the rules. This desire for clarity was evident when, in the 18th century, England codified the rules for horse racing. Likewise, during that same century, the rules and rituals surrounding sumo wrestling in Japan expanded in number and rigor as the game's popularity grew.

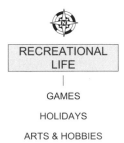

RECREATIONAL
LIFE
|
GAMES

HOLIDAYS

ARTS & HOBBIES

Finally, recreational life builds a group identity among the "players" and "spectators." Thus, 18th-century English theatergoers participated in a common and binding appreciation for well-received stage productions. During the 17th and 18th centuries, it was not unusual for a Native American clan or tribe along the colonial frontier to absorb outsiders (including white captives) into its ranks with the aid of an adoption ceremony. In this case, both natives and outsiders acted as "players" in the performance even though the outsiders must have seen themselves only as "spectators" in a chilling scenario that was all too real.

While recreational activities throughout history share these general characteristics, the particular forms of play that we choose shed light on who we are and what we value. In play, we prepare ourselves for the rest of our lives. For example, games ranging from the Olympics to chess hone our skills for war, while music and art stimulate our creativity. Violent sports ranging from dogfights to boxing steel us to face violence in life whereas holidays and celebrations forge communal bonds that are basic to cooperation at work. In studying the games, holidays, and arts and hobbies that constitute a particular culture's recreational traditions, we can more fully understand the society in its larger contexts.

~*Joyce E. Salisbury and Peter Seelig*

FOR MORE INFORMATION

Huizinga, J. *Homo Ludens: A Study of the Play Element in Culture*. Boston, Mass.: Beacon Press, 1964.

RECREATIONAL
LIFE
|
GAMES
|
England

Japan

New England

Life at Sea

Games

During the 17th and 18th centuries, games were a central part of people's lives in England, Japan, and New England, as well as on Western oceangoing vessels. The varied forms that games took included field and team sports, water games, sports and games performed with animals, and games of chance and of divination. As with most human activities, ethicists and religious dogmatists made pronouncements on certain games and sports, sometimes as advocates and at other times as adversaries.

Games and athletic pursuits frequently took the form of team events. Field games were particularly popular. The spectacular football (soccer) matches that took place in 18th-century England are noteworthy not only for the hundreds of players who participated in them but also for the passions that such games inspired. Tens of thousands turned out for cricket matches, as well. Team sports were also popular in early modern Japan, where games involving deerskin and bamboo balls inspired participants to display whatever skills that they could muster. Players avoided using their hands during these games.

Always a setting for games and sports, water provided a unique context for many recreational and athletic activities. Native Americans living in New England were fond of swimming. In England, those who enjoyed water sports could go boating, fishing, and (during the winter months) ice skating.

Games and sporting events often involved animals. By the 18th century, New England colonists enjoyed horse racing and bear baiting. Japanese samurai (warrior-administrators) flaunted their martial skills in archery tournaments that required the participants, while mounted on a fast-moving horse, to aim at and hit a target. In England, horsemanship acquired a set of codified rules, creating the impression of a formal sport, quite unlike the animal fights that took place within less-reputable circles.

Chance and divination provided the themes for many games in these cultures. Japanese gambling, which derived from efforts to divine future events, was common in cities, and particularly in brothels and sake (rice wine) shops, but was forbidden to peasants. Cards and dice aided gamblers in Japan, England, and New England. Native Americans used stones as dice, and idle seamen played cards and rolled dice aboard ship and in taverns on shore.

Board games such as checkers and chess provided a more relaxed display of talent, while retaining a sense of competition, which is key to any game. In Japan, games for the intellect touched on topics such as literature or military strategy. Backgammon and dominoes furnished sailors and officers aboard ship with a way to relax from the arduous physical demands of their professions.

Although immensely popular, games and sporting events often failed to gain the approval of religious and philosophical moralists. Captains of sailing ships sometimes disapproved of their crew playing cards. In England, there was a good deal of concern over the virtue of games such as horse riding. Nowhere was the prohibitive force of ethics and religion more fiercely felt than in 17th-century colonial New England. Puritans tended to frown on anything that smacked of ritual. In addition, Puritan doctrine identified idleness and use of the imagination with fiendish tendencies, which would result (so the Puritans insisted) from a lack of spiritual vigilance.

Perhaps surprising is the opposite trend that characterized games and religion in Japan. Here, gambling, fortune telling, numerology, and sumo wrestling rested on a strong tradition of Shintō and Buddhist beliefs and practices. Be they games involving teams, water, animals, or chance, such recreational activities reflected the religious and ethical concerns of individual communities.

~Peter Seelig

FOR MORE INFORMATION

The Diagram Group. *The Way to Play: The Illustrated Encyclopedia of the Games of the World.* New York: Paddington Press, 1975.
Hunt, S. E. *Games and Sports the World Around.* New York: Ronald Press, 1964.

ENGLAND

The games that people played in 18th-century England normally centered on exercise, fishing and hunting, team sports, board and card games, and violence.

RECREATIONAL
LIFE
|
GAMES
|

England

Japan

New England

Life at Sea

Again, class membership influenced which games one might consider playing, and participation often depended on society's gender perception (conceptions of the sexes). Not everyone approved of every popular game. A few activities obtained a stamp of approval from morally minded commentators, while other activities, perhaps because of their violence or impropriety, received condemnation.

One slightly controversial game was ice skating. In the winter, people strapped or screwed skates to the bottoms of their shoes and took to the ice. Gentlemen pushed ladies in swings but were cautioned by the *Spectator* to preserve their companions' modesty: "The lover who swings his lady is to tie her clothes very close together with his hat-band before she admits him to throw up her heels." Water sports of various kinds increased in popularity during the 18th century. People swam. For those who preferred to get less wet, one option was pleasure boating on rivers or the Atlantic Ocean, sometimes with the purpose of fishing, picnicking, or participating in or observing rowing competitions.

Fishing was relaxed enough to be considered appropriate for genteel women. A twig pole, a horsehair line, and a little cow brain or a few fish eyes for bait were sufficient for this characteristically calming pastime. Hunting, on the other hand, was a more complex social issue. Hunters faced a strict property requirement, and the rich generally guarded their privileges fiercely. Thus it became suspect for a laborer to own a dog or a gun. Indeed, it was not unusual for some landowners to set out vicious mantraps with which to snare and wound those who trespassed on their property.

Men and women alike rode for pleasure, although women rode sidesaddle, with their legs draped over the horse's left side and their upper body facing forward. The left foot was in a stirrup; the right leg was held up by a support built into the saddle. Men alone were both the jockeys and the principal patrons of horse racing, which came into its own as an organized sport in the 18th century. The Jockey Club, which codified racing rules, was founded in Newmarket in the early 1750s, but continuous records of races were kept as early as 1709.

Not all approved of races. Methodist preacher William Seward denounced them in the same breath with "balls, assemblies, whoredom, and drunkenness," and Parliament passed an act in 1739 designed "to restrain and prevent the excessive Increase of Horse Races." The act was ineffective, and working people continued to flock to the track.

Various team and field sports were popular in England—the newest and most fashionable was cricket. Cricket cut across class and gender lines. Lords, ladies, and laborers alike played the game. Rules were drawn up; gamblers bet furiously on matches; and spectators came in huge numbers (20,000 for a match between Kent and Hampshire in 1772). The "Hambledon men" dominated the game for most of the second half of the century, and the Hambledon women were no slouches either. A 1745 newspaper article reported that "the girls bowled, batted, ran and caught as well as any men could do in that game." Cricket even affected the royal succession when, in 1751, a cricket ball struck the 48-year-old heir to the throne, Prince Frederick, on the head, killing him and enabling his son to become George III.

Other sports included tennis, golf, and lawn bowling. The ultimate crowd-pleasing game, however, was football, in which the teams were each the size of a crowd. Each side might enlist hundreds of players for big interparish matches. Rules varied locally, emphasizing kicking, throwing, and carrying to different degrees; some used a small hard ball, whereas others used a leather-covered bladder.

Most people loved to gamble. They played hazard, a complicated dice game, or EO, a form of roulette. They bet on races, cricket, boxing matches, political events, births, and drinking contests. The government ran and authorized lotteries; indeed, lotteries provided the money needed to found the British Museum and Westminster Bridge. The national lottery existed with varying frequency throughout the 18th century.

Card and board games appealed to servants, King George III, and almost everyone in between. Many people played backgammon, draughts (checkers), cribbage, and chess. Card players enjoyed ombre, a three-person game played without the eights, nines, and tens in the deck; quadrille, a four-person game similar to ombre, overtook it in popularity in the second quarter of the century and was in turn ousted by whist, brag, basset, and put. Other indoor games, which hinged on puzzles and on guessing by an assembled company, included billiards and parlor games akin to charades.

Football, Played at the Marketplace. Football—or, as Americans typically call it, soccer—was a popular 18th-century English sport. © Library of Congress.

Both the torture and killing of animals and fights between humans were a prime source of entertainment. One of the most popular sports was cockfighting. Roosters—their wings and tails clipped and their legs fitted with long sharp spurs—were placed in the ring and pushed at each other until they began to fight. Battle continued until one of the birds stood crowing on its dead opponent's body. The most spectacular competition was the Welsh main, a tournament of 32 birds, with the survivors of each pairing advancing until only one bird was left alive.

Contests between humans were considered good fun, as well. Cudgeling, backswords, and singlestick, all of which involved combat with sticks, ended when blood was drawn. In cudgeling, the combatants each had two sticks, one with which to hit the opponent and one, covered with a bowl-shaped wicker shield, for defense. Singlestick, as the name implies, allowed only one stick per fighter, who agreed to have his unused hand tied behind his back.

Wrestling, like boxing, was a common sport. Although boxing was technically illegal, it survived through aristocratic patronage. In as many as 30 rounds, contestants fought with bare-fisted punches and head butts. Women boxed too, usually fighting other women but sometimes battling men. Some boxers, such as "Gentleman" John Jackson and Daniel Mendoza, became quite famous.

Not all pleasures were violent, of course. People increasingly enjoyed travel and tourism and journeying to scenic locations including medieval ruins, the Welsh mountains, and the Peak and Lake Districts. Poor or rich, there was joy to be had (Olsen, 147–50, 164–68).

To read about sports and games in Chaucer's England, see the Europe entry in the section "Sports and Games" in chapter 7 ("Recreational Life") of volume 2; for

Elizabethan England, see the England entry in the section "Games and Sports" in chapter 7 ("Recreational Life") of volume 3; and for Victorian England, see the Victorian England entry in the section "Sports" in chapter 7 ("Recreational Life") of volume 5 of this series.

FOR MORE INFORMATION

Lynch, J. *Eighteenth Century Resources.* <http://newark.rutgers.edu/~jlynch/18th/>, accessed October 10, 2003.

Malcolmson, R. W. *Popular Recreations in English Society, 1700–1850.* Cambridge, England: Cambridge University Press, 1973.

Olsen, K. *Daily Life in 18th-Century England.* Westport, Conn.: Greenwood Press, 1999.

FRANCE

By the 17th and 18th centuries, there had been so much interaction among the people of Europe that they enjoyed the same games and recreation. See the entry on England in this section for the games the Europeans enjoyed. Readers may also compare these games with those discussed in the entries from England, Spain, and Italy in the section "Games and Sports" in chapter 7 ("Recreational Life") of volume 3 of this series to get a fuller picture of the European games that the French also enjoyed.

RECREATIONAL
LIFE
|
GAMES
|
England

Japan

New England

Life at Sea

JAPAN

Games and sports were popular pastimes for some, but not all, Japanese. Those who lived in the countryside rarely had the time to participate in such activities, which city dwellers were more likely to enjoy, in part because they lived a more leisurely existence and in part because their surroundings comprised all manner of diversionary escapades.

Gambling originated from oracle and divination practices. Japanese commonly believed that the casting of bones, amulets, lots, and other shamanic indicators predicted fortune, thus furnishing a person with insight into the world of the unknown. In Japan, the sometimes perversely capricious *kami*, which were Shintō spirits, purportedly influenced human life through gambling.

In 18th-century Japan, neo-Confucian morality prompted samurai (warrior-administrators) to prohibit gambling among peasants. The punishments for gambling were so draconian that it was practically unknown in the provinces. Peasants were cut down on the spot if they were even suspected of gambling.

In the cities, however, gambling thrived among all classes. Most gambling took place within the Licensed Quarters, where all sorts of games were rife in every brothel, tea shop, and sake shop. A kind of dice was used, as were cards. Geisha (female servant-entertainers) and prostitutes were often used as lure to bring their customers into rigged games.

Predictably, a species of debt collector developed to serve the gambling enterprises. Samurai and *rikishi* (sumo wrestlers) down on their luck naturally gravitated toward such sidelines. Over time, pawnbrokers became very common. The *bakufu* (national military government) frowned on samurai pawning their swords, since these were not only symbols of class and station but family heirlooms, as well.

In a society where shamanic divination was traditionally accepted, it is not too surprising that various kinds of fortune-telling would be common and popular. Virtually every village had at least one diviner. Most were older unmarried females whose occupation it was to fall into a trance in order to "channel" the voices of the *kami* and one's ancestors. There were also "readers" of every omen and sign (tea dregs, animal entrails, and even chicken excrement). They tended to congregate in the (temporarily) dry riverbeds of every large town and city, where the *eta* (hereditary outcastes) resided.

The Daoist *I Ching*, based on the precepts of magic numerology, became very popular in Japan. The 64 possible combinations of six lines of solid or segmented lines were called hexagrams. Each was keyed to a specific cryptic divination in the *I Ching*, indicating the "path" of one's luck, or fortune. Most commonly, one's "fortune" contained ominous warnings of approaching evil that one could avoid by purchasing a cheap amulet or talisman from the selfsame seer. Many of the esoteric and magical symbols of Shintō and Buddhism appeared on these amulets.

Before or after their seemingly endless farm chores, peasant children could play tag, chase, swim, and the like. In the autumn, children played with fireflies and crickets. The latter's chirps (*mushi-kiki*) were considered to be soothing and "lucky." Tiny bamboo cages were made for captured crickets, and small birds were kept for their music. Children played a counting game much like the Western paper-scissors-rock game, as well as a game similar to marbles, but with chestnuts. Tree swings, rock skipping, hide-and-seek, capture the flag, and other such games were familiar to Japanese children in the countryside.

Farm children often received small, carved toys from doting relatives, although not from parents, who feared spoiling their own children. Whistles, flutes, tops, dolls, and other ingeniously wrought items were to be found everywhere.

 Snapshot

Pets in Japan

Japanese enjoyed the company of pets, including caged crickets and fireflies, as well as ponds with carp and goldfish. Aside from Pekinese breeds, dogs were not popular. Cats, on the other hand, were well liked. Particularly fashionable among shopkeepers were cats with one yellow eye and one green eye, representing the twin charms (a kind of "gambling") of gold and silver. (Dunn, 169–70)

At the annual *matsuri* (village festival), young men participated in wrestling matches and tugs-of-war. Thumb wrestling was also popular at *matsuri*. Two opponents would clasp fingers tightly in a kind of handshake and then struggle to see who could pin the other's thumb. A kind of leg wrestling (until recently, known commonly in the West as Indian wrestling) was played to lock the opponent's leg against one's own. A curious game to lift one's opponent off his feet while standing back-to-back was also popular.

Samurai had their own amusements and games. Most samurai played *go* (or *igo*), a warrior's strategy game that can be enormously complex and time-consuming. The principle of the game is to surround the opponent's stones (black or white) with one's own and thereby immobilize, or "freeze," them in place.

Flower cards were very popular among the intelligentsia. A deck consisted of 48 cards, divided into four suits of 12 cards: a bird, flower, butterfly, and poem for each of the 12 months. Another card game required one to remember allusions to 100 famous poems. Incense and perfume games (*kiki-ko*) remained popular among the elite. Contestants would be challenged to name the ingredients of blended odors.

Japanese played several ball games. In the oldest, called *kemari*, a court was marked out with four "trees" in the corners (representing the four seasons and four directions). Without using their hands, participants would then vie to keep a deerskin and bamboo ball aloft. Westerners familiar with hackey-sack would recognize the game. A stick of incense was burned as a timer for the game.

In Japanese field hockey, the object of the first half of the game was to carry, toss, and deposit the team's colored wooden balls into a small (about 18 inches in diameter) net goal while trying to prevent the opponents from doing the same. In the second half, both teams would scramble after one ball. The first team to score a goal won.

Another sport was dog shooting. Mounted archers would surround a dog and shoot rounds of padded arrows in turn to hone their archery skills. Another mounted archery "sport" was usually staged at the Shintō shrines dedicated to the *kami* of war, Hachiman. Mounted archers would gallop full-speed down approach lanes to fire arrows at small narrow targets, a sport requiring tremendous skills in both horsemanship and archery. Winners were said to "be at one with Hachiman."

Sumo (literally, simple dance) began not as a sport but rather as an oracle. It was thought that the *kami* would "answer" questions by favoring one wrestler over another. Shamans presided over the matches, which usually took place on shrine grounds. A simple circle was drawn in the dirt, and the first wrestler to be pushed out of the circle was deemed to have lost.

Troupes of professional sumo wrestlers (*rikishi*) belonged to organized houses (*beya*), which staged tournaments in all the major cities. These *beya* recruited and carefully groomed strapping young men for the sport. By the end of the 18th century, *rikishi* were pampered entertainers, chosen for their size, agility, and strength. Special diets added prodigious girth but shortened the lives of these giants. Former champions were allowed to maintain something of their status, acting as sumo elders.

By the 1740s, regular bouts were scheduled in Edo twice per year, and other tournaments were held in Ōsaka and Kyōto. The traditional rituals of hand clapping to attract the attention of the *kami* and foot stamping to drive away evil spirits now became stylized and obligatory. At the beginning of each day's matches, the wrestlers would parade in a circle, each costumed in a silk apron that was sumptuously embroidered with the crest of their patron daimyō (feudal warlord). Sumo, with its precise rules, professional judges, and printed advertisements, took on all the trappings of a marketable sport.

Eighteenth-century Japanese participated in many types of games and sports, with some sports, such as sumo wrestling, targeting spectators instead of participants. A fixation with gambling and divination, particularly among the wealthy and influential, contrasted with the precious few times during the year that peasants could take part in sports events and games of any kind (Perez, 242–44, 273–74, 276, 278, 280).

To read about sports in Japan in the 20th century, see the Japan entry in the section "Sports" in chapter 7 ("Recreational Life") of volume 6 of this series.

FOR MORE INFORMATION

Dunn, C. J. *Everyday Life in Traditional Japan*. Tokyo: Tuttle, 1969.
Guttmann, A. *Japanese Sports: A History*. Honolulu: University of Hawaii Press, 2001.
Japan Information Network. <http://www.jinjapan.org/index.html>, accessed October 23, 2003.
Perez, L. G. *Daily Life in Early Modern Japan*. Westport, Conn.: Greenwood Press, 2002.
Yamada, H. *Different Games, Different Rules: Why Americans and Japanese Misunderstand Each Other*. New York: Oxford University Press, 1997.

NEW ENGLAND

Unlike their Native American neighbors, colonial New Englanders were deeply ambivalent toward games and sports. On the one hand, recreation was a release from the demands of colonial life; on the other hand, Puritan beliefs made participation in such activities a sign of spiritual waywardness and even of impiety.

In seaside tribal gatherings during the summer and fall, Native Americans typically amused themselves with a variety of games—foot races, recreational swimming, games of marksmanship, and ball games similar to lacrosse. Native peoples in New England also enjoyed games of chance and had several games in which stones were used like dice. Children had their own games and toys, including balls and tops to be spun.

The games and sports that amused the populace in England—bowling, card playing, dice throwing, billiards, shuffleboard, angling, hunting, and horse racing—were familiar to 17th-century New Englanders. We find mention of them in official documents, diaries, and letters. The poetic chronicler of New England life, Edward Taylor, chose games to build his religious metaphors, suggesting that games were commonplace in colonial days. In his poem "The Preface," Taylor writes about bowling in the context of the sun. As for tennis, in the early form of which the players struck the ball with the flat of the hand rather than with a racket, Taylor observes, "I, as Tenis Ball, struck hard upon the ground, Back-bounce with shine." In "Meditation Eighteen," Taylor refers to several games in his effort to develop metaphors for the depraved human heart, mind, and will. Thus, we know that Barley-breaks is a game in which one couple attempts to block two other couples from getting past various lines; pingle is a small, enclosed playing area; and Coursey-Park is a game of chase played by a girl and a boy.

But the religious New Englanders of the 17th century frowned on these games. The Puritans who dominated New England held views of leisure that caused them to discourage most of the games that amused English and Europeans. New Englanders, in general, criminalized many recreational activities.

Three dogmatic biases lay at the bottom of the New Englanders' negative view of most games. First was their suspicion that the faculty of imagination was an agent of the devil, leading to immorality and defiance of God. Second, Puritans believed that idleness was one of the chief sins of human beings and caused people to forget the necessity of hard work and to lapse into immorality. Third, Puritans were biased against amusement because of their fierce disapproval of the Roman Catholic Church and its sacraments and rituals.

For the most part, if people did their work, did not create disturbances, and did not gamble or dishonor the Sabbath, they were left alone to play most games in their own houses. Still, participation in games in public houses was made illegal in 1646:

Upon complaint of the disorders, about the use of the Games of Shuffle-board and Bowling, in and about Houses of Common- entertainment, whereby much precious time is spent unprofitably, and much waste of Wine and Beer occasioned;

It is Ordered by this Court and the Authority thereof, That no person shall henceforth use the said Games of Shuffleboard, or Bowling, or any other Play or Game, in or about any such House.

In 1670, the court, responding to what it saw as an increase in card playing, made the mere possession of cards or dice a crime because it was assumed that the playing of cards necessarily involved gambling. In 1674, under laws relating to soldiering, some individuals expressed concern that members of the militia often gambled away their weapons and ammunition.

Horse racing was also made illegal near towns and major roadways in 1677 because it involved gambling and misspending time, "drawing of many persons from the duty of their particular Callings."

Some New Englanders who "employed" indentured servants frowned upon their absence from the farm, business, or house and as a consequence, drastically curtailed their amusements. The indentured servant's time was not his or her own but belonged to the master. Employers believed that when servants were not actually working, they should be resting up for the next day's labors.

The peculiar New England suspicions surrounding amusements affected colonial children and games. The most apparent instance of Puritan hostility to children's games took place during the early days of the Salem witchcraft episode. In Salem, a group of young girls spent some of their leisure time playing and dancing in the forest. The girls had also played a game of dropping raw egg into cups of hot water to see if the shapes it made suggested something about their future husbands. To a 21st-century mind, this might appear unremarkable, but to Salem Puritans, it was an ominous sign and a deadly combination, as the girls well knew. When confronted, the girls lied to cover up their frolic in the woods, successfully absolving themselves of responsibility by implicating a servant in witchcraft. Thus a whole sequence of horrendous events violently unfolded that divided New England and that resulted in the imprisonment and sometimes in the execution of innocent people and the ruination of literally hundreds of lives. The catalyst for this tragic episode in colonial history was a children's game.

In the 18th century, with the infusion of more urbane Englishmen, games of various kinds became commonplace. Announcements made frequent note of horse races, including one in Cambridge in 1715. Also mentioned were hog racing and bear baiting. New Englanders established a bowling green in Boston in 1700 and openly played billiards and ninepins in the 18th century. In 1720, merchants were selling decks of cards in Boston.

The diary of Samuel Sewall illustrates the overall ambiguity that colonial New Englanders—especially of the 17th-century variety—exhibited toward sports and games. In May 1689, when Sewall was a young man, he made the rounds of a number of taverns and ended up playing ninepins at one of them. In August 1715, some 26 years later, he helped break up a game of ninepins on what was officially referred to as Mount-Whoredom near what is now Louisburg Square on Beacon Hill in Boston (Johnson, 120, 125–27, 130, 140, 166).

FOR MORE INFORMATION

Boorstin, D. J. *The Americans: The Colonial Experience*. New York: Random House, 1958.
Johnson, C. D. *Daily Life in Colonial New England*. Westport, Conn.: Greenwood Press, 2002.

LIFE AT SEA

The sailor needed diversion—known as "idle time"—from the utter and seemingly interminable boredom that he faced at sea. The uncertainty of surviving severe weather, the adventure of the chase, and the danger of capture were high drama indeed, but such excitement could be counted in hours on voyages that lasted three and four years.

Before the temperance movement gained popularity in the middle of the 19th century, taverns and alehouses were in many cases considered respectable men's clubs, and they served not only as public centers for political gatherings, assemblies of merchants or ships' officers, and fertile fields for the hiring of crews and workmen but also as places of entertainment. These establishments provided wholesome diversions in the form of card games, bowling, shuffleboard, music, and singing. Gambling was rampant and socially acceptable.

Cards, dice, dominoes, backgammon, and checkers were popular games among crew members. Watching a game was likely to sustain as much interest as would partaking in it. Sailor Robert Ferguson wrote about a checker game on the *Kathleen*:

All hands except the man at the wheel and those on lookout, stood around watching every move, even the captain. You could have heard a pin drop. The game lasted two hours and Otto won. All the Portuguese stood around with their mouths open. The captain said he

RECREATIONAL
LIFE
|
GAMES
|
England

Japan

New England

Life at Sea

would like to try a game with Otto some day. The cooper told me that our Captain, on the last voyage, beat all the other whaling captains in St. Helena and won fifty dollars.

Checkerboards were likely to be laid out on a piece of painted canvas or on the lid of a sea chest, and the pieces might be made of anything handy, even of buttons from old garments. Amateur craftsmen on board ship fashioned more elaborate, handmade checkerboards, perhaps inlaid with fine woods and ivory, but these were meant to be either sold or given as gifts. Ferguson noted, "For the past few days I have been working on my checkerboard, using pieces of rosewood, ebony satinwood and sandalwood."

Dominoes were especially popular with sailors from continental Europe, but the worldliness of sailors exposed them to many cultures. The austere Protestant background of some New England captains led them to frown upon card playing even though the stakes were more likely to be in tobacco than in shillings or dollars. "I have seen a half dozen seated around a chest a pile of tobacco in the center, greasy cards, playing bluff or all-fours and watching the game as if their very existence depended upon the winning or losing a few pounds of tobacco." Diarist William Whitecar further related a growing alarm among some members of the crew who saw the green hands repeatedly suffering losses at the hands of a certain group of cronies. High words and quarreling naturally followed. Finally, complaints were made to the captain, who offered a bounty of a pound of tobacco for every deck of cards turned into the officers. This strategy was successful, and several decks of contraband cards were thrown overboard.

Monotony, homesickness, and tension were natural outgrowths of a situation during which crews were forced into limited space for extended periods of time. Men welcomed activities that allowed them to focus on the work at hand, relieving the ennui and furnishing them with a detachment that acted as a surrogate for the privacy denied them in incredibly cramped quarters. With mental escape of more importance than the time that an activity consumed, seamen and officers lavished substantial energy and meticulous attention to the pursuit at hand (Volo and Volo, 4, 136, 141, 143).

FOR MORE INFORMATION

Thrower, W. R. *Life at Sea in the Age of Sail*. London: Phillimore, 1972.

Volo, D. D., and J. M. Volo. *Daily Life in the Age of Sail*. Westport, Conn.: Greenwood Press, 2002.

Holidays

During the 17th and 18th centuries, acts of celebration were important for their psychological and social value. Moreover, those who celebrated were from all ranks of society, whether they made their home in sub-Saharan Africa, in colonial Australia, along the frontier regions of colonial North America, on the island nations of England and Japan, in the colonies of New England, or aboard oceangoing vessels. Given the many variations among these cultures' respective holidays, it is interesting to note that cross-cultural types of holidays did, in fact, exist. People celebrated the completion of work, their ancestors, political events, and religious affairs.

Work was such a common and often dreary feature of daily life that the completion of a project merited a festive interruption before proceeding to the next round of labor. The most common work-related holiday was the harvest festival, which was celebrated across cultures. New Englanders recognized the harvest of their crops with a celebration that today has the name of Thanksgiving in the United States. In Africa, the harvest festivals of the Great Lakes region were called *umuganuro*. Native Americans practiced their own rites of thanksgiving, as did the English and Japanese. Indeed, the most celebrated day of the year in Japan was the famous harvest festival, Shukaku. When whaling vessels, which often spent months away from home, met out at sea, the crews would put down their compasses and harpoons to spend a day filled with song, dance, good food, and even better drink. The colonial Australians, upon first arriving in Australia on February 7, 1788, celebrated with abandon the arduous work that made the oceanic trek possible.

The spirits of deceased ancestors acquired a reverence among the masses that is no longer visible in contemporary Western cultures. The Japanese festival of the dead, or *obon*, was akin to Halloween, as the Christian Kongolese practiced it. On this day, Christians in the Congo mixed a celebration of their religious beliefs with open worship of their ancestors.

An excuse to hold a holiday sometimes originated from a political event. In England (and colonial Australia), merrymakers celebrated Guy Fawkes' Day, named after a man who, on November 5, 1605, failed to blow up Parliament. African kings and chiefs frequently integrated themselves into work-related and religious holidays, assigning—by virtue of their established power—honor and tribute to themselves. During times of crisis, New Englanders held community-wide vigils, at which the colonists prayed, fasted, declared their sins, and repented. Happier gatherings followed New England town meetings, when the important business of local government ceded to a more cheerful tone. Along North America's frontiers, Indian communities held ceremonial adoptions for outsiders, who were often settlers whom the tribe's warriors had captured during a raid. These ceremonies were essentially an invitation to the adoptees (who were typically terrified) to be one with the tribe.

Religious holidays were important. Many Africans celebrated traditional Christian or Muslim holidays. For the Muslim Juula of West Africa, Ramadan was a day of fast and prayer, as it has been for so many Muslims around the world. Christmas was a great holiday in England. The Puritans of New England, by comparison, at first refused to celebrate Christmas, claiming that such indulgences desecrated the sanctity of the birth of Jesus.

Holidays related to work, ancestors, politics, and religion dominated the celebratory landscape of many 17th- and 18th-century cultures. Nonetheless, these categories are by no means exhaustive. For instance, Valentine's Day in England was for star-crossed lovers, as was Tanabata in Japan. Perhaps every event—happy or sad—can generate an observance of some kind.

~*Peter Seelig*

FOR MORE INFORMATION

Macdonald, M. R., ed. *The Folklore of World Holidays*. Detroit, Mich.: Gale Research, 1992.

AFRICA

Celebration has represented an important part of every culture, including those of 17th- and 18th-century Africa. Africans celebrated sacred occurrences, honored their ancestors, and marked important times of the calendar and life cycle. In addition, communities gathered for feasts following the completion of important tasks as a way of celebrating jobs well done by the community. During these times, people reaffirmed their identities and renewed bonds with each other, ideally strengthening African communities against the hardships of early modern life.

In West Africa, work itself could become a significant celebration. When a roof needed to be built, men would divide into teams starting from one side of the building. People otherwise uninvolved came to watch and cheer for the competing teams while the workers sang and strove to put the poles in place, sew thatch, or install the supporting framework on the eaves. Following the event, the person whose roof it was held a celebration involving feasting and dancing while people debated the relative merits of the day's achievements compared with similar tasks from the past. In this way, people came together to help those who needed it while taking community pride in their abilities to help the group (July, 115–16).

Another kind of festival common in sub-Saharan Africa was the harvest festival. In most cultures during agricultural festivals, kings and chiefs played important roles as custodians of the harvest, rainmakers, or as symbols of the kingdom itself. In areas with well-developed political systems, such occasions prompted local leaders to reaffirm their loyalty to the state. A typical agricultural festival was the *umuganuro* from the Great Lakes region. The centerpiece of this event was a special meal in which the king and other elites ate sorghum before a new crop. This was called "eating the new year." Special ritual farmers tended the sorghum that the rulers consumed. Chiefs from all around the kingdom attended the ceremony, at which participants of various statures greeted one another with sorghum (for the court), honey beer, cows, and food.

Diviners went among the flocks to determine which bulls should be sacrificed and when the festival should take place. On the day selected, the king and important women from the court moved into a special palace while the ritual farmers prepared a large ball of sorghum paste. The king then ate some and broke the rest into four balls, which he distributed to representatives before having sex with one of the women. Next, he sounded a royal drum, which elicited cries of joy from the assembled throngs. Singers and dancers from each territory would take turns entertaining the king, who gave gifts in exchange for praise poems from the bards (Schoenbrun, 255–56).

When Africans converted to other religions, they adopted the holidays and festivals of the new tradition but often adapted them in ways that made the most sense in their particular culture. Hence, among the Christians of Kongo, Halloween became the holiest day of the year, a day dedicated to commemorating the spirits of the ancestors. Most African societies had ancestor festivals in which the spirits of those departed would return among the living and inhabit the body of a relative who wore a ritual mask dedicated to them. On Kongolese Halloweens, family members gathered to recite the rosary and then formed a candlelit procession that proceeded in the direction of the cemeteries where ancestors were buried. The king observed this day, as well, making a pilgrimage to the graves of past rulers. People placed their candles in circles around the graves, afterward pronouncing another rosary. These processions and vigils lasted throughout the night, before all attended a special mass on November 1, All Saints' Day. People also left a pile of offerings next to an image of a skeleton, which was placed by an altar in the capital's main square. The church then took these offerings (Thornton, 31).

Islam, too, had many festivals, such as the birthday of the Muslim prophet Muhammad and the Eid al-Fitr, or Feast of the Sacrifice, commemorating the day when Ibrahim, the biblical Abraham, offered to sacrifice his son to God. The most important festival, however, remained Ramadan, which, as the holy month dedicated to fasting and prayer, was one of the five pillars of Islam. During this time, people attended the mosque more frequently as they sought to better themselves and to understand God's will. At night, however, when the fast ended among the Juula of West Africa, people feasted while children performed special masquerades in which the older ones directed the younger. On the 27th of Ramadan, the night when Muslims believe that Muhammad received his first revelation, good angels were said to descend on the world. In celebration of this night, the Juula held special dances at which members of different lineages showed off their talents until dawn (Bravmann, 503–5).

African celebrations represented times of community togetherness and the reaffirmation of tradition. People performed their religious observances, seeking to better themselves and to pay homage to that which they believed governed the world. Feasting was common, as people bonded through meals and displayed the pride of their lineages through hard work and the performance of dance and music. Perhaps most important, it was through celebration that people broke the routine of their daily lives and participated in something different, something that led them both to examine themselves and to enjoy what life had to offer.

~Brian Ulrich

FOR MORE INFORMATION

Bravmann, R. A. "Islamic Art and Material Culture in Africa." In *The History of Islam in Africa*, ed. Nehemia Levtzion and Randall L. Pouwels. Athens: Ohio University Press, 2000.

Halsall, P., ed. *Internet African History Sourcebook.* 1996. <http://www.fordham.edu/halsall/africa/africasbook.html>, accessed October 23, 2003.

July, R. W. *A History of the African People.* 5th ed. Prospect Heights, Ill.: Waveland Press, 1998.

Schoenbrun, D. L. *A Green Place, a Good Place.* Portsmouth, N.H.: Heinemann, 1998.

Thornton, J. K. *The Kongolese Saint Anthony.* Cambridge, England: Cambridge University Press, 1998.

COLONIAL AUSTRALIA

Aborigines integrated song, dance, and performance into their spiritual and ritual commemorations and had little concept of them as mere diversion. For the European newcomers, as one contemporary noted, any festivity held an increased importance in their "forlorn and distant circle" (Tench, 66). Although white society was more concerned with the exigencies of everyday survival, it experienced some recreational life.

The first celebration for the early colonists was on February 7, 1788, to mark the end of their arduous voyage to Australia and to mark the British Empire's appropriation of Australian land. Three volleys were fired, the proclamation was read, and European music was played on fifes and drums, as the first governor, Arthur Phillip reviewed the assembly of settlers. The previous evening, a spontaneous party broke out among convicts and officers alike when the convict women were brought ashore. One witness described it as "a scene of debauchery and riot," although the willing participation of the vastly outnumbered women is debatable. At times, the authorities and the clergy fumed about convict "depravity," but sexual excess was an inevitable diversion for many women and men in the isolated community.

Organized entertainment was not introduced for the first decade, although holidays were usually granted in honor of the king's birthday. Such days occasionally brought pardons and emancipation. The first celebration of the king's birthday began with a 21-gun salute. Four male convicts were pardoned and freed; a three-day holiday was then declared for all convicts. Liquor was distributed, and the day ended with bonfires.

Dance was integral to the festivities involving early Australian settlers. Formal dance was first performed as an interlude to theatrical presentations. The first official ball was held about 1800. Informal dance was a part of the life of poorer settlers and convicts. Their celebrations included wedding feasts where the less-privileged colonists danced traditional English folk dances or Irish jigs. In the absence of appropriate venues, dances were often held on board ships at anchor in the harbor. On such occasions, regimental bands played cheerful tunes, and spectators enjoyed a display of fireworks.

Although Governor Phillip had legal authority to establish fairs, the first large gala was not held until 1810, when Governor Macquarie authorized a weeklong fair at Parramatta. Horse racing dominated the event, which also featured foot racing, boxing, and "wheelbarrow" and sack races, two popular 18th-century fairground games. Macquarie actively promoted organized recreation, which, by his time, had begun to assume a momentum of its own, as the penal society embraced every opportunity for recreational life.

At times, holidays featured "prohibited amusements," and cockfighting was an especially popular diversion, as was bare-knuckle fighting between males who competed for a purse and who often fought each other in the absence of formal rules. Horse-match races were held in a similar spirit.

The privileged entertained themselves with musical soirees and card games in the drawing rooms of the fortunate few. For the poor, drinking and gambling offered opportunities of oblivion. Spontaneous celebration included April Fool's pranks. A report in the *Sydney Gazette* in 1804 noted that a group of boys "formed a cavalcade" for the first possible commemoration in the colony of Guy Fawkes' Day.

Anything resembling a holiday, vacation, or off time, in general, afforded colonial Australians with an excuse to attend the theater. The first theater performance in New South Wales took place on June 4, 1789, and was a convict-initiated performance of Farquhar's *The Recruiting Officer*. The 1706 satire was popular throughout the 18th century, and its military theme no doubt influenced the governor's decision to allow the event. The first regular theater performances began on Norfolk Island in 1793. A playhouse was constructed, and monthly productions were staged from May 1793 until January 1794. They were halted after a group of troublesome soldiers precipitated a riot. Theater continued in Sydney intermittently from 1796 to 1798 but was ended because of constant thefts from the vacant homes of the audience. Theater waxed and waned over the following decade.

Because of the constant military presence in the colony, music was often of a martial nature, although naval surgeon George Worgan brought a piano along with the First Fleet. He presented it to Elizabeth Macarthur on his departure in 1791. The first opera performed in 1796 was William Shield's *The Poor Soldier*. Folk ballads and convict laments were sung among prisoners and poorer settlers.

When Elizabeth Macarthur arrived in 1790, she was the first well-educated and cultured European woman in Australia, and she created a social set around her, drawn from her small pool of peers. Preferring decidedly more muted entertainment, these few fortunate women enjoyed the pleasure of bush walks and harborside picnics by day and soirees with their male companions by night. Indeed, the more polished among colonial Australia's population might opt not for a celebratory night life involving raucous parties, but for an evening with the colony's only newspaper, the *Sydney Gazette*, which was a weekly published from 1803 and which, despite being essentially an organ for government orders, featured news and sometimes poetry and puzzles.

~Valda Rigg

FOR MORE INFORMATION

Cumes, J. W. C. *Their Chastity Was Not Too Rigid*. Melbourne: Longman Cheshire, 1979.
Bladen, F., ed. *Historical Records of New South Wales*. Vols. 1–6. Sydney: Government Printer, 1892. Facsimile edition, Marrickville: Southwood Press, 1978.

Jordan, R. *Convict Theatres of Early Australia, 1788–1840*. Strawberry Hills, Australia: Currency House, 2002.

Tench, W. *1788: Comprising A Narrative of the Expedition to Botany Bay [1789] and A Complete Account of the Settlement at Port Jackson [1795]*. Edited by Tim Flannery. Melbourne: Text Publishing, 1996.

Waterhouse, R. *Private Pleasures, Public Leisure: A History of Popular Culture since 1788*. Melbourne: Longman Australia, 1995.

THE COLONIAL FRONTIER OF NORTH AMERICA

The most distinct ceremony of North America's colonial frontiers embraced both Native Americans and settlers. This entry focuses on a thoroughly ceremonial event that was unique to both Native Americans and settlers along the colonial frontier and that involved the adoption by native peoples of non-natives (residents of the colonial settlements). Indians who captured settlers sometimes kept them alive, attempting to integrate them into the clan or tribe as fellow members. Central to this attempt was the adoption ceremony, which, despite many variations, revealed a curious mixture of hostility and compassion.

Native Americans sometimes absorbed captive settlers into the native community. Adoptions were made to make up for demographic losses resulting from war or disease, or to appease those who were in mourning for the loss of a loved one. Warren Johnson, brother to the superintendent of Indian Affairs, William Johnson, noted the practice in his journal: "When the Indians lose a man in action, & chance to take an enemy prisoner, he belongs to the family of the deceased, who take great care of him, & look on him in the same light as on the person lost & even leave him the same fortune."

The adoption process commenced with a ceremony that proved threatening to most captives. Mary Jemison recalled, "During my adoption I sat motionless, nearly terrified to death at the appearance and actions of the company, expecting every moment to feel their vengeance, and suffer death on the spot." The frenzied dancing and "hallooing and yelling in a tremendous manner" proved most intimidating to the abductees. Jemison recalled being engulfed in a circle of squaws who "immediately set up a most dismal howling, crying bitterly, and wringing their hands in all the agonies of grief for a deceased relative." Susanna Johnson recalled, "The figure [of the dance] consisted of [a] circular motion round the fire. Each sang his own music, and the best dancer was the one most violent in motion. The prisoners were taught each a song, mine was, danna witchee natchepung; my son's was nar wiscumpton."

James Smith recorded that his adoption ceremony began with the old chief making a long speech and then presenting him to three squaws, who led him down the riverbank and into the water. "The squaws then made signs for me to plunge myself into the water, but I did not understand them. I thought that the result of the council was that I should be drowned, and that these young ladies were to be the executioners." Eventually, one of the women led him to understand that they meant him no harm, and he surrendered himself to be "washed and scrubbed severely." James was then returned to the council house and given new clothes including "a ruffled shirt, . . . a pair of leggings done with ribbons and beads, porcupine quills, and red hair; also a tinsel laced cappo." Through an interpreter, he was told, "My son, you have now nothing to fear. We are now under the same obligations to love, support and defend you that we are to love and defend one another. Therefore you are to consider yourself as one of our people."

Some captives were surrendered to a ceremonial gauntlet in which members of the entire village hit them with axe handles, tomahawks, clubs, and switches. An ex-captive described the ceremony of running the gauntlet: "There is at the entry of the fort gate a heap of squaws and children who stand ready to receive [the captive] with their sticks, clubs, poles, and fire brands, who lay on with all their force and might till he gets into the wigwam where he is to live." These blows, while real, were not applied in a manner to do mortal harm, however, and in some cases were more symbolic than actual. Young captives were often exempt from this portion of the ritual. Some people believe that the action of Pocahontas throwing her body over John Smith at the moment of his execution was also part of an adoption ritual. Many of these ceremonies have been interpreted as representing the death of a former way of life and a rebirth into the Indian community.

Mary Jemison noted, "In the course of that ceremony, from mourning they became serene—joy sparked in their countenances, and they seemed to rejoice over me as over a long lost child. . . . [A]t the close of the ceremony the company retired, and my sisters went about employing every means for my consolation and comfort." Susanna Johnson reported that "the interpreter came to inform me that I was adopted into his family. I was then introduced to the family, and I was told to call them brothers and sisters." The adoptees were often given gifts such as a new pair of moccasins, a shirt, or a dress.

The papers of William Johnson contain the following remarks, which were attributed to the Shawnee who presented the returning captives at Fort Pitt: "We have taken as much care of these prisoners, as if they were [our] own flesh, and blood; they are become unacquainted with your customs, and manners, and therefore, father we request you will use them tender, and kindly, which will be the means of inducing them to live contentedly with you."

Thus the adoption ceremony signified a momentous integration of settlers into a native community. "Vengeance," "grief," "consolation," and "comfort" were some of the emotions that these ceremonies provoked in both the Indian and colonial participants. Not all captives chose to return to their former communities. Some captives married Indians or other captives and lived the remainder of their lives among their adopted Indian families. Cadwallader Colden, surveyor-general and member of the king's council of New York addressed this fact in 1747: "No arguments, no entreaties, no tears of their friends and relations, could persuade many of them to leave their new Indian friends and acquaintance[s]; several of them that were by the caressings of their relations persuaded to come home, in a little time grew tired of our manner of living, and run away again to the Indians and ended their days with them" (Volo and Volo, 240, 242–44).

FOR MORE INFORMATION

Demos, J. *The Unredeemed Captive*. New York: Vintage Books, 1994.

Volo, J. M., and D. D. Volo. *Daily Life on the Old Colonial Frontier*. Westport, Conn.: Greenwood Press, 2002.

ENGLAND

The celebration of holidays was a cyclical phenomenon that divided the year into distinct parts. The smallest division occurred after each week, the holiday being the weekend or day or days off. The next-smallest division took place from one month to the next. After that, the passage of the seasons inspired anticipation for celebrations associated in some way with the time of year. Holidays embodied numerous motivations for making merry: exhaustion at one's trade, religious sentiment, political or national anniversaries, local commemoration, agricultural turning points, and seasonal developments.

The workweek technically included Monday through Saturday, but in some jobs, where workers were based at home and set their own schedules, there was greater flexibility. In these cases, Sunday's holiday tended to extend into Monday; those who took a long weekend in this manner were said to be observing "Saint Monday." Weavers, cutlers, cobblers, colliers, and a host of other workers spent Monday drinking, gambling, and watching cockfights. In addition, Monday was often the day set aside for the weekly market, conferring a sort of authority on this informal holiday.

For those who honored Saint Monday, there was a price to pay. Taking off an extra day or two meant that Wednesday, Thursday, Friday, and Saturday were days of long and grueling labor. Thus, in these trades, the four days of hard work in a week could last 16 or 17 hours.

Sundays were relatively restful and quiet. Religious organizations policed observance of the Sabbath by prosecuting offenders. Sunday was overwhelmingly the day for church wakes. Trade and most public entertainments were forbidden, and foreign visitors found the Sabbath a somber day; however, even if most theaters and exhibitions were closed, people discovered ways to enjoy themselves. Working people walked to nearby mineral spas, simply milled about in an "unruly and unmannerly" fashion, and then walked home again at night. Others went to church and then rested at home with their families.

Market, churchgoing, and work marked the passage of the week, and other cycles and celebrations marked the passage of months and seasons. For most people, special occasions delineated the year: the king's birthday; regional fairs; the "beating of the bounds," during which a procession marked the territorial boundaries of the parish; birthdays; and trade processions.

Spring brought the culmination of the London season; Parliament's business, which had begun in November, concluded in April, and the social season ended in June. It was the season of Easter, in February or early March, with violent football games in the streets. Other spring holidays were pagan or secular in origin. May 28 was the birthday of George I; May 29 was the anniversary of the restoration of the monarchy in 1660. May Day, May 1, was a day of morris dancing, fertility symbols, flirting, and chimney sweeps' processions.

In the summer, most of the fashionable crowd left London for watering places such as Epsom and Richmond. Those who remained entertained themselves at Vauxhall and at the Royal Academy's art exhibition.

In November, Parliament returned to its business, and the people turned their attention toward the patriotic celebrations of November 5. On that day in 1688, William III landed in Devonshire to oust the Catholic King James II. It was also Guy Fawkes' Day, the anniversary of the failure of Fawkes' 1605 plot to blow up the Houses of Parliament.

Alongside nationally celebrated holidays were local celebrations and gatherings. Although gentry were increasingly suppressing them and entrepreneurs miffed at the loss of work time, gatherings such as wakes, holiday feasts, and fairs were important in the lives of working people. The wake was an annual celebration of the parish church's founding. Often, the feasting and celebration carried over into the following day or week. A fair was a longer revel, lasting two to six weeks, although few people, besides pickpockets and prostitutes, would attend every day. The fair's ostensible purpose was business—selling wool, buying livestock, or hiring servants—but its real business was entertainment. Both wakes and fairs featured any or all of the following: courting, dancing, wrestling, races, eating contests, music, and raffles. Festive foods were available, such as gingerbread, nuts, or roast pork.

Christmas came and went. Twelve days after Christmas, the English celebrated Twelfth Night. February 14 was St. Valentine's Day. And so the year passed, through the darkness of winter and back to spring (Olsen, 115–18, 155–57).

To read about holidays in Victorian England, see the Victorian England entry in the section "Holidays and Festivals" in chapter 7 ("Recreational Life") of volume 5 of this series.

FOR MORE INFORMATION

Brand, J. *Observations on Popular Antiquities Chiefly Illustrating the Origin of Our Vulgar Customs, Ceremonies, and Superstitions.* London: Chatto and Windus, 1900.

Christian, R. *Old English Customs.* New York: Hastings House, 1967.

Lynch, J. *Eighteenth Century Resources.* <http://newark.rutgers.edu/~jlynch/18th/>, accessed October 10, 2003.

Olsen, K. *Daily Life in 18th-Century England.* Westport, Conn.: Greenwood Press, 1999.

JAPAN

During the early modern period, the Japanese year was punctuated by a series of holidays that sometimes inaugurated festivals. These holidays reflected much that was central to the life of peasants and their villages. Seasonal rhythms that affected agricultural activities and religious commemorations were the two most prominent grounds for holding the cyclical holidays of 18th-century Japan.

Amusements and leisure pastimes were rare things for most adults because life was very harsh for most of the country. The only "leisure" time from which peasants profited arose between their never-ending agrarian tasks; and peasants spent that time making items to ease their lives somewhat. Weaving straw and reed baskets, sandals, hats, raincoats, and various mats took up much of the time during the winter. The only real leisure for farmers was at the various harvest-time holidays (*matsuri*), the New Year, and rituals in honor of the tutelary *kami* (spirits).

> *Everyone was required to clean one's house to drive out both ritual pollution and real dirt.*

Throughout the 18th century, the Japanese year was a highly structured round of observances that began with New Year's (*oshogatsu*). In the lunar calendar used in the 18th century, *oshogatsu* began around the middle of January with bonfires at the entrances of the village or *machi* (city wards) to light the way for the *kami*. Everyone was required to clean one's house thoroughly to drive out both ritual pollution and real dirt. Once cleaned, the home received protection from the Shintō holy rope called *shimenawa*, a double-braided straw rope representing the threshold between the sacred and the profane.

Pounded-rice cakes (*mochi*) were added to the special vegetable stews (*zoni*) that celebrants cooked. Ritual decorations were made of special branches. Parents bestowed gifts on their children, and the whole family made a round of visits to honor teachers, patrons, and supervisors.

Traditionally, *oshogatsu* was the time to settle all debts from the previous year—to start the year with a clean financial slate. In some areas, particularly among the samurai (warrior-administrators), people would visit the nearby shrine devoted to the *kami* of war, Hachiman. There, they would buy a ritual white-fletched arrow to ensure good luck for the coming year. It was believed that all of the year's bad fortune would be attached to the arrow, which would then be burned when one bought a new arrow the following *oshogatsu*.

On the 15th day of the first month, the whole country paused to commemorate the anniversary of Buddha's death. Sutras were read around the clock, and for a small gift, priests could be persuaded to think of a person's ancestors during the chanting.

Two weeks later, the first day of spring was observed (corresponding to February 3), prompting another ritual cleansing. People hurled toasted soya beans into the corners of the house and shouted, "Out with the devils!" (*oni wa soto*). Then, one went out into the garden and coaxed the good fortune to come inside by shouting, "In with good luck!" (*fuku wa uchi*).

At the ides of March, Japan celebrated the vernal equinox. Another round of offerings was made to the *kami*, as well as to the Buddha. It was a time to visit and clean the ancestral graves. Traditionally, water was poured over the grave markers to perform a ritual cleaning of all pollution.

In most areas of Japan, March was the traditional rice-planting season, so a festival to "go up into the fields" (*ta ue*) inspired the peasants for the collective work. On auspicious days, local shamans and geomancers performed complex numerological and astrological computations to schedule festivals for the transplanting of rice or to drive insects away.

Among the most colorful of the celebrations was the flower festival (*hana matsuri*), which came in the first week of the fourth month. At this time, villagers trudged up into the nearby hills to picnic and gather wildflowers. This symbolically represented the recruitment of "mountain" *kami* for domestication as "paddy-rice" *kami*. This *matsuri* coincided with the birthday of the Buddha (April 8), when temples held ceremonies at which villagers poured tea sweetened with licorice over Buddhist statues.

The sixth month was the most dangerous cycle in Japan. It coincided not only with the start of typhoon season but also with a period when many diseases circulated in the countryside. The month was full of unlucky days, so people celebrated very few holidays and were rarely married at this time. The summer solstice (June 22) was said to be particularly precarious. A grand purification ceremony (*oharai*) was celebrated at the end of the month throughout the country. Functioning as ritual scapegoats, paper dolls received all of the evils and were then burned at temples and shrines.

The seventh month brought a sense of relief and regeneration. The poignant star festival (*Tanabata*) was celebrated to commemorate the annual conjoining of the star-crossed lovers (Vega and Altair), the herdsman and the weaver. The two had been sentenced to rendezvous in the heavens only once per year.

In the middle of the month, Japanese welcomed their ancestors back into the home at the festival of the dead (*obon*). For two or three days, the whole village feted the spirits with gifts of food, sake, and dances. Priests made most of their income through the sale of amulets during this period. Finally, the now-satiated and contented ancestors returned to the netherworld. Villagers nostalgically gathered at the banks of the river to reminisce as they watched the current carry their ancestors away on bright, floating lanterns.

The eighth month usually coincided with the first weeks of harvest. In this month, regionalism was prominent, as particular areas loosely determined the celebration of various festivals. The most common to the country was moon viewing (*tsukimi*), when the moon was brightest in the heavens. Two weeks later, the harvest festival (*shukaku*) took place once the crop was in the storehouses. Without doubt, this *matsuri* was the most joyous of the year, always celebrated before the tax collectors came to take away the samurais' share of the rice. Often, villagers opened and consumed the last casks of the year's sake production at this time.

The autumnal equinox (*aki no higan*) in the ninth month corresponded to the end of the growing season, and Japanese offered special gifts to the wind *kami* to ward off the end of the typhoon season.

The twelfth month, like the sixth month, was a dangerous time. The country prayed to the water *kami* to overpower evil and to protect the villages from bad fortune. Preparations began for New Year's in the middle of the month, called "the beginning of things." Houses were repaired, evil spirits were exorcised, and the *shimenawa* were strung out at the entrance to protect the house. The winter solstice (December 22) accelerated preparations for the new year. On the last night of the year, visits were made to shrines to expel malignant spirits. Then the religious calendar started all over again with another *oshogatsu matsuri* (Perez, 64–69, 273).

FOR MORE INFORMATION

Dunn, C. J. *Everyday Life in Traditional Japan*. Tokyo: Tuttle, 1969.

Japan Information Network. <http://www.jinjapan.org/index.html>, accessed October 23, 2003.

Perez, L. G. *Daily Life in Early Modern Japan*. Westport, Conn.: Greenwood Press, 2002.

NEW ENGLAND

Native Americans ritualized various ceremonies and holidays with tobacco and powwows, in particular. Puritan colonists, despite their deep Christian beliefs, outlawed the celebration of Christmas during most of the 17th century. Nevertheless, other holidays appeared on the celebratory horizon, including public fasts (more somber than celebratory) and community gatherings that followed the completion of a harvest or the construction of a home. Resistant to the Puritanical interdiction of merriment in New England were Thomas Morton and his Merry Mounters, who made revelry the reason for living. Finally, black slaves in New England recognized the holiday called "election day," which received the patronage of their white masters.

Every garden outside a wigwam included tobacco, which Native Americans seem to have used sparingly and mostly in pipes during social gatherings and for ceremonial purposes. The tobacco plant and the smoke from the plant were considered sacred. In particular, tobacco smoking often symbolized the successful conclusion of an agreement.

Another Native American tradition was the powwow, intended as a psychological defense against various disorders. Tribes stored and donned special costumes for ceremonial dances. In particular, the powwow involved dancing, chanting, and magic. Yet, the native peoples of New England were not image worshipers. Their religious holidays were in evidence in public rites of thanksgiving, prayers for assistance, religious dances, and rites of burial.

Most Christians deemed certain days (Christmas, Good Friday, and Easter) to be holy, and in England, Christmas was a special season of celebration, as were Easter and other religious holidays. But Puritans did not celebrate these days. In discarding all "popish" (Catholic) rituals and sacraments, New Englanders refused to recognize any holy days or to allow the observation of Christmas as a special holiday. Stiff fines were even levied on any member of the colony who was caught celebrating Christmas.

Although they refused to recognize the usual religious holidays, Puritans regularly designated days of prayer for fasting and praise (jeremiads), which were also known as fast days, days of humiliation, or days of thanksgiving. In some cases, as around the time of colony-wide elections, the legislature mandated fast days. At other times (usually upon the instigation of the clergy), the legislature declared fast days in response to serious community crises. The colony records indicate that the legislature declared a fast day for October 19, 1652, as a response to natural, social, and spiritual emergencies—torrential rains and flooding, wars in England, and worldliness and hard-heartedness among the people. With some frequency and throughout the year, officials appointed such days, sometimes as many as one every month.

Later in the 17th century, disputes arose over the power of the legislature to dictate public fast days. The royal governor would, on occasion, refuse to add his authorization for fast days that clerical urging had prompted the legislature to order, especially fasts prompted by the colony's unhappiness with England.

In 1681, with the colonies now firmly under the authority of the British king, the law that had criminalized the celebration of Christmas was repealed. However, year after year, Samuel Sewall faithfully observed with great satisfaction that, at least until 1728, businesses remained open on December 25, an indication that New Englanders were not celebrating Christmas. In November 1712, Cotton Mather delivered a sermon in which he deplored the "Mad mirth," drinking, feasting, and gaming associated with Christmastime revelries. Disapproval of the celebration of Christmas remained a potent force in New England until the Civil War.

The Puritan on the left voices his dislike of Christmas festivities. This religious practice carried over from England to New England during the early years of colonization. © Library of Congress.

Although New England continued to ignore the usual religious holidays, on many other days, by dictate or from custom, the colonial New Englanders gathered together for celebrations that resisted the sobriety of fast days. One such occasion was the local fair, held in many communities and first established by dictate as early as 1633, three years after the settlement of Boston. Days of thanksgiving and election days (when important officials took office) were official occasions for colorful and festive celebration.

Various events occasioned public days for feasting, drinking, and general celebration. These events included weddings, annual town meetings, and the successful completion of a house or a harvest. Nevertheless, an overriding concern with religious propriety discouraged most forms of festive community activities.

For a brief time in colonial New England, there existed a noteworthy exception to this discouragement of entertainments and levity: the 1626 settlement of Mare Mount or, as the Puritans called it, Merry Mount. Located in Massachusetts, not far from the Plymouth settlement, the group had as its leader Thomas Morton, an upper-class Englishman and member of the Anglican Church. This group was anathema to everything the Puritans represented, and although the Puritans had a variety of complaints against the Merry Mounters (who, for example, sold liquor and guns to the Native Americans), it was the Merry Mounters' amusements that so enraged the Puritans.

Morton described their revels in his book *New English Canaan* (1637). They erected what the Puritans called a paganish idol of the Prince of Darkness, a Maypole, and dedicated their revels to the god of love, in anticipation that one day, they would attract women to the settlement. Around the Maypole, the Merry Mounters reveled in all the amusements that the Puritans hated: boisterous laughing, excessive drinking, fervent dancing, theater acting, amorous singing, and drum playing.

In 1628, the Puritans arrested Morton and sent him back to England. When he returned in 1630, they burned Merry Mount to the ground and banished him again.

The amusements of black slaves in New England were largely the same as those enjoyed by whites: quilting bees, barn and house raisings, and fairs on the village common. In addition, black slaves loved meeting together to dance, play violin music, and share stories of Africa.

One institution of amusement was unique to black people in colonial New England. This was a special election day, when slaves and free blacks elected a black governor. With the explicit approval of their masters, slaves and servants fully participated in the celebration. Masters even contributed monetarily to the campaigns of those vying for the governorship and saw to it that their own slaves were handsomely attired and had the use of horses and carriages for the event. Voting usually took place around ten o'clock on the morning of the election, after which time, votes were counted to determine the winner, who assumed a position of some importance as a leader and figurehead of the black community. The declaration of the winner initiated an elaborate inauguration ceremony with extensive feasting and games.

Despite the Puritans' prohibitive distrust of many important Christian holidays—Christmas included—black and white New England colonists, as well as Native Americans, found and made time to attend to spiritual and emotional concerns in a community setting (Johnson, 24–25, 127–28, 130, 139, 140, 154).

FOR MORE INFORMATION

Boorstin, D. J. *The Americans: The Colonial Experience.* New York: Random House, 1958.
Johnson, C. D. *Daily Life in Colonial New England.* Westport, Conn.: Greenwood Press, 2002.

RECREATIONAL
LIFE
|
HOLIDAYS
|
Africa

Colonial Australia

The Colonial Frontier
of North America

England

Japan

New England

Life at Sea

LIFE AT SEA

With all the daily work that had to be done aboard merchant and naval vessels, holidays were not always drawn-out affairs. However, whaling ships were unique in that their voyages increasingly lasted for months and even for years. Hence, certain events served as a pretext for whaling "holidays." Gamming, or the encounter of two whaling ships on the vast seas, occasioned a festive holiday that might last for days. In addition, resting up at foreign ports, particularly the more picturesque ones in the Pacific, provided crews and their families with a chance to shift from work to celebration.

The term *gam* was originally used to describe a school of whales, but it was later applied to the occasion of whaling vessels meeting at sea and visiting. Gamming was an activity unique to whaling—merchant ships had schedules to meet, and naval vessels had their stations to keep and their duties to execute.

It was the extreme length of whaling voyages that made the gam so popular. The intense isolation of these voyages was pleasantly broken when two ships would meet at sea. If both of the captains desired to visit, they would signal each other. As the distance between the ships shortened, the captain and some of the crew of one of the vessels would set out in a boat for the other ship, while the mate and some crew members of the second vessel would visit the first.

The visitors would gravitate to their counterparts on the other ship, officers to officers, crew to crew. All would be besieged with questions about their birthplace, travels, and experiences. Gams lasted from a day to a week. Gamming was a time to share stories, to hear news from home, and to enjoy the company of "fresh faces." It was a time for best clothes and special culinary treats. Tasty foods were customarily abundant during these unforeseen holidays. Before separating, the revelers exchanged books, mail, and newspapers. Gifts of tobacco, pipes, and needed clothing were also freely given.

The gams also served as highlights for women on board ship during the interminable years of a whaling voyage. The most special times for wives and children at sea were when they could "gam" or visit with other ships. Wives of captains who went to sea with their husbands especially welcomed these breaks as a chance to relax and celebrate the very sense of relaxation and release that they occasioned. To facilitate the transportation of a woman to another ship, the cooper would fashion a barrel-like chair with a rope harness, which would deliver the captain's wife safely, if not comfortably. For children, visiting usually also meant candy and gifts.

Another type of holiday unique to lengthy whaling voyages centered on foreign ports where families and crew members had the opportunity to socialize. Honolulu became a major whaling port in the middle of the 19th century with an average of 400 ships per year anchoring there. While ships were refitted, or while they cruised in the cold Arctic waters, many captains' families moved ashore to take up residence in boardinghouses under the palm trees. Some women, who did not sail with their husbands, made the long, arduous journey from home to join them in Hawaii. While in port, these seafaring families established their own little settler community. Days were filled with rides along the beach, picnics, and croquet. Evenings featured dances, suppers, and concerts.

Despite the hard work involved in oceanic travel, those who worked longest, whalers, developed distinctive traditions of celebration, including gamming and vacations in exotic foreign ports (Volo and Volo, 152–53, 169).

FOR MORE INFORMATION

Spence, B. *Harpooned: The Story of Whaling.* New York: Crescent Books, 1980.

Volo, D. D., and J. M. Volo. *Daily Life in the Age of Sail.* Westport, Conn.: Greenwood Press, 2002.

Arts and Hobbies

People during the 17th and 18th centuries found ways to amuse themselves with talents and crafts related to theater, music, the visual arts, and dance. It should not be surprising that the cultural manifestations of these arts and hobbies differed sig-

RECREATIONAL LIFE

|

ARTS & HOBBIES

|

nificantly from one culture to the next. And yet people along North America's colonial frontier, on the open seas, and in sub-Saharan Africa, England, France, Japan, and New England specialized in these same artistic fields, over and over again.

In the world of theater, actors and actresses gained fame for their performances while they obtained notoriety for their offstage antics. England and Japan possessed vibrant theater cultures. During the 18th century, English plays appealed to all classes and tastes, with a keen predilection for brash, lewd, and witty dialogue. Playwrights even considered government to be fair game for their poison pens. Audiences were equally coarse, expressing without hesitation their distaste for a work or performance. Japanese theater had a similar genre. *Kyōgen* acts considered nothing sacred, and *kyōgen* performers would not hesitate to lampoon the more respectable genres in Japanese theater.

Dance could be both a formal and an informal art. In sub-Saharan Africa, dancers trained professionally but made sure that spectators could take part in the physical festivities. Often accompanying or following a marriage, a funeral, or a hunt, African dances possessed spiritual significance. Japanese dance was often indistinguishable from Japanese theater. Morality tales in No theater involved extremely slow and measured movements that complemented haunting, entrancing chants and drumming. The privileged classes in England attended balls and assemblies where they participated in more lively, although no less precise, dances that served the attendees' needs for courtship as much as their artistic aspirations.

Music surfaced in theatrical performances but exerted an extraordinary attraction by itself as well. Sailors found time to take out fiddles, harmonicas, and drums (usually the vessel's supply barrels) and to invigorate the salty air with sweet vibrations. To make the workday more tolerable, sailors sang chanties, the rhythms and lyrics of which adapted to the mood of the crew. In England, such songs were just as popular, but ostensibly more refined tastes opted for opera and chamber music. Africans made music with percussion, string, and wind instruments. In order to arrange some very captivating sounds, Japanese musicians applied their five-note scale to the composition of lutes, chants, drums, and flutes.

The visual arts included etchings, drawings, paintings, sculptures, and carvings. For instance, African Bedu masks were abstract carvings that united distinct realities (male and female, animal and human). The French elite came to appreciate successive visual styles, such as the baroque, which was grandiose in its ornaments; the rococo, which represented a simplified decorative emphasis; and neoclassicism, with its controlled depictions of contemporary and classical scenes. Native Americans along the colonial frontier valued the significance of tattoos. The living skin of the recipient of a tattoo became, in essence, a tableau of black, red, blue, and green patterns.

New England Puritans typically renounced artists as artful, equating imagination with error and sin; but they did find the time (and the desire) to embroider their quilts with curls, curves, lines, and other appealing designs.

Icon painting in Ethiopia, ink-wash paintings and woodblock prints in Japan, and the whalebone and ropework decorations of seamen round out this woefully incomplete record of common arts and hobbies from the 17th and 18th centuries. It is exciting to consider the capacity of the human mind to fashion from tradition and imagination so much pleasing diversity.

~*Peter Seelig*

FOR MORE INFORMATION

Bohlman, P. V. *World Music*. Oxford: Oxford University Press, 2002.

Brown, J. R. *The Oxford Illustrated History of Theatre*. Oxford: Oxford University Press, 1995.

Shiner, L. E. *The Invention of Art: A Cultural History*. Chicago: University of Chicago Press, 2001.

AFRICA

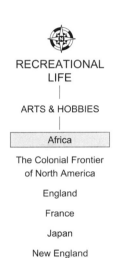

Sub-Saharan Africa's artistic heritage reflects the everyday experiences and perceptions of the continent's many peoples. Many art pieces, such as specially carved pots or furnishings, served to decorate people's daily lives while other objects, such as masks and statues of the ancestors, played important roles in rituals. Although style and content varied from culture to culture, the same types of pieces and aesthetic principles ranged over a wide region. People used art both to spruce up their own surroundings and to signify their status within their community. In this way, art enriched the daily lives of Africans while providing unique forms of expression for cultures and individuals.

In Africa, the usual Western division between the visual and performing arts did not apply. African dances form the best example of this difference, as they combined dance and music with the use of various human-made objects, most notably masks, to achieve the full effect of the performance. Masks took the form of animals, gods, or deceased humans, and they fitted over the faces of performers who, according to some spectators, took on the actual identity of the person whose mask they wore, such as in Anang ceremonies honoring the ancestors. The full artistic value of such masks came through only in performance, during which such factors as the play of light across the mask at different times during the dance greatly impacted the overall effect.

African dances served a number of functions within the community. In some areas, hunters performed dances after a kill to protect themselves from the animal's soul. Other dances marked such occasions as funerals or marriages to symbolize the changes in the community and to honor ancestors. Among the Bemba, when girls reached puberty, people performed a special ceremony called "dancing the girl," at which dancers reenacted such activities as food collection and maize grinding so that the girl could learn her new responsibilities. In the case of dances representing gods or the deceased, the dance allowed people to communicate with the figures represented. Although scholars did not record many of these dances until the 20th century, in their broad outlines they represent a crucial aspect of African artistic traditions that date back centuries (Willett, 44).

Most African dancers received special training, although everyone performed some dances at certain times throughout life. The initiation rituals into adulthood for males represent one example of the prevalence of dance. Other dances were organized according to occupation, as people represented their work to the village and sometimes earned gifts. Under most circumstances, the performers and spectators formed completely separate groups, although in other circumstances (mostly, dances that were primarily for recreation), the members of the audience would spontaneously join the dancers. The social status of dancers varied with the culture, but people usually considered the work of artists as equal to that of most other occupations.

Africans have long categorized musical instruments in many different ways. The Dan of the Guinea coast, for example, divided instruments into two categories: "struck," which includes what Europeans call percussion and strings, and "blown," into which they would have placed brass and woodwinds. Musicians used drums to produce a variety of rich tones during a musical performance. In addition, instruments such as rattles, bells, and hollow logs communicated special types of voices and meanings in performances. People believed that instruments possessed human qualities, and to protect this symbolic bond with the spirit world, musicians often made food sacrifices to their instruments (Stone, 18–19).

This bronze casting from Ife portrays an almost emotionless visage and a pattern of nearly parallel lines that flow vertically and wrap around the chin. © The Art Archive/Antenna Gallery Dakar Senegal/Dagli Orti.

Although some African artists (such as the Ife) used metals from which to craft objects (bronze castings), wood represented the medium most commonly used for carving in Africa; because of decay, however, few masks and statues remain from the 17th and 18th centuries. Nonetheless, those items that have survived reveal a set of aesthetic styles congruent with later centuries. Rather than capture an image at a particular moment in time, African art combined different elements, representing life as a continuum across life categories rather than as a series of units. The Bedu masks, fashioned by people in parts of the Ivory Coast, combined both animal and human and male and female attributes. These masks were made from the roots of the kapok tree and accompanied a costume made of baobab bark. Whereas men sculpted the mask, beat the bark off the tree, and tied everything together, women painted the mask every year before using it (Mack, 116–17).

African statues also transcended categories, featuring the large head of an infant with the body of mature adults. This unusual blend of images represents a portrayal of the complete life cycle, from birth to old age and back again, with newborn infants acquiring existence from the ancestors. Among the Fon peoples of Benin, brass pieces of people and animals were used for decoration and as a means of showing status. Many figurines of the Ashanti of Ghana known as *akua'ba* featured an oval head that was set on a neck with rings representing rolls of fat. The torso possessed very small arms and was either a cylinder or cone featuring breasts and a navel. Women often wore these amulets as fertility figures to induce pregnancy and to ensure a healthy childbirth. In some areas during this period, Africans also began carving statues especially for sale to Europeans (Willett, 162–64; Gillon, 139–40).

One art form important in Ethiopia was icon painting. Many paintings were included in the great church at the holy city of Axum, built in 1665 by the emperor Fasiladas. Much as African dances sometimes conveyed information about the community and the gods, icons depicted saints according to a strict style that conveyed information about their lives and significance. Thus, Saint Gabra Manfus Qeddus appears dressed in feathers and standing patiently among leopards and lions while a bird drinks from his eye. Saint George, on the other hand, rides a horse and spears a dragon to save a woman in a tree. During the 18th century, when workshops for icons and illuminated manuscripts sprang up around the capital of Gondar, artists began signing their works with their own names rather than simply with their patron's (Pankhurst, 59–60).

Other forms of art in Africa involved the objects of daily life. For example, artisans often carved decorative images of animals onto dishes. Dishes that were used for ritual purposes or owned by the rich or powerful had the most elaborate decorations. The Lozi of the Zambezi valley made bowls that often included handles or knobs shaped like animals (Mack, 178).

Men from some communities of southern Africa wore decorated ivory or bone earplugs. Decorative clothing included woven textiles. The people of Madagascar practiced a well-developed art of weaving, although, unfortunately, little is known of its incarnations in the pre-19th century period, when female weavers made fabrics called *lamba akotofahana,* which featured various detailed designs in contrasting colors, for the aristocracy of the kingdom of Imerina (Mack, 198).

People in what is now South Africa also made special headrests, which formed part of a woman's dowry. In this region, a bride would grow an elaborate hairstyle to honor her new husband; she would place her headrest under the neck to prevent her hair from being disturbed. Such headrests often earned the status of ancestral relics, and the body dirt that they retained from generation to generation represented an important link with the past (Mack, 172–73).

Art formed an integral part of the daily life of people through Africa. It played a role in everything from the rituals that regulated passage through life stages to the clothing and other trappings of their routine existence. From music, dance, sculpture, and other media, Africans created a panoply of sounds, images, and impressions that expressed both a sense of beauty and a deeper understanding of the universe. Africans often believed that art objects possessed sacred powers linking them to ancestors; regardless of whether they literally did, these objects kept people in touch with those ancestors' beliefs and traditions and thus played a crucial role in shaping the world as people knew it.

~Brian Ulrich

FOR MORE INFORMATION

Agatucci, C. Central Oregon Community College. *Humanities 211.* 1997. <http://www.cocc.edu/cagatucci/classes/hum211/index.htm>, accessed October 23, 2003.

Diabate, T., and B. Sissoko. *New Ancient Strings.* HNCD 1478, Hannibal Records, 1999. Compact disc.

Gillon, W. *A Short History of African Art.* New York: Facts on File, 1984.

Halsall, P., ed. *Internet African History Sourcebook.* 1996. <http://www.fordham.edu/halsall/africa/africasbook.html>, accessed October 23, 2003.

Mack, J., ed. *Africa: Arts and Cultures.* New York: Oxford University Press, 2000.

Pankhurst, R. *The Ethiopians.* Malden, Mass.: Blackwell, 1998.

Stone, R. M., ed. *The Garland Handbook of African Music.* New York: Garland, 2000.

Willett, F. *African Art: An Introduction.* New York: Thames and Hudson, 1993.

THE COLONIAL FRONTIER OF NORTH AMERICA

Although the frontier settlers of North America found scant time to engage in producing artistic works at a time when food sources, dwelling places, community safety, and spiritual salvation were all in doubt, native peoples in the region benefited from an established practice of arts, including most notably, the production of skin markings (tattoos) and of jewelry.

Indians tattooed various designs on their bodies that remained as long as they lived. On their faces, they impressed figures of snakes, scrolls, lines of tears, and other symbols of importance to them. John M'Cullough, a captive among the Delaware, believed that these "hieroglyphics . . . always denote[d] valor." Jean-Bernard Bossu, a contemporary observer, noted, "If anyone should take it into his head to have himself tattooed without having distinguished himself in battle, he . . . might have the design torn off him, skin and all."

The color most used in tattooing was black. Peter Kalm, who traveled among the Huron, did not recall ever seeing any other. However, he noted, "The men who accompanied me told me that they also use red paint and that black and red are the only colors used." Other contemporary observers described tattoos in red, black, blue, and green—"all bright colors." The blue and green could be made from verdigris, a copper acetate compound, which varies from blue to blue-green to green depending on its various chemical structures. Verdigris was a particularly poisonous compound if taken internally but seems to have had no ill effect when applied to the skin. The red dye came from cinnabar, which the French and English traders called vermilion. The black was made by taking a piece of alder wood, burning it completely, and allowing the charcoal to cool. Gunpowder, being black, was also used on occasion to color tattoos.

In order to pulverize the chosen pigment, Native American tattoo artists usually rubbed it between the hands. They then placed the resulting powder into a vessel of water and allowed the mixture to stand until the powder was well saturated. When the time came to paint some figures on the body, the artist first drew the design on the skin with a piece of charcoal. When a man wanted to have his entire body tattooed, he stretched out on a board, and the tattooer marked out as much of the desired design as could be inscribed in one sitting. The person being tattooed, whether man or woman, would rather die than flinch during the process. The women bore the pain "with the same courage as the men to please them and to appear more beautiful to them." Nonetheless, the operation was bloody and dangerous, as infection could easily set in and cause the subjects to lose their life.

A contemporary journalist noted that to make the image, an Indian tattooer used a needle, "made somewhat like a fleam"—employed by physicians to let blood—or an instrument said to have had several needles fastened together between two pieces of wood:

[They] dip it into the prepared dye and with it prick or puncture the skin along the lines of the design previously made with the charcoal. They dip the needle into the dye between every puncture; thus the color is left between the skin and the flesh. When the wound has healed, the color remains and can never be obliterated. The men told me that in the beginning when the skin is pricked and punctured, it is rather painful, but the smart gradually diminishes and at the expiration of a day the smart and pain has almost ceased.

Native Americans apparently used no form of antiseptic and considered a brief infection to be an expected part of the process. One observer remarked, "[The] blood must flow from the part thus cut by the tattooer's stroke, a swelling follows, forming a scab which falls off after a few days. Then the wound is healed and the tattooing or pattern stands out clearly. The healing takes a shorter or longer time depending on the amount of tattooing done. It is very curious to see a man tattooed in this way, especially when the entire body is tattooed in colors." Another observer noted that in the later part of the colonial period, native peoples gradually abandoned the custom of tattooing.

Finger rings and earrings were popular among Native Americans, even before their contact with Europeans. Naturally occurring copper and gold were in use among Indians for generations. Both men and women used naturally occurring coarse diamonds, garnets, amethyst crystals, and other smooth or polished stones in their jewelry. Soapstone, a soft mineral of gray to green color, was often fashioned into pendants, ornaments, and other geometric shapes by rubbing it with damp deerskin or sawgrass dipped in fine sand. Native artisans could work any stone or bit of metal with an interesting shape into a piece of decoration, and with relative ease, they used a pointed stick dipped in sand with which to bore holes in soapstone.

After European contact, Native Americans quickly acquired brass and silver rings and crosses; medals representative of Catholic saints; large and small bells; pendants cast in the shapes of turtles, bears, and birds; and brass and silver wire. A warrior of the Delaware nation was noted to have had "a large triangular piece of silver hanging below his nose that covered almost the whole of his upper lip." The European traders also supplied items of brass, silver, and tin such as arm plates, wrist plates, ear bobs, and gorgets. The gorget was a metal plate suspended below the throat from a cord worn around the neck. It had a lima bean shape and could be from four to eight inches long. "Both sexes . . . commonly load the parts [of the body] with each sort in proportion to their ability of purchasing them." They were especially fond of these items if they were received as gifts and "would never part with them for the sake of the giver."

Be it a specimen of jewelry or a colorful tattoo, the art of Native Americans along the colonial frontier revealed itself frequently and vibrantly. It would take the colonists many more decades before they, too, could establish an equally extensive and characteristic canon of art (Volo and Volo, 25, 33–36).

FOR MORE INFORMATION

Volo, J. M., and D. D. Volo. *Daily Life on the Old Colonial Frontier*. Westport, Conn.: Greenwood Press, 2002.

Wilbur, C. K. *The Woodland Indians: An Illustrated Account of the Lifestyles of America's First Inhabitants*. Guilford, Conn.: Globe Pequot Press, 1995.

RECREATIONAL
LIFE
|
ARTS & HOBBIES
|
Africa

The Colonial Frontier
of North America

England

France

Japan

New England

Life at Sea

ENGLAND

The arts provided the English people with diversions for the senses. Theatergoers participated in more than just a stage production. There were idolized actors and actresses, saucy and satirical plays, and occasions to come together with one's peers, betters, and inferiors, some of whom got quite rowdy. Music, too, provided people with a feast for the ears. There were simple songs with lively lyrics and singable melodies; there were also refined compositions by some of the great names in classical music. The visual arts, animal shows, puppet shows, and freak shows rounded out pay-and-be-entertained productions. In pursuit of less-formal amusement, people frequented coffee shops, social clubs, assemblies, and balls, or they organized their own clubs, selecting as a theme their favorite hobbies. There was something for everyone.

People of all kinds enjoyed the theater in 18th-century England. The century produced a host of popular plays by George Colman, George Lillo, Hannah More, Sophia Lee, Richard Brinsley Sheridan, and Oliver Goldsmith, but the century's most significant play was John Gay's *The Beggar's Opera*, first produced in 1728. With its lower-class criminal characters, street songs, pointed political satire, and traditional melodies, it was guaranteed to appeal to the working class and to alienate those in power. *The Beggar's Opera* pointed out that poor criminals got hanged whereas rich ones got elected. It was not a message that Prime Minister Robert Walpole wanted to hear on opening night, when he saw himself caricatured as "Robin Bagshot."

Noted actors included Peg Woffington, Anne Oldfield, Catherine Clive, Sarah Siddons, Anne Bracegirdle, Charles Macklin, and Colley Cibber. Greatest of them all, however, was David Garrick, who popularized more natural speech and gestures onstage. Garrick was also the comanager, from 1747 to 1776, of one of the great London theaters: Drury Lane. Another of the great London houses was the Haymarket.

Theatergoers constituted a miscellaneous crowd. The "Persons of Quality" sat in boxes. In the pit, the area at ground level in front of the stage, sat "the *Judges, Wits, and Censurers* . . . the *Squires, Sharpers, Beaus, Bullies* and *Whores.*" Above them, in shallow galleries a few seats deep, sat "the Citizens' Wives and Daughters, together with the *Abigails,* Serving-men, Journey-men and Apprentices."

Theater audiences were often rude. They threw rotten fruit and vegetables at the stage and at other members of the audience. They laughed and talked; and when they found the play to be particularly disagreeable, they rioted. There was nothing passive about attending the theater.

People paid to see other types of performers: magicians, clairvoyants, ropewalkers, clowns, and snake handlers. Spectators flocked to exhibitions of giants, such as the "wonderful tall Essex woman." They showed similar enthusiasm for midgets and dwarfs, hermaphrodites and androgynes, people with bizarre birth defects or missing limbs, "noble savages" from Africa or America, and people who ate fire, cats, stones, or raw flesh.

Music, so often a part of plays and afterpieces, also stood on its own. Opera was popular, with Italian opera dominating the first half of the 18th century. Great composers came to England as well. George Frideric Handel came to stay; later in the century, Wolfgang Amadeus Mozart toured there, as did Joseph Haydn in 1791. Wealthy people also held private parties to hear chamber music played in their homes, while the less well off went to music festivals, sang hymns in church, or joined chamber music clubs or choral clubs. There were songs for particular trades, for literary characters, and for dancing. Songs were often sung in taverns, and imbibing revelers had many lyrics with drinking themes from which to choose. Other songs dealt with love, sex, and courtship.

Displays of unusual or trained animals were always popular. In one act, birds pretended to march with toy guns and then held a mock execution of another bird by firing squad; the "shot" bird fell down on cue and then stood up to march out with his comrades. Various impresarios offered camels, panthers, lions, baboons, and exotic birds for public inspection.

Various other kinds of shows were popular, as well. Waxwork figures of celebrities and historical figures were on display in Mrs. Mills's, Benjamin Rackstrow's, and other less-famous collections. Salmon's, the most notable collection, featured, at various times, the execution of Charles I, the English prophet Mother Shipton (who was rigged to kick each patron on departure), three Cherokee chiefs, and Antony and Cleopatra.

Painters, too, displayed their work. Art enthusiasts admired paintings clustered tightly on the walls at London's Foundling Hospital from 1740 and at the annual Royal Academy exhibition from 1769.

Assemblies and balls offered young people a venue for courtship. The price of admission kept out the extremely poor and sorted people roughly by class, both shunting lesser tradesmen and their ilk to the cheaper assemblies and reserving the genteel city and London assemblies for the wealthy. For genteel young women, it was a heady experience to dance, to be admired, and no doubt, to whisper with friends over the merits of particular gentlemen. Parents of the youthful attendees could supervise chastity while enjoying a hand of cards or a glass of punch and the conversation of their peers.

In time, variations on the ball developed. The type of ball that most terrified moralists, however, was the masquerade. The anonymity of one's dance partner could be arousing, dangerous, or embarrassing, and the masquerade was accordingly embraced by the daring and condemned by the prudent.

Some people enjoyed themselves by finding others with similar interests or temperaments and forming a club. Clubs had existed before, but now they became so popular at every social level that they were a principal aspect of 18th-century English life—although perhaps it is more accurate to say 18th-century male English life: few clubs were open to women. Most clubs were short-lived and casually organized. Some had a specific purpose, whereas others existed purely as an excuse to talk, drink, and gamble.

Lawyers and authors gathered at the Grecian; clergymen at Child's; artists at Old Slaughter's; marine insurers at Lloyd's; stockbrokers at Jonathan's (which became the Stock Exchange in 1773); military men at the Little Devil; and fops at Ozinda's. Another important social club was that of the Freemasons, whose religious tolerance, aura of secrecy, and fashionable, yet diverse, membership made them eminently popular. Some clubs were political in nature. There were scientific and mathematical societies, charitable groups, sports clubs, musical clubs, and gardening clubs. There were other clubs, the chief purpose of which was pleasure. There were literary societies. There were lottery clubs, sodomites' clubs, flagellants' clubs, and book clubs. There was also the Hell-Fire Club for notable rakes. There were even ugly clubs, farters' clubs, and surly clubs.

Given the degree of specialization that the various clubs offered, it seems safe to guess that 18th-century England, and especially London, offered sundry forms of entertainment for all dispositions, ranging from the reform-minded to the connoisseur of theater or music, and from those with a taste for *The Beggar's Opera* to those who craved a view of the "wonderful tall Essex woman" (Olsen, 151–55, 157–60, 163).

To read about the arts and other pastimes in Chaucer's England, see the Europe entries in the sections "Hunting," "Music and Dance," and "Entertainment" in chapter 7 ("Recreational Life") of volume 2; for Elizabethan England, see the England entries in the sections "Outdoor Pursuits" and "The Arts" in chapter 7 ("Recreational Life") of volume 3; and for Victorian England, see the Victorian England entries in the sections "Music" and "Leisure Time" in chapter 7 ("Recreational Life") of volume 5 of this series.

FOR MORE INFORMATION

Lynch, J. *Eighteenth Century Resources*. <http://newark.rutgers.edu/~jlynch/18th/>, accessed October 10, 2003.

Malcolmson, R. W. *Popular Recreations in English Society, 1700–1850*. Cambridge, England: Cambridge University Press, 1973.

Olsen, K. *Daily Life in 18th-Century England*. Westport, Conn.: Greenwood Press, 1999.

Paulson, R. *Breaking and Remaking: Aesthetic Practice in England, 1700–1820.* New Brunswick, N.J.: Rutgers University Press, 1989.

Purcell, H., N. Matteis, and others. *Music in England in the Time of Hogarth.* HMUK 986002, Harmonia Mundi, 1997. Compact disc.

FRANCE

Art of the 17th and 18th centuries falls into three styles: the baroque, the rococo, and the neoclassical. Within these styles, the movements can be loosely grouped into two categories: the art of the nobility (baroque and rococo) and the art of the rising middle class (neoclassical). The art of the French baroque was splendid and monumental in style and size. The rococo, on the other hand, shied away from grand subjects, canvases, and styles and instead represented an attempt to depict intimate experiences. Neoclassical art returned to the monumentalism of the baroque but denounced the values and emphases of both the rococo and the baroque periods. The artistic production of this period thus mirrors the tensions exhibited in politics and culture: tensions stemming from, on the one hand, the focus on the personal glory, elegance, and pleasure that often typified the aristocratic approach to life and, on the other hand, a middle-class emphasis on utility, rationality, and reform.

During the reign of Louis XIV (1643–1715), the French court at Versailles served as the center of artistic life. Unlike the Italian baroque, which was exemplified by church facades and interiors or grand depictions of pious saints, baroque art in France generally served to glorify temporal power. The French baroque was used to ornament museums such as the Louvre and châteaus such as Versailles, while sculpture and portraiture similarly promoted Louis XIV and his reign. With this goal in mind, the Sun King, as Louis XIV was known, founded the French Academy of Painting and Sculpture in 1648, in large part so that artists could be trained to use their skills to enhance even further the king's prestige and reputation.

The aristocracy responded to the death of Louis XIV by revolting against the formalized and academic nature of 17th-century French art. Members of the nobility under the reigns of Louis XV and XVI began to decorate their homes in a more playful, delicate, and intimate manner. The new style became known as the rococo, a term that was derived from the French word *rocaille*, which referred to the rock and shellwork that ornamented aristocratic gardens. Similar to this landscape ornamentation, rococo pieces began to incorporate vines, shells, curves, and pastel colorings. Unlike the grand, vibrant, and geometric baroque, the rococo emphasized surfaces, light, and pastel colors. It was no accident that the decorative arts, ranging from desks to porcelains, were the first to use the new style. Rococo art used the ornamental and relatively unimportant decorative objects of everyday aristocratic life instead of monumental architecture or canvas. Preferring portraits, scenes of daily life, or mythological themes, rococo artists moved away from the historical and religious subjects that had been popular with academic painters.

The painter Antoine Watteau is sometimes referred to as the greatest rococo painter. Watteau's *Departure from the Island of Cythera* (1717) provides a nearly ideal

summary of the new style and its cultural context. A tribute to romantic love, *Cythera* emphasizes romance and elegance rather than martyrs or heroes. According to legend, Venus, the goddess of love, was born on the island of Cythera. Taking this mythology as its inspiration, Watteau's painting shows lovers dressed for a party heading to the island on a secular sort of pilgrimage—to the goddess of love. In the picture, a statue of Venus looks on approvingly while Cupid shoots arrows at the pilgrims. With its iridescent color scheme of pastels and its light-hearted theme of romance and fashionable parties, Watteau's painting embodies the carefree aristocratic style of the rococo.

A reaction against the aristocratic excesses of the baroque and rococo, neoclassical art represented an ostensible return to virtue, as exemplified by simpler and more "classical" forms. In practice, this movement sometimes involved a return to monumental painting, but with historical themes rather than religious ones. Unlike the undulating surfaces of the rococo or the sensuality of the baroque, neoclassical art was controlled, and the movement and placement of its figures seemed calculated and even purposely remote from the viewer. A common theme was obedience to a cause higher than self, such as a nation and ruler.

Neoclassicism is sometimes thought of as a "bourgeois" art form not so much because of these distinctions but because of its ideological affiliation with the French Revolution. One of the most highly renowned neoclassical artists, Jacques-Louis David, portrayed famous revolutionary moments in paintings such as *The Tennis Court Oath* (1791) and *The Death of Marat* (1793). He also played the role of a political figure himself, becoming a member of the National Convention and later, chief propagandist for Napoleon Bonaparte. Although one of David's most famous paintings, *The Oath of the Horatii* (1784), was commissioned by the French king Louis XVI more than five years before the outbreak of the revolution, its style and themes soon transformed it into a symbol of the anti-aristocratic spirit that fed the French Revolution.

The *Oath of the Horatii* illustrates a moment in Roman history when three sons from the Horatii family determined to do battle with three sons from the Curiatii family to settle the war between Rome (home of the Horatii) and Alba (home of the Curiatii). In the painting, the sons swear to their father, who is presenting them with swords, that they will oppose the Curiatii family to save Rome. The men stand to the left of the painting, arms outstretched, taking an oath to uphold liberty. Rather than powdered wigs and embroidered coats, the Horatii wear military helmets, hold spears, and reach for their swords in a military salute. Many French who witnessed the painting saw in it not simply a promotion of the ideals of self-sacrifice and devotion to country but a denunciation of aristocratic frivolity and self-absorption, as well. When David became the official portraitist for Napoleon, he continued to promote revolutionary ideals and used his acute sense of history to portray Bonaparte as the embodiment of the revolutionary ideal. No longer was aristocratic privilege or frivolity acceptable; duty to nation and a bourgeois vision were the most important qualities of didactic and academic art.

~Jennifer J. Popiel

FOR MORE INFORMATION

Conisbee, P. *Painting in Eighteenth-Century France*. Ithaca, N.Y.: Cornell University Press, 1981.

Duro, P. *The Academy and the Limits of Painting in Seventeenth-Century France*. New York: Cambridge University Press, 1997.

Levey, M. *From Rococo to Revolution: Major Trends in Eighteenth-Century Painting*. New York: Norton, 1985.

Lynch, J. *Eighteenth Century Resources*. <http://newark.rutgers.edu/~jlynch/18th/>, accessed October 10, 2003.

Paulson, R. *Representations of Revolution, 1789–1820*. New Haven, Conn.: Yale University Press, 1983.

Roberts, W. *Jacques-Louis David, Revolutionary Artist: Art, Politics, and the French Revolution*. Chapel Hill: University of North Carolina Press, 1989.

Society for French Historical Studies. *H-France, Newsletter about French Culture and History*. 2001. <http://www3.uakron.edu/hfrance/>, accessed October 23, 2003.

Wright, C. *The French Painters of the Seventeenth Century*. New York: New York Graphic Society, 1986.

JAPAN

Music, the visual arts, and theater represent 18th-century Japan's most popular artistic genres outside literature. Distinct from Western traditions, Japanese arts embodied much that was urban and elite in society.

In Japan, musicians used a five-note musical scale, different from the typical Western seven-note scale. Most compositions, which were memorized rather than written down, accompanied other performing activities and therefore never became "popular" to the extent that people went about whistling or humming familiar tunes.

A profusion of musical instruments (many having been skillfully painted, lacquered, inlaid, and carved) were available to Japanese musicians. Lutes and other stringed instruments were very popular, as were various flutes that produced ethereal sounds. The human voice also became an instrument heard in rhythmic chants, shouts, and yells, all of which seemed discordant and cacophonous but which acquired a unique harmony of their own.

By far, the most common instruments were drums. Most were small, handheld drums that accompanied theater performances, but there were many large drums, as well. The drums known as *taiko* were titanic, requiring groups of drummers to play them. Special woods were grown and shaped for these drums, the heads of which were made from the skins of animals. Drums or bells furnished the rhythm for Buddhist chants.

Among the visual arts, ink-wash painting incorporated splashes, blots, and ink washes (hence the name) to suggest the nebulous flash of intuition that was the goal of all Zen meditation. The painters explained that the genre's lack of detail and its use of blank space expressed much more than did the spare form and lines of the ink.

Perhaps the single most dominant artistic style of the period involved as much craft as it did art. The *ukiyo-e* (pictures of the floating world) woodblock prints came about through the combined efforts of the artist who drew the original picture, the artisan who carved the succession of woodblocks, and the printer who carefully matched the colored overlays, all to produce a succession of identical pictures. In 18th-century Japan, the subjects of the prints were the activities and denizens of the Licensed Quarters. Prints were commissioned as theater playbills, advertisements, illustrations for inexpensive books, and curios and souvenirs.

Of the several distinct traditions in 18th-century Japanese theater, No was certainly the most formal and "proper." Kabuki and *joruri-bunraku* were more popular among the common people, particularly the *chōnin* (city folk).

Based on Buddhist moral principles, the No style obeyed formalized conventions requiring an opening introductory scene wherein the principal character appears first as a ghost relating his personal story as a cautionary moral tale. The long recitations were delivered in rhythmic chants accompanied by offstage drums and a chorus. The principal actors "danced" their roles to give visual effect to the performance, but the dances involved very little body movement except for the stamping of the feet. In contrast, the *kyōgen* interludes between No scenes were as lively and ribald as No was proper and static.

The *kyōgen* were most likely the early attempts of minor actors to entertain the audience while the major actors changed costumes between scenes. The *Kyōgen* involved bawdy visual puns and slapstick comedy, sometimes even satirizing the foregoing No scene. By the 18th century, the *kyōgen* had become more popular and prominent than the No plays themselves.

The themes of Kabuki plays were neo-Confucian moralistic in content. The typical story involved *chōnin* struggling with the pressures of social obligation (*giri*), as they became involved in love affairs (*ninjo*) that inevitably doomed both lovers. Love-suicide (*shinju*) of the star-crossed lovers was often the remedy.

Elaborate and lavish costumes became the norm in Kabuki. Brightly colored lush silks and sumptuous brocades attracted the attention of the crowds. Makeup evolved, as well. The traditional whiteface was limned with bright colors to emphasize and exaggerate facial expressions: for example, red colors were to emphasize anger, and only heroes used blue facial lines.

Sitting with the musicians on the side of the Kabuki stage was a narrator, who clarified and expanded upon the actors' lines. The standard musical instruments included *biwa,* drums, gongs, and flutes that produced eerie, ghostly sounds.

The major Kabuki companies signed their major actors for 11-month contracts. A major actor made a huge salary based on his popularity from the previous season. The major companies vied with each other to sign the most popular ones, and financial backers often tied their support to the actors employed.

The plays themselves were marathon performances that frequently lasted all day. Meals, light snacks, and drinks of all kinds were served during the performances. Wealthy patrons purchased the choice block audience areas (there were no actual "seats") and used them to entertain their family, friends, and clients. The attention of the audience would be riveted when major actors entered the scene but wandered when minor characters dominated the stage.

Using woodblock prints of famous scenes as playbills, theater companies advertised heavily. Actors were encouraged to engage in sexual affairs and to spend lavishly on geisha (female servant-entertainers) and prostitutes to remain in the public eye. Many restaurants paid to have actors dine at their establishments. Wealthy *chōnin* and sometimes thinly disguised daimyō (feudal warlords) and samurai (warrior-administrators) mixed with top actors, high-ranking geisha, and prostitutes in this nocturnal demimonde. Occasionally, when scandals became too common, the *bakufu* (national military government) or local daimyō would send in censors, and a few samurai would be humiliated, a few *chōnin* dispossessed, and a few theater owners fined or admonished, all to the entertainment of the general populace.

Bunraku puppetry became a crowd favorite in part because the puppets could do things on stage that were impossible for human actors: puppets could fly, they could turn into animals, and they could suffer decapitation. Puppets could also say things for which actors would be imprisoned.

The artisans who made puppet heads carefully carved them from a single block of special wood, hollowing out the interior, which received almost as much attention as the outer part. Toggles and strings enabled the puppeteer to manipulate the movement of several parts of the face. Eyes were made to roll, blink, and even move independently of each other, creating the expression of extreme rage and frustration: the cross-eyed stare. Eyebrows could arch and knit, lips could part to bare teeth, and tongues could even protrude. The puppet-actors, however, did not "talk." All dialogue was delivered by one stage-side narrator who changed the timbre and cadence of his voice to allow for the differences of male-female and old-young styles of speech. The musical accompaniment was similar to that of Kabuki.

The haunting sounds of lutes, the stylized and almost-surreal concentration of No performances, and the exceptional talents of Bunraku artisans and puppeteers, especially in their metropolitan and elite manifestations, can only furnish the uninitiated with a fleeting sense of this important category of existence in 18th-century Japan (Perez, 189–90, 277, 285, 290–92, 295–99).

FOR MORE INFORMATION

Inoura, Y. *The Traditional Theater of Japan.* Tokyo: Japan Foundation, 1981.
Japan Information Network. <http://www.jinjapan.org/index.html>, accessed October 23, 2003.
Japanese Melodies. Yo-Yo Ma and Masami Nakagawa. 039703, Sony, 1985. Compact disc.
Living Treasures of Japan. Vestron Video. Produced by Thomas Skinner. Videocassette, 1988.
Malm, W. P. *Japanese Music and Musical Instruments.* Tokyo: Tokyo University Press, 1959.
Perez, L. G. *Daily Life in Early Modern Japan.* Westport, Conn.: Greenwood Press, 2002.

NEW ENGLAND

Although New Englanders certainly possessed and developed their own artistic genres, it is also true that a discussion of the arts and hobbies of these people reveals,

more often than not, their negative views of art and their attempts to suppress or forbid it. That is to say, an analysis of New Englanders and their artistic imaginations inevitably ends in a discussion of the artistic genres that New Englanders outlawed or discouraged.

England in the 17th century was a country of thriving arts, but the religious dissenters who dominated New England held views of the imagination that prompted them to discourage most of the arts that the English and Europeans enjoyed. New Englanders' suspicion of many artistic genres was grounded in their view of the creative imagination, from which literature, painting, and music spring. Most New Englanders regarded the imagination as an agent of the devil, which, through appeals to human imagination, led people to commit all manner of sinful overt actions, as well as sins of the mind and heart.

Moreover, these same New Englanders regarded the imagination with suspicion because it was not checked and limited, as were other human faculties. For instance, Puritans argued that while the intellect (reason) checked the drives that derived from the emotions (passions), the imagination was completely immune from any inhibitions. Thus, by conjuring up erroneous visions (of dragons and monsters, for example), the imagination led people to embrace falsehoods. William Perkins, one of the most influential English writers in colonial New England, wrote that "the Imagination of mans heart is evil even from his youth."

The imagination was dangerous for another reason. Through the use of the imagination, a person could pretend to create a world of his or her own. Such an artist committed the worst of all possible sins: the sin of attempting to be like "God the Creator."

Art was also discouraged because it promoted idleness, regarded as one of the worst sins in colonial New England. Art not only led one into immorality; it diverted one's attention from work in one's God-given calling—work that was required to keep the New England communities from collapsing.

Puritan leaders in the Massachusetts area completely banned most performing arts, and especially theater, until 1793. Throughout the 18th century, authorities inevitably arrested traveling actors and threw them out of town not only in Boston and New Haven but in Philadelphia and Albany, as well. The exception to this practice involved private theatricals staged by and for British troops stationed in New England.

In 1646, the colonies prohibited public houses from conducting dances, which constituted another performance art, as well as a social entertainment. Two dancing masters tried to introduce dancing to Boston in November 1685 and were promptly thwarted in their attempts, one of them fleeing Boston in July 1686. Both were subject to stiff fines that would be canceled if they agreed to leave the colony.

In Europe and England, the Roman Catholic and Anglican Churches had been and continued to be great sponsors of graphic and musical arts; but colonial New England, founded on Puritan doctrine, tolerated no such religious art. Largely as a reaction to the rich ornamentation of the Roman Church, the dissenters who settled New England repudiated all symbolic and decorative art within their houses of worship. They considered any statue or painting in the "meetinghouse" to be popish

(Catholic) idolatry. As a consequence, colonial artists depicted virtually no biblical scenes in colonial paintings.

The chief pictorial art produced in 17th-century New England was portraiture. Few figures of stature or wealth in New England died without having had their portraits painted. Sometimes these portraits were single figures, and sometimes they were family group portraits.

The meetinghouse in New England was cleansed of traditional church music as well as of art. Puritan leaders banned any kind of instrumental music from their establishments and permitted only the vocals that were the intoning from *The Bay Psalm Book*.

Throughout the 17th century, most of New England's artistic impulse went into the decoration of ordinary household objects, such as quilts, coverlets, and other linens. The artists of this genre were women, and the artistic instrument was the needle rather than the paintbrush. From this tradition, Nathaniel Hawthorne, the great 19th-century American author and son of prominent 17th-century Puritans, developed his novel *The Scarlet Letter* about a seamstress who becomes a representative of the artist and a target of Puritan prejudices.

Mention of the arts in 17th-century colonial New England gives rise to the mention of forbidden activities and objects more than to any reference to a thriving and diverse collection of paintings, sculpture, dance, theater, or song (Johnson, 119–21, 123).

FOR MORE INFORMATION

Johnson, C. D. *Daily Life in Colonial New England*. Westport, Conn.: Greenwood Press, 2002.

Wright, L. B. *The Cultural Life of the American Colonies*. New York: Harper and Row, 1957.

LIFE AT SEA

With relatively little space and even less material with which to create art, mariners nonetheless had a tradition of inventive practices related to the visual arts, music, and even theater.

Many sailors and officers, both on merchant ships and naval vessels, practiced the art of scrimshaw, the most elaborate examples of which involved scraping, sanding, soaking, and carving whale teeth. The sailor then finished the scrimshaw piece by depositing ink, paint, or the juice of tobacco, berries, or tar in the incised lines. Each tapering tooth ranged from five to eight inches tall. Sailor artists ornamented walrus tusks with scenes of naval engagements, classical images of Greek mythology, and engravings of military heroes. Some designs were born of the fertile imaginations of the artist. Others were copied from periodicals or books.

The most common scrimshaw products were busks (center bodice stays used in women's foundation garments), pastry crimping wheels, work boxes, knitting needles, thimbles, clothes pins, toys, dice, and dominoes from whalebone. Officers and

the more literate among the crew designed sealing devices, lead pencil holders, and straight-edges.

Shipboard needs required sailors to be skilled with ropes. Experienced sailors were also proficient at the practical knots of their calling. Decorative ropework was an outgrowth of everyday seamanship, as it was somewhat natural for sailors to embellish the knots with pleasing adaptations that produced an artistic effect.

Fancy ropework had the advantage of requiring few tools. A knife with a spike was all that was essential. A few nails would be driven into a board or spar for more complicated woven mats and rings. Books on seamanship from the 18th century discuss decorative ropework.

Every ship had a kind of unofficial song leader, or "chantyman."

Knot makers fashioned rope ladders, decorative chains, bracelets, tablemats, shoes, and buttons. Chest handles were a matter of particular pride, as a sailor's chest was his sole personal property on a voyage. Sailors who were familiar with fancy ropework created gifts for loved ones by fashioning domestic fancies, such as picture frames, from complex knots.

Sailors were especially partial to all kinds of music. During the dogwatches, the sailors not on duty would gather and sing or dance to whatever musical accompaniment was available. Although there was little room in such tight quarters for extraneous items, seamen were known to have commonly brought aboard both fiddles and concertinas. Harmonicas, pipes, and penny whistles took up little space in a sailor's ditty bag. In the absence of any instrument, oceangoing musicians would impress barrels into service as drums. Wiser and more compassionate captains appreciated the psychological value of music and used it to maintain good morale.

Music provided much more than pure entertainment for the crew. Work songs were an integral part of shipboard labor in the merchant service, although they were seldom used aboard naval vessels. Songs or chants provided the rhythm needed for an efficient team effort among the crew when setting sails, hauling cargo in or out of the hold, or raising the anchor. Thus, every ship had a kind of unofficial song leader, or "chantyman." In addition to a fine voice and a good set of lungs, the chantyman needed a singular sense of timing and an instinctive feel for the mood of the men. The chantyman would sing out a line of the song, and the sailors would follow with the chorus. A well-chosen song that fit the task at hand and suited the spirit of the crew could inspire the hands to peak efficiency.

A far different kind of singing took place in the forecastle, where the sailors sang for themselves. These tunes were often bawdy and recreational in nature and were sung during the watch below, on deck during dogwatches, and during any leisure time from which a sailor might profit. These songs were traditionally accompanied by whatever instruments were available.

Sailors also composed lyrics. These usually had a narrative quality, tended toward the sentimental or romantic, and were infused with a sense of the vastness and the power of the sea. The combination of these three traits provided sailors with an outlet for their feelings of deep inner sadness, their longing for loved ones, or a general awareness of the proximity of death. Often, the subject of the song was dramatic, relating tales of shipwreck, storms, mutinies, or violent death.

Many other songs began by fixing the chanted or sung tale in a certain time and place. Lyrics routinely identified crew members by position, if not by name, and the supposed original composer sometimes received prominence aboard the vessel.

The isolation of the sea demanded that sailors be creative in furnishing their own entertainment. Some crews produced their own theatricals. Finding costumes and scenery had its challenges, although the audience was likely not to be too demanding in this respect. Accounts exist, however, of plays complete with drop curtains, footlights, and props that included even a door with knockers. Slapstick and melodrama were particularly popular. Stellar acting and stimulating scripts were unnecessary, and some performances were given kudos simply for organization and presentation.

The variety of interests, skills, and hobbies on which seamen drew both to pass their off-duty time and to express themselves was limited only by the number of men who went to sea. Scrimshaw, decorative ropework, chanties for every occasion, and even theatrical performances were the most prominent artistic pastimes that sailors of the period explored and refined. These pastimes did, however, share their popularity alongside other skills. Reports survive of a captain who ardently knitted a pair of slippers, one who cross-stitched a pin cushion, and another who was so proficient at net lace that he completed a bedspread on every voyage (Volo and Volo, 136–41, 143–44, 146–47, 153).

FOR MORE INFORMATION

Bryant, Jerry. *Roast Beef of Old England: Traditional Sailor Songs from Jack Aubrey's Navy.* CD5001, ESS.A.Y, 2000. Compact disc.

Laffin, J. *Jack Tars: The Story of the British Sailor.* London: Cassel, 1969.

McCracken, P. *Maritime History on the Internet.* 1995. <http://ils.unc.edu/maritime/home.shtml>, accessed October 23, 2003.

Thrower, W. R. *Life at Sea in the Age of Sail.* London: Phillimore, 1972.

Villiers, A. *Men, Ships, and the Sea.* Washington, D.C.: National Geographic, 1973.

Volo, D. D., and J. M. Volo. *Daily Life in the Age of Sail.* Westport, Conn.: Greenwood Press, 2002.

RECREATIONAL LIFE: WEB SITES

http://instructional1.calstatela.edu/dfrankl/CURR/kin375/k260ch11.htm

http://witcombe.sbc.edu/ARTHLinks.html

http://www.cricket.org/link_to_database/ARCHIVE/CRICKET_NEWS/2000/JUN/037354_CI_13JUN2000.html

http://www.origami.as/home.html

http://www.origami.gr.jp/People/OKMR_/history-e.html

http://www.fruitlands.org/onlinelearning/ch1.htm

8

RELIGIOUS LIFE

The human world is made up of more than the material and social environments that surround us. Throughout history, people have left records of their recognition of and longing for something larger than themselves, and this desire to transcend daily life forms the basis for people's religious faith. Religions have two intertwined components—belief and rituals—and the second derives from and preserves the former. Thus, through careful enactments of rituals, the faithful believe that they can rise above the mundane realities of day-to-day life, and historians find that the study of religious practices offers a window into people's spiritual beliefs.

Religious beliefs have served to help people make sense of the natural world—from its beauties to its disasters. For example, both an ancient Egyptian pharaoh (Akhenaton) and a medieval Christian saint (Francis of Assisi) wrote magnificent poetry praising the blessings of this world. In addition, both the Buddha and the Hebrew scriptures' Book of Job address the deep sufferings of this life. In these ways, religion has always helped people to make sense of the world that surrounds them. Religious beliefs were central to each of the cultures discussed in this volume. Hoping to elucidate the origins and ends of things, followers of many faiths, including the Copts of Ethiopia, the Catholics of New France, the Methodists of England, the Huguenots of France, the Puritans of the Massachusetts Bay Colony, and the Zen monks of Japan, drew from their respective religious beliefs, hoping to reach a spiritual understanding of themselves and the world around them.

Alongside religious beliefs, religious rituals serve the needs of society. The faithful reinforce their social ties by worshiping together, and sociologists of religion argue that religion is the symbolic worship of society itself. Coordinated acts of piety have always served to bind communities closer together by uniting people in a common expression of devotion. In this respect, the function of ritual practices among the 17th- and 18th-century cultures discussed in the entries that follow is no different. Sub-Saharan Africans, colonial Australians, North American colonists and Native Americans (including New Englanders and frontier communities), English, French, and Japanese identified religious beliefs, as well as sacred places where one could, through the performance of certain rituals, come closer to transcending the world of everyday things. Frequent participants in these rituals were spiritual mediators

RELIGIOUS LIFE

RELIGIOUS BELIEFS
RELIGIOUS PRACTICES

such as priests, ministers, shamans, and monks. Because religion was a symbol of belonging, those who did not belong—perhaps because of their differing religious beliefs or practices—often suffered social marginalization and even exile, torture, or death.

The intimate relationship between religious beliefs, rituals, and societies makes the study of religious life a fruitful one. Through the study of religious life, we can learn about how people have viewed the natural and supernatural and how rituals have organized people's daily lives. At the same time, we can glimpse the deep longing in the human soul, a longing that has generated some of the noblest—and cruelest—works of humanity.

~Joyce E. Salisbury and Peter Seelig

FOR MORE INFORMATION

Smart, N. *The World's Religions.* Cambridge, England: Cambridge University Press, 1998.

Religious Beliefs

During the 17th and 18th centuries, people's religious beliefs shaped, to a great extent, people's views of the world. Although such beliefs varied significantly, sub-Saharan Africans, settlers and Indians along North America's frontiers, English, French, Japanese, and New Englanders exhibited certain shared values. Commonalities included the belief in one God, or at least in a chief deity; the notion of a god as creator; the conviction that certain humans possessed a privileged relationship with the spiritual world; and a belief that some kind of release from misery was possible.

Muslims and Christians traditionally conceived of one and only one God. Certainly, the Anglicans, Catholics, Methodists, and Dissidents—all of whom were self-professed Christians—considered there to be but a single God. Outside these sects, which constituted the main religious communities in England and France, as well as of the North American colonial frontier and New England, traditional Muslims held that only one God existed—Allah. And yet many Muslims living in sub-Saharan Africa combined the traditional tenets of Islam with their own traditional beliefs, creating belief systems that accounted for the existence of multiple gods. Often, Muslim Africans south of the Sahara identified Allah with their most prominent traditional god, while maintaining a significant place for lesser deities.

Therefore, the monotheistic belief in a single God, distinct from the surrounding world, was not representative of traditional sub-Saharan African religions; nor was monotheism representative of Japanese or Native American religious convictions. In Japan, the traditional and amorphously organized religion of Shintō allowed for a dizzying array of spirits that derived their existences from kinship groups. Worthy of note, however, is the spiritual hierarchy that exerted a powerful influence over Japan during the early modern period. Belonging to the preeminent Japanese kinship group, the Yamato, was the sun goddess Amaterasu-omi-kami, the preeminent Japanese spirit.

The cultures that are covered in this volume typically attributed a creative power to one or more of their gods. Among Christians in Africa, colonial North America's frontier communities, England, France, and New England, the notion of a single God that created the world is key. For instance, both Puritan covenant theology and its infrequent bedfellow Deism emphasized a God that single-handedly created a world and set it in motion. Native Americans in New England and along the frontiers believed that the creator, far from being distinct from the world, suffused all nature with its spiritual presence.

In Africa, communities such as the Ethiopians, the Kongolese, the Wolof of Senegambia, the Yoruba, the Ashanti, and the San of Kalahari all held the doctrine that the world had an origin and that this origin had, as its source, a creator god or gods. The Yoruba of southern West Africa believed in a pantheon of gods, the *orisha*, and that a cooperative effort among its deities resulted in the creation of the Earth, souls, and bodies. Elsewhere, Africans told of other creator gods, including Kaang and Mulungu.

Some people claimed (or were thought by others) to possess special religious powers that constituted a kind of privileged access to the spiritual world. By helping to bridge the gap between the world of gods, deities, and spirits, the belief in such individuals was central to the effectiveness of the overall belief system. In England, inspirational Methodists such as John Wesley and George Whitefield gave impassioned orations with which to motivate listeners and spectators. Methodists in New England were also prominent, as were Puritan ministers, who encouraged a general conviction during the 17th century that a necessary condition for salvation was the intervention of a Puritan minister.

In Japan, a strong faith in the capacity of shamans, geomancers, and diviners to predict future events placed them in a curious position of influence, particularly among peasants. In France, militant Catholics known as Jesuits established themselves as a powerful repressive tool in the struggle against both Protestantism and renegade forms of Catholicism. African Muslim leaders, called marabouts, were instrumental in maintaining and spreading information about Islam. Some of these Muslims acquired such a pronounced degree of reverence during their lives that they attained a kind of sainthood. Called *walis*, they healed the ailing, judged the accused, predicted the future, and cursed their foes.

Many, although not all, of the religious beliefs discussed in the following entries reveal a preoccupation with salvation. Whereas the Anglican Church in England was generally regarded as more interested in questions of material and political influence than in questions of the soul, other Christian sects stressed not only the corruption that blighted people's souls but the possibility that some were or could be saved. Puritans routinely reminded themselves and others that the mind, will, and hearts of all humans—without exception—were corrupt. Puritans believed that a very few Puritans who underwent a process called justification could be among the "elect," that is, among the saved. Significantly more optimistic were Quakers, who held that every person could find salvation on his or her own, thanks to an inner light that each possessed.

In a related way, Buddhists throughout Japan held that human desire prompted the vain and illusory quest for happiness. Because of reincarnation, people could live out this painful cycle over and over again, until they grasped the truth of existence and shook off the chains of desire.

Religious beliefs provided individuals from many cultures with a profound spiritual framework that enabled them to develop an understanding of their origins, their lives, and their futures.

~*Peter Seelig*

FOR MORE INFORMATION

Smart, N. *The World's Religions*. Cambridge, England: Cambridge University Press, 1998.

RELIGIOUS LIFE

RELIGIOUS BELIEFS

Africa

The Colonial Frontier
of North America

England

France

Japan

New England

AFRICA

In much of Africa during the 17th and 18th centuries, religion was the cornerstone of all life and inseparable from the routines, joys, and problems of daily existence. Traditional African religions derived from a mythology and worldview that also gave rise to people's sense of history and social order. African religious beliefs sprung from the material of daily life and often changed over time as new beings from the spirit world were discovered to possess more power. Islam and Christianity, as they developed in Africa, took on many of these same tendencies and combined during this period in different ways with other belief systems in a process called "syncretism."

All traditional African religions postulated the existence of a high god who created the world and who is often unknowable and inaccessible. Along with this god, countless lesser gods were believed to be involved with natural processes, important places, and social customs and institutions, gods to which people looked for aid in different areas of life. These gods and the myths surrounding them formed part of a community's oral tradition, which also included stories of the community's history, their traditional ways of doing things, and even politics and government, essentially infusing everything that an African did with some degree of religious significance.

During the 17th and 18th centuries, the Yoruba, a people who have lived in southern West Africa from what is now Nigeria to the Ivory Coast, worshiped a pantheon of gods known as *orisha*. Olorun, the *orisha* of peace, harmony, justice, and purity, ruled the sky and all things that were white, such as bones and clouds. Whether Olorun was male, female, or both varied from village to village. According to tradition, Olorun asked his son Orishala to create the Earth at Ile-Ife, traditional seat of the Yoruba kings. Orishala failed, however, and Odudawa finished the job. The god Odudua created the human body, and Olorun the soul. Another important god was Shango, the god of thunder, who was portrayed with a double axe on his head. He is the ancestor of the Yoruba leaders. Ogun, the god of iron, also enjoyed a wide following because the Yoruba used iron in so many different areas of life.

One important god from the Ashanti pantheon, also from West Africa, is the trickster Anansi, known as the "spider god." His father, the wise and all-knowing high god Nyame, ordered him to fetch rain during fires and to set the boundaries of flooding rivers. The Ashanti believed that Anansi created the first human, into whom Nyame breathed life. The San of the Kalahari Desert believed in a high god named Kaang, who created the world and who is present in all things. When the first man he created disobeyed him, Kaang sent fire and destruction into the world and moved his home to the top of the sky. Much of East Africa believed in a creator god named Mulungu, a god of the sky who spoke in thunder.

Although most Africans believed in life after death, they did not typically believe in a heaven or hell. Usually, the spirits of the dead simply remained part of their clan or village and were honored as elders. In that sense, concern for the afterlife represented more a part of family life than religion, as Europeans knew it. The spirits of the dead retained all their characteristics and ties to the living and had much influence in all areas of life. People looked to traditional rituals and priests to help them communicate with both gods and ancestors and to seek their intercession in daily life.

After these traditional beliefs, Islam was the most important of sub-Saharan African religions during the 17th and 18th centuries. Almost all the people of the Mediterranean coast and the Sahara Desert professed faith in Islam, and Muslim communities were also important along the Swahili coast and in the states and villages of West Africa. The Wolof in Senegambia claimed that they had been Muslims since the beginning of time. Muslim leaders in West Africa were known as marabouts—these included Qur'an reciters, people who transmitted the traditions of Muhammed's life, scholars of Islamic law, and local Sufi hermits and organizers of Sufi lodges.

This Yoruba statuette praises worship of Obatala, the *orisha* of creativity. Werner Forman/Art Resource, NY.

Many marabouts were eventually revered as *walis* or "friends of God." Sometimes regarded as a sort of sainthood, *baraka* was the divine grace that God bestowed on those who had lived especially pious lives and who had performed the Sufi spiritual exercises. With this *baraka* came the power to give blessings to others, to heal their wounds, to foretell events, to judge controversies, and to curse enemies. In these and other ways, marabouts and *walis* and the Muslim communities to which these prominent followers of Islam belonged became part of the existing African religious fabric, as they demonstrated the same kinds of connections to the spirit world as the traditional African priests. After death, a *walis's baraka* was believed to pass to the tomb, which became a place of pilgrimage. In this way, Islam came to have shrines across the African landscape, as did the traditional religions.

In accepting Islam, Africans did not really abandon their traditional religions; rather, they simply added Islam to them. People identified the God of the Qur'an with their own high creator gods and saw nothing wrong with continuing to seek the aid of traditional minor deities. The most significant difference between Islam and other African religions was the Qur'an, a text written in Arabic and, according to Muslims, untranslatable. Because of this exclusiveness, even non-Muslims came to see Arabic as a sacred language and venerated the Arabic script.

Christianity also had a long history in Africa. During the 16th and 17th centuries, Ethiopia and Kongo became the continent's two most important Christian kingdoms, although missionaries sought to spread the faith wherever they went. Ethiopia had become Christian during the fourth century, whereas the religion came to Kongo with the Portuguese in the 16th century. Each kingdom, however, developed a different version of Christianity.

Ethiopians followed the Coptic branch of Christianity, and their *Abuna*, or patriarch, was always an Egyptian appointed by the patriarch of Alexandria. The Copts were Monophysites who believed that Jesus had only a divine, and not a human, nature. The negus, or ruler of Ethiopia, was also the official head of the church. Ethiopians possessed an understanding of concepts such as the sacraments and sainthood similar to those of the Eastern Orthodox Church. One unusual feature, however, was that in Ethiopia, Pontius Pilate, who oversaw the Crucifixion, was regarded as a saint.

The case of Kongo, the other large Christian kingdom, reveals how Africans retained their own identity even when adopting "imported" beliefs. During the 16th and 17th centuries, Catholic missionaries had succeeded in converting most of the country, and the Kongolese kings were protectors of the faith. Nonetheless, people continued to believe in the presence of their late ancestors and in different nature spirits. The church fought with limited success to pass these traditional roles over to Catholic saints, especially to St. Anthony and St. Francis of Assisi. In 1704, a religious leader named Dona Beatriz Kimpa Vita claimed to have been possessed by the spirit of St. Anthony. She denounced the European priests for misleading the people and taught that Jesus was a Kongolese and that Christianity had originated right there in Kongo. Two years later, she was burned at the stake as a heretic, but her teachings lived on.

African religious practices came in many different forms, ranging from local cults dedicated to features of the landscape under a high God, to larger, world religions that brought with them a complex, written theology and distinct culture. Choosing from this spiritual smorgasbord, Africans based their selections on the perceived power of different religious traditions to meet their religious needs, whether these needs concerned an intervention to find a marriage partner or the desire to adopt a tradition that connected them to a larger community. In doing so, they preserved their own religious culture into which other religious beliefs could be incorporated.

To read about religion in Africa in the 20th century, see the Africa entry in the section "Religion" in chapter 8 ("Religious Life") of volume 6 of this series.

~*Brian Ulrich*

FOR MORE INFORMATION

Biallas, L. J. *World Religions: A Story Approach*. Mystic, Conn.: Twenty-third Publications, 1991.

Halsall, P., ed. *Internet African History Sourcebook*. 1996. <http://www.fordham.edu/halsall/africa/africasbook.html>, accessed October 23, 2003.

King, N. Q. *Religions of Africa: A Pilgrimage into Traditional Religions*. New York: Harper and Row, 1970.

Levtzion, N. "Islam in Africa to 1800: Merchants, Chiefs, and Saints." In *The Oxford History of Islam*, edited by J. L. Esposito, 475–507. Oxford: Oxford University Press, 1999.

Fung, K. *Africa South of the Sahara*. 1994. <http://www-sul.stanford.edu/depts/ssrg/africa/guide.html>, accessed October 23, 2003.

Ogot, B. A., ed. *General History of Africa*. Vol. 5. *Africa from the Sixteenth Century to the Eighteenth Century*. Paris: United Nations Educational, Scientific, and Cultural Organization, 1992.

Scheub, H. *A Dictionary of African Mythology*. New York: Oxford University Press, 2000.

van Beek, W. E. A., T. D. Blakely, and D. L. Thomson, eds. *Religion in Africa: Experience and Expression*. Portsmouth, N.H.: Heinemann, 1994.

THE COLONIAL FRONTIER OF NORTH AMERICA

Unlike many European settlers, Native Americans exhibited little antipathy toward the concept of wilderness. Native American religion accepted a relationship between humanity and the natural world and bordered on a love of nature. Its followers recognized humanity as one with all living things. Moreover, for them, the wilderness did not connote evil and disorder but a natural order and the very essence of deity. It should not be surprising, therefore, that European explorers, missionaries, and settlers failed to understand the Native Americans' spiritual relationship with and pious regard for the land.

The religions of the Iroquoian, Algonquian, and many other woodland Indians were dualistic. Good and evil existed in the world, and the objective of humans was to please friendly spirits and to mollify unfriendly ones. The Iroquois believed in a creator, Orenda, who embodied the health and creativity of nature. The spirits of maize, beans, and squash—the "Three Sisters"—were examples of how the Iroquois assigned spiritual personality, or manitou, to all the material objects around them.

With the exception of a few Catholics who settled in Maryland, the English who came to America were almost all Protestants, but they represented a large number of discrete, if not mutually antagonistic, religious sects. Protestants, in general, found the Catholic Church unacceptable in its hierarchical beliefs and practices. However, Protestants disagreed among themselves. For instance, Puritans were Protestants who believed that the Church of England (the Anglican Church), although Protestant, was a corruption of true Protestantism and barely distinguishable from the Catholic faith. The belief system of the Puritans displayed a greater emphasis on spiritual purity and unbending piety than on the Church of England's espoused beliefs in hierarchy and ornate ritual. Thus, adherents of the Church of England, or Anglican Church, dominated the colonies of Virginia, Delaware, and even Maryland.

The Scotch-Irish who came to America were nearly all Presbyterians. The Scotch-Irish Presbyterians in general subscribed to the belief that the organization of church government, in order to be correct, had to eliminate the episcopacy (the system of bishops) used in both the Catholic Church and the Church of England. In this, the Scotch-Irish traced many of their ideas to those of John Knox, who had made efforts to establish Presbyterianism as the Church of Scotland. Having pushed the Irish Catholic population out of Ulster, in the northeast of Ireland, these Scots acted on their own brand of rigidity, avoiding the Puritans and despising the tolerant Quakers for their faith in pacifism. On the frontier, the tough-minded Scotch-Irish unabashedly believed that Scripture foreordained them to take their land from the Indians, by force if necessary.

Quakers, drawn by William Penn's assurance of religious toleration, initially settled in Pennsylvania. George Fox and Margaret Fell established Quakerism in 17th-century England. Quakerism was a radical religion that attracted these generally independent people by preaching the virtues of the family as the basic disciplining and spiritualizing authority in society, as opposed to that of magistrates and church prelates.

The Germanic settlers were Protestants and divided into Lutherans and many related Pietist sects including Moravians, Mennonites, and Methodists. German Baptists (Dunkers) existed in small numbers throughout the colonies and were, on the whole, sober and collected, valuing the beliefs of simplicity, justice, and mercy. They believed that true Christians should attempt to follow the beliefs of the early Christian Church, advocating complete immersion in water for baptism, for which they became known as "Dunkers." German Baptists eschewed religious and denominational controversies as unchristian, preferring pleasing, contemplative, and reaffirming sermons over those that espoused dogmatic confrontation and brutal orthodoxy.

Finally, the Dutch, the Flemish Walloons, and the French Huguenots were Protestant dissenters and nonconformists who drew from the ideas of the theologian and activist John Calvin. Walloons were French-speaking Calvinists from the southernmost provinces of the Spanish Netherlands. The Huguenots were Protestant refugees from within France. Along with the Dutch, these groups shared the conviction that the Catholic Church did not adequately represent Christian principles. Both the Walloons and Huguenots were thus targets of the relentless persecution of the Catholic regimes of Spain and France, respectively. These Protestants tended to remain in those regions of the English colonies that Holland had originally colonized.

The Catholic faith dominated New France (present-day Canada). Initially, the sole spiritual ministers of the colony were to be Jesuits, a powerful order of Catholics that emphasized education, charity, and missionary work and that aimed to establish Catholicism as the one legitimate Christian church in North America. Crown policy ensured that the settlers were wholly Roman Catholics. No one whose devotion to the Catholic Church was suspect was allowed to emigrate to New France. Among the English, a hatred of Catholics, and of Jesuits in particular, was deep-seated and engendered from an early age. When studying the events that took place on the frontiers in this era, one should not underestimate the themes of anti-Catholicism and anti-Protestantism.

As zealous missionaries, the French Jesuits hoped to convert the native population to Catholicism. However, many Native Americans only partially accepted Cathol-

Catherine Tekakwitha was an Iroquois who converted to Catholicism in New France. Reprinted from M. Bacqueville de la Potherie, *Histoire de l'Amérique Septentrionale . . .* Paris, J.-L. Nion et F. Didot, 1722.

icism, whereas the missionaries were attempting to extract from them a total acceptance of the Roman faith and a complete abandonment of traditional native beliefs.
The spread of Catholicism in New France had limited results, at the very most. Even
less successful were the largely abortive efforts of the English to bring Protestantism
to the native peoples along the Anglo-American frontiers. Missionaries in the region
came too late and with too little vigor to tie the Indians to Protestant dogma.
Moreover, the Protestant faiths in general seem to have lacked much of the mysti-
cism and ceremony that drew Native Americans to Catholicism.

In the earliest years of black slavery, the new arrivals from Africa depended heavily
on their own tribal religions and cultural practices. With time, many African religious practices came to be fused with Christianity. Yet white English society deemed
the simplest vestiges of African culture to be pagan, innately evil, and inconsistent
with Christianity. In New England, among the Puritans, even the remotest hint of
aboriginal religious practice brought charges of witchcraft, incarceration, torture, or
worse. White ministers, therefore, absolutely forbade blacks from retaining even the
simplest forms of African culture and strove to eliminate completely any cultural
memories from among blacks living in the New World.

Religious beliefs were central to the historical development of the old colonial
frontier. Protestants rejected Catholicism not only in Europe but in New France, as
well. Protestants themselves splintered into Anglicans, Puritans, Presbyterians, German Lutherans and Pietests, and the Calvinist Dutch, Walloons, and Huguenots.
To varying degrees and with different reactions, these Christian sects typically dis-
dained Native American and African religious beliefs, occasionally attempting to
eliminate them through missionary work (Volo and Volo, 2–3, 44–45, 51, 55–56,
64, 67, 103, 106, 108, 110–11, 113).

FOR MORE INFORMATION

Bourne, R. *Gods of War, Gods of Peace: How the Meeting of Native and Colonial Religions
Shaped Early America*. New York: Harcourt, 2002.

Volo, J. M., and D. D. Volo. *Daily Life on the Old Colonial Frontier*. Westport, Conn.: Greenwood Press, 2002.

ENGLAND

There was a good deal of popular support for the idea of religious belief among
Anglicans, Catholics, and Dissenters alike in 18th-century England. Their beliefs,
however, tended toward the confrontational and represented a general lack of religious fervor, as well as a distinctly politicized emphasis on secular organizational
methods. For most of the century, with the singular exception of the success of
Methodism, the nation seemed to linger in a state of spiritual inertia. Clergy, who
seemed more interested in tithes and fox hunting than in hellfire and salvation,
bored Anglicans. And without the motivating force of fierce, organized persecution,
even Dissenters grew increasingly lax.

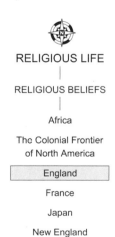

Anglicans were, in the eyes of the law, those who subscribed to the Thirty-nine Articles of the faith and who took Anglican communion. They were the majority of the people as a whole: the *Anglican* Church, the Church of *England*. To be anything but a member of the established church was by definition to be un-English. Higher education at Oxford and Cambridge, government posts, and the governing corporations of towns were still closed to non-Anglicans. Anglican clergy could preach anywhere they liked, whereas Dissenting ministers could only occupy the pulpits of licensed Dissenting chapels. Even the basic unit of local government, the parish, was identical to the basic unit of the religious hierarchy. The most telling sign of Anglican supremacy at the local level concerned the fact that non-Anglicans had to pay tithes, a kind of tax, to the parish priest.

The Anglican preoccupation with political power, financial solvency, and relative supremacy among competing sects was not unusual for the time. The 18th century was a uniquely secular age, an age in which reason and science were given unprecedented importance. The occasional brave soul even declared him- or herself an atheist. Throughout the 18th century, people of all kinds noted, usually with dismay, the lack of faith around them.

Numerous rival sects were eager to take advantage of the Anglican Church's lassitude; however, the most visible rival was in many ways the least able to seize its opportunities. Since the 16th century, the Church of England had been waging a war of public relations against "papists" (Catholics), and it had quite decisively won. Papists were almost universally believed to be superstitious, treasonous, and idle (owing to the larger number of religious holidays in the Catholic calendar). Although toleration was fashionable in some circles, anti-Catholic bias remained strong and gained support in light of the Jacobite attempts in the first half of the 18th century to return a Catholic monarch to the British throne. Thereafter, anti-Catholicism waned somewhat with the failure of the Jacobite cause.

It was not Catholicism that attracted those on the Anglican fringe but Dissent, and the most successful new Dissenting or Nonconformist sect of the 18th century actually began as a part of the Anglican Church. Brothers John and Charles Wesley, with other divinity students, founded the Holy Club at Oxford in 1729 and were joined in 1732 by George Whitefield. They developed a system of devotion, charity, and evangelism that came to be known as Methodism. In 1739, Whitefield failed to gain access to a pulpit from which to preach his unorthodox views, but he turned the setback into an advantage, taking his message directly to the people in a series of open-air sermons. John Wesley joined him in field preaching, delivering about 40,000 such sermons between 1739 and 1791 and traveling nearly 25,000 miles on his journeys through England. John Wesley—a Tory, a royalist, and for most of his life a stout opponent of Dissent—insisted that Methodists attend Anglican services. Only in 1784, seven years before his death, did he begin ordaining his own priests, in defiance of the Anglican Church.

John Wesley's vision was of poor, itinerant, evangelist priests and spiritually enthusiastic, even ecstatic, congregations. Sermons, full of the agonies of hell and the unfathomable joys of heaven, frequently prompted intense emotional displays among participants, and it was not unusual for enemies of the new sect to emphasize the supposed frenzies of worshipers.

If the Church of England primarily served the gentry, and Methodism the poor, Dissent aimed at the prosperous and growing middle class. In general, Dissenters were Whiggish and urban and were likely to be professionals, intellectuals, entrepreneurs, weavers, and reformers. Because Dissenters also had to pay tithes to the Anglican parish priest, regardless of whether they attended his services, Dissenting ministers often received paltry pay and had to take second jobs.

The sheer number of openly practiced faiths in England, particularly in London, was both dazzling and baffling to contemporaries. There were Congregationalists (or Independents) and Baptists, who doubled in number between 1750 and 1790; Quakers, noted for their plain dress, their use of "thee," and their tendency, shocking for the time, to let women preach; Moravians, who inspired the Methodists in the 1720s but split from them in the 1740s; Sandemanians; Antinomians; Swedenborgians; Muggletonians; Unitarians, whose liberal faith—popular with scientists, writers, and educators—rejected miracles and the Trinity; Presbyterians, from whose ranks Unitarians originally emerged; Lutherans; Calvinists; and Arians.

Eighteenth-century England was a religious nation, in that almost everyone subscribed to a faith and submitted on a daily basis to the influence of religion. It was, however, a nation inclined to secularism, with science, an overall lack of interest in worship, a largely indifferent government, and the materialism of the Anglican clergy each playing a part in the heyday of "rational religion." Minority religions achieved few civil rights victories during the century; however, the degree of religious freedom that existed in 18th-century England was no small achievement (Olsen, 280, 284–88).

To read about religion in Chaucer's England, see the Europe entries in chapter 8 ("Religious Life") of volume 2; for Elizabethan England, see the Catholicism and Protestantism entries in chapter 8 ("Religious Life") of volume 3; and for Victorian England, see the Victorian England entries in chapter 8 ("Religious Life") of volume 5 of this series.

FOR MORE INFORMATION

Jacob, W. M. *Lay People and Religion in the Early Eighteenth Century*. New York: Cambridge University Press, 1996.

Lynch, J. *Eighteenth Century Resources*. <http://newark.rutgers.edu/~jlynch/18th/>, accessed October 10, 2003.

Olsen, K. *Daily Life in 18th-Century England*. Westport, Conn.: Greenwood Press, 1999.

Rupp, E. G. *Religions in England, 1688–1791*. New York: Oxford University Press, 1986.

FRANCE

The 17th and 18th centuries in France, as in the rest of Europe, were host to extremes in faith and belief. On the one hand, French rulers began to prize political

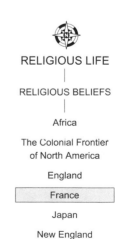

RELIGIOUS LIFE
|
RELIGIOUS BELIEFS
|
Africa

The Colonial Frontier
of North America

England

France

Japan

New England

gains over warfare inspired by denominational difference. However, the Counter Reformation also continued to influence religious practice. The Jesuits, a quasi-militaristic religious order that was founded to combat the spread of Protestantism, paired with kings who attempted to enforce religious uniformity. And even as rationalist intellectuals became more secular, Christian groups feuded over power, influence, and the path to salvation.

In 1598, Henry IV had issued the Edict of Nantes, which promised religious toleration for the Protestant minority in France, the Huguenots. An attempt to end the wars of religion that were sweeping across France, the Edict promised that Huguenots would have judicial protection, freedom of worship, and the right to defend themselves against aggression. This was a major step toward religious toleration in France. While Henry IV's successor, Louis XIII, destroyed most of the political and military protections of the Edict, the Huguenots maintained freedom of religious practice. Louis XIII also entered the Thirty Years' War in an attempt to weaken the power of the Habsburg family, the other major Catholic power on the continent. Protecting the international interests of Roman Catholicism was demonstrably less important to the king of France than was furthering the interests of his state. In his political doctrine of *raison d'état*, the chief minister of France, Cardinal Richelieu, confronted the topic of the state and its priorities and stridently defended the justification of national self-interest as a law possessing greater importance than religious conformity. This way of thinking demonstrated the elevation of secular standards for decision making above doctrinal squabbling.

However, in 1685, Louis XIV promulgated the Revocation of the Edict of Nantes, which led to the persecution, imprisonment, and expulsion of Huguenot artisans and merchants throughout the kingdom. Louis XIV's desire for religious uniformity targeted not only Protestants but also certain Catholics. The Jansenists, a Catholic group that agitated for reform, came under particular attack. Louis XIV was especially hostile to this group because its beliefs resembled Protestantism insofar as its adherents emphasized individual faith and the depravity of human nature. Unlike Henry IV, Louis XIV believed that total unity, even within spheres of Catholic belief and practice, was a necessary foundation for a successful state. Influenced as he was by the orthodoxy of the counter-reforming Jesuit order, Louis XIV was even willing to decimate the resources of the nation by expelling wealthy Protestant artisans and influential Jansenists to achieve this unity.

The growing attempt on the part of the state to enforce orthodoxy sparked its own backlash. Philosophers had begun questioning religious beliefs and practices even before the Edict of Nantes. The sun-centered universe proposed by the Copernican theory called the literal accuracy of the Bible into question and changed the earth-centered universe of the medieval world into a system in which the role of humanity was much less central.

Soon, Isaac Newton tied the universe into one coherent whole that remained in perpetual motion through the power of gravity. According to Newtonian science, the universe was a machine that ran on its own principles, independent of the God who created it.

Of further importance to religious beliefs were the ideas of Enlightenment philosophers who not only popularized the theories of Copernicus and Newton but also argued that if everything was matter in motion in the Newtonian world, then human life itself should be explicable by laws such as those that explained physical movement. Social sciences such as economics, sociology, and political science were thus born as a way of understanding the laws of human society. This mechanistic view of the universe led philosophers to revise Christian beliefs into a religion that they called Deism. According to Deism, God was analogous to a great watchmaker who manufactured the universe, wound it up, set it in motion, and then left it to run according to the principles of motion that had been determined in the process of creation.

Because philosophers argued that these rational principles were not merely applicable to physical objects but to social phenomena as well, human beings could understand God by means of their reason. No longer were religion and "superstition" part of the equation; people would not need to have recourse to religious explanations or doctrines to know how they ought to behave. It was in this context that Voltaire could utter his war cry of *Ecrasez l'infame!* or "Destroy the infamous thing," by which he meant, most notably, the Catholic Church and its single-minded enforcement of a particular set of beliefs.

In an equally serious attack on traditional religion, Enlightenment writers such as Pierre Bayle argued that it was necessary to subject religious beliefs to rational standards. In his *Historical and Critical Dictionary* (1697), he asserted that people ought to discard doctrines or dogmas that clashed with "natural understanding," even if the authority of Catholic scripture supported such beliefs. In another shock to 18th-century sensibilities, Bayle also claimed that morality was not dependent on religion; he claimed, for example, that there could be atheists who would be just as moral as devout Christians.

As greater portions of society promoted the tolerance of varying religious beliefs, a debate over the basis for morality became ever more relevant. If the Deists and Bayle were correct, morality ought not to be based on the Bible or tradition but on natural laws as revealed by social behavior. A growing interest in the moral codes of non-Western societies also demonstrated that different societies had different standards for moral

This engraving of a scene from a Paris brothel portrays the perceived moral laxity between men and women following the Thermidorean reaction. The larger, older woman in the center plays cards while either distributing or receiving a key. Unknown artist. © Perry Casteneda Library.

and immoral behavior. The existence of this social diversity led a number of Enlightenment philosophers to advocate a range of positions founded on moral relativism.

Just as the changing political winds of France had led to the Revocation of the Edict of Nantes, the country's growing secular influence led in its turn to political and religious upheaval. French Revolutionaries (deeply influenced by Voltaire's critique of the power of the Catholic Church and its " superstition") tried to destroy the Church. In its place, they promoted a belief in the "Supreme Being," which was not a Catholic God, but a Deist creator, removed from the universe. Civil war broke out between Catholics who defended their faith and Revolutionaries who wanted to create a new world. There followed a period known as the Thermidorean reaction, during which time many French perceived a weakening of religious morality and a strengthening of "loose behavior." These tensions were formally resolved only with Napoleon's Concordat, in which it was agreed on the one hand that Catholicism was "the religion of the majority of the French" and on the other hand that the official policy of the state was to reflect a toleration of other religions.

~Jennifer J. Popiel

FOR MORE INFORMATION

Doyle, W. *Jansenism: Catholic Resistance to Authority from the Reformation to the French Revolution.* New York: St. Martin's Press, 2000.

Hacken, R. *The History of France, Primary Documents.* 1996. <http://www.lib.byu.edu/~rdh/eurodocs/france.html>, accessed October 23, 2003.

Lund, R. D. *The Margins of Orthodoxy: Heterodox Writing and Cultural Response, 1660–1750.* New York: Cambridge University Press, 1995.

Lynch, J. *Eighteenth Century Resources.* <http://newark.rutgers.edu/~jlynch/18th/>, accessed October 10, 2003.

McManners, J. *Church and Society in Eighteenth-Century France.* Vols. 1–2. New York: Clarendon Press, 1998.

Trevor-Roper, H. R. *The Crisis of the Seventeenth Century: Religion, the Reformation, and Social Change.* New York: Harper and Row, 1968.

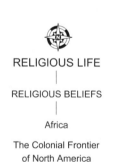

RELIGIOUS LIFE

|

RELIGIOUS BELIEFS

|

Africa

The Colonial Frontier
of North America

England

France

Japan

New England

JAPAN

The religious life of 18th-century Japan was a complex amalgam of traditions that included Buddhism, neo-Confucianism, and Shamanism. The primary tradition, however, was an indigenous conglomeration of folk beliefs.

Prior to the 16th century, Shintō (the way of the gods) was very much a chaotic set of regional and localized belief systems that coexisted almost independently of each other. In the prehistorical past, fictive kinship groups (*uji*) created spirits that were to act as guardians of a local area. These spirits (*kami*) coexisted with, sometimes influenced, and at other times were influenced by humans, animals, and other life forms.

The preeminent *uji*, the Yamato family, chose for its *kami* the ideal example of fertility and life: the sun. When the time came for Japan to write its history, the imperial Yamato house appointed its *kami*, the sun goddess Amaterasu-omi-kami, the chief deity of all Japan.

Shintō featured neither a divinely inspired canon of either precepts or moral obligations nor a hierarchically organized priesthood. Instead, Shintō was a hodge-podge of regional taboos, rituals, folklore, and superstitions. Until the 17th century or so, no attempts were made at systemization, rationalization, or organization. And yet Shintō survived in the face of the infinitely more sophisticated Chinese systems, becoming a part of every Japanese ritual ceremony and festival.

Shintō did provide Japanese with an intense connection to their environment. Inextricably linked to the very being of Japanese was every aspect of their cosmic flora, fauna, and geologic surroundings. Everything shared the same life force; everything could be, and perhaps latently was, *kami*. Japanese farmers were constantly reminded of the mysterious, imperfectly understood verities at the heart of the agricultural rhythms of life.

The *kami*, themselves, were as flawed as was humanity. Good spirits and bad spirits alike were capricious, hungry, suspicious, jealous, and greedy. Humans needed to cajole, flatter, trick, and bribe the *kami* to avert catastrophe. And even then, no outcome was certain.

Buddhism was as philosophically sophisticated as Shintō was simplistic. It abounded in written canons in several languages (notably, Sanskrit and Chinese). During its millennium of experience in China, it had acquired a complex moral system and an elaborate priestly hierarchy. When the efforts of charismatic Buddhist missionaries (*ubasoku*) from Korea significantly contributed to the inculcation of Buddhism into Japanese culture, the religion intertwined with local Shintōist beliefs. Soon, Japanese considered *kami* to be local manifestations of Buddhas; Buddhist religious practices subsumed Shintō superstitious and purification rituals.

Essentially, Buddhism affirms that life is a painful illusion. Humans are doomed to an endless cycle of painful incarnations until they rid themselves of attachment and desire (which cause the pain). The path to release is through the realization of the preceding truths. Know and you will be released; but therein lies a cosmos of interpretation and contention. What is truth, and how shall we know it?

In 18th-century Japan, there were perhaps hundreds of schools of truth within Buddhism. Zen and the various so-called Amida Pureland sects held that single invocations of religious formulaic chants were sufficient for salvation. Perhaps 70 to 80 percent of those who professed to be Buddhists at the time were adherents of Pureland Buddhism.

Confucianism is properly considered a secular social and political philosophy rather than a religion. However, it was treated very much like a religion in 18th-century Japan, particularly in its neo-Confucian incarnation. It was essentially the chief moral system for the society and constituted the ideal of the samurai (warrior-administrator) class. Neo-Confucianism became virtually inextricable from Buddhism in the early modern period, and the chief adherents and scholars of neo-Confucianism were Zen monks.

The Chinese philosopher K'ung Fu-tzu elaborated the basic tenets of classical Confucianism in the fifth century B.C.E. He taught that society properly reflects the harmonious cosmos and that the best expression of social hierarchy corresponds to normal family relationships, including the filial piety that governs relations between father and son. Women, being naturally more emotional than men, require benevolent protection, and children need moral nurture and education.

The 12th-century philosopher Chu Hsi posited a system of reforms that became known as neo-Confucianism, called *Shushi* in Japan. As practiced in 18th-century Japan, neo-Confucianism maintained that the best division of society corresponds to four hereditary socioprofessional classes. At the summit were the samurai, whose moral rule was a consequence of their superior education. Below them were the peasant farmers, whose agricultural production was of great value. Beneath the peasants were the artisan-craftsmen, who manufactured goods for the benefit of everyone. Merchants, relegated to the bottom of the social hierarchy, purportedly contributed little to society except the movement of goods from areas of production to areas of demand.

Buddhism played an integral role in the reinforcement and diffusion of neo-Confucian truths. The semiofficial orthodoxy of virtually every Buddhist priest and monk was that one's karma determined one's social station in the next life. Proper behavior helped to work off one's karma so that in the next life, good souls were incarnated as samurai and that immoral people were reborn as merchants, *eta* (hereditary outcastes), or even animals. Obviously, this was a powerful religious and philosophical reinforcement for social control.

If anything, the core of Shintō was systematic compared with the shamanistic beliefs of 18th-century Japan, and yet the two religious cultures merged. Magic, geomancy, and divination were tightly bound up in the superstitions fate-oriented mentalities of Dao and even Shintō.

"The Way" (Dao) is best maintained when complementary opposites are balanced in nature. The cosmic binaries of light-dark, dry-moist, male-female, high-low, ethereal-earthy, and so on affect everything and are, of course, affected by everything else. When the elements are in balance, the cosmos is in harmony. The essential goal of humanity is to discover how best to maintain that harmony—hence, the need for diviners and geomancers.

Shamanistic ideas melded almost effortlessly with essential Shintō. Peasants believed that just as the *kami* of Shintō required appeasement, so too did virtually any change in life, such as travel, marriage, adoption, purchase, and so on. Shamans could divine the future and determine auspicious times by consulting with one's ancestors. Shamans also practiced the art of spell and hex removal. Indeed, anyone who experienced a run of extraordinarily bad fortune could, and often did, consult a shaman for a remedy. Charismatic practitioners, who might very well be both a Daoist geomancer and a Shintō diviner, made their livelihood based on success and perceived efficacy.

The religions of 18th-century Japan were somewhat chaotically fused together, without ever really losing their individual characteristics. Shintō was characteristically untidy in its "system" of beliefs but essentially reflected a belief in spirits that were a mixture of good and bad and that could affect the future of humans. More systematic in its beliefs was Buddhism, which asserted that life is forever painful unless one renounces desire. Neo-Confucianism, more a political philosophy than a religion, laid out the theoretical justification for Japan's social hierarchy during the period. Finally, shamanism was a diverse set of vague beliefs in the power of prediction (Perez, 11, 38–40, 42–44, 49, 51–53).

To read about religion and morality in Japan in the 20th century, see the Japan entries in the sections "Morality" and "Religion" in chapter 8 ("Religious Life") of volume 6 of this series.

FOR MORE INFORMATION

Bellah, R. N. *Tokugawa Religion: The Values of Pre-Industrial Japan.* Glencoe, Ill.: Free Press, 1957.

Japan Information Network. <http://www.jinjapan.org/index.html>, accessed October 23, 2003.

Perez, L. G. *Daily Life in Early Modern Japan.* Westport, Conn.: Greenwood Press, 2002.

Yusa, M. *Japanese Religious Traditions.* Upper Saddle River, N.J.: Prentice Hall, 2002.

NEW ENGLAND

Religious beliefs contributed to every imaginable facet of daily life in colonial New England. Puritans, who constituted the region's dominant religious group during the 17th and early 18th centuries, crafted an interpretation of scripture called covenant theology, which provided an explanation for Eden, the Fall, human sinfulness, the role of Jesus Christ, and the salvation of a very few of the damned. By the end of the 17th century, several trends were contributing to the decline of Puritan influence, including intervention from the British government and an internal split within the body of Puritans. Long before the arrival of the colonists, however, there existed a strong tradition of native beliefs among New England tribes.

The Native Americans' view of nature, which is also to say their religion, was largely the same throughout New England. They viewed nature as a whole, refusing to consider any one part, including humankind, as greater or more sacred than another. A tree was to be looked on as just as sacred, meaningful, and important as a human being. Some aspect of the Creator dwelled in birds, bears, wolves, stones, and flowers. Native Americans viewed themselves as sharing the earth with other animals, which they saw as brothers.

Their gods lived in many natural elements—for example, the sea, thunder, wind, and rain. One colonist counted 37 such gods sacred to the people of the Narraganset.

Religious beliefs decided all else in colonial New England life. The Puritans who dominated colonial New England were committed to the establishment of a "godly" state in the New World, a theocracy in which church and state were virtually the same.

According to Puritans, each turning point in God's relationship with humans is expressed as a "covenant," or "contract." A contract is an agreement wherein one party promises to act in a specified way toward a second party, which, in turn, must act in a specified way toward the first party.

In God's covenant with Adam, God's part of the bargain was to provide humans with a protected place to live—the Garden of Eden. According to believers, concepts such as change and adversity left this special place untouched. Adam's part of the bargain was to praise God and obey him, specifically by avoiding the fruits of the Tree of Life and the Tree of the Knowledge of Good and Evil. As long as Adam obeyed God, God was obligated to keep Adam in paradise.

God kept his part of the bargain by providing Adam and Eve with a paradise, but Adam and Eve broke the contract. Satan, in the form of a snake, approached Eve, convincing her that if she and Adam ate of the forbidden fruit of the Tree of Knowledge, they would be greater than human; they would take on the power of God. Adam and Eve ate the fruit of the Tree of Knowledge.

With humanity's breach of the covenant of works, God's attitude toward humanity underwent a cataclysmic transformation because—according to the Puritans—God now became enraged. Indeed, wrath became God's fundamental quality. He would no longer tolerate humans in his presence. Hence, the Puritans would never describe God chiefly as a God of love and benevolence. Rather, God contained all things: hate and love, mercy and justice, light and dark, pride and humility.

As a result of the breach, three things utterly changed: the physical world, human nature and destiny, and God's relationship with humankind. In the first place, nature—the physical world, which, in the Garden of Eden, had been a perfect mirror of the divine—became a distorted and partial image of God.

As bad as was the change in physical nature, the alteration in human nature was worse. Every faculty of the human being "fell," that is, was ineffably corrupted. First, the human mind fell: people were never again able to grasp full knowledge of God or things divine. More than that, their will—their ability to make choices—was paralyzed. Worst of all, their hearts became defiled. They became capable of, and even desired, to commit every possible horrible sin. In the Puritans' view, this condition, known as natural depravity, was true of every person for all time, including even the tiny unborn infant and the most pious, charitable saint.

As for human destiny, Adam and Eve and all other people who came after them would now suffer, grow old, and die. After they died, they would inevitably go to hell.

God, for his part, decided that because of human disobedience, he would never again enter into any kind of covenant at all with humankind and would never again enter into a covenant of works with anyone.

Cotton Mather was a prominent Puritan minister who, toward the end of the 17th century, attempted to revitalize a fear of sin among New England's colonial population. Mather's influence revealed the political power that Puritan clergymen wielded. © Bettmann/CORBIS.

In the Puritans' interpretation of Scripture, however, something happened that gave *some* human beings something of a respite. Jesus Christ, the Son of God, appeared in human form. Because God would never again enter into a contract with humankind, Jesus, in his great compassion for the human race, made his own contract with God on behalf of all people. And because God would never again bind himself with a covenant of works that required of him contractual actions, the new covenant would be a covenant of grace, which placed no obligations on him. By virtue of this new covenant, God was free to do whatever he wanted to do, never to be contractually bound to provide benefits.

In exchange for Jesus' self-sacrifice, however, God agreed to "elect" (or choose) a very few human beings for salvation; that is, he would save them from going to hell. Such fortunate people were known as members of God's elect. In the strictest interpretation of Puritan doctrine, there was absolutely nothing one could do to become a member of the elect if God, before the beginning of time, did not choose one; and absolutely no way existed according to which one could ever positively know whether someone was a member of the elect.

By the end of 17th century, Puritanism, although still powerful enough in 1692 to fuel the Salem witchcraft trials, was in decline. The British introduced the much more ornate Anglican Church (the official Church of England) to New England and forced the Puritans to tolerate other religious denominations.

Puritanism itself splintered in the 18th century. Puritan clergy had always professed the need for a crucial balance between head and heart. Some clergymen came to emphasize emotions, becoming part of the Great Awakening, a movement that energized Congregationalism with revivals. Unlike the older Puritans, the followers of the Great Awakening practiced religion at highly charged, emotional meetings. Interestingly, the Great Awakening was meant to be a revitalization of Puritanism; in reality, however, the movement invigorated other Protestant churches, including the Baptists and emerging Methodists.

Other clergymen and parishioners came to emphasize the intellect over emotions. These Christians evolved into the strong Unitarian church of New England. As the name implies, they did away with the idea of the Trinity. They also greatly modified or entirely dropped Puritan ideas of salvation by election and grace alone.

To understand the beliefs of Puritanism is crucial if one is to grasp the spiritual element of daily life in colonial New England, which for so long held sway over the actions and thoughts of many colonists and which continues to resound in American culture (Johnson, 4–8, 13–14, 136).

FOR MORE INFORMATION

Cowing, C. B. *The Saving Remnant: Religion and the Settling of New England.* Urbana: University of Illinois Press, 1995.

Johnson, C. D. *Daily Life in Colonial New England.* Westport, Conn.: Greenwood Press, 2002.

RELIGIOUS LIFE

Religious Practices

Between 1600 and 1800, the religious practices of sub-Saharan Africans, colonial Australians, settlers and Native Americans along the North American colonial frontier, English, Japanese, and New Englanders reveal a threefold preoccupation with places of worship, hierarchies of religious officials, and the placement and treatment of minority or marginalized religious communities. An understanding of these themes in a cultural and cross-cultural context will facilitate an appreciation of the differences and similarities that marked some of the cultures discussed in this volume.

Places of worship tended to divide between locations that ostensibly served only the devotional wants and needs of a given population (churches, temples, meeting-houses) and those that featured secular, as well as religious, functions (homes). In England, the Anglican Church (the Church of England) laid emphasis on the importance of churches, sometimes more for the wealth and stature that they afforded a parson and his parish than for the godliness that they could encourage among parishioners. Colonial Australians saw St. John's Church and St. Phillip's Church erected early in the 19th century. Along the colonial frontier of North America, the French took great pride in their "cathedral," Notre Dame de la Paix (1657). On the Protestant side of the frontier, missionaries established "praying towns" and brought Native Americans there to be converted.

Meetinghouses in New England often lacked the elaborate architecture and ornate fixtures that characterized Anglican churches across the Atlantic. Puritan colonists during the 17th century had little choice but to attend the two daylight services that meetinghouses held every Sabbath. During these gatherings, organ music, signs of the cross, and kneeling were not allowed. Furthermore, Puritans practiced only two sacraments—holy communion and infant baptism—and Puritans insisted that holy communion, or the act of consuming wine and a wafer, amounted to a symbolic representation, and not a literal transformation, of the blood and body of Jesus.

During the 18th century, Japanese who desired to worship spirits in the tradition of Shintō (indigenous folk beliefs) could visit relatively large, if not elaborate, shrines, which were rather commercialized. Indeed, one could purchase talismans at such a shrine's entrance to enhance the piety of the visit. Buddhist temples also graced the Japanese landscape. Characteristically green, with tiled roofs that curved up at the eaves, the interiors of these temples offered visitors lavish visions of painted ceilings, gold-leaf designs, and elaborate carvings.

Designated places of worship often occupied a portion of a household's interior. Among the Ashanti, every home contained a small shrine dedicated to the high god Nyame. This shrine involved a preset arrangement of a bowl, white cloth, tree branch, and assorted objects. Japanese peasant households had similar shrines, referred to as "god-shelves," where offerings of food indicated an effort to please and appease ancestral spirits.

Some religions developed hierarchies of religious officials who had various titles and obligations. In England's official church, the Anglican hierarchy included bishops, parsons, clerks, churchwardens, and curates. Here, wealth and social status played a significant role in determining who occupied what position and received what promotion. In Africa, the Muslim reformer Sidi al-Mukhtar al-Kunti sought to resurrect what he considered a lack of discipline; to this end, he created an order of reformers who spread his beliefs south of the Sahara.

In the case of Anglo-Australia, a mixed bunch of commandants, governors, magistrates, chaplains, and other officials took part in the regulation of the colony's religious practices. Puritan New England's religious hierarchy comprised a confusing number of positions variously referred to as officers, ministers, clergy, and pastors.

Officers as a whole included teaching elders (who educated the church members), deacons (who saw to the church's financial needs), and tithing men (who kept order during church services). Along North America's colonial frontier, parish priests in New France and shamans among the native communities played important roles in governing their respective peoples' spiritual practices.

All the societies treated in this volume encompassed not one but many religious communities. The differences between the communities were sometimes within a broader religious community. Christian communities in England and New England, for example, comprised numerous sects that were often sharply at odds with one another over beliefs and practices. The resulting hierarchy of Christian communities inherited and built on existing discriminatory practices. Catholics in England suffered from uneven treatment biased in favor of Anglicans. Thus, if one were Catholic, one could not vote, hold public office, possess weapons, or purchase land. It is of little surprise that given this harsh penalization of Catholics, their numbers substantially diminished over the 18th century.

A marginal exception to Anglican intolerance concerned England's and colonial Australia's Jewish populations, which benefited from several formal and informal exemptions from discriminatory laws. England was a country where enlightened pluralism therefore existed but did not extend far enough to obliterate widespread prejudice. Nor was prejudice in England's colonies in New England any better. In fact, the Massachusetts Bay Colony's 17th-century government and religious establishment were much likelier worse on this count than were England's.

Interestingly, Japanese tended to mix—rather than exclude—the various elements of Shintō, Buddhism, and neo-Confucianism with one another, the conflation of which created a dependence of sorts among the three faiths.

Given the extraordinary diversity of religious practices that characterized cultures in sub-Saharan Africa, colonial Australia, the North American frontier, England, Japan, and New England during the 17th and 18th centuries, one cannot fail to note that certain themes that were related, for example, to places of worship, hierarchies of religious officials, and treatment of religious difference repeatedly exemplified important trends in daily religious practices.

~Peter Seelig

FOR MORE INFORMATION

Smart, N. *The World's Religions*. Cambridge, England: Cambridge University Press, 1998.

AFRICA

African religious practices were as diverse as African religion itself. In traditional African religions, a number of means existed for contacting the spirit world and honoring both gods and ancestors. Muslims followed the dictates of Islamic law, recited the Qur'an, and sought to mirror Islamic principles in their daily lives. Christians, too, found a number of ways to express their faith and regularly performed

RELIGIOUS LIFE
|
RELIGIOUS PRACTICES
|

church-established rituals. Through these practices, Africans of the 17th and 18th centuries sought to relieve suffering and to regulate their social order, while in some cases preparing for a new life to come.

The religious practices of the Ashanti of West Africa were typical of many of the practices in traditional African religion. Each house had a shrine to the high god, Nyame, which was usually kept indoors behind a white cloth. This shrine consisted of a bowl set in a tree branch. In this bowl, believers placed different sorts of objects, such as feathers, bones, and eggs, which the god could inhabit when he wished. In times of need, whether from hunger, disease, or social difficulties, the family would make sacrifices here, usually of food, and seek the god's assistance.

The Ashanti priests were essentially channels through which the gods communicated with their followers. People became priests when a god seized them and they began hearing voices and speaking incomprehensible gibberish. If this occurred around a shrine or at the funeral of another priest, people assumed that the god had called them. Sometimes new gods appeared, prompting the construction of a new shrine with a new priesthood. Once a person's religious calling was "determined," the future priest served seven years as an apprentice and during that time learned the lore of curing illnesses, the ritual dances necessary to summon a god, and the skills needed to communicate with the many deities. The new priest then had to become possessed by a god as part of a test, answer questions from other priests, and demonstrate an ability to divine things from scattered stones or string (McLeod, 57–60).

> *People became priests when a god seized them and they began hearing voices.*

Many African peoples used masks bearing a god's likeness as part of the ritual to communicate with that god. Some used masks to communicate with ancestors. On those special occasions when a community honored its ancestors, chosen intermediaries would don the masks of their ancestors, the spirits of which would promptly take possession of the intermediaries, who were not, at such times, held accountable for committing a crime or wronging an individual because, after all, it was really the ancestor spirit that was "possessing" and thus "governing" their actions. Both gods and ancestors were vital parts of a community and involved themselves in daily life not simply to help their friends but also to hurt those who had angered them.

Muslims in sub-Saharan Africa inherited a rich tradition and culture that they shared with people across North Africa, the Middle East, Central Asia, and throughout the Indian Ocean basin. Muslims studied the *shari'a*, or holy law, which served as a guide to daily life, recited the Qur'an, and performed the five ritual prayers each day. Much as followers of traditional African religions sought the aid of the divine through a priest, so too did Muslims through those possessing *walaya*, or a nearness to God similar to sainthood. Pilgrimage to saints' tombs became an important feature of African Muslim life.

One duty important to every Muslim involved the obligation to advance the faith in the world and within oneself, often called *jihad*. Sidi al-Mukhtar al-Kunti, who lived in the Sahara during the 18th century, felt that he had been born during a time of decadence and that God had chosen him to renew and strengthen the faith for the future. To that end, he founded a Sufi religious community where individuals could strengthen their own faith and serve as an example to others. He organized his community around both the kinship networks of his own Kunta people and the master-disciple relationships that formed the basis of organized Sufism. Born into a world of trans-Saharan caravan traders, he taught his followers to earn their own wealth and to avoid a dependence on charity. At a number of centers scattered around the Sahara, people gathered to study and perform the designated Sufi rituals that would bring them closer to God. Sidi al-Mukhtar himself became the real pillar of the community, as students came from far and wide to learn his ways, and pilgrims brought him gifts, which he redistributed in support of his work. During his lifetime, Sidi al-Mukhtar's order spread throughout Mauritania, the Niger River Valley, Guinea, the Ivory Coast, and the highlands of Senegambia (Coulon and O'Brien, 36–43).

African Christianity featured the same basic rituals as its European counterpart, but with scattered differences. In Ethiopia, which had a very old Jewish tradition, mass took place on Saturday, and male infants were circumcised. Monasticism was also an important ideal of Ethiopian spirituality, as it was in Egypt. In Kongo, the priest put salt on a person's tongue during baptism, which the Kongolese believed kept away the evil spirits. A baptized person was said to have "eaten salt." Saints often assumed the role held by ancestors in traditional African religions. Kongolese Christians also took Portuguese names, all of which began with Dom or Dona. Some missionaries objected to these cultural differences, but they persisted nonetheless (Thornton, 17).

Africans looked to religion in all aspects of their daily lives. Gods and other spirits became involved in family affairs, money matters, health, and the weather. People who were connected to religious powers, whether Christian priests, Muslim marabouts, or traditional African spirit mediums, wielded great influence in society, as a whole. The sacred was as much embedded in the landscape as in everyday life. Household shrines, sacred groves, and the tombs of religious figures became centers of sacred power. Even when confronted with a new, influential religion from the outside world, Africans shaped the new beliefs to their own ends and understood it through the lens of their own cultures, thus demonstrating how their own traditions could adapt to new situations.

To read about religion in Africa in the 20th century, see the Africa entry in the section "Religion" in chapter 8 ("Religious Life") of volume 6 of this series.

~Brian Ulrich

FOR MORE INFORMATION

Coulon, C., and D. B. C. O'Brien, eds. *Charisma and Brotherhood in African Islam*. Oxford: Clarendon Press, 1988.

Fung, K. *Africa South of the Sahara*. 1994. <http://www-sul.stanford.edu/depts/ssrg/africa/guide.html>, accessed October 23, 2003.

Halsall, P., ed. *Internet African History Sourcebook*. 1996. <http://www.fordham.edu/halsall/africa/africasbook.html>, accessed October 23, 2003.

King, N. Q. *Religions of Africa: A Pilgrimage into Traditional Religions*. New York: Harper and Row, 1970.

McLeod, M. D. *The Asante*. London: British Museum Publications, 1981.

Thornton, J. K. *The Kongolese Saint Anthony*. Cambridge, England: Cambridge University Press, 1998.

van Beek, W. E. A., T. D. Blakely, and D. L. Thomson, eds. *Religion in Africa: Experience and Expression*. Portsmouth, N.H.: Heinemann, 1994.

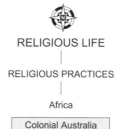

RELIGIOUS LIFE
|
RELIGIOUS PRACTICES
|
Africa

Colonial Australia

The Colonial Frontier
of North America

England

Japan

New England

COLONIAL AUSTRALIA

Although numerous religions were present during the 1788–1810 period of colonial Australian history, few of them enjoyed the recognition or approval of authorities. In practice, Anglicanism enjoyed official primacy, especially the evangelical kind that the colony's first two chaplains, Richard Johnson and Samuel Marsden, made a point of practicing.

When Johnson arrived as the colony's first chaplain, he possessed useful farming skills and teaching experience and so was well suited to offer pastoral nourishment to his unusual congregation. Johnson came to Australia with 4,000 Bibles and religious tracts provided by The Society for the Propagation of the Gospel and The Society for Promoting Christian Knowledge. While Johnson and others showed respect for and interest in Aboriginal society, they failed to appreciate the depth of their spiritual life. Perhaps because of difficulties with his own flock, Johnson did not attempt to convert Aborigines but exhorted settlers to set an example for the "poor unenlightened savages."

Johnson attended to the needs of the settlers with kind devotion and yet was perplexed at their irreligious tendencies. He claimed that "most of them would sell their souls for a glass of grog" (a type of alcohol) and had "no concern for religion." When the second fleet arrived in 1790, thereby relieving the colony's distress, Johnson delivered a sermon "full of gratitude and solemnity." In 1806, when news arrived of the English victory at Trafalgar, a service of thanks was conducted. However, Thanksgiving did not become a feature of Australian religious practice.

Although religion was not one of the immediate priorities of the colonial authorities, officials quickly realized that public worship could serve as a muster. Convicts were ordered to attend weekly services, which became a convenient forum for the propagation of official declarations. These services also provided authorities with an opportunity to monitor the convicts' material circumstances perhaps more than to monitor their spiritual well being. Many individuals, including officers and soldiers, resisted compulsory attendance. Still, a failure of the less fortunate to attend worship resulted in their punishment. The practice of linking religion with social order continued, as, in 1798, colonial officials ordered licensed public houses to close during the hours of Divine Service; and in 1810, Governor Macquarie prohibited Sunday work, making it the colony's official Sabbath.

Although some governors adopted a less-rigorous approach to public worship, others demonstrated more zeal. On Norfolk Island, when no Protestant clergy was available, Commandant Phillip King conducted services himself. In 1789, he ordered that unless illness prevented attendance, those absent would be fined a day's rations and that a second offence would attract corporal punishment. At a time when Catholic priests were absent from the island, King allowed a condemned man to have the company and counsel of two Catholics during the eve of his execution.

Samuel Marsden arrived in Australia in 1794 to assist Johnson in his spiritual duties, succeeding him in 1800. Marsden was also a farmer and, like Johnson, received an appointment to be a magistrate. Unlike Johnson, however, Marsden displayed excessive zeal in his decided preference for the lash, once ordering the flogging of Irish convicts merely as a result of government suspicion of an uprising. For such actions to be associated with a man of God was widely noted, earning him the hatred of the Irish and the historical sobriquet of the "flogging parson."

The merging of spiritual and legal duties was a constant source of tension. As late as 1810, the Reverend William Cowper, assistant chaplain, wrote to Macquarie declaiming the use of a church building for court hearings. He reminded him of the 88th Canon, forbidding their use for "Temporal Courts and Musters." In 1794, Marsden's wife, Elizabeth, lamented the lack of "religious society" and spiritual discussion in the colony, asserting that the lack of a church building was making religion there seem "contemptible." Finally, in 1803, St. John's Church at Parramatta was consecrated, and St. Phillip's, named after the first governor, was consecrated on Christmas Day of 1810. A Presbyterian chapel was not begun until 1809. With Marsden's blessing, Rowland Hassall and a handful of missionaries from Tahiti introduced organized private worship to the colony when they began devotion meetings marked by piety and fervor.

A View of Sydney Cove, an 1804 engraving by Francis Jukes from a drawing by Edward Dayes. This picture of Sydney reveals the expansion of the British settlement there. On the right are a hospital, convict housing, and a church tower. The dock is in the center. On the far left atop the hill is the governor's mansion. Notice the Aborigines in the foreground. Francis Jukes, *A View of Sydney Cove,* an601689. The Rex Nan Kivell Collection, National Library of Australia.

Although official attitudes to Catholics remained trenchant, some in authority took a more tolerant view. In 1792, five Catholics appealed for a priest without success. Nevertheless, by 1802, the authorities relented. Catholics were ordered to register with Father James Dixon, who was permitted, although under strict regulations, to conduct services that April. Dixon had to swear not to allow "seditious conversations." Services were to be conducted at nine in the morning, rotating on a three-weekly order between Sydney, Parramatta, and the Hawkesbury area. People were forbidden to worship outside their districts, and a strong police presence at each service persuaded the priest to fulfill his mandated obligation to see to each worshiper's orderly return home. In March 1803, King (now governor) reported to England that Dixon's efforts "had the most salutary effects on the number of Irish Catholics" who, he noted, made up 25 percent of the population. After the Castle Hill uprising in 1804, in which many Irish participated, colonial officials temporarily suppressed Catholic services. In 1806, Governor Bligh allowed Catholic schooling to commence.

At least eight Jewish convicts arrived in the First Fleet, but fewer than 50 Jews resided in the colony in 1800. The first free Jewish settlers did not arrive until 1816 and did not organize their rites in public ceremonies. Records exist of authorities showing some sensitivity at times of difficulty for the Jews, who were permitted to swear their oaths on the Old Testament when giving evidence. In 1803, a Jewish man under sentence of death was prepared for burial "by a person of his own profession." Jewish prayers were offered at the gallows, and such a religious statement is thought to have been the first public expression of the Jewish faith in the colony.

Although religious practices were ultimately a matter of personal choice, many people, including Aborigines, Jews, Catholics, and groups without their own religious officials, preferred to remain outside the sacraments of the Church of England. For many others, religious practice was a matter of compliance.

To read about the religious beliefs of Aboriginal Australians, see the Australian Aboriginal entry in the section "Religious Beliefs" in chapter 8 ("Religious Life") of volume 1 of this series.

~*Valda Rigg*

FOR MORE INFORMATION

Bladen, F., ed. *Historical Records of New South Wales*. Vol. 7. Sydney: Government Printer, 1901. Facsimile edition, Marrickville: Southwood Press, 1978.

Carey, H. *Believing in Australia: A Cultural History of Religions*. St. Leonards, Australia: Allen and Unwin, 1996.

Johnson, R. *An Address to the Inhabitants of the Colonies Established in New South Wales and Norfolk Island*. 1792. Australiana Facsimile Editions No. 22. Adelaide: Libraries Board of South Australia, 1963.

Levi, J. S., and G. F. J. Bergman. *Australian Genesis: Jewish Convicts and Settlers, 1788–1850*. Sydney: Rigby Limited, 1974.

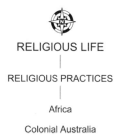

RELIGIOUS LIFE
|
RELIGIOUS PRACTICES
|
Africa

Colonial Australia

The Colonial Frontier
of North America

England

Japan

New England

THE COLONIAL FRONTIER OF NORTH AMERICA

Although Native Americans regarded their environment with great piety, their practical application of these beliefs was not as devout. Thus, in line with their daily life of hunting, chopping, and burning, Native Americans along the frontier generally took from the environment around them until it was exhausted. They hunted and fished until the game would no longer support them. They burned the forest underbrush to open the woods for the hunting of game. They girdled trees to kill them and farmed the land until it refused to yield. Then they moved on without attempting to revitalize the area.

As for religious rituals, the Green Corn celebration was of immense importance to the Shawnee, Creek, Choctaw, Chickasaw, and other tribes of southeastern North America. It lasted from four to eight days and was an occasion for amnesty and absolution. The ceremony involved purging oneself to cleanse the body and the lighting of new fires in the hearth to cleanse every home. A more striking aspect of native religion was cannibalism. The traditional term that other nations used in reference to the Mohawks meant "man-eaters." The ritual eating of an enemy was an attempt to assimilate the power of the victim no less than the consumption of a deer or bear was thought to provide fleetness of foot or great strength. The practice of cannibalism does not seem to have died out until the late 18th century.

Shamans played a significant role in all these religious practices. However, they were not priests or ministers in the European sense. Hunters and warriors would consult shamans because shamans had many spirit helpers and had shown wisdom in the past. Among the Ojibwa and Chippewa of the western Great Lakes, there was an actual priesthood known as the Midewiwin, or Great Medicine Society. These priests, both male and female, possessed various degrees of competency that required training and initiation.

Most Catholic settlements in New France featured no resident priest. The number of Frenchmen in New France was so small, possibly no more than 3,000, that it was impossible to assign a priest to each of the scattered settlements and farmsteads. Consequently, the available clergy were assigned to parishes comprising many hundreds of square miles of wilderness territory. A parish might reach for 50 miles along a river and a day's walk into the interior, for it was largely by canoe that the priest made his spiritual visits to his flock. Under these conditions, he managed to minister to his entire flock three or four times a year.

Built in Quebec in 1633, the first church in New France was destroyed by fire seven years later, and its replacement was not undertaken for a decade thereafter. The new building, Notre Dame de la Paix, was opened in 1657. Although only 100 feet long and 30 feet wide, it was described as "a cathedral made of stone, . . . large and splendid." To the tiny French community of Quebec, the edifice was a tremendous achievement. With its gold and silver ornaments, statues, and stained glass, Notre Dame stood in sharp contrast to the churches of the other districts of New France.

The French crown Christianized the native population for the practical purpose of encouraging Indians to carry a religious war to the English frontier settlements. Thus, English settlers widely believed—and not without supporting evidence—that the Jesuits of New France actively incited the Indians to take up arms against the English frontier settlers because of the latter community's Protestantism. The French civil authorities viewed the missions as the equivalent of outposts guarding the main avenues to New France. On the other hand, New Englanders tended to designate the French missionary activity as mere subversion of native allegiance and displayed little understanding of the dedication of the Jesuits to the conversion of souls.

Along the frontier, Protestant missionaries also resided, and their practices were as innately rigid as were their beliefs in propriety and good form. For example, some Protestant missionaries forced Native Americans into "praying towns." Here, the Protestants looked upon the customary wardrobe, ornaments, and language of the Indians with scorn and insisted on the eradication of such "savagery." Even the English-leaning Iroquois viewed the French as more accepting of Indian ways. "Brother," said an Onondaga diplomat to the English, "you must learn of the French [priests] if you would understand, and know how to treat Indians. They don't speak roughly; nor do they for every little mistake take up a club and flog them." Many of the Indians who converted to the Protestant faith seem to have taken every opportunity to revert to their traditional religion in much greater numbers than did those who sought to become Catholics.

Quakers, however, made notable inroads among Native Americans. Perhaps their relative success was at least a partial consequence of their tolerance. As a case in point, Quakers devoted themselves to their religious duties by creating nearly autonomous moral households. Everything in the Quaker household—wives, children, and business—was subjected to a familial order based in morality. The Quaker community enjoined every member of each family to assume the burden of incorporating religious, civic, and economic virtues into daily household activities. Outside authorities such as an intolerant established priesthood, an authoritarian upper class, or even a pedantic university system were considered "not only unnecessary but even pernicious." In applying their principles, Quakers rigorously applied their religious and spiritual beliefs to very concrete human relations. They radically reorganized their church from one that required the performance of a series of external disciplines and the reception of a well-prepared sermon, as was the case with other Protestant settlements, into one in which the silent meeting and a personal conversion took precedence.

Practicing their religious beliefs meant that Native Americans, Jesuit missionaries, Protestant evangelists, and Quaker pacifists had an opportunity to stray from or draw near their guiding principles. Perhaps not surprisingly, it was common for pious declarations to occupy a tenuous, even incongruous, position opposite the reality of religious practices. It is precisely this tension between sincerity and expediency that accounts for the environmental degradation, territorial conquest, and religious intolerance that often characterized the Native American, French, and English application of spiritual ideals (Volo and Volo, 45–46, 55, 58, 62–63, 68–69, 109).

FOR MORE INFORMATION

Bourne, R. *Gods of War, Gods of Peace: How the Meeting of Native and Colonial Religions Shaped Early America.* New York: Harcourt, 2002.

Volo, J. M., and D. D. Volo. *Daily Life on the Old Colonial Frontier.* Westport, Conn.: Greenwood Press, 2002.

ENGLAND

Religiously, England was an anomaly. It had a state-sanctioned church, like France, yet, unlike almost every other nation in Europe, it allowed minority religions. However, it stopped short of the policy of the Netherlands (and later, of the United States), which was to allow complete freedom of worship. England still imposed civil or financial penalties on Catholics, Jews, Moravians, Methodists, Quakers, and all other non-Anglicans.

In the Anglican Church, the parson's duties were not particularly onerous. He performed marriages, christenings, and funerals; delivered a sermon each Sunday;

visited the sick and dying; and socialized with the local squire. The parson usually received help from three types of assistants: a clerk, who recorded baptisms, marriages, and deaths; two lay churchwardens, who supervised church property; and often at least one curate, a low-paid member of the clergy. All too often, the bulk of the parson's duties actually fell on the curate, who worked hard and lived meanly.

Bishops—who occupied a position above that of the parson—were responsible for overseeing the functions of the diocese, ordaining clergymen, and licensing curates. They also had the right to sit in the House of Lords. Aristocratic families constituted a disproportionate number of positions at this level of the Church but were never in the majority.

The Church of England's governing body, Convocation, was dismissed in 1717 and, for all practical purposes, remained dissolved for the rest of the century. The ecclesiastical court system, which dealt with such matters as marital separations and nullifications and which regulated the conduct of clergy, was on the wane.

Part of the Anglican Church's problem was that it consisted in large part of men who wanted genteel status and a good annual income, rather than of men who felt a genuine calling. To be sure, the average clergyman was a worldly man, concerned with his income and status, enjoying a glass of good wine, and perhaps not above buying a little smuggled tea. Only a few were truly scandalous or eccentric. And as England's population underwent profound changes in the 18th century, with the number of people growing overall and their distribution shifting, there arrived a situation where simply too few churches were in the right places.

Anti-Catholicism was widespread and virulent in 18th-century England. Even late in the century, the law treated Catholics unequally. They paid a double land tax. They could not hold public office or military commissions. They could not succeed to the throne of England. They could not vote or own weapons. They could not purchase land—they could even be forced to forfeit their property. Not surprisingly, English law treated Catholic priests as felons.

In 1778, the Catholic Relief Act removed these last three disabilities. Scots rioted so vigorously against the act that officials could not enforce it. In England on June 2, 1780, anti-Catholic protestors quickly turned violent, and for nearly a week, a mob burned and pillaged the homes, chapels, and businesses of Roman Catholics.

In the face of such hatred, Catholics could hardly hope to capitalize on the inertia of the established church. Maintaining numbers alone was difficult. In 1720, England had 115,000 resident Catholics; by 1780, there were only 69,000. Late in the century, English society came to associate Catholicism with Irish laborers working in England, thereby identifying a marginalized religion with a marginalized people.

When the 18th century began, there were four main groups of "Old Dissenters": Presbyterians, Congregationalists, Baptists, and Quakers. The laws regarding Dissenters, as was the case with those regarding Catholics, granted members of the sect tolerance but not full civil rights. The Toleration Act gave them the right to establish their own chapels, although they still had to pay Anglican tithes. They could also (unlike Catholics) set up their own religious academies, carry weapons, and vote. The Test and Corporation Acts barred those Catholics who were unwilling to take Anglican communion once a year from holding public office. By the end of the century, Dissenters had grown increasingly impatient with Parliament for failing to award them equal citizenship.

Another Protestant religion was Methodism, which, as it operated under John Wesley, was thoroughly autocratic. An appointed leader headed each "class" of a dozen or so worshipers. The classes belonged to larger "bands," segregated by sex and marital status, which sent delegates to an annual conference. The design of the conference did not lend itself to discussion or debate but rather to the issuance of decrees by the ardent preacher John Wesley.

Methodism was quite successful in large part because it targeted the groups usually overlooked by the tithe-conscious church—the supposedly "ungovernable," the poor, workers, servants, and women. Methodism was well established by the end of the century: there were only 24,000 Methodists in 1767, but 77,000 by 1796. The number perhaps seems small, but Methodism's rapid growth unsettled the majority.

Sunday Morning Bible Reading at the Cottage Door, by Alexander Carse. Bible reading among the less affluent was a common religious practice throughout Great Britain. © National Gallery of Scotland.

Eighteenth-century England was also home to perhaps 20,000 Jews, most of whom lived in London's East End. Most upper-class Jews were Sephardim; most lower-class Jews were Ashkenazim. They were specifically exempted from certain laws that would have required compliance with Anglican ritual, such as the Marriage Act of 1753, and from time to time, despite laws to the contrary, they even held public office. Even though anti-Semitism probably declined over the century, there were still numerous instances of Jews being "hooted, hunted, cuffed, pulled by the beard and spat upon."

Not all religious practices involved one religion's tendency to discriminate against another religion. Religious concerns manifested themselves in formal ritual and more familiar activities. Conspicuously discernible in the daily lives of people of all faiths were religious tracts, pamphlets, magazines, sermons, novels, chapbooks, and almanacs, as well as the Bible. Even though the church or chapel was no longer the sole center of community social life, the chief holidays were still those associated with the church—Good Friday, Easter, Christmas, Twelfth Night, and Shrove Tuesday. For most, the Sabbath was Sunday, and most work and travel ceased on this day.

The religious practices of 18th-century England were not readily distinguishable from the politics of religious discrimination. At the center of this grab for obedience was the Anglican Church—the Church of England. It, along with Parliament and many English, continued a tradition of open hostility toward Catholics, Methodists, Dissenters, Jews, and other religious minorities. At the same time, the members of each of these religious groups could practice their particular religion, despite legal and societal restrictions. It appears that 18th-century England offered the faithful a strange mixture of tolerance and intolerance that, on balance, was relatively enlightened for its day (Olsen, 281–89).

To read about religion in Chaucer's England, see the Europe entries in chapter 8 ("Religious Life") of volume 2; for Elizabethan England, see the Catholicism and Protestantism entries in chapter 8 ("Religious Life") of volume 3; and for Victorian England, see the Victorian England entries in chapter 8 ("Religious Life") of volume 5 of this series.

FOR MORE INFORMATION

Jacob, W. M. *Lay People and Religion in the Early Eighteenth Century*. New York: Cambridge University Press, 1996.

Lynch, J. *Eighteenth Century Resources*. <http://newark.rutgers.edu/~jlynch/18th/>, accessed October 10, 2003.

Olsen, K. *Daily Life in 18th-Century England*. Westport, Conn.: Greenwood Press, 1999.

Rupp, E. G. *Religions in England, 1688–1791*. New York: Oxford University Press, 1986.

FRANCE

Like other Europeans, the Catholic French had a long tradition of established religious rituals. See the Catholicism entry in the section "Priests and Rituals" in chapter 8 ("Religious Life") of volume 3 of this series for a discussion of the rituals that persisted well into 18th-century French life.

JAPAN

Religious practices in Japan during the 18th century included much that occurred in the presence of shrines and temples. Indeed, pilgrimages to these sites constituted one of most intriguing and revealing Japanese religious practices of the early modern period.

In Japan, the shrines that served the purposes of Shintō (indigenous folk beliefs) were large in total number but very limited in actual construction. The shrine was usually a small rustic affair. The wood used to make the shed was not even stripped of bark, and not a few of these edifices were little more than bunches of tree limbs lashed together to form a crude shelter for the offerings to the *kami* (spirits).

A crude, lattice fence or sometimes paper or straw ropes set the "holy" area around Shintō shrines apart from their surroundings. The traditional *torii* gate of a single crossbeam that was mounted on two uprights led directly to a fount of water where worshipers ritually cleansed themselves before approaching the "worship sanctuary" (*haiden*).

Within the *haiden* might be another structure called "chief sanctuary," the place where the *kami* visited or lived, and where some symbolic object (a mirror, paper, rock, or anything "awe-inspiring") represented them.

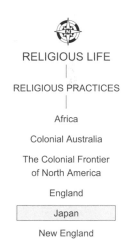

Sometimes, there was no *haiden* because a mountain, a craggy boulder, a strangely shaped tree, or a river was the *kami*. Whatever the designation, worshipers approached such sites individually or sometimes in a small group. There were no prescribed prayers, no accepted rituals, and no mandatory ceremonies. Very often, there were no priests or caretakers about.

At the smaller local shrines, worshipers offered gifts to the *kami*, such as rice cakes (*mochi*), balls of cooked sticky rice, or straw sandals. The offering was to be earnest.

There were perhaps a thousand or so more substantial buildings for Shintō shrines in the entire country. These shrines, built high off the ground, included thatched or planked roofs with protruding crossed exterior beams, and residences for priests. The unpainted wood weathered naturally.

At the larger and more elaborate Shintō shrines, worshipers purchased tiny, wooden placards called *ema* (literally, horse pictures). The *ema* harked back to an earlier age when horses were actually sacrificed to the *kami*. One could purchase small, inexpensive talismans, which one would then affix to the lintel of one's home to ward off evil.

The Buddhist temple intimately and organically assimilated to the life of the people. Small Shintō shrines shared space with every Buddhist temple, and *kami* "guarded" virtually every temple in Japan.

Bell pulls and small lattices played Shintō and Buddhist roles alike. The sound of the bells or gongs caught the attention of both the Buddha and the resident *kami*. The smoke of incense was more Buddhist, but Shintō also used it as part of its symbolic ablutions.

Green is the color for Buddhist temples. The distinctive architectural aspects of these constructions included enormous tiled roofs that turned gracefully upward and thick tree-sized posts that were joined to the roof beams with wooden joints. Enclosed with sliding or folding wall screens, the interior consisted of wide, polished planks of wood and the altar area, where one or more statues of the Buddha stood. The ceiling displayed ornate, gold leaf designs or sumptuous painting or carvings. Atop Buddhist temples often stood tall, elaborately carved pagodas, which channeled the eye and the soul upward toward heaven. Monks and priests lived, ate, studied, and otherwise worked in surrounding buildings.

At home, most peasant families kept a "god-shelf" (*kamidana*) where they could commune with ancestors and *kami*. The first portion of a meal was frequently placed on this shelf in order to honor the *kami*. Japanese typically hung talismans and amulets in the northeast quarter of residences (no home had an entrance that faced the northeast) because of the widespread belief that evil spirits approach humans from that direction.

In the countryside, shamans probably lived on the cusp of social respectability. Many were principally agrarians who supplemented their incomes by performing a few spiritual tasks throughout the year. Japanese consulted them for advice on such important events as marriage, planting, harvesting, purchases, and so on.

Travel for religious purposes had a long and rich tradition in Japan. By the 18th century, many well-established pilgrimage routes crisscrossed Japan. The most famous and perhaps the most spiritually prestigious site to visit was the Shintō shrine at Ise. Many daimyō (feudal warlords), while on *sankin-kotai* ("alternate attendance" between the daimyō's regional domains and the capital of Edo), would make a side trip there at least once in their lives.

Pilgrims would dress in special white robes and sedge hats and would carry straw sandals and walking sticks. Often, monks would ink a magic Sanskrit letter on a pilgrim's robe. Pilgrims were expected to buy talismans and amulets for their family, friends, and neighbors.

At several times during the century, a kind of madness overtook entire regions, and whole villages spontaneously set off for Ise. In the space of two months (April 9 to May 29, 1705), for instance, an astounding 3,620,000 visited Ise. This was more than 12 percent of the total population of Japan. These outbursts of religious hysteria frightened the daimyō and *bakufu* (national military government) but were never destructive or politically dangerous.

Some people spent their entire lives wandering from one holy place to another, surviving by begging from other pilgrims or from ordinary travelers on the road. Nuns engaged in pilgrimages, as well. That wandering monks, beggars, and nuns could proceed along the roads to visit holy sites, both crude and ornate, testifies to the commonness and importance of pilgrimages and religious practices in 18th-century Japan (Perez, 40–42, 47, 52, 120–22, 306–7).

To read about religion and morality in Japan in the 20th century, see the Japan entries in the sections "Morality" and "Religion" in chapter 8 ("Religious Life") of volume 6 of this series.

FOR MORE INFORMATION

Bellah, R. N. *Tokugawa Religion: The Values of Pre-Industrial Japan.* Glencoe, Ill.: Free Press, 1957.

Japan Information Network. <http://www.jinjapan.org/index.html>, accessed October 23, 2003.

Perez, L. G. *Daily Life in Early Modern Japan.* Westport, Conn.: Greenwood Press, 2002.

Yusa, M. *Japanese Religious Traditions.* Upper Saddle River, N.J.: Prentice Hall, 2002.

NEW ENGLAND

The Puritans who immigrated to the New World from England were the absolute rulers of the principal New England colonies—Massachusetts Bay, Plymouth, Hartford, and New Haven—and their religious beliefs shaped every aspect of daily life in colonial New England for more than 200 years. Their religion determined who was allowed to vote (in most colonies, only church members), the laws that were enacted (to enforce church attendance by all citizens and to exclude other denominations and dissenting doctrines), the clothes that colonists might wear, the entertainments that they tolerated, their attitude toward work, and all other aspects of practical existence.

RELIGIOUS LIFE

RELIGIOUS PRACTICES

Africa

Colonial Australia

The Colonial Frontier
of North America

England

Japan

New England

For the New England colonists, the practice of religion required a hierarchy of formal religious practitioners. Thus, the earliest settlers of Plymouth, Salem, and Boston prioritized the establishment of churches that were independent entities and that operated under the supervision of officials who identified themselves variously as church officers, ministers, clergy, and pastors.

One category of church officer was the teaching elder, who reinforced doctrine and disciplined members of the congregation, visiting and warning those who were behaving unacceptably. Another category, the church deacon, was the business officer, who received church offerings and distributed church funding to the minister and church members who were in need. Tithing men, another class of church officer, were chiefly responsible for keeping order in the meetinghouse. To awaken any dozing parishioners, tithing men used a long rod, on one end of which was a feather and on the other end a ball. Thomas Scott, a worshiper in Lynn, Massachusetts, was once so abruptly awakened from his loud snoring that he leaped up and knocked the tithing man to the floor.

Legal documents from New England prove that government encouraged the union of church and state by requiring all citizens of the Massachusetts Bay Colony to attend church, even though most of the ordinary people who emigrated were likely not Puritans. The simple fact of attending a church did not indicate church membership. Only a small percentage actually obtained church membership, which was a privileged position in that only members were allowed to vote or hold office.

Securing church membership was usually an arduous process. First, candidates revealed to the officers of the church their desire for church membership. The elders and the minister then examined each candidate to determine whether his or her knowledge or religious experience merited a recommendation of membership. If the candidate passed the first examination, the congregation reported any moral failings related to the candidate or testified to the candidate's good character. The examination concluded with the candidate's profession of faith and a vote of the congregation.

Each congregation closely scrutinized the faith and behavior of its members. In order either to move from the area or to join churches in other locations, for example, church members needed the permission or recommendations of the congregation.

Churches held two services on Sunday, both during daylight hours. All the Sunday services followed a prescribed pattern. The minister began with an extemporaneous prayer of about 15 minutes, followed by the minister's or teacher's scriptural reading and an explanation of it. Next was the singing of psalms, the only hymns allowed in the early Puritan churches. The service, at the heart of which was a one-hour sermon, concluded with a prayer and a blessing from the teaching elder.

📷 *Snapshot*

Keeping Warm in Colonial New England Churches

During the early part of New England's colonial history, churches were not heated. The bitterly cold air became a problem for churchgoers, with their feet suffering most of all. Among the solutions were

• wolfskin bags, nailed to the seats, in which parishioners could snuggle their feet,

• open invitations to dogs, who lay on their owners' feet, keeping them warm,

• portable foot stoves, which were made of metal and contained hot coals, and

• noon-houses, where churchgoers rushed during the noon intermission to heat themselves by a fire. (Earle, 374–75)

Besides the two services on the Sabbath, at least one other instructive church meeting was held each week. Not infrequently, every day of the week offered a church meeting of some kind.

Neither the sign of the cross nor kneeling was part of Puritan ceremony, and church officials permitted no organ, piano, or other instrumental accompaniment during the service. Furthermore, the Puritan church recognized only two sacraments: holy communion and infant baptism. Puritans did not, as did Roman Catholics, believe in transubstantiation—that the wine of holy communion became the blood of Christ and that the wafer became the body of Christ. Puritans did not consider marriage a sacrament; thus magistrates, not clergymen, performed the marriage ceremony. Neither last rites nor religious burials for the dead were sacraments.

One role that was dear to the clergy and that gave them power over the lives of everyday citizens was their responsibility (they believed it was their chief responsibility) to prepare church members for the experience of justification—that is, for a journey to hell. Elect and nonelect alike were said to profit from such a journey. For the elect, justification was necessary for those who wanted to secure their election or salvation. The nonelect could also benefit from such a journey. Although a journey, according to Puritans, would not change the fact of one's eternal damnation, it could make life easier for that person in the here and now. For instance, the nonelect could benefit from fewer deaths in the family, less illness and pain, fewer community catastrophes, and above all, less spiritual pain.

To fulfill their role, clergy composed nightmarish sermons on the wickedness of humanity. In 1741, Jonathan Edwards delivered his famous sermon, "Sinners in the Hands of an Angry God," to parishioners in Enfield, Connecticut. Edwards's successful representation of hell generated such groaning and loud weeping in the audience that he had to ask attendees to quiet down so he could finish.

Some members of the religious community, Cotton Mather among them, strongly believed that it was the duty of Christians to convert the slaves to Christianity. Some masters taught their slaves to accept a lowly position in life and insisted that it was God, rather than slave owners, who enslaved blacks. A few masters argued that Christianizing the slaves would make them more manageable and submissive because doctrine would teach them that obedience to a master was equivalent to obedience to the Christian God.

But other members of the community strongly objected to conversion of slaves on several grounds, all of them economic. Any slave who converted to Christianity would be forced to attend church on the Sabbath, and his or her work would be lost to the master at such time. Furthermore, many whites believed that Christianity gave black slaves a "false" sense of equality, which made them less malleable and therefore less marketable. Some whites worried that to permit slaves to join the church could give them grounds to argue for suffrage. However, the argument that bothered most religious New Englanders concerned the biblical warning that no Christian could hold another Christian in bondage. Thus, to convert a slave to Christianity and retain him or her as a slave was a violation of God's Word.

The first clergymen, by the force of their characters, held absolute power over their congregations and their communities. When the force of character was insufficient to command control, the clerical response was to legislate its authority. By the 18th century, as Puritanism was declining sharply, many prominent ministers became absolute despots who ruled over congregations that often resented the control. Nevertheless, the emphasis on Puritan religious practices, at least in its 17th-century New England form, continued its irregular, though unmistakable, decline in status for the remainder of the colonial period (Johnson, 17–19, 22–23, 25, 27–29, 154–55).

FOR MORE INFORMATION

Earle, A. M. *Home Life in Colonial Days*. New York: Macmillan, 1928.
Foster, S. *The Long Argument: English Puritanism and the Shaping of New England Culture*. Chapel Hill: University of North Carolina Press, 1991.
Johnson, C. D. *Daily Life in Colonial New England*. Westport, Conn.: Greenwood Press, 2002.
Salem Witch Museum. 1996. <http://www.salemwitchmuseum.com/>, accessed October 23, 2003.

RELIGIOUS LIFE: WEB SITES

http://etext.virginia.edu/salem/witchcraft/home.html
http://www.wsu.edu:8080/~dee/TOKJAPAN/TOKJAPAN.HTM
http://www.bbc.co.uk/worldservice/africa/features/storyofafrica/index_section6.shtml
http://www.c18.rutgers.edu/li/religion.html
http://www.sonoma.edu/history/reason/religious.html.htm
http://www.loc.gov/exhibits/religion/rel02.html

PRIMARY SOURCES

WATKIN TENCH, DESCRIPTION OF THE FIRST ENGLISH
CRIMINALS TRANSPORTED TO AUSTRALIA, FROM A
COMPLETE ACCOUNT OF THE SETTLEMENT AT PORT
JACKSON ON NEW SOUTH WALES (1791)

In this passage, Watkin Tench relates his observations of Australia's early criminal inhabitants, who had been transported from England to this island continent
as punishment. Not incidentally, this group of "pickpockets," "footpads," "highwaymen," and "ruffians" of both sexes put their "perverted genius" to good use
in their new home.

SOME OBSERVATIONS ON THE CONVICTS, 1791

A short account of that class of men for whose disposal and advantage the colony
was principally, if not totally, founded, seems necessary.

If it be recollected how large a body of these people are now congregated, in the
settlement of Port Jackson, and at Norfolk Island, it will, I think, not only excite
surprize, but afford satisfaction, to learn, that in a period of four years few crimes of
a deep rye, or of a hardened nature have been perpetrated: murder and unnatural
sins rank not hitherto in the catalogue of their enormities: and one suicide only has
been committed.

To the honour of the female part of our community let it be recorded, that only
one woman has suffered capital punishment: on her condemnation she pleaded
pregnancy; and a jury of venerable matrons was impanelled on the spot, to examine
and pronounce her state; which the forewoman, a grave personage between 60 and
70 years old, did, by this short address to the court; "Gentlemen! she is as much
with child as I am." Sentence was accordingly passed, and she was executed.

Besides the instance of Irving, two other male convicts, William Bloodsworth, of
Kingston upon Thames, and John Arscott, or Truro, in Cornwall, were both eman-

cipated, for their good conduct, in the years 1790 and 1791. Several men whose terms of transportation had expired, and against whom no legal impediment existed to prevent their departure, have been permitted to enter in merchant ships wanting hands: and, as my Rose Hill journals testify, many others have had grants of land assigned to them, and are become settlers in the country.

In so numerous a community many persons of perverted genius, and of mechanical ingenuity, could not but be assembled. Let me produce the following example:— Frazer was an iron manufacturer, bred at Sheffield, of whose abilities, as a workman, we had witnessed many proofs. The governor had written to England for a set of locks, to be sent out for the security of the public stores, which were to be so constructed as to be incapable of being picked. On their arrival his excellency sent for Frazer, and bade him examine them; telling him at the same time that they could not be picked. Frazer laughed, and asked for a crooked nail only, to open them all. A nail was brought, and in an instant he verified his assertion. Astonished at his dexterity, a gentleman present determined to put it to farther proof. He was sent for in a hurry, some days after, to this hospital, where a lock of still superior intricacy and expence to the others had been provided. He was told that the key was lost, and that the lock must be immediately picked. He examined it attentively; remarked that it was the production of a workman; and demanded ten minutes to make an instrument "*to speak with it.*" Without carrying the lock with him, he went directly to his shop; and at the expiration of his term returned, applied his instrument, and open flew the lock. But it was not only in this part of his business that he excelled: he executed every branch of it in superior style. Had not his villainy been still more notorious than his skill, he would have proved an invaluable possession to a new country. He had passed through innumerable scenes in life, and had played many parts. When too lazy to work at his trade, he had turned thief in fifty different shapes; was a receiver of stolen goods; a soldier; and a traveling conjurer. He once confessed to me, that he had made a set of tools for a gang of coiners, every man of whom was hanged.

Were the nature of the subject worthy of farther illustration, many similar proofs of misapplied talents, might be adduced. . . .

A leading distinction, which marked the convicts on their outset in the colony, was an use of what is called the *flash*, or *Kiddy* language. In some of our early courts of justice, an interpreter was frequently necessary to translate the deposition of the witness, and the defence of the prisoner. This language has many dialects. The sly dexterity of the pickpocket; the brutal ferocity of the footpad; the more elevated career of the highwayman; and the deadly purpose of the midnight ruffian, is each strictly appropriate in the terms which distinguish and characterize it. I have ever been of opinion, that an abolition of this unnatural jargon would open the path to reformation. And my observations on these people have constantly instructed me, that indulgence in this infatuating cant, is more deeply associated with depravity, and continuance in vice, than is generally supported. I recollect hardly one instance of a return to honest pursuits, and habits of industry, where this miserable perversion of our noblest and peculiar faculty was not previously conquered.

Those persons to whom the inspection and management of our numerous and extensive prisons in England are committed, will perform a service to society, by attending to the foregoing observation. Let us always keep in view, that punishment, when not directed to promote reformation, is arbitrary, and unauthorized.

From Charles M. H. Clark, ed., *Sources of Australian History* (New York: Oxford University Press. 1965).

ST. JOHN DE CRÈVECOEUR, EXCERPT FROM *SKETCHES OF EIGHTEENTH-CENTURY AMERICA* (COMPOSED IN THE YEARS PRECEDING THE AMERICAN WAR OF INDEPENDENCE)

In his book *Sketches of Eighteenth-Century America,* the Frenchman St. John de Crèvecoeur provides a rhetorically appealing, if overly sentimental and simplified, depiction of the self-reliant, hardworking, and daring type of man that the British North American colonies seemed to be producing in substantial and consistent numbers.

REFLECTIONS ON THE MANNERS OF THE AMERICANS

Let us view now the new colonist as possessed of property. This has a great weight and a mighty influence. From earliest infancy we are accustomed to a greater exchange of things, a greater transfer of property than the people of the same class in Europe. Whether it is occasioned by that perpetual and necessary emigrating genius which constantly sends the exuberancy of full societies to replenish new tracts; whether it proceeds from our being richer; whether it is that we are fonder of trade which is but an exchange—I cannot ascertain. This man, thus bred, from a variety of reasons is determined to improve his fortune by removing to a new district, and resolves to purchase as much land as will afford substantial farms to every one of his children—a pious thought which causes so many even wealthy people to sell their patrimonial estates to enlarge their sphere of action and leave a sufficient inheritance to their progeny.

No sooner he is resolved than he takes all the information he can with regard to the country he proposes to go to inhabit. He finds out all travelers who have been on the spot; he views maps; attentively weighs the benefits and disadvantages of climate, seasons, situation, etc.; he compares it with his own. . . .

When near the spot, he hires a man, perhaps a hunter, of which all the frontiers are full, and instead of being lost and amazed in the middle of these gloomy retreats, he finds the place of beginning on which the whole survey is founded. This is all the difficulty he was afraid of; he follows the ancient blazed trees with a sagacity and quickness of sight which have many times astonished me, though bred in the woods. Next he judges of the goodness of the timber by that of the soil. The humble bush which delights in the shade, the wild ginseng, the spignet, the weeds on which he treads teach him all he wants to know. He observes the springs, the moisture of the earth, the range of the mountains, the course of the brooks. He returns at last; he has formed his judgment as to his future buildings; their situation, future roads, cultivation, etc. He has properly combined the future mixture of conveniences and inconveniences which he expects to meet with. In short the complicated arrangement of a great machine would not do greater honour to the most skilful artist than the reduction and digesting of so many thoughts and calculations of this hitherto obscure man.

He meets once more the land-proprietors; a new scene ensues. He is startled at the price. He altercates with them, for now he has something to say, having well explored the country. Now he makes them an offer; now he seems to recede; now wholly indifferent about the bargain; now willing to fulfill it if the terms are reasonable. If not, he can't but stay where he is, or perhaps accept of better offers which have been made to him by another person. . . .

He departs with all his family, and great and many are the expenses and fatigues of this removal with cows and cattle. He at last arrives on the spot. He finds himself suddenly deprived of the assistance of friends, neighbours, tradesmen, and of all those inferior links which make a well-established society so beautiful and pleasing. He and his family are now alone. On their courage, perseverance, and skill their success depends. There is now no retreating; shame and ruin would infallibly overtake them. What is he to do in all possible cases of accidents, sickness, and other casualties which may befall his family, his cattle and horses, breaking of the implements of husbandry, etc.? A complicated scene presents itself to the contemplative mind, which does the Americans a superlative honour. I have purposely visited many who have spent the earliest part of their lives in this manner; now ploughmen, now mechanics, sometimes even physicians. They are and must be everything. Nay, who would believe it? This new man will commence as a hunter and learn in these woods how to pursue and overtake the game with which it abounds. He will in a short time become master of that necessary dexterity which this solitary life inspires. Husband, father, priest, principal governor—he fills up all these stations, though in the humble vale of life. Are there any of his family taken sick, either he or his wife must recollect ancient directions received from aged people, from doctors, from a skilful grandmother, perhaps, who formerly learned of the Indians of her neighborhood how to cure simple diseases by means of simple medicines. The swamps and woods are ransacked to find the plants, the bark, the roots prescribed. An ancient almanac, constituting perhaps all his library, with his Bible, may chance to direct him to some more learned ways. . . .

But here this great resource fails in some measure, at least with a great many of them, from the weakness of their religious education, from a long inattention, from the paucity of instructions received. Is it a wonder that new rules of action should arise? It must constitute a new set of opinions, the parent of manners. You have already observed this colonist is necessarily different from what he was in the more ancient settlements he originally came from; become such by his new local situation, his new industry, that share of cunning which was absolutely necessary in consequence of his intercourse with his new neighbours.

From Hector St. John de Crèvecoeur, *Sketches of Eighteenth-Century America, More "Letters from an American Farmer,"* ed. Henri L. Bourdin, Ralph H. Gabriel, and Stanley T. Williams (New Haven, Conn.: Yale University Press, 1925), 66–78.

BISHOP JEAN'S ORDINANCE AGAINST DRUNKENNESS AND IMPURITY, QUEBEC, CANADA (1690)

In this 1690 ordinance regarding "drunkenness" and "impurity," Jean, bishop of Quebec, warns his peers in New France that danger to the colony derived not only from the English settlers and their Iroquois allies but also from the "great evils" found within New France itself. To promote purity, the bishop suggests that fewer absolutions be granted.

Jean, by the mercy of God and the grace of the Holy Apostolic See, Bishop of Quebec. To all our dear Brothers, the *Cures,* Missionaries and Confessors of our Diocese, Greeting and Blessing.

God having inspired us to make a visit of our diocese with all the care of which we are capable, he also gave us the strength needed to execute this enterprise so difficult and perilous at a time when our enemies are attacking us on all sides. That which touched us most in the visits and missions we made in the towns and in the country was to see that our temporal miseries are nothing in comparison with the spiritual miseries with which our diocese is depressed. Having known perfectly our flock, we thought we would have no enemies to fear except the English and the Iroquois; but God having opened our eyes to the disorders in our diocese, and having made us feel more than ever the weight of our charge, we are obliged to recognize and confess that our most redoubtable enemies are drunkenness, impurity, luxury, and slander, and that we must employ all our forces to conquer them. After having prayed a long time before God to obtain from him the light and the suitable remedies for such great evils, it has come to us in our thinking that in order to stop drunkenness it would be proper that the confessors would not give absolution to those who intoxicate the savages or the French unless they give to the poor churches, the hospital or other works of piety according to the advice of their confessor, all the gain that they had made by this drink, leaving to them only the liberty of retaining that which the drink cost them so that they might be able to satisfy their merchants, it being quite easy through the obligation that we impose on the confessors of giving this penance to those who wish to lose their souls to satisfy their greed, to make known to the tavern-keepers and to others who trade in drinks that they must use with moderation the liberty that is accorded to them to trade, which is only permitted to them to the extent that they are able to guarantee the use that is made of it.

Regarding impurity which we consider as one of the principal causes of the punishments that God sends us, we cannot exhort you too much to take great care of the absolutions that you give when those who are in the habit of sinning address themselves to you, realizing that there is nothing which gives more occasion to impenitence for immoral acts than the facility that they promise to find in the confessors, to be absolved of them as often as they present themselves at confession, without placing themselves under any penalty of reform.

Regarding luxury which touches so near lewdness, we desire that you hold principally to three things: the first is, that you take great care to study and eradicate in the persons in your charge the attachment that they have for vanity, without regard to the pretexts that the ornaments which they wear to satisfy such vanity can be worn without mortal sin; for however difficult it is to decide how far one can go in this matter without committing mortal sin, there is nothing, however, more easy to lose oneself than the disposition of wishing to be vain as much as one can without sinning mortally, and nothing more certain for the confessor than to judge that a soul cannot do anything for her salvation and for her protection when she is in such a disposition.

The second thing is that you examine with attention if the attachment which is found in the fair sex for the ornaments is not an occasion of impurity; for in this case, that which would otherwise be venial becomes mortal. Now, it is very important to remark that there is hardly a person to whom vanity is not an occasion for impure glances or words, and that there are few of these vanities which do not expose one to hearing discourses against honour, and to suffer even criminal liberties. In a word, vanity opens all the doors of the soul, that is to say, all the senses to the demon of impurity. A vain woman finds herself daily in company where modesty is attacked by the eyes, ears, touch, imagination and by all the senses, her vanity being a signal for all lewdness to gather about her. That is why we do not believe that you should, nor that you can, give absolution to vain persons, to whom their vanity is an occasion for mortal sin whether their ornaments are in themselves criminal or not.

The third is that you do not content yourself that your penitents are dressed modestly when in church or when they approach the sacraments; but that you inform yourself further how they are dressed in their own homes; for we have known that several women and girls do not scruple to have the throat and shoulders uncovered when they are at home and we have even encountered them in this state. Now, in order to declare distinctly our intention on this matter, we forbid you expressly from absolving girls and women who have their necks and shoulders bare, whether inside or outside their homes, or who have them covered only with a transparent veil; and in regard to the communion, presenting the blessed bread, the offering and collections which are made by girls and women in the churches, we renew all that which has been ruled before by our predecessor in his *mandement* of February 26, 1682, and we desire that following the Apostle, the girls appear veiled, that is to say the head covered in church.

From S. D. Clark, ed., *The Social Development of Canada* (Toronto: University Press of Toronto, 1942).

LETTERS TO *GENTLEMAN'S MAGAZINE* (1731, 1733)

Gentleman's Magazine, which was perhaps the most influential English publication of its kind during the 18th century, contained articles devoted to a wide range of topics. It frequently featured articles from another publication, the *Universal Spectator*, which featured among its many pieces a popular advice column. The following letters reflect England's growing appreciation for mutual affection and respect within the institution of marriage.

ADVICE TO THE MARRIED

Joseph Spruceby acquaints Mr. Stonecastle in a Letter, that he loves every thing about him exceeding neat and clean. Two Years ago he married, chose his Wife neither for Beauty nor Fortune, but because she was a good Housewife. Soon after they were married, to his great surprise, she became an arrant Slut, and all his persuasions to the contrary being ineffectual, therefore complains to the *Spectator*.

Penelope Gentle addresses the *Spectator*, and sets forth, that before Marriage, her Husband told her he did not smoke, upon her declaring she had an unconquerable aversion to Tobacco. But of late takes 2 or 3 Pipes before he goes to Bed; by which his Breath becomes so disagreeable, that it makes her sick, and fears it may occasion her utter Dislike of him, and prejudice his Health, it not being good for him. This she dreads, but as he is a sensible good natur'd Man, a sight of her Letter in the *Spectator*, may produce an happy Effect.

In answer to these, Mr. *Spectator* observed, that a great deal of Complaisance, as well as Affection, is necessary to render the Marriage State agreeable; that 'tis very ungenerous to break the Promises of Courtship; that it is a Matter of more Importance for a Woman to make herself amiable after, than before Marriage; gives an ingenious Reason why so many Marriages are unhappy, because the Women employ more pains to make Nets than Cages.

AFTER SOME REMARKS ON THE AUTHORITY OF PARENTS, MR. STONECASTLE INSERTS A LETTER FOR THE SERVICE OF A YOUNG LADY, TO THE FOLLOWING PURPORT

Sir,

I am the only Child of a Gentleman of strict Virtue and honour. From my Infancy, till of late, he has treated me with the utmost Fondness, which I have always acknowledged by a dutiful Behavior. Being of a tender Constitution, I have resolved upon a single Life, and refused several Matches without his being uneasy at it. But a certain Gentleman has lately so insinuated himself into my Father's good Opinion, that he commands me absolutely to marry him, tho' his Person, Tempers, and Morals are my utter Aversion.

About a week ago he din'd with us. After Dinner I retir'd with a Relation to another Part of the House, where I endeavoured to divert her and myself on the

Harpsichord. As soon as the Gentleman was gone, my Father came to us in a violent Fury, broke the Harpsichord, tore my Books, and said a thousand bitter Things to me, protesting, since I would not marry at his Desire, he would force me to it; I fainted away; which, I suppose, occasion'd my Friend to say something on my Behalf, for which he rashly told her he never more desir'd to see her at his House, and would take Care that I should not be troublesome at hers. An Incivility he would have been ashamed of at another Time. Alas! How is he alter'd! What cruel Sufferings do I undergo! My Constitution is too weak to bear them long, and Death is my Choice rather than this hateful Marriage. When my Father reads this Letter, I hope he'll be sensible of some Compassion, and cease to persecute me. I am, &c.

Mr. Stonecastle observes on the Case of his Correspondent, that her Noncompliance is not an Act of Undutifulness, but Self-preservation, and that forcing a Child to marry, is contrary to Reason, as well as the natural Liberty of every Creature. This he illustrates by the following Instance.—A friend of mine had an advantageous Offer made him for his Daughter; on his acquainting her with it, She in a respectful Manner, beg'd his Excuse. The Father was greatly disappointed; but soon found his Daughter was pre-engag'd to another of a much inferior Fortune. At this he was under much Concern, but instead of a rigorous Treatment, used the kindest Arguments to persuade her to like that which he judg'd most for her Advantage; whilst with Tears she intreated him not to press her to a Marriage that must make her very miserable, assuring him she would never marry without his Leave. Finding how her Intentions stood, the indulgent old Gentleman sent instantly for the Lover, and joyned their Hands, here, Sir, says he, I give you my Daughter, even without your asking: Let that, however, not lessen but inhance the Gift: She might have been *Great* elsewhere; but, remember, I give her you to make her *happy*.

From E. A. Reitan, ed., *The Best of the Gentleman's Magazine* (Lewiston, N.Y.: E. Mellen Press, 1987), 164–66.

JOHN HAMPDEN, DESCRIPTION OF A PUBLIC EXECUTION IN LONDON, FROM AN *EIGHTEENTH-CENTURY JOURNAL* (1774)

The following entry for Saturday, July 2, 1774, is a vivid account of the events preceding a public execution in England. Notice how the arrest of a pickpocket enabled the author to transform a summary of the events into a denunciation of the frequency and ineffectiveness—as he saw it—of capital punishment in 18th-century England.

Saturday, July 2nd.

Early in the morning [yesterday] the prisoners [who were to be executed] employed themselves in singing psalms and other acts of devotion. Exactly at seven o'clock they were brought from the cells into the Press-yard, in order to the taking off their irons.—Jones trembled as if his frame was dissolving, while Hawke appeared, if not with unconcern, with a fortitude very unusual. While the irons were taking off, an acquaintance of Hawke accosted him with a "How d'ye, Billy?"—which the other replied to with cheerfulness, and enquired after an old acquaintance whom he had heard was indisposed. From Newgate to the place of execution Hawke behaved with much calm resignation, while Jones prayed and wept incessantly. When they came within 200 years of Oxford Street Turnpike, Hawke looked round him, as if he rather wished than feared the journey at an end. When they arrived at the place of execution about 20 minutes were spent in devotion, and then they were tied up. A number of pigeons were now thrown into the air, as were others at stated periods during the melancholy ceremony. About a minute before they were turned off Hawke kicked off his shoes with great violence, and at the instant the cart moved he drew up his knees to his breast, so as to fall with a violent jerk, which almost instantly deprived him of life. There was a hearse in waiting, with a handsome black coffin with yellow nails, on which was the following inscription:

MR. WILLIAM HAWKE,
Died July 1st,
1774
Aged 24

Hawke has desired that a tombstone may be erected to his memory, with an epitaph from a stone in Stepney Churchyard, beginning thus:

"Adieu, vain world! I've had enough of thee!"

Just as the unhappy men were turned off, a young fellow, a shoe-maker by trade, was detected picking a gentleman's pocket of a gold watch, and consigned to the care of the constables, who carried him before a magistrate.

Much has been said with great humanity and truth on the dreadful frequency of executions at Tyburn, and nothing is more evident than that they have very little effect in restraining men from committing depredations on the public. A reformation in our criminal laws has been long and loudly called for: In the opinion of the celebrated H. Fielding Esq., the lives of those executed are thrown away. It is not so much the severity as the certainty of punishment which deters men of bad morals. He who is about to commit a robbery estimates the numbers whom the jury will not convict from a proper reluctance to hang men for a petty act of pilfering, those who escape, because no evidence but the most certain will convict for a capital offence, with the numbers who are pardoned at the report, where it is become a kind of maxim to hang none but those who have been guilty of repeated offences, and laughs at the danger when there are so many chances of escaping. The beneficial effects of the severities of Pope Sextus the Fifth must convince every man that legal severity is real mercy. Our Laws should be carefully reviewed and the number of capital offences greatly lessened; but when that is done, the sentence of the law should be the voice of fate.

From John Hampden, ed., *An Eighteenth-Century Journal, 1774–1776* (London: MacMillan, 1940), 181–82.

ARTHUR YOUNG, EXCERPTS FROM *TRAVELS IN FRANCE DURING THE YEARS 1787, 1788, AND 1789* (1787 AND 1789)

The eve of the French Revolution was a tumultuous time. The selection excerpted here is from that period as seen through the eyes of an English traveler, Arthur Young. Young was a gentleman farmer who captured great detail and provided contrasts between English and French customs and tradition. Note the information given concerning the physical qualities of the French countryside.

[October 23, 1787] Again to Versailles. In viewing the king's apartment, which he had not left a quarter of an hour, with those slight traits of disorder that showed he lived in it, it was amusing to see the blackguard figures that were walking uncontrolled about the palace, and even in his bedchamber; men whose rags betrayed them to be in the last stage of poverty, and I was the only person that stared and wondered how the devil they got there. It is impossible not to like this careless indifference and freedom from suspicion. One loves the master of the house, who would not be hurt or offended at seeing his apartment thus occupied if he returned suddenly, for if there was danger of this the intrusion would be prevented. This is certainly a feature of that good temper which appears to me so visible everywhere in France. I desired to see the queen's apartments, but I could not. "Is, her Majesty in it? No. Why then not see it as well as the king's?" Ma foi, Monsieur, c'est une autre chose.

Ramble through the gardens, and by the grand canal with absolute astonishment at the exaggerations of writers and travelers. There is magnificence in the quarter of the orangery, but no beauty anywhere; there are some statues, good enough to wish them under cover. The extent and breadth of the canal are nothing to the eye, and it is not in such good repair as a farmer's horse pond. The menagerie is well enough, but nothing great.

[October 25, 1787] This great city [Paris] appears to be in many respects the most ineligible and inconvenient for the residence of a person of small fortune of any that I have seen, and vastly inferior to London. The streets are very narrow, and many of them crowded, nine tenths dirty, and all without foot pavements. Walking, which in London is so pleasant and so clean that ladies do it every day, is here a toil and a fatigue to a man, and an impossibility to a well-dressed woman. The coaches are numerous, and, what is much worse, there are an infinity of one-horse cabriolets, which are driven by young men of fashion and their imitators, alike fools, with such rapidity as to be real nuisances, and render the streets exceedingly dangerous, without an incessant caution. I saw a poor child run over and probably killed, and have been myself many times blackened with the mud of the kennels. This beggarly practice, of driving a one-horse booby hutch about the streets of a great capital, flows either from poverty or wretched and despicable economy; nor is it possible to speak of it with too much severity. If young noblemen at London were to drive their chaises in streets without footways, as their brethren do at Paris, they would speedily and justly get very well threshed or rolled in the kennel. This circumstance renders Paris an ineligible residence for persons, particularly families that cannot afford to keep a coach—a convenience which is as dear as at London. The fiacres—hackney coaches—are much worse than at that city; and chairs there are none, for they would be driven down in the streets. To this circumstance also it is owing that all persons of small or moderate fortune are forced to dress in black, with black stockings.

[Young was in Paris during the early sessions of the Estates General in 1789. On June 28 he left the capital to visit the eastern and southeastern provinces.]

[July 12.] Walking up a long hill to ease my mare, I was joined by a poor woman, who complained of the times, and that it was a sad country. Demanding her reasons, she said her husband had but a morsel of land, one cow, and a poor little horse, yet they had a franchar (forty-two pounds) of wheat and three chickens to pay as a quitrent to one seigneur; and four franchar of oats, one chicken, and one franc, to pay to another, besides very heavy tailles and other taxes. She had seven children, and the cow's milk helped to make the soup. "But why, instead of a horse, do not you no keep another cow?" Oh, her husband could not carry his produce so well without a horse; and asses are little used in the country. It was said, at present, that something was to be done by some great folks for such poor ones, but she did not know who nor how, but God send us better, car les tailles et les droits nous ecrasent.

This woman, at no great distance, might have been taken for sixty or seventy, her figure was so bent and her face so furrowed and hardened by labor, but she said she was only twenty-eight. An Englishman who has not traveled cannot imagine the figure made by infinitely the greater part of the country women in France; it speaks, at the first sight, hard and severe labor. I am inclined to think that they work harder than the men, and this, united with the more miserable labor of bringing a new race of slaves into the world, destroys absolutely all symmetry of person and every feminine appearance. To what are we to attribute this difference, in the manners of the lower people in the two kingdoms? To government. . . .

Among Arthur Young's observations can be found the author's description of *capitaineries*. The term refers to the sentries who safeguarded areas of land on which the hunting of abundant game was, under the monarchy, reserved for the French nobility and clergy. Peasants strongly objected to this regulation because they had to submit to the free ranging animals and birds, which were an inaccessible source of food and a risk to peasants' crops.

The capitaineries were a dreadful scourge on all the occupiers of land. By this term is to be understood the paramountship of certain districts granted by the king to princes of the blood, by which they were put in possession of the property of all game, even on lands not belonging to them; and what is very singular, on manors granted long before to individuals so that the erecting of a district into a capitainerie was an annihilation of all manorial rights to game within it. This was a trifling business in comparison to other circumstances; for in speaking of the preservation of the game in these capitaineries it must be observed that by game must be understood whole droves of wild boars, and herds of deer not confined by any wall or pale, but wandering at pleasure over the whole country, to the destruction of crops, and to the peopling of the galleys by wretched peasants who presumed to kill them in order to save that food which was to support their helpless children.

From Arthur Young, *Travels in France during the Years 1787, 1788, and 1789* ed., Jeffry Kaplow (New York: Doubleday 1969), 76–78, 144, 441.

SHINPU KENCHIKU-O, ACCOUNT OF A PEASANT UPRISING IN JAPAN, FROM *A RECORD OF HOW THE FOUR ORDERS OF PEOPLE IN MIMASAKA RAN RIOT* (1727)

Composed in the months that followed a peasant uprising in a western Japanese province, this 1727 chronicle reveals the risks that many Japanese peasants were willing to take to counter an "untenable" situation. Increased taxes and corruption were identified as the causes of the uprising. In the end, Japanese forces captured and crucified the peasant leaders.

This force numbered over eight thousand rebels, over one hundred of them armed with hunting guns or pop guns used to frighten birds, the rest armed with board hunting spears, bamboo spears, hatchets, and axes. Each vying to be first, they advanced like a landslide. They pursued and captured the boats being loaded at the Kuse district warehouse and confiscated the rice. (It was commonly claimed that no one knew who the rebels were.) Then they took the rice to the town of Kuse, where they set a guard over it.

Thereafter they marched on the Kuse warehouse agents, where they sent a message to the sake brewer, Tsukadaniya Taroemon, telling him to hand over his government rice. Before he could finish replying that "for me, on my own, to hand over the rice I hold in trust for the government would be unthinkable," several hundred men had smashed up his front door and lattices with their axes and hatchets. Unable to withstand them, Taroemon fled.

The rebels sent a similar message to the warehouse agent Yamaguchiya Kaneda Rokurozaemon living in the same town. Mr. Kaneda was a mere townsman, but he understood the logic of what the peasants were doing so he handed them the keys to the warehouse.

"There is nothing in there but my own property," he said as he got out of their way.

After that, the people's commander Amakusa Tokisada ran around giving these orders to his forces: "Do not cast covetous eyes upon the accumulated wealth of this district. Our enemies are the country samurai. Do not confuse them with our wealthy neighbors."

That same night the peasant forces divided at Odankoge. One troop of over a thousand rebels led by men from Doi, Yamane, Omori, Hinata, and Maga marched on the home of the country samurai in Meki, Fukushima Zenbei. With their axes and hatchets they shattered his front door to smithereens. They hauled out and smashed up his coffers, chests, tools, dishes, household utensils, weapons, and harnesses.

In the midst of this, one peasant said, "Here we have a helmet. Well now, would it be so difficult to smash that up?" All the other peasants laughed.

Fukushima was a country samurai experienced in the ways of the world. Not being one to underestimate a situation, he secretly opened his back gate and hid himself in a mountain forest. His entire family, including his wife and children, also escaped.

"We have realized our long cherished desires," the peasants shouted. Having set their minds at ease, they withdrew.

Rumors ran rampant that Fukushima had been really greedy, wrongfully charging 30 to 50 percent interest on loans of rice and grain. Besides, he had taken great pride in being a country samurai.

Another troop of over one thousand led by men from Higuchi, Shinjo, Tagucki, Mikamo, Kuroda, Kanayama, and Fumoto swept all before them in marching on the home of the deputy district headman Chujiro, who lived in the same district. With their axes and hatchets they shattered and smashed his front door and the doors inside. Chujiro valued his life. He flew through the back door to vanish no one knew where. The troops broke in the house. They put a match to his furnishings, sliding doors, buckets and bowls, and old clothes for a bonfire to ward off the cold of the night. This was so everyone would later remember how he had been punished by heaven. . . .

At dusk on the fifth, two intendants, Yamada Bunhachi and Miki Jinzaemon, arrived in Kuse and summoned the people's army. Afraid that they might be taken hostage, no one appeared. Instead they sent a message saying, "If you have business with us, go to Odankoge, where the peasants will outline their position." It being beyond their power to do otherwise, the other magistrates went to Odankoge, where the peasants surrounded them on all sides. . . .

The two magistrates listened to them. "You're absolutely right. As you have requested, we will retract the supplementary notice raising taxes, and we will allow you to pay 86 percent of the regular taxes demanded in this year's tax bill. We will abolish the district and deputy district headman, replace the village headmen, and leave it up to you to choose whomever you please for messenger service. Debtors and creditors will negotiate their terms face to face. We will cancel your obligation to repay the rice you borrowed from the domanial authorities. Right now we will distribute to every peasant present a day's ration of rice. The former village headmen are to let us know how many there are." Since they were talking about over thirteen thousand peasants who would each receive five *go*, they realized that even 120 bales of rice would not be enough.

The poor peasants each returned to his own district, leaving behind those ordinary peasants who had become the new messengers and those who had taken the lead in being the spokesmen. The spokesmen and the magistrates then exchanged written promises, but this was all a plot on the part of the magistrates to learn the names of the leaders for the future.

From Anne Walthall, ed., *Peasant Uprisings in Japan: A Critical Anthology of Peasant Histories* (Chicago: University of Chicago Press, 1991), 92–95.

KAIBARA EKIKEN, EXCERPT FROM COMMON SENSE TEACHINGS FOR JAPANESE CHILDREN

Influential during the 18th century, the Japanese scholar Kaibara Ekiken (1630–1714) composed a short text entitled *Wazoku Doshikun* (*Common Sense Teachings for Japanese Children*), in which reading, writing, and arithmetic often seem of secondary importance in relation to the teaching of virtuous behavior. Also of note is the separation of boys from girls and the academic prioritization of youth from "high-ranking families."

EDUCATION OF CHILDREN

(a) For the children in their sixth year

In January when children reach the age of six, teach them numbers one through ten, and the name given to designate 100, 1,000, 10,000 and 100,000,000. Let them know the four directions, East, West, North and South. Assess their native intelligence and differentiate between quick and slow learners. Teach them the Japanese syllabary (*kana*) from the age of six or seven, and let them learn how to write. . . . From this time on, teach them to respect their elders, and let them know the distinctions between the upper and lower classes and between the young and old. Let them learn to use the correct expressions.

(b) For the seventh year

When the children reach the age of seven, do not let the boys and girls sit together, nor must you allow them to dine together. . . .

(c) For the eighth year

This is the age when the ancients began studying the book *Little Learning*. Beginning at this time, teach the youngsters etiquette befitting their age, and caution them not to commit an act of impoliteness. Among those which must be taught are: the daily deportment, the manners set for appearing before one's senior and withdrawing from his presence, how to speak or respond to one's senior or guest, how to place a serving tray [*shokuzen*] or replace it for one's senior, how to present a wine cup and pour *sake* and to serve side dishes to accompany it, and how to serve tea. Children must also learn how to behave while taking their meals. This includes how to accept *sake* and side dishes from one's senior, and how to greet prominent people at dinner parties. Teach them also how to conduct themselves at tea ceremonies:

Children must be taught by those who are close to them the virtues of filial piety and obedience. To serve the parents well is called filial piety [*ko*], and to serve one's seniors well is called obedience [*tei*]. The one who lives close to the children and who is able to teach must instruct the children in the early years of their life that the first obligation of a human being is to revere the parents and serve them well. Then comes the next lesson which includes respect for one's seniors, listening to their commands and not holding them in contempt. One's seniors include elder brothers, elder sisters, uncles, aunts, and cousins who are older and worthy of respect. The way of a man is to observe the virtues of filial piety and obedience, and the children must be taught that all goodness in life emanates from these two funda-mental virtues. . . .

If the parents permit their children to hold other people in contempt, and take pleasure in their antics, the children will lose a sense of distinction between good and evil. They may view such antics lightheartedly, and cannot get out of their bad habits even after they become adults. They fail to become good children to the parents, or good younger brothers to the older brothers. They will be impolite, unfilial and disobedient. These are caused by the foolishness of parents who en-courage their children in evil-doing. As the children grow older, teach them to love their younger brothers and to be compassionate to the employees and servants. Teach them also the respect due the teachers and the behavior codes governing friends. The etiquette governing each movement toward important guests—such as standing, sitting, advancing forward, and retiring from their presence—and the lan-guage to be employed must be taught. Teach them how to pay respect to others according to the social positions held by them. Gradually the ways of filial piety and obedience, loyalty and trustworthiness, right deportment and decorum, and sense of shame must be inculcated in the children's minds and they must know how to implement them. Caution them not to desire the possessions of others, or to stoop below one's dignity in consuming excessive amounts of food and drink. They must know at all times a sense of shame. . . .

Once reaching the age of eight, children must follow and never lead their elders when entering a gate, sitting, or eating and drinking. From this time on they must be taught how to become humble and yield to others. Do not permit the children to behave as they please. It is important to caution them against "doing their own thing."

(d) From the spring of the eighth year

On this spring, calligraphy lessons on the square-style [*kaisho*] and cursive-style [*sosho*] writings must begin. . . . Teach them the basic lessons in reading. Avoid the *Classics of Filial Piety, Little Learning,* and the Four Books which have long sentences. They are difficult to memorize and not interesting [to the children who may as a result] form an adverse opinion on learning. First of all, select short sentences, which are easy to read and comprehend. Then let the children learn them by rote memory.

(e) For the tenth year

At the age of ten, let the children be placed under the guidance of a teacher, and tell them about the general meaning of five constant virtues and let them understand the way of the five human relationships. Let them read books by the Sage and the wise men of old and cultivate the desire for learning. Select for them, those books which are easily understood and which are suitable for moral instruction. The important passages must be clearly explicated for their benefit. Thereafter gradually expand their readings to include the *Little Learning,* and the Four Books and Five Classics. When not engaged in reading, teach them the literary and military arts. Generally, the public starts instructing the children in calligraphy at the age of eleven. I think it is too late. Unless children are taught from an early age, their hearts will become desolate, and their minds wild. They will dislike the teachings, and acquire a lazy habit. So teach the children early in life. . . .

(f) For the fifteenth year

Fifteen is the age when the ancients began the study of the *Great Learning.* From this time on, concentrate on the learning of a sense of justice and duty [*giri*]. The students must also learn to cultivate their personalities and investigate the way of governing people. This is the way of the *Great Learning.* Those who are born in the high-ranking families have the heavy obligations [*shokubun*] of becoming leaders of the people, of having people entrusted to their care, and of governing them. Therefore, without fail, a teacher must be selected for them when they are still young. They must be taught how to read and be informed of the ways of old, of cultivating their personalities, and of the way of governing people. If they do not learn the way of governing people, they may injure the many people who are entrusted to their care by the Way of Heaven. That will be a serious disaster. Other people too, depending on their social status, have some work to do in the governing of the people. Therefore they must acquire knowledge concerning their work. Even though one may be born without a good mind, he can comprehend the general outline of the *Little Learning* and the Four Books. If he is intelligent, he must study widely and know many other things.

(g) At the twentieth year

In olden days in China, when children reached the age of twenty, a capping ceremony was held to celebrate their coming of age [*genbuku*]. The word *genbuku* means to put a cap on the head. In olden days, in Japan too, both the court nobles and samurai placed ceremonial caps [*koburi eboshi*] on those who reached the age of twenty. . . . Once the *genbuku* ceremony is completed, the children become adults. From that moment on, they must discard their former childish way, follow the virtues of the adult society, reach out everywhere for knowledge, and act in an exemplifying manner.

From David John Lu, ed., *Sources of Japanese History*, vol. 1 (New York: McGraw-Hill, 1974), 247–50.

WILLIAM BRADFORD'S ACCOUNT OF THE MURDER OF A NARRAGANSETT BOY AT PLYMOUTH PLANTATION, FROM *OF PLYMOUTH PLANTATION, 1620–1647* (1638)

In the year 1638, a violent event unfolded in the New England colony of Plymouth Plantation. A group of settlers participated in the fatal stabbing of a Narragansett boy, from whom a handful of valuables was stolen. The offenders were captured, and it was incumbent on William Bradford—who was a frequent governor of Plymouth Plantation, although not in 1638—to resolve the situation to the satisfaction of the victim's family and friends.

This year Mr. Thomas Prence was chosen Governor.

Amongst other enormities that fell out amongst them; this year three men were after due trial executed for robbery and murder which they had committed. Their names were these: Arthur Peach, Thomas Jackson and Richard Stinnings. There was a fourth, Daniel Cross, who was also guilty, but he escaped away and could not be found.

This Arthur Peach was the chief of them, and the ringleader of all the rest. He was a lusty and a desperate young man, and had been one of the soldiers in the Pequot War and had done as good service as the most there, and one of the forwardest in any attempt. And being now out of means and loath to work, and falling to idle courses and company, he intended to go to the Dutch plantation; and had allured these three, being other men's servants and apprentices, to go with him. But another cause there was also of his secret going away in this manner. He was not only run into debt, but he had got a maid with child (which was not known till after his death), a man's servant in the town, and fear of punishment made him get away. The other three complotting with him ran away from their masters in the night, and could not be heard of; for they were not the ordinary way, but shaped such a course as they thought to avoid the pursuit of any. But falling into the way that lieth between the Bay of Massachusetts and the Narragansetts, and being disposed to rest themselves, struck fire and took tobacco, a little out of the way by the wayside.

At length there came a Narragansett Indian boy, who had been in the Bay a-trading, and had both cloth and beads about him—they had met him the day before, and he was now returning. Peach called him to drink tobacco with them, and he came and sat down with them. Peach told the other he would kill him and take what he had from him, but they were something afraid. But he said, "Hang him, rogue, he had killed many of them." So they let him alone to do as he would. And when he saw his time, he took a rapier and ran him through the body once or twice and took from him five fathom of wampum and three coats of cloth and went their way, leaving him for dead. But he scrambled away when they were gone, and made shift to get home, but died within a few days after. By which means they were discovered. And by subtlety the Indians took them; for they, desiring a canoe to set them over a water, not thinking their fact had been known, by the sachem's command they were carried to Aquidneck Island and there accused of the murder, and were examined and committed upon it by the English there.

The Indians sent for Mr. Williams and made a grievous complaint; his friends and kindred were ready to rise in arms and provoke the rest thereunto, some conceiving they should now find the Pequots' words true, that the English would fall upon them. But Mr. Williams pacified them and told them they should see justice done upon the offenders, and went to the man and took Mr. James, a physician, with him. The man told him who did it, and in what manner it was done; but the physician found his wounds mortal and that he could not live, as he after testified upon oath before the jury in open court. And so he died shortly after, as both Mr. Williams, Mr. James and some Indians testified in court.

The Government in the Bay were acquainted with it but referred it hither because it was done in this jurisdiction; but pressed by all means that justice might be done in it, or else the country must rise and see justice done; otherwise it would raise a war. Yet some of the rude and ignorant sort murmured that any English should be put to death for the Indians. So at last they of the Island brought them hither, and being often examined and the evidence produced, they all in the end freely confessed in effect all that the Indian accused them of, and that they had done it in the manner aforesaid. And so, upon the forementioned evidence, were cast by the jury and condemned, and executed for the same, September 4. And some of the Narragansett Indians and of the party's friends were present when it was done, which gave them and all the country good satisfaction. But it was a matter of much sadness to them here, and was the second execution which they had since they came; being both for willful murder, as hath been before related. Thus much of this matter.

From Wilcomb E. Washburn, ed., *The Indian and the White Man* (New York: New York University Press, 1964), 310–12.

MUNGO PARK, EXCERPT FROM THE ACCOUNT OF HIS EXPLORATIONS IN WEST AFRICA, FROM *TRAVELS IN THE INTERIOR DISTRICTS OF AFRICA* (1794)

In late May 1794, Mungo Park sailed from England to Africa, where he spent two years exploring, in particular, the Niger River and the famous city of Timbuktu. He also encountered the slave trade during his travels. Park returned to Africa in 1805 and traveled up the Niger to its source, but he was attacked by members of the region's indigenous population and was never heard from again.

April 19th. The long wished-for day of our departure was at length arrived; and the Slatees [black slave traders] having taken the irons from their slaves, assembled with them at the door of Karfa's house, where the bundles were all tied up, and every one had his load assigned him. The coffle [caravan] on its departure from Kamalia, consisted of twenty-seven slaves for sale but we were afterwards joined by five at Maraboo and three at Bala, making in all thirty-five slaves.

When we departed from Kamalia, we were followed for about half a mile by most of the inhabitants of the town, some of them crying and others shaking hands with their relations, who were now about to leave them; and when we had gained a piece of rising ground, from which we had a view of Kamalia, all the people belonging to the coffle were ordered to sit down with their faces towards Kamalia. The school-master, with two of the principal Slatees, pronounced a long and solemn prayer; after which they walked three times round the coffle, making an impression in the ground with the ends of their spears and muttering something by way of charm. When this ceremony was ended, all the people belonging to their coffle sprang up, and without taking a formal farewell of their friends set forward. As many of the slaves had remained for years in irons, the sudden exertion of walking quick with heavy loads upon their heads occasioned spasmodic contractions of their legs; and we had not proceeded above a mile before it was found necessary to take two of them from the rope, and allow them to walk more slowly until we reached a walled village, where some people were waiting to join the coffle.

As we proposed shortly to enter Jalonka wilderness, the people of the village furnished us with great plenty of provisions and on the morning of the 21st we entered the woods. During this day's travel, two slaves, a woman and a girl, were so much fatigued that they could not keep up with the coffle; they were severely whipped, and dragged along until about three in the afternoon when they were both affected with vomiting, by which it was discovered that they had *eaten clay*. This practice is by no means uncommon amongst the Negroes; but whether it arises from a vitiated appetite, or from a settled intention to destroy themselves, I cannot affirm. They were permitted to lie down in the woods, and three people remained with them until they had rested themselves; but they did not arrive at the town [where we were camping] until past midnight, and were then so much exhausted that the Slatees gave up all thought of taking them across the woods in their present condition.

April 24th. As soon as day dawned we set out, and traveled the whole morning over a wild and rocky country. A woman slave, who had refused victuals in the morning, began to lag behind, and complain dreadfully of pains in her legs. Her load was taken from her and given to another slave and she was ordered to keep in front of the coffle. About eleven o'clock as we were resting by a small rivulet, some of the people discovered a hive of bees in a hollow tree, and they were proceeding to obtain the honey, when the largest swarm I ever beheld flew out, and, attacking the people of the coffle, made us fly in all directions. When our enemies thought fit to desist from pursuing us, it was discovered that the poor woman above mentioned, whose name was Nealee, was not come up; and as many of the slaves in their retreat had left their bundles behind them, it became necessary for some persons to return and bring them. They likewise brought with them poor Nealee, whom they found lying by the rivulet. She was very much exhausted and had crept to the streams, in hopes to defend herself from the bees by throwing water over her body; but this proved ineffectual; for she was stung in the most dreadful manner.

When the Slatees had picked out the stings as far as they could, she was washed with water, and then rubbed with bruised leaves; but the wretched woman obstinately refused to proceed any further; declaring that she would rather die than walk another step. As entreaties and threats were used in vain, the whip was at length applied; and after patiently bearing a few strokes, she started up, and walked with tolerable expedition for four or five hours longer, when she made an attempt to run away from the coffle, but was so very weak that she fell down in the grass. Though she was unable to rise, the whip was a second time applied, but without effect; upon which Karfa desired two of the slaves to place her upon the ass which carried our dry provisions; but she could not sit erect. The Slatees, however, were unwilling to abandon her, the day's journey being nearly ended; they therefore made a sort of litter of bamboo canes, upon which she was placed and tied on it with slips of bark: this litter was carried upon the heads of two slaves.

In this manner the woman was carried forward until it was dark when we reached a stream of water, at the foot of a high hill; and here we stopped for the night. As we had only eaten one handful of meal since the preceding night, and traveled all day in a hot sun, many of the slaves were very much fatigued; and some of them *snapped their fingers*, which among the Negroes is a sure sign of desperation. The Slatees immediately put them all in irons; and such of them as had evinced signs of great despondency, were kept apart from the rest, and had their hands tied. In the morning they were found greatly recovered.

April 25th. At day-break poor Nealee was awakened; but her limbs were now become so stiff and painful, that she could neither walk nor stand; she was therefore lifted, like a corpse, upon the back of an ass; but as Nealee made no exertion to prevent herself from falling, she was quickly thrown off, and had one of her legs much bruised. Every attempt to carry her forward being thus found ineffectual, the general cry of the coffle was *kang-tegi*, "cut her throat"; an operation I did not wish to see performed, and therefore marched onwards with the foremost of the coffle. I had not walked above a mile, when one of Karfa's domestic slaves came up to me, with poor Nealee's garment upon the end of his bow, and exclaimed *Nealee affilita* (Nealee is lost). I asked him whether the Slatees had given him the garment, as a reward for cutting her throat; he replied that Karfa and the schoolmaster would not consent to that measure, but had left her on the road; where undoubtedly she soon perished, and was probably devoured by wild beasts. . . .

On the 30th we reached Jallacotta, a considerable town. Here one of the slaves belonging to the coffle, who had traveled with great difficulty for the last three days, was found unable to proceed any further: his master proposed therefore to exchange him for a young slave girl, belonging to one of the townspeople. The poor girl was ignorant of her fate until the bundles were all tied up in the morning, and the coffle ready to depart, when, coming with the other women to see the coffle set out, her master took her by the hand, and delivered her to her new owner. Never was a face of serenity more suddenly changed into one of the deepest distress; the terror she manifested on having the load put upon her head, and the rope fastened around her neck, and the sorrow with which she bade adieu to her companions was truly affecting.

From Rhoda Hoff, ed., *Africa, Adventures in Eyewitness History* (New York: Walck, 1963), 39–43.

WILLIAM CORNELISON SCHOUTEN, EXCERPTS FROM THE ACCOUNT OF HIS VOYAGE AROUND CAPE HORN, FROM *THE RELATION OF A WONDERFULL VOIAGE MADE BY WILLIAM CORNELISON SCHOUTEN OF HORNE* (1615)

> For Europe's nation-states, maritime exploration was an essential precursor to the exercise of mercantile and naval power. The entries that follow are an account of the Dutchman William Cornelison Schouten and his voyage around Cape Horn and entrance into the Pacific. His disturbing encounters with native populations serve to remind the reader of the momentous changes that European ocean exploration brought about.

Upon the 14 of June 1615 we sailed out of the Texell, and the 16 of the same month, being in sight of Dunkerk, passed between Dover and Callis. . . .

The 28 we left Plymouth and sailed with a north north-east wind and fair weather, and the 29 the Master and Merchant of the *Horne* came aboard the *Unity* to agree together about order to be taken upon the 4 of July, for sharing of our victuals, according to the manner and custom used in ships that sail long voyages, where they deliver the sailors their meat and drink by weight, and measure, to every man alike and according to his quality.

The 4 of July, according to the aforesaid resolution, it was ordered that every man should have a can of beer a day, 4 pound of biscuit, and half a pound of butter (besides sweet suet) a week, and five cheeses for the whole voyage.

The 8, being under 39 degrees and 25 minutes our carpenter's mate died . . .

The 19 as we were busy about both the ships to make them clean, and burned reeds under the *Horne*, the flame of the fire suddenly got into the ship, and presently took such hold thereof that in the twinkling of an eye, it was so great that we could by no means quench it, by reason it lay 50 foot dry from the waterside, and by that means we were constrained to stand still, and see it burn before our eyes, not able to do anything to save it.

The 20 at a high water we launched the *Unity*, into the water again, and went to the *Horne* and quenched the fire, but the ship was burnt clear down to the water. The next day when we had cast the water out of that part of it that was left, we saved all the wood, ironwork, anchors, ordnance, and what else that was to be gotten and put it into our ship.

The 20 we were under 53 degrees, and guessed we were about 20 leagues southward from the Straits of Magellan. . . .

Then about noon we were under 54 degrees and 46 minutes. There we saw an innumerable number of penguins and thousands of whales, so that we were forced to look well about us, and to wind and turn to shun the whales, lest we should sail upon them.

The 25, in the morning we were close by the east land, which was very high and craggy, which on the north side reacheth east south-east, as far as we could see, that land we called States Land, but the land that lay west from us, we named Maurice Land. We perceived that on both sides thereof, there were good roads, and sandy bays, for on either side it had sandy strands and very fair sandy ground. There are great store of fish, penguins and porpoises, as also birds and water enough, but we could see no trees . . .

There we saw extreme great sea mews, bigger of body than swans, their wings being spread abroad, were each of them above a fathom long. These birds being unaccustomed to see men, came to our ship, and sat thereon, and let our men take and kill them. . . .

The 12 [February] our men had each of them three cups of wine in sign of joy for our good luck, for then the Straits of Magellan lay east from us: the same day by advice of all our counsel, at the request of our chief Merchant, the new passage (by us discovered between Mauritus Land and the States Land), was named the Straits of le Maire, although by good right it should rather have been called William Schouten's Strait, after our Master's name, by whose wise conduction and skill in sailing, the same was found. . . .

The 14 in the morning, we saw another island right before us, about seven leagues distant from us . . . and made towards it. . . . Then ten or twelve canoes came to our ship, but we would not let them come aboard, but showed them friendly countenance, and bartered with them for four flying fishes, for the which we gave them some beads, which we let down by a rope at the stern of the ship, and they taking them tied the fishes to the rope, and we pulled them up. In the meantime our shallop sounded along by the land, which they in the canoes seeing, presently made towards it, and being close by it, at first spake unto the men, but withal compassed them about with fourteen canoes, and therewith some of them leaped overboard, thinking to fall upon the shallop, or to draw it away with them, which our men perceiving, shot with their muskets among them (there being six muskets, and other arms, cutlasses and pikes in the shallop), and therewith killed two of the indians as they sat in their canoes, whereof one presently fell dead overboard, the other sat still with his hand wiping off the blood upon his breast, but at last fell likewise overboard: the rest in the canoes, were thereat in so great fear, that in all haste they made away, at which time we saw many men standing upon the shore, that cried and made a great noise. But for that we there could find no fit anchoring ground, we took our shallop in again, and went forward on our voyage, holding our course south-west, the better to get to the south, hoping there to find firm land. . . .

The 16 in the morning we sailed in with our ship between both the islands, and anchored at 9 fathom, where we had good lying. After noon our boat and shallop rowed to the lesser island, to fetch some coco-nuts, and burned 2 or 3 of the indian's houses, whereupon they that dwelt in the other island began mightily to cry and make a noise, but durst not come to us, for with our ordnance we shot along the shore, and into the wood, that the bullets entered into it with thundering noise, whereat the indians fled, and durst not once look out. About evening our men came aboard again, and brought so many coco-nuts, that everyone of us had three nuts for his part. That night there came of the indians aboard our ship to make peace with us, with him bringing one of our men's caps which before fell off his head in the skirmish. Those people are clean naked, their privy members and all.

The 14 [October] in the morning, we saw Java, and that day sailed by Tuban.

The 23 we set sail, and the 28 went by Jakarta, where we anchored without the island, there we found three ships of Holland. The *Horne*, the *Eagle*, and the *Trou*, and 3 English ships. The next night, one of our men died, which was the first man that died that voyage in the *Unity*, besides 2 more that died in the *Horne*, the one John Cornelison Schouten, our Master's brother, in the south sea, and one about the coast of Portingale. So that until then, there died but 3 men in both the ships, and then we had left 84 men living, all indifferently well.

From Donald Macintyre, *The Adventure of Sail, 1520–1914* (London: Elek, 1970), 91–96.

THE SLAVER BARBOT'S ACCOUNT OF THE SLAVE TRADE, FROM "A DESCRIPTION OF THE COASTS OF NORTH AND SOUTH GUINEA" (EARLY 18TH CENTURY)

Barbot, a French slaver and the author of this text about the maritime commerce in slaves, wrote on the topic with great clarity and concision. Throughout the document, Barbot voices his opinion that his fellow slavers and he were "very nice" in their efforts to keep the slaves alive and passive during the Middle Passage.

As to the management of our slaves aboard, we lodge the two sexes apart, by means of a strong partition at the main mast; the forepart is for men, the other behind the mast for the women. If it be in large ships carrying five or six hundred slaves, the deck in such ships ought to be at least five and a half or six foot high, which is very requisite for driving a continual trade of slaves: for the greater height it has, the more airy and convenient it is for such a considerable number of human creatures; and consequently far the more healthy for them, and fitter to look after them. We build a sort of half-decks along the sides with deals and spars provided for that purpose in Europe, that half-deck extending no farther than the sides of our scuttles, and so the slaves lie in two rows, one above the other, and as close together as they can be crowded.

The Dutch company's ships exceed all other Europeans in such accommodations, being commonly built designedly for those voyages, and consequently contrived very wide, lofty, and airy, betwixt decks, with gratings and scuttles, which can be covered with tarpaulins in wet weather; and in fair uncovered, to let in the more air. Some also have made small ports, or lights along the sides at proper distances, well secured with thick iron bars, which they open from time to time for the air; and that very much contributes to the preservation of those poor wretches, who are so thick crowded together.

The Portuguese of Angola, a people in many respects not to be compared to the English, Dutch or French, in point of neatness aboard their ships, though indeed some French and English ships in those voyages for slaves are slovenly, foul, and stinking, according to the temper and the want of skill of the commanders; the Portuguese, I say, are commendable in that they bring along with them to the coast, a sufficient quantity of coarse thick mats, to serve as bedding under the slaves aboard, and shift them every fortnight or three weeks with such fresh mats: which, besides that it is softer for the poor wretches to lie upon than the bare deals or decks, must also be much healthier for them, because the planks, or deals, contract some dampness more or less, either from the deck being so often washed to keep it clean and sweet, or from the rain that gets in now and then through the scuttles or other openings, and even from the very sweat of the slaves; which being so crowded in a low place, is perpetual, and occasions many distempers, or at best great inconveniencies dangerous to their health: whereas, lying on mats, and shifting them from time to time, must be much more convenient; and it would be prudent to imitate the Portuguese in this point, the charge of such mats being inconsiderable.

We are very nice in keeping the places where the slaves lie clean and neat, appointing some of the ship's crew to do that office constantly, and several of the slaves themselves to be assistant to them in that employment; and thrice a week we perfume betwixt decks with a quantity of vinegar in pails, and red-hot iron bullets in them, to expel the bad air, after the place has been well washed and scrubbed with brooms: after which, the deck is cleaned with cold vinegar, and in the daytime, in good weather, we leave all the scuttles open, and shut them again at night.

It has been observed before, that some slaves fancy they are carried to be eaten, which makes them desperate; and others are so on account of their captivity: so that if care be not taken, they will mutiny and destroy the ship's crew in hopes to get away.

To prevent such misfortunes, we use [sic] to visit them daily, narrowly searching every corner between decks, to see whether they have not found means, to gather any pieces of iron, or wood, or knives, about the ship, notwithstanding the great care we take not to leave any tools or nails, or other things in the way: which, however, cannot be always so exactly observed, where so many people are in the narrow compass of a ship.

We cause as many of our men as is convenient to lie in the quarter-deck and gunroom, and our principal officers in the great cabin, where we keep all our small arms in a readiness, with sentinels constantly at the door and avenues to it; being thus ready to disappoint any attempts our slaves might make on a sudden.

These precautions contribute very much to keep them in awe; and if all those who carry slaves duly observed them, we should not hear of so many revolts as have happened. Where I was concerned, we always kept our slaves in such order, that we did not perceive the least inclination in any of them to revolt, or mutiny, and lost very few of our number in the voyage.

It is true, we allowed them much more liberty, and used them with more tenderness than most other Europeans would think prudent to do; as, to have them all upon deck every day in good weather; to take their meals twice a day, at fixed hours, that is, at ten in the morning, and at five at night; which being ended, we made the men go down again between decks: for the women were almost entirely at their own discretion, to be upon deck as long as they please, nay even many of the males had the same liberty by turns, successively; few or none being fettered or kept in shackles, and that only on account of some disturbances, or injuries offered to their fellow-captives, as will unavoidably happen among a numerous crowd of such savage people. Besides, we allowed each of them betwixt their meals a handful of Indian wheat and mandioca, and now and then short pipes and tobacco to smoke upon deck by turns, and some coco-nuts; and to the women a piece of coarse cloth to cover them, and the same to many of the men, which we took care they did wash from time to time, to prevent vermin, which they are very subject to; and because it looked sweeter and more agreeable. Towards the evening they diverted themselves on the deck, as they thought fit, some conversing together, others dancing, singing, and sporting after their manner, which pleased them highly, and often made us pastime; especially the female sex, who being apart from the males, on the quarter-deck, and many of them young sprightly maidens, full of jollity and good humour, afforded an abundance of recreation; as did several little fine boys, which we mostly kept to attend on us about the ship.

We messed the slaves twice a day, as I have observed; the first meal was of our large beans boiled, with a certain quantity of Muscovy lard, which we have from Holland, well packed up in casks. The beans we have in plenty at Rochel. The other meal was of peas, or of Indian wheat, and sometimes meal of mandioca; this provided in Prince's Island, the Indian wheat at the Gold Coast; boiled with either lard, or suet, or grease, by turns: and sometimes with palm-oil and malaguette or Guinea pepper. I found they had much better stomachs for beans, and it is proper fattening food for captives; in my opinion far better to maintain them well, than Indian wheat, mandioca or yams; though the Calabar slaves value this root above any other food, as being used to it in their own country: but it is not at certain times of the year to be had in so great a quantity as is requisite to subsist such a number of people for several months; besides that they are apt to decay, and even to putrify as they grow old. Horse-beans are also very proper for slaves in lieu of large beans: there is good plenty of them in Great Britain, which, as well as the other beans, will keep, if well put up in dry vats or casks.

We distributed them by ten in a mess, about a small flat tub, made for that use by our coopers, in which their victuals were served; each slave having a little wooden spoon to feed himself handsomely, and more cleanly than with their fingers, and they were well pleased with it.

At each meal we allowed every slave a full coco-nut shell of water, and from time to time a dram of brandy, to strengthen their stomachs.

The Dutch commonly feed their slaves three times a day, with indifferent good victuals, and much better than they eat in their own country. The Portuguese feed them most with mandioca.

As for the sick and wounded, or those out of order, our surgeons, in their daily visits betwixt decks, finding any indisposed, caused them to be carried to the Lazaretto, under the forecastle, a room reserved for a sort of hospital, where they were carefully looked after. Being out of the crowd, the surgeons had more conveniency and time to administer proper remedies; which they cannot do leisurely between decks, because of the great heat that is there continually, which is sometimes so excessive, that the surgeons would faint away, and the candles would not burn; besides, that in such a crowd of brutish people, there are always some very apt to annoy and hurt others, and all in general so greedy, that they will snatch from the sick slaves the fresh meat or liquor that is given them. It is no way advisable to put the sick slaves into the long-boat upon deck, as was very imprudently done in the *Albion* frigate, spoken of in the description of New Calabar; for they being thus exposed in the open air, and coming out of the excessive hot hold, and lying there in the cool of the nights, for some time just under the fall of the wind from the sails, were soon taken so ill of violent cholics and blood fluxes, that in a few days they died, and the owners lost above three hundred slaves in the passage from St Tome to Barbados; and the two hundred and fifty that survived, were like skeletons, one half of them not yielding above four pounds a head there: an oversight, by which fifty per cent of the stock or outset was lost.

Much more might be said relating to the preservation and maintenance of slaves in such voyages, which I leave to the prudence of the officers that govern aboard, if they value their own reputation and their owner's advantage; and shall only add these few particulars, that though we ought to be circumspect in watching the slaves narrowly, to prevent or disappoint their ill designs for our own conservation, yet must we not be too severe and haughty with them, but on the contrary, caress and humour them in every reasonable thing. Some commanders, of a morose peevish temper are perpetually beating and curbing them, even without the least offence, and will not suffer any upon deck but when unavoidable necessity to ease themselves does require; under pretence it hinders the work of the ship and sailors, and that they are troublesome by their nasty nauseous stench, or their noise: which makes those poor wretches desperate, and besides their falling into distempers through melancholy, often is the occasion of their destroying themselves.

From Donald Macintyre, *The Adventure of Sail, 1520–1914* (London: Elek, 1970), 117–19.

CUMULATIVE INDEX

Boldface numbers refer to volume numbers. A key appears on all verso pages.

language, **4:**202–4; lineage, **4:**366, 368; literature, **4:**202–4; map (18th Century), **4:**15; marriage, **4:**30–32, 46–47; masks, **4:**445, 446; material life, **4:**237–38; matrilineal societies, **4:**46–47, 368; men, work of, **4:**47; merchants, **4:**331; military service, **4:**403; musical instruments, **4:**446; nuts, **4:**240; paintings and drawings, **4:**447; palm, **4:**240; percussion instruments, **4:**446; poetry, **4:**203; political centers, **4:**330; polygamy, **4:**30; professions, **4:**153–54; religion, **4:**134, 330–31, 464–69, 483–86; rural life and agriculture, **4:**135; seniority of offspring, **4:**369; shrines, **4:**484; slaves in, **4:**370–71, 403–4; social status, **4:**330, 370; social structure, **4:**368–71, 446; sorghum, **4:**430; spirits, **4:**221; "stateless societies," **4:**348–49; statues, **4:**446–47; storytelling, **4:**202–4; taxes, **4:**136; textiles, **4:**121; trade, **4:**134–36; trading posts, European, **4:**331; vegetables, **4:**240; warfare, **4:**402–4; weapons, **4:**403–4; weaving, **4:**447; women, **4:**46–48; work celebrations, **4:**430; yams, **4:**240

Africa (20th Century): AIDS, **6:**294–95; alcoholic beverages, **6:**323–24, 331–33; beer, **6:**331; charcoal, use of, **6:**194; Christianity, **6:**601, 602; courts and judges, **6:**432–33; crimes, **6:**432; discrimination, **6:**193; diseases, **6:**293–95; drink, **6:**323–24, 331–33; economic life, **6:**86, 124–25; education, **6:**124, 194, 196, 212–14; education of women, **6:**86; ethnic composition of, **6:**25; family life, **6:**178; government workers, **6:**124; health and medicine, **6:**193, 260, 293–95; historical overview, **6:**25–26; holistic medicine, **6:**293; independence movements, **6:**25–26; Islam, **6:**433, 601, 602; language, **6:**178, 212; law and crime, **6:**431–34; literacy, **6:**87; men, **6:**177; mining, **6:**125; missionaries, **6:**601; music, **6:**178; ovens, **6:**194; political life, **6:**178; religion, **6:**601–3; religious education, **6:**214; religious rituals, **6:**293–94, 331; running, **6:**510; rural life and agriculture, **6:**86, 123, 124, 177; science, **6:**193–95; sports, **6:**509–11; taboos, **6:**293–94; taxes, **6:**124; trade, **6:**86; travel and transportation, **6:**193; unemployment, **6:**178; universities, **6:**213; urban life, **6:**125, 162, 177–79; witch doctors, **6:**293; women, **6:**85–87; women, work of, **6:**86, 332; work, **6:**111, 123–25. *See also* Colonial rule of Africa

Afterlife. *See* Death, burial, and the afterlife

Afternoon tea, **5:**240

Agamemnon, **1:**378

Agassiz, Louis, **5:**152–53

Age of marriage: Byzantium, **2:**63; China (Tang Dynasty), **2:**40, 45, 84; Europe (Middle Ages), **2:**40, 41; Islamic World (Middle Ages), **2:**85–86; Middle Ages, **2:**39–40; Vikings, **2:**44

Age sets, **4:**369

Agincourt, Battle of, **3:**13

Aging. *See* Old age

Agnosticism, **6:**572–73

Agora, **1:**97, 103–4

Agricultural Adjustment Act, **6:**436–37

Agriculture. *See* Rural life and agriculture

A-Group Nubians, **1:**13, 149–50, 259, 312, 354, 387

Aguadores, **5:**245

Aguateca, **3:**167

Aguilar, Geronimo de, **3:**21

Ah atanzabob, **3:**45

Ahaws, **3:**294–95

Ah Cacau, **3:**353

Ah chembul uinicob, **3:**269

Ah Chicum Ek, **3:**372

Ah cuch cabob, **3:**296

Ahmed, **3:**292

Ah kulebob, **3:**296

Ahmose, **1:**374–75

AIDS: Africa (20th Century), **6:**260, 294–95; India (20th Century), **6:**287; United States (1960–90), **6:**282–84

Aid to Families with Dependent Children (AFDC), **6:**130

Aigina and minting of coins, **1:**134

Airplanes: invention of, **6:**184; World War I, **6:**4, 461–62

Air pollution, **6:**363

Air traffic controllers fired by Reagan, **6:**132

'A'isha (wife of Muhammad), **2:**86, 157

Aja, **4:**347

Ajax, **1:**396

Akhenaton: economic life, **1:**96; palaces of, **1:**93, 95; poetry by, **3:**359; religious beliefs, **1:**6, 453, 458–59, 475

Akiko, Yosano, **6:**238

Akkadians. *See* Mesopotamia

Akua, **2:**308

Alaska. *See* Inuit

Albania: independence, **5:**392; Ottoman Empire, war against, **3:**12

Albanian language, **3:**166

Alberini, Marcello, **3:**179

Albert (Prince of England), **5:**33, 300, 413

Alberti, Leon Battista, **3:**212

Alcabala, **3:**275

Alcalá de Henares, University of, **3:**176, 211–12

Alcaldes, **3:**287

Alchemy: Europe (Middle Ages), **2:**160. *See also* Magic and superstition

Alcibiades, **1:**47, 66, 267, 413

Alcoholic beverages: Africa (20th Century), **6:**323–24, 331–33; China (Tang Dynasty), **2:**217–18; Civil War soldiers, **5:**224; England (15th & 16th Centuries), **3:**237, 238–40; England (17th & 18th Centuries), **4:**261–62; 15th & 16th Centuries, **3:**237; films depicting drinking (1920–39), **6:**518–19; Hindus and, **5:**252; India (19th Century), **5:**54, 252–53, 442; Islamic World (Middle Ages), **2:**283; Islamic World (19th Century), **5:**468; Japan (20th Century), **6:**324, 330; Jews and, **3:**245; life at sea (17th & 18th Centuries), **4:**267–68; Middle Ages, **2:**196, 213; Muslim prohibition on, **2:**206–7, 219; Muslims and, **3:**237, 245; **5:**252; Native Americans (colonial frontier of North America), **4:**258–59; New England, colonial, **4:**265–66; North American colonial frontier, **4:**258–60; 17th & 18th Centuries, **4:**256–57; Spain (15th & 16th Centuries), **3:**240; United States (Civil War era), **5:**383; United States (1920–39), **6:**307; United States (1960–90), **6:**328–29; United States (Western Frontier), **5:**124, 126, 251; Vikings, **2:**398. *See also* Ale; Beer; Prohibition; Wine

Alcoholism. *See* Drunkenness

Alcoman, **3:**104

Alcuin, **2:**5

Aldrin, Edwin, **6:**188

Ale: China (Tang Dynasty), **2:**103, 217–18; England (15th & 16th Centuries), **3:**237, 239; England (Victorian era), **5:**239, 240; Europe (Middle Ages), **2:**198, 214; Vikings, **2:**202

Alencar, José de, **5:**427

Aleppo, **3:**261

Alexander, Eveline, **5:**236

Alexander of Tralles, **2:**188–89

Alexander the Great: death of, **1:**6; economic life, **1:**135; Indian campaign of, **5:**14; **6:**8; military conquests, **1:**5, 8, 11, 178, 381; time of conquests, **3:**299

Alexandria, **1:**88

Alexiad (Komnene), **2:**62

Alexios I, **2:**404

Alexis I Comnenus, **2:**19

Alfonso d'Aragona, **3:**10

Alfonso the Battler, **3:**287

Alfred of England, **2:**147–48

Algebra, **1:**219; **2:**165

Algeria, French control of, **6:**230

Al-Ghazal, **2:**57

Algonquians (17th & 18th Centuries): longhouses, **4:**332; religious beliefs, **4:**469; social structure, **4:**372; tribal government, **4:**350; villages, **4:**332. *See also* Native Americans (colonial frontier of North America)

Alguacil mayor, **3:**287

Ali, **3:**368–69

'Ali, **2:**15

Ali, Muhammad (Cassius Clay), **6:**497, 504, 505

Alice's Adventures in Wonderland (Carroll), **5:**181, 193, 282

Aligarh Muslim University, **5:**455

'Ali ibn Abi Talib, **2:**457

Alimentation, **1:**43

Alimony, **1:**40. *See also* Divorce

al-Jahiz, **2:**319

Alkmaionidai, **1:**25

Allada, **4:**347

Allah, **5:**16, 453, 467–68

Allemande, **3:**346

Allende, Isabel, **6:**77

All I Really Need to Know I Learned in Kindergarten (Fulghum), **6:**227

All Quiet on the Western Front (film), **6:**520

All Saints' Day, **5:**417

All Souls' Day, **5:**417

All Souls' Feast, **2:**456

All that Heaven Allows (film), **6:**38

All the Year Round (magazine), **5:**190

Allyoscas, **3:**314–15, 328

Ally Sloper's Half-Holiday (joke book), **5:**191

Almanacs: Aztec, **3:**140; Maya, **3:**127, 137–38, 202

al-Mas'udi, **2:**138

Almehenob, **3:**269, 278

Almodovar, Pedro, **6:**515

Almshouses in United States, **5:**385

al-Mu'tasim, **2:**317, 319

al-Mutawakkil, **2:**320

Alpacas: Inca, **3:**2, 105, 107; Latin America (19th Century), **5:**288

Alphabets: Chinese alphabet, **2:**167; Cyrillic alphabet, **2:**19, 167, 427; **3:**166; development of, in 15th & 16th Centuries, **3:**157–58; Egypt (ancient), **1:**175; England (15th & 16th Centuries), **3:**160; Glagolitic alphabet, **3:**166; Greece (ancient), **1:**177; Ottoman Empire, **3:**165–66; Roman alphabet, **2:**171–72, 176; Rome (ancient), **1:**190; runic alphabet, **2:**171–72; Semitic alphabet, **3:**165; Slavic alphabet, **2:**167

Ares, 1:382, 470, 481

Argentina: beef, 5:98; cattle, 5:133; "dirty wars," 6:481; Falkland Islands dispute with Britain, 6:479; government, 6:385, 387; immigrants, 5:98; wheat, 5:98. *See also* Latin America *entries*

Arghun Khan (Mongol ruler), 2:246

Arguedas, Alcides, 5:158

Ariès, Philippe, 2:77

Ariosto, Lodovico, 3:206, 213

Aristocracy: China (Tang Dynasty), 2:242, 306–7; England (Victorian era), 5:109, 112–13; Europe (Middle Ages), 2:54, 81, 198, 224, 236, 258, 302–4, 322, 368, 379, 460; France (17th & 18th Centuries), 4:453, 454; Middle Ages, 2:301–9, 377; 19th Century, 5:218; Polynesia, 2:299, 308–9; Vikings, 2:304–5

Aristophanes: domestic life, 1:35, 59, 67; economic life, 1:145; intellectual life, 1:187, 202; material life, 1:255, 267; political life, 1:398; recreational life, 1:426, 427

Aristotle: on economic life, 1:126, 127; on health and medicine, 1:283, 296–98; importance to Europe (Middle Ages), 2:157, 159–60, 161; importance to Islamic World (Middle Ages), 2:165; intellectual life of, 1:226; philosophies of, 1:411; on political nature of humans, 1:327; 2:287; 3:267; 4:343; 5:305; 6:369; on slavery, 1:111, 113; writing of, 1:178, 226

Arithmetic. *See* Mathematics

Arkamani I, 1:355

Armenian language, 3:166

Arminius, 1:387

Armor, military. *See* Weapons

Armstrong, Edwin, 6:244

Armstrong, Lance, 6:499

Armstrong, Neil, 6:188

Army. *See* Military service

Army Nurse Corps (U.S.), 6:62

Army of the Potomac, 5:58, 200

Arnow, Harriette, 6:222

Arpilleras, 6:77

Arranged marriages: Egypt (ancient), 1:23; England (17th & 18th Centuries), 4:36; France (17th & 18th Centuries), 4:209; Greece (ancient), 1:44; India (19th Century), 5:39; India (20th Century), 6:32, 46, 136, 590; Japan (20th Century), 6:49; Middle Ages, 2:30; Rome (ancient), 1:26. *See also* Marriage

Arrogation, 1:53

Arrowroot, 2:212

Arson: England (15th & 16th Centuries), 3:302; England (Victorian era), 5:333

Art: Africa (17th & 18th Centuries), 4:445–48; ancient world, 1:230–41; Australian Aboriginals, 1:240–41; Aztec, 3:353–56; China (Tang Dynasty), 2:11; Egypt (ancient), 1:232–37; England (15th & 16th Centuries), 3:341–44; England (17th & 18th Centuries), 4:450–53; France (17th & 18th Centuries), 4:453–55; Greece (ancient), 1:237–39, 519; Inca, 3:3, 357–58; Italy (15th & 16th Centuries), 3:346–48; Japan (17th & 18th Centuries), 4:455–57; Jesus Christ in, 3:340; life at sea (17th & 18th Centuries), 4:459–61; Maya, 3:350–53; Mesopotamia, 1:230–32; Native Americans (colonial frontier of North America), 4:448–49; New England, colonial,

4:457–59; North American colonial frontier, 4:448–50; Nubia, 1:240; Oaxacan Civilization, 3:3; Olmec Civilization, 3:3; Ottoman Empire, 3:348–50; Rome (ancient), 1:239–40; 17th & 18th Centuries, 4:443–48; Soviet Union, 6:233, 234–35; Spain (15th & 16th Centuries), 3:344–46; United States (1940–59), 6:15. *See also specific types such as Icons, Painting, and Sculpture*

Art, religious. *See* Religious art; Temple art; Temple statues

Artemis, 1:56–57, 58, 480

Arthasastra, 1:352, 353

Arthritis: Europe (Middle Ages), 2:181; United States (1940–59), 6:275; Vikings, 2:184

Articles of War (17th & 18th Centuries), 4:399

Artificial sweeteners, 6:312

Artillery: England (Victorian era), 5:371; United States (Civil War era), 5:357

Artisans. *See* Craftsmen

Art of Cookery Made Plain and Easy, The (Glasse), 4:246

Art of Courtly Love, 2:301

Art of Love (Ovid), 1:203

Art of War, The (Sun-Tzu), 2:344, 354

Arts and crafts movement in England, 5:439

Aryans, 1:11

Asante, 4:16

Ascension Day: Italy (15th & 16th Centuries), 3:134; Spain (15th & 16th Centuries), 3:134

Ascot horse race, 5:113

Ashanti religion, 4:467, 484

Ashley, William, 5:124, 230

Asian Americans, discrimination against, 6:16–17, 150, 151

Asipu, 1:283, 284

Askeri, 3:291

Asoka, 1:11, 85, 353

Aspartame, 6:329

Aspasia, 1:67

Aspelta, 1:355, 467

Assam tea, 5:248, 252

Assassinations: India (20th Century), 6:10, 47, 79; Israel, 6:483; Japan (20th Century), 6:493, 600; Latin America (20th Century), 6:592; United States (20th Century), 6:152, 380, 449, 476

As Seen on TV: The Visual Culture of Everyday Life in the 1950s (Marling), 6:340

Assemblies in England (17th & 18th Centuries), 4:451–52

Assembly lines: automobile manufacture, 6:115, 357–58, 360; 20th Century, 6:110, 111, 131

Assur, 1:159, 456, 471

Assurbanipal, 1:287

Assurnasirpal II, 1:3, 342

Assyrians. *See* Mesopotamia

Asthemia, 5:208

Astor, John Jacob, 5:125, 127

Astrolabes, 2:282, 285

Astrology: ancient world, 1:525; Europe (Middle Ages), 2:160; India (ancient), 1:216; Mesopotamia, 1:219, 526, 528–29

Astronomy: ancient world, 1:525; Aztec, 3:185, 189; Egypt (ancient), 1:211; England (17th & 18th Centuries), 4:175; Europe (Middle Ages), 2:148–49, 151, 159–60; Greece (ancient), 1:225, 226; Inca, 3:141, 142; India (ancient), 1:216; Islamic World (Middle Ages), 2:147, 166; Maya, 3:136, 189, 201, 383; Mesopotamia, 1:209, 219, 221, 528–29; North American colonial frontier, 4:173; 17th & 18th Centuries, 4:169; Vikings, 2:152, 162

Astrophil and Stella (Sidney), 3:209

Atahuallpa, 3:22

Atatürk, Mustafa Kemal, 6:423

"A" tents, 5:254, 257

Atheism: Soviet Union, 6:596; United States, 6:572–73

Athena, 1:479, 480

Athenian Empire. *See* Greece (ancient)

Athens, ancient, 1:101, 102–5; coins of, 1:135; foundation date, 1:213; grain and food importing by, 1:139; guardian god of, 1:479; housing, 1:276–77; Ionian origin of, 1:333; literacy, 1:178, 187; plays of, 1:201, 425; population of, 1:333; priesthood eligibility, 1:493; professions, 1:188; rescue from Visigoth attack on, 1:463; roads, 1:161. *See also* Greece (ancient)

Atherton Company, 4:411

Athletics. *See* Sports

Atmiya Sabha, 5:66

Atole, 3:246–47

Atomic bomb. *See* Nuclear weapons

Atomic Energy Commission, 6:364

Aton, 1:458–59

Attention deficit disorder (ADD), 6:281–82

Attention deficit hyperactive disorder (ADHD), 6:281–82

Attics, 5:263

Attorneys: England (15th & 16th Centuries), 3:271; England (17th & 18th Centuries), 4:158–59, 392; England (Victorian era), 5:111; Japan (20th Century), 6:431; Soviet Union, 6:395

Atum, 1:475

Aucassin and Nicolett, 2:485–88

Aud (Unn the Deepminded), 2:56

Auden, W.H., 6:219, 225

Augers. *See* Diviners

Auguraculum, 1:496

Augustus Caesar: arches and temples erected by, 1:106, 107, 483, 505, 523; death of, 1:497; education of, 1:189; empire of, 1:10; on gladiator shows, 1:443; on literature, 1:203; marriage laws, 1:48, 50; Meroities opposition to, 1:389; military conquests, 1:151, 356; on military size, 1:383; on public morality, 1:71; on slavery, 1:115, 116; statues of, 1:239; superstitions of, 1:534; urban life, 1:99; on wills, 1:368; on women's role, 1:36, 37

Aum Shinrikyo, 6:600

Aun's disease, 2:90

Auschwitz, 6:406–8, 488

Australia, colonial: agriculture, 4:50, 102, 106–8; alcoholic beverages, 4:257–58; animals, 4:170–71; botanical study, 4:170–71; Botany Bay settlement, 4:21; bread, 4:242; cattle, 4:242; chaplains, 4:486; churches, 4:487; civil rights, 4:387; courts and judges, 4:386–87; crimes, 4:386–88; crops, 4:106–7; dance, 4:432; drink, 4:257–58; drinking water, 4:257; English settlements, 4:21; fairs, 4:432–33; fauna, 4:170–71; flogging, 4:388, 487; food, 4:49, 51, 242–43; games, 4:432–33; government, 4:50; governors, 4:386–87; grain crops, 4:106–7; hats, 4:286, 303; historical overview, 4:22; holidays and festivals, 4:432–34; insurrections, 4:388; laborers, 4:287; law, 4:386–89; maize, 4:106–7; map of (1606-1818), 4:20; marines, 4:286; marriage, 4:32–33; material life, 4:237–38; meat, 4:242; men, work of, 4:49–50; men's clothing, 4:285–87; men's roles, 4:48–52; military service, 4:387–88; music, 4:433; navigational exploration, 4:171; plows, 4:106; professions,

Banquets

Canzoniere (Petrarch), **3:**213

Capac Raymi, **3:**52, 88, 142, 391

Cape Horn, account of sea voyage (1615), **4:**519–21

Capes: Aztec, **3:**233; Maya, **3:**231; Spain (15th & 16th Centuries), **3:**228

Capital punishment. *See* Death penalty

Capone, Al, **6:**326

Capping, **2:**84

Capra, Frank, **6:**521

Caps: England (Victorian era), **5:**285; nightcaps, **5:**282; United States (Civil War era), **5:**276

Captain Blood (Sabatini), **4:**218

Captains: British Royal Navy, **4:**365, 383; merchant vessels (17th & 18th Centuries), **4:**362

Captives: Native Americans (colonial frontier of North America), **4:**389–90, 418, 434–35; Native Americans (colonial New England), **4:**411. *See also* Prisoners of war

Captives as slaves: ancient world, **1:**108; China (Tang Dynasty), **2:**316; Mesopotamia, **1:**109, 373; Middle Ages, **2:**310; Polynesia, **2:**290, 300, 366; Rome (ancient), **1:**114; Vikings, **2:**314

Captivity narratives of North American colonial frontier, **4:**205–6

Caracol, **3:**120

Caradeuc de la Chalotais, Louis-René, **4:**191

Carapulcra, **5:**245

Caravans: China (Tang Dynasty), **2:**138–39; India (ancient), **1:**148; Mesopotamia, **1:**78, 141, 156, 157, 158; Spain (15th & 16th Centuries), **3:**112. *See also* Trade

Cárdenas, Lázaro, **6:**172, 371, 385

Cardinals, **3:**364

Cards: development and spread of, **2:**369; England (15th & 16th Centuries), **3:**315, 317–18; England (17th & 18th Centuries), **4:**421; Europe (Middle Ages), **2:**372; Italy (15th & 16th Centuries), **3:**315, 323; Japan (17th & 18th Centuries), **4:**424; life at sea (17th & 18th Centuries), **4:**428; New England, colonial, **4:**426; Spain (15th & 16th Centuries), **3:**315, 321; United States (Civil War era), **5:**429; United States (Western Frontier), **5:**433

Cargo. *See* Shipping

Carillo, Joaquin, **5:**333

Carlisle Indian School, **5:**161, 170

Carlyle, Thomas, **5:**10

Carmichael, Stokely, **6:**152, 448–49

Carnatic music, **5:**424, 425

Carnival: Italy (15th & 16th Centuries), **3:**63, 135, 322, 347; Latin America (19th Century), **5:**416–17; Spain (15th & 16th Centuries), **3:**135

Caro, Miguel Antonio, **5:**341

"Carolingian miniature," **2:**169

Carolingians, **2:**2, 32, 148. *See also* Europe (Middle Ages)

Carols, **2:**388

Carpenter, Helen, **5:**487–88

Carpenter, Scott, **6:**187

Carpentry: England (Victorian era), **5:**110; Europe (Middle Ages), **2:**267; Islamic World (Middle Ages), **2:**273; Mesopotamia, **1:**120

Carpet. *See* Floors and floor coverings

Carpini, Friar Giovanni Di Plano, **2:**245, 265, 342

Carrara, **3:**99

Carrera, Rafael, **5:**378

Carriage dress, **5:**284

Carroll v. U.S. (1925), **6:**416

Carrom, **5:**441

Carson, Kit, **5:**46, 87

Carson, Rachel, **6:**17–18, 224

Carter, Richard, **5:**206

Carthage, **1:**10

Cartier, Jacques, **4:**9

Cartography: Greece (ancient), **1:**227; Mesopotamia, **1:**221

Cartoons, animated, **6:**521

Cartwright, Alexander, **5:**399

Carvel-built hulls, **4:**324

Carvings: Africa (17th & 18th Centuries), **4:**445, 446; Rome (ancient), **1:**106; Vikings, **2:**100–101. *See also* Stone carvings

Castanets, **3:**346

Caste systems: India (ancient), **1:**117, 329, 337–39; India (19th Century), **5:**26–27, 42, 52, 118; India (20th Century), **6:**57, 126, 135–37, 140, 155, 316, 343; Islamic World (19th Century), **5:**26; Latin America (19th Century), **5:**17

Caste War (Latin America), **5:**379

Castiglione, Baldasar, **3:**213, 413–14

Castile: historical overview, **3:**1, 10; language and writing, **3:**161; music, **3:**345; taxes, **3:**275; universities, **3:**175–76; wheat, **3:**95. *See also* Spain *entries*

Castilian language, **3:**161–62, 218

Castillo, Bernal Diaz del, **3:**421–22

Castillo, Ramón, **5:**378

Castles: Edo (17th & 18th Centuries), **4:**337; Europe (Middle Ages), **2:**224–25; Japan (17th & 18th Centuries), **4:**408; Middle Ages, **2:**223, 301; Windsor Castle, **5:**141

Castramentation, **5:**255

Castration, **1:**62, 64, 286. *See also* Eunuchs

Castro, Fidel, **6:**8, 371, 480

Catalán language, **3:**161–62

Cataloguing and classifying: Greece (ancient), **1:**226; Mesopotamia, **1:**219–20

Cataluña: houses, **3:**256; language, **3:**161

Catapults, **2:**361

Catechism: England (15th & 16th Centuries), **3:**172; Italy (15th & 16th Centuries), **3:**38; Latin America (19th Century), **5:**471

Catfish, **5:**228

Cathedral schools: Europe (Middle Ages), **2:**148–50; Vikings, **2:**152, 153

Catherine of Siena, **3:**55

Catholic Church: Australia, colonial, **4:**487; celibacy, **2:**31, 33; diplomatic recognition of Vatican by U.S., **6:**586; dissent in Europe (Middle Ages), **2:**411; dissent in United States (1960–90), **6:**586; education funding and, **6:**200; England (17th & 18th Centuries), **4:**471–72, 491; film industry and, **6:**520; Japan (20th Century), **6:**600; Jews and, **6:**141–42; Latin America (19th Century), **5:**19, 469–72; Latin America (20th Century), **6:**43, 591–93; legal jurisdiction (Middle Ages), **2:**328–29, 434; Middle Ages, **2:**2, 4, 160, 410, 433–36; Native Americans (colonial frontier of North America), **4:**470–71; New France, **4:**470–71; seven sacraments of, **2:**411; social activism in Latin America (1960–90), **6:**592–93; Soviet Union, **6:**597; split from Greek Orthodox, **2:**407, 409, 425–26; United States (Civil War era), **5:**309, 458, 459; United States (1920–39), **6:**36, 569; United States (1960–90), **6:**579;

Vatican II and ecumenical changes, **6:**577, 581, 592. *See also* Catholicism *entries*

Catholicism (France), **4:**355

Catholicism (Spain, Italy, England): angels, **3:**363; baptism, **3:**380–81; Bible, **3:**379; bishops, **3:**364; cardinals, **3:**364; confession, **3:**380, 382; confirmation, **3:**380–81; Crucifixion, **3:**362; deities, **3:**362–64; devils, **3:**363; English separation from, **3:**15; Franciscans, **3:**364; holy orders, **3:**380, 382; Jesus Christ in, **3:**362; last rites, **3:**380, 382; Latin, **3:**379; marriage, **3:**31; mass, **3:**379; matrimony, **3:**380–81; Messiah, **3:**362; Ottoman Empire, **3:**166; *Pater Noster*, **3:**132, 364; Pentecost, **3:**363; priests and religious rituals, **3:**364, 380–82; Protestantism, opposition in Spain, **3:**344; religious beliefs, **3:**361, 362–64; Resurrection, **3:**362–63; sacraments, **3:**20, 380–82; sacrifices, **3:**363; saints, **3:**363; sins and sinners, **3:**363; Trinity, **3:**363. *See also* Popes

Catholic Worker, **6:**574

Catlin, George, **5:**103

Cato the Elder, **1:**115, 299

Cat-o-nine-tails, **4:**400

Cats in Victorian England, **5:**440

Cattle: Africa (17th & 18th Centuries), **4:**105; Australia, colonial, **4:**242; Byzantium, **2:**209; India (ancient), **1:**85; India (19th Century), **5:**252; Latin America (19th Century), **5:**133; Latin America (20th Century), **6:**314; Mesopotamia, **1:**77; Nubia, **1:**259; Rome (ancient), **1:**85. *See also* Livestock

Cattle drives, **5:**106–7

Cattle stations in Latin America, **5:**267

Catullus, **1:**70–71, 203

Caudillos, **5:**325, 326, 377, 378, 379

Causes and Cures (Hildgard of Bingen), **2:**477–78

Caute, David, **6:**527

Cavagliere, **3:**276

Cavalry: Africa (17th & 18th Centuries), **4:**403; England (Victorian era), **5:**371; United States (Civil War era), **5:**357

Cave dwellings of China, **2:**229

Caves as housing (colonial New England), **4:**280

Caviar, **2:**209

Caxton, William, **3:**209

Celebration. *See* Holidays, festivals, and spectacles

Cellars, **5:**262

Celler, Emmanuel, **6:**71

Cemeteries, **5:**29. *See also* Tombs; Tombstones

Cempoala, **3:**22

Cenote of Sacrifice, **3:**47

Censor, Roman, **1:**337

Censorship: China (19th Century), **5:**323; Europe (20th Century), **6:**218; film industry, **6:**518, 520, 531, 532–33; India (20th Century), **6:**531; Japan (20th Century), **6:**237; McCarthyism, **6:**377; music, **6:**552–53; Soviet Union, **6:**233, 234–35, 256, 532–33, 536, 552–53; United States (1940–59), **6:**38; World War II films, **6:**525

Census data: for Soviet Union, **6:**23; for United States, **6:**13

Centaurs, **1:**335

Centuries, **1:**351

Centurions, **1:**384

Cephalus, **1:**521

Cerberus, **1:**520

Cereal crops. *See* Grains

Cerén, **3:**250, 262

Cervantes Saavedra, Miguel de, **3:**206, 210–12, 410–11

C-Group Nubians, **1:**13, 312, 387

Eskimos. *See* Inuit

Espionage: Communist spies in U.S., **6:**376, 378–80, 527; Japan (17th & 18th Centuries), **4:**358; Soviet Union, **6:**427

Esquires, **3:**271

Essay on National Education or Plan of Study for Youth (Caradeuc de la Chalotais), **4:**191

Estates and inheritances: Byzantium, **2:**63; England (Victorian era), **5:**113; Europe (Middle Ages), **2:**52; Greece (ancient), **1:**45; India (20th Century), **6:**58; Latin America (20th Century), **6:**45; Mesopotamia, **1:**53–54, 110; Mongols, **2:**38; North American colonial frontier, **4:**82–83; primogeniture, **2:**31, 32–33; Rome (ancient), **1:**367–68, 522; Vikings, **2:**34

Estates-General, **4:**5

d'Este, Cardinal, **3:**337

d'Este, Isabella, **3:**229

Este family, **3:**8

Estudio de Madrid, **3:**175

Eta, **4:**17, 159, 378–79; **6:**160

Ethel: The Fictional Autobiography (Nason), **6:**379

Ethics. *See* Morality

Ethiopia (17th & 18th Centuries): Coptic Christianity, **4:**468; icon paintings, **4:**447; literature, **4:**203; religious practices, **4:**485; social structure, **4:**370. *See also* Africa *entries*

Ethnicity: Africa (17th & 18th Centuries), **4:**329–30; British Royal Navy, **4:**382; Japan (17th & 18th Centuries), **4:**328; Mesopotamia, **1:**330; North American colonial frontier, **4:**372–73; 17th & 18th Centuries, **4:**367. *See also* Discrimination; Social structure

Eton: cricket, **5:**402; schools, **5:**113

Etruscans, **1:**9, 350

E.T.—The Extra Terrestrial (film), **6:**529

Etymologies, The (Isidore of Seville), **2:**180

Euboulos, **1:**103

Eucharist: Catholicism (Spain, Italy, England), **3:**379–81; Christianity (England, Spain, Italy), **3:**206; Europe (Middle Ages), **2:**410; Jesus Christ, **3:**381; Protestantism (England), **3:**366–67, 379, 382–83

Euclid, **1:**226

Eudokia Makrembolitissa, **2:**63

Eugenics (Latin America), **5:**158

Eunuchs: Byzantium, **2:**30, 70, 74–77; China (Tang Dynasty), **2:**11, 30, 70, 71–72; Islamic World (Middle Ages), **2:**30, 70, 72–74; Mesopotamia, **1:**65; Middle Ages, **2:**30, 69–77. *See also* Castration

Euripides, **1:**201–2, 426, 428, 462, 480, 532

European Acquaintance (DeForest), **5:**188

European colonialism. *See* Colonial rule *entries*

Europe (15th & 16th Centuries): barley, **3:**236; barley break game, **3:**58, 317; bread, **3:**236; diet changes after European conquest of Americas, **3:**221–22, 236; diseases **3:**166, 188; handkerchiefs, **3:**221; kirtles, **3:**223; Lord's Prayer, **3:**77; merchant class, **3:**269; middle class, **3:**269; painting, **3:**340; peasants, **3:**91, 157, 223, 285, 339; underwear, **3:**221; violins, **3:**340; wheat, **3:**236. *See also specific countries*

Europe (Middle Ages): abbesses, **2:**51, 54; abortion, **2:**42; acrobats, **2:**395, 396; adultery, **2:**42, 434; age of marriage, **2:**40, 41; ale, **2:**198, 214; annulment of marriage, **2:**41, 42; apprentices, **2:**53, 97–98, 182, 322; archers, **2:**346, 369; aristocracy, **2:**54, 81, 198, 224, 236, 258, 302–4, 322, 368, 379, 460; astronomy, **2:**148–49, 151, 159–60; backgammon, **2:**372; bagpipes, **2:**387; bakers, **2:**97; barbers, **2:**182; bathing, **2:**181; bear, **2:**378; bear baiting, **2:**371; beards, **2:**257, 260; bedrooms, **2:**30; beds, **2:**30, 267, 268–69; beer, **2:**214; brandy, **2:**213, 215; bread, **2:**97, 198, 199; bridges, **2:**134; brigands, **2:**346, 348; brooms, **2:**269; bubonic plague, **2:**183; burgers, **2:**320; calendars, **2:**148, 450; candles, **2:**268, 269–70; cannons, **2:**350; canon law, **2:**329, 434; canvas, **2:**247, 249; carpentry, **2:**267; castles, **2:**224–25; cathedral schools, **2:**148–50; cheese, **2:**52, 199; chemistry, **2:**160; chess, **2:**371–72; childbirth, **2:**79; children, **2:**79–81, 122; children's games, **2:**371; churches, **2:**441–43; cider, **2:**215; clergy and priests, **2:**258, 289, 290, 409, 433–36, 460; clothing, **2:**235, 237–40; clothing materials, **2:**239–40, 247, 248–50; cockfighting, **2:**371; colors, **2:**250; combs, **2:**260; communes, **2:**320; contraception, **2:**42; cooking utensils, **2:**269; cosmetics, **2:**259; cotton, **2:**248; craftsmen, **2:**226, 322; crimes, **2:**134; crossbows, **2:**346; dance, **2:**388–89; death and the afterlife, **2:**458, 459, 460–62; death penalty, **2:**326; deer, **2:**379; dental care and problems, **2:**182, 183; dialects, **2:**168; dice, **2:**367, 369, 372; dinner, **2:**201; diseases, **2:**181; divorce, **2:**41, 42; dowry, **2:**41; drink, **2:**198, 199, 214–16; drinking water, **2:**213, 215; eating habits, **2:**199, 224, 268; eating utensils, **2:**269; education, **2:**148–52, 159; education of priests, **2:**149, 150; education of women, **2:**149; entertainment, **2:**396–97; epilepsy, **2:**181; estates and inheritance, **2:**52; ethics, **2:**159; fabrics, **2:**248–50; fairs, **2:**98–99, 132, 135, 395, 396; famine and starvation, **2:**124; fasting, **2:**200; fertilizer, **2:**123; festivals and holidays, **2:**148, 151, 449, 450–52; feuds, **2:**31; fever, **2:**181; fire, **2:**276; fish, **2:**200; floors and floor coverings, **2:**224, 268; food, **2:**124, 197, 198–201, 277; footwear, **2:**238; fortifications, **2:**225; freeholders, **2:**312–13; friars, **2:**434; fruits, **2:**200; fur, **2:**238, 250; furnishings, **2:**268–70; gambling, **2:**372–73; games, **2:**369, 370–73; geometry, **2:**149, 160; glass, **2:**277; gloves, **2:**238; grains, **2:**123, 198; grammar, **2:**148, 150, 151; grapes, **2:**123; guilds, **2:**96–98, 277, 320–21; hair, **2:**257, 258, 259; hats, **2:**239, 257, 258; headdresses, **2:**239; health and medicine, **2:**151, 179–83, 198; helmets, **2:**349; herbs and spices, **2:**200, 201; heroes, **2:**169; historical overview, **2:**1–5; honey, **2:**80, 200; honor, **2:**31; hose, **2:**237, 238; housing, **2:**223–26; human waste disposal, **2:**123; hunting, **2:**198, 379–80; illegitimate children, **2:**292; infant care, **2:**80; infant mortality, **2:**79; iron, **2:**124, 275, 276; jousts, **2:**367, 370; kinship, **2:**32–33; landowners, **2:**52, 123, 303, 312–13; language, **2:**167, 168–70; laundry, **2:**239; law, **2:**32, 151, 327–29; leather, **2:**238, 239, 276; leprosy, **2:**181; life expectancy, **2:**88, 183; lighting, **2:**269–70; linen, **2:**239–40, 247, 248–49; literature, **2:**146, 169–70; lunch, **2:**201; manors and manor houses, **2:**123–24, 290, 291; map of, **2:**3; marriage, **2:**41–43, 434; mathematics, **2:**147, 148, 151, 160–61; meat, **2:**197, 198, 200; men's clothing, **2:**237–38, 239; merchants, **2:**226, 290, 322; metalworking, **2:**277; middle class, **2:**302, 322; midwives, **2:**79; military service, **2:**344; milk and dairy products, **2:**52, 198–99, 215; mirrors, **2:**259; monasteries, **2:**180, 432, 433–36; monastic schools, **2:**148–49; monks, **2:**258, 433, 434–35; music, **2:**149, 151, 386, 387–89; mustaches, **2:**257, 260; names, **2:**79; needlework, **2:**54, 149; nuns, **2:**53–54, 258, 434–35; old age, **2:**87, 88–89, 183; oral tradition, **2:**169; peasant revolts, **2:**311; peasants, **2:**122–24, 223, 290–91, 302, 312–13; personal appearance, **2:**258–60; philosophy, **2:**159–60; physicians, **2:**182; physics, **2:**159, 161; playing cards, **2:**372; plays, **2:**396–97; poetry, **2:**169, 170; political life, **2:**159, 311; poor persons, **2:**323; prostitution, **2:**50; punishment, **2:**326; raptors, **2:**380; reading and writing, **2:**148–49, 169; recreational life, **2:**181; recycling, **2:**277; religion, **2:**396–97, 410–12; religious buildings, **2:**440, 441–43; religious ceremonies and festivals, **2:**386; retirement, **2:**86, 88; revenge, **2:**31; roads, **2:**134; robbery, **2:**134; rodents and vermin, **2:**181, 183; roofing, **2:**224, 225, 277; rural life and agriculture, **2:**52, 122–24, 277, 290–91; school curriculum, **2:**147, 151; science, **2:**159–61, 182; scurvy, **2:**181; serfs, **2:**289, 292, 310, 311–13, 321; servants, **2:**323, 346; sheep and goats, **2:**247; shellfish, **2:**200; shields, **2:**349; shipping, **2:**135; shirts, **2:**237, 238; sieges, **2:**345; silk, **2:**249; slaves, **2:**310, 311; social structure, **2:**201, 289, 290–92, 321–23; songs, **2:**169, 387; sports, **2:**370–73; storage, **2:**269; sugar, **2:**200; sumptuary laws, **2:**236, 302; supper, **2:**201; swimming, **2:**135; tables, **2:**268; tattos, **2:**258; taxes, **2:**133, 135; teachers, **2:**150–51; technology, **2:**275–77; tennis, **2:**370; theater, **2:**395; theology, **2:**151; tombstones, **2:**460; tools, **2:**269, 275–76; torture, **2:**326; toys, **2:**80; trade, **2:**96, 132, 133–36, 320; travel and transportation, **2:**96, 133–34, 215; trials, **2:**327; underwear, **2:**238, 239; universities, **2:**146, 148, 150; urban life, **2:**53, 96–99, 321–23; vegetables, **2:**123, 124, 198, 199, 200; veils, **2:**239, 259; warfare and weapons, **2:**345–51; warriors, **2:**289, 290, 302; water mills, **2:**275, 277; weaving, **2:**52, 249–50; weights and measures, **2:**97; wet nurses, **2:**79–80; wheat, **2:**123, 196; whey, **2:**199, 215; wild boars, **2:**377–78, 379; wills, **2:**240, 328, 434; wimples, **2:**239, 259; windows, **2:**223, 225, 268, 269; wine, **2:**214–15; witnesses, **2:**326, 327; women, **2:**30, 41, 50, 51–54, 122, 124, 149, 182, 238, 239, 258–59, 310, 380; wool, **2:**135, 240, 247–48, 249–50; work hours, **2:**98, 450; wrestling, **2:**369, 370

Europe (17th & 18th Centuries): Africa, commercial relations, **4:**2; seaports, **4:**340; sea power of nations, **4:**362. *See also specific countries*

Europe (20th Century): anti-Semitism, **6:**140–45; censorship, **6:**218; colonialism, **6:**9, 25; epidemics, **6:**260; film, **6:**512–15; food during World War I, **6:**301–2; health and medicine, **6:**62–63, 260, 261–70; influenza, **6:**62–63; literature, **6:**217–20; middle class, **6:**110; painting, **6:**217–18; poetry, **6:**217, 218; religion, **6:**604–6; sports, **6:**497–500; technology, **6:**349–56; travel and transportation, **6:**498; work, **6:**111–14. *See also* Holocaust; *specific countries*

Indigo

6:316; hospitals, 6:287; housing, 6:300, 334, 343–45; humors of the body, 6:286; hygiene, 6:589; independence, 6:371; infant mortality, 6:45–46; language, 6:388–89; literature, 6:228–30; malaria, 6:287; marriage, 6:32, 33, 46, 78, 104, 156, 590; meat, 6:316; men, 6:57–59; menstruation, 6:104; mosques, 6:343; mythology, 6:79, 228; old age, 6:47, 58; patriarchy, 6:57–59, 78; patrilineages, 6:46–47; political life, 6:10, 78; poultry, 6:316; poverty, 6:388; railroads, 6:255, 389; rape, 6:79; religious beliefs, 6:568, 588–91; religious purification, 6:316; religious rituals, 6:46–47, 58, 104, 316; rice, 6:301, 315–16; riots, 6:389; rural life and agriculture, 6:334; schools, 6:344; shrines, 6:345; slums, 6:344; social structure, 6:135–37; sons, 6:45, 47, 58, 103–4; sports, 6:509; tea, 6:301, 316; technology, 6:254–55; temples, 6:343, 589; urban life, 6:334, 344–45; vegetarianism, 6:316; wells, 6:344; wheat, 6:301, 316; widows, 6:79, 156; women, 6:78–80, 156, 611–12

Indigo, 5:132

Indra, 1:352

Industrial Revolution in England, 5:8

Industry: Africa (17th & 18th Centuries), 4:120–21; China (19th Century), 5:115, 156; England (17th & 18th Centuries), 4:2, 123–26, 124; England (Victorian era), 5:92–93, 109, 300; Great Depression, 6:164; India (19th Century), 5:77, 291, 301; Japan (17th & 18th Centuries), 4:126–28; Latin America (20th Century), 6:170–71; life at sea (17th & 18th Centuries), 4:130–32; New England, colonial, 4:13, 128–30; North American colonial frontier, 4:121–23; 17th & 18th Centuries, 4:118–32; United States (Civil War era), 5:2–3; United States (20th Century), 6:110, 114–16

Indus Valley civilization. See India (ancient)

Infant care: England (Victorian era), 5:239–40; Europe (Middle Ages), 2:80; Middle Ages, 2:78. See also Child care; Wet nurses

Infanticide: Egypt (ancient), 1:56; Greek and Roman, 1:57, 58, 6:141; Japan (17th & 18th Centuries), 4:74–75; Mesopotamia, 2:64; Polynesia, 2:68; Vikings, 2:81–82

Infant mortality: England (15th & 16th Centuries), 3:33, 75; Europe (Middle Ages), 2:79; Greece (ancient), 1:46, 59, 295; India (19th Century), 5:77; India (20th Century), 6:45–46; Islamic World (Middle Ages), 2:85, 318; Latin America (20th Century), 6:314; Mesopotamia, 1:52; Spain (15th & 16th Centuries), 3:77; 20th Century, 6:88; United States (Civil War era), 5:29; United States (1920–39), 6:67; Vikings, 2:34, 81

Infections. See Diseases

Infertility. See Childless couples

Infidels in Islamic World (19th Century), 5:447

Infirmaries, 5:390. See also Hospitals

Inflation: England (15th & 16th Centuries), 3:93, 111, 271; United States (1920–39), 6:436; United States (Western Frontier), 5:61

Influenza: England (15th & 16th Centuries), 3:189; England (Victorian era), 5:209; Europe (20th Century), 6:62–63; Spain (15th & 16th

Centuries), 3:194; United States (1920–39), 6:272

Inheritance. See Estates and inheritances

In-line skates, 6:505

Inns: Greece (ancient), 1:162; Rome (ancient), 1:164

Inoculation. See Vaccination

Inquisition, 2:326, 411. See also Spanish Inquisition

Insanity. See Mental illness and treatment

Insecticides, 6:260, 275

Insects: China (Tang Dynasty), 2:205, 206; United States (Western Frontier), 5:105, 254. See also specific insects

Insider trading (Japan), 6:400–401

Institutes of the Christian Religion (Calvin), 3:366

Insulae, 1:280

Insurance: England (Victorian era), 5:350–51; long-term care insurance (Japan), 6:292. See also Health insurance

Integration. See Civil rights movement; School desegregation

Intellectual life: ancient world, 1:169–241; China (Tang Dynasty), 2:11; 15th & 16th Centuries, 3:155–220; France (17th & 18th Centuries), 4:56–58; Middle Ages, 2:4, 145–94; 19th Century, 5:149–216; 17th & 18th Centuries, 4:167–236; 20th Century, 6:181–298. See also Art; Literature

Intercalary month: India (ancient), 1:216; Mesopotamia, 1:209; Rome (ancient), 1:214

Intercourse. See Sexuality

Internal Security Act of 1950, 6:376

International Workers of the World, preamble, 6:619–20

Internet, 3:155; Japan (20th Century), 6:259

Interstate Highway Act of 1956, 6:362

Inti, 3:53, 376–77, 391–92

Intifada, 6:483

Inti Raymi, 3:391

Inuit: breast feeding, 6:321, 322; cancer, 6:322; childbirth, 6:296; children, 6:50–51, 107; Christianity, 6:603; colonial rule, 6:402; cooking methods, 6:367; discrimination, 6:161; diseases, 6:295–96; education, 6:196, 214–15; environment, 6:296, 321–22; family life, 6:33, 50–51; food, 6:302, 320–22; fur trade, 6:347; government, 6:401–4; health and medicine, 6:261, 295–96, 295–98; historical overview, 6:26–27; housing, 6:51, 346–48; hunting, 6:321; kinship, 6:402; language, 6:214–15; life expectancy, 6:296; literature, 6:239–41; mercury and, 6:302; missionaries, 6:603; music, 6:557–58; names, 6:50; newspapers, 6:240; Nunavut land claims agreement (1993), 6:620–22; old age, 6:51; patrilineages, 6:50; poetry, 6:239; pollution, 6:296, 321–22; religion, 6:603–4; shaman, 6:295; social activism, 6:604; technology, 6:349, 367–68; tuberculosis, 6:296; writing, 6:239–40

Inuit Circumpolar Conference, 6:403

Inuktitut language, 6:214–15, 239, 240–41, 403

Inupiat Ilitqusiat, 6:604

Inventions: England (17th & 18th Centuries), 4:176–77. See also Science; Technology

Investiture Controversy, 2:328

Invisible Man (Ellison), 6:441

Invitation to an Inquest: A New Look at the Rosenberg and Sobell Case (Schneir), 6:380

Ionian Rationalism, 1:225

Ionians, 1:225, 333; vs. Dorians, 1:333. See also Greece (ancient)

Ionic architecture, 1:504–5

Iormungand, 2:412

Iowa cattle drives, 5:106

Iqbal, Muhammad, 6:229

Iran, 3:20; European colonialism in, 5:353; government, 6:390–91; language, 6:390; revolution, 6:11; war with Iraq, 6:11; women's roles, 5:37

Iran hostage crisis, 6:392

Iraq, 3:20, 164; European control, free from, 6:483; invasion of Kuwait, 6:478; war with Iran, 6:11. See also Islamic World (Middle Ages)

Ireland, 3:235, 340; Dublin, founded by Vikings, 2:99; towns founded by Vikings, 2:99

Iron: China (Tang Dynasty), 2:275, 280; England (17th & 18th Centuries), 4:176; England (Victorian era), 5:300; Europe (Middle Ages), 2:124, 275, 276; Islamic World (Middle Ages), 2:275; Italy (15th & 16th Centuries), 3:99; Maya, 3:351; New England, colonial, 4:129; Vikings, 2:100, 126

Iron Age, 1:122, 371. See also Mesopotamia

Irons, electric, 6:335

Ironworkers (Japan), 4:409

Iroquois: confederation of tribes, 4:348; New France, 4:10; religious beliefs, 4:469; social structure, 4:372; tribal government, 4:349; villages, 4:332

Irrigation: Byzantium, 2:130, 284; China (Tang Dynasty), 2:127, 197; India (19th Century), 5:14, 302; Islamic World (Middle Ages), 2:282–83; Maya, 3:102; Mesopotamia, 1:75, 78, 79; Nubia, 1:87

Irving, Washington, 5:348

Isaac, Jorge, 5:196

Isabel de Valois, 3:211

Isabella, 3:10, 176, 287, 288, 345

Isadore of Seville, 2:169

Isherwood, Christopher, 6:219

Ishmael, 2:418, 424

Ishtar, 1:471, 488, 510

Isidore of Seville, 2:180–81

Isidoros of Miletus, 2:285, 447

Isis, 1:289, 430, 475, 476, 477

Isla Cerritos, 3:7

Islam: Africa (20th Century), 6:433, 601, 602; alcoholic beverages and, 3:237, 245; 5:252; charity, 6:595; Christianity, relationship with, 6:11; death, burial, and the afterlife, 3:43; ethical behavior as part of, 2:409; fasting, 6:595; founding of, 2:12, 417–25; 5:16, 467–68; 6:10; guilds, 3:119; Hindu vs. Muslim feud in India, 6:9, 10; India, Muslim conquest of, 6:8–9; India (19th Century), 5:466; Jews, relationship with, 2:421; 6:11; life cycles, 3:30–31; Mongols and, 2:429; monotheism, 3:361; Ottoman Empire, 3:65; pork and food restrictions, 2:207–8; 3:241, 245; 6:316; prayers, 5:454, 456, 468, 469; 6:595; prophets and prophecy, 6:594; rituals, exclusion from, 3:30–31; Soviet Union, 6:23, 597; views on women, religion, slaves, and war, 5:494–96; women's dress, 5:287. See also Five Pillars of Islam; *Hajj*; Muhammad; Qur'an (Koran); Sharia; Shi'ites

Islamic World (Middle Ages): abandonment of spouse, 2:49–50; age of marriage, 2:85–86; alcoholic beverages, 2:283; archers, 2:358; astronomy, 2:147, 166; banks and banking, 2:143–44; banquets, 2:85; bathhouses, 2:232; beds, 2:273; board games, 2:401; bride-price, 2:47, 62; bubonic plague, 2:85; camels, 2:129, 142; carpentry, 2:273; chairs, 2:267, 273; chess, 2:369; childbirth, 2:423; children, 2:84–86; circumcision, 2:85; civil wars, 2:357; clothing, 2:243–45; coffee, 2:219;

1:202–5; 17th & 18th Centuries, 4:200–218; Silver Age, 1:204; Soviet Union, 6:216, 219–20, 233–36, 551; Spain (15th & 16th Centuries), 3:210–12; 20th Century, 6:215–41; United States (Civil War era), 5:182–88; United States (1940–59), 6:216, 220–26; United States (1960–90), 6:226–28; United States (Western Frontier), 5:188–89; Vikings, 2:172. *See also specific genres, titles, and authors*

Lithium carbonate, 6:281
Little, William, 5:421
Little Big Horn, Battle of, 5:87
Little Dorrit (Dickens), 5:185
Liturgies, 1:145
Live Aid concerts, 6:548
Livers, reading of. *See* Entrails, reading of
Livestock: Byzantium, 2:131, 209; England (15th & 16th Centuries), 3:57; England (17th & 18th Centuries), 4:112; New England, colonial, 4:117; North American colonial frontier, 4:109–10; Spain (15th & 16th Centuries), 3:112
Living National Treasure system (Japan), 6:556
Livingstone, Robert R., 5:347
Livy, 1:205, 214, 553–55
Li Yuan, 2:7. *See also* Gaozu (emperor of China)
Li Zicheng, 5:322
Llamas: Inca, 3:2, 105, 107, 144, 249, 391–93; Latin America (19th Century), 5:288
Loans: Buddhist monasteries (Middle Ages), 2:439–40; England (17th & 18th Centuries), 4:139–40. *See also* Banks and banking
Local government: England (17th & 18th Centuries), 4:353–54; Japan (17th & 18th Centuries), 4:357–59
Locke, John, 4:57
Locro, 3:249
Locusts, 1:76, 287
Lode mining, 5:299
Loewenberg, Peter, 6:305
Logbooks of seamen, 4:217
Log cabins, 4:273
Loggia, 3:251, 257
Logic: Europe (Middle Ages), 2:159–60; Islamic World (Middle Ages), 2:165, 166; Vikings, 2:152
Loincloths: Aztec, 3:47, 50; Inca, 3:53, 88; Maya, 3:231
Loki, 2:412
Lolita (Nabokov), 6:38, 222
Lombard, Carole, 6:525
Lombard dialect, 3:163
Lombard kingdom, 2:2
Lombardy, 3:99
London, Herbert, 6:542
London (19th Century): County Council, 5:140; estates, 5:113; growth of, 5:81, 135; Metropolitan Board of Works, 5:141; pollution, 5:135; population, 5:140; work, 5:111
London (15th & 16th Centuries): Flemish people in, 3:109; lawlessness, 3:331; Parliament, representation in, 3:286; physicians, 3:190; population, 3:108; theater, 3:108, 207, 342
London (Middle Ages): fortification, 2:108, 110; government, 2:98, 110; population, 2:322; urban life, 2:109–12, 321
London (17th & 18th Centuries), 4:333–36; death penalty, 4:393; law enforcement, 4:392; neighborhoods, 4:335; public execution account (1774), 4:506–8; water supply, 4:334
London Bridge, 2:110
London Journal, 5:191

London Times, The, 5:142, 192
Longbows: English use of (Middle Ages), 2:346, 350; Japan (17th & 18th Centuries), 4:409
Long hose, 3:224
Longhouses of Algonquians, 4:332
Long Shadow of Little Rock, The (Bates), 6:443
Long-term care insurance (Japan), 6:292
Long Walk Home, The (film), 6:442
Looms. *See* Textiles; Weaving
Looting of conquered nations: Mesopotamia, 1:317, 370–71, 372–73; Vikings, 2:352
Lord Lieutenant (Victorian England), 5:321
Lord Macarthy, 5:130
Lord's Prayer: England (15th & 16th Centuries), 3:178; Europe (15th & 16th Centuries), 3:77; in Latin and English, 3:364
Lorica segmentata, 1:399
Lotteries (England), 4:421
Lotto, 5:431
Louis XIII (king of France), 4:355–56, 474
Louis XIV (king of France), 4:5, 356, 453, 474
Louis XVI (king of France), 4:5
Louisiana Purchase, 5:6, 125, 343, 347–48
Louisiana sugar, 5:121
Louis IX (King of France), 2:4
Louis the Pious, 2:149
Lounging attire (Civil War era), 5:276
Love: marriage, and (17th & 18th Centuries), 4:28; New England, colonial, 4:62
Love poetry: Europe (Middle Ages), 2:170; Rome (ancient), 1:203
Lovering, Joseph, 5:152
"Lover's lane," 6:34
Lowry, Edith, 6:575
Loyalty of Free Men, The (Barth), 6:527
Loyola, Ignatius, 3:210
Loyola, Martin Garcia de, 3:24
Luba rulers, 4:348
Lucca, 3:289
Lucretia, rape of, 1:36
Lucy, Autherine, 6:443–44
Ludendorff, Erich, 6:5
Lull, Ramon, 2:88
Lumière brothers, 6:513, 530
Lunacharskii, Anatolii, 6:208–9, 233
Lunar calendar: Greece (ancient), 1:213; India (ancient), 1:216; Mesopotamia, 1:208–9. *See also* Calendars
Lunar festivals: China (Tang Dynasty), 2:450, 454; Mesopotamia, 1:436
Lunch: England (Victorian era), 5:219, 240; Europe (Middle Ages), 2:201; Latin America (20th Century), 6:315; Ottoman Empire, 3:244; United States (Western Frontier), 5:234. *See also* Meals
Lunda kingdom, 4:348
Lung cancer and disease: England (Victorian era), 5:210; United States (1960–90), 6:279
Lungis, 5:286
Luo society, 4:348–49
Lupercalia, 1:441; 2:303
Lustration, 2:455
Lutes: description of, 1:422; Europe (15th & 16th Century), 3:340, 343; India (ancient), 1:432; Vikings, 2:389
Luther, Martin, 3:19, 365, 379
Lutheranism, 3:361, 365, 382
Lutherans: North American colonial frontier, 4:470; United States (Civil War era), 5:457
Lu Xun, 5:182, 195
Luxury items, trade in: ancient world, 1:139; Dutch in 17th and 18th Centuries, 4:151; Mesopotamia, 1:140; Middle Ages, 2:135,

136, 138, 196, 206; Nubia, 1:149; Rome (ancient), 1:146; Silk Road, 2:138–39, 248
Lu Yu, 2:217
Lychee, 2:205
Lyman, Mary, 6:574
Lynching: United States (1920–39), 6:140, 148–49; United States (Western Frontier), 5:332–33
Lynd, Robert and Helen, 6:569, 570, 572
Lynge, Augo, 6:241
Lyrical composition by sailors (17th & 18th Centuries), 4:460–61
Lysenko, Trofim, 6:191
Lyubery, 6:554

Maat, 1:344, 476
MacArthur, Douglas, 6:494
Macarthur, Elizabeth, 4:433
Macaulay, Thomas, 6:155
Macdonnel, John, 5:124
Macedonia, 1:8, 383; 5:391–92
Machado de Assis, Joachim Maria, 5:197
Machi, Tawara, 6:238
Machiavelli, Niccolò, 3:177, 213, 415–16
Machine guns (World War I), 6:4, 350, 351–52
Machines (ancient Greece), 1:227, 427
Machismo, 6:55, 57, 77
Machu Picchu, 3:204
Macintosh computers, 6:252
Mackenzie, Charles, 5:123
Mackenzie, Kenneth, 5:126
Macquarie (governor of colonial Australia), 4:432–33, 486–87
Madhhab, 2:419–20
Madonnas, 3:277
Madrasa, 2:157
Madres de Plaza de Mayo, 6:77
Madrid (15th & 16th Centuries): Cervantes in, 3:212; economic life, 3:112–13; gambling, 3:321; houses, 3:255–56; theaters, 3:333; universities, 3:176. *See also* Spain (15th & 16th Centuries)
Madrid Codex, 3:214
Maestros, 3:277
Magazines: England (17th & 18th Centuries), 4:208; England (Victorian era), 5:191–92, 439; *Gentleman's Magazine*, 4:505–6; United States (1960–90), 6:227; on Vietnam War, 6:473–74
Magic and superstition: ancient world, 1:524–35; China (Tang Dynasty), 2:400; Greece (ancient), 1:524, 532–34; Inca, 3:392–93; Japan (17th & 18th Centuries), 4:87, 423; Mande (17th & 18th Centuries), 4:154; Mesopotamia, 1:283, 284, 524, 525–31; Rome (ancient), 1:524, 534–35
Magic lanterns, 5:430
Magistrates: China (19th Century), 5:323; New England, colonial, 4:397–98
Magna Carta, 2:4, 288, 328; 3:284–86
Magnetic compasses and ocean navigation, 4:180–81
Magnifici, 3:277
Magyars, 2:2
Mahabali, King, 5:415
Mahabharata, 1:13, 207; 5:465; 6:228
Mahavira, 5:416
Mahavir Jayanti, 5:416
Mahayana Buddhism, 5:465
Mahdi, 2:468
Mahfouz, Naguib, 6:232
Mahishasura, 5:414
Mail delivery: England (17th & 18th Centuries), 4:208; England (Victorian era), 5:142–43;

Japan (17th & 18th Centuries), **4**:322; Japan (20th Century), **6**:259; seamen, **4**:217

Mailer, Norman, **6**:220–21

Mair, **5**:37, 39

Maize: Australia, colonial, **4**:106–7; Aztec, **3**:104, 221, 237, 248; Inca, **3**:2, 221, 237, 248–49; Latin America (19th Century), **5**:133, 245, 246, 247; Maya, **3**:100–102, 221, 237, 246; United States (Western Frontier), **5**:230; Vikings, **2**:126

Makar Sankranti, **5**:415

Makeup. *See* Cosmetics

Makioka Sisters, The (Jun'ichirou), **6**:237

Malaeska, the Indian Wife of the White Hunter (Stephens), **5**:187

Malaria: England (15th & 16th Centuries), **3**:189; Europe (15th & 16th Centuries), **3**:166; India (19th Century), **5**:253; India (20th Century), **6**:287; Italy (15th & 16th Centuries), **3**:196; New England, colonial, **4**:88; United States (1940–59), **6**:275

Malatesta family, **3**:8

Malcolm X, **6**:152, 448, 595

Male prostitution, **1**:67–68

Malaria, **1**:295

Maliki, **3**:65

Malil, **3**:262

Malintzin, **3**:168

Mallorca, **3**:161

Malls, shopping, **6**:169–70

Malnutrition: England (17th & 18th Centuries), **4**:225; Latin America (20th Century), **6**:314; seamen, **4**:234; United States (1920–39), **6**:307; United States (1960–90), **6**:313

Malpractice. *See* Medical malpractice

Malta Knights of Saint John, **3**:276

Mama-Cocha, **3**:376

Mamaconas, **3**:72, 187, 390

Māui, **2**:177–78, 469

Mama Ocllo, **5**:417

Mama-Quilla, **3**:376

Mamluks, **2**:317–18, 319

Manahuatzin, **3**:399

Manchu Dynasty, **5**:453

Manco Capac, **3**:109, 126, 282, 402–4; **5**:417

Manco Inca, **3**:23

Mandal Commission Report (India), **6**:156

Mandamiento, **5**:134

Mandarins, **2**:296, 454

Mandel, Yelena, **6**:159

Mandela, Nelson, **6**:433

Mandelshtam, Osip, **6**:233

Mande (17th & 18th Centuries), **4**:153–54

Mandeville, Bernard, **4**:143–44

Mandulis, **1**:468

Manhattan Project, **6**:184, 185, 469

Manic depression, **6**:281

Manioc: Inca, **3**:105; Maya, **3**:246

Mannes, Marya, **6**:97, 565

Man Nobody Knows, The (Barton), **6**:572

Manorialism, **2**:290, 291, 311

Manors and manor houses: England (15th & 16th Centuries), **3**:253; Europe (Middle Ages), **2**:123–24, 290, 291; Middle Ages, **2**:301; Spain (15th & 16th Centuries), **3**:95

Manslaughter, **3**:302. *See also* Homicide

Mansour, **2**:117, 118

Mantas: Aztec, **3**:233; Maya, **3**:231

Mantillas, **3**:223, 227

Mantle, Mickey, **6**:503

Mantua: Countess of, **3**:229; Duke of, **3**:339

Manturcalla, **3**:391–92

Manuductio Ad Ministerium (Mather), **4**:214

Manufacturing industry: England (17th & 18th Centuries), **4**:123–24; Europe (Middle Ages), **2**:276; North American colonial frontier, **4**:121–22

Manumission, **1**:115

Manus marriage in Roman Empire, **1**:48–49, 50

Manu Smriti, **1**:338

Manzikert defeat of Byzantium (1071), **2**:356

Mappa mundi, **1**:220–21

Maps: Africa (18th Century), **4**:15; Australia (1606–1818), **4**:20; Aztec Empire, **3**:12; Byzantine Empire, **2**:18; China (19th Century), **5**:12; China (Tang Dynasty) divided into three kingdoms (Wei, Shu, and Wu), **2**:9; China under Tang dynasty, **2**:8; Crusades, **2**:14, 16; England and Wales (16th Century), **3**:4; England (1789), **4**:3; England (Victorian era), **5**:9; Europe and Mediterranean (Middle Ages), **2**:3; France (1789), **4**:3; Greece (ancient), **1**:7, 225; Inca Empire, **3**:17; India (ancient), **1**:12; India (19th Century), **5**:15; Islamic World (Middle Ages), **2**:13; Japan (1550–1853), **4**:18; Latin America (19th Century), **5**:18; Maya, **3**:13; Mesopotamia, **1**:2, 155, 220; Mongol conquests, **2**:21; Oceania (Middle Ages), **2**:24; oceanic trading routes (17th Century), **4**:8; Ottoman Empire, **3**:19; Paris (Middle Ages), **2**:113; Proclamation Line of 1763, **4**:11; Renaissance Italy, **3**:9; Rome (ancient), **1**:9; Spain (16th Century), **3**:7; United States (19th Century), **5**:5; United States (Western Frontier), **5**:5; Vikings in the North, **2**:6. *See also* Cartography

Maqlû, **1**:525

Maquahuitl, **3**:233

Marable, Manning, **6**:153

Marabouts (17th & 18th Centuries), **4**:347, 467

Maracatú, **5**:416

Marathon, Battle of, **1**:379

Marble, **3**:99

Marcheses, **3**:276

March on Washington, 1963, **6**:447

Marcian (Byzantine emperor), **2**:426

Marconi, Guglielmo, **6**:241, 243

Marco Polo: on Mongols drinking koumiss, **2**:221; trading journey to Mongols, **2**:22, 94, 133, 140, 363; *Travels of Marco Polo,* **2**:481–83

Marcus, Greil, **6**:540–41

Marcy, Randolph, **5**:488–90

Marduk, **1**:456, 471, 472, 474

Mare Mount settlement, **4**:441

Margaret (queen of England), **3**:13

Mari, **1**:140

María (Isaac), **5**:196

Marianismo, **6**:55, 75, 77

Marine Corps, **6**:64

Marines (British Royal Navy), **4**:365

Maris, Roger, **6**:503

Marjoram, **4**:223

Marketplaces: Byzantium, **2**:106; China (Tang Dynasty), **2**:101–3; Europe (Middle Ages), **2**:98, 133; Greece (ancient), **1**:97; Islamic World (Middle Ages), **2**:104–5; Mesopotamia, **1**:91

Marling, Karal Ann, **6**:340

Marlowe, Christopher, **3**:206, 208, 209, 342

Mármol, José, **5**:197

Marquess of Queensberry, **5**:403

Marquis and marchinesses: England (15th & 16th Centuries), **3**:271; Italy (15th & 16th Centuries), **3**:276; Spain (15th & 16th Centuries), **3**:274

Marriage: Africa (17th & 18th Centuries), **4**:30–32, 46–47; ancient world, **1**:39–50; Australia, colonial, **4**:32–33; Australian Aboriginals, **1**:28; Aztec, **3**:32, 49–51; Catholicism (Spain, Italy, England), **3**:31, 380–81; China (19th Century), **5**:447; China (Tang Dynasty), **2**:45–47; England (15th & 16th Centuries), **3**:33; England (17th & 18th Centuries), **4**:35–38, 55; England (Victorian era), **5**:27, 34, 64–65, 110, 352, 373, 462; Europe (Middle Ages), **2**:41–43, 434; Greece (ancient), **1**:44–47; Hindu, **6**:590; Inca, **3**:32, 53–54; India (ancient), **1**:38; India (19th Century), **5**:27, 39, 53, 286; India (20th Century), **6**:32, 33, 46, 78, 104, 156, 590; Islamic World (Middle Ages), **2**:39, 47–50; Islamic World (19th Century), **5**:27, 37, 447; Italy (15th & 16th Centuries), **3**:39–40, 61, 347; Japan (17th & 18th Centuries), **4**:38–40; Japan (20th Century), **6**:49; Latin America (20th Century), **6**:43; love and (17th & 18th Centuries), **4**:28; Maya, **3**:45–46; Mesopotamia, **1**:21, 22, 40–43; Middle Ages, **2**:30, 39–50; Native Americans (colonial frontier of North America), **4**:34; New England, colonial, **4**:40–43, 62; New South Wales, **4**:32; North American colonial frontier, **4**:33–35; Ottoman Empire, **3**:42–43, 65; Protestantism (England), **3**:31; Rome (ancient), **1**:36, 47–50, 69, 385; seamen, **4**:43–45; 17th & 18th Centuries, **4**:27–45; slavery, **5**:27; slaves in colonial America, **4**:42; Spain (15th & 16th Centuries), **3**:35, 59; United States (1920–39), **6**:35; United States (1960–90), **6**:39; United States (Western Frontier), **5**:27; Vikings, **2**:43–45. *See also* Annulment of marriage; Brother-sister marriage; Dowry

Marriage contracts: China (Tang Dynasty), **2**:45; Europe (Middle Ages), **2**:41; Middle Ages, **2**:40

Marriage of slaves: Mesopotamia, **1**:110, 489; New Orleans, **5**:28

Mars, **1**:483

Marsden, Samuel, **4**:486–87

Marshall, John, **5**:366

Marshall, Thurgood, **6**:442

Marshall Plan, **6**:469

Martens, **5**:122

Martial arts in Japan, **4**:410

Martial games: England (15th & 16th Centuries), **3**:331; Inca, **3**:328; Italy (15th & 16th Centuries), **3**:315, 321–22; Spain (15th & 16th Centuries), **3**:315, 320

Martial sports in Europe (Middle Ages), **2**:370

Martine, Arthur, **5**:274

Martineau, Harriet, **5**:63

Martín Fiero (Hernández), **5**:196

Martín Rivas (Blest Gana), **5**:197

Martyrs, Muslim, **2**:457

Marx, Karl, **3**:207, 360; **5**:485–87

Marxism, **6**:137

Mary (queen of Netherlands), **4**:2

Mary I (queen of England), **3**:15, 409

Marye, Etienne-Jules, **6**:512

Maryland: government (17th & 18th Centuries), **4**:350–51; slavery in, **5**:86, 121

Mashkan-shapir, **1**:91

Masia, **3**:256

356, 387–89; wild animals, hunting of, **1**:259, 405, 416; wine, **1**:87, 259; women's clothing, **1**:312–13

Nuclear energy: Japan, **6**:192; United States (1960–90), **6**:364–65

Nuclear family, defined, **1**:21

Nuclear threat, **6**:40, 183. *See also* Cold War

Nuclear weapons: invention of, **6**:183, 184; United States (1939–45), **6**:468–69, 493

Nudity: 15th & 16th Centuries, **3**:223; Greek art, **1**:237–38. *See also* Sexuality

Nullification crisis (United States), **5**:313–14, 316

Numbers: Arabic numerals, **2**:165; Aztec, **3**:85, 140, 151; England (15th & 16th Centuries), **3**:160; Maya, **3**:136–37, 200–202; Mesopotamia, **1**:173, 218; Roman numerals, **2**:165

Numina, **1**:454–55

Nun, **1**:475

Nunavut Territory: creation and government of, **6**:403; land claims agreement (1993), **6**:620–22

Nuncheon, **2**:201

Núñez, Rafael, **5**:341

Nuns: Buddhism, **2**:432; Civil War hospitals, **5**:201; convents (Byzantium), **2**:64; Europe (Middle Ages), **2**:53–54, 258, 434–35; Latin America (20th Century), **6**:591–92; Middle Ages, **2**:51

Nur al-Din, **2**:359

Nuremberg Trials, **6**:404, 410–12

Nurses: England (Victorian era), **5**:110; Soviet Union, **6**:290; World War I, **6**:61–62

Nursing homes, **6**:383

Nut (Egyptian goddess), **1**:475, 476

Nutrition: development of field of, **6**:302–3; United States (1920–39), **6**:307–8; United States (1960–90), **6**:310–11, 312

Nuts: Africa (17th & 18th Centuries), **4**:240; Byzantium, **2**:209; China (Tang Dynasty), **2**:204, 206; Greece (ancient), **1**:255; India (19th Century), **5**:53–54, 244; Vikings, **2**:203

Nuzi: women's role, **1**:30–31. *See also* Mesopotamia

Nyamakala, **4**:154

Nye, David E., **6**:358–59

Oath of the Horatii, The (David), **4**:454

Oaxaca, Valley of, **3**:3

Oaxacan Civilization, **3**:3

Obelisks (Mesopotamia), **1**:231

Observation and experimentation: Australian Aboriginals, **1**:229; China (Tang Dynasty), **2**:164; Europe in Middle ages, **2**:161; Holocaust victims, **6**:409, 410; Islamic World (Middle Ages), **2**:167

Obstetrics. *See* Childbirth

Oca, **3**:105

Occupations. *See* Professions and occupations

Oceanic exploration and travel: England (17th & 18th Centuries), **4**:7–9; map (17th Century), **4**:8; 17th & 18th Centuries, **4**:1–2, 7, 315

Ocelotl, **3**:233

Ochpaniztli, **3**:69, 186

O'Connor, Flannery, **6**:221

O'Connor, Sandra Day, **6**:74

Ocopa, **5**:245

Octavian, **1**:10. *See also* Augustus Caesar

Odin, **2**:399, 412, 413–14

Odoric of Pordenone, Friar, **2**:266

Odyssey: on death, burial, and the afterlife, **1**:520; educational role of, **1**:188; on magic, **1**:533; on money, **1**:134; on slavery, **1**:111, 112; stories of, **1**:200, 481; on travel and transportation, **1**:161; on women, **1**:33–34

Oedipus the King (Sophocles), **1**:200

Office of Economic Opportunity, **6**:381

Officers. *See* Military officers; Naval officers

Office work, **6**:117

Ogden, Peter Skene, **5**:47, 49

Oghul Qaimish, **2**:65, 246

Ögödei, **2**:221, 246, 343, 363, 428

OGPU (Unified State Political Administration), **6**:426

Oil: Japan (17th & 18th Centuries), **4**:249; lighting in Spain (15th & 16th Centuries), **3**:256; Nubia, **1**:259. *See also* Olive trees and olive oil

Okitsuga, Tanuma, **4**:18

Olaf Sigurdson (Viking king), **2**:7

Olaf Skotkonung (Viking king), **2**:137, 415

Olaf Tryggvason (Viking king), **2**:137, 279, 374, 397, 415

Old age: China (Tang Dynasty), **2**:87, 90–92; England (17th & 18th Centuries), **4**:84; Europe (Middle Ages), **2**:87, 88–89, 183; Greece (ancient), **1**:297; India (20th Century), **6**:47, 58; Inuit, **6**:51; Japan (17th & 18th Centuries), **4**:86, 359; Japan (20th Century), **6**:292; life at sea (17th & 18th Centuries), **4**:89–92; medical care (United States 1960–90), **6**:382–83; Mesopotamia, **1**:287; Middle Ages, **2**:86–92; New England, colonial, **4**:88–89; North American colonial frontier, **4**:82–83; Rome (ancient), **1**:297; 17th & 18th Centuries, **4**:80–92; Vikings, **2**:87, 89–90

Old Bailey, **5**:336

Old English, **3**:159

Old Jules (Sandoz), **5**:31–32

Oligarchy in India, **1**:353

Oliphant, Margaret, **5**:191

Oliver Twist (Dickens), **5**:181, 185, 190

Olive trees and olive oil: Byzantium, **2**:130, 208, 284; Greece (ancient), **1**:83, 144, 255, 440; Islamic World (Middle Ages), **2**:206; Italy (15th & 16th Centuries), **3**:243; Rome (ancient), **1**:85, 99, 256

Ollamaliztli, **3**:315–16, 326

Ollo podrida, **3**:241

Olluca, **5**:246

Olmec Civilization, **3**:3

Olmstead, Frederick Law, **5**:421

Olmstead v. U.S. (1927), **6**:416

Olympic Games: Africa (20th Century), **6**:510; England (Victorian era), **5**:402–3; Europe (20th Century), **6**:499; Greece (ancient), **1**:6, 63, 66, 211, 381, 411–13, 479; reinitiated in 1896, **6**:498; South Africa ban, **6**:511; 20th Century, **6**:498; United States (1960–90), **6**:506–7

Omecihuatl, **3**:373

Omens: ancient world, **1**:524–25; Aztec, **3**:218, 354; China (Tang Dynasty), **2**:164; Greece (ancient), **1**:379; Inca, **3**:393; Mesopotamia, **1**:272, 285, 436, 526–28; Polynesia, **2**:364, 365. *See also* Diviners; Entrails, reading of

Ometecuhtli, **3**:373

Ometeotl, **3**:341, 354, 373–74

Omeyocan, **3**:139, 373

Onam, **5**:415

"On Being Brought from Africa to America" (Wheatley), **4**:215

One Day in the Life of Ivan Denisovich (Solzhenitsyn), **6**:234

One Flew over the Cuckoo's Nest (film), **6**:281, 528

One Hundred Days of Reform of 1898 (China), **5**:324

Ongghot, **2**:428

Only Yesterday (Lewis), **6**:12

Onsen, **4**:229

On the Origin of Species by Means of Natural Selection (Darwin), **5**:154

Opera: Latin America (19th Century), **5**:426; New York Opera Association, **6**:547

Opium: China (19th Century), **5**:131, 375–76; England (Victorian era), **5**:207; India (19th Century), **5**:54, 442; Latin America (19th Century), **5**:246

Opium War: causes of, **5**:375; Chinese defeat in, **5**:323; effects of, **5**:130; foreign influence resulting from, **5**:176; historical overview, **5**:13; start of, **5**:132, 355; Taiping Rebellion resulting from, **5**:452

Oppenheimer, J. Robert, **6**:184, 185–86

Oracle of Pachacamac, **3**:392

Oracles: ancient world, **1**:485; Greece (ancient), **1**:493–94; Mesopotamia, **1**:530

Oral tradition: Australian Aboriginals, **1**:192; Europe (Middle Ages), **2**:169; Middle Ages, **2**:145–46, 167; Polynesia, **2**:23, 25, 176; Vikings, **2**:172

Oratory (ancient Rome), **1**:191, 203, 205

Orchestras: Latin America (19th Century), **5**:427; United States (1920–39), **6**:245

Ordeal by Slander (Lattimore), **6**:376

Ordeals to determine innocence/guilt: Europe (Middle Ages), **2**:327; Vikings, **2**:330

Order of Santo Stefano, **3**:276

Ordinary seamen on merchant vessels (17th & 18th Centuries), **4**:363

Oregon Trail, **5**:6, 487–88

Oresme, Nicole, **2**:161

Oresteia, **1**:200–201

Orfeo, **3**:213

Organically grown food, **6**:312

Organized crime (Soviet Union), **6**:430

Organized labor: Latin America (19th Century), **5**:326. *See also* Labor unions

Organ transplants, **6**:277

Orhan, **3**:180

Oriental Acquaintance (DeForest), **5**:188

Origen, **2**:70, 76

Orisha, **4**:466

Orlando furioso (Ariosto), **3**:206, 213

Orlando innamorato (Boiardo), **3**:206, 213

Orphanages (England), **5**:35, 389

Orphics, **1**:520

Ortaoyuno, **3**:350

Ortega, Aniceto, **5**:426

Ortenberg, David, **6**:158

Orthodox Church. *See* Greek Orthodox Church; Russian Orthodox Church

Osaka (17th & 18th Centuries), **4**:144–45, 337

Osamu, Dazai, **6**:237

Oshogatsu, **4**:438

Osiris: death of, **1**:289; description of, **1**:476; family of, **1**:475; as god of the dead, **1**:476, 507, 512; Set's feud with, **1**:471

Osman, **3**:10

Ostia, **1**:147–48

Ostraka, **1**:178–79, 188

Ostrogothic kingdom, **2**:2

Other America, The (Harrington), **6**:120, 129, 380

Otogi-zoshi, **4**:213

Otomies, **3**:5

Otranto, **3**:12

separation of religion and education, **6:**200; writings, **6:**375

Roosevelt, Franklin D.: anti-discrimination efforts by, **6:**140, 151, 375; atomic bomb's development and, **6:**184; election of 1932, **6:**371, 372; failure to rescue Holocaust Jews, **6:**560–62; fireside chats of, **6:**15, 246, 373, 374; foreign relations prior to entering World War II, **6:**466; on home ownership, **6:**162; on job discrimination, **6:**375–76; leadership of, **6:**15; McCarthy opposition to, **6:**376; political life, **6:**373; racial or ethnic-based actions by, **6:**140; second inaugural address of, **6:**14. *See also* New Deal

Roosevelt, Theodore, **5:**90; **6:**54, 371

Root, Waverly, **6:**309

Ropework of seamen, **4:**460

Rosas, Juan Manuel de, **5:**325, 378

Rosenberg, Alfred, **6:**412

Rosenberg, Julius and Ethel, **6:**378–80

Ross, Major, **4:**387

Rosser, Thomas, **5:**57

Rotis, **5:**243; **6:**316

Rotten boroughs, **4:**354

Rounders, **5:**397, 399

Roundups, **5:**88–89

Rousseau, Jean-Jacques, **4:**210

Rowing: England (Victorian era), **5:**401; Greece (ancient), **1:**126; Rome (ancient), **1:**400; United States (19th Century), **5:**399

Roy, Arundhati, **6:**229–30

Roy, Ramohun, **6:**229

Royal Albert Hall, **5:**142

Royal and Pontifical University (Mexico), **5:**180

Royal clothing: Egypt (ancient), **1:**222–23, 347; Mesopotamia, **1:**317; Nubia, **1:**313, 314

Royal colonies (17th & 18th Centuries), **4:**350

Royal decrees and edicts: Mesopotamia, **1:**360; Mongols, **2:**342

Royal Exchange (England), **5:**139

Royall, William B., **5:**205, 332

Royal Military Academy (England), **5:**372

Royal Naval College (England), **5:**374

Royal Navy. *See* British Royal Navy (17th & 18th Centuries)

The Royal Commentaries of the Incas (Vega), **3:**425–27

Royalty: Egypt (ancient), **1:**331; Latin America (19th Century), **5:**117; Mesopotamia, **1:**330, 509. *See also* Kings; Pharaohs; *specific king or member of royal family*

Royce, Josiah, **6:**564

Royce, Sarah, **5:**59, 91

Rubber blankets of Civil War soldiers, **5:**254, 258–59, 294

Rubber (Latin America), **5:**133

Ruede, Howard, **5:**103, 206, 207, 261, 278

Ruffin, Edmund, **5:**314

Rugby: England (Victorian era), **5:**401; Europe (15th & 16th Centuries), **3:**315; schools, **5:**113

Rugs. *See* Floors and floor coverings

Ruizong, **2:**10, 58

Rum: Latin America (19th Century), **5:**245; New England, colonial, **4:**265–66; World War I soldier ration of, **6:**306

Rum Corps, **4:**22

Rum Rebellion (Australia), **4:**22, 258, 388

Runaway servants in colonial New England, **4:**398

Runaway slaves: China (Tang Dynasty), **2:**317; Fugitive Slave Law, **5:**308; Mesopotamia, **1:**109, 489; Rome (ancient), **1:**114; underground railway, **5:**58, 140, 382

Rune stones, **2:**82, 171

Rune stories, **2:**34

Runic alphabet, **2:**171–72

Running: Africa (20th Century), **6:**510; England (Victorian era), **5:**402–3; United States (19th Century), **5:**397, 398–99; United States (1960–90), **6:**503, 504, 507. *See also* Footraces

Running shoes, **6:**503

Rural Electrification Administration, **6:**438

Rural life and agriculture: Africa (17th & 18th Centuries), **4:**103–6, 135, 241, 430; Africa (20th Century), **6:**86, 123, 124, 177; ancient world, **1:**74–88; Australia, colonial, **4:**50, 102, 106–8; Australian Aboriginals, **1:**260; Aztec, **3:**102–4; British colonies, **4:**12; Byzantium, **2:**64, 129–31, 284; China (19th Century), **5:**94, 115; China (Tang Dynasty), **2:**93, 126–28, 315; derivation of word "agriculture," **1:**83; England (15th & 16th Centuries), **3:**57, 92–94; England (1914–18), **6:**303, 304–5; England (17th & 18th Centuries), **4:**4, 55, 102–3, 110–13, 112; England (Victorian era), **5:**92–93, 109, 111; Europe (Middle Ages), **2:**52, 122–24, 277, 290–91; France (1914–18), **6:**304; Germany (1914–18), **6:**303; Great Depression, **6:**162, 164; Greece (ancient), **1:**82–83; Inca, **3:**104–8; India (ancient), **1:**85–86, 257–58; India (19th Century), **5:**291; India (20th Century), **6:**334; Islamic World (Middle Ages), **2:**93, 128–29, 282; Italy (15th & 16th Centuries), **3:**97–99; Japan (17th & 18th Centuries), **4:**17, 60, 113–15, 177, 377–78, 437–38; Japan (20th Century), **6:**162, 176; Latin America (19th Century), **5:**96–97, 246–47; Latin America (20th Century), **6:**101, 102, 135, 170–72, 314; Maya, **3:**99–102; Mesopotamia, **1:**75–80, 221; Middle Ages, **2:**93, 121–31, 309; Native Americans (New England, colonial), **4:**62; New Deal programs, **6:**436–37; New England, colonial, **4:**13, 102–3, 116–18; North American colonial frontier, **4:**53, 108–10, 173, 373–74; Nubia, **1:**86–88; Olmec Civilization, **3:**3; Rome (ancient), **1:**83–85, 115; 17th & 18th Centuries, **4:**102–18; Soviet Union, **6:**172–75, 317–18; Spain (15th & 16th Centuries), **3:**94–97; Toltec Empire, **3:**5; 20th Century, **6:**161; United States (Civil War era), **5:**2, 3, 86; United States (1920–39), **6:**128, 273, 307; United States (1940–59), **6:**119–20, 128, 334; United States (Western Frontier), **5:**103; Vikings, **2:**55–56, 57, 125–26, 294

Rus, **2:**5

Ruse, James, **4:**107

Rush, Benjamin, **5:**151

Russell, Bertrand, **5:**177, 452

Russell, Charles, **5:**107

Russell, Osborne, **5:**48, 230

Russian Orthodox Church, **2:**427; Communist repression of, **6:**596–97

Russia (post-Soviet Union), **6:**22

Russia (pre-Soviet Union): Cyrillic alphabet, **3:**166; historical overview, **6:**1–2, 21; workers and revolution, **6:**112

Rustin, Bayard, **6:**442

Rustling, **5:**88

Ruth, Babe, **6:**497, 501

Ruxton, Frederick, **5:**231

Rynok, **6:**318

Ryounosuke, Akutagawa, **6:**236

Sabatini, Rafael, **4:**218

Sabbath: England (15th & 16th Centuries), **3:**130, 341; England (17th & 18th Centuries),

4:436, 492; German immigrants to United States, **5:**138; Greece (ancient), **1:**438; Jews, **6:**141; New England, colonial, **4:**98, 482, 486; slaves required to attend Church, **5:**86. *See also* Sunday

Sacajawea, **5:**410

Sacbe, **3:**120

Sacco, Nicola, **6:**414–15

Sacerdos, **3:**380

Sachem, **4:**360

Sackbuts, **3:**343

Sack of Rome (1527), **3:**179

Sacraments: Catholicism (Spain, Italy, England), **3:**20, 380–82; Latin America (19th Century), **5:**471; Protestantism (England), **3:**365–66, 382

Sacred stories: Aztec, **3:**399–402; Christianity (England, Spain, Italy), **3:**395–97; Inca, **3:**402–4; Maya, **3:**397–98. *See also* Creation stories; Mythology

Sacrifices: ancient world, **1:**485; Catholicism (Spain, Italy, England), **3:**363; Greece (ancient), **1:**438–40, 492; India (ancient), **1:**449; Jesus Christ, **3:**379; Jews, **3:**363; Mesopotamia, **1:**436, 486; Rome (ancient), **1:**442, 444, 447, 448, 498–99; Vikings, **2:**305, 314, 452–53. *See also* Human sacrifices

Saddam Hussein, **1:**102

Sadanobu, Matsudaira, **4:**18

Saddlers, **5:**110

Sadr-i azam, **3:**292

Safavid Empire, **3:**20, 164, 291, 367

Saffron, **2:**201

Saga of Bosi, **2:**389, 390

Saga of the Orkney Islanders, **2:**389

Sagas of Icelanders: on cult celebrations, **2:**453; on drinking, **2:**398; on families, **2:**34; on homosexuality, **2:**44; on marriage, **2:**43, 44; on the settlement of Iceland, **2:**172; on widows, **2:**56

Sahagún, Bernardo de: on Aztec game playing, **3:**327; on Aztec temples, **3:**387; on Aztec women's role, **3:**68, 424–25; Aztec world view communicated to, **3:**375; on human sacrifice, **3:**423–24; records collected by, **3:**207; writings and teachings of, **3:**217–19

Sahal, **3:**294

Sahara Desert tents (17th & 18th Centuries), **4:**270–71

Sailing and Fighting Instructions, **4:**218

Sailors: England (15th & 16th Centuries), **3:**110, 189; England (Victorian era), **5:**374; Greece (ancient), **1:**334; Vikings as, **2:**162. *See also* British Royal Navy (17th & 18th Centuries); Life at sea *entries*; Navy

Sails (17th & 18th Centuries), **4:**325

St. Louis and refusal of Cuba & U.S. to accept Jewish refugees, **6:**6–7, 560, 562–63

Saint Augustine, **3:**344

Saint Francis of Assisi, **3:**135, 359

Saint Godric, **2:**132

St. James's Square, **4:**335

Saint John of the Cross, **3:**162

St. Lawrence River, **4:**316–17

Saint Mathias' Day, **3:**305

St. Paul's Cathedral, **2:**111; **5:**139

Saints: Byzantium, **2:**210; Catholicism (Spain, Italy, England), **3:**363; Latin America (19th Century), **5:**471; Vikings, **2:**184

Saint Stephen, **3:**344

Saint Teresa, **3:**162

Saivas, **6:**588

United States (1850–65)

1:396–98; Islamic World (Middle Ages), 2:357; Japan (17th & 18th Centuries), 4:408–10, 409; Mesopotamia, 1:392–93; Middle Ages, 2:4, 344–45; Mongols, 2:362–63; Native Americans (colonial frontier of North America), 4:404; North American colonial frontier, 4:405–6; Nubia, 1:387; Polynesia, 2:364–65; Rome (ancient), 1:398–400; 17th & 18th Centuries, 4:401–2; Soviet Union, 6:488–89; 20th Century, 6:349; United States (1940–59), 6:119; Vikings, 2:352–53, 373; World War I, 6:4, 349–55. *See also* Guns; Warfare; *specific type of weapon*

Weather: Australia, colonial, 4:171; Greece (ancient), 1:295. *See also* Natural disasters

Weaving: Africa (17th & 18th Centuries), 4:447; Byzantium, 2:63–64; China (19th Century), 5:94; China (Tang Dynasty), 2:272, 315; Europe (Middle Ages), 2:52, 249–50; India (19th Century), 5:302; Middle Ages, 2:248; Polynesia, 2:254; United States (Western Frontier), 5:278; Vikings, 2:55–56. *See also* Textiles

Webster, John W., 5:152
Webster, Noah, 5:160, 164
Wedding ceremonies. *See* Marriage
Wedding dresses of Civil War era, 5:272, 274
Weekends, 4:436
Wei (Chinese Empress), 2:58–59
Weightlifting in ancient Rome, 1:414
Weights and measures: China (Tang Dynasty), 2:102; Europe (Middle Ages), 2:97; Islamic World (Middle Ages), 2:105
Weisbrot, Robert, 6:152, 449
Weiser, Conrad, 5:122
Weld, Theodore D., 5:56, 187
Welfare: England (Victorian era), 5:388–89; Great Depression, 6:165; United States, 6:129–30
Weller, Edwin, 5:429
Wellington, Duke of, 5:8
Wells: Greece (ancient), 1:278; India (20th Century), 6:344; United States (Western Frontier), 5:260; Vikings, 2:228. *See also* Drinking water; Water supply
Wells Fargo, 5:62
Wergild, 2:35, 328, 330
Wernher der Gartenaere, 2:488–91
Wesley, Charles, 4:472
Wesley, John, 4:472
West Africa (17th & 18th Centuries): agriculture, 4:104; explorations by Mungo Park, 4:516–19; housing, 4:271; work celebrations, 4:430. *See also* Africa (17th & 18th Centuries)
Westerns (TV shows), 6:97–98
Westinghouse, 6:244–45
Westminster Abbey, 2:109
Westminster Hall, 5:112
Wet nurses: China (Tang Dynasty), 2:83; England (Victorian era), 5:239; Europe (Middle Ages), 2:79–80; Middle Ages, 2:78
Whaling (17th & 18th Centuries): black slaves, 4:130; description of process, 4:130–31; holidays, 4:442–43; letter writing, 4:217; marriage, 4:43; nations engaged in, 4:119; New England, colonial, 4:129–30; seaports, 4:443; try-works, 4:130
Whaling (Vikings), 2:202, 381
Wharves. *See* Seaports (17th & 18th Centuries)

Wheat: Argentina (1914–18), 6:304; Australia, colonial, 4:106–7; Byzantium, 2:196, 208; Castile, 3:95; England (15th & 16th Centuries), 3:92; England (1914–18), 6:303, 304; England (Victorian era), 5:238; Europe (15th & 16th Centuries), 3:236; Europe (Middle Ages), 2:123, 196; France (1914–18), 6:303, 304; India (20th Century), 6:301, 316; Islamic World (Middle Ages), 2:206; Italy (15th & 16th Centuries), 3:242; Latin America (19th Century), 5:97–98, 133, 245; Middle Ages, 2:196; Spain (15th & 16th Centuries), 3:95, 112. *See also* Grains
Wheatley, Phillis, 4:215
Wheelbarrows, invention of, 2:274, 281
Wheeled vehicles: Greece (ancient), 1:160; Mesopotamia, 1:154
Wheelwrights, 5:121
Whey: Europe (Middle Ages), 2:199, 215; Vikings, 2:202
Whig Party (United States), 5:307, 308
Whigs (England), 4:2, 352
Whippings. *See* Corporal punishment
Whiskey: Japan (20th Century), 6:330; Latin America (19th Century), 5:246; United States (Western Frontier), 5:409
"Whiskey blanc," 4:259
White, E.B., 6:224
White, José, 5:427
White Birch (*Shirakaba*) School, 6:237
Whitecar, William, 4:428
White-collar crime: Soviet Union, 6:430; United States (1960–90), 6:418
White-collar workers (United States), 6:116–17
Whitefield, George, 4:472
Whitfield, James M., 5:345
Whitney, Eli, 5:302
Whitsun: England (15th & 16th Centuries), 3:130; England (Victorian era), 5:412
Whittier, John Greenleaf, 5:56, 382
Whittling, 5:429
Who Spoke Up (Zaroulis and Sullivan), 6:475
Why Change Your Wife? (film), 6:512, 518
Widows: China (Tang Dynasty), 2:91; Church care for, Middle Ages, 2:87; England (15th & 16th Centuries), 3:56; England (Victorian era), 5:285, 480; Greece (ancient), 1:47; India (19th Century), 5:286; India (20th Century), 6:79, 156; Italy (15th & 16th Centuries), 3:40; Japan (17th & 18th Centuries), 4:40; life at sea (17th & 18th Centuries), 4:91; Maya, 3:45; Mesopotamia, 1:31; New England, colonial, 4:88–89; North American colonial frontier, 4:82–83; Ottoman Empire, 3:64; Spain (15th & 16th Centuries), 3:60; Vikings, 2:56
Widukind, 2:415
Wife's role. *See* Family life; Marriage
Wigs: England (17th & 18th Centuries), 4:291; Puritans, 4:297–98; 17th & 18th Centuries, 4:285
Wigwams, 4:279
Wild animals: entertainment of killing, Rome (ancient), 1:446; Europe (Middle Ages), 2:377–78; importing of, Rome (ancient), 1:148; Nubian hunting of, 1:259, 405, 416. *See also specific type (e.g., Bear)*
Wild boars, 2:377–78, 379
Wildcats, 5:122
Wilde, Oscar, 5:10
Wildfowl, 3:238
Wilhelm II, Kaiser, 6:3, 6
Wilkinson, James B., 5:234
William II (king of England), 2:109, 110

William III (king of England), 4:350–51
William the Conqueror, 2:109, 344; 3:12
William of Malmesbury, 2:184
William of Normandy. *See* William the Conqueror
William of Orange, 4:2
William of Rubruck, 2:65, 66, 191, 220, 245, 265
Williams, Roger, 4:361
Williams, Tennessee, 6:37, 38, 221
Williams, William Carlos, 6:225
Wills: England (15th & 16th Centuries), 3:33; Europe (Middle Ages), 2:240, 328, 434; Italy (15th & 16th Centuries), 3:40–41; North American colonial frontier, 4:82; Rome (ancient), 1:367–68; Spain (15th & 16th Centuries), 3:60. *See also* Estates and inheritances
Wills, Maury, 6:503
Wilson, Woodrow, 6:370, 371
Wimbledon, 5:402
Wimples, 2:239, 259
Winchell, Walter, 6:246, 248
Windmills: Australia, colonial, 4:172; Byzantium, 2:284; spread of (Middle Ages), 2:93, 145, 275; United States (Western Frontier), 5:260
Wind on United States Western Frontier, 5:104
Windows: China (Tang Dynasty), 2:223, 231; England (Victorian era), 5:262; European castles (Middle Ages), 2:225; Europe (Middle Ages), 2:223, 268, 269; Greece (ancient), 1:277; Japan (20th Century), 6:346; Mesopotamia, 1:271; Rome (ancient), 1:279; Spain (15th & 16th Centuries), 3:36, 59, 255; United States (1940–59), 6:340; Vikings, 2:227
Windsor Castle, 5:141
Wine: Byzantium, 2:208; China (Tang Dynasty), 2:217; England (15th & 16th Centuries), 3:239–40; England (17th & 18th Centuries), 4:262; England (Victorian era), 5:240, 242; Europe (Middle Ages), 2:214–15; 15th & 16th Centuries, 3:237; Greece (ancient), 1:58, 83, 266–68; India (ancient), 1:258; Italy (15th & 16th Centuries), 3:243; Latin America (19th Century), 5:245; Mesopotamia, 1:263, 273; Middle Ages, 2:213; Mongols, 2:221; Muslim prohibition on, 2:206–7, 219; Nubia, 1:87, 259; Prohibition, 6:324–25; Rome (ancient), 1:85, 256, 269; Spain (15th & 16th Centuries), 3:95–96, 241; World War I soldier ration of, 6:306
Winn, Marie, 6:250
Winthrop, Theodore, 5:188, 318
Wisdom literature (Mesopotamia), 1:194–96
Wise, Henry A., 5:315
Wise, John, 5:310
Wishart, David J., 5:46
Wister, Owen, 5:87
Witchcraft: England (15th & 16th Centuries), 3:302; Italy (15th & 16th Centuries), 3:198; New England, colonial, 4:397, 426. *See also* Magic and superstition
Witch doctors, 6:293
Witching Times (DeForest), 5:188
Witnesses: ancient world, 1:358; Europe (Middle Ages), 2:326, 327; Mesopotamia, 1:359
Wittenberg, 3:19
Wives, life of. *See* Family life; Marriage
Wizard of Oz, The (film), 6:520, 521
Wobblies, 6:619–20
Wolves, 5:119, 122
"Woman marriage," 4:31
"Woman question" (France), 4:56–58

ABOUT THE CONTRIBUTORS

General Editor

Joyce E. Salisbury is Frankenthal Professor of History at University of Wisconsin–Green Bay. She has a doctorate in medieval history from Rutgers University. Professor Salisbury is an award-winning teacher: she was named CASE (Council for Advancement and Support of Education) Professor of the Year for Wisconsin in 1991 and has brought her concern for pedagogy to this encyclopedia. Professor Salisbury has written or edited more than 10 books, including the award-winning *Perpetua's Passion: Death and Memory of a Young Roman Woman*, *The Beast Within: Animals in the Middle Ages*, and *The West in the World*, a textbook on western civilization.

Volume Editor

Peter Seelig is an independent scholar with a bachelor's degree in the humanities from the University of Wisconsin–Green Bay. He continues to study topics in history, language, and philosophy. Following a year spent teaching in France, he has been working as a university-level logic tutor and proofreader in Madison, Wisconsin. He is also a freelance editor and an author of educational supplements.

Additional Contributors

Jennifer J. Popiel, University of Wisconsin–Green Bay
Paula Rentmeester, University of Wisconsin–Green Bay
Valda Rigg, Macquarie University Australian History Museum
Brian Ulrich, University of Wisconsin–Madison

We also acknowledge the following authors of Greenwood Publishing's "Daily Life through History" series, whose books contributed much to entries in the current volume:

Claudia Durst Johnson, *Daily Life in Colonial New England*, 2002.
Kirstin Olsen, *Daily Life in 18th-Century England*, 1999.
Louis G. Perez, *Daily Life in Early Modern Japan*, 2002.
Dorothy Denneen Volo and James M. Volo, *Daily Life in the Age of Sail*, 2002.
James M. Volo and Dorothy Denneen Volo, *Daily Life on the Old Colonial Frontier*, 2002.